Mark Morris: Musician—Choreographer

Mark Morris: Musician—Choreographer

Stephanie Jordan

DANCE BOOKS

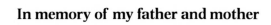

In memory of my father and mother

First published in 2015
by Dance Books Ltd.,
Southwold House, Isington Road, Binsted, Hampshire GU34 4PH

ISBN 978-1-85273-175-5

Cover photograph:
Mark Morris at work in the studio. © Chantal Regnault, 1988

Contents

Illustrations

Acknowledgements

Writing about a choreographer as alive and celebrated as Mark Morris is not only exciting—it is also challenging, even daunting. How could I reconcile his different opinions with my own and maintain critical distance while relishing special access to archive material? How could I accept that he would not stop making interesting work, even going against his own grain, just as I reached a point of closure and was tempted to make grand generalisations? But in Morris's case, these were challenges that rapidly proved their worth as I embarked upon this seven-year research project. He could not have been more gracious in offering as many interviews as I wished for—some very extended, trusting me enough to allow me into classes and rehearsals, while answering patiently outstanding questions as the writing neared completion, never pressuring me to hurry my work. Back in 2005, meeting Morris for the first time as I researched for my previous book *Stravinsky Dances*, I soon learnt that he was hugely inspiring to interview, compressing what could well have been an hour's conversation into fifteen minutes of highly specific, intriguing responses, not just about his own work, but about aesthetics in general. The idea of a book on the musical aspect of his work immediately suggested itself.

Nor has Morris imposed upon my views within this book. Just as Joan Acocella wrote in her brilliant critical biography of 1993: 'The book is in no way authorised.' Morris simply read the whole manuscript for accuracy before it went to print and corrected a few errors.

Executive Director Nancy Umanoff gave me similar freedom, while reading the manuscript very carefully—endnotes included. She has a formidable memory for everything relating to the Mark Morris Dance Group (MMDG), covering the archive that she herself initiated in 1986 as well as an ever-expanding present. This not only means history and facts, but also artistic views and creative interpretations of the past, often goading me to think around a problem, and including vital suggestions about increasing the book's accessibility to a non-academic public. It was she who came up with the idea of a website of film clips to support my analyses of Morris's dances. I am very grateful to both Morris and Umanoff for allowing this to happen: it enlivens my contribution immeasurably.

As time progressed, I treasured more and more the welcome and help that I received from the MMDG operation as a whole. There were the administrative staff who helped me access research resources, made contacts for me, prepared visual material for publication and arranged tickets to performances, first Alex Pacheco, later Sarah Horne, Jenna Nugent, Moss

Allen, Karyn LeSuer and Anni Turkel. Ever patient with my countless requests, they supported me with huge commitment and imagination.

Turning to others whom I interviewed, I acknowledge the artists other than Morris himself, who were highly articulate about their practice in collaboration with him. First are the dancers from past and present, who offered important insights into the subtleties of their performance, ranging from detailed relationships to notes and beats to rehearsal techniques and creative strategies of their own: especially Joe Bowie, Tina Fehlandt, Lauren Grant, John Heginbotham, Penny Hutchinson, David Leventhal, Bradon McDonald, Amber Star Merkens, June Omura, Michelle Yard and, guesting with MMDG, Mikhail Baryshnikov. Then there are the musicians, composers and performers, associated with Morris during various stages of his career: Herschel Garfein (the composer), and performers Emanuel Ax, Harriet Cavalli, Linda Dowdell, Colin Fowler, Jane Glover, Ethan Iverson and Page Smith.

Rehearsal director Matthew Rose has a rare understanding of musical, as well as dance, technicalities, and provided invaluable, precise rhythmic detail. His knowledge greatly informed my notated examples. Johan Henckens, MMDG's Technical Director, opened my eyes (and ears) to the niceties involved in staging musicians as well as dancers, the intensely important hidden side of a dance company's choreomusical practice. Ellen Highstein also proved immensely helpful in her account of Morris's teaching at the Tanglewood Music Center.

I benefited hugely from the advice of a group of expert critical readers who scrutinised most of my book between them, particularly Helen Julia Minors, who, with her rare knowledge of both music theory and dance, checked my methodological approach and the detail of my analysis, also Helena Hammond, Lawrence Zbikowski, Simon Morrison, and Matthew McDonald. I am immensely grateful to Elizabeth McClean for her meticulous editing of the complex chronology of Morris dances. My grateful thanks too to Joan Acocella for her generosity in allowing multiple quotations from her own book on Morris.

This project would never have happened without the support of several organisations. I was offered a Research Fellowship from the Leverhulme Trust and a grant to bring the book to completion from the British Academy jointly with the Leverhulme Trust. My own University of Roehampton also supported me in allowing me time to research and write. Nor do I forget my inspiring discussions with staff colleagues and graduate students on whom I have tested my ideas over the years in tutorial and during my courses in Music and Dance. I am grateful too for opportunities to talk about Morris's work outside Roehampton, especially at the Universities of

Michigan, Oregon (at Eugene) and Auckland, and outside the academy, to audience members from two ballet companies who feature Morris's work in their repertory, Pacific Northwest Ballet and San Francisco Ballet. Just Radio gave me refreshing opportunities to present two BBC broadcasts featuring Morris's work.

I am of course greatly indebted to my production team, with whom I once again have enjoyed working: Paul Terry, for his skill in documenting music examples integrated with dance information, Liz Morrell, for her elegant work and great patience as editor and designer, also indexer Katharine Stimson. Finally, thanks to David Leonard of the great publishing house Dance Books, for supporting me yet again in the progress of a monograph that turned out to be an exceptionally complex production. He maintains the highest standards for dance, and I could not wish for a more sympathetic, flexible and author-friendly publisher.

Just as for my other three books, I had considerable encouragement from my musician parents, who have always taken a keen interest in my work. Sadly, however, neither was able to witness the publication of this book. It has to be dedicated to their memory. As always, with a sound critical eye, yet with immense generosity and a terrific sense of humour, my husband Howard Friend undertook to read and comment upon the entire manuscript. His contribution has been invaluable. I promised him that this one would not be quite so long as the last.

Stephanie Jordan, December 2014

Introduction

'Choreographer Mark Morris... has done more to revive interest in, to dignify and illuminate classical music to a broad audience than any conductor or musician of the last 20 years...' The year was 2000, and Helen Wallace, editor of *BBC Music Magazine*, signalled the achievements of one of the most celebrated American choreographers working today.[1] Long before this, the Mark Morris Dance Group (MMDG) had achieved international standing. Since its formation in 1980, the company had spent three years (1988-1991) at the Brussels opera house Théâtre Royal de la Monnaie, enjoying sumptuous musical resources. They were now back home in New York and just about to make the momentous move into their current impressive home in Brooklyn, the Mark Morris Dance Center (in 2001). Here, there was not only a permanent rehearsal base for his dancers—and musicians, but a school with a menu of dance classes for all, and live music everywhere, even the sound of singing, loud singing... probably the choreographer himself breezing through the corridors. But Wallace's statement also signifies specific recognition within the UK, Morris's musicality viewed from the perspective of the country outside the US that has most regularly embraced his company work and musical collaborations.

Probably of all contemporary choreographers, Morris is the one most often cited for emphasis on musical values. In this respect, although he runs a modern dance group, he follows in the ballet tradition of George Balanchine in the US, and less frequently recognised, Frederick Ashton in the UK. With music central to his rapid rise to international eminence, Morris has also developed a fervent following of music-lovers and an exceptional standing within the music profession: working in opera as well as dance (including The Metropolitan Opera, New York City Opera, English National Opera and the Royal Opera, Covent Garden), sought out by outstanding performers (such as Yo-Yo Ma and Emanuel Ax) and reviewed frequently by the music press. In 2013, he became the first artist outside the music profession itself (after, among others, Igor Stravinsky, Pierre Boulez, Esa-Pekka Salonen and Simon Rattle) invited to be Music Director of America's Ojai Music Festival. He is now a conductor, too, of his own music ensemble and others. He has also made eighteen ballets, including eight for San Francisco Ballet.

Morris's commitment to live music has been essential, a rare priority for a modern dance company anywhere. Liveness is about much more than sound quality. It introduces the challenges of variability between performances and opportunities for mutual embodiment between dancers and musicians, physical sensations enhanced by presence and sometimes visual contact. Of its kind, Morris's company is perhaps unique in having its own music ensemble while also performing regularly with large orchestras and 'star' soloists. But it is important that Morris not only engages with 'classical' music. His musical selections are remarkably catholic: alongside, for instance, Bach, Beethoven, Satie and Lou Harrison, the wry wit of the Scottish poet-singer Ivor Cutler, the prog-rock of jazz trio The Bad Plus, as well as country-western, pop-Indian and traditional Balkan styles. The musical precision and flexibility of his dancers is also formidable.

A less frequently observed feature, but a central topic of this book, is that Morris, through his work, asks us a string of fundamental questions about the role of music in dance, while probing the possibilities for relationships between the two media. Although dance is nearly always music-and-dance, and the centrality of music within dance has long been considered an unquestionable fact of life, we rarely stop to think about the nature of the inter-relationship, which might lead us to imagine new practices as well as to understand the variety that already exists. In discussing these matters, I use the convenient, and now regularly-heard term 'choreomusical', coined by Paul Hodgins in 1991.[2] (Morris himself has begun to use the term over the last few years.) The simpler term 'musical' has been over-used in dance and has encouraged simplistic responses, as if a choreographer or dancer either *is*, and to her/his advantage, or *is not*. But musicality is not one simple thing. Perhaps it is better to ask questions about what precisely is going on *choreomusically* and the effect of what is going on.

Sometimes, it is possible to talk about different 'choreomusical styles', for instance, in general terms, how the relations with music in Balanchine's work differ from those in the work of Ashton, Antony Tudor, or the more distant figure of Merce Cunningham. Yet Morris cannot be pinned down to one clear style quite so easily. He borrows from various existing methods and styles, and adds still more of his own. This makes choreomusical style itself a reflexive phenomenon, an opportunity for commentary on the past: a phenomenon that emerges as a series of discourses alongside the other discourses offered up by a work. His borrowing from tradition might link Morris with a number of other recent choreographers who have been labelled 'postmodern', although he may well be unique among them in borrowing so extensively within the choreomusical domain.

We might consider here one such discourse or method. It is the one with which Morris has frequently been associated, so-called 'music visualisation', sometimes, unfortunately, at the expense of all others. This practice refers directly back to an early twentieth-century modern dance form initiated by the American dancer-choreographers Ruth St Denis and Ted Shawn (Denishawn). Morris has sometimes used the term himself. But the visualisation procedure has been criticised by a number of dance writers. For several reasons, this critical stance now needs to be reconsidered. First, there is the breadth of Morris's approach to music, which demands recognition and in relation to which, just one of these, music visualisation, should be carefully contextualised. There are more basic questions: why should this method be considered a problem? Do our values say more about us than about the work itself? Is visualisation simply one thing, or can it occur in a variety of forms? Returning to the generic question about what goes on and what effect it produces, now let us ask: what is being visualised and how, and what is the effect in each particular instance of visualisation?

In 2000, in *Moving Music: Dialogues with Music in Twentieth-Century Ballet*,[3] I used the term 'music visualisation' in order to explain and apply a conceptual framework or method for thinking about music and dance. It was applied during discussions of ballet choreographers, and mostly in terms of structure. In the current book, after situating it within a historical context, I use the concept more sparingly. Since *Moving Music*, and as demonstrated in *Stravinsky Dances: Re-Visions across a Century* (2007),[4] I have become increasingly interested in how choreomusical relations release meaning (including irony) and emotional resonance. Always experimenting, jumping ahead, Morris's work encourages us further in this direction. But, unusually, he also prompts us to consider our cognitive processes when watching and listening. In this way, Morris might be seen to have prompted developments within choreomusical theory. Theories of conceptual blending and empirical, scientifically-based studies of how we process hearing and seeing provide important supplements to existing methods of analysis.

Ironically, it took some time before I felt any urge to write about Morris, and probably, as much as anything, the reason was to do with his new, daring, widely-ranging, approaches to music. But one of the most exciting discoveries from this project was awareness of my own prejudices and having them challenged. In the 1970s and 80s, my principal inclinations as a critic and scholar (backed by continuing dance training) were towards the work of Cunningham and the post-Cunningham British choreographers (like Richard Alston, Siobhan Davies and Rosemary Butcher), as well as towards ballet.[5] Relatively uncritical at that stage, I believed that there should always be a measure of independence between music and dance, driven by the Cunningham-Cage formula, but also by the extraordinary contrapuntal ingenuities of Balanchine. Probably as a result of a second background in music, I retained a strong interest in formal structures: of dance and music and, most important of all, the combination of both.

Like a number of other British writers at the time, I was not ready for Morris's first London Dance Umbrella performances of 1984 and 1985— not ready for his rude muscularity and voluptuous fleshiness, never more clearly manifest than on his own big, baroque body.[6] The manner in which he took ownership of the music was also alarming, so fearless, even invasive, it seemed, not only snatching up its detail—here was none of the independence that I inclined towards—but also taking an uncivilised pleasure in its secret, sensual interiors. By the mid-90s, things had begun to change. I was now fascinated and eager for the challenge. I became a regular at performances both in the UK and later in the US and, during the long *Stravinsky Dances* project that began soon after the millennium, embarked on a study of two small pieces: one was the early *Frisson* (1985), set to Stravinsky's *Symphonies of Wind Instruments*, and the other, Morris had just premiered, *Candleflowerdance* (2005), to the *Serenade in A*. I was hooked. My background in formal analysis still proved useful, for Morris's work regularly lends itself well to that. Thus, having grown to admire Morris's passionate misbehaviour and threat to sanctimonious civility, and having been deeply moved by the extreme tenderness that frequently hides within his musical response, I came to write this book.

A great deal of inspiring Morris-specific literature already existed, led by Joan Acocella's seminal and highly illuminating biography (1993, covering the early part of his career),[7] and the edited collection on his most celebrated work *L'Allegro, il Penseroso ed il Moderato* (2001).[8] Morris has also provoked a considerable body of insightful criticism—and still does—by, for instance, Arlene Croce, Robert Greskovic, Deborah Jowitt, Wendy Lesser, Alastair Macaulay, and again, Acocella, beyond the scope of her book.

Given, however, that Morris is increasingly celebrated for his use of music, it seems high time that this aspect of his work should be scrutinised further as the subject of detailed study. To start us off, Acocella included an excellent music chapter within her book. But it is the dance and music academics who have made the running with this task, from Denmark, Inger Damsholt, from the UK, Rachel Duerden, Sophia Preston and myself and, working in the US, Daniel Callahan, Alice Miller Cotter and Hamish Robb. Some of these writers are trained in both music and dance. They use structurally-based analytical methods, but these are thoroughly integrated with interpretative strategies, the discussion of broader issues such as aesthetic and gender implications and acknowledgement of historical context. This all happens at a time when choreomusical studies in general are increasing, and extending their range of topics and historical coverage. It is worth pointing out that, over the last ten years, there have been at least twelve international conferences on the subject, others devoted to the topic of music and the body, and several related publications.[9] Much of the work cuts across boundaries and informs my own.

While this book continues in the line established by earlier writers on Morris and is fundamentally an analytical and critical study of Morris's work, it also sets his works within the context of several histories: his own up to the present—given that Acocella's book ends in 1993—the artform of dance in general, and, specifically, the history of choreomusical style. I have also seized the opportunity to document Morris's working processes, partly because they provide additional insights into his work, partly because such information about an established choreographer could be helpful to others, in the manner of tools that might be used, or modified for use, or that might stimulate other processes. Information about process I have used carefully in relation to analysis, as much as possible after undertaking several viewings of a dance, aware that, while such information might provoke useful new ways of thinking about dance, enriching our potential for experience, it might also bias, or limit, our interpretation of the piece in hand. But these processes also form part of Morris's history.

The analyses in this book cover a wide range of choreomusical tactics. I have also been led by dances in which the choreomusical content sustains interest after many viewings; unsurprisingly, many of these are among the finest in Morris's repertory. (So my selections do not map simply onto those of Acocella: I spend little time, for instance, on *Dogtown* and *Lovey*, which make their point by succumbing to, or totally ignoring, the pummelling rock beat of Yoko Ono and Violent Femmes respectively.) Some dances get more detailed treatment than others, inasmuch as they have more to contribute to the Morris 'story', like the two landmark ensemble works of the Brussels years *L'Allegro* and *Dido and Aeneas* and the 2006 full-evening symphonic enterprise *Mozart Dances,* but also much smaller-scale pieces, like the early *Vacant Chair* and *One Charming Night* and the 2007 *Italian Concerto.* This is not to deny the value of works that are less 'choreomusical' and more about other matters. Having said this, it is important that I do consider 'other matters', the larger dance context, in order to make sense of the choreomusical treatment in the dances that I analyse.

Today, although there are many Morris dances to choose from, and a good proportion of these have been revived, the touring repertory does not tell the full tale: by 2014, a total of 183 works, ballets, operas, and pieces for MMDG and other ensembles. In undertaking this research project and in order to make my selection, I made it my business to look at every piece on film. I have seen many of these works live as well.

To date, DVDs of just four Morris dances are commercially available: *L'Allegro* (1988), *Dido and Aeneas* (1989), *The Hard Nut* (1991) and *Falling Down Stairs* (1997). The MMDG archive, which was established in 1986 by the now Executive Director Nancy Umanoff and is housed at the Mark Morris Dance Center, contains other films (videos and DVDs) of nearly all Morris's dances. (Most of these are also available for public viewing in the Jerome Robbins Dance Division of the New York Public Library.) Many dances have been recorded more than once at different periods in the history of MMDG and in different venues (most often the Brooklyn Academy of Music, Jacob's Pillow, Massachusetts, and Zellerbach Auditorium, Berkeley).

It is as well to remember that film represents just one performance interpretation of a work and is already a kind of translation of it. The footage from the 1980s and 1990s of Morris's dances is often of poor technical quality. In recent years, the recording quality is much improved and his dances have been captured in both long-shot, covering the full stage, and close-up, attending to the detail of individual dancers. Nor are films reliably exact in capturing choreography. Sometimes, they include errors or agreed changes made between performances. There may also be problems with musical synchronisation—the tiniest shift in time can have major impact, or a musical tempo that is too fast or too slow might affect the accuracy of movement detail. It is always wise to consult multiple sources, if they are available, in order to see beyond the errors and changes and, as far as possible, into the 'text' that lies behind a single performance. Here, for dances analysed in detail, I have examined all available film material. Still, film is no substitute for the 'feel' of live performance, and Morris himself is the first to recognise this. Adequate recordings of Morris's ballets have been less easy to access than those of his own company works, but there is evidence that the breadth of his approach to music is already represented by his work for MMDG; only one ballet has been chosen for detailed analysis.

Apart from a few exceptions, Morris does not have his work notated. There is one early Benesh score by Wendy Walker of *Drink to Me Only with Thine Eyes*, created for American Ballet Theatre (1988). Then, there is the Labanotation of *All Fours* (2003), an experiment initiated by the Dance Notation Bureau in New York and, a decade later, of *Crosswalk* and *Spring, Spring, Spring*. These meticulous, detailed scores, all by Sandra Aberkalns, provide invaluable information for anyone analysing a dance or, indeed, for the rehearsal directors of the future.

While films and live performances naturally occupy central position for analysis, other sources have proved essential, including further MMDG archive material: press reviews, interviews, programmes, music scores (often containing choreographic annotations). The archive also contains audio recordings of interviews with Morris—surely one of the most interviewed choreographers on this earth—Question and Answer pre- and post-performance sessions and oral histories provided by those who have worked with him over the years. An exciting development: the archive itself appeared to expand during my project as memories were jogged and staff uncovered materials that had hitherto lain hidden away.

I conducted many interviews myself, twenty in total, with Morris. (Unless otherwise indicated, these are the Morris interviews referred to in endnotes.) The Morris interviews commenced in 2005 with discussions of his *Frisson* and *Candleflowerdance* for *Stravinsky Dances*. They continued for the current volume between 2009-13, roughly three a year (see p. 489 for a list of dates), taking place on the East and West Coasts of the US, in London and Madrid, focusing on MMDG live performances in these various venues as well as on the broader content of the book. I do not indicate precise dates in endnotes, because referenced ideas often recurred across interviews, even if in different contexts, and several later meetings included straightforward fact-checking prior to the re-drafting of chapters. Exceptionally, where Morris's thinking clearly developed over time, I have highlighted this.

It was important also to include the perspective of Morris's dancers (from MMDG over the years, and the Russian star Mikhail Baryshnikov) and of a range of collaborating musicians (composers, class/rehearsal pianists, conductors and performers). Soon, I learnt to understand the importance of reaching beyond the artists to consult Morris's management and technical personnel, and his promoters, to hear about the defining practicalities behind the Morris enterprise and, in the case of Umanoff, to discover more about the history behind everything, not only the dances. (As with Morris, unless otherwise indicated, I conducted all of these other interviews.)

Accessing every archive interview with Morris that I could find, I became aware of how his attitudes and practices have changed over time, but very soon realised that he suffered having to answer the same questions repeatedly and to respond to the perennial observations of his 'bad-boy' or 'loud-mouth' image. In haste, he seemed also to provide reductive answers to the more complicated and interesting questions. But Morris knows what he is doing. He once told me that in Q and As, every so often, he will let out a tiny new gem of information, in the manner of a drip-feed, but no single individual could possibly be mobile enough to catch all these occasions.

Writing this book, I was on different ground from most other interviewers: Morris seemed to enjoy sharp focus and detail and my job was to 'read' the recordings carefully and critically. Yet, as well as confirming what I believed to be true, he introduced inconsistencies. Were these the result of faulty memory, or interpretation of the past differently in the light of the present?

Did Morris re-image a piece when coaching a revival, renewing the dance for himself and his dancer? Was he, or was he not, thinking conceptually about his setting of a Mozart fugue? Sometimes, I had to recognise that he and I, the interviewer, simply thought differently about choreomusical relations.

The one aspect of his creative practice that Morris does not talk about is the meaning of his dances: he will not provide an interpretation. There is the occasional slip, after a dance is finished, but never enough for a programme note and, for years, these have been banished. He wants his work to be open to multiple interpretations, again, not to limit us. Besides, a choreographer's spoken intentions do not provide *the* right way into a work. Instead Morris talks very willingly about the background to a work and another major preoccupation: structure. Documenting the thoughts of the living always requires a special sensitivity and is inevitably beset with dangers. But Morris offers the bonus of being exceptionally articulate about musical matters, and so are his dancers. Certainly, in this book, I would like to have other voices heard behind my own selection of quotations and line of argument.

Engagement with practical activities beyond performance has been invaluable, like watching company class, which I recognised as a musical training, not simply a means for building technical proficiency. Morris's class combinations are structured to teach dynamics and phrasing to music. But I also learnt from trying out movement myself, a kind of 'sketch learning' of moves and phrases to music. I am convinced that this can inform choreomusical analysis. The result is hearing and seeing better, partly because the business of practical learning draws us into detail, highlighting distinctions and dramas within the work far more than distanced watching of film allows. I am especially grateful to John Heginbotham[10] for teaching me the central solo in *Italian Concerto* (originally made for Morris himself), a process that provided many insights into imagery and relations with music, not only within this piece but also crossing into others.[11] I also undertook study of Balkan dance forms, in particular Bulgarian and Macedonian dance, in order better to understand the choreomusicality lying within Morris's early training.

The book partly follows a chronological scheme and is partly thematically-based. But the chapters also stand independently and do not have to be read in the given order. They can be used for reference as much as for any linear story of Morris's choreomusical development.

There are three Parts, covering the context of Morris's work, a framework for analysing dance, and analyses of the dances themselves. The first three chapters, Part 1, comprise new background documentation. In Chapter 1, I set the scene with a musical biography covering Morris's career since his childhood training in the 1960s and 1970s, the formation of MMDG in 1980, and the period from then to the present. Chapter 2 documents Morris's working processes and collaborative practices with his dancers and musicians. Chapter 3 reflects upon the historical context of choreomusical relations, looking at the past practices with which Morris engages and in relation to our current understanding.

Part 2, which is Chapter 4, constitutes a discussion of the conceptual basis for watching and listening. Here, I suggest how we can theorise choreomusical relations, drawing from previous work in this area, including technical discussions of music and dance, as well as developments prompted by the diversity of Morris's work. The framework is potentially applicable to a great deal of other repertory by other choreographers, and written with this in mind. This chapter in particular could well be read independently, perhaps after more familiarity with Morris's dances, used for reference alongside the analytical discussions or with a view to further theoretical exploration.

The following chapters, Part 3, address the dances themselves, divided into three periods. Chapter 5 covers the early dances (1980-88), a period of broad experiment, encompassing 'real' music visualisations, the borrowing of musical principles, the 'angry dances' introducing connotational disjunctions between music and dance, dances based on systems, as well as dances pursuing independent strategies and influenced by the methods of Merce Cunningham (e.g. *Ten Suggestions, Fugue, Marble Halls, Gloria, The Vacant Chair, One Charming Night, Not Goodbye, Frisson,* the collaborations with the composer Herschel Garfein).

After this, I cover Morris's period at the Monnaie in Brussels (1988-1991), with detailed analysis of his two most celebrated large-scale works, *L'Allegro* and *Dido and Aeneas* (Chapters 6-7), followed by a survey of the range of other work produced during this period, from his *Nutcracker* setting, *The Hard Nut,* to his single, silent work *Behemoth* (Chapter 8).

The last group of chapters covers the broadest timespan (1992-to present). Chapter 9 explores work that is strongly led by narrative, in the conventional sense, most of it plot-based, Morris's settings of two well-known, full-length ballet scores (*Sylvia* and *Romeo and Juliet*), and his growing commitment to opera direction. In Chapter 10, I consider experiments crossing narrative (in a less conventional sense) with 'abstract' musical form. All of these dances use vocal scores: in other words, they are text-based (*Four Saints in Three Acts, Bedtime* and *Socrates*). Chapter 11 is unique in focusing on a single composer, the West Coast American Lou Harrison, a series of eight dances set to his music, including one, *Rhymes with Silver,* that Morris and Harrison devised together from scratch. Perhaps Morris's most important choreomusical development of this later period is his frequent use of symphonic-scale concert scores, many of them non-programmatic and consisting of several musical movements. Examples analysed in Chapter 12 cover scores ranging from the eighteenth to the twentieth century: *Rondo, V, Rock of Ages, Italian Concerto, All Fours* and *Empire Garden*. This chapter also includes an examination of Morris's *Spring, Spring, Spring,* his setting of Stravinsky's ballet score *The Rite of Spring* as a symphonic, formal enterprise. Chapter 13 is devoted to Morris's most substantial exploration of this kind, the full-evening *Mozart Dances,* which comprises settings of two concertos and a sonata.

My book aims to be useful both to scholars and students (undergraduate and postgraduate) of dance, music and interdisciplinary studies and to a broader audience of dance and music enthusiasts. I also hope that it will reach the professions of dance and music, choreographers, composers and performers who are interested in exploring the extended possibilities for 'working' dance with music that Morris's dances suggest.

Readers are invited to approach the topic of musical and dance structure at a variety of levels. I have not ventured into the extremes of esoteric musical analysis. Technical discussion, however, is regularly employed in order to reveal the complexities of choreomusical relationships, to uncover the links, for instance, between formal device and meaning: accurately applied technical terms imply precision in communication. Thus, there are examples in music notation as well as examples that show dance-rhythmic information in musical notation, very much a short-hand compared with actual dance notation (for example, Laban or Benesh), but with the major advantage of easy cross-reference between music and dance. Readers are also encouraged to listen to the music independently from watching a dance, and some may wish to access music scores as well. This makes particular sense for Morris's work because he burrows into musical detail so frequently: when dance film is unavailable, the music itself tells a considerable part of the story.

Finally, a ground-breaking website is connected to the book. This allows direct access to clips of much of the choreography discussed and sometimes to the precise film recordings used for my analyses: http:// markmorrisdancegroup.org/jordanbookclips. The website may be modified after the publication of the book so, before tackling any analysis, readers are advised to check it for the most up to date collection of clips. It is hosted by MMDG, whose umbrella site is in itself an invaluable supplementary resource, comprising further clips, interviews, chronologies, a variety of written material and a Photo Gallery. Perhaps the biggest advantage of the film clips is that they present material never before available for study and that can be looked at in ways other than my own. However 'you', the reader, come to Mark Morris's work, my principal aim through such illustrative examples is to enable a strong, direct engagement with the dance and its music.

PART 1
THE CONTEXT

1

Setting the Scene:
Morris's Career as Musical Journey

Introduction

In 1985, Morris was already clear: 'As a dancer I'm a musician. As a choreographer I'm a musician.'[1] By 2010, he made the point even more strongly by reversing the statement: 'I am a musician and my medium is dancing.'[2] Many times along the way, Morris had confirmed his reliance on music as his starting-point: 'what it's all about. It's not that I'm driven to make up dances. It's that I'm driven to listen to music and to present music to people... [3] I love music better than dance, basically. I also think it's better. Higher standards.'[4]

These claims are driven by Morris's deep-seated belief in the aesthetic superiority of music. 'All art constantly aspires to the condition of music': the nineteenth-century English essayist Walter Pater's statement is now a cliché.[5] But Morris likes to quote him, because he believes in the cliché and tries to demonstrate it through his choreography. Looking back, Linda Dowdell, the first musical director of the Mark Morris Dance Group, is convinced that dance for Morris has always been fundamentally his *hommage* to music.[6] Meanwhile, David White, director of New York's Dance Theater Workshop, where Morris presented some of his early choreography, noted the unusual musical erudition within his makeup: the 'music-scholar guy' amongst a 'car-crash of personalities...this working-class guy... this folk-dance guy and this gay guy, and they've all washed up into the same body'.[7]

But has any other choreographer publicised himself quite so boldly in this manner? Morris's stance is unusual. George Balanchine, to whom Morris has often been likened from a musical point of view, immediately comes to mind: a trained musician, perhaps *the* model musician-choreographer, certainly one of the most admired by Morris himself. Balanchine was similarly deferential about what music could do and dance could not and about music being the foundation for dance activity. Both choreographers, too, have operated analytically as regards musical structures. Yet their backgrounds were quite different. Balanchine trained in piano, composition and music theory at the Petrograd Conservatory of Music alongside his studies of ballet, and we learn that, soon after his arrival in America in 1933, he was still filling in time 'freshening up on counterpoint and harmony with his friend, the composer Nicolas Nabokov'.[8] During his career as a choreographer, he continued to develop his knowledge of music theory, and remained an active pianist and composer of the occasional song or piano miniature: according to his friend, the violinist Nathan Milstein, 'he sight-read freely'.[9] Throughout his life, too, he made his own piano transcriptions of orchestral scores, which enabled him to get to know the music better, from the inside. Morris does not match Balanchine in terms of formal musical education and professional training, his knowledge being largely self-driven; nor has he ever learnt to play an instrument fluently. Still, he has probably been the more ambitious and greedy for new musical experiences of all kinds.

Despite the lack of conventional musical training, for instance, Morris has been fascinated for a long time by the formal emphasis of music, its traditional tendencies towards the systematic, abstract and 'mathy'. Characteristically, by the mid-80s, he was regularly referring to himself as a 'structure queen'.[10] All this means that, when moved to choreograph a piece of music, he approaches it analytically (sometimes even in the manner of a music theorist), with rigorous attention to detail and complexity, and to the movement of music as rhythm. When the music is written down, he undertakes a close reading of the score, which he continues to refer to as he works in the dance studio. It also means that he goes to music (much more than to choreography) for his structural models and that he applies musical terms when discussing his dance practice. There is no question that he is fully confident and precise when conversing with musicians and in communicating musical information to his dancers.

Morris is exceptionally well-read about music. For any new score that he sets, of whatever period or style, he steeps himself in the literature on the composer and on the specific piece, including published analyses. He has read the writings of a number of composers: like Virgil Thomson's autobiography and Leonard Bernstein's introduction to musical appreciation *The Joy of Music*. He has studied music criticism, such as *Shaw on Music* (the collected writings of Bernard Shaw) and *The Rest is Noise* by today's *New Yorker* critic Alex Ross—a tour of the landscape of twentieth-century music, including popular music, and its confluence with social, political and cultural forces—a breadth that suits Morris well. Frequently he refers to Charles Rosen's seminal work *The Classical Style*, a discussion of the language and structures of classical period music, as witnessed through the achievements of Haydn, Mozart and Beethoven. He purchased a copy in the 1980s; it stimulated his early ideas about form. Another favourite is Roger Shattuck's *The Banquet Years*, an assessment of the modernist avant-garde at the turn of the twentieth century, including music, with a chapter on Satie, a composer set by Morris on several occasions.[11]

Morris's assertions about how he sees himself have been matched by the esteem in which he is held by musicians. Today, many embrace him as a musical colleague, one of the finest around, acknowledging that he has influenced greatly their own musical understanding. Acclaim comes both from those who have worked regularly with him, like the fine pianists Ethan Iverson and Colin Fowler, and more occasional superstar collaborators, like the cellist Yo-Yo Ma and pianist Emanuel Ax (who, significantly, have sought to maintain their connections with him). 'If he played the piano', says Ax, the premiere pianist for *Mozart Dances*, 'he'd be one of the great pianists of the world';[12] on another occasion: 'he probably would have been a fabulous conductor if he weren't a dancer'.[13]

Perhaps more surprisingly, the stars, not only Morris's regular musicians, are prepared to enter into *his* personal vision as he assumes primary responsibility for their interpretation of the music. Like a musical director himself, Morris is as clear about how the details of a score should be shaped as he is about the shaping of his choreography. Such detailed interpretative control by a choreographer is extremely rare. Yet Morris is known to respect, and negotiate with, musicians as artists more than most choreographers do.[14] That helps, and even if some might find such control invasive, others have gone out of their way to work with him, often accepting that a modern dance company cannot afford their usual fees. Was even Balanchine quite so engaged with the musical performance aspect of the dance event? Morris talks much more about his working processes than his predecessor ever did.

Appreciation for Morris extends to music audiences, and his Executive Director Nancy Umanoff explains that reaching them was always a part of the company's marketing strategy: 'Musicians *always* appreciated Mark more than dance people did'.[15] For years, they have gone in their droves to see him, sometimes primarily to hear unusual musical choices rarely heard in concert or for which no recording is available, sometimes interested in re-thinking music they know as a result of seeing it choreographed. As one young music critic Kathryn Bacasmot recently put it:

> When you attend a MMDG show, you basically get two shows for the price of one... Through the compliment of physical movement one might perceive new metanarratives in old favourites...[16]

Morris's need to get closer to the production of music in order to converse more intensely with it reveals itself in another way: since 2006, his forays into conducting. There is evidence that he had wanted to do this from as far

Mark Morris conducting *Gloria* at BAM. © Stephanie Berger, 2006

back as March 1995.[17] It signals another side to Morris's engagement with music, which is not about being the music scholar engaged in research and structural rigour, but about the immediacy of physical experience. Life for Morris has always been full of singing, and singing and dancing *together*, just as often happens in folk dance which, as we shall see, is an important part of his background. Singing is still a part of his natural rehearsal behaviour, as well as whistling and clapping musical rhythms, or tapping his fingers in perfectly executed counterpoint.

Morris often talks about being powerfully moved by music, describing his gut responses to sheer sound quality or timbre. His language is strong. Music can be 'thrilling' or 'shocking', he says, or it can drive him 'insane':

I am tickled pink by musical structure—the permutations and the logic. But music is actually about sound, and sound makes me absolutely crazy. The first chord of something can knock me out.[18]

Here, he uses the examples of organ music and choral singing:

Organ music doesn't transfer to recording. There isn't a sub-woofer that makes a 32ft pipe sound like a 32-foot pipe. You don't even hear it. It moves you viscerally. That's what I like. There's nothing like the first chord that the chorus sings in the opera, it's like—WOW—and those are people and they're doing it right now, and there's spit and fatigue and maybe some halitosis involved, but it's an animal action.[19]

Morris especially loves the direct contact with the physical, sounding body that the voice affords:

Singing is like dancing. It's the body, the body in the world, with nothing in between, no instrument between.[20]

He also treasures subtlety, remarking, for instance, that, in today's iPod culture, people rarely experience the true quietness of chamber music. In an article on the piano 'as miracle', he communicates a special effect:

The sound of decay as a chord dies out always thrills me. I hear a sharpening of pitch as the overtones resonate up and away.[21]

And on the few occasions, like this, when he has written for publication, Morris's subject tends to be music, not dance. Such musical qualities, big and small, come across most powerfully in live performance, and Morris demands no less than full power. By the time he was fifteen years old, he knew that live music was his ideal,[22] although, for financial reasons, whether it be so important to them or not, many modern dance groups over the years have had no choice but to rely on recorded music. Today, Morris has his own music ensemble, a core group of regular musicians supplemented by others as necessary.

Such is the importance of live music to Morris that he chose to address a 1998 Midwest Arts Conference on the topic.[23] Three different experiences he described as profound examples of the 'fact and mystery' aspects of live performance that consume him to this day. First there was the 'startling physical fact' of the 'whomp' of a bass drum in a street parade hitting his stomach when he was a small boy—it seemed to communicate some kind of important message. Also as a child, he was enraptured by his first experience of counter-tenors and plainchant as he sat alone in the dark of Seattle's St Mark's Episcopal Cathedral. Years later, there was Janet Baker's 'ravishing voice' speaking to him in languages that he did not understand but conveying the essential message of love. These became the grounds for arguing why live music is so essential and, importantly, Morris's terms are as much about physical sensation as about feeling and emotion:

Because we need to. Because of biology. Because we are beings who crave touch. Because we are human animals who need that specific danger inherent in the fact and the mystery of live performance; the danger of truth...

Live music *is* music. A recording is a simulacrum, an aide-memoire, maybe a guide or learning tool. But music is in the flesh and in the moment, and it joins together those who hear it in a way that's both ancient and inexplicable. Individuals listening together and feeling less alone.

Liveness has broader implications, the inevitable element of risk, challenge and play in performance tugging away at very precisely rehearsed interpretation. The ephemerality of a single performance Morris sees as a cause for relish rather than dismay:

Some people only work to recorded music because it's so reliable and exactly the same every time, which is exactly why I don't. Wouldn't you rather have live people doing something? A recording of a performance is a recording of a performance. It's not the performance.[24]

He finds a useful parallel in opera, where no one ever puts up with a recorded orchestra or hears the orchestra as mere accompaniment.

There is history behind this view. Back in 1959, in her choreographic primer *The Art of Making Dances*, American modern dance pioneer Doris Humphrey wrote with fervour:

Canned music is undeniably *déclassé*. Musicians will sniff and carp, and audiences, though not so ivory-towerish, certainly do react better to the immediacy of live music.[25]

The composer Barbara White, who works with dance today, goes so far as to suggest that recordings can 'anaesthetise' a choreographer's musical response. Frozen, intractable sounds might even 'seem to dominate, to *determine* the dance... Faced with a musical "collaborator" offering all the warmth and responsiveness of an inflatable sex doll, choreographers may well decide that they "don't care" about the sound.'[26]

Morris's huge range of musical choices is highly unusual. Again, there is a sign of the 'car crash of personalities', and a particular openness to the 'low' as well as the 'high'. He has never subscribed to the hard and often hierarchical distinctions between the classical and popular, the scored and un-scored. (In the same spirit, he refers to his performances as 'shows' and to instrumental ensembles as 'bands'.) Additionally, his knowledge of the repertoire is vast, so that he can employ rarely heard music, and resorts only very occasionally to items from the canon. His eclecticism is neatly encapsulated within the selections from his own record collection for four radio programmes—'Music I want you to hear' (2009): pieces of Lou Harrison (the contemporary composer whose music he has worked with most frequently), baroque music, songs featuring female vocalists from India, Egypt, Portugal and the US, and finally, country-western examples. Iverson, his music director 1998-2002, sums up his attitude as fundamentally democratic—'relating to all music as if it's a folk music'.[27] No matter what tradition it comes from, music can thrill and fill him with awe. At the same time, he hears it as a robust and naturally integrated part of his everyday life and communion with others.

Given this range of interest, it is hardly surprising that music has always been Morris's main field for research and expressive exploration: it is mainly through music that we understand his personal journey as an artist.[28]

In the Beginning: Dance and Music Together

From early days—he was born in 1956 in Seattle—music and dance existed alongside each other for Morris, immediately central to his life as both work and pleasure. His expanded family (grandparents, parents and sisters) were all instrumental in his artistic development, remarkably active amateur enthusiasts who entertained themselves not only with home-grown music and dance, but also theatre events and films. No one was didactic or rigid. No one was concerned with the respective merits of different genres of art, or of high or popular forms. All were seen as interesting and fun.

His mother and father had courted through dancing to the big bands that visited Seattle, and father Bill would play the double organ or piano at home while his children sang along or danced the favourites that he liked to dance himself: such as 'Charmaine', 'Mood Indigo', 'Harbor Lights', 'Sweet Sue', 'Sentimental Journey'.[29] There was always a lot of singing, for instance, on the family's long road-trips, or when Bill took Morris to the local Presbyterian church to sight-sing in Welsh for song-fests. Behind him all the way in encouraging his passion for dancing was his mother Maxine, and she remained so throughout his later career. Of Morris's two best friends during his high school years (and still close to him), one was a dancer, Penny Hutchinson, who became a long-time member of his company, the other a cellist, Page Smith, who has played for his dances and still works professionally in the Seattle area (including with the orchestra of Pacific Northwest Ballet).

Important to him as well was the rich cultural milieu of Seattle, while he lived in a neighbourhood with both black and Asian families. There is also the fact that people in Seattle look more to the American West and across the Pacific than to the closely tied traditions of the American East Coast and Europe. (This may be a general feature of West Coast mentality, like the informal flow between high art and popular culture.) Morris had Fijian, Samoan and Japanese friends, all of whom introduced him to their distinctive cultural traditions. [30] This was long before today's terms 'multi-culturalism' and 'world music' achieved common usage.

Seattle also hosted stimulating activity from within western cultural traditions. Morris remained a regular at the Episcopal Cathedral, listening to the music at compline and attending piano recitals and concerts by the Seattle Symphony and North West Chamber Orchestra. He remembers that his passion for opera commenced in grade school, on seeing a performance of Donizetti's *L'Elisir d'amore*. One summer, aged sixteen, he saw the whole of Wagner's Ring cycle—the Seattle Opera is famous for performing all four of these operas back to back. [31] The city was an important stop-off for visiting artists and companies. As a teenager, Morris took himself to the big ballet companies that passed through, the Joffrey Ballet and Béjart's Ballet of the 20th Century (his favourites), as well as Pennsylvania Ballet, and Nureyev's performances (which he did not like). He saw modern dance too: the companies of Martha Graham, Paul Taylor and Alvin Ailey.

Yet making and performing art, doing it yourself, was as important to Morris as watching and listening to others, if not more so. Very young, he created solos for himself to the *1812 Overture* (Tchaikovsky) *Carnival of the Animals* and *Danse Macabre* (both Saint-Saëns). Then, aged eight, he was taken to see José Greco's flamenco troupe and decided immediately that he wanted to become a flamenco dancer. At that time in Seattle, training in Spanish dancing could be found at the Verla Flowers Dance Arts Studio, amongst an extraordinary range of other styles: in her biography of Morris, Joan Acocella lists ballet, tap, acrobatics, Hawaian, Tahitian, jazz, 'creative', ballroom, baton twirling and fencing. [32] Immediately recognising Morris's talent and determination, Flowers took him on scholarship and tailored for him a diverse and demanding curriculum of activities. She signed him up for ballet and character dance lessons, and got him a paid job as a Russian dancer with Seattle's Russian Balalaika Orchestra (he was with them for three years, from the age of eleven) as well as a one-week stint in a children's group with the touring Bolshoi Ballet. Still a child, he was taken by her to audition for Greco's summer school and was accepted. Flowers' annual studio recitals all featured Morris, and, such was his precocity, at the age of thirteen, he began teaching for her.

It was at this time that Morris enrolled in one of his most consuming and seminal dance activities, with the Koleda Folk Ensemble. This was a group that specialised in Balkan dances (Romanian, Bulgarian, Macedonian, Serbian and Croatian) and rehearsed five or six nights a week for performances in schools and colleges. Being part of the group instilled within Morris principles that have remained important ever since: that dancers should look like ordinary human beings in communion with one another, and that dancing is a participatory act to be shared with, rather than performed *at*, others. Today, MMDG dancer David Leventhal suggests that Morris's roots in folk dance aesthetics and structures still bear as strongly as ever upon the 'look, logic and rhythmic foundation' of his dances.[33]

Koleda work was highly sophisticated musically. Flamenco dancing had already exploited Morris's natural aptitude for rhythm with its rapid play between beat and offbeat and polyrhythms between hands and feet. But the rhythmic complexities of Balkan dances encouraged him to master odd metres like 11, 7 or 5 in a bar (see pp. 116-7). They are the kind of dance that might also find you singing and moving at the same time. Morris read these rhythms as potential choreographic material—they gave him an appetite for nuance that has deeply informed his own work. Later, in 1973-74, he paid a nine-month visit to the Balkans and Spain for further dance study and observation.

Morris's first exposure to modern dance (Martha Graham, Isadora Duncan and José Limon techniques) came when he was fifteen, but still then as only one part of provision at the summer dance camps run by Seattle's First Chamber Dance Company (1971-72). Modern dance, like ballet, was never central to his training or vision in these early years: it was simply one strand out of many within an extraordinarily rich educational experience. Dance camp offered opportunities to watch films, both ballet and modern—like Graham's 1959 *A Dancer's World*—stimulating a voracious appetite for dance history. This was the occasion when he encountered the dance accompanist Harriet Cavalli. She later played for the classes he taught at the University of Washington (Seattle) and collaborated with him as arranger and performer brought in specially for *Canonic 3/4 Studies* (1982). They have stayed in touch ever since, and in 2001 he wrote a cover note for her book *Dance and Music: A Guide to Dance Accompaniment for Musicians and Dance Teachers*.[34]

Morris's father Bill taught him to read music, although he largely taught himself to play, or rather find his way around, the piano, which he says he can still do today, even if badly.[35] It was only when he was sixteen that Morris took a few proper lessons, but times were hard, and the family could not afford for them to continue. In the meantime, he bought sheet music from the local music shop and Salvation Army centre and picked his way through piece after piece, a wide range—CPE Bach, Gottschalk, Hindemith, Fauré, Gershwin, Satie, Shostakovich, Tcherepnin and Walton. Some of this music he later choreographed, like the Gershwin *Three Preludes* and Tcherepnin Bagatelles, Op. 5. A lot of it he shared with Smith as regular after-school activity. She played one hand while he played the other, or she would play the cello while he accompanied her.

Self-taught as he was, the piano was central to Morris's life. Following the catastrophic fire that burnt down his family home, including the piano, in 1971, Morris immediately spent his own seventy-five dollars on a replacement.[36] But he was a fearless experimentalist as well. One day he set about 'preparing' his piano, inserting tacks and paper into the mechanism, with no idea that the composer John Cage had set the precedent.[37] Another time, he strung up a rope and hung from it objects that he could bang as percussion accompaniment. He was never the typical piano student, patiently practising scales or learning correct fingering. His priority was to get to know more music and more about music.[38] He listened avidly to the radio as well, and bought records that offered journeys into other territories such as South Indian and country-western music.[39]

Morris also loved to sing folk songs, rounds and madrigals and play rhythm games with his peers, Chad Henry (a writer and music theatre composer), Smith again, and sister Maureen. Smith remembers their break times at junior high school: 'He would stamp out one rhythm with his feet and another with his hands. Or I would be the drone, keeping a steady rhythm, and he would try out things over it—a four to a three, or something like that. So we'd just walk around the playground, stamping and clapping, until recess was over.'[40] Clearly, from an early age, he was already fascinated by music, not only as rhythm, but also as assemblage of different voices or parts, as contrapuntal intricacy. So we hear about his nascent interest in Bach, whom he later dubbed 'God's favourite composer':[41] Smith and he learnt to whistle the two-part Inventions, keyboard miniatures that have haunted him across his career and that have been picked up and put down by him several times, never fully realised through choreography.

As luck would have it, Morris attended Franklin High School, which had a strong reputation for the arts, music included.[42] There, he was a keen member of the school choir and came across Vivaldi's Gloria, which he later set, his first major choreography to baroque music. Having so much sight-reading experience at the piano, he discovered that he was strong at sight-singing as well. The school offered him music theory lessons. There were opportunities to study the rudiments of harmony and counterpoint— he recalls using the classic primer on this by Walter Piston—the rules for baroque figured bass, how to write in the style of Bach chorales, all standard components of western music theory training.[43] Today, he admits that he has forgotten the detail of these studies, but the principles have undoubtedly served him well.

First Steps in Choreography

Morris demonstrated his rapidly growing musical sophistication as soon as he turned to choreography. This began in 1971, when he was fifteen and, in her biography, Acocella lists seventeen dance entries from then until 1976, when he went to New York to embark on his career as a professional dancer. He made dances for Flowers' recitals, local high school plays and children's theatre groups, wherever opportunities arose. The first listed, for one of the recitals, deserves special mention. *Boxcar Boogie (Piece by Piece)* used a very ambitious, off-the-wall mix, music by Jacques Lasry, Conlon Nancarrow, Harry Partch and Steve Reich. The selection came off a single promotion record called 'The Wild Sounds of New Music' (Columbia Masterworks BTS 17, USA). Morris selected Reich's minimalist *Violin Phase*. From Nancarrow, he took one of the player piano (pianola) studies with complex, mechanically-ordered tempo relationships between musical lines in canon (No. 7). He used Nancarrow's music again later in *Etudes modernes* (1981) and *Jr. High* (1982).

The other two musical selections are significant for using home-made instruments that introduced fresh sonorities. Lasry, a French composer, used metal instruments or 'structures sonores' (c. 1964) devised by the brothers Bernard and Francois Baschet, one an engineer, the other a sculptor. But the West Coast American Harry Partch proved of special, lasting interest to Morris, so much so (and the same with Nancarrow), that he bought every recording of his work that he could find, and watched films and read about him.[44] The reading included Partch's own book *Genesis of a Music*, which documented his theory and practice.[45] Well-established as a leading member of the West Coast counter-culture by the 1960s, Partch was an intriguing figure. Possessed by radical ideas of personal freedom (for ten years during the depression he lived as a hobo) and of fusion between the arts and the body, he believed that musicians should return to an ancient primitive state that he termed 'corporeality'. This led naturally to an interest in dance and, in 1952, he created a three-movement work entitled *Plectra and Percussion Dances (An Evening of Dance Theater)*.

Partch was ready to dispense with the whole of western musical tradition. Much more interested in the alternative musicality of speech, he held in particular disdain the didactic conceptual model of standard equal temperament tuning (see p. 360). Instead, he immersed himself in the 'pure' tuning of the traditional Greek modes and in microtonal structures, becoming especially famous for his 43-note scale. Partch also constructed his own instrumentarium, creating variations on existing instruments, like an adapted viola with a long neck and a version of the lyre-like Greek Kithara, and incorporating 'found' materials such as bottles, artillery cases, hubcaps, and cloud chamber bowls.

All this fascinated Morris, opening his ears to intervallic relationships and timbres well beyond those of Western classical music as well as supporting his unruly inclinations. Perhaps experience of Partch stimulated his own percussion experiments with found objects while he played the piano. In *Boxcar Boogie*, Morris used Partch's *Castor and Pollux*, the second movement of *Plectra and Percussion Dances*.[46] The same score he choreographed again in 1980 for a dance that used the musical title. He set Partch's *Barstow* (1941) in a 1973 dance of the same name—a vocal score incorporating a hobo graffiti text 'Eight Hitchhiker Inscriptions' (Morris counts this as his first important dance); and finally his 'Studies on Ancient Greek Scales' from *Eleven Intrusions* (1946) in the 1998 dance *Greek to Me*.

In his pre-professional period, Morris worked with other unusual choices, like sixteenth-century French traditional music using crumhorns (for *Renaissance*, 1972), and the acidic fourth movement of Bartók's Fourth String Quartet (for *Ženska*, 1974, which was later inserted into *All Fours* (2003)). Less surprising, given his training, he arranged a number of Spanish dances to traditional music. Yet it is important that, from early in his career, Morris rarely looked for music written specifically for dance. In this respect, he followed the broader traditions of musical choice, including concert music, that had opened up in both ballet and modern dance in the early twentieth century (see pp. 80-1).

Already, as often as he could, Morris brought in live musicians to accompany his choreography, and this included two occasions when he had composed the music himself. In 1972, he wrote a score for a dance called *Mourning Without Clouds*, for two flutes, two clarinets, violin, viola and cello, and a chorus of six. At that time, he had no idea about the distinctions between written and concert pitch, or that the same written note C would sound as C on the flutes but as B-flat on the transposing clarinets. The result, he says, 'was terrible but it was way better than what I had in mind'.[47] In 1974, for *In Pruning My Roses*, he wrote a piece for cello and piano to precede a movement from a Shostakovich cello sonata. Smith was the cellist for both compositions. Although Morris is embarrassed by these early forays into musical composition, Smith remembers *Mourning* as reminiscent of the style of twentieth-century French composers like Satie or Jean Françaix. Impressed by these efforts, she wishes that he could have continued further as a composer.[48]

Occasionally, Morris expresses regret that he had so little in the way of piano lessons.[49] On the other hand, just as his unconventionally skewed dance training had a positive impact, it is quite likely that self-motivation made Morris what he is musically, and to advantage. Finding his own way, freed from the strictures of institutional training, meant that he could spend more time getting to know the musical repertoire and its technical aspects. He could also maintain that special, joyful immediacy of response, ever to be 'thrilled', 'shocked' or 'driven crazy' by what he heard.

Thanks to a work study programme that accounted for his multiple extra-curricular dance endeavours, Morris graduated early from high school, which meant that he could then concentrate on his career in dance. He made his trip to Europe (1973-74), then returned to Seattle, embarking on ballet classes with a respected local teacher Perry Brunson (for whom Cavalli played) and continuing to make dances and teach. But he soon knew that he had to leave for New York in order to gain the most challenging professional experience. He set off from the West Coast in January 1976 and then, apart from one dance *Brummagem* (to Beethoven, 1978, for Pacific Northwest Ballet), stopped making dances for four years. Instead, he grasped opportunities to get work as a dancer, with the companies of Eliot Feld, Lar Lubovitch, Hannah Kahn, and Laura Dean. All those he danced with used music regularly as a basis for their choreography, although this was a time when many of the more radical choreographers did not see this as the way forward. Music was also key to the work of the choreographers Morris auditioned for unsuccessfully—Twyla Tharp and Paul Taylor. Kahn taught him the most: her work demonstrated the structural rigour and understanding of musical principles that he sought for his own work. But with Dean, in 1982, overlapping with the formation of his own company, he toured India and Indonesia, which fuelled an interest in Asian music that lasts until this day.

The New Professional—and a New Dance Group 1980-88

The Mark Morris Dance Group (MMDG) was formed in 1980, and presented its first performance at the Merce Cunningham Studio in New York. That programme included revivals of *Barstow*, *Ženska* and *Brummagem* as well as premieres of *Dad's Charts* (a solo for Morris himself) and *Castor and Pollux*. On the basis of this show, Morris's company was invited to appear at Dance Theater Workshop, New York's most influential centre for experimental dance; it became his regular New York venue for several years.

The story of Morris's meteoric rise to fame across this first decade has often been told. Suddenly, at the tail end of the American dance boom of the 1970s and early 1980s, a bright new voice arrived on the scene. Crucially, in 1983, the influential *New Yorker* dance critic Arlene Croce gave Morris a glowing review all to himself.[50] The following year, he appeared for a sold-out and widely-acclaimed season at the prestigious Next Wave Festival of the Brooklyn Academy of Music (BAM). He was already remarkably prolific, staging as many as nine, be they mainly short, dances in 1983, ten in 1984, and proving his versatility by working in a number of different modes.

Morris borrowed ideas from the more abstract, systems-based work of experimental choreographers he came across in New York, such as Trisha Brown and Lucinda Childs, yet much of his work was quite different: it contained narrative reference (of a non-linear kind) and was about people and feelings. He also introduced a certain comfort of recognition through links with the past. As Acocella suggests, he turned back to the history of American modern dance for inspiration, and to the various manners of its pioneers—their interest in the exotic Other, their heroism, exalted states and inner turmoil.[51] He borrowed, too, from their movement vocabularies as he saw fit. But he renewed these sources for the 1980s, introducing curious clashes of reference and strange mixtures of anger and humour. The musical component of his work was soon noted as special, particularly as he frequently talked about translating music in interviews. Indeed, by about 1987, some bad press had begun—for some critics, the music was *too* noticeable, the choreography *too* closely tied to it.[52] But this musical practice had a history in early American modern dance (see pp. 76-7).

MMDG started out as an informal group of friends, ten in total, although at first they were rarely contracted to perform as such. Two of Morris's longest and most ambitious works, for the full company, were only shown in New York: *Gloria* (Vivaldi, 1981) and *New Love Song Waltzes* (Brahms, 1982). But that all soon changed after late 1984, when Barry Alterman became manager[53] and company touring rapidly increased (across the US and to Europe—after a brief 1984 trip for three dancers to London's Dance Umbrella). Now, the dancers all came together much more regularly. (During this period, the company had its two main seasons in New York and Seattle. Feeling alien to the New York environment and much of its dance scene, however, Morris elected to make his home base back in Seattle between 1984 and 1988.) Nancy Umanoff was invited to deal with financial matters, joining as managing director officially in 1986: she became Executive Director in 2000, retaining this title while moving into the senior position after Alterman's departure from MMDG in 2006. Morris and company were fast movers. In 1986, the Public Broadcasting Station (PBS) made him the subject of an hour-long *Dance in America* television programme—he was only thirty.[54] During MMDG's visit to Stuttgart in 1987, Gérard Mortier, Director of the Théâtre Royal de la Monnaie in Brussels, saw a performance, which led directly to the next stage of Morris's career. Mortier immediately invited the group to move from the US to

Brussels, and, for three years, MMDG was the Monnaie's resident dance company.

Choreographing Music: The Next Stage

During the first period of his company's existence, Morris's music choices continued along the path established during his teens. This is no standard list for dance: it displays an enquiring mind and rare knowledge of the repertoire. Baroque and twentieth-century music he turned to most frequently, using some of the following composers more than once. They are listed here in their chronological order:

Baroque: Purcell, Couperin, Vivaldi, Domenico Scarlatti, Handel, JS Bach, Pergolesi, CPE Bach.

Eighteenth- and nineteenth-century: Haydn, Mozart, Sri Tyagaraja (the distinguished Indian composer), Beethoven, Schubert, Verdi, Brahms, Ponchielli.

Twentieth-century: Satie, Tcherepnin, von Dohnányi, Bartók, Stravinsky, Virgil Thomson, Henry Cowell, Gershwin, Poulenc, Partch, Shostakovich, Françaix, Nancarrow, Lou Harrison, Harold Budd, Herschel Garfein.

The selection here of American West Coast contemporary composers is noteworthy—not only Partch, but also Cowell, Budd, and Harrison, who became a regular collaborator during Morris's later career.

Morris also moved beyond 'classical' music. He chose country-western, popular contemporary Indian and Thai music that he had come across during his first visit to South Asia with Laura Dean, traditional songs from Romania and Tahiti, parlour songs, organ music of the kind played at skating rinks (like Milt Buckner for *Dad's Charts*), and, on a couple of occasions, raucous rock songs—by Yoko Ono and the folk punk group Violent Femmes.

There was a gradual reduction in work to 'popular' music and an increasing use of baroque music during this period. *Gloria* (Vivaldi, 1981) was Morris's first baroque setting while, as Acocella has computed, between the years 1985 and 1988, he choreographed at least two baroque pieces a year. The passion for this period of music has remained with Morris. He loves its dance rhythms (which he finds in every work, even those not intended for dance), its rigour and systematic tendencies, alongside its emotional expressivity.[55] It has to be stressed, however, that he rarely responds to it, or indeed any other old music, with a sustained period sense in the choreography. For him, this is simply music of today. Johann Sebastian

Bach is, for him, the ultimate in music, especially in powerful large works like the B Minor Mass and St Matthew Passion that Morris says he would never choreograph. In this early period, he set Bach once, the Concerto in C minor for two harpsichords, for *Marble Halls* (1985). Morris says that Handel, another favourite, taught him structure: in 1985, he made the solo *Jealousy* for himself to a chorus from the musical drama *Hercules*, which three months later became part of a series of settings entitled *Handel Choruses*. The same year, he came across Handel's oratorio *L'Allegro, il penseroso ed il moderato*, which made a deep impression. The recording he heard was by the Boston early music group Banchetto Musicale conducted by Martin Pearlman.[56] Morris's setting of this score came in 1988: it was his first Brussels premiere.

The 1980s were an especially exciting time for baroque music in general, springing from the energetic early music movement that had begun some years earlier. Morris was fully aware of this development, and the music scholar within him was excited by the ideas and controversies that it provoked. Period instruments produced fascinating new sounds, which Morris typifies as 'rustic...dangerously direct...less mannered',[57] while 'authentic' period styles of performance practice introduced a new, bracing aesthetic. He was particularly inspired by the work of the English pioneer David Munrow and his Early Music Consort (formed with Christopher Hogwood). Since the 1960s, Munrow had travelled widely abroad, unearthing unusual instruments from a variety of cultures, which gave him ideas as to the kinds of instrument used in the medieval and Renaissance periods. The ease with which Munrow moved between folk and high culture was something Morris shared: he could make connections with his own Koleda practice and liked the fact that Munrow was 'wild...not precious'.[58]

The early music movement was one of those rare phenomena based on academic research but immediately able to capture the public imagination. In this instance, the original scholarship produced a cascade of further ideas, some of these undermining the original authenticity principles. By the 1980s, there were those who aimed towards a pure text, likened to cleaning the dirt from paintings in order to get at an original,[59] while others felt that musical eloquence and personal stamp should not be relinquished in the interest of stylistic authenticity. There were others still, led by the musicologist Richard Taruskin, who considered that the ambitions of the purists were fundamentally false and more a reflection of the dry twentieth-century aesthetic (promoted by Stravinsky, for example) than of any real past. Key publications that fuelled the debate were the 1984 issue of *Early Music*, which contained a group of articles under the title 'The Limits of Authenticity' and Nicholas Kenyon's edited collection *Authenticity and*

Early Music (1988, drawn from a symposium at the Oberlin Conservatory of Music),[60] both including contributions by Taruskin.

Morris used live period instruments for the first time in 1986, for an all-baroque programme with the St Luke's Chamber Ensemble conducted by Michael Feldman at the Brooklyn Academy of Music (BAM) (*Marble Halls* (Bach) and two premieres, *Pièces en Concert* (Couperin) and *Stabat Mater* (Pergolesi)). When Morris took this programme to Ottawa, the recordings he used followed the same philosophy, for instance, Trevor Pinnock's account of the Bach Concerto for two harpsichords for *Marble Halls*.[61] This was the year when Hogwood, then at the Academy of Ancient Music (Cambridge), took up directorship of the Handel and Haydn Society in Boston. It is little known that Hogwood was initially billed to conduct the first performance of *L'Allegro*, in 1987, in collaboration with dancers from Boston Ballet, the idea then being that the orchestra would be fully visible on a raised platform above the stage.[62] So Morris was, even at this point in his career, connected with one of the biggest names in the business. But collaboration with Hogwood was delayed for some years: the *L'Allegro* project shifted to Morris's own company in Brussels a year later, with different musicians. Within his own repertory, Morris had already used a Hogwood recording in *Love, You Have Won* (Vivaldi, 1984) with English soprano Emma Kirkby, his favourite singer during the 1970s and early 1980s. He was deeply impressed by Kirkby's 'white tone', and refers to her as the 'boy soprano, the voice of early music' at that time. Later, he went to hear her live in concert in Seattle. But he also became interested in the more 'bizarre, dramatic' style of another English singer Glenda Simpson.[63]

It is noteworthy that half of Morris's musical choices during this period were vocal music. Acocella suggests that no other Western choreographer since the Renaissance has such a record.[64] This interest is probably partly because of his background in the singing dances of Spain and the Balkans, also because he loves direct contact with the physical, sounding body that singing affords (see p. 19). But words open up further possibilities by providing a programme.[65] They can, if the choreographer chooses, be matched in mime, or in much less detail, in either case, offering another structural principle, alongside that of the music.

At this stage, Morris showed a clear preference for using short pieces of music, or scores comprising a series of short sections (like *Gloria*). Many of his songs to popular music, for instance, have simple, economical structures. Still, on several occasions, beginning in his teens, he used long, multi-movement sonatas, concertos and trios containing complex musical forms: for instance, the Bach Concerto in *Marble Halls*; Poulenc's Sonata for Clarinet and Piano—in this case borrowing the musical title for his dance;

the second and third movements of Beethoven's piano trio Op. 11 in B-flat major for *Brummagem*; and the Shostakovich cello sonata—the second movement for *In Pruning My Roses*, and all but the first movement for *Vestige* (1984).

Morris continued to teach himself choreography through musical principles. *Gloria* he saw as a lesson in counterpoint and SATB (Soprano, Alto, Tenor and Bass) vocal organisation, both of which structural principles could be used as a starting point for choreographic construction. He made a series of studies. There was *Canonic 3/4 Studies* (1982), to piano miniatures by Czerny and others, selected and arranged by Harriet Cavalli to sound like music for ballet class. Morris created this dance at a summer workshop in Seattle as an essay in 3/4 time—he was practising for *New Love Song Waltzes* choreographed later the same year.[66] There were also studies in movement vocabulary, *Caryatids* (Harold Budd, 1983) and *Slugfest* (in silence, 1984) as preparation for, respectively, *The Death of Socrates* (Satie, 1983) and *Championship Wrestling After Roland Barthes* (Herschel Garfein, 1984). In these instances, the working process guaranteed freedom from detailed musical structure. All the time, too, Morris sharpened his skills in score reading.

Two of Morris's biggest challenges came with specially-written scores by Herschel Garfein. *Forty Arms, Twenty Necks, One Wreathing* (1984) was commissioned by the prestigious American Dance Festival (ADF, in Durham, North Carolina) for its Young Choreographers and Composers in Residence Program. Morris chose to work with Garfein after listening to a variety of tapes submitted for the residency programme.[67] This collaboration led to the trilogy *Mythologies* (1986) based on polemical essays by the French philosopher Roland Barthes: first *Championship Wrestling*, then *Soap-Powders and Detergents* and *Striptease*. The full trilogy premiered in Boston and was later presented in New York and revived for Brussels. It was commissioned by Dance Umbrella, Boston and supported by a 'New Works' grant from the Massachusetts Council on The Arts and Humanities. *Mythologies* used taped-synthesized as well as live music, while *Soap-Powders* required an orchestra and four solo singers. Collaboration is always expensive, and the two men made the most of these funded opportunities.

Garfein was just out of the New England Conservatory, influenced at the time primarily by the late music of Stravinsky and Aaron Copland, and by Karlheinz Stockhausen's *Gesang der Jünglinge* (1956). 'Mark was completely un-phased by the complexity,' Garfein recalls, 'which was bigger than anything else he'd undertaken to date'.[68] The choreographer simply set to work, fast. In both cases, he had to choreograph while the music was still being created (literally from scratch, or from tapes prior to orchestration), and there were times when Garfein came up with the goods very late. As for *Striptease*, dancer Tina Fehlandt recalls: 'It wasn't choreographed musically because we didn't have the music. Things were incredibly fluid until the last minute.'[69] But Garfein's lateness is not at all unusual amongst composers, as Morris was to discover later.

The Garfein experience taught Morris two important lessons: that he could make a virtue out of the particular resources (including time) available to him when working on a new dance, and that he could learn new things— for instance, about choreomusical independence—in the process. Garfein appreciated Morris's flexibility:

> Part of Mark's brilliance lies in fully acknowledging the forces available to him—whether musical, theatrical, choreographic—and then working without excuse or apology to fully realise a piece within the allotted time and for the particular venue.[70]

On a few other occasions, not having access to a musical score resulted in a certain independence from the music. Sometimes, this was simply a question of money, as with the 1983 *Death of Socrates*—the French publishers were asking for something in the region of 150 dollars for the Satie score.[71] When it came to *Frisson* (1985), set to Stravinsky's *Symphonies of Wind Instruments*, Morris could not afford the hire cost of a perusal score. So, in these circumstances, he worked solely through listening to recordings. On a couple of occasions too, and only in this early period, Morris was led by an idea *before* choosing his music, in other words, he found music to suit an existing concept. For *One Charming Night* (1985), he wanted to make a vampire dance after reading Anne Rice's *Interview with the Vampire* and then found Purcell songs to set alongside it. Another time he wanted to make a dance alluding to a party. He already knew a Trio by Jean Françaix, not especially fine music, certainly not part of the canon, but decided that it would suit his dance theme—*My Party* (1984)—very well.[72]

Occasionally, Morris choreographed for companies other than his own. Beginning in 1986, he created his first ballets, for Boston Ballet, Joffrey Ballet and, for American Ballet Theatre—one of his most successful ever, a piano ballet *Drink to Me Only with Thine Eyes* (Thomson, 1988). He worked with Seattle Opera, in 1986 creating a 'Dance of the Seven Veils' for Richard Strauss's *Salome* (in which Josephine Barstow stripped down to a G-string) and the 'Ballabili' for the Triumphal Scene of *Aïda*, and in 1988, dances for their *Orpheus & Eurydice* (the first of his three settings of Gluck's score). He also directed their production of *Die Fledermaus* (Johann Strauss II, 1988). In 1987, he commenced his collaboration with the experimental director Peter Sellars, providing dances for Houston Opera's production of *Nixon in*

China. It was his first encounter with the composer John Adams, with whom he collaborated on two later opera and ballet productions.

As for using live music, there was often no way at this stage in his career that Morris could afford it. (Today, well-established, he claims that if you want something enough, you find a way of getting it.) Involving touring as well as employing musicians, it is very expensive. Obviously, for music that only exists in recording, this was never an issue and, indeed, Morris always preferred to use music intended for recording if he could not count on live music.[73] But he was already fully committed to the principle of liveness and, by the mid-80s, two factors complemented each other usefully: his growing interest in baroque music and rapidly developing reputation. By this point, he was beginning to attract the professional connections and funding that made live music a reality.

To begin with, a pianist would play for just one item on a programme, or a pianist and one other musician. The first all-live music concert took place in Seattle in 1984, when Page Smith organised a group of musician friends to support the MMDG: *My Party* (Françaix), *Prelude and Prelude* (Cowell), *Love, You Have Won* (Vivaldi) and *She Came from There* (Dohnányi). The musical requirements were a soprano, harpsichord, and string trio (violin, viola and cello). Garfein brought with him a mixed ensemble of six musicians for *Forty Arms* at ADF. As for larger instrumental forces, the ballet and opera companies had their own permanent orchestras, but opportunities improved for MMDG itself. Alea III, the Contemporary Music Ensemble of Boston University played for the premiere of *Mythologies* (conducted by Theodore Antoniou); later, Garfein himself conducted a similar ensemble at the Manhattan Center Ballroom in New York.

Other music groups were eager to collaborate, like St Luke's Chamber Ensemble (conducted by Michael Feldman) for the 1986 performances at BAM. It is a group that Morris has worked with on many occasions since. Then, for the premiere of *Strict Songs* (Harrison, 1987), the Seattle Men's Chorus was enlisted. This dance completed a richly-resourced live-music BAM programme in 1988: after *New Love Song Waltzes* (Brahms), *Fugue and Fantasy* (Mozart, orchestrated), *Sonata for Clarinet and Piano* (Poulenc) and *One Charming Night* (Purcell). A group of solo singers was hired, and the Orchestra of St Luke's and New York City Gay Men's Chorus brought in for the second and last items.

The Music World: Key Contacts

Meanwhile, Morris acquired an influential circle of artist friends and collaborators who played an important part in his career for many years. There was the mezzo-soprano Lorraine Hunt (later Hunt Lieberson), who became his favourite of all singers, with a richer voice than Kirkby, and who remained a regular collaborator with MMDG until her death in 2006. Her first appearance with Morris's company came in 1988 when she sang in the BAM *New Love Song Waltzes*, followed soon by *L'Allegro*, *Dido* and *Mythologies* in Brussels (she was originally billed to take the title role in Morris's 2007 production of Gluck's *Orfeo* for the Metropolitan Opera). But Sellars, the theatre/opera director, was the lynchpin. Morris met him when the MMDG performed at the 1985 PepsiCo Summerfare at SUNY Purchase (a campus of New York's state university) and Sellars directed Handel's *Giulio Cesare* (Hunt's operatic debut). In 1987, Morris choreographed for his *Nixon in China* and in 1988, a rock 'n' roll dance to the Fandango in the Act III Wedding Scene of *Le Nozze di Figaro*. This was the period when Sellars directed his famous trilogy of Mozart Da Ponte operas: *Così fan Tutte*, *Don Giovanni* and *Figaro*.

Through Sellars, Morris met Craig Smith, the conductor of *Giulio Cesare*. Smith was Artistic Director of Emmanuel Music in Boston, a collective of local singers and instrumentalists founded by him at Emmanuel Church. There, he led performances of the complete cycle of Bach cantatas, the first of their kind in the US, later extending his range to perform other genres of music, including operas, several by Handel (their first productions in the US) and Mozart. Prompted by Sellars, Smith joined Morris for two years at the Monnaie in Brussels, conducting performances of *L'Allegro* and *Dido*. The two men maintained a strong friendship and professional relationship until Smith's death in 2007; Smith also frequently conducted and toured internationally with MMDG. Other regular singers with Sellars featured in Morris's own oratorio/opera productions, like the baritone James Maddalena, and soprano Jayne West, who joined Morris during the Brussels years. But undoubtedly Sellars' most influential gesture in driving forward his friend's career was to suggest to Mortier that Morris take over at the Monnaie in Brussels. Years later, in 2006, it was Sellars again who forged the connection with the Vienna New Crowned Hope Festival for the premiere of *Mozart Dances*. (Through him too, Morris encountered designers whom he continued to work with in his later career, for sets Adrianne Lobel, and lighting James F. Ingalls.)

Towards the end of this period, Morris reached the point when he needed to work with a regular pianist for rehearsals and performances as well as company technique class. This was an important moment within his musical practice. It is a much more efficient and flexible arrangement to work with a pianist than to a fixed tape, and Morris was, after all, moving away from using recordings in performance. During his teaching stints at the University of Washington in Seattle, he had enjoyed working with Linda

Dowdell as his accompanist. Even if not conservatory-trained, she was a strong musician and, unlike many conservatory musicians, had the skills to improvise for class—which is always useful for expanding stylistic range and interlocking with dance combinations in different ways. She could also sight-read well and perform from existing scores. When the move to Brussels was settled, Morris invited Dowdell to play for the SUNY Summer Workshop in 1988 and for the opening rehearsals there of *L'Allegro*. Although Brussels offered him a rehearsal pianist, he insisted on bringing her with him.

In this early period, as we will see later, Morris tried out many different kinds of music and choreomusical tactics, while continuing to develop his musical skills. He was highly experimental, racing enthusiastically from one new experience to another. Within eight years, he choreographed some sixty pieces.

Brussels and Baryshnikov: Summer 1989-91

Morris's Brussels 'story' has been told so many times that it hardly needs repeating: about MMDG turning into one of the largest modern dance companies in the world, the luxurious conditions afforded by public subsidy, huge music resources and rehearsal opportunities (a large orchestra as well as choir, the main reason why Morris accepted the invitation), a beautiful baroque opera house theatre (the Monnaie) with excellent technical facilities, a massive design budget, and a physical home with several rehearsal studios.[74] Probably no other modern dance company in the world had such facilities. Yet it was a situation full of tensions—critics often antagonistic towards Morris's choreographic style (the French and Flemish feuding amongst themselves[75]) and judging him against his predecessor Maurice Béjart, Morris's brutally honest public behaviour as a gay man and outspoken artist, not to mention the internal strife between the Morris team (which included Alterman and Umanoff) and the Monnaie bureaucracy. There were also tensions within the new, much enlarged Monnaie Dance Group/Mark Morris. From twelve experienced dancers, the company expanded to twenty-seven upon its arrival, with many younger recruits. Contracts ran for three years from summer 1988 to summer 1991.

Despite the difficulties, some of the best works that Morris ever made came out of this period, and the Brussels experience has had a lasting effect on MMDG operations ever since. Faced with a totally new, enlarged situation for working, Morris thought big and his ambition immediately paid off. He continued to develop his musical skills, and on a larger scale. His first two Brussels pieces *L'Allegro, il Penseroso ed il Moderato* (to the Handel oratorio allegorising different states of human mind and feeling) and *Dido and Aeneas* (a dance setting of Purcell's opera) turned out to be the most acclaimed of all his dances, and premiered within a few months of each other. *L'Allegro* is widely regarded as one of a mere handful of top-rank dance masterpieces of the twentieth century. *The Hard Nut*, however, the last piece that Morris made in Brussels, a 1970s period setting of *The Nutcracker*, turned out to be the only unqualified success there. All three of these works have remained staples of his repertory, the first two performed at least once a year, often more, except for one six-year gap in *Dido* scheduling which happened when Morris stopped dancing the role of Dido himself, while *The Hard Nut* is a regular Christmas favourite. It is worth considering that Morris would probably never have had the financial backing to premiere *L'Allegro* and *The Hard Nut* back home in the US. Once he had made these works, he owned them both for future use. When he left Brussels, he was allowed to purchase at a good price and take with him the sets and costumes of all the dances he made for the Monnaie.

Larger-scale as Morris's pieces were during the Monnaie period, they were fewer in number given the time available, eleven in total, and, in addition, two opera productions. He made three of these dances outside the Monnaie, one for the Paris Opera Ballet (*Ein Herz*), and two for the White Oak Dance Project (*Motorcade* and *A Lake*), his joint venture with the Russian ballet superstar Mikhail Baryshnikov. (White Oak took its name from the plantation which was owned by the philanthropist Howard Gilman and which housed the dance project.) Work made outside the Monnaie is highlighted in the following list:

1988 *L'Allegro, il Penseroso ed il Moderato* (Handel)
1989 *Dido and Aeneas* (Purcell)
Love Song Waltzes (Brahms)
Wonderland (Schoenberg: *Accompaniment-Music for a Motion Picture*, Op. 34; *Five Orchestral Pieces*, Op. 16)
1990 *Behemoth* (without music)
Going Away Party (Bob Wills and His Texas Playboys—songs)
***Ein Herz* Paris Opera Ballet (Bach Cantata BWV134)**
Pas de Poisson (Satie—*Cinéma*, symphonic interlude from *Relâche*)
***Motorcade* White Oak Dance Project (Saint-Saëns Septet in E-flat major, Op. 65)**
1991 *The Hard Nut* (Tchaikovsky's 'The Nutcracker')
The Death of Klinghoffer (John Adams—opera directed by Peter Sellars, choreography by Morris)
***A Lake* White Oak Dance Project (Haydn Horn Concerto, No. 2 in D)**[76]
Le Nozze di Figaro (Mozart—opera directed by Morris)

Baryshnikov had just left his job as Artistic Director of American Ballet

Theatre and was keen to work with Morris again after his ABT commission *Drink to Me Only with Thine Eyes*. So he joined the MMDG for the premieres of *Wonderland* and *Pas de Poisson*, and would have danced the role of Young Drosselmeier in *The Hard Nut*, had he not been injured.[77] Meanwhile, in 1990, Morris and he set up White Oak as a small company of mature dancers. Morris created new pieces, rehearsed work from his existing repertory for the new company and helped select the dancers (in its third, 1991 tour, he danced himself). White Oak shared Morris's principle of having live music as often as possible and although, after 1991, he became less central to it, Morris made further solos for Baryshnikov over the years: *Three Preludes* (Gershwin, 1992), *Three Russian Preludes* (Shostakovich, 1995) and *Peccadillos* (Satie, 2000). (White Oak folded in 2002, by which time it was a mixed repertory company.) In 1990, the collaboration with Baryshnikov, as well as creation of *L'Allegro*, became the subject of a London Weekend Television *South Bank Show*.[78]

Most of the Monnaie works made use of the extended live musical resources now available to Morris. Several used orchestral scores: *L'Allegro* and *Dido* needing chorus and solo singers in addition, and *Wonderland* requiring as many as ninety-five musicians (the only time the work was repeated after Brussels, in New York in 1990, a recording had to be used). There was one silent piece *Behemoth*, the only large piece that Morris has ever made without musical accompaniment, a stark construction lasting thirty-eight minutes. *The Hard Nut* was Morris's first use of a ballet score with a narrative already built into it. If he has always tended to choose music not written for dance, he says that he chose this score partly because it had been overused—as muzak as well as in concert suites and traditional ballet—and that he wanted people to hear it in a new way. He conceived of the score in a more scholarly and purist manner than usual, having it played in the tempos intended by Tchaikovsky and complete, with everything in the correct order. (*The Hard Nut* was filmed for PBS television during this period, broadcast in 1992.) Only one piece was made to a recording during Morris's stay at the Monnaie, and that, too, became a favourite: the funny-melancholy *Going Away Party* to the western swing songs of Bob Wills and His Texas Playboys. For one week in 1990, Morris devised a special programme called 'Loud Music', which used recorded music throughout: *Ballabili*, *Going Away Party*, *Lovey* (1985, heavily amplified, to the folk punk Violent Femmes) and *The "Tamil Film Songs in Stereo" Pas de Deux* (1983). There was one ironic exception, which Morris calls 'the loudest of all'—the silent *Behemoth*—which was noisily interrupted by the ambient sounds of 'throat-clearing' and outdoor 'ice-cream trucks'.[79]

Morris revived a number of works from his existing repertory to show in

Brussels, performing them in other European countries and bringing them back to the US each year during seasonal breaks. His new *Love Song Waltzes* was sometimes set to follow the older *New Love Song Waltzes*, the two Brahms scores (*Liebeslieder* and *Neue Liebeslieder*) paired as Balanchine had done back in 1960, although billed in reverse order. Morris also seized the opportunity to experience several older pieces with live music, for the first time, *Frisson*, the very popular *Gloria* and, once again, after BAM in 1986, *Stabat Mater*. The situation was quite different when MMDG toured in America or around Europe. Then, again, except for *L'Allegro* and *Dido*, which have always been performed with live music, this was a rarity.

Morris encountered a new range of European musicians during this period, not only those regularly contracted to the Monnaie. For *Gloria*, the small ensemble known as the John Strange Singers was brought over from the UK (conducted by Craig Smith, with Lorraine Hunt and Jayne West as the soprano soloists). Several opportunities to work with baroque period-instrument specialists presented themselves. There was the conductor Philippe Herreweghe and the orchestra of his Collegium Vocale Ghent, who played for a 1989 Monnaie programme including *Marble Halls, Love, You Have Won* and *Stabat Mater*, and later with his choir La Chapelle Royale and the Freiburger Barockorchester for the 1991 performances of *L'Allegro* at the Théâtre des Champs-Elysées in Paris. Two months later, for the Paris performances of *Dido*, MMDG collaborated with Les Musiciens du Louvre from Grenoble, then conducted by Marc Minkowski. In the meantime, in 1990, Morris met his future collaborator, the British conductor Nicholas McGegan. He had taken over directorship of San Francisco's Philharmonia Baroque Orchestra in 1985 and led the first New York performances of *L'Allegro* and *Dido*. (McGegan has conducted these works many times since.)

With his own close band of musician friends, Morris also enjoyed informal musical activities. He remembers vividly that, within a week of arriving in Brussels, he hosted a sing-along with Dowdell, Garfein (composer of *Mythologies*) and Hunt in his apartment. The project was shape-note singing, a mainly sacred American genre of the eighteenth and nineteenth centuries that was especially popular in the south and owed a great deal to country folk music.[80] Morris adored the full-throated, lusty style and, as usual, the experience of community that it offered. No matter that it was not received as classical high art.

Dowdell was promoted to the position of Musical Director of MMDG during this period. Her job had grown from merely playing for class and rehearsal. As she once admitted: 'What happened to me is really strange. I am not a world-class musician.'[81] When on tour, she occasionally played for performances as well (in New York, Boston and Vienna, all in 1990), although the Monnaie provided other pianists for its own seasons. By then, too, she was coaching musicians, preparing them to work alongside Morris's choreography, sometimes travelling ahead on tour in order to do so. During 1990-91, she expanded her activities to become pianist and Music Director for White Oak.

Closer to music: Forwards as an institution 1992-

In Brussels, the manner in which Morris talked about his aesthetic principles began to change: 'I'm into classical thinking now,' he announced in a 1990 interview during one of his visits to the US, 'not ballet, you understand, but classicism'.[82] The label 'classicist' he continues to use today, citing Balanchine and Cunningham as his main choreographic inspirations and stressing that he no longer needs to make work of the angry-joking kind. During this later period, he has been more concerned with processes of refinement and paring down to essentials, especially getting deeper into musical matters. Thus, he said in 2001: 'Instead of doing everything, I try to see if I can do as little as possible and get a really streamlined, efficient result. I don't mean that to sound cold, I just want it to be clear.'[83] More recently, however, he has moderated this stance yet again: as for *Socrates* (Satie, 2010), getting to the ultra-essential, but then adding layer to layer, 're-embracing complexity' after simplicity.[84]

Morris returned from Brussels a highly experienced, internationally recognised artist. He had been watched and eagerly supported by many critics from outside Belgium during this period (especially those from the US and the UK), and by then had a prolific track record and a large repertory to offer. Today, MMDG is over thirty years old and the total number of Morris's dances performed by the group is 136. Approximately 20-25 dances are held as current repertory, the pool of dances drawn upon in any single season. The company remains large, although smaller than in Brussels (on average eighteen dancers). The scope of MMDG touring continued to increase after Brussels: around the US every year, to western Europe and Canada occasionally (most often to the UK, where national tours have often accompanied London seasons), but also, from time to time, further afield: Australia, Israel and New Zealand (all twice), Brazil, Hong Kong, Japan, Russia, Bermuda and, most recently, China, Cambodia, Timor-Leste and Taiwan. Both then and now, *L'Allegro*, supported by local orchestras, and, to a lesser extent, *Dido*, have been the mainstay of the repertory, the pieces that people most want to see if they are new to Morris, and the pieces most likely to lure people back. (Indeed, *L'Allegro* inspired a woman in New Zealand to leave money in her will to MMDG.) In 1993, Acocella's book came out—at the age of thirty-seven, Morris was ready for a biography—and in 2001, the luxurious and beautiful tome of photographs and essays on *L'Allegro* was published.

If Acocella proposed that Morris and company became an institution during the Brussels years,[85] that status was doubly assured in 2001 with the opening of the Mark Morris Dance Center in Brooklyn, which remains his home base. Here, there is not only a suite of studios and company offices, but also a main studio performance space for informal showings (the Martha Duffy Performance Space), large enough to house full-scale opera as well as MMDG rehearsals. There is a school, too, which is not a conservatoire aiming to produce professional dancers, but rather a local dancing school based on the open principles that Morris grew up with in Seattle. It welcomes children of all ages as well as adults, provides an education in dance styles of many kinds (including a ground-breaking programme in dance for people with Parkinson's Disease) and has a live music policy throughout. No other modern dance company in the US enjoys such a well-appointed and spacious environment for work.

After the millennium, there were some key changes in the manner in which the company operated. Morris himself began to stop regular dancing. With age, warming up the body for performance takes longer, and, he said: 'When I looked around the stage, I thought, *I don't even know these people. I feel like the crazy-scary uncle.*'[86] He performed the major role of Dido for the last time in 2000. As time went on, he began to take on 'older-man' roles, separating himself from his group of dancers, as the 'lech' in a bar in *From Old Seville* (Requiebros, 2001) and in a series of solos: *Peccadillos, Serenade* (Harrison, 2003) and the slow movement of *Italian Concerto* (Bach, 2007). In 2012, he took the role of Dr Stahlbaum (father of Fritz and Marie) in *The Hard Nut*. He remains a wholly charismatic dancer, light, tender and wicked. But he spends his time on other creative activities: more ballets, more music-related teaching, and more opera—since Brussels, he has worked with major companies such as English National Opera, the Royal Opera, New York City Opera and The Metropolitan Opera (now directing as well as choreographing). In 2006, Matthew Rose, MMDG member from 1997, became his assistant, soon to be titled Rehearsal Director, the position he still holds. Sometimes, dancers (occasionally former dancers returning 'home'), have taken on some responsibility for reviving dances or coaching roles—understanding the intentions and innuendo lying behind the movement, although Rose's role has increased inasmuch as he now has first-hand experience of all new repertory.

Promoting Liveness

In 1996, the MMDG live music policy was made public, but Umanoff stresses that it came about logically and organically. The company always used live music, whenever possible. Even in the 1980s, as we have seen, there might be a pianist for one item on a programme or a pianist and one other musician. But from 1996, liveness has happened at every performance and for nearly every work performed. Morris wrote his speech on the subject in 1998 (see p. 19) and has continued to mention the policy in just about every interview since. Exceptions are rare, occasional pieces set to orchestral scores and the few works that only exist in recording, like *The "Tamil Film Songs in Stereo" Pas de Deux* (1983), *Deck of Cards* (1983, to popular songs) and the 2012 *A Wooden Tree*, to songs written and performed by the Scottish poet-singer Ivor Cutler. Even the very popular *Going Away Party* was performed live for the big 25th anniversary celebrations of MMDG in Brooklyn (2006) by the country swing band Western Caravan, except the cover band did not have the trademark style of the late career of Bob Wills and His Texas Playboys, and Morris reverted to the original recording after that.[87] *Dancing Honeymoon* (1998), a medley of songs popularised in the 1920s and 30s by Gertrude Lawrence and Jack Buchanan, started off using the original recordings, but was later transcribed for piano, drums, violin and soprano.

The MMDG Music Ensemble was officially formed in 2004, indicating the growth in its status: biographies were included for the first time in the company's twenty-fifth anniversary programme (2006). Again, this formation was entirely organic, the 'Ensemble' name applied retrospectively. Under Dowdell, there was already a core group of musicians who would accompany MMDG as the repertory demanded, but by now this had grown to a touring group of five to seven players. The Ensemble has always operated very flexibly as core members within a larger 'pool', sometimes functioning as an orchestra, for instance in performances of *Gloria*, *Dido* and the 2006 *Hard Nut* at Bard College, upstate New York. In 2013, the Ensemble played an especially prominent role at California's Ojai Music Festivals (the year when Morris was Music Director, see p. 48), a total of thirty-one members performing independently in concert as well as with MMDG, as soloists, in small groups and as an orchestra. Another sign of their standing is that their biographies are now normally integrated with, not separately listed from, those of the dancers in programmes. Ensemble members are of a very high standard, with strong international professional careers outside their work for Morris, and frequently singled out for critical praise.

Although every effort is made to bring into being the projects that Morris is passionate about, whatever resources are required, MMDG programming, especially where touring is concerned, is directly affected by the number of musicians who can be covered financially (fees, travel and accommodation). Such practical considerations involving the live music component are a major factor determining what Morris pieces are seen, where, and how often. So there are piano shows, or piano and violin shows, and bigger shows still when other possibilities present themselves. For instance, when the group toured the UK for five weeks (eight venues) in autumn 2009, they could field a pianist Colin Fowler and violinist Georgy Valtchev, while the standard Bob Wills recording was used for *Going Away Party*. In the centre of the tour, however, for the four performances in London, the original two players were supplemented by five singers and, to make up a string quartet with Valtchev, three more string players.

In 1997, 1998 and 2001, the MMDG were able to tour the US and UK regularly with the six/seven strong early music group ARTEK (Art of the Early Keyboard) and 458 Strings from New York. This was for one dance, *I Don't Want to Love* (1996; set to Monteverdi madrigals)—in addition to MMDG Music Ensemble members—and it is a rare example of an external group touring with MMDG. But the financial requirements of this ensemble were relatively modest, and the late 90s was a period when fee expectations in the arts were lower, and higher funds available, than today (it was the 'dotcom' era). Following the 2009 recession, when the financial situation became far more difficult, the company has returned to performing more one-night stands and in venues (offering relatively low fees) that they would have turned down ten years ago. Still, they were able to take both the MMDG Music Ensemble and the choir of Trinity Church, New York with them to Moscow in 2010. A grant from the Trust of Mutual Understanding supplemented the fee from the presenters, but, most importantly, Trinity was inspired by the opportunity and willing to share the financing of the expedition.[88]

It is a stroke of good fortune that one of Morris's most popular pieces, *Grand Duo* (1993), has a score (by Harrison) requiring the modest resources of violin and piano. On the other hand, at one time, you would have been forgiven for suspecting that *Frisson* (1985; to Stravinsky's *Symphonies of Wind Instruments*—scored for woodwind and brass) was either not a good piece or that Morris had lost interest in it. This is not at all the case. Rarely has this unusual instrumental ensemble been practically feasible, especially as it fits just one item on any programme. *Frisson* has been revived to live music only at the Monnaie (1988) and at the Tanglewood Music Center (2003 and 2011, see p. 49), very successfully on both occasions.

Each of Morris's leading musicians has had a slightly different work profile, it seems, according to their skills and interests, while feeding changing individual needs. Fowler, who has been with the MMDG Music Ensemble since 2006, now occupies central position, not only performing, but acting as rehearsal pianist and Music Director, preparing other musicians for final rehearsals and performances. He is also a conductor, in company rehearsals, and, for the first time, in performance: in 2013, *Mozart Dances*, at the University of Texas, Austin. He maintains a separate professional career as a pianist, organist, church Music Director and college professor.[89] 'I'm a better musician through knowing him,' Fowler says of Morris.[90]

Dowdell continued as the first Music Director until 1998, having added to her responsibilities the hiring of musicians and occasional conducting in 1997: *Dido* in Seattle, *Gloria* at BAM, and, on several occasions, *Lucky Charms* (Ibert, 1994), including Ohio State University, Berkeley and Boston. Iverson then took over the role of Music Director (1998-2002). Like Dowdell, Iverson could improvise on the piano, so he too played for company class. But he came from a very different background, with a range of other skills that suited Morris well at this point in his career. Fundamentally un-schooled musically, Iverson was already a highly accomplished jazz pianist, but now keen to train himself into the classical requirements needed for MMDG Music Ensemble work. He also undertook arrangement of music for Morris, as in *Dancing Honeymoon*, when he had fun (and so did the dancers) adding different details to the violin part from one show to the next.[91] There was *Zwei Harvey Tänze* (1999) too, an improvised solo for Morris to Iverson's florid, cinematic rendering of 'Laura' by film composer David Raksin, followed by his own Boogie Woogie composition 'Flatbush Stomp'.

Iverson composed for the cross-cultural *Kolam* (2002), alongside the tabla extemporisations of Zakir Hussain and arrangements of George Brooks. Although it is never mentioned in programmes, he also composed one of the numbers for *Foursome* (2002), a work for four men set to piano pieces by Satie and Hummel. Iverson wrote in the style of Hummel—a private joke with Morris, although, today, he says, he can no longer tell which is by him and which by the real Hummel! Iverson left MMDG in order to extend his career with The Bad Plus jazz trio. He returned, however, in 2004 to create a score for *Violet Cavern*, which MMDG and the trio performed until 2008, and again in 2013 and 2014 with the trio's version of Stravinsky's *The Rite of Spring*, chosen by Morris for his setting *Spring, Spring, Spring*.

Cellist Wolfram Koessel took over as Music Director from 2004-8, after which he modified his position, remaining responsible for hiring musicians while expanding his independent professional career. Today, MMDG musicians are no longer expected to take on so many different roles as they did in the past. Again, the leading criterion is to have live music of the highest standard, and with musicians suited to particular contexts.

One further point is worth making about the programming of music in MMDG performances today. Umanoff observes a recent shift in the stance of company presenters: their increasing demand to be involved in programming discussions. She gives two examples. One recent presenter felt that *All Fours* (2003, to a Bartók String Quartet) was too 'adventuresome'. After much persuasion, the MMDG changed the order of the programme so that the Bartók came second rather than first. On another occasion, a presenter was desperate to have *V* (2001, to Schumann's Quintet for piano and strings) end the programme rather than *Grand Duo*. She had heard rave reports of *V*. But the Schumann considerably increased the music costs. In the end, the venue paid the difference.[92]

The Music World Comes to Morris

At the same time as Morris developed his own live music ensemble, the music world outside his MMDG 'family' began to secure its relationship with him and play a much more important role in company operations. Over the last twenty years, members of the American music press have taken him on as one of their own—like John Rockwell (*The New York Times*), Richard Dyer (*Boston Globe*) and Alex Ross (*The New Yorker*). Several academics with interests crossing music and dance began to write about his work: he is the only contemporary choreographer to have attracted major attention of this kind. Since the millennium, he has received two major music awards: in 2006, the WQXR Gramophone Special Recognition Award, and in 2010, the Leonard Bernstein Lifetime Achievement Award for the Elevation of Music in Society. Evidence too of the profound enthusiasm of the music world are the strong relationships established with organisations promoting concerts and opera, as well as with specific music ensembles.

Cal Performances at University of California, Berkeley was the first of these organisations, directed since 1986 by conductor Robert Cole until his retirement in 2009. Cole originally got to know Morris (and Sellars) at the PepsiCo Festivals of the 1980s. MMDG first performed in Berkeley in 1987 but, after their return from Brussels, became annual visitors. In 2002, Berkeley became their official second home, which means that they have sometimes appeared there twice or three times a year, including for regular Christmas seasons of *The Hard Nut*, although recently, just once a year. When, in 1996, Morris looked for a conductor for *Hard Nut*, Cole jumped at the opportunity: he was regular conductor of the work until 2010 (including in New York—in 2002 and 2010—and London in 2004). Berkeley was able to provide Morris with more than one orchestra, for different purposes: the Berkeley Symphony for *Hard Nut* and, for early music,

McGegan's Philharmonia Baroque Orchestra. But MMDG also suited Cole's ambition to broaden audiences, which they did in a manner unmatched by any other dance company. He told critic Allan Ulrich in 2001:

> It has been a happy marriage. Mark and I were made for each other. And, more than any other dance artist, he has increased our visibility. He attracts a much wider audience than most modern choreographers. We found, oddly, that our chamber music subscribers are strongly drawn to Mark.[93]

The close relationship with MMDG and Cal Performances continues under its current director Matías Tarnopolsky, who is also from a music background.

While Cal Performances has offered the most stable points on the Morris schedule as regards collaborations with orchestras and local choirs, there have been many other opportunities for events demanding large musical resources, continuing through to the present. Links have existed since the 1980s with the Brooklyn Philharmonic Orchestra at BAM, St Luke's in the New York area and, until his death in 2007, Craig Smith and Emmanuel Music in Boston. In 1995 came the first of several opportunities to stage *L'Allegro* in Manhattan, at Lincoln Center's New York State Theater (with the New York Chamber Society and Pro Arte Chorale, under Smith's direction). Seattle, Morris's home town, has remained especially supportive, the Seattle Symphony accompanying *L'Allegro* in 1994, and three different programmes annually 2008-10.[94] Here too, the Northwest Chamber Orchestra (with Page Smith playing cello continuo) and Choral Arts North West accompanied *Dido* in 1995 (with Dowdell conducting). Special, one-off collaborative opportunities arose too, such as the invitation from Christopher Hogwood in Boston for Morris to direct as well as stage dances for Gluck's *Orfeo*. This was the Italian version of the French *Orphée et Euridice* for which Morris first staged dances in Seattle in 1988. Supported by the Handel and Haydn Society period orchestra, the new production toured the US and concluded its run at the 1996 Edinburgh Festival.

Some of the most substantial invitations have come from the UK, indeed the Edinburgh Festival claimed Morris for six years running, 1992-7. (His company was by then too large for small venues in London like The Place Theatre. Morris was unhappy with the alternative facilities offered him at Sadler's Wells Theatre, and the company did not perform there until 1999, after its rebuilding as a new, bigger theatre, now London's major dance house.) Edinburgh gave the first performances of *Dido*, *L'Allegro* and *The Hard Nut* in the UK, in 1992, 1994 and 1995 respectively. It also presented two of his large-scale opera productions, *Orfeo* in 1996 and, in 1997, the premiere of Rameau's *Platée* with the Royal Opera (conducted by McGegan).

Morris showed several mixed repertory programmes in Edinburgh, and these were very generously supported. *I Don't Want to Love* was a 1996 Festival commission, introducing the spectacularly dramatic Monteverdi interpretations of Rinaldo Alessandrini's Concerto Italiano (see p. 66). On the same programme appeared the South Bank Gamelan Players, imported from London to perform Lou Harrison's score for *World Power* (1995). Edinburgh also offered Morris the services of the Emperor String Quartet in 1995 and, in 1993, a roster of world-class singers performing the two sets of Brahms' *Love Song Waltzes*—Amanda Roocroft, Felicity Palmer, John Mark Ainsley and Thomas Allen. Strong local ensembles were brought in: the Royal Scottish National Orchestra, Scottish Chamber Orchestra and Schola Cantorum of Edinburgh. In both 1992 and 1994, Morris was honoured with the Edinburgh International Critics Award, and in 1995, with the Scotsman/Hamada Trust Festival Prize.

When, in 1997, Morris's collaborations with the English National Opera (ENO) at the London Coliseum began, his association with the Edinburgh Festival abruptly ended. For him, opportunities often arise as others disappear. Here, apparently, Brian McMaster, Festival Director, was under pressure not to bring the same people back every year, especially if they also had a strong profile in London. It could be said that Morris shot himself in the foot with his own success.

Noticing that the two most celebrated of Morris's works called on operatic resources, ENO asked for those pieces, as part of their own season, offering their own singers (off stage) and orchestra in return. *L'Allegro* was, as so often, the first work to be scheduled, in 1997, introducing Morris to Jane Glover, a conductor who has worked regularly with him ever since. Then there was a double bill with *Dido* and the premiere of Virgil Thomson's *Four Saints in Three Acts* (2000), another opera in which only dancers appeared on stage and the subject of a second *South Bank Show*.[95] Finally, in 2006, Morris staged Purcell's *King Arthur*, for which he and Glover together developed an edited version of the score. She conducted further performances of *L'Allegro* at the Coliseum in 2010, borrowing the ENO Orchestra again for the occasion (this time with the New London Chamber Choir).

Morris understood, with good reason, that full-evening works set to orchestral scores are especially attractive to audiences. Two further 'large project' opportunities came to him from music presenters, this time with premieres in the US, but in co-production with international partners. The first, *Mozart Dances* (2006), was co-commissioned by Lincoln Center for the Performing Arts, the Barbican Centre, London, and the New Crowned Hope Festival, Vienna. Settings of two piano concertos and a four-hand piano sonata, and a collaboration with the pianist Emanuel Ax, it continues to be a success with audiences and critics. The project has attracted fine orchestras, such as the Academy of St Martins in the Fields in London and Camerata Salzburg in Austria. To a more mixed reception, Bard College commissioned *Romeo & Juliet, On Motifs of Shakespeare* in 2008, a co-production with a number of American and British producers including Cal Performances and the Barbican. Prompted by Leon Botstein, the conductor and President of Bard, this production was a collaboration with musicologist Simon Morrison, Professor at Princeton University, using the original 'happy-ending' version of Prokofiev's score. Since the premiere with the American Symphony Orchestra, *Romeo & Juliet* has been conducted by Stefan Asbury (enlisting the London Symphony Orchestra at the Barbican). Asbury has since become one of Morris's closest musician colleagues, like Glover and, in former times, Smith.

After 2000, several well-established music festivals began to embrace Morris, marking their first collaborations with dance. The Mostly Mozart Festivals at Lincoln Center have included him every year since 2002 (starting with *L'Allegro* and hosting this work again in 2005 and 2010); it was they who first presented *Mozart Dances*, using their own orchestra, conducted by Louis Langrée, the festival's Music Director. Chicago's Ravinia Festival has also hosted MMDG, drawing on the local orchestra Music of the Baroque for performances of *L'Allegro* (2005, conducted by McGegan) and *Mozart Dances* (2007, conducted by Glover, Music Director of this ensemble since 2002).

In 2013, Morris became the first non-professional musician invited to be Music Director of California's annual summer Ojai Festivals, the main one in Ojai itself (the 67th), and then the smaller version (Ojai North!) on the Berkeley campus a week later (under the auspices of Cal Performances). He had an entirely free rein to choose the programme, and his approach was innovative, focusing on the West Coast American 'school' and its link with dance, indeed history of dance. Thus, amongst a broad range of music intended for concert performance, there was music by Henry Cowell written for the modern dance pioneers Martha Graham and Doris Humphrey, by John Cage for Cunningham, and other scores more recently used by Morris himself and danced by MMDG at the Ojai Festivals—by Cowell, Harrison and Charles Ives (a kindred spirit from the East Coast). Audiences also had a chance to hear Harrison's Concerto for Organ with Percussion Orchestra, which Morris is keen to choreograph in the future, several pieces by the Alaskan-based, 'environmental' composer John Luther Adams, as well as a number of gamelan items from the Berkeley-based ensemble Sari Raras. In total, thirty-seven events took over the entire town of Ojai: concerts, dance performances, workshops, talks, as well as karaoke (with a live band), social dance sessions and two appearances of the local high school marching band. The Festival bore Morris's indelible stamp.

Ojai Artistic Director Thomas Morris welcomed Morris as a musician-choreographer who offered a route to hearing and understanding festival events from a fresh perspective. One enthusiast at the main festival described the dance performances in the *Los Angeles Times* as:

> Quite a unique visual enhancement to the contemporary Chamber music and a great introduction to modern dance... I'm sure the Dance Group enhanced the music experience for a large number of concert attendees.[96]

Yet Morris stated repeatedly that he did not aim to 'teach a lesson', rather simply to share music that he loves.

Annually since 2003 (except 2006 and 2014), operating in conjunction with the Tanglewood Music Festival and Boston Symphony Orchestra, the Tanglewood Music Center has explored its own mode of collaboration with Morris. It has commissioned new pieces[97] and given Morris a chance to present work with instrumental ensembles that are hard to resource in any other circumstances (including revivals of *Frisson*, set to Stravinsky's *Symphonies of Wind Instruments*). It provides unique opportunities as well for musicians and dancers to explore each other's art-forms and for Morris to coach early-career professionals (see p. 60). He and his company remain the Festival's only featured dance artists. Collaboration outcomes have exceeded expectations. On several occasions, Tanglewood Fellows have accompanied MMDG performances at the nearby Jacob's Pillow Festival later in the summer, and some have become members of the MMDG Music Ensemble.[98] The choreographer has also directed operas at Tanglewood without using dancers. In 2011, he undertook Milhaud's three 1927 *Opéras-minutes: La délivrance de Thesée, L'enlèvement d'Europe, L'abandon d'Ariane*, satires on classical themes, each lasting less than ten minutes. Using Tanglewood students, the operas formed part of 'An Evening of Opera and Song' directed by Morris, in heroic, formal style, and interspersed with baroque vocal numbers for contrast—by Monteverdi, Carissimi and Handel. Then, in 2013, he directed Benjamin Britten's Noh-inspired 1964 church parable *Curlew River*, here joining together singers and instrumentalists on stage.

Morris sees opera, like dance, as an expanded form of music. In most cases when the opera world approaches him, he creates the choreography on his own company, although other dancers may take over after the premiere season. His considerable body of work in opera may have come about partly as recognition of the natural link between early opera and dance,[99] but also because of a recent trend in opera practice to make productions more physically fluent.

Following the Sellars collaborations and those with Hogwood, McGegan and ENO, Morris was commissioned to direct a third *Orfeo* production in 2007 for The Metropolitan Opera, conducted by James Levine, a Haydn opera *L'Isola disabitata* (*The Desert Island*, 2009) for Gotham Chamber Opera (without dancers), after which Herschel Garfein invited him to workshop sections for a 2009 project based on Tom Stoppard's play *Rosencrantz & Guildernstern Are Dead*. The Met *Orfeo* proved especially successful, revived in 2011 and chosen for international cinema distribution in 2009 during the 'Live from the Met,' series. *Orfeo* performances resulted in further work with the two star singers who held the title role, soprano Stephanie Blythe who joined MMDG for Morris's *Dido and Aeneas* (2011 and 2012) and counter-tenor David Daniels, who, in 2012, invited Morris to create movement for MMDG dancers 'around' his Princeton University solo recital.

Increasingly, as this aspect of his career develops, Morris is invited to select the operas that interest him rather than taking on someone else's idea. For example, the Haydn opera was his own choice, and so was Handel's *Acis and Galatea* (in Mozart's more colourful arrangement), a 'through-danced' production that premiered in Berkeley in 2014 (with McGegan's Philharmonia Baroque) before further performances in Boston and Lincoln Center, New York.

Meanwhile, Morris continues to make ballets, fourteen since Brussels, for companies based in North America. He is interested in ballet not only for its vocabulary and forms, but also for musical reasons. For a start, as a tradition that is far more frequently led by music than modern dance, ballet usually guarantees large live music resources and sometimes unusual scorings that would hardly be feasible for his own touring group (like the four saxophones needed for Glazunov's Quartet in *Up and Down* (Boston Ballet, 2006)).

Since 1994, Morris has built a particularly strong rapport with San Francisco Ballet, for which he has made eight pieces to date, including a full-length production of *Sylvia* (Delibes, 2004). In 2009, the company presented its first all-Morris triple bill: *A Garden* (Couperin, arranged Richard Strauss, 2001), *Joyride* (Adams, 2008) and the especially popular *Sandpaper Ballet* (Leroy Anderson, 1999). Many of Morris's ballets have been revived and re-staged on other companies, including several abroad: such as Pacific Northwest Ballet, Houston Ballet, The Washington Ballet, and abroad, The Royal Ballet (Covent Garden), English National Ballet, Dutch National Ballet, Grand Théâtre de Genève, and Royal New Zealand Ballet.[100]

On a couple of occasions, Morris has made dances for folk ensembles, in 1994, *The Office* (Dvořák), for the Ohio-based Živili—Dances and Music of the Southern Slavic Nations (later staged for MMDG), and in 2012, *Carnival* (Saint-Saëns) for Philadelphia's Voloshky Ukrainian Dance Ensemble.

A Cellist and a Pianist

Another development during this period was collaboration with individual star artists. The singers Hunt Lieberson, Blythe and Daniels have already been mentioned, but otherwise, Morris has enjoyed especially interesting dialogue with two instrumentalists. The cellist Yo-Yo Ma approached Morris when looking for projects to broaden his experience. Having chanced upon Morris's second *South Bank Show* in 1990, Ma asked Morris to take part in a series of multimedia performances (for television) of the Bach Cello Suites. Ma also commissioned ice dancers (Jane Torvill and Christopher Dean), film-makers, a garden designer and a Kabuki artist. Morris picked Suite No. 3, which became *Falling Down Stairs* (1998, winner of an Emmy Award, after filming in 1994). (In the meantime, in 1993, Ma joined MMDG for a performance of *Mosaic and United* (Cowell)). *Falling Down Stairs* has also been performed live since 1997, most recently with Ma in 2011, at the Tanglewood Festival. Seated on a plinth, Ma features as a central figure within the visual experience. He was totally consumed by this work, which, he admits, changed his view of the Suite indelibly. On the subject of playing alongside the dancers, he admitted that 'it sounds like a cliché, but working with them actually changed my life'.[101]

At this point in his career, Ma was also driven to learn about music outside the western, classical repertoires in which he had been trained: 'It comes from my anthropological background', he says, referring to his studies at Harvard University.[102] So, in 1998, he founded the Silk Road Project, an arts and educational organisation inspired by the historic trading routes as a metaphor for multicultural and interdisciplinary exchange. Such a project seemed especially urgent to him after the events of September 11, 2001. It was also close to Morris's interests. The choreographer had already invited him to be the premiere soloist in Harrison's score for *Rhymes with Silver* (1997), which drew on a diversity of cultural sources (see Ch. 11). Ma then performed in another, western-classical project: *The Argument* (1999, to Schumann's *Fünf Stücke im Volkston* for cello and piano), at which point he joined MMDG for a full programme including *Falling Down Stairs* and *Rhymes*. Ma later introduced Morris to the renowned tabla player Zakir Hussain, after which Morris initiated the *Kolam* collaboration (2002). This involved Ma in improvisation, a new experience for him, and, at the premiere, he also played in the Schumann Quintet for *V*. Later that year, he toured Japan with the MMDG, drawing from the expanded repertory that they had by then built together.

Yo-Yo Ma and Mark Morris in conversation, during the filming of *Falling Down Stairs*.
© Cylla von Tiedemann, 1994

The pianist Emanuel Ax, a friend and professional colleague of Ma, was likewise ready to shift into new musical directions. He had seen the *Falling Down Stairs* film and, after a performance of *V* at Jacob's Pillow, Umanoff remembers him enthusing to Morris: 'I'd do anything with you. [He was] bowled over'.[103] So the 2006 *Mozart Dances* collaboration slipped into place, with Ax playing two Mozart concertos, joined by his wife Yoko Nozaki for *Double*, set to the Sonata for Two Pianos. In 2009, he joined Ma in the Tanglewood premieres of *Visitation* (to Beethoven's Cello Sonata No. 4 in C major, Op. 102, No. 1) and *Empire Garden* (to Charles Ives's Trio for Violin, Cello and Piano, S.86). The two musicians had asked Morris to select a sonata for them to work on, which turned out to be the Beethoven, whereupon Morris agreed, the deal being that they must take on the Ives as well. Ma and Ax repeated these two pieces at the Mostly Mozart Festival in New York (2009), when they both joined in a performance of *V*.

Umanoff feels sure that the respect of Ma and Ax, their excitement in learning from Morris's interpretations, entering into his personal vision of the music, boosted his confidence as a musician immeasurably.[104] As the Ma and Ax works entered the regular repertory, their roles have been taken by other well-known artists, the cellist Matt Heimowitz, and pianists

Ursula Oppens, Garrick Ohlsson and Russell Sherman. Colin Fowler and Yegor Shevtsov from the MMDG Music Ensemble have been enlisted when just the first two parts of *Mozart Dances* have been programmed, the Sonata and the Concerto K. 413 in the piano and string quartet scoring.

Star performers often play a central role within theatrical performance. It seems likely that both audiences and presenters expect them to be on show—after all, their names sell tickets. Ma, for instance, was exposed on stage, even if at the side, on several occasions, and *The Argument* involves direct dialogue, even an element of confrontation, between him and the dancers. Dance begins to blend with concert performance in such circumstances.

Musical Choices: Continuity and Change

During his later career, Morris explains how his musical choices for choreography have shifted: even less music with a straight ethnic base— although he sustains himself with regular visits to India (six since 1996); no rock—for him, it is too rhythmically regular; and very little new jazz— although Iverson has begun to interest him in this form. He never uses the minimalist style popular with his choreographer contemporaries, and finds much nineteenth-century programme music 'too bossy'.[105] Otherwise, his enthusiasms are as broad as ever, provided, he says, that he has some kind of 'hook' to excite his creative energies, such as melodic surprises, strange harmonies, missing beats or odd phrase lengths.[106] Structural details stimulate both his intellectual and emotional imaginations.

At Morris's apartment, there is a large collection of recordings— especially of Bach, Stravinsky and Shostakovich—all the complete works. Whenever a new Handel opera release appears, he buys it. Various oddities confirm the breadth of his musical interests and his fascination with the sheer sound quality:

> I have a bunch of music written for glass harmonica, which is hard to find, but it's interesting and irritating and you want to have it in your collection. I have a Theremin recital and I have shape-note hymns from the south [see p. 39], and I have gypsy music. I don't have the collected works of Beethoven because I hear those. I buy stuff that I can't hear.[107]

In 2012, with *A Wooden Tree* (which included a role for Baryshnikov), he surprised audiences by suddenly side-tracking from classical choices to the songs of Ivor Cutler. Yet there is a lot of music that he likes listening to that he would never want to choreograph.

While Morris retains a passion for baroque music, he now uses it much less in his choreography. Since 2000, there has only been Purcell's *King*

Arthur (2006)—and for ten years he waited before he could set it—*Italian Concerto* (Bach, 2007), his third production of the Gluck opera *Orfeo* (2007) and *Acis and Galatea* (Handel, 2014). There has also been a loosening in his approach to baroque performance style, coinciding with similar changes within the world of musical performance. In Morris speak, early music style is 'much groovier, less anal-retentive... It's like things can swing again.' Yet he knows what matters most to him today: 'Although I am generally a big fan...I am sceptical...[108] Forget about purism, it's bullshit... I want high quality, but I don't care if it's amplified or abridged. I want it to be real and engaging and interesting.'[109]

Today, both 'original' and contemporary instruments are acceptable to Morris, as well as ensembles of different size. Indeed, he welcomes change as a refreshing opportunity, just as he can appreciate radically different interpretations in concert performance.[110] He is ready, too, to shift the 'affect' of the music, as the occasion or performance venue suggests, 'warming it up' or 'cooling it down'.[111] Sometimes, the bracing, 'rustic' edge simply works better. Robert Cole considered that the sound quality and balance of McGegan's period orchestra at the Berkeley performances of *King Arthur* were better than at the ENO London premiere.[112] As for McGegan, he says that his musicians actually play better when working with MMDG: 'They can feel it.'[113]

Using less baroque music has also meant using less vocal music, but perhaps this is because increased opportunities to work in opera helped satisfy Morris's need for words. Instead, he has edged towards nineteenth-century music a little more, including two works apiece to Schubert and Schumann, and four to Beethoven. At the same time, his enthusiasm for twentieth-century American composers remains as strong as ever.

It is important that, during this period, Harrison became Morris's main composer-collaborator, although there was only one commission as such: *Rhymes with Silver* (1997). Morris made in total eight pieces to Harrison scores, more than to any other composer, starting with *Strict Songs* in 1987 and ending with *Serenade*, premiered just after the composer's death in 2003. Set to the eponymous violin and piano score, *Grand Duo* (1993) became one of the strongest, most popular pieces Morris has made: it is usually billed as the thrilling closing number on a programme. The two artists had much in common. Like Partch, who was a friend, Harrison had corporeal leanings, and had even undertaken some dance training. 'Music is a song and a dance', he used to say, fervently believing that the two art-forms belong naturally to each other.[114] Like so many West Coast composers, Harrison offered Morris the unaffected pan-culturalism that had attracted him since his childhood. He looked still further West across the Pacific, fascinated by Asian music, its fresh sonorities and variety of tunings—other than the equal temperament of western music. Again like Partch, he was an instrument-maker: he constructed his own gamelan. Working in relative obscurity for many years, outside the East Coast mainstream, eventually, in the 1990s, Harrison achieved wide recognition as one of America's most important twentieth-century composers. Morris has proudly compared his relationship to Harrison with that of probably the most celebrated composer-choreographer collaboration of the twentieth century: 'I think Harrison is to me what Stravinsky was to Balanchine'.[115]

The temperament issue exercises Morris to this day. Equal temperament he calls 'the greatest crime against music',[116] adjusting as it does 'pure' intervals so that all musical keys sound reasonably well (or not so well) on fixed-pitched instruments such as pianos. 'Reasonably well' is not good enough for Morris. Always open to new sound experiences, he likes to explore alternatives, for instance, in returning to Partch's studies on ancient Greek scales in *Greek to Me* (1998) and entering the *Kolam* collaboration with Ma, Hussain and Iverson. Once the Silk Road Project was underway, he was delighted to find Ma experimenting with new tunings in his cello playing.[117]

This later period is also one when, with developed skill and confidence, Morris began, not only to take on complex scores of 'symphonic' proportions, but to work intensely with their structural detail: multi-movement scores by, for instance, Bach, Bartók, Beethoven, Ives, Mozart, Schumann, and Villa-Lobos. Never before had he allowed such musical structures, expanded through the addition of his choreography, to tell their story. With *Mozart Dances*, he went furthest in this direction, setting an evening of three-movement scores, full of allusions, but never projecting any literal, linear narrative. Looking across the dance repertoire, perhaps the work most like it in form is Balanchine's *Jewels* (1967), set to substantial works by Fauré, Stravinsky and Tchaikovsky, another evening of what are essentially three large-scale plotless pieces.

Music actually written for dance still does not feature very often amongst Morris's choices. The big ballet scores are often too programmatic for him, although, just as he had done earlier with *The Hard Nut*, he made exceptions with *Sylvia* (2004) and *Romeo & Juliet* (2008). On the other hand, Milhaud's *La Création du monde* (the 1923 Ballets Suédois score that he borrowed for *Cargo* (2005)) is a relatively unfamiliar one-act score and consequently more easily able to adapt to new subject matter, here inspired by the cargo cults of the South Pacific. But Morris believes that most dance music is simply not good enough in quality.

When he made his first Chopin piece *Sang-Froid* (2000), using a series of piano miniatures, Morris was determined to avoid the conventional balletic associations of such miniatures, from, for example, Fokine's *Les Sylphides* (1908) and Robbins' *Dances at a Gathering* (1969). Thrilled by the 'fearless' Iverson, the jazz player 'courageous enough to play Chopin', he spotted new possibilities:.

> I don't like a real romantic reading of Chopin; I like it much fiercer ... [Chopin is] too often seen as pastel and sentimental. My intention was to purge it of those qualities, which is also why I chose the title I did [which translates as 'cold blood']... I find it extremely advanced and rigorous and great. It sounds like it was written a hundred years after it was.[118]

Only occasionally has Morris edited music, and when he has, the cuts have been big and bold, never short passages or phrases that disrupt local musical continuity. In the early days, he would sometimes omit one or more musical movements from a multi-movement score, as in the Shostakovich Sonata, Beethoven Trio and Bartók Quartet (see p. 32). Now, he rarely does this, although he did remove the fourth movement of Harrison's *Grand Duo*, to the unhappiness of the composer (see p. 372): 'It would have made the dance too long' was the reason.[119] Then, in *The Office* (1994, Dvořák), he used only the A section of an ABA final movement, because he wanted it to 'stop short'. The cut makes the ending of this dance especially bleak and uncertain. He went along with Iverson's suggestion for *The Argument*, set to Schumann's *Fünf Stücke im Volkston*. The original last movement made a weak conclusion, so they agreed to close with a repeat of the opening movement. Morris also reversed the order of the four piano pieces when he set Samuel Barber's *Excursions* (2008, borrowing the musical title). On the other hand, the editing of baroque scores (as Morris did in *L'Allegro*) is generally accepted practice, despite the presence of carefully researched versions of several scores from this period.

Given the size of Morris's output, we might expect more choreographer-composer collaborations, in the literal sense, as commissions from scratch. There have been very few: just the early two with Garfein; *Home*, with the country music singer Michelle Shocked and bassist Rob Wasserman (1993), a project initiated by company manager Barry Alterman; *Rhymes with Silver* with Harrison (1997); and a ballet *Joyride* for San Francisco Ballet with Adams (2008), who was already familiar to him from the operas *Nixon in China* and *The Death of Klinghoffer*. A Broadway show *The Capeman* (1998) was devised with Paul Simon, with whom, as choreographer, Morris greatly enjoyed working, although there were several changes of director before he finally came on the scene, and the show flopped, panned by the critics.

At least a couple of ideas never came to fruition. In 1999, another

Alterman initiative, there was a plan for a piece with the celebrated American jazz pianist Herbie Hancock, a project that BAM was keen to support. In 2000, the New York City Opera at Lincoln Center agreed to stage, with Morris as director, an opera *Young Caesar* by Harrison.[120] Based on a homosexual encounter during Julius Caesar's adolescence, this was a revision and extension of an earlier puppet opera score. It was eventually realised in 2007, after the composer's death, but not with Morris.

Violet Cavern has an especially interesting history. Morris had worked the piece thoroughly to *Visions de l'Amen* (1943) by Messiaen, only to be thwarted when the composer's widow refused to allow choreography to his religious music. The simple solution was for the three Bad Plus musicians (Iverson's band) to write a score instead, for the most part based on the rhythmic structures of the Messaien.[121] This was the method that John Cage had resorted to in similar circumstances, replacing Satie's *Socrate* with his own *Cheap Imitation*, as accompaniment to Cunningham's appropriately titled 1970 dance *Second Hand*.

The importance of collaboration has often been over-stated. It is as if a kind of myth has evolved about the meeting of minds, although it can push an artist into new, unexpected and potentially fruitful directions. As Balanchine and Frederick Ashton were to discover, and indeed many other choreographers unable to commission because of lack of funds, the use of existing music is not necessarily any less challenging or more conservative a mode of enquiry. With existing music, there is more time for un-pressured, intensive private study, the chance to get to know and use the detail of a full, completed score and to listen to a range of recordings. Time was a problem during the collaborations with both Garfein and Adams, when music was often completed very late. At one point, Morris literally ran out of music during the making of *Joyride*—whereas he had kept to schedule, Adams had not.[122] With Harrison, there was no such nightmare over schedule for *Rhymes with Silver*. Instead, after Morris's big cut in *Grand Duo*, he playfully subverted the whole concept of collaboration, providing Morris with a 'kit' of possibilities so that he could edit, select and determine the order of events and overall length himself.

The *Home* collaboration was different yet again, the score constructed from a number of songs and instrumental interludes for step-dancing. Morris explains: 'We had several sessions together, and Michelle and Rob would propose things and then I would say what I needed. I ended up being pretty editorial, having a lot of say about how things happened with tempo and with structure and the length of things and bridges—more than I expected to.'[123] Crucially, Morris had a good deal of control.

Morris's closest associates have clear views on how he operates best. 'If there's a whiff of collaboration that's not a great thing,' says Iverson. 'Mark is most comfortable with long-dead composers or long-finished scores. Hence *Rhymes*, which is not as good as *Grand Duo*. And *Violet Cavern* was OK, but not one of the greatest works of Mark or Bad Plus.'[124] After the Adams experience, Umanoff decided: 'Mark really needs the music to be done—completed—not a simultaneous collaboration'.[125] We can let Morris have the last word:

> My management says that I'm not good at collaborating with people but that's not entirely true. It is just that I often have a strong idea about what I want, which limits what can happen with a collaborator...I don't work with composers very often partly because it's so arduous and you never know what you're going to get.

Besides, he adds: 'There's so much fabulous music already.'[126]

Umanoff believes that the lack of collaborators also betrays how Morris engages with other people:

> There is a comfort level for Mark, in all collaborations. How many people have designed costumes and lights for Mark? You can count on one hand. The collaborator pool is small. The comfort level with regulars allows him to create and be who he is...and that includes his music ensemble.[127]

Conductor and Teacher

Working with those he knows well and feels comfortable with has certainly eased Morris's pathway as a conductor. His mentors are all regulars and friends: first Smith, then Glover, and later Asbury. One reason for taking up conducting is his interest in getting another perspective on music and revitalising his interest in old repertory, for example, he recalls the 'gorgeous viola line in the Triumphing Dance [*Dido*] that I had forgotten'.[128] But when he jokes about wasting time training others to copy his own interpretations, he is also making a serious point about getting things right and key values: like his commitment to 'reducing what people think needs punching out for dance...hemiolas, dissonances and terminal retards'.[129]

Umanoff testifies to an extraordinary shift in his outlook as he approached this new challenge of conducting:

> For *Gloria* he rehearsed every afternoon on the road. Mark would practise with a couple of people for twenty to thirty minutes each time, whoever was available [instrumentalists from the Ensemble or even dancers operating as singers]. The same with *Dido*. It was humbling. He *studied*. He asked for feedback. When making dances, he is not looking for feedback,

rather a compliment. For the first time, I saw him genuinely looking for advice, support, assistance, encouragement from the players. 'Do you need me to give you more? Do you see the downbeat? Am I doing OK?' It was stunning! He was learning again. I felt he hadn't in this way for a very long time, he hadn't taken a class (aside from his own) in years... It was a long time since I had seen him so generous of spirit, and vulnerable. And it was intentional that he should practise with people he'd actually be conducting from the pit—in his comfort zone. He had more rehearsals than anyone [else] would ever get.[130]

Morris's conducting debut took place in 2006 with *Gloria*, followed in 2007 by *Dido*. By 2008, he felt ready to direct people outside of his Ensemble, and the first occasion was a performance of *Dido* with the Pacific Symphony Orchestra and University of California, Irvine Chamber Singers (although still with Fowler and Koessel at the centre as continuo). In 2011, he conducted Berkeley's period orchestra Philharmonia Baroque in *Dido*. At one point, he toyed briefly with the idea of trying his hand at *The Hard Nut*, but instead, in 2012, took on the challenge of a full programme in New Haven, Connecticut, including *A Lake* (to Haydn's Horn Concerto), *Jesu Meine Freude* (1993, to the Bach motet) and *Gloria*, accompanied by the Yale Choral Artists and Collegium Players. The following year, he conducted for the first time in situations without any dance: for the Bach series at Trinity Church, *Jesu Meine Freude* and the double-chorus motet *Fürchte dich nicht*, then a read-through of Telemann's *Water Music* with the period instrument ensemble at the Juilliard School, and a performance (including the audience) of the short vocal *Exaltation* by Carl Ruggles during the Ojai Festivals.

Morris is also interested in new kinds of teaching involving music, beyond the statutory dance technique class for his company. In 2013, for instance, he co-taught with Iverson a course for UK choreographers and composers at Dartington Hall (the Rambert Dance Company Masterclass for Choreographers and Composers), with dancers from the Rambert and Richard Alston companies. Undoubtedly as the result of his own reputation as a musician, the music world has come up with a number of imaginative ways of using him. He did more than conduct the Telemann read-through at Juilliard. Ara Guzelimian, the Provost and Dean, recalls him compelling his students to consider performance as a 'creative' rather than 're-creative' act, breaking their habits and pushing them to extremes. Finding their initial playing so flawless as to be dull, Morris stressed the physical basis of musical expression, experimenting with tempo—having them play as fast as possible, or 'just uncomfortably' slow, and with 'corporealisation'—having them stand up, stomp and sing, in order to feel sound within their bodies.[131]

Morris's most longstanding commitment as teacher has been at the

Tanglewood Music Center (the Boston Symphony Orchestra's academy for advanced musical study) where, every year, some 150 young musicians who have just embarked, or are about to embark, on their professional careers study as Fellows in parallel with the Orchestra's summer season. Ellen Highstein, director of the Center, says that her strategy in inviting Morris and MMDG to be in residence every year since 2003 (except 2014) is to get the Fellows to think 'out of the box', to enjoy 'experiences which are outside those that are standard at most conservatories'.[132] 'The fact that [Morris] works in dance, and that therefore they get to work with dance, is surprising and interesting for them,' she confirms, 'but far less important than the fact that he's a great musician.'

So the Fellows have learnt short sections from the dance repertory that they will later accompany—for instance, from *Marble Halls*, *Falling Down Stairs*, or *Lucky Charms*—and, watching the dances, gain understanding of how they are constructed in relation to a score and how dancers embody musical phrasing. The dancers have absorbed techniques from them in turn, learning, for instance, Steve Reich's *Clapping Music* (a score that Morris has not choreographed) and sections from Harrison's *Rhymes with Silver*. Morris has regularly offered a castanets session to the percussionists, taught from his point of view as a trained Flamenco dancer, and another for the composers, on stage presentation and taking a bow. But coaching Fellows in their own musical interpretation is central. Highstein explains the niceties:

> They may re-think the way they approach a phrase. Phrasing should be specific rather than general. A phrase has to take its time, which has to do with weight and breathing, things that are essential when dancing, when working with the whole body; Mark understands and brings this essential awareness to the musical gesture.[133]

> It's the same thing with overall structure as with the detail of a phrase— the performer can find different ways of highlighting development and change by bringing a deeper awareness of the musical gesture when deciding how something should be played.[134]

Brutally honest and enthusiastic, ever free from institutional constraints, Morris has clear opinions about the downside of current professional training in music and what he offers instead:

> This experience makes musicians better. Way better! ...I'm the enemy of the conservatory, because it kills music. Nobody gives a damn about intonation. It's not about that. Imagination has been wrung out of these people, and it's tragic. Really, musicians have lousy rhythm.[135]

Morris coaching Tanglewood Music Fellows. © Johan Henckens, 2004

When he premiered Stravinsky's *Renard* (2011) at Tanglewood, Morris had to cajole the impeccably schooled musicians to loosen up:

> I asked one young, fabulous percussionist, 'Could you please play this as if you are not a good drummer?' I wanted the overture to sound like it was being played by a broken-down Salvation Army band. The singers had a hard time performing glissandos; they were so careful it always sounded like scales. I told them that it's meant to slide around.[136]

For soprano Anne-Carolyn Bird, class of 2003 and 2004: 'Ever since I worked with Mr. Morris... I've heard concerts differently, even without dancers there. I hear more layers in the music. Something just woke up in my ear.'[137] Counter-tenor José Lemos claimed that 'from Mark and the dancers I've learned to listen to what the music tells me instead of paying so much attention to what I am trying to tell it'.[138] On the other hand, a Bartók specialist, the cellist Norman Fischer, joined Morris in coaching the Fourth Quartet for *All Fours* and summarised the distinctions between their approaches:

Musicians and dancers start from different points of departure. I am listening for clarity, articulation, balance, the energies and characters of the music. Mark is fed by the personality of each musical moment, which he responds to in a primal way.[139]

Morris has also taught within a more academic, musicological context. In autumn 2010, he was invited by Princeton University to co-teach a 'Modernism in Music and Dance' course (with Simon Morrison). The course was concerned mainly with dance and twentieth-century music, Morris's own repertory in particular, occasionally taking off to discuss topics such as the musical approach of Balanchine and Cunningham, or Disney animation as music visualisation. Understandably, Morris's impatience with conceptions of music as dry and technical re-emerged strongly in this context. He spoke, for instance, of his own 'emotional reaction' to the Bartók of *All Fours*, to the visceral, violent quality of sound that most of the music literature fails to discuss. Morrison recalls the choreographer constantly urging the students to 'have passion' as they approached their analytical assignments, to start the research process working from what they *felt* most strongly about.[140] Always, Morris seeks the immediate response, for people to be moved.

None of these developments during Morris's professional career has occurred as a result of strategy, except the targeting of music audiences. All have happened naturally and organically in the context of finding a way for Morris to do what he needs to do—whether that be big projects that require a lot of planning and resources, or smaller ones that demand much less, whether to satisfy his keenness to direct more opera, or to encourage his joy in teaching and coaching musical interpretation. Nevertheless, the result stems from imagination to grasp opportunities and maximise potential. It means that today, within a highly original style of choreomusical exchange, Morris is the lynchpin, a musician-choreographer who feeds, supports and challenges his fellow musicians, as much as he needs them to nourish his own work. At this point, we turn to the immediacy of Morris's working processes, and those of his dancers and musicians, to the detail of their exchange.

2

Towards Performance: Process and Practice

While information about the working processes of choreographers is rarely documented systematically, understanding Morris's processes and those of his collaborating dancers and musicians is highly revealing. An intricate network of social and artistic practices has evolved over the years, and knowing about them enlivens our perceptions as we watch and listen, while demonstrating the importance of detail and precision within his choreography.

In common with probably all other choreographers who base their work on music, Morris listens many times to a piece of music that he plans to use (almost invariably existing music), and to as many recordings as he can find. Since his early career, as often as he can, he also works with the musical score—a much less common procedure amongst choreographers—marking it up and colour-coding it as a kind of analytical aide-memoire. From the Brussels period onwards, his reading skills developing all the time, Morris's enthusiasm for intensive score analysis increased, and he began to share more information in interviews about his working methods.[1]

By the late 1990s, Morris's live music policy by then firmly established, scores gave him the freedom to develop his *own* view of a piece of music. 'He's like a great conductor', says the pianist Emanuel Ax, who first worked with him on *Mozart Dances* (2006), 'They'll all hear a lot of recordings, but they'll find their *own* vision.'[2] Yet Morris often shifts tactics, adopting different approaches at different stages of the creative process: listening and reading the score, reading only, listening only, constantly refreshing his perspective, a methodology that leads to detailed personal musical interpretation. Then, the choreographic process begins.

Morris's creative procedures vary considerably. Often, though not always, he will choreograph directly on to specific phrases or sections of music, not necessarily starting at the beginning of a score. Or he might make up passages of movement in silence, then move ideas around, spin variations on them, draw from the dancers' improvisation, or, very occasionally, introduce verbal instructions to his dancers that guarantee a varied response. 'Turn, run, kick, point, look', for instance, are the specific ingredients for one part of his Bach piece *Falling Down Stairs* (1997; Bourrée 2). In such cases, he fits the movement to the music after it has been made. Given his firm grasp of musical timing, Morris has many options. Occasional passages he leaves free from one performance to the next, to provide a deliberately rough and disorderly impression, for instance, large sections of the Act 1 party scene in *The Hard Nut* (1991) or the Witches' choreography in *Dido and Aeneas* (1989). But there are still firm rules for the dancers to follow. Meanwhile, Morris encourages his dancers to listen to recordings, to get to know the real instrumentation, beyond the piano rehearsal reduction, even to carry out research outside the studio. Sometimes he invites them to examine the score.

Morris refines his personal musical interpretations through the medium of his rehearsal pianist, to whom he provides guidance well beyond the issues of tempo that normally exercise choreographers and dancers. As well as ideas about when to slow down or speed up the music (not necessarily keeping strictly to score tempo indications), he selects accents and musical lines to emphasise. Undoubtedly, the act of making choreography also affects his relationship to, and understanding of, the music, a point rarely considered. A two-way process begins. The movement he comes up with may well suggest new tempos, inflections and emphases in the music.

His tempo observations are fascinating: 'Dance choreographically fast is different from musically fast', he says. He is naturally inclined towards detail, wanting both to hear and see it. For instance, he asked for the slower, articulated, 'deliberate drive of a scale' in the Beethoven sonata (for *Visitation* (2009), at the start of the Adagio movement) rather than a swift, single gesture, a glissando. Choreographing had developed his understanding of the music and, when cellist Yo-Yo Ma and pianist Emanuel Ax arrived to play for final rehearsal, Morris asked them to slow down their interpretation accordingly.

In the case of *Renard* (Stravinsky, 2011), Morris initially choreographed to many of the rapid sub-beats, parsing (and counting) 5 in bars of 5/16. But then, in order to maintain a rapid musical tempo, he changed his mind and chose to bring out the larger long-short rhythm (5 divided into 3+2). A contrasting example: Page Smith, solo cellist for *Kammermusik No. 3* (Hindemith, 2012, for Pacific Northwest Ballet), recalls that Morris asked the orchestra to slow the tempo for the two fast movements. In the first of these, especially, Morris wanted to articulate the musical detail in his choreography and asked the musicians to forget the 'big three' (in a bar) of the time signature.[3] Here, significantly, the speed of the dance movement allowed the overall impression of tempo to remain fast.

Today, when members of the MMDG Music Ensemble are brought into rehearsal, Music Director and principal pianist Colin Fowler takes the lead and conveys information from earlier working processes. Morris himself then directs a final music rehearsal before the dancers and musicians come together. He regularly coaches and advises instrumentalists and singers, his occasional conducting being a natural extension of this. He might advise string players, for instance, to change to another string for a particular effect, or to bow up or down, or instruct singers on diction. Although context is crucial, when there is a choice, he normally asks for the powerful harmonic clash of appoggiaturas through a clearly sustained tie or strong beat accent, rather than introducing the lighter dissonance of a grace note. He is also insistent about musicians being on time with opening downbeats (an especial problem, he perceives with string players) and singers timing diction so that words, which often relate directly to the choreography, are clearly heard.

When it comes to baroque scores, Morris makes many musical decisions, in the manner of any baroque music conductor. Depending on the size of the orchestra, the type of theatre in which a performance takes place and the players available, he decides whether or not to use a harpsichord for the continuo, or a theorbo instead (a large, plucked, lute-like instrument), or to double the cello with the bass. Dido's 'Ah! Belinda!' aria (Scene 1), for instance, he prefers to have played on cello alone with no other instrument. He also makes decisions about ornamentation and recitative practice, whether to re-strike chords or let them segue through a passage.

As often as possible, Morris invites his performing musicians to watch the choreography first before accompanying it. The dancers learn each other's parts too, which is unusual in traditional choreographic practice. (Morris also works out his own solos on other dancers.) All artists knowing what their colleagues are doing—and across music and dance—is, he insists, essential to a coherent, engaged ensemble, understanding what they are all making together and alive to change within the moment of performance.

This ability to live and respond in the moment is crucial, and, as much as he develops his own views, Morris does not present a blueprint for interpretation. He is not like Jerome Robbins, for instance, who used to press for a fixed text, from both the dancer and the accompanying musician. Robbins was apt to listen to lots of recordings and settle on one as if it was the only possible interpretation.[4] This represents an extreme position. Similarly Hans van Manen choreographed precisely to the Christoph Eschenbach recording of Beethoven's *Hammerklavier Sonata* (for *Adagio Hammerklavier* (1973)),[5] while Pina Bausch kept the same Pierre Boulez recording as the model interpretation for conductors of her *Rite of Spring* (1975).[6] Morris operates quite differently. He keeps his new pieces fluid and open to change for as long as he can before a premiere and, although he has overall control, there is often an element of negotiation with his musicians.

Fowler emphasises his receptivity: 'he is not dictatorial', nor does he say that 'it must be a certain way.'[7]

Morris remembers one rare occasion when he abandoned his own musical interpretation. It was at the Edinburgh Festival premiere of *I Don't Want to Love* (1996), set to Monteverdi madrigals for tenor voices and performed by Rinaldo Alessandrini's group Concerto Italiano. A single female aria 'Lamento della ninfa' occurs near the end, like a 'nervous breakdown' or 'mad scene', says Morris, and the soloist Rossana Bertini sounded 'crazy, psychotic'. The stage rehearsal was like 'scat singing'—she improvised wildly beyond the boundaries of the score, not at all how he had imagined the song. But he was thrilled by its 'weirdness'. At the last minute, an indication of his own flexibility and commitment to the live situation, he seized the opportunity to inject new spontaneity into the dance and go with the singer, and set about adjusting his choreography accordingly. He describes this as the most radical experience he has ever had with musical interpretation.

Frequently, there are distinct advantages in working with regular MMDG musicians, fine musicians in their own right who have had time to build up a sophisticated relationship with Morris and his dancers. Ethan Iverson, the jazz pianist who was MMDG Music Director from 1998-2002, stresses the rhythmic aspects that brought him close to Morris. 'Putting the rhythm first', or in jazz vocabulary, having 'swing' or 'groove', is, he suggests, what classical musicians usually think about last of all, privileging instead melody and rubato or, in the case of singers, the meaning of a text.[8]

Iverson observes the unusual vibrancy of Morris's dance classes and rehearsals, their clear, sustained rhythmic impetus stemming from his robust inclinations. This is how Morris sings, which he does often, vigorously, no matter what the style of music. Yet at the same time, both men clearly register fermata (written pauses on specific notes or chords) and rests, sometimes extending these further than usual. A moment from the ballet class parody *Canonic 3/4 Studies* (1982) provides an especially good example. Keen to enliven the rhythmic content by exaggerating a break in the speed of motion, Iverson made a jump look like 'a gasp... Sometimes it is good to elongate a note to a ridiculous point theatrically... I can hear Mark saying "This note is supposed to last *too* long".'

The point here is dramatic as well as rhythmic. On the other hand, Morris condemns the tradition in ballet of destroying musical logic:

> Ballet, unfortunately, usually gets bent out of shape. The coda in *Swan Lake* Act III [the Black Swan/Prince Siegfried pas de deux] stops five times and is in a different tempo every time it starts... for him and then her. It's like, wait a minute. And then they stop and take a bow in the middle.[9]

Ethan Iverson at the toy piano, with Mark Morris, in *Peccadillos*. © Stephanie Berger, 2001

In Morris's ballet-based technique class, egos that demand multiple *pirouettes* and high jumps at the expense of musical tempo and phrase endings must be left behind.

Iverson remembers several occasions when he made musical suggestions to Morris while the choreography was being made. One comes from *Sang-Froid* (2000), during a Chopin Nocturne, when the dancers evoked statues: 'My favourite part in that dance,' says Morris, 'is where nobody moves for way too long'.[10] Iverson responded by playing the passage as quietly as possible, as if to put 'no dance' into the music as well, thereby increasing the sense of contrast when the dancing started again. He was the one who suggested repeating the first movement of Schumann's *Fünf Stücke im Volkston* at the end of *The Argument* (1999) because he felt that the original last movement made a very weak ending. The repeat begins attacca, with no pause after the preceding movement, and deliberately slowly, 'like a machine slowly cranking back into life', and then gets faster to project motion towards a climactic conclusion. It was Iverson's idea too that the first account of the music should contain big pauses, while the second should be run together.[11]

Sometimes, an intense relationship between dancers and musicians that has developed during rehearsal allows for repartee and deep connection between them within performance—they can surprise and tease each other.

Such playfulness is most likely to happen during solos, on a one-to-one basis, with the musician watching the stage carefully. Unusually for a dance pianist, Iverson learnt everything by heart (except for Harrison's *Grand Duo*, 1993), so he could regularly watch what was happening on onstage, and MMDG's technical director Johan Henckens devised especially for him a rope of white lights behind the keyboard.[12] Using piano music is immediately advantageous: the most direct route from earliest rehearsal to performance.

Fowler singles out a passage for Lauren Grant in the first movement of 'Eleven' (the opening part of *Mozart Dances*), when he plays (from the pit) a trill leading to a high note, three times (bars 132-35) while she flourishes an arm, steps up on to her toes and pauses on each high note. They used to vary the tempos from one performance to the next. A few bars later, Grant moves upstage, turns round to a big descending scale passage, then stops on a big arrival chord throwing her arms out sideways in a dramatic pose (bar 143). Sometimes Fowler would subvert the moment by making the chord almost inaudible, his reason: 'It's Mozart and it's supposed to be fun!'[13] Grant remembers one performance when 'he practically made me laugh on stage, the way he played that chord...I really had to listen'.[14] Such flexibility between performers develops over time, with shared experience, and sometimes you sense conversation between parties, sometimes embodiment, which can work in both directions: the dancer 'possessing' or identifying with a particular musical instrument, and vice versa.

Morris's choreography also offers musicians the opportunity to develop new insights into scores, especially those that are not standard concert repertory, like Bartók's Fourth String Quartet (for *All Fours*, 2003) or Charles Ives's Trio for Violin, Cello and Piano (for *Empire Garden*, 2009). A series of dance performances, far more of them than are likely in concert, encourages this exploration, but so does the particular experience of working with dancers and with Morris's particular musical interpretation. Even guest soloists Ma and Ax, far less accustomed to adapting to someone else's interpretation than Morris's regular musicians, had to be open to new points of view. Both are insightful about their work with Morris.

Ma recalls his impressions of working with dancers for the first time on *Falling Down Stairs*, the television collaboration that he had initiated (see p. 51). He came with considerable baggage, already very familiar with Bach's Cello Suites, but his enthusiasm was renewed:

> Their union of mind and body was of a kind that I've rarely experienced. I was just bowled over. The dancers are not reading scores—their body *becomes* the score.[15]

So Ma began to interpret the Bach through the bodies dancing before him, almost in the manner of a kinetic score: 'I actually think of the choreography as living notes.'[16]

The collaborative process involved Ma sending sample recordings of his playing to Morris while he was on tour and a continuous process of negotiation between them from one rehearsal to the next. The choreographer noticed that Ma immediately started to play the Bach Cello Suite in a radically different way. For instance, he took the Sarabande slower, with an accent on the second beat and 'springing' the rhythms, in other words re-connecting with its dance origins. Ma discovered that he could work interactively with MMDG, that he and the dancers could read off each other, and that he learnt a new sense of timing from the dancing body:

> Like at one point, at the end of the Courante, one of the dancers has to jump off the plinth, which is fairly high up, and she has to land in the arms of basically four or six people. So the way she sort of runs up that set of stairs and jumps down determines how I'm going to end the Courante.

Gravity sometimes determined timing. On the film documentary, Ma notes:

> Bodies have to follow the natural laws of gravity and so, if somebody launches themselves up in the air, you know the timing and the feel it takes before they land again. And that gives me a sense of timing of what I have to do.[17]

Sometimes, Ma's musical accentuation was determined by the choreography. He recalls the dancers in the Sarabande turning on the spot during a trill, and stopping on a C-sharp in the bass:

> You can choose to avoid that and go for the top line, but the way he choreographed it, and he said that to me, 'Well, this has to go to the C-sharp, you really have to emphasise the bass.'[18]

The moment discussed is in Part 2 of the Sarabande's binary form, the first time round in the music (bars 12-13). On the other hand, Grant remembers *discovering* a particular moment of eye contact with Ma near the start of the Gigue. She delighted in bursting out of the wings and prancing towards him: 'we allowed that joy to happen'.[19]

To Ax, understanding Morris's 'absolutely encyclopaedic knowledge of classical music',[20] it was no surprise that one of the concertos chosen for *Mozart Dances* (No. 11 in F major, called 'Eleven' in the dance) was relatively obscure and new to him. He describes how Morris initially went through the Mozart, not using technical musical language, rather getting across in enthusiastic lay terms his idea of the dynamic progression of the piece and its key signposts: 'A lot of the time, it's a very different vision from most musicians I know.' There was no question, however, but to 'try to get into his sound world and his conception of the piece'.[21] The process of spontaneous creativity he likened to working with a composer, except that 'I've almost never had a back-and-forth. The most I've gotten is that maybe John Adams will send me four bars and ask, "Is this playable", and I'll say yes or no.'[22] With Morris, the collaborative dynamics were more intense than usual, and the experience 'totally original...illuminating and exciting', always fuelled by 'an overriding desire from both sides...to come together'.

Most of the *Mozart Dances* choreography had been completed by the time Ax arrived for rehearsals, but the concerto cadenzas had not yet been put together and here, Morris mostly went along with Ax's existing timing. Ax explains a point of transition where Morris gave way to his interpretation:

> At the end of K. 595 Finale [in B-flat major, 'Twenty-Seven'], I like to come out of the cadenza by playing the theme slightly slower, in a more ethereal way than before. Now Mark originally had a dance going on with four couples, but when I wrote him about my tempo, he wrote back to say he'd change the choreography. Instead, he'd take three couples out, leave one couple, and bring the other three back in when I got louder.

Yet there were restraints:

> Mark had very particular things that he wanted to happen musically. He'd say, 'Look, can you wait on this fermata a really long time, and don't play that run so fast', and so forth. And I try to comply so that it sounds as though I want to do these things, and try to make them sound natural. I'm always happy to try anything different, and not be stuck with having to have an interpretation be a certain way. It's exciting. I used to play the cadenzas a lot quicker than I do in this performance, but Mark's slower tempos work so beautifully and logically—they just sound good.[23]

Indeed, Morris often asked for slower tempi than Ax was used to, particularly in slow movements, like the one in the Concerto K. 595:

> It was much slower than I had ever played it before, but that's fine, and I now love to play it this way![24]

In the middle movement of the Piano Concerto K. 413 for 'Eleven', the accompaniment figure assumed a new identity, suddenly, a tick-tick rhythm. Both the conductor Louis Langrée and Ax were surprised by this but, again, found it totally acceptable alongside the dance. Langrée said:

> I wouldn't have imagined it like that, but it is beautiful. It is like something very distant...musically, it will be more vertical, like a Swiss clock.[25]

At least one idea Ax recalls as too good to lose from his own concert

Emanuel Ax and Mark Morris in conversation during rehearsals for *Mozart Dances*.
© Amber Star Merkens, 2006

performances. Six bars before the end of the 'Double' second movement (to the Sonata in D K. 448 for two pianos—the second piano played by Yoko Nozaki), there is a passage of demisemiquavers that could be read as the continuation in elaborated form of a phrase already begun. But Morris heard it differently, as a new beginning, and highlighted this by changing the dancers' movement pattern at this point. He therefore encouraged the two pianists to make a split-second break before the elaboration and to clarify the division by shifting into soft dynamics (in the score, there is no indication of dynamic change). Ax is certain that they would now take that particular interpretation into concert performance.

As for Beethoven's Fourth Cello Sonata in *Visitation*, Ax and Ma had played it together for twenty-five years or more, but Ax recalls that they almost re-learnt it to suit Morris's vision. The choreographer sought a less romantic performance—the opening theme, for instance, less 'Sturm und Drang' than they were used to, inclinations that may well have stemmed from his own, different associations with early music style.

Having live music also entails important technical decisions, about where to place the musicians, never to be 'in the way' or blocking the audience's view, Henckens insists, but still to be in close rapport with the dancers.[26] Sometimes, there is a conflict of interest when an ideal set-up for MMDG may involve the presenter selling a block of seats as limited view or simply not allowing them to be booked at all. In terms of sight-lines, singers, who stand high in the pit, are especially hard to position: MMDG operates with a range of solutions to suit different dances and venues.[27]

For several pieces, musicians are 'choreographed' to be on stage as part of the theatrical action and consequently more central to audience experience: towards downstage right, angled so that they can see the dancers and vice versa. Such was the case for Ma in *Falling Down Stairs* and *The Argument*, when he engaged directly with solo dancers literally in front of him, but also for Iverson at a toy piano in *Peccadillos* (Satie, 2000) and a guitarist and percussionist in *Serenade* (Harrison, 2003). (Morris dislikes placement of the piano more obtrusively, upstage centre, although this does happen for *Drink to Me Only with Thine Eyes* (1988).[28]) Especially when relationships with dancers are intense, musicians, whether in the pit or onstage, not only need to see the dancers, they *like* to watch what is going on. They may indeed turn away from the audience in order to see the stage more easily, which may not be so appealing to those who watch them. Henckens recalls: 'When we toured *Rhymes with Silver* [Harrison] with Yo-Yo, marketing people hated when he would move his chair and music stand up against the pit rail, effectively disappearing from view but enabling himself to see the stage.' Exceptionally, video monitors were used by Ax and Nozaki for the two-piano Sonata in *Mozart Dances* ('Double'), because they were too low in the pit to see the dancers.

Henckens regularly introduces sound enhancement, but 'as little as possible—Mark loves none at all—to balance things out'. The piano, for instance, often comes across as too loud accompanying a singing voice, which consequently needs support, and, in the case of *Grand Duo*, in order to hear 'the fight between piano and violin', the violin needs boosting. But the main reason for miking the pit is to provide sound for the onstage sound monitors used by the dancers (and singers in the case of operas).

Meanwhile, it is crucial that Morris has developed a group of dancers who are also, in their own way, musicians, able to think musically, to hear and embody detail, and to nuance their relationship with music in many different ways. That, if anything, is what the troublesome word 'musicality' could mean when applied to dancers, and the MMDG dancers are rightly celebrated for it. Some have experience of playing an instrument, many can follow the outline of a score; all of them have learnt a lot more about music from working with Morris.

Morris has devised techniques to ensure this special rapport with music.

The use of a live pianist in rehearsals, surprisingly rare for modern dance companies, is invaluable preparation for dancers. No musician ever plays exactly the same twice. It means too that Morris can work bar by bar and slow the music in order to attend to detail, to follow, for instance, an elusive quiet inner line or bring out an accent, just as a musician might. Recordings are used occasionally in rehearsal, to familiarise dancers with the real instrumentation, but mainly at a later stage in the creative process, or for revivals when, for obvious reasons, they are usually recordings taken from MMDG performances. Significantly, each recording is treated as only one possible version, never one recording for too long, never for the dancers to become over-accustomed to one single interpretation.

Indeed, in the spirit with which he conducts his own practice, Morris guarantees that his dancers do not get stuck in habitual patterns of behaviour, rather that they listen acutely, ready to take on the challenge of each performance as a unique event. Rehearsals involve a variety of tactics beyond the dancing, like listening without moving, counting a rhythmic framework—although ultimately, counting never takes precedence over listening—even singing, which encourages the dancers to forget the beat and attend to melody, phrase and breath. The idea is to develop rich understanding. 'The company knows every piece of music cold', Morris once boasted, and gives the example of *Dido and Aeneas*:

> We can rehearse the whole dance with piano accompaniment while we sing the entire piece. We sing it horribly but we can do every bit of it, every nuance, in very bad baroque style.

And of another opera:

> Once we were in dress rehearsal for *The Death of Klinghoffer* [Adams, 1991]...with a full orchestra, giant chorus and extras. At one point everything broke down—the orchestra fell apart and the chorus stopped dead. The dancers, however, kept singing this extremely complicated John Adams piece while they danced. It made the conductor so mad he could hardly speak. Isn't that fabulous? It cracked me up.[29]

The language of rehearsal often incorporates musical concepts, and MMDG dancers are familiar with them all--tonality, modulation, counterpoint, instrumentation, hemiola, standard formal structures like fugue, sonata form and ABA. It is almost a point of principle (music and dance being equal partners) that Morris darts between both languages when referring to cues:

> I can say to the dancers, 'We're starting from the development section of the first movement.' Or I can say to the pianist, 'We're starting when those

two enter.' It can go either direction. That way nobody's accompanying anybody else. We're doing the same thing at the same time. That's my goal if I'm doing an opera, if I'm working with a ballet company, or if I'm with my own company. I don't want part of it to run the other part of it.[30]

Early 1980s film footage, the 'ancient style', as Morris calls it, provides evidence that MMDG members were even then far more accurate with rhythmic information than dancers in most other companies. As in good folk dancing, the rhythm of the feet was secure, although the placement of the body in space was much freer than it is in today's style. Although Morris's company classes are primarily aimed at preparing the body and refining its technical capabilities, they too provide occasions to explore rhythm. His exercises often try out a variety of options, as he alters the timing and dynamics of weight change in relation to strong and weak beats of the musical bar. To take an example, in one class, a memorable allegro combination began with a multiple *pirouette*, so (said Morris) that the dancers could get it over with and stop worrying about its difficulty.[31] But it was phrased as an anacrusis (or upbeat) introduction before the initial musical downbeat, which is not the traditional context, and like the sudden eruption of a fountain, a very familiar move was wonderfully renewed. It felt as if I was seeing it for the first time.

Movement to musical event or beat can also be sharp/staccato or smooth/legato, imprinted lightly or with considerable energy, laid back or anticipatory, and all the stages in between these opposites. Again, Morris explores a wide range of possibilities. Such nuance will be further discussed in Chapter 4. For now, the point about temporal precision and collaboration between forces is important. Most of the time, Morris wants his dancers to move precisely *on* the beat, the instant that the note sounds, and without any waiting around on either side:

It's not like the pistol starting runners—it's the pistol and the runners starting at the same time. You don't hear it and respond. The person pulling the trigger is doing the same job as the person doing the *piqué*... You take the step off into nothing, and that's what all live performance does every night, even if you think it's crap, even if they're bad, even if the show's crap, that's still so, so admirable.[32]

We turn now to a discussion of the historical context of Morris's choreomusical approach.

3

Choreomusical History...and the Question of 'Music Visualisation'

Morris came out boldly on the subject of history in the 1986 *Dance in America* programme devoted to his work: 'I like to think that I've built on what's gone before me...I certainly refer to it. And I don't know if that's homage or plagiarism. But I use things I like. And I often like things that have been done before.'[1] Such interest in heritage suggests a link with the movement of postmodernism.

Although this book is not the place to explain postmodernism in any detail, a brief, preliminary discussion of it in relation to history is useful to an assessment of Morris's choreomusical procedures. The term has carried many different meanings for dance over the years. Yvonne Rainer started to use it for dance in the early 1960s, in a chronological sense, implying that, as a founding member of New York's Judson Dance Theater, she was of the generation after modern dance. Soon, postmodern dance came to be associated with minimalism, pedestrian movement and systematic formal tendencies that encourage the viewer's self-conscious awareness: a distancing, discursive enterprise tied to commentary upon the basic nature of dance. There were also the techniques of bricolage and radical juxtaposition of diverse images and representations, making us work conceptually and aware of issues of representation. The historical sense of the term postmodern is the one generally accepted across the arts, and the one that resonates most readily with Morris's work. But it too can be combined with distancing tactics, as commentary, or irony.[2]

At the same time, it is important that Morris's work has not always been seen as postmodern commentary. In the early 1990s, for instance, Robert Bordo, a painter who designed four pieces for Morris, vigorously refuted any idea that his work was of this kind:

> Mark is innocent, tremendously. He's not an insider. He doesn't go through any of this sort of cultural mediation that you see today. He doesn't want to deconstruct Balanchine. He wants to be a great artist and make great human dances as he sees fit. He's not self-willed. He doesn't have a vehicle or an angle or a strategy. He has a gift.[3]

Joan Acocella changed her mind about Morris's position. In a 1988 article, she made a valiant stab at placing Morris precisely in terms of postmodernism. She had just observed the reference to 'baroqueness' within his predominantly contemporary setting of the Chaconne in Gluck's *Orpheus & Eurydice* (for the Seattle Opera):

> And so we have the postmodern experience: the retrieval, the juxta-position, the irony, the experience of distance, the meditation on representation.[4]

Yet, in her 1993 book, Acocella did not continue to argue the case for postmodernism, instead, she articulated a 'profound disagreement with the main line of postmodern art'.[5]

As for Morris himself, while he prefers not to have labels attached to his work, he has applied the term postmodern loosely to some of his dances: he did so, for instance, in several interviews that I had with him. For the purposes of this book, it seems particularly appropriate to use it as a historical concept, for his borrowings include choreomusical methods. And the method with which he has been most strongly associated—even controversially—is 'music visualisation'.

In this chapter, I outline the history of choreomusical relationships within modern and postmodern dance, in order to contextualise the reception and understanding of this aspect of Morris's work over the years. But I focus on the music visualisation concept—it is hardly a single method—because it came to occupy such a central position within discussion of Morris's work and because it is useful to address early on the complex aesthetic questions that it raises.

The term 'music visualisation' stems from the early American modern dance pioneers Ruth St Denis and Ted Shawn (Denishawn). It was coined around 1917 for their own music-based dances, but also applied to others, for instance, those by their student, the choreographer Doris Humphrey. (Morris knew some of these dances from old archive films seen during his early visits to the Jacob's Pillow Dance Festival in Massachusetts.[6]) Sometimes, and almost invariably derogatorily, the term 'mickey-mousing'—which hardly needs explanation—has been used as an alternative to 'music visualisation'. Technically speaking, when applied to choreography, these terms refer to the use of formal equivalences between music and dance. These have settled as conventions over the centuries although they are partly cognitively based—like pitch relating to height of movement, or the matching of rhythm, accents and counterpoint (all concepts shared across the two arts), or, in terms of form itself, the duplication of repetition and variation structures across music and dance. St Denis stressed the abstract properties of visualisation:

Music Visualisation in its purest form is the scientific translation into bodily action of the rhythmic, melodic and harmonic structure of a musical composition, without intention to any way 'interpret' or reveal any hidden meaning apprehended by the dancer. There is a secondary form of music visualisation, which naturally has not our keenest interest, wherein we definitely superimpose dramatic ideas or arbitrary dance forms which seem to relate themselves closely to the composition in emotional colouring, structural outline, rhythmic pattern, and general meaning.[7]

Visualisation is often assumed to refer to dance complementing musical affect as well as structures, in other words, what is perceived as the mood or spirit of the music.

In Morris's case, the term 'music visualisation' (or the same concept worded differently) used to be applied relentlessly, to the point of tedium, even to the extent that critics felt compelled to mention that Morris was not doing this as much as usual, or that *other* critics had spotted that Mouse on *other* occasions. Certainly, pronounced, extended examples of visualisation (in a formal sense) occur during all stages of Morris's career. Yet it is important that they still differ in their details and appear sporadically, and much of Morris's output is choreomusically quite different.

Early during his professional career, Morris's musicality was noticed instantly by many critics, and Morris would refer in interview to his musical approach almost invariably in terms of translation, parallelism, doing what Bach did, the dance being the same as the music, and sometimes, 'music visualisation'. This could be misleading as well as a philosophical impossibility. Then, by about 1986, the practice of visualisation was seen as a problem by some critics. Clive Barnes (the *New York Post* critic, here writing for the British magazine *Dance and Dancers*) found Morris's work Disneyesque:

When I say, as I must say here, that a choreographer is 'mickey-mousing' I mean, somewhat inelegantly, that he is keeping too strictly to the beat of the music for the surprise of the art.[8]

Laura Shapiro in *Newsweek* wrote: 'Too often his choreography shows us nothing more than the notes printed on the page.'[9]

Later in his career, Morris began to talk far less about simple translation, rather, he would emphasise, as he still does today, that he visualises a piece of music *from his own point of view*, and makes distinctive choices in the process.[10] Or his descriptions of method are vaguer still. Understandably, he has a tendency to simplify matters in quick interviews. But in some cases, as we shall see, what Morris hears seems to have encouraged distinctly oppositional tactics.

He once told Acocella: 'People forget that somebody actually choreo-graphed what Mickey Mouse does.' She provides a precise example to illustrate this, asking why, if music can determine dance movement, the 'visualisations' by Balanchine and Morris of the same *Love Song Waltzes* (Brahms) look entirely different from each other.[11] In other words, choreographers might visualise the same musical details, but in different ways, or they might select different details for visualisation. Furthermore, if we consider how dances get made, once choreography is added to music, most choreographers are likely to experiment with dance values outside the remit of music, to extend in directions beyond mere 'visualisation'.

Yet the idea that music visualisation is Morris's most characteristic approach to music, and potentially problematic, stuck hard for a long time. Drawing attention to the preoccupation of *other* critics, Karen Campbell began her 2005 review by referring to them 'hurl[ing] the charge of "mickey-mousing" at the music visualisation in much of Mark Morris's choreography'.[12] The next year John Rockwell noted that 'he is frequently praised and castigated for his sometimes slavish mimesis to music'.[13] It is around this time that critics began to drop the topic, but this is not because Morris had significantly changed his ways.

Certainly, one of the reasons why Morris has undertaken visualisation is his interest in earlier modern dance practices. Asked about influences, at the 'Meet the Choreographer' session during London's 1986 Dance Umbrella, Morris immediately replied 'Denishawn'.[14] On another occasion, invited to talk about his 1981 Tcherepnin solo *Ten Suggestions*, he said: 'I just wanted it to be music visualisation,' completely up-front about his purpose, and, on borrowing their practice with props: 'What do you do with a hoop? You jump through it. What do you do with a ribbon? You swirl it. What do you do with a chair? You sit on it.'[15] Thus, he could share the delight in musical forms of the early modern dance pioneers and reflect upon their romantic aspirations and dreams of unity with great music.

Simply walking on the plain tick-tick of musical beats, a relatively frequent characteristic of Morris's choreography, has often been referred to as a kind of music visualisation. Indeed, it seems that rhythm in general is key in determining whether a dance is perceived as a visualisation, far more than relationship between pitch and movement level. Morris would have been used to this walking on the beat from his folk dance background, which could be one reason too why he became passionate about Indian classical dance, a genre driven by precise beat. Called upon to justify his need to work with music in this way, he is adamant that: 'People around the world, except for some super cerebral modern dance types, dance *to* music [my italics]. Dancing to music is necessary, it's somatic, it's part of the human body.'[16]

Morris's longstanding love for the animation form, for Mickey Mouse himself, is also significant. Disney he mentions alongside his other models: Merce Cunningham, George Balanchine and Busby Berkeley, and when Mindy Aloff wrote her book *Hippo in a Tutu: Dancing in Disney Animation* (2008), Morris was the obvious choice for a foreword:

> For my entire career, I have been accused of the dreaded sin of 'mickey mousing' the music (as if music itself contained an embedded dance that needed only a cryptographer to release it to the world). I figure that somebody brilliant taught us all how to watch dancing and music and recognise the bond between the two. I love it when sound and sight are saying the same irreducible thing. The inevitable. That's what Disney does. From the very early *Silly Symphonies* (my favourites)... via the great *Fantasia*, I marvel at the variety of choreographic invention and aptness. What a remarkable resource of whimsy, fantasy, art!... [And it was] the place where I first heard Rossini and Mendelssohn and Schubert.[17]

Notice that Morris refers to the 'inevitable': when something is highly enjoyable, we often feel (irrationally) that no alternative is possible.

As for relations between sound and film, it is noteworthy that Morris singles out for special mention the early *Silly Symphonies* (from 1929 into the 1930s) and *Fantasia* (1940), which were led by existing scores (whereas the early Mickey Mouse shorts were a separate series generally led by animation). Many of these music-led animations introduce alternatives to the punchy Mickey stereotype, although that too is still present in *Fantasia*'s *The Sorcerer's Apprentice* (Dukas).[18] They are also a lesson in different choreomusical approaches for different expressive effects, and Morris most probably learnt from them. Many were sourced in live dance in the first place.

With the animations, again, there is the issue of choice. For example, there are many different ways of using beat and downbeat. You see visual syncopations and hear musical beats in *Lullaby Land* (1933) and *Flowers and Trees* (1932), often staccato but sometimes more legato (as in the seductive swaying of one tree lady), or something more subtle still, like the dancing on top of (just before) the beat in the carioca of *Cock o'the Walk* (1935). Or you catch lots of things at the same time: polyrhythms. Sometimes movements are 'arhythmic', swimming smoothly across the music, like the rocking bed in *Lullaby Land*, or simply shaking you out of the complacency of a regular pattern. At other times, there is a legato 'drag' effect, a kind of rubato that makes you feel the 'moment' of event continuing on after its onset—as with the *Water Babies* ((1935), specifically mentioned by Morris in his foreword) when they travel merrily through air and water, or the *Goddess of Spring*

(1934), who is nothing but a Revived Greek dancer in sandals.[19] That 'drag' is a relative of the larger curves and breaths that we enjoy in some parts of *Fantasia*'s *Nutcracker Suite*. Here, the Disney team, rather than articulating distinct rhythmic events, caress us with the lightness and flow of dewdrop fairies, cobwebs, blossoms and wind-blown leaves: this is a world where gravity does not exist.

In an insightful article entitled '"As if they didn't hear the music", Or: How I learned to Stop Worrying and Love Mickey Mouse', the composer Barbara White sets out to establish why the concept of visualisation or mickey-mousing is still considered such a problem for dance. She pays especial attention to the *practice* of choreography and musical composition. Mickey Mouse, White suggests, is usually invoked as an absence or normative presence against which certain artists have rebelled and 'in Jungian fashion, the denial of the shadow ultimately serves to enlarge its power'.[20] (She emphasises that no choreomusical alternatives have ever gained any equivalent power: 'what is interesting in this renunciation of synchronisation is not the value being espoused, but the failure to espouse any value at all'.[21]) White lays the blame for this odd situation on anxieties about power relations between the media—the anxieties of the choreographer reacting to, and constrained by, music written before the choreography, rather like those of the composer when writing for film (in these circumstances, usually entering the game in second place). It is generally agreed that one of the two collaborating art-forms is boss: rarely are terms like compromise or cooperation used. But White also suggests that there is anxiety about the intensity and loudness (metaphorically-speaking) that we experience in moments of synchronisation: a kind of 'overhearing' as 'sound and movement join together in glorious excess'.[22] Once again, this perception is cognitively based: scientific experiments confirm such special intensity from cross-modal synchronisation, although not in terms of any value judgement about the phenomenon itself.

Pursuing further the 'problem' of music visualisation, it is useful to go back in history, and first of all to the beginning of the twentieth century. There, we find a number of precursors to modern dance aside from Denishawn putting music first, usually using existing, concert music, in both the US and Europe: Isadora Duncan, expressing the *geist* or spirit of the music; the Swiss music pedagogue Emile Jaques-Dalcroze, whose movement-based 'eurhythmics' method was built upon a lexicon of equivalents between music and what he called 'moving plastic'; and the Russian choreographer Fedor Lopukhov, who attempted to develop a 'symphonic ballet' and a theorisation of principles of choreomusical integration (even claiming that dance could match musical sonata form). The root of these ideas is the essentially romantic theory of organicism, wholeness, a long-standing tradition in the arts of transcending dualities. The drive for wholeness is also manifest within the centuries-old tradition of synthesis of the arts leading to the nineteenth-century theatrical *Gesamtkunstwerk* principle of Wagner (which was later the underlying principle of Diaghilev's Ballets Russes). But the choreographers and dancers of the early twentieth century saw music as a liberating force as well—offering structural models that contained in-built motion, an alternative to plot-driven form—and as a vital quality ingredient, offering seriousness and depth to dance.[23]

Soon, however, the tables were turned. Some choreographers viewed music with suspicion and instead sought autonomy and power for dance, alongside new structural relationships between music and dance. This is akin to the growing tendency within modernism across the arts to focus on the materials of the individual medium. Influenced by parallel contemporary developments in Central Europe (with Mary Wigman a leading figure), a number of silent dances were created by American modern dance choreographers from the 1920s into the early 1930s. By the 1930s and 1940s, another theory of music and dance prevailed, greatly encouraged by the writings of John Martin (dance critic of *The New York Times*).[24] As Humphrey put it later in her seminal choreographic primer *The Art of Making Dances* (1959):

> The dance must have something to say of its own, and a mere visualisation of the music is not sufficient justification for bringing it to birth.[25]

> The dance should be related to, but not identical with, the music, because this is redundant—why say in dance exactly what the composer has already stated in music?—and because the dance is an entirely different art, subject to physical and psychological laws of its own.[26]

For a while, music was required to serve dance and was composed specifically for it. In some cases, thanks to a new culture of 'house' dance composers, including Morris's later collaborator Lou Harrison (see p. 365), it was composed after the dance. Ironically, this often turned out to be a kind of music visualisation in reverse, with movement detail now matched regularly by the music that came after it. The dance critic Edwin Denby proclaimed:

> It is no fun seeing a dancer dance smack on his *Gebrauchsmusik*, and he looks as dramatic doing it as a man riding an electric camel.[27]

The new theory overlapped with the old, as schools of music interpretation and visualisation continued to operate. It itself was toned down by the 1950s. But, by that time, Merce Cunningham had sprung upon the scene, turning the tables yet again, advocating the absolute opposite to wholeness, total independence between music and dance, both conceived entirely (or virtually entirely) separately. The Judson Dance Theater and Grand Union artists of the 1960s and 1970s pursued Cunningham's questions further, pushing again into the foreground issues of power, this time as the primary conceptual content of the work. The climax was Rainer's famous manifesto, delivered as a tape accompaniment within her 1968 *Performance Demonstration*:

> ...I would like to say that I am a music-hater. The only remaining meaningful role for muzeek in relation to dance is to be totally absent or to mock itself. To use 'serious' muzache simultaneously with dance is to give a glamorous 'high art' aura to what is seen. To use 'program' moosick or pop or rock is to generate excitement or coloration which the dance itself would not otherwise evoke.

> ...I simply don't want someone else's high art anywhere near mine... I don't collaborate...Furthermore, I am all for one medium at a time.[28]

In line with this thinking, when Rainer *did* use music, she used it deconstructively, in the postmodern sense of commentary (see p. 75). She made an issue of the distance between plain, matter-of-fact pedestrian movement and the conventionalised sentiment of high romantic or popular music, for instance, Berlioz's *Requiem* in *We Shall Run* (1963), and Henry Mancini's 'The Pink Panther' as an interlude in *The Mind is a Muscle* (1968).

Meanwhile, firm rules for good behaviour continued, in other words, for what works as an acceptable relationship between music and dance. From the standpoint of today, it might indeed seem strange that the dance philosopher Selma Jeanne Cohen, writing in 1962, could be so confident about the right way to do things, indeed that there is such a thing as a right way. She writes, not as a practitioner, but as a theorist advocating maturity for dance, as befits an 'intelligent' audience:

> The relationship [between music and dance] must be clearly perceivable, yet not so simple that it offers no challenge to the intelligent observer... Music visualisation did not last. It was not interesting. It said the same thing as the music and nothing more. It made no comment.[29]

Today, we might interpret these developments across the twentieth century as a kind of linear progress myth: the ascent of independent choreomusical relationships over time as signal of the progress of dance as an independent art.

When Morris first arrived in New York in 1976, he perceived that the main trends amongst current postmodern choreographers were conceptual dance: the kind that was reflexive and discursive, and dance that was minimalist (and sometimes pedestrian) in movement content. Dance often happened in silence or was accompanied by verbal discourse. But not everyone had given up on music. There were obvious exceptions: Laura Dean, with whom Morris danced, and who sometimes composed her own music for her trademark spinning dances; Meredith Monk, a composer-singer as much as dancer in her holistic and idiosyncratic brand of theatre productions; and Twyla Tharp, whose interest in a casual, popular-dance style of virtuosity led her back into music during the early 70s. Others used music primarily for reference, experimenting with the effects of dissociation of music from dance and with collage principles.

It is certainly an exaggeration to suggest that Morris was exceptional in his embrace of music when he started showing choreography in New York in 1980. The older New York postmodern 'club' (as he used to call it), who had once cleansed their dance of music, were now eagerly grasping what it offered as fresh stimulation, structural possibilities included—like Trisha Brown (choreographing Bach or Laurie Anderson) and Lucinda Childs (using György Ligeti, Philip Glass or John Adams). Music was now a strong ally in their choreographic progress. The next generation of postmoderns wanted music from the start. As Jim Self put it, 'Yvonne Rainer said no to all those things [spectacle, music]...And I felt like saying yes.'[30]

Yet Morris *was* different, an outsider to them all, with his very different dance and music background. In terms of his movement language, he still used the 'basic, natural' body stance of the postmoderns, and, as we shall see later, he sometimes adopted their systems and game structures (see pp. 160-7). Musically-speaking, however, he was a world apart, in terms of range, of both musical selections and approach. These included in-depth analysis of musical structure as well as much freer choreomusical relationships and a relatively traditional view of music and dance as aesthetic expression. He also made audiences listen more acutely than most of his contemporaries. In this respect, he was more like Balanchine of the ballet world than any other modern dance choreographer, for Balanchine too had made dances that were closely allied to musical detail. In particular, his *Symphonie Concertante* (Mozart, 1947) and *Allegro Brillante* (Tchaikovsky, 1956) could well have been accused of the same 'dreaded sin' of mickey-mousing.

Given this history, it is not surprising that Morris's return to music visualisation has faced opposition. Breathing space between media has become the 'correct' choreomusical style, and the old way is seen as alien and 'excessive', even sometimes as a 'renunciation of imagination'[31] or showing us 'nothing more than the notes printed on the page'. Perhaps too, the link with 'other' culture is seen as problematic: the traditions of social dance and non-western forms, and of animations with their technological representation of the world.

It is useful at this point to consider the nature of the audience watching and listening to Morris's work. For a dance company, as mentioned earlier, Morris's music following is exceptionally large. So, are we musician or dancer, music lover or dance enthusiast, and what impact do our identity and background have on our experience of Morris's choreomusicality? Let us first consider how some musicians have approached his work.

In a 1990 essay on Mozart opera, Carolyn Abbate and Roger Parker discussed Morris's setting of the composer's *Fugue and Fantasy* (1987, see pp. 132-4), as matching the SATB (soprano, alto, tenor, bass) counterpoint and fugue entries, and its rhythm and pitch. In other words, they suggested exact duplication of the fugue structure:

> The audience found this hilarious...But the laughter went deeper, engaged a more complex aesthetic intuition. In the end, the audience was made to mock redundancy. The dance was too exact an inscription of the music... Correspondence—a classical aesthetic category—had become *laughably* absolute. By engendering banality, predictability, and ridicule through such precise means, Morris subverted a fundamental assumption that all of us bring to 'reading' ballet: that gesture and motion should be generated by and correspond to music.[32]

As for the last statement, conceptual polemic is very much of today (see p. 75), but does this not also sound like musicians putting their own art-form first and assuming how 'all of us' read dance? Presumably, Abbate and Parker knew nothing of the earlier debates within the dance fraternity about the autonomy of dance. Does their view say more about them than the work? Morris himself denies the intention that they read into his work.

Other musicians confirm that their dance experiences relate first and foremost to their own art-form. They also speak in the old terms of dance, as if it should be a translation of music.[33] The British pianist Susan Tomes writes in her book *Out of Silence* of her problems with dance:

> So often, particularly with classical ballet, I feel a sense of frustration that the dancers' steps are not actually to the music, but merely run in parallel with it. I'm all too aware of the way they have rehearsed their movements in the studio using spoken rhythms ('And one-and-two-and-point-and-turn,' etc.)... Even today at dance programmes I often feel I'm hearing one set of rhythms from the dancers' feet pattering on the wooden floor of the stage, and another set emanating from the musicians in the orchestra pit. The dance steps are superimposed on the music, but don't truly arise from it. In some crazy way it makes ballet seem unmusical.[34]

For Tomes, Morris proved an exception. So too for *New Yorker* music critic Alex Ross, although he soon learnt that the musical point of view was not necessarily the only one. He writes of his early cultural education:

> The few dance performances that I did see caused discomfort: the movements of the dancers seemed at odds with the rhythm and the structure of the music. Ignorant of the distinct vocabulary of dance, I expected music to dictate the terms of the engagement.[35]

It could be argued, however, that one role of dance *is* to illuminate music to musicians, music-lovers as well as to dance-lovers, to give them a new experience of music, and in some cases, music that they already know. To reiterate a suggestion made in Chapter 1, perhaps a MMDG dance performance is also a concert.

There is one further point to be made about the stance of musicians. Although many are clearly moved and excited by their Morris experience, it is significant that their specific comments on his work are virtually all about structure, focusing on moments of correspondence, the duplication of musical structures in dance. Conductor Jane Glover welcomed the choreographic clarification of the music in *V* (Schumann, 2001) and recalls the approval of a colleague: 'This is like watching an analysis class...there is sonata form, described for you'.[36] Another conductor, Christopher Hogwood, came out with some of the richest clichés of all. Here is how he enthused about his collaboration with Morris on the 1996 *Orfeo*: 'Mark's dance is almost an exact translation of the music. One would be hard pressed to think of another way of doing it. It has such great invention, yet it seems very inevitable.'[37] (Again, the word 'inevitable' elides with the concept of value.) He had been deeply impressed by the televised Vivaldi settings in *Love, You Have Won* (1984, to a recording that he himself had conducted): 'When (soprano) Emma Kirkby sang a trill, the dancers danced a trill[38]... every musical gesture and ornament was reflected in what he did. I thought it was incredibly perceptive.'[39]

Recently, Ross too, despite admitting earlier ignorance of the 'distinct vocabulary of dance', was unequivocal in his praise of Morris's 'music dances', because they were revealing about the music. So he wrote in a 2011 blog:

> The Hummel piece, *Festival Dance*, struck me most of all, because it's another uncanny instance of Morris's ability to illuminate abstract instrumental music through gesture and motion... As so many classical types have commented over the years, Morris and his crew tell you as much about the inner life of musical form as any panel of analysts, and they're a lot more fun. You see the contrasts between the principal

themes, the contours of phrases, the development of motifs, the interplay of counterpoint, the demarcation of longer paragraphs, the nuances of emotion buried in each modulation or cadence. Best of all was the acting out of folkish rhythms in the finale of the Hummel: I said to myself, '*That* is what the music is about.' I seriously believe that all conservatory students should be required to see Morris's work: they will learn to play more intelligently and more vividly.[40]

He too considers *V* a classic Morris 'music dance', and *All Fours* (2003) he claims, was like hearing Bartók's Fourth String Quartet with 'the lights switched on'.[41]

No criticism is intended here. Rather these comments emphasise how musicians, coming from a long tradition of structural analysis and debate, privilege these values far more than dance specialists. They indicate as well the inadequacy of words to explain the experience of form as exhilarating revelation. Musicians are accustomed to the systematic unfolding of ideas and a degree of predictability through the use of repetition-based models such as fugue and sonata. These have nothing to do with lack of imagination. Quite the opposite: they inspire imagination. The music literature is full of material on this subject. The dance literature is not. Looking at the duplication of musical structures from a dance history point of view, however, we can now understand the anxiety, why the 'overhearing' and 'excess' have not been seen as positives.

Aside from those who are specialists in music or dance and carry with them all the theoretical and historical baggage that has grown up around these two media, we should also consider members of MMDG's broader audience. These are the lay people, some of whom do not necessarily attend regular performances of either dance or music. As Nancy Umanoff suggests, some of them may well 'hear, navigate, or better understand music through Mark's dances'.[42] The opposite may also be true, that some are better able to navigate their way through a dance via its music.

I have focused in this chapter on the music visualisation 'problem', because it became central to the discussion of Morris's work and controversial, and because he too has so often been forced to justify it in quick-fire interviews. If it is no longer such a regular topic for discussion today, it is significant that some of his most intense visualisations, like *Ten Suggestions* and *V*, are still thriving as regular repertory. As part of his history, Morris still wants us to see them, he believes in them, and we cannot be sure that he will not make any more of this kind of work in the future. Yet, as we shall see, visualisation is not even half the story, nor is it necessarily the most interesting one to tell. The concept dominates our memories: anxiety has at the same time enlarged its power and diminished the power of what else goes on in a dance by Morris and of his other approaches to music. Of these, there are many, and they too borrow from the history of choreomusical relations.

In the final analysis, Morris's project has been to question the foundations of choreomusical practice (for a broad music-and-dance audience). He asks us to think about our habits and history, what we have grown to accept as rules, then to be open to his surprises, to develop our musicianship as well as our dance literacy, to think beyond the norms of western high art dance, and to listen and watch more closely.

PART 2
WATCHING AND LISTENING
TO DANCE

4

A Framework for Analysis

Introduction

It is useful at this point, before discussing Morris's individual dances, to consider how we might talk meaningfully about relationships between music and dance. How can we conceptualise meetings between music and dance in a way that preserves their full richness and diversity?

For many years, relationships between music and dance have been discussed in deliciously polite and vague terms, not untouched by anthropomorphism—with reference sometimes to happy marriages (going back at least as far as Guillaume Du Manoir in 1664[1]), sometimes to total unity as an ideal, sometimes to civilised debate. Just occasionally, as mentioned in the last chapter, someone dares to propose total independence. But what does all this really mean? How do we process cross-modal information in the form of two artistic media? Quite apart from the underlying value systems implied, what do unity, civilised debate and total independence mean in practice?

Here are some thoughts on watching and listening that engage with the complexity of Morris's dances[2] and inform the analyses that follow. Some readers, on the other hand, may prefer to work the other way round, addressing the analyses of dances first and using this chapter for reference. Or they may wish to use the chapter for later in-depth exploration of an underpinning, specifically choreomusical, analytical framework. Several routes through the book are possible, and several ways of using this chapter.

These are exciting times: intermedia theory is developing fast. Encouraged too by the diversity within Morris's work, the approach here is to draw from a multi-stranded theoretical base, like an analytical toolbox, ready for selective use of its contents, and always as appropriate to a particular dance speaking to us in a particular way. The theory will be regularly supported by examples from Morris's work. While stressing the relevance of method to his specific context, I suggest that the various ways of thinking about choreomusical relations outlined here might also be useful to a broader dance repertory, extending well beyond the work of a single choreographer.

A fundamental concept is that there is always some kind of relationship when music and dance are put together. This seems obvious in the case of Morris's work, where relationships are carefully set up and manipulated, but it is equally true of the work of Merce Cunningham and John Cage, who famously created dance and music totally independently, in other words, made no attempt to 'manage' relationships between the two media (other than being familiar with each other's general style and philosophy).

At the same time, as Allen Fogelsanger has observed, we still tend naturally to conceive of music and dance as either going, or not going, together.[3] We are also naturally inclined to find, or work at finding, coherence or pattern, although there may be times when this is so rarely possible that we lose interest in pursuing this line (as in the work of Cunningham and Cage, when we grow to accept what comes our way from one moment to the next). To expand from the previous chapter, we even sense a number of apparent formal equivalences that have settled as conventions over the centuries and that have led us to imagine that music can be 'visualised' (or not). Dance equivalents, for instance, have at various times made sense for all the following musical categories: rhythm and form; dynamics; texture (for instance, comparing the organisation of dancers with thick or thin instrumental layout or polyphonic/homophonic structures); pitch contour; staccato and legato articulation; timbre (using established associations between a dancer or particular gender and an instrument or instrumental group); energy pattern (large-scale patterns of tension and relaxation).[4]

Supporting the idea that relationships of opposition are also relationships, just as much as relationships of equivalence, the composer-theorist Barbara White adds the point that there is never, in any case, one without the other. There is always an element of simultaneous opposition as well as equivalence, at least due to the disciplinary incongruity—congruence and incongruence, similarity and difference, and various kinds of similarity and difference,[5] so much so that words like similarity and difference often seem hopelessly inadequate. Furthermore, just as White proposes, we have to go to precise examples within precise contexts in order to spell out these dilemmas and pleasures in any meaningful way, to go beyond the question of *whether* music and dance meet each other or not, to ask *where* or *how* they meet.[6]

We need also to take into account that we as audience construct shape and meaning just as music and dance construct shape and meaning together. Our backgrounds and prior experience are crucial in determining how we listen and watch. Are we more musician or dancer? Our personal awareness is never quite the same as anyone else's. We are also likely to find ourselves favouring different stimuli at different moments, our attention shifting fluidly between the two media, and perhaps the same stimuli perceived differently from one day to another.

Both shape and meaning are referenced here. Structural and semantic concerns are inextricably connected, although the emphasis shifts. The chapter moves from ideas about semantic content, to ideas about structure (borrowing from traditional music theory). Structure is not some dry, schematic phenomenon. It is important that, even if Morris says that audiences do not need to know about the structure and mechanics of his pieces, we can experience a tremendous aesthetic thrill when seeing something rigorously wrought as well as expressive and intellectually stimulating in other ways. (Besides, he enjoys talking about structure himself.) Finally, we turn to more body-based, sensual phenomena, the crucial issue of embodiment that is especially hard to rationalise in words.

Another basic concept used here is that music and dance operate in dynamic interaction. They are both seen as subject to change rather than static entities, operating within a mechanism of interdependence rather than maintaining the hard binary of parallelism versus counterpoint.[7] We are dealing with a composite form, music and dance. Whilst we might still be able to trace the separate development of the two media, these two sensory planes now meet to affect each other and to create a new identity from their meeting.

A number of theorists from outside dance have contributed to the development of theories of dynamic interaction involving music, with an emphasis largely on semantic content. Film music theory has been especially useful. In 1947, recognising the inadequacy of the term parallelism, Hanns Eisler made suggestions for a more mobile and multivalent approach to description:

> From the aesthetic point of view, this relation is not one of similarity, but, as a rule, one of question and answer, affirmation and negation, appearance and essence. This is dictated by the divergence of the media in question and the specific nature of each.[8]

Leading from this, in 1980, Claudia Gorbman proposed the concept of 'mutual implication', music and image working together in a *combinatoire* of expression'.[9]

Since then, in 1990/94, Michel Chion has introduced the useful concept of 'transsensorial perception' that cuts across the usual boundaries between the senses. He refers to these senses as 'channels' or 'highways' more than 'territories' or 'domains'. Thus the visual can convey the aural (even if the visual dimension is still central) and vice versa:

Silent cinema, in the absence of sync sound, sometimes expressed sounds better than could sound itself, frequently relying on a fluid and rapid montage style to do so. Concrete music [*musique concrète*], in its conscious refusal of the visual, carries with it visions that are more beautiful than images could ever be.[10]

Chion's ideas resonate with the Gilles Deleuze and Félix Guattari cultural model of 'deterritorialisation' and 'nomadisation', a model also used by dance philosopher Michel Bernard, who argues the case for dance and musicality as roving vehicles for possible sensorial conjunction.[11]

The American modern dance pioneer Doris Humphrey was one of the first to acknowledge the important, active role of music in determining how dance movement is read. In her primer *The Art of Making Dances*, she explains that music can:

...distort the mood. Suppose the dancer has a sequence arranged which is quite serious, a small segment of one of life's major encounters. Accompany this by trivial music which patters along without any depth of feeling. The result is that the dancer does not become stronger by contrast; rather he seems empty, silly and pretentious. Such is the power of the sound to set the mood. This same sequence, accompanied by jaunty, slightly jazzy music, can make the dancer look cynical; he is pretending to be serious, but actually it is all bluff, and he believes in nothing. The variations on this kind of thing are endless.[12]

Humphrey advocated trying out the juxtaposition of the same dance material with different musical accompaniments, testing out the effect of the musical changes. Interestingly, Morris gave a similar assignment at the Dartington Masterclass (2013, see p. 59), when composers and choreographers separately created a hundred seconds of material and then examined the result of different combinations of movement and sound. Humphrey observed that in some circumstances the effect was more of separation or disjunction between music and dance, in other words, of two opposing voices, with music speaking from outside the dancer:

If soft sound supports strong movement and vice versa, a curious effect is produced. The music seems to be antagonist; the figure of the dancer fights to be strong without encouragement; and in his more vulnerable moods the music seems to seek to destroy and dominate him.[13]

Yet, whether or not we perceive music and dance as disjunct, our experience of each is inevitably changed by their meeting.

A related point is that nearly all Morris's dances have been made to existing musical scores, which has particular implications for our understanding of those dances, especially if we are familiar with the scores before seeing the choreography. Each of those scores has developed its own tradition of historical and cultural reference. Each too is subject to freedom from the composer's supposed intentions and renewed through the choreography set to it, informed by new dance and cultural contexts. Thus, our perceptions of the music might well be changed by its association with dance, and perhaps to lasting effect. For instance, we might literally hear notes that we have not noticed before, or a particular instrumental line might suddenly emerge more strongly. Movement seems to seek out related properties in the music and vice versa, and new meanings emerge from their point of contact. The consequence or underside to this is that other aspects of the music and dance are hidden from view or erased. Together, the two media can even create a new shape through time.

All these intermedia proposals clearly acknowledge our cognitive capacities as human beings. We now turn to recent intermedia research involving music that considers these cognitive capacities more systematically. This research draws especially from linguistic theory that has been influenced by cognitive science's discoveries about the nature of mind.

Crossing Domains

Nicholas Cook's *Analysing Musical Multimedia* (1998) is an important contribution to intermedia studies, putting forward a general theory of how potentially *all* different media—music, words, moving pictures, dance—can work together—in theatre, commercials, film and music video. In keeping with his emphasis on issues of denotation, Cook proposes metaphor as a viable model for cross-media interaction, with 'enabling similarity' at its root, the possibility of the 'transfer of attributes', which results in the creation of new meaning.[14] He draws from the literary theory first proposed by George Lakoff and Mark Johnson in 1980, according to which, given 'enabling similarity', we can map across two conceptual domains and understand a target domain in terms of a source domain. For instance, we can understand love (target) in terms of war (source) within the metaphor 'Love is war' because the two concepts have attributes in common: they involve more than one party, and, in certain circumstances, love can absorb from war the concepts of conquest, strategy and siege. But the metaphor, Lakoff and Johnson would say, 'gives love a new meaning'.[15]

Aside from his application of linguistic theory in assessing a multimedia work as 'a distinctive combination of similarity and difference',[16] Cook puts forward three basic and potentially overlapping models of multimedia interaction: conformance, where there is direct congruence and no element of incompatibility, a concept associated with theories of synaesthesia; contest, a more dynamic concept indicating essential contradiction and potential for irony, the media 'vying for the same terrain, each attempting to impose its own characteristics upon the other...each medium strives to deconstruct the other, and so create space for itself';[17] complementation, a kind of mid-point between these two extremes. In what he terms a relationship of contest, Cook proposes the kind of relationship that results from opposition, connection through a primary disconnection, as in punning (which is often introduced between visuals and music in commercials), but the issue of connection/disconnection can arise in far less connotationally loaded contexts, where there is loud music to very gentle dance, strong movement to soft sound and so on.

Theory from cognitive science and linguistics has more recently been applied, and in more developed form, by Lawrence Zbikowski, in most detail within song contexts, crossing music with text.[18] To summarise the theory in relation to dance and music, let us first consider a simple example (to which I will return later), the commonly understood metaphorical link between pitch and spatial patterning, in terms of 'up' and 'down'. The conceptual metaphor at the root of this link between pitch and spatial patterning is: PITCH RELATIONSHIPS ARE RELATIONSHIPS IN VERTICAL SPACE.[19] This conceptual metaphor in turn relies on the pre-conceptual VERTICAL image schema that is grounded in our everyday bodily experience.[20] Our natural capacity to stand upright leads to embodied experiences when seeing upright objects--like trees and poles, or moving objects like rising escalators or water; or moving our own bodies, as in climbing up or going downhill; or, via kinaesthetic empathy, watching the rise and fall of dance movement on stage. Meanwhile, an underlying 'invariance' principle operates, which proposes that 'the best cross-domain mappings are those that preserve as much of the image-schemata structure of both target and source domains as possible'.[21] Thus, Zbikowski argues, we are able to make the link between pitch and space because they are both continua that can be divided into discontinuous elements, with points along each continuum, degrees of 'up' or 'down'.[22] There are:

> correlations between musical pitches and points in vertically-oriented space, and between relationships between pitches and relationships between points in space (such that one pitch can be 'higher' than another).

And Zbikowski continues:

> Once this framework has been established it is but a short step to a characterisation of the succession of pitches in terms of a motion between points in space.[23]

But it is important that the notion of spatial patterning mapping on to pitch is not natural or universal within human understanding. To some extent, it is culturally-based, and is most likely prevalent in the west because it reflects Western music notation systems. It also reflects the apparent sources of vocal sounds in our bodies: the chest for low sounds, nearer the head for high sounds.[24] Yet what we consider 'high' or 'low' is, for instance in Java and Bali,[25] considered small or large (which reflects the fact that small things vibrate at a higher rate than large things). In the West, however, we do not find it hard to understand this small-large paradigm (as an alternative to the high-low one), because of our experience of the sounds that emanate from physical objects and animals of different sizes.[26] Thus, it makes sense that in Camille Saint-Saëns' *Le Carnaval des animaux* (a piece set by Morris in 2012) his elephant is characterised by the double bass and his aviary by the flute. Both these metaphorical paradigms have implications for Morris's *Dido and Aeneas* (1989), even to the degree that a mezzo soprano seems to be a more suitable accompaniment to Morris the dancer than a soprano, because of his size, not just because one of the characters he portrays is the *low*-minded Sorceress. But there is yet another paradigm to consider. Music imagery experiments demonstrate that rise in pitch can also be associated with distancing and acceleration, and pitch fall with approaching and, more surprisingly, turning left.[27]

On stage, matters are more complicated still. Up-down/rise-fall do not relate directly to the small/large paradigm because of the law of perspective and our understanding of upstage and downstage. Our eye-line rises as the dancer moves away from downstage. At least until she reaches stage centre, she appears to increase in size and power, an effect further exaggerated if the stage is raked, in other words sloped upwards away from the audience. Yet we must always consider the bigger context of a dance-music event when applying these paradigms. Sometimes choreographers make use of them, sometimes they disrupt them, and at various times consciously or unconsciously.

Since the mid-90s, the rhetorician Mark Turner and linguist Gilles Fauconnier (followed again by Zbikowski in music) have explored metaphor within a more complex framework, blending concepts from different domains (two or more) to create a further, new, domain, and forming a conceptual integration network (CIN).[28] This theory too can be usefully applied to dance and music. Blending, by its nature, means something more than the sum of parts. The CIN structure is also more interactive, less determined by movement in one direction, from source to target (as in moving a spatial source concept—like verticality—on to the target of music). There is again a kind of 'invariance principle' at work, now called 'generic space', which could work for any of the paradigms mentioned above. For instance, the generic space behind 'rising' and 'falling' in dance and music could comprise continua with the possibility of discontinuous elements and the verticality schema. Now, bringing dance and music together, this might result in a blended space in which we perceive either relatively congruent or relatively non-congruent relationships between what we see and hear, rising and falling occurring at the same or at different times. Such differences in relationship give rise to meaning and lead through elaboration into human concerns, like agreement and opposition, or compliance and resistance, beyond, that is, simple ideas about note patterns and movements in space seeming to relate or not to relate. Or the concepts of high and low alone (in instances where music and dance 'match') can connote such things as joy and despair, or life and death.

Below is a diagrammatic representation of the CIN principle in its simplest form:

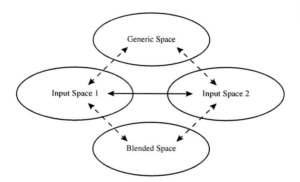

The arrows in the diagram are double-headed because, as Zbikowski explains, 'under certain circumstances, structure may also be projected from the blended space back into the input spaces, and from the input spaces back into the generic space'.[29] For instance, the idea of vertical motion in music and dance symbolising forces that can complement or resist each other in a particular context could make us think differently about vertical motion in either music or dance in other contexts. This in turn might also affect how we think about vertical motion in general.

A prime example in this book to illustrate conceptual blending is Morris's setting of the famous Lament from Purcell's *Dido and Aeneas*. There is an extended analysis of the whole work in Chapter 7. Here, I present summary examples to illustrate the theory in action and move quickly towards the blend, referring to the two input spaces of dance and music. The new CIN works from a shared 'generic space' that 'contains' the concept of Dido preparing to die, her heart broken by Aeneas who has now departed. Part of my analytical approach was to work back to the input spaces, watching the dance in silence, to reinvigorate my ideas about what could be brought into the blend. Already, of course, there was a blend between music and text, and Purcell had introduced repetitions of his own into the text, for the purposes of stress, to suit his interpretation of the story.

A key feature of the music is the 5-bar ground bass that is heard eleven times and is like a second strand within the music in dialogue with, and moving relentlessly against, the vocal line.

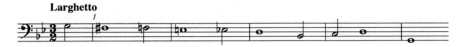

Ex. 4.1 *Dido and Aeneas*, Purcell, Lament, bars 1-5, bass line.

First, the choreography 'fleshes out' the music (and especially the vocal and bass lines) as a conduit for human subjectivity. Dido becomes a moving human being, and the ground bass line becomes a much enriched 'voice', carrying a variety of human traits. It is matched by the dancing chorus and, as such, represents the speech of courtiers, cupids and conscience. In the instrumental postlude to the Lament, the dancing Dido and the chorus illustrate the resolution between voice and accompaniment, completing the blend as it were.[30]

By reflecting melodic contour and phrasing in selected places, the dance increases the particular emphasis suggested by Purcell. He elected to repeat Dido's pleas that her confidante Belinda should not be troubled and should remember her, stressing that remembrance of her, living in the memory, should resist the finality of her physical death. Morris's choreography further highlights these pleas. It illustrates too the metaphorical connection between pitch relationships and vertical space. A number of key movements embody the vertical dimension. In this context, however, the connection between dance and music speaks of the tension between living and dying (for which vertical space is yet another metaphor). The dance component greatly increases the tension, being visual and literally using the 'earth' to which Dido refers.

At the same time, there is a compelling, pervasive element of resistance within this blend. The dance movement not only draws attention to pitch change (or lack of it), it is also influenced by that change. First, there is a resistance to the downward pull of the accompaniment. But enlargement is another, second form of resistance. Both Parts 1 and 2 of Purcell's Lament are repeated, but, on both occasions, Morris chose to make bigger, rather

Dido and Aeneas, Postlude to the Lament, Mark Morris (Dido), with hands in 'fate' position.
© Petra Bober, 2000

than simply repeat, his choreographic statements. Most strikingly, in the Part 2 repeat, Morris hugely increases his upward reach at the melodic climax, the climax of the entire Lament, by both running all the way upstage and mounting a balustrade. Later, we will discuss even more intense examples of resistance, as oppositional resistance, in other examples of Morris's work (see, for example, *The Vacant Chair*, pp. 154-7).

Multiple Voices

The *Dido* example illustrates the concept of 'voice' operating within Morris's work—'voice' as speaking to us from within the music, in the form of both the vocal line and the ground bass, mapping on to Dido and her community. Another example in which separate musical voices have been taken over by dance is *Gloria* (Vivaldi, 1981, see pp. 138-45), where Morris regularly duplicates the SATB organisation in his casting plan. But distinct media are also frequently conceived of as independent voices, potentially saying different things when assembled alongside each other. Nijinska, for instance, conceived of her *Les Noces* choreography as a 'voice' distinct from Stravinsky's music.[31] Another example: in social dance situations, musicians and dancers play both with and against each other in dialogue, the voices of performers operating again through their respective media.

Let us now examine the voice concept in more detail, as a basis for further understanding of Morris's work. It has been debated widely within music theory, especially in the work of Edward T. Cone (*The Composer's Voice*[32]), Carolyn Abbate (*Unsung Voices*[33]) and Lawrence Kramer.[34] It is perhaps significant that, just as Morris has used a high proportion of vocal music, Cone, Abbate and Kramer have all incorporated many vocal music examples in their writings. All these scholars reject the Romantic notion of art as manifestation of the creator's single personality or soul and think of voice instead as a flexible concept.

Cone refers to the persona (or more precisely *a* persona, one of potentially more than one) of the composer evident from within a single work.[35] His stance remains fundamentally composer-centred. But his position is one that post-structuralism has long since questioned. Critiquing Cone's monological approach, Abbate (drawing from Mikhail Bhaktin) refers instead to 'potentially multiple musical voices that inhabit a work'. She also focuses on these as 'certain isolated and rare gestures...that may be perceived as modes of subjects' enunciations', and that 'distance us from the sensual matter of what we are hearing, that speak across it'.[36] In accordance with the post-structuralist idea of 'voice' as fundamentally illusory in a wishful sense, Kramer characterises the concept as the 'feeling of a continuous plane of intentionality'.[37] Yet he says that voice must be understood 'not as cause but as effect',[38] and that we should be careful to recognise it for what it really is: 'a rhetorical strategy meant to humanise the impersonal agency that we hear in music'.[39]

Leaving aside the problematic, composer-centred aspects of Cone's theory, his work has proved useful in opening up the 'voice' discussion and particularly in highlighting a variety of other possible personae that can be found in music, like the literal voice in song as opposed to the piano accompaniment, the various singing characters as opposed to the orchestra in opera, the solo instrumentalist in a concerto, or the various instrumental lines in a fugue or other kind of polyphonic work. In each case, the total musical construct (formed by the interaction between the components mentioned) is considered by Cone to be the complete musical persona or the composer's persona. But, as we will see later, the term 'voice' could be applied to the 'topics' in instrumental music as well, specific musical styles bringing particular connotations into a score, as in the scores used in *Mozart Dances* (see pp. 438-9).

It is a useful coincidence that one of Cone's main musical examples is Schubert's familiar *Erlkönig*, a song that Morris set as one of three Schubert songs in *Bedtime* (1992, see pp. 341-7). The story is based on Goethe's poem about a man and his son riding home at night in a storm. A spirit, the Erlking, tempts the boy to come away with him. The father does not see him and ignores the frightened boy, but when he arrives home, he finds the boy dead in his arms.

Cone first looks at Goethe's ballad, a series of stanzas, and suggests that, within it, the number of 'voices' can be read in at least four different ways: from just one, the narrator who quotes the three characters, to five, an interlocutor, a responder and the three characters who speak for themselves.[40] But Schubert's song presents a quite different scenario. Cone concludes that the reading of four voices from the text, the narrator and three characters, is the one that works best in this other context, but with the accompaniment equivalent to another narrative voice.[41] He also argues the particular relationship here between the composer's voice and the singing voice. The vocal line has special power as it absorbs text and gives us perhaps the strongest impression we ever have of a human being, a 'dramatic character' or 'protagonist', actually speaking to us.[42] The composer's voice, however, according to Cone, may still be the dominant presence, influencing this vocal persona (who is logically unaware of this) as well as the 'mute' piano accompaniment. In *Erlkönig*, the accompaniment refers to the environment of the character, depicting stormy night music, but also symbolically suggesting the outer world impinging strongly upon the character and his reaction to this impingement.[43]

Cone proposes that the composer makes the poem his own, by appropriating the music: 'by turning it into music. What we hear in a song, then, is not the poet's persona but the composer's.'[44] But Kramer makes the useful point that Cone does not include the voice of the poet within song, arguing that in most songs, 'the poetry and music will pull the voice in different directions, and the more so to the extent that the listener takes the text seriously'.[45] So conflict and resistance are involved. The music may absorb the poetry smoothly, but not necessarily so, and indeed, as he intimates, previous experience plays its part, just as knowing a piece of music before watching a dance set to it inevitably affects our experience (see pp. 94-5).

As for Morris's treatment of *Erlkönig*, we should first bear in mind the obvious, that the work now involves his 'voice' too. Yet I do not go so far as Cone probably would, to say that Morris's 'voice' is now the central, dominant authority, even if, as the last creative voice to enter the fray, he has changed matters radically. Later analysis will demonstrate how Morris's characters as dance 'voices' interact with what Goethe and Schubert came up with before him. Sometimes, the dance voices map directly on to the four voices of the song, but at other times Morris blurs the boundaries between his characters and extends them into other phenomena such as the wind, the fog and the horse. So, pulling into other, new directions, he disrupts what may previously have seemed like coherent voices.

The voices within instrumental music are another important source for Morris, not only singing voices. A compelling example occurs in the central movement of *All Fours* (2003, to Bartók's Fourth String Quartet): a dialogue between the first violin and cello, first in inverted canon, later (from the end of bar 59, see Ex. 4.2), straight canon, 'visualised' by a couple who seem like 'parents', sharing the stage with their two 'children'. The violin and cello speak as one with each of them respectively (the cello as the man, then the violin as the woman). I have already suggested that Morris sees a large proportion of music as drama, as do some of the composers he sets, not simply for its abstract values. A clear illustration is this kind of treatment of instrumental voices as subjectivities, or, as Kramer would see these, as examples of 'humanised impersonal agency', either because Morris feels that this is what they already are, or because he makes them so with his choreography. Compared with dance, music is relatively open in its capacity for meaning, yet, even without a programme attached, it is never entirely abstract (see Chs. 12, 13). Morris makes that meaning more specific: he grounds it.

Considering application of the 'voice' concept to dance, Cone raises the interesting question as to whether the musical accompaniment is to be understood as heard by, or as part of the consciousness of, the dancer:

Ex. 4.2 *All Fours*, Bartók, Fourth String Quartet, third movement.

The character [Cone refers to dance with story] portrayed by the dancer is conscious of his *actions*, realistically interpreted, but he is only subconsciously aware of his *dancing*, which is both a formalisation and an expressive amplification of his natural gestures. In the same way he is subconsciously aware of his accompaniment.[46]

Yet dancers can sometimes show conscious recognition of their music, even in plotless choreography. On many occasions during Morris's choreography, a dancer draws our attention to the music. Morris does this in several solos for himself, for instance in his 1994 *Rondo* to Mozart, adopting a knowing, self-conscious performance manner as he 'shows' the musical detail in his body. It is one of his performance 'styles'. But there is another especially good example near the beginning of the 'Double' section of *Mozart Dances* (2006, to the Sonata in D for Two Pianos, K. 448) when the soloist (originally Joe Bowie) stands still, turning upstage, then towards the audience, and making isolated gestures to two isolated high notes (each of them E, decorated by a preceding grace note, bars 35 and 37). He attaches himself precisely to Piano I: these decorated Es are the only thing happening in the Piano I score at this point. It is as if he suddenly addresses us directly: 'Let me bring out for you this tiny moment in the music *and* I'm fully aware that I'm mickey-mousing!' In another sense, he embodies, or 'becomes', the voice of the piano. The opening hand gesture is small and rather like the pianist's actual motion when producing the original musical gesture.

Ex. 4.3 *Mozart Dances*, Sonata in D for Two Pianos, first movement.

Processing Sound and Motion: The Phenomenon of Capture

Formal relationships operating in a less discursive and personal manner—for instance, in the domains of structure through time, rhythm or pitch—can still lead to meaning. There is, for instance, the phenomenon of movement exaggerating musical events (which, heard alone, may be barely perceptible) and thus influencing our perceptions of the music. In psychology, this phenomenon is known as 'visual capture', although it has been described aptly by psychologist Lawrence E. Marks as one medium 'sopping up' attributes from another.[47] In other words, visual stimuli are strong enough to influence people to perceive simultaneously presented auditory stimuli as related. The phenomenon can work in the opposite direction too, as 'auditory capture', sound stimuli affecting our perception of visual information. 'Capture' relates to Chion's notion of *added value* in film. This is:

the expressive and informative value with which a sound enriches a given image so as to create the definite impression, in the immediate or remembered experience one has of it, that this information or expression 'naturally' comes from what is seen, and is already contained in the image itself.[48]

A scientific experiment by Kathleya Afanador (and colleagues) provides a dance example of 'auditory capture'.[49] The experiment suggested that different musical tempos may change our perceptions of the speed of dance movement so that it looks faster or slower than it really is.

A solo that Morris made for himself to the central movement of Bach's *Italian Concerto* (2007, see pp. 402-11) provides a good illustration of the reverse 'visual capture'. The solo is like a metaphor for a thought process and unlike what people usually associate with Morris, for he is relatively hands-off here with musical details such as pitch and rhythm, often ignoring them. On several occasions, however, shared accents turn into structural signposts, moments in the score pulled out of their melodic surroundings by dance movement, as if 'frozen' out of their context, and thus afforded additional impact. For instance, Morris shows us a distinctive lunge and swing out backwards with an arm. Each time, he draws upon a syncopated leaping interval in the melody line, and the leaps become larger and more urgent. Here is another instance when 'up' in music can (metaphorically, and through Chion's concept of 'transsensorial perception', see pp. 93-4) connote distance (away from place or goal), not simply height in the vertical dimension (see pp. 96-7).

There is a degree of mutual enhancement here between music and dance. The argument for visual capture is that the physical movements at these particular points are especially powerful (or, in science language, 'salient') within their context. They stand out from their context, as major accents, more so than the 'accompanying' musical syncopations, which are part of the regular style of the unfolding long, long melody. And this 'freeze phenomenon' (another concept from psychology)[50] undoubtedly disturbed the expectations that I had from already knowing the music by itself. I also experience a sudden 'lift' or 'tension' within my body when I encounter these moments: they structure my experience of the whole solo. But it is important that their effect draws from music and dance *together*. This is an example of the two media *together* creating a new shape through time (see p. 95). Such moments of common accent contribute to interpretation, suggesting sudden realisation or crystallisation emerging from the thought process or murmuring subconscious in this particular solo.

'Capture' can extend in time beyond mere accented moments. An example of this comes in Young Drosselmeier's solo (Tempo di Tarantella) in the Act 2 pas de deux of *The Hard Nut*: he welcomes the clarinet interjections within the flute melody by changing from jumps to tiny steps in short-long rhythm just at these points.

Ex. 4.4 *The Hard Nut*, Tchaikovsky [*The Nutcracker*], Young Drosselmeier's solo. L and R indicate 'left' and 'right' steps.

Watching more traditional settings of the same music, we may never be aware of these changes of orchestration.

With regard to the direction of 'capture' and the power of one medium over another, the current view on how we perceive rhythm and the phenomenon of pulse or beat is intriguing. Morris claimed recently: 'people don't see rhythm, not nearly as well as they hear it'.[51] He probably meant hearing *and* feeling kinaesthetically. So when we watch dance and think we feel dance rhythm, we might really be feeling musical rhythm? Various experiments, but which do not use the body as the visual source, have demonstrated entrainment to heard beat as the norm when aural and visual beats move out of synchronisation.[52] But is this always the case? What about stepping, or stepping in particular ways? Do we know enough about the power of the body? Morris's own work suggests that movement can profoundly alter our sense of musical rhythm and tempo (see p. 64).

To date, there is little scientific research on dance and music that addresses formal concerns such as these. Looking to the future of choreomusical analytical theory, however, the discipline of cognitive science (including neuroscience) could well help us understand how we process hearing and seeing within a dance context. It is interesting, for instance, that, within the field of philosophy (including aesthetics), the boundary between the conceptual and empirical has become more porous in recent years: current philosophy is now informed by cognitive science.[53] In the choreomusical field, a raft of scientific experiments readily suggests itself, such as testing our perception of aural and visual beat and their respective strengths, or our kinaesthetic response to conditions of choreomusical congruence and incongruence. Morris's work, as much as anyone's, calls for further work of this kind: it is clear that he himself thinks deeply about audience perception. Having said that, working towards an integrated approach would seem crucial, in other words, empirical work taking into account cultural issues, our aesthetic judgements, as well as the varying dance and musical experience of those who participate in this kind of experiment.

Structures through Time

In terms of temporal structures, many existing concepts from music theory can be applied within choreomusical analysis. The concept of *unit hierarchy* refers to the combining of smaller units of notes or moves (the microform) to form larger units, and the continuity between these units up to the level of the macroform, which is the whole piece. In music, an established nomenclature exists for units that are either part of specific forms (for instance, exposition, variation, episode, fugue subject) or common to all tonal forms (phrase, period, theme or motif). These named musical units are very important for locating dance material within analytical discussion. For in dance, there is no such fixed nomenclature, except the titles for individual dance numbers (e.g. variation), and motif, the term for an arrangement of movements (spatial and temporal) that is characteristic of, and particular to, a work. The term 'phrase' has been frequently used for dance, but in a variety of ways, and rarely defined. I use it here to convey the idea of a short dance unit, but will clarify what this means within a particular context.

In many styles of dance, including, to some extent, Morris's, symmetrical units of structure together form a larger unit. These derive from the symmetrical structures of much eighteenth- and nineteenth-century music, especially music written for dance, but also from the structure of the body. Often, a musical unit is repeated or answered by a unit of related length; the dance unit is repeated on the same or opposite side of the body.

The concepts of *mobility* and *closure* refer to the processes of continuity and breaks in continuity that define units and articulate music and dance at various levels. They are widely used in music and literature and are well-suited to dance too. Broadly speaking, these processes are deeply intertwined, but mobility can be said to derive from developmental devices, and closure from separation in time (sustainment or rest), completion of a progression (like the end of a pathway, or a musical cadence), or a major change that marks off as finished what has just been seen or heard. Simple, immediate repetition without rest or break has dual mobility/closure characteristics, indicating continuity through relationship to what has just been seen or heard, while closing off the previous material. There are also different degrees of mobility and closure.

Music and dance often play off against each other in terms of mobility and closure. A choreographer or dancer can choose to draw attention to the long line of a section of music or to dissect the music in order to show its internal units. Matching musical closure in dance appears to emphasise the effect of closure, to reinforce the sense of completion (just as matching accents reinforce emphasis).

Return is a particular form of closure. Signalling a concluding or terminal event, return articulates larger structural units and provides a major effect of closure, a sense of coming-home stability. We see this in any number of musical forms, such as sonata (the section called recapitulation after the exposition and development of material), ternary (ABA) and rondo (ABACA etc.), and the effect of closure is especially strong if the recapitulation is an exact repeat of what happened before, and in the home key. Similarly in dance, return can be made more or less exact as repetition or variation, and as a result more or less emphatic. Whether or not the choreographer decides to match a musical return is important. Dealing with sonata form structure, for instance (see Chs. 12, 13), Morris can choose to create a more or less powerful sense of return by repeating the familiar movements and formations of the exposition with the music, from the beginning of the recapitulation and onwards (the most powerful), or by introducing change: variations on the original movement, additional layers of material, fresh casting, or new spatial arrangements. Masking the straight emphatic return can give the impression of openness and continuing progression, rather than resolution or finality, instability rather than stability. It is a matter of degree, and the structural choice can have a decisive effect upon our experience of closure and resolution.

As well as the organisation of material into units, *tonality* plays a central role in determining structure across a vast history of western music, from the Renaissance, through the nineteenth century and, to some degree, into the present. It is a force therefore within the majority of Morris's musical choices. (There is no simple equivalent in dance.) This book is not the place for discussing the huge variety and complexity of codes for chordal progressions based on the western major and minor scale. Most important here is to stress the fundamental drama within tonality, the move from and back to a point of stability, that supports, or drives, thematically-based musical structures. A tonal piece of music starts in a home key, the tonic key, which is rooted in the first note of the scale that forms the foundation of a score. Thus, to take an example from the Morris repertory, F is the tonic of Mozart's Concerto No. 11 in F major, which opens *Mozart Dances*, and the score begins in the key of F. Then there is a move to one or more other keys, each clinched by a cadence, a marker point, or punctuating gesture, of closure. Most often, these keys include the dominant, the key based on the fifth note of the tonic scale, traditionally associated with the culmination of a sonata form exposition. Thus, C is the dominant key of the F major Concerto and after its arrival within the exposition, the music moves into other keys and then back again, at the point of recapitulation, to the home (tonic) key and to stability.

Talking Rhythm

An immediate point of contact between music and dance, rhythm is another fruitful basis for examining structural relationships. In both cases, it reaches us via a part of the brain connected with motor function. Here, I still find it useful to hold on to the notion of parallelism (or 'visualisation') and counterpoint between music and dance. The principle used is that music and dance are two simultaneous voices operating sometimes with, sometimes against, each other through matching or crossing accents or metres, with the term counterpoint reserved for those occasions when accentual or metrical patterns conflict. I steer away from hard binary opposition, however, acknowledging instead a continuum of possibility, weakening and strengthening effects of rapport and disjunction (according to the frequency and force of crossing accents). This notion of counterpoint is grounded in evidence from social dance traditions, of the play between musicians and dancers (as independent voices) that invites interpretations of tension, anxiety, chase and competition.[54]

Even within situations that might be interpreted as prime examples of rhythmic parallelism or music visualisation, it is important to consider the distinctive manner in which music and dance operate. Fundamental differences between dance and music emerge when we consider speed as rate of rhythmic events (notes or moves). Physical limitations determine that, in a given period of time, the maximum number of events possible is smaller in dance than in music. In order to create an effect of parallelism, changes in musical speed can be reflected in a generalised rather than precise fashion. It is also possible to reflect broad contrasts in continuity, in other words, whether musical notes form a continuous series or are broken with rests.

Furthermore, speed changes are more likely to be obvious within a single dance movement than within a single musical note. A dance movement, by its very nature, has slowing and quickening built into it. Take a simple step, which is only relatively simple—it is nuanced in many different ways in Morris's style—and consider how much happens before and after the impulse of weight change that marks a point in time. In the same way, even when the phrase beginnings and endings in music and dance seem to correspond, there is often overlap, a blurred synchronisation, energies awakening and trailing to repose at different times. Dance constantly fluctuates in speed, and because of this, the effect of rubato in dance, the slowing, delaying and then catching up with the beat, can arise from within as well as across individual moves.

In terms of the shared principles of beat and metrical framework, music rhythm theory is the basis of the system of structural categories proposed here for dance: again, the field has developed a much more thorough detailing of concepts and of their interrelationship than exists for dance. Music theory also suggests that we engage with rhythmic structure as drama, responding to its capacity to build and defeat expectations, to the effects of syncopation as a feature of instability forced against stability, and again to patterns of mobility and closure that suggest tension and release. In other words, as suggested earlier, rhythm, like other formal principles, gives rise to meaning. Crucially, these rhythmic categories, together with their implications for meaning, can contribute directly to choreomusical analysis: patterns of interaction can be observed, demonstrating that musical and dance features can both reinforce and contradict each other.

A summary follows of the rhythmic categories that I use and which are explained in more detail in *Moving Music*.[55] The rhythmic categories (again respecting distinctions between media) can be divided into three strands. After this tabulation, some of the concepts are given more detailed explanation and related to examples from Morris's work:

> 1. Categories that refer to duration and frequency: note or move (the basic unit of duration in dance and music); beat (or pulse); rubato/breath rhythm (the kind of rhythm which avoids or plays against a motoric beat); speed, for instance, tempo (the rate of beats), the rate of consecutive notes or moves, harmonic rhythm (the rate of harmonic change), or the rate at which space is covered.
>
> 2. Categories of stress, or accent: the stress of single notes or moves, for instance, metrical accents (the accent of downbeat, the first beat of the bar, or strong relative to weak beat); rhythmic accents (when a movement or note stands out through lasting longer than those around it); dynamic accents (accents produced by physical energy in both dance and music).
>
> 3. Categories referring to the grouping of sounds or movements through time, the interaction of 1 and 2: metre, metrical hierarchy, hypermetre, polymetre (the use of different metres simultaneously); units (of grouped notes or moves that are not necessarily congruent with metrical structure), downbeat and upbeat (pick-up) units (terms that indicate beginning at the bar-line or before it, with an anacrusis).

Strand 1 includes the rate of consecutive notes or moves (as opposed to tempo, the rate of beats). Morris often plays with this concept, finding a dance beat different from, but mathematically related to, the one in the music (e.g. twice, or half, as fast), also using it as an opportunity to give the impression of slowing or speeding up when the musical tempo/speed remains more level (see p. 64). An example comes from *Dido and Aeneas*: the 3/4 chorus 'Thanks to these lonesome vales'. Morris's dancers start out in quick running steps to the quaver beat, faster than the crotchet pulse of the music, but later he adds lines of dancers in counterpoint to them, now walking to each crotchet (see p. 240, Ex. 7.4).[56] (The principle here relates to that of *metrical hierarchy*, which is discussed below.)

One of the most sophisticated examples, however, of this play between music and dance can be found in *The Argument* (1999, to Schumann's *Fünf Stücke im Volkston*), a dance for three couples. The duet that Morris made for himself and Tina Fehlandt is both the most tender and the most upsetting. The musical tempo is *langsam* (slow), but to the same, repeated 7-bar musical phrase, we see two extremes within the choreography. First, Morris introduces short dance beats, giving the illusion of a quicker tempo than the music, then later he utterly subverts this approach with jaw-dropping molto adagio. His space-devouring allegro phrase casts soft triplet steps at quaver rate over the musical 2/4 (Morris makes this both silky and relaxed, but also passionate, a miraculous combination). Later, there is a devastating incident when Fehlandt cautiously holds on to his arm and opens both of hers into a window through which she stares out at us. The pair do not look at each other; it is as if she no longer belongs to his world. Then she quietly slips in front of him, still looking away—minimal motion, slower than *langsam*, and all dance beats abandoned.

A witty demonstration of harmonic rhythm, on this occasion an emphatic acknowledgement of musical structure, emerges within Morris's setting of Chopin in *Sang-Froid* (2000). During the creative process, rehearsal pianist Ethan Iverson noted for him the only place 'where the harmony changes on every beat', in other words, quickening to crotchet rate sixteen bars before the recapitulation (bar 53 in the 'Winter Wind' Etude, Op. 25, No. 11). 'Well, I'd better make the most of it,' joked Morris: 'since it's a well-known fact that I'm the most musical of choreographers.'[57] So he did and, at that precise point, the dancers take eight deliberate strides, one for each harmony.

To illustrate stress (strand 2) in relation to metre, I turn to Dido's first aria 'Ah! Belinda' (the second part). When she sings 'I languish', the dancing Dido makes a series of strong, staccato gestures, on the upbeat (a preparation), then on the downbeats of bar 29 (straight arms before her, palms together), of bar 30 (the arms raised over the head, palms still together), and finally on the second beat of the same bar 30 (the arms separated).

Ex. 4.5 *Dido and Aeneas*, Dido's aria, 'Ah! Belinda'.

Dido's dynamic stress here is not prompted by the music. Choreographing the last gesture to the second beat of the bar turns it into a rhythmic accent (the position lasts for two beats), while also creating syncopation, an accent crossing what you hear in the music by taking weight away from the main, downbeat accent. Additional syncopations follow to the next line of words, 'Yet would not have it guess'd', crossed wrists over the head with tilts of the body from one side to the other (left and right, twice), occurring on the downbeat (three times) and then on the weaker beats 3 and 2.

Ex. 4.6 *Dido and Aeneas*, Dido's aria, 'Ah! Belinda'.

It is normal for us to make sense of music and dance in terms of patterns of linked or grouped beats, notes and moves (strand 3). When we consider the linking of beats, we are dealing with the concepts of *metre* and *metrical hierarchy*. If the fundamental metrical unit is the bar (measure), which groups beats in twos, threes, fours, and so forth, with a metrical accent at the beginning of each group, similar grouping and accenting is seen to occur at sub-bar and broader levels, the hierarchy extending from the length of the smallest note or movement values. We find shifting lengths of beat as well, for instance, as crotchet, quaver or semiquaver, the time signature written accordingly as a number over 4, 8 or 16. But let us take as an example a bar of 6/8, which is a grouping of two beats (dotted crotchets). Each bar contains two sub-bar groupings of three quavers. Then, several bars (four in the example) might group together into *hypermeasures*, each one lasting one hyperbeat.

Ex. 4.7 An example of a hypermeasure, comprising 4 bars in 6/8 metre.

Metrical accents feel stronger the broader the level in the hierarchy; in other words, they are strongest at the hypermetrical level. *Hypermetre* does not always exist in music and dance, but when it does, it is usually regular and perceived either as a result of regular notes or moves every two or more bars, or successive units grouping notes or moves, each unit of equal length (two bars or more), most strongly when dance and musical material repeats, exactly, or with an element of variation. Hypermeasures can sometimes indicate musical phrases ending with cadences. In the 8-bar example from *Mozart Dances* (the 'Double' section that was referred to earlier, see p. 105, Ex. 4.3), we sense hypermeasures of 2 or 4 bars in length, defined here by repetition and varied repetition. There is a clear similarity across the first three 2-bar units, and precise repetition (like re-starting from the beginning) in bars 5-6. In classical western music prior to the twentieth century, groupings of 2- and 4-bar hypermeasures are by far the most common. They are especially strong in music written for dance (in the nineteenth-century ballet classics and in the dances in *Dido*), also in a great deal of recent popular music (for instance, in the American gospel and country music of Morris's *Songs That Tell a Story* (1982) and *Going Away Party* (1990)).

As befits what is most useful to each medium, dancers and musicians often count differently, dancers at a slower rate than musicians. In dance, the counts used in rehearsal sometimes demonstrate the grouping of bars into a hypermetrical structure, but straight four-square constructions often need no counting at all, they are simply felt instinctively in the body. Nor are MMDG counts necessarily fixed, and they are often dropped once dancers are familiar with movement material. The dance counts that appear within the examples in this book are my own, drawn from analysis, although informed by a general knowledge of MMDG practice.

Morris engages frequently in *metrical counterpoint*. By far the most common examples in his work are 'hemiola' effects taken (as well as the term) from baroque music practice, 6 beats divided simultaneously into three 2s and two 3s across two voices or parts, or, in Morris's case, across dance and music. A good example is the opening, signature theme of the duet/chorus 'Fear no danger' from *Dido*, when after throwing their arms up and over their heads with a big jump on the spot, matching the vocal rhythm (bars 1-2, 6 musical beats divided into two bars of 3/4), the dancers do a knee bend and little jump on to the heels in second position, three times (bars 3-4, again 6 musical beats divided into two bars of 3/4, while the movement is now divided into three 2/4 bars).

Ex. 4.8 *Dido and Aeneas*, Duet/chorus, 'Fear no danger'.

But there are many examples of other kinds of metrical crossing, to different effects: a delightful gently bouncing travelling step in 3s for the couples against the straight 4s in the music in the last song of *Going Away Party* ('When you leave Amarillo') and, unusually, a 5-count gestural pattern that opens the Triumphing Dance in *Dido*, over the music in 3/4 (with hints of 2/4, see pp. 246-7).

Normally, metrical counterpoint happens in Morris's choreography when it does not appear in the score. The idea stems from the stamping and clapping games that he played with Penny Hutchinson in his childhood (see p. 22). As a teenager watching Pennsylvania Ballet in Vancouver, he was beside himself, too, joyful and laughing, when he spotted the famous three lines of counterpoint in the last movement of George Balanchine's 1941 *Concerto Barocco* (bars 41-47): the music in 3/4 (counted here in accordance with the quaver-rate dance pulse), **1** 2 3 4 **5** 6, and two different groups of women: one group with repeating 4-count units—three jumps on pointe, followed by a leg extension to the side, and the other group breaking away into a 3-count version (with just two jumps on pointe) of the same motif. The result is, as Acocella describes, 'a fantastic machine'.[58] But Morris has a penchant for machines himself (see p. 149), and Balanchine's metrical crossings provided a useful model—no other choreographer has used this device so frequently. Morris, however, does not introduce more extended metrical units, like 5s and 7s, as often as his predecessor.

Sometimes, Morris mixes together several devices to create a delicious pattern of dialogue. Here is an example from *Festival Dance* (2011), the opening line dance step of Hummel's final Rondo movement barred as 2/4 in the music. There are several points of independent accentuation. In the music, there is a syncopation on the B in the melody (bar 2), but the dance does not follow suit. On the other hand, there is a special dance accent at the halfway point in bar 4 (beat 2)—a sharp curve forwards of the body—which is not prompted by anything in the music. Furthermore, the dancers now pause in this curved position, so that the fourth dance bar becomes 3/4, which is followed by two hopping step patterns in 3/8, before reconciliation with the musical metre 2/4 in bar 7.

Ex. 4.9 *Festival Dance*, Hummel, Piano Trio No. 5 in E major, Rondo.

The 1997 *Rhymes with Silver* collaboration with Lou Harrison contains an exceptional amount of metrical counterpoint. My example is the 'Prince Kantemir' section (named after a Moldavian prince), part of which was taught me by John Heginbotham (see p.8). Here, Morris sometimes fits, sometimes crosses, the written musical metre and the metrical grouping within bars.[59] Harrison introduces a 4-bar percussion ostinato pattern with two bars of 5/8, each subdivided rhythmically to articulate counts 1-3-5 (bars 1-2), then 1-3-5-7 (bar 3 in 7/8) and 1-4-7 (bar 4 in 9/8). In dance phrase 1, Morris follows Harrison's rhythmic outline. But in dance phrase 2, to the repeat of the ostinato, he weights his own rhythms slightly differently, in bar 2, favouring count 4 (instead of 3) and re-structuring the sub-metre of 7/8 (bar 3) as 1-4-7. Then, by introducing dancers in lines of three following different rhythmic/metrical patterns, Morris builds a texture of several rhythmic layers across the stage. It is significant that this dance was influenced by the Balkan models that Morris experienced when growing up in the Koleda Folk Ensemble (see pp. 22-3). This is demonstrated not only by the asymmetrical rhythms and metrical counterpoint, but also by the movement style, with the occasional bounce on the supporting leg and the

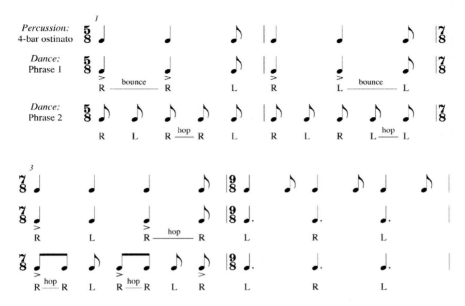

> = accents made by steps and arm movements

Ex. 4.10 *Rhymes with Silver*, Harrison, 'Prince Kantemir'.

arms swinging forward and back on certain steps, held together by the little fingers.

It is useful to consider further the implications of Morris's Balkan experience and to examine Balkan rhythmic asymmetries in more detail, for their effect as much as for their construction. Looking beyond Morris's work, take, for instance, the Macedonian Žensko Beranče step in the pattern 3+3+2+3+2,[60] forming a bar of 13/16 and the Bulgarian Kopanitsa analysed as 2+2+3+2+2 adding up to 11/16.[61] The semiquaver lowest common denominator refers to a very quick division which is best conceptualised in the flexible terms of sub-metrical grouping, into 'long' and 'short' units.

Much Balkan music and dance is not based on a mathematically regular unit long enough to register and hold on to in a series of what ethnomusicologists have called isochronous units.[62] Rather, our dancing bodies grow to feel secure meeting the irregular pulses that group together the tiniest divisions like the semiquavers of the examples given. So this is music that you do not (and should not) count, but rather feel within the body. The effect is striking: 'Looking as though you quiver, but it's really internal', Morris once described how it felt.[63] His friend, the dancer Penny Hutchinson, at one a time a trainee Koleda member herself, confirms the distinctive feel of the style. 'It makes you shimmer,' she says. 'It's sexy.'[64] Both could well have been referring to the excitement of the rapid bounce and lift of the body and the tiny shifts between 'long' and 'short' timing in Balkan style. It is significant too that the 'counting' that accompanies the learning of Balkan dances often relates to the number of steps in a sequence rather than to regular beat. This too reflects organicism, the experience of acceleration and deceleration, rather than of a mathematical beat framework for movement.

I suspect that this freedom at the most detailed rhythmic levels, which became second nature to Morris during his early training, could be a reason for his nuanced experiments with classical western musical rhythms. It could also explain his occasional impatience with the complexity of notated scores, 'all this insanity', he calls it, speaking specifically of *Nixon in China* (1987) when he would question John Adams: 'Did you have to put in a bar of 1/8 right here? Is that necessary? Come on! Isn't that the same as a comma?'[65] The point is that Morris heard and felt the 1/8 primarily as a short extension. Ultimately, it is big, deep physical response that means most to him. He conceives of all music as a communication between physical bodies, as precise communication, never merely as a computational, metrical and score-based operation. Regular metre in western music, for him, means the possibility of rubato, and likewise in the dance that goes with it.

A subtle example is Morris's setting of the second Dvořák Bagatelle in *The Office* (1994), a disturbing piece in which, one by one, members of a community are ordered to leave by a besuited woman (or man) carrying a clipboard. Dvořák's scoring is for two violins, cello and harmonium. The movement here, rather than the music, contains the rhythmic interest. It is a line dance, with a limping sideways step repeated to stage left, then continuing to stage right, forming one long phrase, with the right foot (the left on the return journey) stepping down and across in front of the body. Morris repeats the same step at different speeds. The passage as a whole accelerates and then slows again, with hints along the way (bars 3, 6 and 7) of 2 beats in the dance against 3 in the music.

The key issue here is that the acceleration and deceleration in the dance is magnified by rubato, beyond straight contact with the musical beats. (The notation in Ex. 4.11 cannot reveal this degree of nuance.) At the slow speed, there is a strange lingering, a resistance or holding back with the weight as the step down is taken, and a sense of catching up on the quick, high steps in the centre of the phrase. At the end, there is a lazy, relaxed swing of the right leg in preparation for a repeat of the journey. As Morris puts it, this gesture is the kind of move that 'folk dancers can do and highly trained professional dancers have a harder time with'.[66] Suddenly the plainest step pattern looks subtle, both perceptually and emotionally. I tried out the passage myself with the music in order to test this out. The unusual, easy quality of the

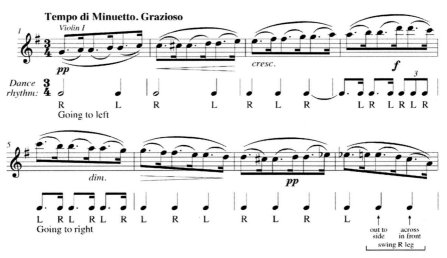

Ex. 4.11 *The Office*, Dvořák, Bagatelle, No. 2.

leg swing, allowing the gesture of a leg or arm to happen on the music, but without accentuation, turns out to be another aspect of Morris style. It is a quality seen in some of the slower Balkan dances. In most western theatre dance styles, on the other hand, gestures have an impulse attached, to start them off or to mark their point of arrival.

Morris's approach to beat deserves further discussion, for it affects even the simplest step. Dancer David Leventhal explains: 'In Mark's world, the dancers are required to shift their relationship to the beat depending on what kind of specific approach Mark wants. There's no universal way to hear it, and so you're always on your toes.'[67] Beat is a concept that is not about a point, but rather about a length, in time: for Morris, it has a 'front', a 'back' and the more familiar centre, which he simply calls being 'on' it. 'It's not about a click-track,' he says.[68] The critic Edwin Denby thought similarly when he compared the New York City Ballet style of dancing 'on top of the beat...they can take the exact lift of the upbeat to dance on' with the Royal Ballet's tendency to 'follow the beat, follow it with a tiny lag'.[69] But Morris style involves both strategies, as well as the one most frequently used, being 'on' the beat. 'Lazy rhythm' is an occasional instruction, when Morris wants his dancers to relax 'at the back of the beat', as is the opposite, 'at the front'—'anticipate...be ahead of it'. There is a link here with popular music specialist Richard Middleton's notion of 'groove' in music, using for beat the more 'substantial' image of a mound or hill, taking up 'a little real estate'.[70]

A fascinating example of Morris's nuanced attitude to beat occurs in the central section of Morris's *Mozart Dances* (Double, to the Sonata in D for Two

Pianos, K. 448) when a circle of men just walk slowly, downstage, across and back upstage again. Of course, the musical beat was there to use in the first place, but now they soften the percussiveness of the piano by pushing off the back foot *on* the beat and changing weight smoothly just *after* it. 'The beat is suspended,' Morris explains. He also uses the image of 'lurching'.[71] Here, it is as if the dancers lengthen our sense of beat most powerfully and, for men, unusually gently. The result is profoundly moving.

Embodiment

I return at this point to the subject of musical embodiment. Today, a range of writing refers overtly to the body or the 'carnal' in music, which is especially relevant to Morris's own experience of music (see pp. 18-20), and one reason why he likes to put the dancing body alongside it. Cook, for instance, proposes that we 'might speak of the feel of the sounds in the fingers or gut', something that is hard to explain in words—and neither science, nor hard theory, at least currently, can help us—yet that is powerfully concrete and deeply 'known' within our bodies.[72] In her book *Boccherini's Body: An Essay in Carnal Musicology* (2006), Elizabeth Le Guin suggests that, as listeners, 'we join our eighteenth-century counterparts in "reading" apparently sonic events for imagistic or tactile associations'[73] and, writing from her experience as a professional cellist:

> No music I have ever played seems to invite and dwell upon *the nuances of physical experience* [my italics] as does Boccherini's: one can count on tiny variations of position, weight, pressure, friction, and muscular distribution having profound structural and affectual consequences.[74]

These ideas complement Roland Barthes' theories (in his well-known essay 'The Grain of the Voice' (1972)[75]) that 'body' can be transmitted directly from the body of the musician performer, to become an embodied musical feature. He calls for the return to an aesthetics of musical pleasure, '*jouissance*' (with all the erotic connotations of that word), after years of performance as execution. Thus, he admires the voluptuousness and physicality of the Russian church bass, of the baritone Charles Panzera (as opposed to pristine Dietrich Fischer-Dieskau). In terms of instrumental voice, he rejoices over the physicality of Wanda Landowska's playing, in contrast with the 'petty digital scramble, of so many harpsichordists...As for piano music,' he goes on, 'I know at once which part of the body is playing —if it is the arm, too often, alas, muscled like a dancer's calves, the clutch of the fingertips (despite the sweeping flourishes of the wrists), or if on the contrary it is the only erotic part of a pianist's body, the pad of the fingers whose "grain" is so rarely heard'.[76]

I suggest that there is a parallel here with Morris's movement style, its visceral nature, indulgence of weight, and exposure of the 'pad' or 'grain' of the sensual, pliant bare foot (as opposed to hard, tight muscle, often in shoes). Coded, formal vocabularies, as in ballet and Merce Cunningham's work, often project a glistening surface muscularity that distances the audience as much as it is impressive and even spectacular. Morris's dancers are instantly more friendly—they stand like normal, un-stylised human beings, have mass, flesh and, we imagine, internal substance—and make no attempt to disguise any of these things. This is possibly why audiences so often say they would like to get up on stage and join them.

One particular dance theatre genre makes the point about the 'body' in music with special force, the kind that introduces the doubling of singers and dancers/mimes in the same roles, as in a number of pieces by Morris (like *Dido*, or *Erlkönig* in *Bedtime*, when the singer becomes a series of different characters). The effect is especially strong when singers are visible, even more so when they are seen moving on stage (as in Gluck's *Orfeo*, see pp. 294-8). Here, there is the most direct link between the body of the dancer and the body of the musician. As Morris once said, justifying his unusually large repertoire of choreography to vocal music, and wanting more body: 'Singing is like dancing. It's the body, the body in the world, with nothing in between, no instrument between.'[77] Indeed, singing has an intensely visceral edge, emanating from *inside* the body. Now, the doubling device, even though there is a sense of visual separation—a voice literally seen outside as well as heard speaking through the dancer and her voice—has the potential to forge quite the opposite, a powerful empathetic connection. The bond, for instance, between the singing and dancing Didos, is physically deepened as it were, and presence enlarged (doubled).

There is fresh nuance here to that old cliché of 'music visualisation' as sound seems to insinuate itself into the dancer's private spaces and by proxy into the spectator as well. Or, in a reading that gives the performer more agency, the dancer listens acutely, and responds. But the effect can sometimes be of mutual possession rather than two-way dialogue, of a dancer inhabiting and being inhabited by a musical line, breathing with the swell of sound, touching a note, opening our ears so that we relate what we see and feel in our bodies from the dancer to what we hear.

It is important that I have embodied material from Morris's work myself while analysing it, literally experimenting through movement, 'doing dance', in most cases, a kind of 'sketch learning' of moves and phrases to music rather than full, stylistically accurate rendering of the choreography. Morris's solo from his *Italian Concerto* is the outstanding example of this, learnt with the choreographer's agreement from John Heginbotham, in 2011, and at the same time, the phrase from *Rhymes with Silver*. The experience led to further thoughts of my own about the structure and meaning of these dances. But I also 'sketched' out the whole of the Lament from *Dido* and numerous other phrases of material. I remain convinced that this kind of experience can inform choreomusical analysis,[78] seeing it as comparable to the practice of many music analysts (probably those who are the most interesting): they edge towards the piano as a natural part of their working process. (Indeed, it is pertinent that today, increasingly, music analysts view performance itself as an analytical act.[79]) The result of such 'sketch learning' is hearing and seeing better, partly because the business of practical learning draws us into detail, highlighting distinctions within the choreography far more than distanced watching allows. At the same time, we feel more strongly the dynamics and drama of music and movement, grasping information that film sources, and especially those of poor quality, tend to disguise. We might even 'interpret' ourselves, working in the spirit of a creator, a participant in the process of bringing into being the work analysed, discovering points of relationship between what we do and what we hear that we might never have experienced from watching a performance. Thus, we get a modest glimpse of what Morris's dancers must experience, the 'voice' of the performer.

Towards the Performance of Analysis

It is appropriate that on this most physical note, the survey of this analytical toolbox draws to a close, save for a few suggestions as prelude to the actual practice of analysis. First, a reminder, readers are strongly encouraged to keep in touch with the MMDG website of film clips attached to this book before approaching each analysis (http://markmorrisdancegroup. org/jordanbookclips) and to check the up to date list of clips available for viewing. They are also advised to keep in touch with the umbrella MMDG website with its invaluable visual resources, photographs, additional film material, as well as written items. Those who are less familiar with rhythmic aspects of music and dance may want first to practise their skills, and I recommend starting with two dances analysed in Chapter 5: *I Love You Dearly* and *Canonic 3/4 Studies*. Readers are also encouraged to refer to musical scores (where possible) and to listen to musical recordings, especially important when film material is not available. On the other hand, a useful tip for clarifying dance rhythm on film is simply to turn the music off and watch in silence.

As so much of Morris's choreography converses with musical structure and its detail, the music itself tells a major part of the whole story. For a basic introduction to musical score reading and theory, two books are valuable in being written specifically with dancers in mind: *The Muncey Music Book*, and Katherine Teck's *Ear Training for the Body*, which involves direct exploration through movement, concepts immediately put into practice. Approaching music theory from the point of view of the musician or music lover is Eric Taylor's two-part *AB Guide to Music Theory*.[80]

My final point has to be about keeping in touch with the real, live theatre experience of dance and the provisional nature of all analysis. Musicologist Stephen Walsh once pointed out that '[music] analysts tend to look at music as segments of score that are static before their eyes, but performers have always to consider the way that music reaches the ears in time'. His example is Stravinsky's *The Rite of Spring*, which, he notes:

> has come down to us, after all, as a concert work with a beginning, a middle and an end and internal continuities that sustain it through the not inconsiderable lapse of more than half-an-hour on the clock.[81]

Walsh's point can easily be transferred to dance. We might remind ourselves of how dances are intended to be experienced. An audience member at a performance probably sees a dance once only, all the way through without a break, allowing certain moments to be forgotten, others to be emphasised and remembered, as an evolving whole, not as a choreomusical structure. In the case of *Italian Concerto*, which was something of an experiment in methodology, I avoided reading the musical score until late on during research, and I used it then largely as a means of checking observations. I wanted to keep my reactions to sound and visual motion as fresh as possible, undisturbed by knowledge of the kind of deep structures that come only from close interrogation of the score and detailed cross-referencing. Initial reactions are of the utmost importance. Sometimes, I even stage *forgetting* a dance, leaving breaks between viewings and, if at all possible, not getting fixed on just one recorded dance performance (a problem that dance analysts constantly face).

The circularity of procedure in the development and application of analytical method is also interesting. Seeing and hearing have generated methodological concepts in the first place, which in turn have generated seeing and hearing more and more distinctively. Then, while use of a method can be revealing about a dance, application of it can also lead to its own refinement. The dance speaks back to us again and we must let it do so. Living with the fluid and the uncertain is both exhilarating and true. Analysis is a creative act, another kind of performance.

PART 3
THE DANCES

Period 1: 1980-88

5

Early Dances

In Chapter 1, the first part of Morris's professional career was characterised as a period of exuberant experiment—he tried his hand not only at setting different kinds of music but also at employing many different approaches to it. Ironically, therefore, although this is the period when Morris spoke most vociferously about translating and *being* music, it is also the time when some of his work most obviously contradicts such statements. The dances discussed here betray a vigorous, unsentimental approach to music and a fascination with rhythm stemming from Morris's background in Balkan dance and Flamenco. Some are among the most exciting dances that he ever made.

The first MMDG programme, presented at the Merce Cunningham Studio in New York (1980), already confirms variety of approach. To take examples from the five pieces, both old and new, there was *Barstow* (1973), its movement largely driven by the 'found' graffiti inscriptions quoted in Harry Partch's score; *Brummagem* (1978) (originally for Pacific Northwest Ballet), featuring sudden outbursts of intricate steps and obsessive gestures alongside a Trio by Beethoven; and the new *Castor and Pollux* (1980, also to Partch), a kind of stylised folk ritual with rhythm patterns constantly shifting both within and between music and dance.

Selected clips of dances that will now be analysed can be found on the MMDG website: http://markmorrisdancegroup.org/jordanbookclips.

'Real' Music Visualisations?

Not one of the dances in this first programme could be labelled a music visualisation if we adhere rigidly to the original Denishawn principle (see pp. 76-7): the reflection of musical structural detail to such an intense degree that it seems to be the raison d'être for a piece. For now, let us keep this principle in mind. A year later, 1981, there was what might be called a *real* music visualisation, *Ten Suggestions*, to the Bagatelles Op. 5 (Ten Pieces for Piano) by the Russian composer Alexander Tcherepnin. But it did not set a trend. Pieces by Morris clearly belonging to this genre can be counted on the fingers of one hand, a tiny number out of some sixty dances created between 1980 and 1988. Sometimes, even then, we find this intensity within only one section of a dance. After *Ten Suggestions*, it can be found in *The "Tamil Film Songs in Stereo" Pas de Deux*—a small part of it (film music, 1983), *Love, You Have Won* (Vivaldi, 1984), *Marble Halls* (Bach, 1985) and the fugue of *Fugue and Fantasy* (Mozart, 1987). In every other respect, these dances are very varied. Since this early period, dances of this kind have been even fewer and farther between. It is perhaps most significant that there have been any at all.

Perhaps the most interesting and sophisticated from the early group is *Ten Suggestions*, the solo that Morris made for himself. It has been revived several times on other dancers, Mikhail Baryshnikov (who danced it within the repertoire of the White Oak Dance Project), Peggy Baker, another White Oak dancer, and, after a fifteen year break, in 2011, Amber Star Merkens and 2013, Dallas McMurray. The analysis here is based primarily on the recording of Morris himself dancing it in 1981.[1]

As Morris said in a 1986 interview (see p. 78), *Ten Suggestions* was a piece that he clearly intended as a 'music visualisation', a reference to dance history, also as a manifestation of dance clichés that once had truth in them. So it incorporates the props of visualisation pioneers like Ruth St Denis and Doris Humphrey—a hoop, a ribbon and a chair.[2] It is the lyricism of this women's genre that seems to interest him here—not the hard and often tedious rhythmic approach of Ted Shawn[3]—also the romantic aspirations and dreams of unity with great music associated with the genre. Assumed by a man in pink silk pyjamas however, their kind of dance is immediately made strange and gently humorous. The feminine side emerges as Morris trips daintily to the beat, like a young ballet girl holding her skirt (his pyjamas), rippling the ribbon joyfully to the exuberant, high melody and charming us with deftness of execution. You marvel at the precision and lightness of a big man doing such moves.

Yet, if Morris sometimes seems to insinuate himself into the spirit of a pioneer American woman dancer, at other times there are impressions of a child's innocence—and these were, after all, pedagogical pieces by a budding composer, or of male figures of a certain sensitivity—a Pierrot or a Chaplin—all of them here in a private place of fantasy. One of the Bagatelles is a march; so Morris dons a pith helmet and marches, jauntily. At the very end, he leaps up on to the chair, triumphantly hitting a high note, but his hands cover his face, an image of shock, fright or perhaps a kind of hysterical ecstasy. (Different performances suggest different meanings here.) The dramas stop, and all the fleeting characters, including Morris himself, dissolve into one...then blackout.

Morris tells us that the piece sprang from his own improvisations—at first, the props were not linked to any particular Bagatelle.[4] It settled over time, but only up to a point, as is clear from comparison between the 1981 recording and those of Morris's performances during the 1990s. Each performance has different details, those of the 1990s decidedly more forceful and melodramatic, as if playing for laughs. I am drawn particularly to the lighter-touch early performance.

Morris arrives on stage suddenly and spectacularly during the last two bars of Bagatelle No. 1, with a presto triple *pirouette* that ends frozen in a crouch. He proceeds to make a number of proposals about what the various Bagatelles mean to him. While much of the attachment to musical detail, its pitch contours, rhythmic variety and repetitions (immediate and at a distance), seems casual and pleasantly naive, elsewhere, a striking awkwardness engenders sympathy. There are times when full body manoeuvres underline a determination to articulate minutiae. Morris refers to this (and particularly the business of props) as 'showing the effort of music visualisation'.[5]

The dance proper begins (No. 2, Con vivacita) as Morris somersaults (once) to a brittle, staccato motif (heard twice) encompassing, like the somersault, a small range, three semitones. Back up in crouched position, Morris softly releases his downstage foot and the wisp of a hand and your ear turns to the chords that start to plod (again staccato) in the accompaniment. These are odd, non-dancerly movements, in fact Morris looks more like some four-legged creature than a human being and you can easily identify with the discomfort of undertaking such moves. They constitute the main theme of the dance. When the foot and arm gestures become larger and more marked, like isolated body parts generating a life of their own, you seem to hear the accompaniment more clearly. Later the foot becomes a motif—a little kick in standing position—to a single low chord, which exaggerates its lowness and isolation. Foot equals bass, no doubt at all now, and again, it sharpens our hearing of the musical event. So too the props acquire a life of their own, as their manipulation causes a sudden switch of attention away from the body, like the push of the hoop (No. 4, Lento con tristezza) or the scissors snipping the ribbon (No. 6, Allegro con spirito), the culminating actions of their respective Bagatelles.

In Tcherepnin's score, there are many striking passages of pitch ascent and descent and series of accents, and Morris likes to highlight these further, showing them as 'rattles' or twitches up and down through his body, anything from exclamatory hand gestures beckoning skywards down to the shake of a foot. Sometimes, he makes a legato descent seem even more so, with a long controlled sink to the floor (No. 7, Vivo), or a pointed finger traces the direction of motion (No. 10, Presto)—as if you could possibly mistake it—or the gay ribbon is flung high in the air and then beyond human control. All this looks both slightly ridiculous and exciting: when things happen fast, we can hardly keep up with them.

One of the most intriguing dances is based around the chair (No. 5, Dolce). The first image is of Morris sitting on it, pulling his feet up and down to the oscillating up-down left-hand accompaniment. This gives the impression of a wider musical interval than it really is. At the ends of bars 1 and 2, his bottom rises in response to the melody (in the right hand), and when the melody rises still further in bars 3 and 4, he gets up, turns round and steps half-way up on to the chair, then back down again as it falls.

Ex. 5.1 *Ten Suggestions*, Tcherepnin, Bagatelles, Op. 5, No. 5.

Later, the dance frees itself from the chair, tempted by the music: higher pitch (and spatial) regions are engaged. Morris returns to the lower registers (and to sitting on the chair) towards the end. But there is a touch of ambiguity—each time Morris puts his feet down, he rises just a little off his bottom—like a see-saw effect—as if when something goes down, something else has to go up. Morris often likes that kind of twist within the vertical paradigm (see pp. 96-7), especially when it involves both matching and contradicting direction of pitch. Finally, the musical oscillation is inverted (down-up), at which point he heaves *both* feet *and* bottom up and down together, then turns round to hop up and down, hands supporting him on the chair, another version of the see-saw.

At the end of No. 7, Morris repeats one of the long, slow falls, as mentioned earlier, but the final chord tips upwards. This is another example of the see-saw, and here a big surprise.

It is important that Morris's approach to the musical detail is selective. You cannot visualise everything; even the attempt to do so would look ridiculous. The crucial point is that the real moments of visualisation stand

Ten Suggestions, the 'chair' dance, Mark Morris. © Tom Brazil, 1992

out very strongly, like dance 'marks'. Indeed, so much is this the case, you might well think there are more of them than there actually are. You also grow to expect these 'marks', and when the music repeats without them, there is a sense of loss.

Nevertheless, *Ten Suggestions* is not at all like a music visualisation of the early twentieth century. It is imbued with what Acocella calls a 'double-sidedness that is absolutely fundamental to his vision, an ability to see and express two opposing aspects of an experience simultaneously'.[6] Where she suggests double-sidedness—and this is a recurring theme in her reading of Morris—I am inclined towards multi-sidedness, multiple voices. There are already hints of several personalities hiding in the work, and the piece darts between each. Together, these voices speak of another, over-arching voice that maintains critical distance and recognises the loss of innocence, one that is strengthened by Morris's ploy of taking time out between numbers: tidying his sleeves in preparation for the next dance, observing and listening to the clatter of the hoop as it settles to rest on the floor, or just being himself. If the piece is funny—'showing us the effort of music visualisation' recognises a fundamental absurdity—it is also serious, fundamentally respectful, Morris sharing with us his impossible ambition to embody an unbelievable truth as well as the sheer pleasure of dancing to this music. This kind of commentary upon, and ironic distance from, a borrowed source, links Morris with a prevailing concept of postmodernism (see p. 76). It is also because *Ten Suggestions* moves into areas beyond merely 'copying' musical detail, using this as just one device alongside other, dance values, that it stands out as such a remarkable early work.

Occasionally, Morris has used the visualisation tool even more strictly. Perhaps the most extreme example is also the simplest, the short mnemonics section within *The "Tamil Film Songs in Stereo" Pas de Deux*, a piece that tells the story of a lesson given by a tyrannical dance teacher.[7] From a street vendor in Singapore, Morris picked up the recording, the soundtrack from an Indian film about a singing lesson, and he had the idea for a parallel in dance. To each note of the Indian raga, in western speak, C, D-flat, E, F, G, A-flat, B, C, he attached a particular mnemonic syllable—uttered in an especially irritating, whining manner by the female pupil—and fixed a different pose to each syllable/note. Dressed in blue lycra tights—teacher Morris demonstrates for his hapless pupil Penny Hutchinson to copy him (cod Western modern dance style, including a Graham contraction). (N.B. Unless otherwise indicated, I refer in all my analyses to the dancers who premiere Morris's works.) Morris shows the sequence growing from a simple scale, ordering the notes/moves in different ways, sometimes encompassing intervals more ambitious than scalewise motion, in retrograde and inversion ('ma ma, pa pa, dha dha, pa pa, ma ma, pa pa, dha dha, ni ni'), but the same moves always represent the same notes. He doubles up the time, once, then again, as is conventional in Indian dance, in a hilarious mixing, a true presto body-twister, of two cultural practices.

Far more sophisticated, yet quite as strict, was his setting in 1987 of Mozart's Fugue in C minor for two Pianos, K. 426. This was created as a prelude to the Fantasia in C minor for Piano, K. 475, which visualises large musical gestures in the kind of drama about imagined demons in a downstage 'Fateful Corner' that was common in early modern dance.[8] The Fantasia outstays its welcome, but the Fugue is a tiny gem, four minutes of non-stop hectic activity. The score follows the standard form of a fugue, with a series of subject entries—for four 'voices', episodes featuring other material, subject inversions and rapidly overlapping vocal entries (strettos). Fairly early on, once all the musical ideas have been stated, the dance, also for four 'voices', virtually writes itself. It is a miraculous system.

Each of the dancers has a chair as home base, all four in a line arranged to match the 'gender' of instrumental voices and in the order, reading left to right:

Soprano   Tenor   Alto   Bass

Choreographically, the musical voices are matched perfectly throughout in terms of motivic organisation, pitch and rhythm (although shifts of key are not an issue): a leaping interval, one that falls, a tight three-note gesture, a repeating note hammered out staccato, a trill. When the fugue subject is inverted, so the dance moves get inverted too.

The key to the interest of the system lies in the movement ingredients and arrangement of the line-up. Bass man sits down to start it off and all his colleagues watch the neighbour on their left in readiness for action. Then Mozart takes over.[9] Few choreographic liberties are taken, although dancers get to stand up from time to time. By the end, when a buzzing semiquaver accompaniment starts up, they are allowed to somersault out into the space, run round and return to base.

To the trill, the seated dancer pulls her feet off the floor and shakes them. Denishawn theory stated, with no irony, that trills 'may be visualised as a whirl, or a vibration throughout the body accented in the arms and hands, or a ballet *emboît* [quick little steps on the toes]'.[10] Morris devised his own eccentric version, which gives an idea of the madness of the piece. There are also impatient stampings, determined fists, throwing the arms up in despair—as if saying 'heaven help me'—or lying back in exhaustion and shielding the eyes—'I can't take any more'. Although you cannot possibly absorb all the information, there are moments that command your attention. A few moves, like the foot trills, turn into dotty messages passed quickly from one dancer to another. Occasionally, pairs of dancers team up, as near the end, when the 'soprano' and 'tenor' get together just as the music instructs them. Finally, they and the other two voices play fugue subject and inversion off against each other.

As in *Ten Suggestions*, all this adds up to something bigger than structural ingenuity. The fugue principle becomes metaphor for a battle or fierce competition, the orderly kind with rules, but fundamentally aimless all the same. It is also about the business of any performing art, playing your own part, struggling with yourself, while being responsible to the group. In that respect, it can be terrifying as well as hilarious: 'people laugh at the desperation of others', says Morris.[11] Building a crescendo of tension, the Fugue reaches a bizarre, broken climax, the team all set to split. Morris also explains the piece as conceptual polemic, a means of 'de-deifying' what he considers a 'clumsy Mozart attempt' at a fugue (see p. 84).

Another kind of Morris visualisation involves words, and there are many dances of this kind, the very early *Barstow* (Partch, 1973), *Songs That Tell a Story* (Louvin Brothers, 1982) and *Lovey* (Violent Femmes, 1985), where mime gestures enlarge and confirm what you hear from the singer. Some of these dances are also interesting musically. *Love, You Have Won*, Morris's setting of Vivaldi's solo cantata *Amor hai vinto*, RV 651 is one. (He made it to the Emma Kirkby recording, which is featured in the 1986 *Dance in America* documentary.[12]) Communicating a man's passion for the nymph Chloris, the cantata is structured as two recitatives, each followed by an aria. Morris sets it as a duet for two men in loose white shirts. During the recitatives, the two dancers mirror each other and mime ideas such as the arrow of Chloris's beauty, the cold blood circulating within the man's veins, and the torment within his mind. The arias are strict Da Capo, ABA, starting as solos for the first A section, and turning into duets, the cue for the new arrival to spin a web of decoration alongside his partner, following the baroque musical convention of decorated repeats. The structure of each recitative and aria is exactly the same:

Recitative	duet in mirror formation
A	solo [originally Guillermo Resto for the first aria, and Morris for the second]
B	duet
A	duet

Within the arias, there is still occasional reference to the words, to being tossed like a boat amongst high waves (unsteady lurching upstage), looking out (a hand raised to the forehead, as if towards a harbour or shore), or finally, to the dream of requited love, the calming sea (hands forming waves of diminishing size). The approach to musical ornaments and melismas is especially interesting, shown as *pirouettes* (lots of them), little *cabrioles* (beaten steps—a form of decoration borrowed from early ballet), extra skipping (fidgety) transition steps, a flowery operatic gesture, the gentle shimmer of a hand, or grand flourish of a leg. Sequential musical repetitions are followed as a matter of course. But there are some counter-moves, a huge full-body gesture or stub of the foot without any accompanying musical accent, a step in three counts crossing the metre of one of the instrumental interludes. Once again, Morris uses vocabulary associated with women: there are lots of steps high on the toes.

If this dance description sounds a trifle silly, there is indeed something silly about extreme baroque elaboration. Back in 1984, Alastair Macaulay worried that *Love, You Have Won* jokes about the music 'in a manner I found condescending'.[13] Yet he enjoyed the 'sweet strength' of Morris's vision and was 'touched' by the gestures of its two 'renaissance choirboys'. Just a few years later, more accustomed to Morris's manner of doing things, he was excited by the ambiguities within the dance: 'You no sooner laugh, however, than you're touched. The relish Morris finds in Vivaldi's rhetorical flourishes gets under your skin....'[14] Indeed, the vigour of performance and construction is clear demonstration that Morris takes the music seriously. Once more, this is not straightforward music visualisation in the manner of Denishawn: there is gentle ribbing of, as well as respect for, the tradition.

The last music visualisation example *Marble Halls* is a muscular, tick-tick-style dance, with body parts operating somewhat robotically—what you see is what you get—but odd things suddenly happen, the dance wanders off course from time to time. (The piece was originally made for the men of the Batsheva Dance Company, later staged on MMDG.) Set to a three-movement Bach concerto (BWV 1060), *Marble Halls* explores relationships between soloists and a large group, as equivalent to solo instruments and orchestra. The piece has been performed both with the original scoring for violin and oboe and with Bach's transcription of the solo parts for two harpsichords.[15] Morris prefers the transcription because the two harpsichords sound like 'machines, so clattery and strange',[16] just what he wanted for rigorously systematic choreography. *Marble Halls* is also *hommage* to Trisha Brown,[17] reminiscent of her *Glacial Decoy* (1979), in which dancers drop out into the wings as the choreography surges from one side of the stage to the other. The title comes from a popular and often-quoted nineteenth-century opera aria 'I dreamt I dwelt in marble halls'.[18] Morris had the image of dancers emerging from behind huge columns.

Tina Fehlandt, who danced in the work for many years, and now stages it, clarifies the schematic deployment of dance forces in relation to the music. In the first movement, a line of four dancers reaching from up- to down-stage centre 'represents' the string orchestra, while the trios flanking on both sides cover the solo instruments. Orchestral tuttis are visualised by both the central line and one or more of the outside groups. In the second, slow movement, there are two lines, broadly-speaking six dancers across the back representing the accompaniment and four soloists dancing the solo instruments in front. The last movement shows the soloists (now down to one man and one woman) occupying the central area of the stage, again dancing the solo instruments, while the tutti group tend to work on the stage diagonals.[19]

In both outer movements, the music follows standard ritornello concerto form, in which an introductory tutti section returns in part or whole, and in different keys, at various points during a movement, interspersed with different material. Continuing in the mode of visualisation, Morris staples dance movement to the musical material. This is especially clear in treatments of the main 8-bar tutti theme of the first movement. It is in two halves. The opening (bars 1-4) and its response (bars 5-8) later become separated, but the dance material associated with both halves always returns fixed as in the original form, and so does the material associated with fragments that break away from this theme.

This main theme also sets the scene in reflecting pitch and rhythm very closely, starting with arms pressing down to one side on beats 1 and 3 (of 4/4 time) and going up again with leg lifts on beats 2 and 4 (bars 1-2). Yet, just as the musical material is differently nuanced on repeat (bars 3-4), starting one tone lower, in bars 3-4 we see that the dancers' arms are the same as before, but the leg moves in retrograde, up on beat 1 instead of 2, down on beat 2 instead of 1. This makes for another of Morris's favourite seesaw twists embracing up-down contradiction, within the body and between the dance and the music, a variant on visualisation of his own devising.

Later, Morris treats us to hopping and turning variations of this main dance theme (always when the same musical material repeats) and to a fragmented account that takes the movement of bar 2 down to the ground to match a scalewise descending musical sequence. In the first movement, there is also a recurring leg kick step on three beats against four in the music, performed by the trios, sometimes in canon at two beats to make matters even more complicated. A common pulse remains, linking score and choreography, but this is a clear step away from visualisation technique. Sometimes, Morris plays with pulse and tempo (rate of pulse). In the first movement, he digs into the music for both slow and fast pulses, at crotchet and quaver rates, giving the impression of an overall change of speed. In the second (in 12/8 time), he introduces all three rates: dotted crotchet, quaver and semiquaver. It is significant, however, that these changes are not prompted by musical change (see pp. 111-12).

Of quite a different order is the strong sense of motivic unity and economy of material across all three movements of *Marble Halls* choreography. Again, this is not the case in the score, even though the principle itself comes from music. In *Marble Halls*, thematic restrictions are such that you would be hard put to find any new dance material in the last movement: just familiar moves assembled in new ways.

One of the most striking features of *Marble Halls* is the response to isolated passages of harmonic stasis, one or two in each movement. In the first, there are two sudden shifts to a sustained dominant ninth chord. As the choreographic 'equivalent', the dancers stand rooted to the spot, their arms snaking and writhing around their bodies (bars 50-2 and 96-8),[20] visually, a startling metamorphosis, a sudden disturbance. The same visual disturbance occurs once in the last movement, to a long dominant pedal chord—a sudden shift of behaviour by the central couple, while the group surround them as if honouring totems. Morris's choreography makes these musical passages seem even stranger. He weaves a variant on the same gestures into the language of the second movement.

Another intriguing example of crossing musical boundaries is an isolated, syncopated hopping sequence (like a talisman) that only fits the musical accentuation (almost exactly) when we see it in the last movement. Here, it is expanded into a 4-bar sequence.

Ex. 5.2 *Marble Halls*, Bach, Concerto in C minor for Violin and Oboe, BMV 1060, third movement.

In the first movement, the hopping is over in a flash, a one-bar intrusion (bar 60). A single man in the central line strikes out with it, while everyone else falls into a crouch. In the second, a woman performs it adagio and legato, literally lifted through it. It occupies just half of a slow bar (24), the outstanding point of harmonic stasis in this movement. So the occurrence in the final movement is like a resolution, at least a structural resolution: only now is it fully absorbed into the continuity, tempo and language of the piece.

Let us now consider other references to music visualisation in Morris's repertory of this early period, as temporary strategies, visualisation taking its place within a larger choreomusical context. First, we go back in time to *Gloria* (1981/revised 1984), one of the most popular works that Morris has ever made and the first dance that he conducted.[21]

Gloria

Two especially valuable and provocative analyses of *Gloria* already exist: Acocella's account of its use of music and interpretation (in her 'Heaven and Hell' chapter), including apt descriptions of the step motifs that permeate the dance; and Inger Damsholt's detailed discussion of its choreomusical aspects.[22] *Gloria* was the Vivaldi score that Morris sang at school and which provided him with invaluable insider's experience. His own colour-coded miniature score confirms his thinking as a choreographer, for he highlights selected lines of material—solo singers and instrumentalists, SATB (soprano, alto, tenor, bass) choral parts, and occasionally other musical details that he intended to emphasise. Morris's setting was televised in abridged form for *Dance in America*.[23] *Gloria* takes its text from the Catholic mass. Its layout is as follows:

1. Gloria in excelsis Deo
2. Et in terra pax hominibus
3. Laudamus te
4. Gratias agimus tibi
5. Propter magnam gloriam
6. Domine Deus, Rex coelestis
7. Domine Fili unigenite
8. Domine Deus, Agnus Dei
9. Qui tollis peccata mundi
10. Qui sedes ad dexteram Patris
11. Quoniam tu solus sanctus
12. Cum Sancto Spiritu

In notes that he wrote at the time of the 1984 revision, Morris stated that *Gloria* 'borders on the devotional'.[24] Taking its cue from the text, it is a celebratory statement that speaks of people in plain, grey street clothes, from any time or place, who are sinners, penitents, secure within a community and of being saved. Much of Morris's setting is, as Acocella says, 'friendly', full of joy and fun, and, for the final 'Amen', all the participants fall to earth in a big cross formation (X meaning Christ).[25]

All involved, however, have to suffer before reaching heaven, and the dance opens with the disturbing image of a man crawling on his stomach (dead legs implied), and a woman jerking forwards beside him—the 'leg-iron' walk. (I borrow from Acocella's motif descriptions.) Even more disturbing is his rise, only to fall again—then total blackout as the voices shout 'Gloria! Gloria!' and for the remainder of this first section of the work. In Morris's account of it, the music seems to sound as ferocious as it is joyful. This is the same fall to earth, 'locked' in your mind from this point onwards[26] that we see at the end of the work, at that point a reminder of sin, of the difficulty of the progress towards heaven. So it is perhaps not such a clean resolution, the ecstatic fall to earth, as Acocella suggests. 'Double-sidedness' pervades *Gloria* from start to finish, and Acocella's assessment of the relations with Pergolesi in Morris's *Stabat Mater* (1986) can well be applied to the earlier piece. *Stabat Mater* is punishing to an extreme, formal and faceless as much as it contains terrifying, anguished and uncomfortable moves, and Acocella hits upon a tension between forces, an unresolvable distance from the music that speaks of postmodernism (see pp. 75-6):

> Morris's tactic is to locate a membrane between the noble and the not-noble, and then to press hard on both sides at the same time. For me, the membrane never breaks; the two elements never blend. In *Stabat Mater*, when the dancers drop one another—smack, splat, on the floor—as an image of betrayal and loss, I am conscious of the TV-land brutality of the action, and I see it as a sort of challenge to Pergolesi's tender cantata, a test of it.[27]

A similar challenge to music can be observed in parts of *Gloria*.

It is useful at this point to summarise Damsholt's reading of the piece. While acknowledging the devotional aspect of the work, she focuses almost exclusively on its choreomusical aspects. The reason is that, for her, the central subject of *Gloria*, is a self-reflexive strategy, the act of choreomusical perception. Indeed, she estimates that this is the subject of all Morris's work and observes no fundamental difference in aesthetic approach between *Gloria* and *Ten Suggestions*.

In order to demonstrate this, Damsholt draws from music visualisation theory and the longer history of choreomusical practices (see Ch. 3). She incorporates recent metaphor theory, especially the concepts associated with 'up-down' (using the vertical paradigm, see pp. 96-7) and of 'a voice is a dancer', which achieves particular significance given Morris's contrapuntal explorations. She also suggests that Morris reflects on the act of reading a dance in the manner of a musical score: from left to right, following the tracks and activities of dancers as if they were operating on musical staves, and 'seeing' SATB, from a pair of sopranos upstage to a pair of basses downstage. She gives a compelling reading of 'Propter magnam gloriam', arguing here that, while material defined as Subject, Motif, Bridge and Closure moves mainly from left to right (taking the audience point of view), a Return phrase moves back to the left, reminding the 'reader' of turning pages or glancing back to the left side of a page.[28]

A further stage to Damsholt's argument is her focus on Morris's *Gloria* as choreomusical polemic, using Michel Foucault's theoretical construct—'the rule of the tactical polyvalence of discourses'.[29] In essence, for her, Morris's work questions all choreomusical practice, by re-presenting one of the most problematic and outmoded—music visualisation, then treating it playfully and providing alternatives as connection through opposition. The result is that we can no longer be seduced by the old method:

> Morris's work not only reinforces the aesthetic of music visualisation, but by means of exaggeration and simultaneous choreomusical counterpoint exposes it as a hindrance, a stumbling-block, and a necessary starting point for new creative strategies, establishing the conditions for a new discourse of dance scholarship.[30]

This is an interesting argument, again one in tune with postmodernism, although Morris himself never worked with this intention in mind.[31] Let us now apply the readings of Acocella and Damsholt to a section from *Gloria* that demonstrates music visualisation principles very clearly.

In 'Laudamus te', the third section of the work, Morris clearly parallels the musical ritornello form, here with instrumental sections flanking, and forming interludes amidst, an aria for two solo sopranos. Two dancers (women) map on to the two soprano lines, at the opening, for instance, where the voices enter in canon, and later in close proximity, performing the 'Suzie-Q' hip and foot counter-twist, which can be compared to the proximity of voices in parallel thirds. They also visualise a trill (bar 67) with a shake through the body and hands, corresponding with one of St Denis's definitions of trill (see p. 133). Their material imitates very explicitly the melodic and rhythmic features of the vocal material. Two other dancers (a man and a woman—so there can be no gender parallelism here) take the ritornello sections, and are associated with rapid motion across the stage diagonals, either running, or performing a hopping 'heel-clicking' motif. But this motif takes 3 counts (3/8) across 2/4 in the music, one of several simple examples of metrical counterpoint in *Gloria*, which Damsholt reads as an example of opposition. Taking up her polemical argument, Damsholt concludes that

> *Gloria* transmits and produces the power of music visualisation, but it also undermines visualisation and exposes it, renders it fragile, and strips it of its seeming ability to command movement.[32]

Towards the end of 'Laudamus te', a swing and sideways lean are set against a kind of leap-frog, which Damsholt reads as another parallelism:

> The first and second sopranos exchange parts—accordingly, the 'soprano' and ritornello dancers switch roles, with the former taking the leapfrog

pattern and the latter the swinging and leaning pattern.[33]

Acocella and I read this section differently from Damsholt. Acocella already harbours doubts about some of Morris's visualisations: 'The music [at times] is reduced to a set of rules and the dance becomes simply an obeying of those rules, with nothing to tell us beyond the fact that the choreographer knows how to read the score.'[34] But she believes that, at the end of 'Laudamus te', Morris wants 'to enlarge the stage picture and the sentiment', and her main point is that the two pairs of dancers now *share* material simultaneously and link as a quartet:

> Shedding their former identity, these 'orchestral' dancers now join the two 'vocal' dancers, working in counterpoint to them. So where, before, we had one dancer per voice, now we have one two-dancer dance per voice. Okay, but now comes a twist. In the music, the orchestra enters and the voices cease. What will he do now? Will he make the vocal dancers exit? No. They let the orchestral dancers join in their section; in return they now get to join in the orchestral dancers' section....Morris has built a wing onto Vivaldi's house, because he wanted to expand and complicate the dance.[35]

I suggest a further kind of sharing and expansion. At the end, all four dancers in a line repeat the full opening statement to the same orchestral music, down the diagonal and up again. At the same time, Morris turns this line-up into a ragged, complicated stage picture. He stops their heel clicks at different times, landing them on different legs and facing opposite directions, and ends with a very tight canon back up the diagonal, each entry one beat after the last. In his own way, he takes on the musical principle of sequence here (material repeating at different pitch levels), but adds to it the principle of counterpoint that has been a strong feature earlier in 'Laudamus te'.

It is in this dance material, too, that we find yet one more of Morris's awkward see-saws, in a strange, effortful *arabesque* that involves shooting the back leg upwards while the body and head pull in the opposite direction downwards. Acocella reads this as Morris 'showing us what the sense of the divine is really like for human souls...We get a Brueghelesque image: weight, bulk, mass, something distant from the divine and therefore, in its reach for the divine, truly moving.'[36] Normally in such circumstances, the body pull would determine the focus of attention, but here there is a definite tension, especially as a high note captures the upward direction of leg and face. The musicality of the moment doubles the awkwardness of the action.

The expansion towards the end of 'Laudamus te' forms part of the logic of *Gloria* as a whole. At this point, we will look beyond the short-term structure of the dance and its parallelism (or opposition) with music. Allowing other values to take over, other readings become possible and reflect the richness of Morris's choreomusical approach.

It is possible to rationalise some of Morris's strategies as maintaining continuity or building energy through *Gloria,* that is, more obviously than the music does alone. On a couple of striking occasions, the choreography moves at a faster speed than the music suggests. Musically, 'Gratias agimus tibi' is a very slow 6-bar prelude to 'Propter magnam gloriam' (with a fermata—a pause mark——at the end of the third and sixth bars indicating the ends of two utterances of the text). But Morris sets separate, freely-timed solo phrases within each bar and for each word, and on three different dancers (the bars are accordingly separately colour-coded in his working score). The combined effect of presto movement and shifting dancers greatly increases the pressure, especially through each sustained chord. Later, at the end of the Largo 'Domine Deus, Rex coelestis', a 'crippled' woman falls to the ground, is healed, and then races joyfully through a solo that assembles together a large number of familiar dance motifs. Again, none of the moves fits the detail of musical structure.

We might also sense a growth in confidence across *Gloria,* towards a more hopeful conclusion. Release from detailed, simultaneous visualisation techniques symbolises this process. The final section 'Cum Sancto Spiritu' takes off, literally, across the stage and into the air. Musically, this is the only real fugue in the piece, with a subject and more rapid counter-subject entering half a bar later, but Morris has not created an equivalent dance fugue. Instead, he scores a series of canons (three), all forged out of the same material.[37] Morris speaks of harmony across the dancing group and the music, by adhering clearly to the contrapuntal principle, and still, from time to time, contacting the rhythms and entries of the subjects. But these canons quickly give the impression of additional 'voices' bursting into operation. Everyone is eager, as it were, to have her own say, taking charge independently in a texture of co-existence. So there is more of a crowd as well as more individuals in the crowd, and there are additional 'sub-canons' of heel-kicking and leaping across the stage. The vision is utopian.

Near the end of 'Cum Sancto Spiritu', Morris shifts gear momentously, despite the motion of the music. He introduces a series of spectacular dives to the floor, flying across the stage, a happy variant to the earlier painful stomach crawl. The dancers dive one by one, an arrival every two bars (a somewhat arbitrary contact with the score), and each then joins in the slow building of a pyramid formation behind those who follow. So the structure here is determined entirely by the dance, not by the sound of the music. There is a mass halt (end of bar 69). All this reinforces by contrast the climactic final statement of the dance theme, the return of allegro, culminating in the

Gloria, 'Cum Sancto Spiritu', the 'dive' section. © Tom Brazil, 1989

fall to earth and the X formation—itself a canon and a means of sustaining intensity through the final fermata chord.

Nothing as 'tied' to musical structure as 'Laudamus te' and 'Propter magnam' occurs in the second half of *Gloria*. Morris's use of the 'voice is dancer' metaphor loosens by Section 7 'Domine Fili unigenite'. Here, dance ideas still stem directly from the musical rhythms (not pitch this time), and especially striking are the pervasive jaunty short-long patterns, and the contrasting sustained events, one note and one gesture per bar. Association between SATB voice lines and groups of two or three dancers inhabiting four positions on stage is a foundation of the choreography, but various devices make it hard for an audience to hold on to this scheme. Two dancers move from one group to another, groups carry on moving even though their voice line is no longer active, and part of the 'crippled' woman's solo from 'Domine Deus, Rex coelestis' suddenly finds itself amongst group material upstage.

It is likely that we expect to find these SATB associations by this stage—the style of the piece from its opening encourages this. But any such expectations are soon defeated: our attention is drawn much more to the unpredictable departures and arrivals between groups and to the brief correspondences or moments of harmony across all of them. Sudden unisons between colleagues within such a complicated game, the sheer mental relaxation that they offer, are a huge pleasure—the rest is exhilarating.

Turning now to section 10 'Qui sedes ad dexteram Patris', a ritornello form aria for alto solo, we find far more counterpoint in the dance than in the music, within and across pairs, and in a ragged group of individuals hopping, turning and leaping across the stage at beginning and end. There is also far more coming and going—and of a larger number of people—than the musical scoring would suggest. The raggedness is a foil for some of the most extended passages of rapid sequential repetition in the work. Damsholt suggests that we still have expectations of a dance fugue by the time we reach Section 12 'Cum Sancto Spiritu', expectations that turn out to be frustrated,[38] but I am not sure that, by this late stage of *Gloria*, we have any reason to predict such a tidy relationship.

The dance presence often expands the expression of community inherent in the score, introducing more individual voices with thoughts to express. This is the case, we have seen, in 'Cum Sancto Spiritu': more dance voices, in addition to those visualising parts in the music, and more solo voices. So a choral group has a second identity, it can also be understood through dance as a group of individuals. Movement sometimes humanises the voices of instruments too, like the brass in 'Cum Sancto Spiritu', a row of leaping dancers embodying the sound (bar 16), and the oboe in 'Domine Deus, Rex coelestis', which engages in a duet with the soprano and initiates a dance for two women (bars 27-31). (Morris coloured the oboe and soprano lines separately in his working score.) The choreography also undermines the strict demarcations of gender in the SATB arrangement, as Morris readily sets men dancing to women's voices and vice versa. Dance makes more things seem possible, more democratic, a larger number of opinions heard, and it blurs the distinction between sung passages and instrumental interludes.

Similarly, movement enhances the sense of lightness and heaviness in the music, expanding the possibilities of affect. The treatment of sequential repetition in the music is a good example of this, so often in wave-like motion, descending before ascending to a higher point, or ascending before falling lower, visualised by a soloist or a pair of dancers as question and answer. I cannot read one dancer's repeating fall and rise in 'Domine Deus, Rex coelestis' (bars 19-21) as Damsholt does, fundamentally humorous, in order to exaggerate the visualisation process for self-reflexive purposes. Rather I read it as an expression of labour, of throwing oneself to the ground in despair, or of getting stuck in a groove. At other times, for instance, in 'Qui sedes', it does seem more like a game, competitive within a partnership, and your attitude towards it may change—you watch exactly the same move again and again and, a while after it causes you to smile, a sense of desperation begins to set in. The most extreme sequence in 'Qui sedes' occurs when a couple upstage settle down beside each other and alternate moving up and down many times (from bar 107, six times each, twelve in total). First, they seem doggedly determined to keep going. Then, they accelerate—after bar 116, getting up and down takes two bars instead of three. When they rise to their feet, the tone lightens and they start leap-frogging up and over each other (bar 124, see 'Laudamus te'). (This whole sequence was quite different in 1981. Now it is much simpler, more repetitive, and much more fun.)

At the same time as the joy, there are frequent intrusions, reminders of the awkward language with which *Gloria* began: like the pelvic thrust and crotch grip of 'Et in terra pax', the jerky walks of the huddle of penitents pushing into the musical beat (or at random) during 'Domine deus, Rex coelestis', or, near the end of the finale, a single bar of spasmodic movements (bar 71) 'waking up' from the unison halt. Could this ever be called translation or *being* the music? Did Morris *ever* think of it that way? Previous choreography to baroque music tended to stress graceful, elegant movement, like Paul Taylor's *Aureole* (1962) and *Esplanade* (1975) or Balanchine's *Concerto Barocco* (1941). In the 1980s, Acocella says, Morris's awkward movement to the 'fine old classical music' that puts audiences in 'worshipful mood' confused people into thinking that he was joking.[39]

Both Acocella and Damsholt tend to use visualisation as their yardstick for assessing choreomusical behaviour (and for rationalising everything else as simply not visualisation). They work within the boundaries that Barbara White noted as she pressed for alternatives (see p. 92). To be fair, music visualisation undeniably stands out in the memory—and it is interesting how often it is the most intense instances of this that people single out in their writing. Damsholt's own main example, for example, is 'Propter magnam' and, in a very descriptive critique for *Drama Review*, Laurie Lassiter singled this section out too, as well as 'Laudamus te'.[40] Yet there is a lot more to be said about what is not music visualisation in Morris's work, and there are other ways of thinking about choreomusical processes, suggested by the particular unfolding of a particular piece, in other words, by considering these processes within a specific context.

Borrowing Musical Principles

On several occasions so far, I have touched upon Morris's use of musical principles, as opposed to the simultaneous mirroring that happens in music visualisation. Those principles are one of the most important guides across his work as a whole, and Morris himself was very clear about this. For instance, in 1985:

> I deal with choreography from a musical point of view. Even if my work doesn't relate directly to the score that I'm using, or if I'm not using one, it's still structured musically, because I think that way makes sense.[41]

During these early professional years, Morris often mentioned that baroque music taught him how to structure choreography, 'perfect architecture', he called it, and Handel, he used to say, taught him most of all.

In similar vein, he admired the structural legibility of Haydn and, notably, Charles Rosen's account of it in his seminal book *The Classical Style: Haydn, Mozart, Beethoven* (1971).[42] Although Morris did not undertake his major explorations of classical period forms until much later in his career, Rosen's work taught him principles that he was already keen to use.

It was in this period too that Morris developed his skills in using musical techniques of repetition, development and variation, and of contrasting textures, polyphony and homophony. He also learnt about irregular phrasing structures, setting up and confounding expectations, the effects of prolongation and telescoping of time, and tonal drama: how modulation, for instance, might 'open up' or 'darken' mood.[43]

One principle underlies all the others: structural coherence, a theoretical concern that has had a long tradition in music and has preoccupied Morris across his entire career.[44] Taken to an extreme, coherence can mean strict economy, making a lot out of very little basic material. 'I'm just trying to do what Bach did', Morris once said. 'He takes a very small amount of material and goes crazy with it.'[45] He was also impressed by Haydn's 'monothematic' experiments, his belief that every part of a musical form should be motivically related.[46] Morris once explained to an interviewer:

> I'll take a rhythmic motif that appears somewhere in the music, and I'll make up a step that echoes it. Then I'll put that same step in places where it doesn't belong—or change the rhythm of it. And it can become another movement later on. It's an artifice that allows me to tie a piece of dancing together in the way I feel the music is tied together—like the tonal architecture which you don't hear immediately, but understand if you listen to a piece for a long time.[47]

Music also taught Morris counterpoint, not only how to invest his choreography with distinct 'voices', but also how to work the counterpoint rhythmically, expanding upon the valuable knowledge gleaned from his folk dance training. By the 1980s, he was already a commmitted 'rhythm nut', describing his juvenalia as 'rhythmically based and packed solid; not a quarter [crotchet] rest in the score was skipped'.[48] From now on, rhythmic counterpoint became an integral part of his style.

Some pieces that Morris made during this early period could indeed be said to be *about* cross-rhythms. An example is the solo *I Love You Dearly*, choreographed in 1981, the same year as *Ten Suggestions* and *Gloria*, set to three traditional Romanian songs. Let us look in detail at the first dance, which is based on the principle of variation, performing material at two different speeds (unprompted by musical change) or shortening or lengthening it. The modern dance style (origin unspecific) is nuanced by 'folk' stepping and swinging movements, and metres and phrases constantly cross. My analysis is based on the 1981 performance by Nora Reynolds. There are four song verses, the first three similarly structured musically, as three different phrases, ABC, each comprised of two similar sub-phrases of 8 fast counts (total 16 counts). (The fourth verse is an extension of the first three.) There is also an instrumental introduction and refrain. On the other hand, the choreography, divided into verses as follows, shows considerable variation in structure, and after verse 1, no longer fits the regular lengths of musical units:

Instrumental introduction 8 counts
Dance Verse 1.
a. 1 slow phrase: 16 counts = 16
a. 1 as fast phrase (double time, performed twice): 2 times 8 counts = 16
a. 2 the start of a.1 (performed three times): 3 times 5 counts, plus 1 count transition = 16
Music: A = 16, B = 16, C = 16

Instrumental refrain: the dancer turns and walks round to starting position: 2 times 8 counts =16

Instrumental introduction 8 counts
Dance Verse 2.
a. 3 a variation of a.1 fast version, ending differently: 3 times 8 counts = 24
b. 3 times 4 counts =12
c. 3 times 4 counts, the third time with syncopation =12
Music: A = 16, B = 16, C = 16
Instrumental refrain (as above): the dancer turns and walks round to starting position: 2 times 8 counts = 16

Instrumental introduction 8 counts
Dance Verse 3.
a. 1 slow phrase: 16 counts (as in 1.) =16
a. 4 2 new counts added on to the front of a. 3 (double time, performed twice): 2 times 10 counts = 20
a. 5 4 times 3 counts = 12
Music: A = 16, B = 16, C = 16

Instrumental refrain (as above): the dancer turns and walks round to starting position: 2 times 8 counts =16

Instrumental introduction 8 counts
Dance Verse 4.
a.3 3 times 7 counts, and a continuation so that the last 7 counts are extended

to 10 = 24
b. c. a. recapitulation, but now moving freely over the musical beat and extending into the dance refrain = 49
Music: A = 16, B = 16 C = 16, C = 16 and 9-count extension (= 73 counts)

The sheer variety and balance between the expected and unexpected in this little solo makes it fun. The refrains of the third song/dance in *I Love You Dearly* contain a jolly mathematical puzzle. The dancer bumps her heels up and down, then steps to the beat, accumulatively the first time round and crossing the music, in phrases of 4, 5, 6, 7 and 8 counts. She reverses the procedure at the end of the second verse, then starts the last refrain with the music, only to hint at another accumulation as the song closes.

Doubling time in choreography is a feature of Indian dance and music. Morris used the technique in *"Tamil Film Songs"* and *O Rangasayee* (1984). The second of these two dances was an exceptionally ambitious and well-received work of this period, a 23-minute solo danced by Morris to an Indian raga by the eighteenth-century composer Sri Tyagaraja, sung by the celebrated female artist M. S. Subbalakshmi. Acocella describes it as looking like 'the dark side of the moon....' showing Morris, in a loin-cloth, 'descending further and further into some consuming inner state, both grotesque and ecstatic'.[49] He had studied the music since his days dancing in Laura Dean's company and, in his setting—as well as references to Indian iconography and dances—there were reminiscences of her spinning dances and the repetitive structures of minimalists such as Lucinda Childs. The solo was rigorous in its theme and variation structures and mathematically very complex, with phrases constructed in irregular lengths, like 7 or 10 counts, against the 'square' temporal organisation of the music.[50]

Unusually, in the case of *My Party* (1984), to Jean Françaix, the concept of the dance came first to Morris, before the music. Here, the music already contains much in the way of syncopations and metrical games (for instance, 6/8 becoming 3/4, and vice versa), and it prompted still more of this in the choreography, in the form of counterpoint. All this makes a major contribution to the party: metrical crossings thoroughly embedded within the basic language of this piece. Again, Morris developed from a musical principle.

He did too in his work for American Ballet Theatre *Drink to Me Only with Thine Eyes* (1988, to an assortment of Etudes by Virgil Thomson). Here, there are exceedingly exaggerated moments of music visualisation: the ballet opens with a striking landing from a jump into a motif fifth position *plié* (arms over head, hands crossed at the wrists), smack on a sforzando chord. Later, in the Tango (No. 10), there are perfectly and unusually 'timed' slow *pirouettes*, tick-tick-tick, to upbeats 2, 3, 4, before the working leg is extended into second position on the next downbeat 1 (a short-short-short-long rhythm). The phenomenon was inspired by the super-controlled virtuosity of Baryshnikov, who danced at the premiere. But there are countless examples of 2 against 3 or the reverse in this work, indeed this is its style, prompted by the ambiguity already in the music. The most intricate section is No. 5 (Oscillating Arm—Spinning Song), where the music is written in 6/8, the bass sounds like 2/4, and the dance follows patterns of 2/4 and 3/4.

Morris's *Drink to Me Only* explores ballet as a democratic, flexible phenomenon without the usual concentration on couple relationships, but it also offers a totally fresh musical perspective. There is a requirement to start and finish movement on time, also possibilities for dancing fast (still on time) to slow music, the final dance based on the title tune illustrating this last point particularly well. There are many canons too, alternatives to traditional ballet unison. Morris's musicality contributes to the democracy —again, everyone has an individual voice.

Morris's penchant for canons is closely related to his interest in rhythm. For this, a special study *Canonic 3/4 Studies* (1982) set him on his way, to piano music arranged by his class pianist Harriet Cavalli, taken largely from an obscure Russian musical compilation.[51] The idea was that the study would be preparation for choreographing *New Love Song Waltzes* (Brahms, 1982), but Morris later discovered that not all the pieces were waltzes. Nor did the music feature canons.

Canonic 3/4 Studies is a parody of ballet class, an over-the-top account of the boisterous romance and hackneyed indulgence of its most conservative accompaniment, and there is even a cheeky addition—Cavalli hit a bell on her piano to cap the end of a phrase in the 'Hotel Bell Waltz' (as they nicknamed it), with music by Moritz Moszkowski. (Morris once got to hit the bell himself.) That is one of the numbers here that recalls Balanchine's *Agon* (1957)—the dancers, whether women or men, all wear his familiar practice-clothes costume of white top and black tights. A few numbers might also spoof ballet timing, especially its often-excessive rubato. In one number, Morris's group hold *arabesques*, suspending for as long as possible before stumbling off balance. In another, a woman quietly wanders through a little solo barely attached to the music, like a sleepwalker.

Canonic 3/4 Studies, however, is mainly concerned with canon structures, of the kind that are full of articulated beats and accents. In such structures, when you assemble the 'machine' and set the metre of the second person against the first, you feel a cross accent, a form of syncopation, and a tension from experiencing a downbeat twice in quick succession. Morris allows you to catch the flow of a phrase and then disrupts it by jolting your attention towards the next person in the canon, and then on to others further down the line.

Beats are also dissected in different ways by the choreography. The opening number of *Canonic 3/4*, a solo for Morris, shows off his personal skill in coordinating different rhythms on different parts of his body. His right arm moves upwards (U) on beat 1, then down (D) twice, like a conductor, at crotchet rate, then three more times down as a triplet, moving to the right, finally faster still (he gave the image of a ball bouncing faster and faster of its own accord[52]).

Ex. 5.3 *Canonic 3/4 Studies* (no composer's name given), dance No. 1.

Morris does exactly the same pattern again with his head, moving to the left, and then with his right leg, to the right. But the fun has barely begun. He then makes a circle and starts all over again, this time overlapping ('canonising') the three statements by one bar, so the head dovetails with the arm (going in opposite directions) and the leg with the head.

The third number 'Bolero' is hilarious, formed from hardly any material— the kind of thing that Morris is very proud of—just a few plain walks then jumps up and down on the spot. There are three parts, the woman always leading off with the man following behind, first in canon at one bar (three beats), next just two beats after her, finally only one beat behind. This now means that when they jump, they go up and down at different times, yet another version of the 'see-saw' in the vertical dimension—except on the last note, he catches and freezes her up in the air, to our delight.

In the middle of No. 7, a frantic 3/8 Czerny study, we see the most complex canon of all, with five dancers in a line. This, more than any other number, would have taught Morris how canons drive the perceptions of the viewer, how they worry, excite and even suggest chaos by change of level, direction of focus, body part (feet, arms, shoulders, head) or the addition of syncopations. Actions constantly grab the eye and distract us from catching the larger pattern. Morris developed two sequences of material, the second involving more body parts than the first, and ended up running both together down a line with dancers alternating between sequences. No. 7 is one of many noisy, stamping dances that he created during this early period—the kind that Hutchinson remembers used to hurt her legs.[53] Morris wanted rhythm to be clear, and one way was to make it audible as well as visual.

The structural layout, showing the length of each statement in slow counts (each slow count covering two bars of 3/8), is as follows:

Statement 1 unison: 4 counts
Statement 1 in canon, reading right to left down the line of dancers (from the audience viewpoint): 4 counts
Statement 1 (variation) in canon, drawing from the first half of the material, making a full turn on the spot in stages, reading right to left down the line of dancers: 8 counts
Statement 2 unison: 4 counts
Statement 2 in canon, reading right to left down the line of dancers: 4 counts
Statements 1 and 2 in canon, alternating dancers: dancer 1 on the right does statement 1 then 2, the neighbouring dancer does statement 2 then 1 in canon one beat later, and so on: 8 counts
The dancers run upstage one after another, to repeat statement 1 (variation) in canon, drawing from the first half of the original material: 8 counts

When he came to choreograph *New Love Song Waltzes* (1982), Morris was ready to explore a very different kind of canon, and a very different attitude to 3/4 metre. He was moved by Brahms's intimate settings of fourteen love-poems adapted and translated into German by Georg Friedrich Daumer (for piano—two pianists and four solo singers). A final, fifteenth poem is by Goethe, and turns away from the plight of lovers to appeal to the Muses for solace. Balanchine had choreographed the same music in 1960 in the pairing *Liebeslieder Walzer* and *Neue Liebeslieder Walzer* (Morris was to choreograph this earlier score in 1989, see pp. 281-2.) *New Love Song Waltzes* is about individuals within a community, their passion, pain, yearning, and the love that overwhelms them both emotionally and physically. Morris builds his choreography according to the feelings and broad images evoked by the poems, rather than to the specifics of the German that most non-German-speaking audiences would not understand. Unlike Balanchine's settings, which look back to nineteenth-century romanticism, he refers to what we understand as contemporary experience.

The choreography here flows more freely than in any piece so far described, as if a river of sensuality takes over, the dancers allowing their weight to drop into and merge with the bodies of their companions. A different musicality prevails, much less about the detail and controlling, driving impetus of beat and the separation of rhythmic events. Morris got that out of his system in *Canonic 3/4*. There is an outstanding pliancy in the footwork of *New Love Song Waltzes*, a major contrast with the stamping dances of this period.

Certainly, there are some choreographed steps to the beat, including hemiolas (see p. 114) and syncopations, but there are rarely any straight triplets or occasions for waltzing. Instead, we relish the luscious swinging steps lifting out of the big downbeats, and the touches of 'lazy rhythm' (see p. 119) that suggest a resistance to emotion. The main rhythmic style of this piece stems from lyricism and melody. There is also a lot of plain running and walking through the beat. It seems right therefore that walking like this, in a spiral, leads to the conclusion of the dance. Beats make time stop, very briefly. Stepping to beats articulates them further, and the stopping. Step through them and time keeps moving on.

The canons in *New Love Song Waltzes* demonstrate this different kind of rhythm, with their long winding progress between musical 'seams' that are formed by harmonic hiatuses or cadences. Consider the two canons in No. 7,

Ex. 5.4a *New Love Song Waltzes*, Brahms, Op. 65, No. 11, 'Alles, alles in den Wind', first phrase.

Ex. 5.4b *New Love Song Waltzes*, Brahms, Op. 65, No. 11, 'Alles, alles in den Wind', second phrase.

'Vom Gebirge Well' auf Well" ('From the mountains, wave upon wave'). The first is 15 bars of non-stop activity for nine dancers massed together, taking turns in a 3-bar phrase that begins with wheeling arms—like waves. They start off in small groups, but not as neighbours, so they look unruly. As soon as they finish the 3-bar phrase, they repeat it. The second canon lasts for 11 bars and creates a greater sense of mobility in both horizontal and vertical planes. The basic phrase here is much longer, zig-zagging through the entire group, the arm-wheeling now leading into a big roll to the floor, legs flung into the air (like a breaking wave) before each dancer rises up again.[54]

Several other large group numbers show people engaged in diverse activities, a turbulent stage picture. Then suddenly, all coalesce into harmonious agreement. There are climaxes where couples cling passionately and, as if making love (Nos. 8 and 13), or, in the final dance, to the only truly contrapuntal song, there is an extended moment of homophony and unison dance and the sentiment peaks too at this point.

The rhythmic attack and patterning of No. 11 'Alles, alles in den Wind' ('All, all is lost to the wind', see Exs. 5.4a and b) is highly unusual. The dancers leap across the space and out into the wings—like the wind. The first phrase is immediately airborne and finishes cut-off in mid-air on count 3 of the bar (the end of a 4-bar musical phrase). The second (6 bars long) pursues its own rhythmic pattern with 2s against 3s in the music, then two low, syncopated squats (D) on either side of a climactic jump straight up on the downbeat with arms flung high (U). It is also surprising in overlapping by one beat the start of the next musical phrase.

You gasp at the rhythmic and technical virtuosity of both phrases, genuine resolution only coming with the landing or exit from the stage. But No. 11 is an exception, one of the shortest numbers, and its hectic and unsettling rhythm is definitively calmed during the four songs that follow.

So far, all the pieces discussed have entered, even if obliquely, into what might provisionally be called the 'spirit' of the music—its programme, or the kinds of meaning conventionally attached to it. But a handful of Morris's pieces do anything but this.

Angry Dances

Morris was angry during this early period of his career, he told Acocella, about the dishonesty of bourgeois respectability and about his own spirituality.[55] While he harboured religious feelings, he was at the same time ambivalent and embarrassed about his private direction. He made a number of dances that confronted this uncertainty and frustration.

Probably his most infamous piece was *Lovey*—which shows dancers engaging in overt erotic behaviour with naked dolls. It bewildered some and offended others. Did it represent child abuse? some asked. Morris himself claimed that the dance was about people failing to 'relate' and punishing what they felt closest to—he had watched his niece thrashing her own doll.[56] But these were souls all the same, even if they were lost souls. Morris also questioned the euphemistic sexual manifestations that are conventional in dance, with people in leotards, as he put it, operating ten feet apart.[57] *Lovey* had fierce music by country-punk group Violent Femmes and the choreography matched its statement in a straightforward manner.

Of special interest here are the pieces that use more subtle musical enquiry as a means of achieving heavy, bitter irony. One of these was *The*

Vacant Chair (1984), a solo setting of three American parlour songs. Their message is Christian, reflecting sorrow and regret, as well as commenting on the beauty of nature. But Morris turns each song on its head—especially alarming for American audiences who are most familiar with them—by bringing to the stage an image of the unbeliever, the lost or dead one, who is inconsolable, humiliated and out of control, and who cannot be part of a good, sweet community. Morris's statement seems clearly against the spirit of the music, although some viewers may feel more sympathetic towards the voice behind the song than Morris was at the time. Morris choreographed the solo for himself.

The setting is dark, and in the spotlight is a music stand with the drawing on it of a chair (the vacant chair, later a tree, and then a bed). The first song is about a young man who has died during the American Civil War, is mourned, but also revered for his heroism. He leaves a vacant chair. Stripped down to his underpants, Morris wears a grocery bag over his head, which confounds him at every turn—he reaches out, stumbles, and falls to the floor again and again. The third song is one of sweet melancholy about the departure of a friend at the end of a happy day, but the dance breaks down into increasingly wild crashing about the stage. Finally, Morris knocks over the music stand.[58]

The second song 'Trees' (words by Joyce Kilmer, 1913; set by Oscar Rasbach, 1922) is especially intriguing musically. A kind of conceptual blend operates (see pp. 97-8). Both trees and men live, and they die, which is Morris's additional concept. They also stand upright, embodying the vertical dimension. Otherwise, this is a confrontation, or contest, of ideas, a nasty pun. Here, the solo dancer represents a tree growing towards God, but as a 'gnarled' and distorted body, with his back to the audience, carrying in his hands, as leaves, the torn-in-two grocery bag of the previous song. Here is the full poem, with italics showing the words that are stressed in the song setting and, in brackets, notes reached in the melody line at these points. The two-part form of the music is indicated:

[Piano introduction]

PART 1
I think that I shall never see
A poem lovely as a tree.
A tree whose hungry mouth is *prest* [E]
Against the sweet earth's flowing *breast* [rise to G-sharp];
A tree that looks at God all day,
And lifts her leafy arms to pray;

PART 2
A tree that may in summer wear
A nest of robins in her hair;
Upon whose bosom snow has lain;
Who intimately lives with rain.
Poems are *made* [G-sharp] by fools like me,
But only *God* [drop to C-sharp] can make a tree.
[Piano postlude]

Part 1 of the song ends with a full cadence, but with the vocal line stopping on the mediant (the third note of the scale, rather than the first, the tonic), preventing a sense of full closure. 'Prest' and 'breast' are the two climaxes (melodic and dynamic), on E and G-sharp respectively, the second being the higher and bigger of the two. The second part begins like the first, but continues with variation. The climaxes emerge later and are larger in volume and dramatic impact, though reversed in order of size, on 'made' (G-sharp, again the bigger of the two) and then 'God' (C-sharp).

The large trajectory of the dance is that the man rises and falls, describing life, growth, and a death. This shadows the large trajectory of the song, although *it* has a serene ending, as a statement of Christian belief, not a death. So too are shadowed the two climaxes in Part 1, which are painful to watch, seen from behind the man's body, his right elbow raised sharply, and then his left, higher still, countering the legato of the music but showing the higher pitch.

Yet the treatment of musical climax in Part 2 is quite different. After the man shudders and sways under the weight of 'snow' and pushes to and fro as if in a storm ('rain'), he drops the 'leaves' to the climactic words 'made' and 'God' (his right, then left, side pulling upwards again).[59] This is a wholly dry, passive subversion of the passionate vocal line (the leaves fall downwards), and object-driven (the fallen leaves suggest disappearance of human agency, total annihilation of human dynamics), cutting cruelly across any feeling generated up to this point. On 'God', however, the left side of the man's body still pulls upwards, a final, pathetic resistance, far less strongly supported musically than before, by the lower, pathetic C-sharp. The intensity of the oppositional component within this short dance stems from both the conflict within the up-down paradigm and the non-congruent dynamics and imagery, *despite* the blend factor, the common factor of life/ death and the verticality of both men and trees. The visceral, nakedly physical embodiment of voice deepens the expression of anguish.

The other two songs in *The Vacant Chair* include stamping. Anger again? The oddest thing is that the stamping relates very strictly to musical structure. In the first song, the man could be a soldier trying, in this absurd, blinded situation, to map out the rhythm of a march. But the last? Why in such circumstances—a terrifying lack of physical control—should there be any musical control whatsoever? Here, you have a particularly anachronistic opposition between the wild stumbling—which the critic Deborah Jowitt once described as 'butchering the beat'[60]—and utterly precise adherence to musical phrase and metrical divisions. How could anything so visually chaotic fit so neatly in time? It is as if some other mind works through the man's legs and feet. Similarly, in the earlier *Jr. High* (1982) Morris's reflections on his school experiences, he ranges from pensive gestures to increasingly fierce outbursts, but his trainers always step exactly on the 'chaotic' accents of Conlon Nancarrow's jangling Studies for Player Piano. In both cases, precision jars.

People used to laugh at *The Vacant Chair*, which Morris never could fathom. They might have remembered him, from other pieces, as a very funny dancer. But the only laughter that really makes sense for this dance, at least today, is the laughter of discomfort, on confronting opposition.

For different reasons, people have laughed at *One Charming* Night (1985), another anti-religion dance, this time a mocking melodrama, and another rare instance of an idea for a dance coming before its music. Anne Rice's 1973 novel *Interview with the Vampire* was the inspiration, and Morris gave himself the role of a hero vampire dressed as a cleric in a smart black suit: 'the most fleshy and lewd and unctuous of fiends' wrote Macaulay.[61]

The cleric vampire seduces a young girl, the lightest of his dancers, tiny 'paper cup'[62] Teri Weksler. At the beginning, she waits, yearning for him, her attention glued to an upstage wing. Then he arrives, teasing, enchanting and possessing her. He sucks her blood, she sucks his in return, and the dance ends with him carrying her off.

There is already an odd mixture of musical sources, a devious collage, even though all the music is by Purcell. Some items are secular—'Be welcome then, Great Sir' (1683), an ode to King Charles II with political intent from *Fly, Bold Rebellion*, and two songs from *The Fairy Queen* (1692) (after Shakespeare's *A Midsummer Night's Dream*): from Act 2, Secresy's song as Titania sleeps—'One Charming Night', and from Act 5, a song from the final celebrations of marital happiness—'Hark! The Ech'ing Air'. The final song, the most extended, is sacred, in praise and wonder of God, to the words of William Fuller Lord-Bishop of Lincoln:

Lord, what is man, lost man,
That Thou shouldst be so mindful of him?
That the Son of God forsook his glory, His abode,
To become a poor, tormented man!

One Charming Night, Mark Morris and Teri Weksler. © Beatriz Schiller, 1985

Here, the double irony is that the words are the cleric's sermon preached to the girl.[63] Yet the torment in the dance is really one of mounting sexual desire, not of suffering sin, and the final 'hallelujah!' is the celebration of a truly terrible triumph. 'Charming' soon reads as bitter sarcasm. Morris felt that the strange other-worldly timbre of counter-tenor voice and acidic harpsichord continuo would work well, and wanted contrast, speaking specifically of the last number: 'I thought that it was important that the music be...godly, in order for the dance to be evil enough.'[64]

Much of the time in *One Charming Night* we find detailed response to musical structure, and there is especially rigorous deployment of motifs for purposes of unity, images that are shared as the pair draw closer. In 'Hark! The Ech'ing Air', each has a solo that turns into a duet with one shadowing the other. Morris's own vampire characterisation develops musically, too. He arrives stealing from nineteenth-century romantic ballet—his entry dance begins with nine light, bouncy jumps from Giselle's wili solo, easing into each beat. *One Charming Night* is, after all, a variation on the dangerous erotic fantasies of that era. Later, the flourish of legs in a *gargouillade* (a fancy ballet jump) displays his growing assertiveness. A striking moment opens Morris's 'Hark' solo, his leg shooting up to a high accent, while his body dips downwards—the old see-saw again and here, a perfectly apt image of duplicity. But he soon becomes impatient, with noisy, stamping syncopations in a secret upstage corner to long winding melismas, then in canon behind the girl's soundless miming of Cupids clapping their wings, echoing her as the song suggests. Meanwhile, 'clap, clap, clap' sings the counter-tenor.

During the pivotal 'Lord, what is man' recitative, the counter-tenor's eerily voluptuous voice smoulders in demonic minor mode, singing of death, while the dancing turns into action. But it is only when the hymn of praise begins and regular beat returns that the dastardly deed takes place. Morris heaves with passion, devouring her, forcing himself most brutally on to every downbeat. God and the devil are not so far apart after all.

One Charming Night sucks its strength from directly opposing the original spirit of the music. Here is another example of conceptual blending gone awry, and the more ungodly the narrative, the less balletic and the more overbearing Morris's cleric vampire. He is the ultimate visualiser of music as rhythm, ideal exemplar of Barbara White's 'glorious excess' (see p. 80), except that there is a profound distortion of the music's meaning—it is a horrible dance.

The tone of contact between movement and music in these examples is crucial. 'Blunt' is a word often used about Morris's dynamics. For he can exert an especially hard pressure upon structural congruence. In some dances, the more he pushes the dance into the music, with forceful, staccato gestures and duplication of repetitions, the more we sense a struggle to break apart rather than any blending into harmony. In a few dances, this works the other way round, with big music playing against diminutive dance resources. *Handel Choruses* (1985) is an instance of this, a crowd of singing voices all but overpowering the solo figures on stage. When these figures rise in turn from the floor, from the dead as it were, they still respond significantly to musical detail as if sucked in by, or struggling to match, its force. Whichever way round, this is music visualisation in high definition, another route to double- or multi-sidedness, and White may well be right, it can be hard to take: uncomfortable, angry-ironic, indecent, beyond 'glorious excess'. This could be another reason behind the problems that some people have had with Morris's approach to music—the assault factor.

Daniel Albright hits the nail on the head with his analysis of the exaggerated 'homophony' in Hindemith's 1919 setting of Oskar Kokoschka's play *Mörder, Hoffnung der Frauen* (*Murderer, the Hope of Women*). His observations could well be applied to Morris's angry dances. A work, he writes, that seems in every way to be unified may fall apart. It could well result in

> ...a kind of overdetermination and overemphasis, which may in turn lead to a kind of ironising, which may in turn lead to the disaffiliation of the very arts that are trying to cooperate.

Thus, Albright says, the 'shrieks' in *Mörder, Hoffnung der Frauen* turn into 'smirking caricatures of shrieks'.[65] In these circumstances, he finds them inappropriate, but this need not necessarily be so.

There is a similarity here with Acocella's image of the membrane pressed on both sides (between two opposites in *Stabat Mater,* see p. 139).[66] The membrane never breaks, but nor do the two opposites ever blend. Morris's particular use of pressured structural congruence between music and dance in this early period could have been one of his most distinctive features as an artist. According to the terms of postmodernism, big connection means big distance.

As a footnote to these angry dances, I suggest that big connection also resonates with the revival of a baroque aesthetic (the 'Neo-baroque') during the 1980s, Morris's formative period as a professional choreographer. Let us situate Morris's work alongside what are generally considered baroque tendencies linking the original seventeenth-century period with the present. There are the characteristics of enlargement, of exceeding the norm: rhetoric (the bold, full-on statement made with neither embarrassment nor recoil); underlining and redundancy (visualisation of musical structures, with the addition of mime to reinforce the period concept of word painting in music); elaboration; and a kind of noisy abundance. But there are also characteristics of transgression, instability, sensual ecstasy, the violent, contorted, grotesque, and badly-behaved.[67]

These transgressive characteristics emerge especially strongly in Morris's early work, his muscular solo presentations, the naked upper body, contorted, and massive, in his settings of Handel's chorus *Jealousy* (1985) and the parlour songs of *Vacant Chair,* the in-your-face nudity of *Striptease* (1986), and the violence and bad behaviour of *Lovey, Dogtown* (to Yoko Ono, 1983) and *One Charming Night.* But, as we will see, vestiges remain in much later dances and opera productions (see p. 298). All this suits Morris's personality—he is not a moderate person.

Systems

Morris would not be Morris, forever in search of variety and new challenges, if he had not done the opposite to such violent statements in other work. That, indeed, seems to be the case with the cluster of early dances driven by systems, another way of achieving structural rigour that releases very different kinds of choreomusical relationship. (Significantly, the music of Handel and Bach he called 'a perfect system'.[68]) We have encountered Morris's attraction to systems already in the visualisations that virtually write themselves: like the Mozart *Fugue*, the first movement of *Marble Halls*, and the *"Tamil Film Songs"* phrase generated by the notes of a scale. At other times, Morris chose to work in freer relationship with music. For instance, although they follow a musical principle, some of his canon systems evolve relatively freely between musical cue points some distance apart (as in *New Love Song Waltzes* No. 7). Or Morris simply used the abstract frame of metre and pulse, rather than the actual flesh of the music, to guide his choreography (as in the thrilling series of dives, one every two bars, regardless of anything else in the music, near the end of *Gloria*).

If the need for structural rigour was deep-seated and driven by Morris's passion for music, it was also a point of contact with a number of postmodern choreographers whose work he came across in New York. He readily admits his interest in the 1970s systems work of Lucinda Childs and Trisha Brown (see p. 28). *Deck of Cards* (1983), his dance about a soldier who uses the characters in a pack of cards to remind himself of Biblical figures and events, is constructed like one of Brown's accumulations, with moves growing in number (1, 1 2, 1 2 3, 1 2 3 4 and so on). One of the dance refrains in *I Love You Dearly* was an accumulation structure too (see pp. 146-8). The dance historian Sally Banes would have theorised these dances as developments from 'analytic' postmodern dance,[69] the kind that seeks the detached stance of the spectator, rather than enveloping her or him in emotion or sensuality. In analytic work, dance structure and the spectator's self-awareness in grasping that structure are thrust into the foreground. Nevertheless, much of Morris's work of this kind still reflects the spirit of the music that he chose, incorporating a touch of more traditional aesthetics and, in the case of *Deck of Cards*, of narrative.

A good example of this systems approach is Morris's *Not Goodbye* (1982), a trio set to three traditional Tahitian songs, described by him at the time—he even used the term—as 'a real formal study, a postmodernist arrangement of phrases'.[70] The three songs together last for five minutes, but the dance happens in real time, regardless of the beginning and end of the songs: three different, independent solos in three spots side by side on the stage, each solo in three stages, exactly one minute in each spot. The dance structure is as follows, reading dancers A, B and C spatially, from the viewpoint of the audience:

Minutes
1.   A
2.   A   B
3.   A   B   C
4.   B   C
5.   C
A= Mark Morris   B=Teri Weksler   C=Rachel Brumer

Dancer A re-appears at the end of the dance (again, from the right of the audience) ready to start the pattern all over again—as in 'not goodbye'.

The Tahitian touch lies in the dancers' appearance and the manner in which they ease into the music. They are all bare-breasted (Morris and two women) in sarongs, and share a gently swinging, undulating style, 'fake Polynesian dancing', Morris calls it,[71] although each performs different solo material. This is the poetry. Otherwise *Not Goodbye* is a cool, time-space construction, with rules for the progression of each solo. The first stage is for hands and head, while the dancer sits on the floor. The second brings the same dancer to standing, mainly facing upstage, but 'as if your face is on the back of your head and there is a necktie on your back', while focusing on the legs. The last stage is the most active, the 'fully formed phrase', bringing the whole body into focus.

Such structural independence from the music was unusual for Morris, though not for Merce Cunningham and many other postmodern choreographers. Morris's inclination is to make us more aware of the choreomusical. Consider, for instance, *Prelude and Prelude* (1984), to a duet for violin and harpsichord, played twice, to a duet by Henry Cowell. The first time round, a line of six dancers with fans, blue on one side, gold on the reverse, change positions on every slow beat, moving the fans to cover different parts of their bodies or to extend them out into space. They start and finish in unison. But try, if you dare, to make sense of the constantly shifting patterns of matching (across two or three people) and counterpoint in the centre of the dance. In fact, their material is yet another 'old-style' accumulation, with the possibility here of starting at any point in the structure or of performing the positions in retrograde order. Morris explored the potential for counterpoint and fixed the final choreography. Meanwhile, as the violin starts up, a lone woman breaks out of the line—biting on the fan between her teeth, pressing on in 'a solo full of inelegant steps: sumo wrestler squats, backward falls that leave her with her legs splayed in the air'.[72] But such is her dignity, her solo speaks to you poetically. She does not respond to the detail of the music or to its moment of recapitulation, she seems instead to embody the *sound* of the violin.

The second time the music is played, the woman takes the place of the line-up and the line-up dancers take over her solo in a ragged canon with sporadic synchronisations. Choreomusically, Morris appears to have taken an analytical, conceptual turn, inviting us to question what is solo and what is accompaniment. The woman and the violin were soloists to begin with, and the jagged actions of the group with their fans went well with the 'clattery' harpsichord. But after that, the connections seem to work either way round: you still remember the violin as the 'voice of the woman'. Towards the end of Cowell's Prelude, the harpsichord copies a descending scale motif from the violin, which blurs still further the division between solo and accompaniment. Interestingly, in 2013, Morris set another Cowell duet, his *Suite for Violin and Piano*, and again, the two instruments are humanised, especially as you can relate them (loosely) to the couple on stage. The piece is called *Jenn and Spencer*, after the two MMDG dancers for whom it was made.

Two points arise from these examples. The first is that, by taking an arbitrary structural decision, Morris lost a good deal of authorial control. He let things happen and, as Cunningham surely did, learnt from the result. The second is about a different concept of time for, in both dances, Morris turns his back on traditional hierarchical, climax/release structures and developmental, goal-oriented progression. This links him with the work of other postmodern choreographers of the period. It also connects him with Asian music (and West Coast American music influenced by Asian styles) and the contemporary questioning of western, tonally-based forms and manners of conceptualising music (see Ch. 11).

The humanities scholar and occasional writer on music, Edward Said, is especially illuminating about this other concept of time. In his book *Developing Variations*, he celebrates the virtues of non-authoritative, non-coercive musical forms (unlike sonata form, see pp. 385-6), that are about being in, rather than getting through, time. Said's examples range widely, from the variations of late Beethoven to Eastern models. Of particular interest, he mentions Umm Kulthum, the famous exponent of classical Arabic song, whom, it happens, Morris later highlighted in his selection for the radio programme 'Music I Want You to Hear' (2009, see p. 20). Said describes Kulthum's structures and timing:

> Her peculiar rigour as performer derived from an aesthetic whose hallmark was exfoliating variation, in which repetition, a sort of meditative fixation on one or two small patterns, and an almost total absence of developmental (in the Beethovenian sense) tension were the key elements. The point of the performance, I later realised, was not to get to the end of a carefully constructed logical structure—working through it—but to luxuriate in all sorts of byways, to linger over details and changes in text, to digress and then digress from the digression.[73]

Morris reconciles his interest in western developmental tonal forms with radically different alternatives.

This other, flat sense of timing could be the main reason why critic Arlene Croce did not take to Morris's *The Death of Socrates* (1983), set to the third, final section of Satie's *Socrate* (1918). (Morris was so haunted by this score that he choreographed a second dance to the full *Socrate* in 2010. Croce described the piece as 'a parched and static vista peopled by boys in Greek tunics. As a picture, it had life and thought; its intentions were clearly stated. But as a dance it was inert.'[74] The impact on Jowitt could hardly have been more different. For her, it was 'elegiac and quite beautiful...We see the simple grave gestures echo around the space—the way ideas of a master might appear in the discourse of a disciple.'[75]

The choreography covers the part of Satie's score that deals with Socrates' death in prison surrounded by his friends, his final conversation with his jailer and the drinking of poison. The words are from Plato's 'Dialogues', translated into French by Victor Cousin and considerably abbreviated by the composer. Morris used Satie's version for orchestra and soprano soloist.[76] The score has been described by Roger Shattuck as 'utterly *white* music, which denies its own existence as it goes along by an absolute refusal of development'.[77] With its modal basis, there is no harmonic drive or progressive sense of time. Meanwhile, the vocal line is melodious, but contains no memorable tune as such, and is designated '*en lisant*' ('as if reading'), to encourage distanced, unemotional delivery. The accompaniment is very independent, often based on short, repetitive one-bar motifs, as in the progressions of four triads spanning a tetrachord—the 'Socrates motif'—that open this part of the score.[78] Yet, if the overall manner is even, there are sudden shifts within the score, 'wipes' followed by fresh starts, and a few loud, emphasised moments that arise from nowhere. Even small changes create high drama in such restrained circumstances, although these markers inevitably disappear as rapidly as they came into being.

Morris's choreography is in harmonious relationship with the music insofar as it is ritualistic and slow to unfold, but its language often seems hard-edged in comparison: frozen hieratic shapes and predominantly two-dimensional, angular movement including flexed ankles and wrists. It is also highly schematic choreography, a manner not at all determined by the 'flesh' of the music. 'Super-mathy', Morris calls it. 'I shudder to use the term postmodern, but it was.'[79] The six men enter one after another in a series of solos that start lying on the floor, then cross the space in a grid pattern. Three of them work the up- and down-stage axis, three move from stage right to left, they all form a brief unison, return to their solos and finally leave the

Death of Socrates, Rob Besserer. © Tom Brazil, 1983

stage one by one. Built in the same movement style, the slow openings of the solos are all different and relatively brief. Other phrase material is shared. The second phrase is medium length and faster, the third longest of all and, in both of these, the movement relates to, and dissects, the musical beat. After a while, you can predict how the larger form of the dance will work itself out, as it functions palindromically in terms of both phrase order and spatial organisation. (Morris, as we will see, loves palindromes and forms with a central core, see pp. 391, 412.) The last person to start, downstage right with the slow phrase (the very tall Rob Besserer), ends with the same phrase upstage left. The unison in the middle passage is a 'red herring', outside the system.

This schematic structure is largely the result of Morris choreographing on this occasion without a score, allegedly because he could not afford to buy one (see p. 33). So he counted the music from start to finish, 590 counts in total (295 bars of 4/4, each divided into 2 counts), and organised the dance's time structure mathematically, again as an almost perfect symmetry. He made a chart of this structure.

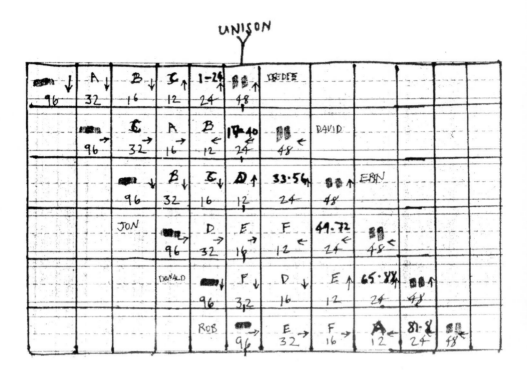

Death of Socrates—Facsimile of Morris's own chart

The numbers represent the number of counts in each phrase unit and the arrows indicate the direction of travel for each member of the cast. For instance, 'Dee Dee' (Guillermo Resto) begins with a phrase of 96 counts (directed downstage) and continues with a 32-count phrase performed three times (adding up to 96 counts), while David Landis performs his opening 96-count phrase (towards stage left). Resto continues with six 16-count phrases (again totalling 96 counts), then 12-, 24- and 48- count phrases (always assembled into 96-count units). The diagram shows how the dance builds to a central unison and then reverses the process. The performers referred to are: Rob Besserer, David Landis, Erin Matthiessen, Jon Mensinger, Donald Mouton and Guillermo Resto.

There are twelve sections, as well as the central unison, an introduction of 5 bars (10 counts) and a coda of 2 bars (4 counts). The six solos (each 96 counts long) start as follows: at bars 6, 30, 54, 78, 102, 126. The central unison occurs from 137 to 160, and the departures happen at 174, 198, 222, 246, 270. Unsurprisingly, the seams of dance and music rarely meet, not just the solo divisions, but also shorter units of material, so the effect is of letting things happen, of 'air' between what you see and hear, and of enhanced drama when chance structural meetings occur. (Morris tested out the movement vocabulary in *Caryatids*, earlier the same year, to a rhythmless score by Harold Budd.)

The unison centre is an especially powerful section. It is the point of maximum scale, the 'voices' of all six dancers joining as a community (which the scheme set up), but it is also the occasion when we learn that the death is imminent. A few moments are highly emphatic: the *pianissimo* 'adieu' of the kindly jailer telling Socrates that he is about to fetch the poison—all the dancers bow (bar 146)—and the *fortissimo*, ominous ascending tetrachord when the tearful jailer departs (bar 154). Another moment that stands out is at bar 222, when Socrates drinks the poison—*forte*-staccato—one of the most traditionally harmonised passages in the entire score. (It also happens to coincide with one of the solo departures.) In these emphatic moments, the music 'holds' movements that are by now familiar.

So there is still poetic content in this dance, as much as it is highly schematic. The sudden moments of enlargement contribute to this and include the final image: to the musical oscillation of the two-bar coda, Besserer, who remains, seated upstage, moving one hand down and up like a curtain over his face. As if closing the eyes of a dead person is how Morris explains this,[80] but it is also an image of disappearance, a final contact with the narrative of the score. The music does not finish: it just stops.

Cunningham Connections and Collaboration with Herschel Garfein: In Pursuit of Independence

Much of what Morris learnt from *The Death of Socrates* went into *Frisson* (1985). Set to Stravinsky's fundamentally static *Symphonies of Wind Instruments*, this was also made without access to the score. But by this time Morris had undergone a conversion to the work of Merce Cunningham. Hitherto, he had been a regular at Cunningham concerts, but was known sometimes to boo them. Morris recalls that he suddenly saw the light and 'fell apart'[81] in 1984 when he encountered *Quartet* (1982: to a score by David Tudor), actually an intensely moving quintet featuring Cunningham as a much older, outsider figure. *Frisson* was Morris's acknowledged tribute, although it never looks like a Cunningham piece.

The full live wind ensemble being hard to muster, *Frisson* is rarely performed. Morris used a recording for the premiere at Dance Theater Workshop, New York. The only other performances (with live music) have been at the Théâtre Royal de la Monnaie, Belgium (1988) and at Tanglewood (2003 and 2011). The piece is nine minutes long. Stravinsky wrote the music in 1920 and revised it in 1947; the following choreomusical analysis uses the 1947 score.[82]

Once again, working primarily from sound without a score turned out to be key to the particular style of this work. Unusually too, the movement was created in blocks, perhaps a subconscious link with Stravinsky's style of distinctive blocks of material, separated by breaks or disruptions. The tempo and distribution of the choreography were then adjusted to fit the music. But Morris does not emphasise the point by matching musical blocks simultaneously in his choreography and, although some connecting points are specified, other movement is not nailed to sound and can fit the music differently at different performances. Likewise, the timing between the performers, as a simultaneous duet and trio, or a solo alongside a quartet, can vary. Those very tactics allow for the spaciousness of the composite work: opportunities, sound spaces for us literally to hear the dance, the thud of a step in an awkward manoeuvre or of a landing from a fall—and the opposite, many visual pauses that then turn our attention full on to the music. Like the score, the time sense of the choreography is mainly static: it leads in no clear direction.

A limited number of movement ideas recur many times in different contexts—distinctive positions and clusters of activity—but Morris organises them quite differently from the musical structure. The movement fragments are like kaleidoscopic particles rather than the structural interpolations or pillars within the music[83] and, unlike in the music, none of them conspicuously drops out to give more space to others. Nor do we associate particular moves with particular musical ideas. Once more, sound and movement coexist with plenty of 'air' between them. Relations with the score are a good deal more specific and planned than in Cunningham's totally independent work, but the freedom from sound detail is strikingly similar in effect.

Other aspects of the choreography are reminiscent of both *Socrates* and Cunningham. There is the factual performance manner, the decentred use of the stage and multi-directional facings, the autonomy of each of the performers (the three women and two men, all in leotards), operating alone or in shifting combinations. Morris describes the attitude behind the execution: 'Report over there and do this. When you're done with that go over there and do this.'[84] The movement style is chunky, sturdy and sculptural, emphasising angles within body designs—not a curve or soft wrist to be seen—but with an element of suspension and precariousness (which the title *Frisson* complements nicely).

One or two images are plain and stable, like a wide second position (arms and legs, straight or in *plié*), often occasion for tentative matching across the group. But most moves are uncomfortable. There are many versions of standing on one leg and getting into the position fast with no time to find balance, like one knee raised at a right angle in front of the body and an arm covering it with a parallel line, or the lower leg bent up behind the body, the opposite arm straight forward, while the head twists an awkward 90 degrees to the side. Morris sought 'wrongnesses' to extract a particular intensity of concentration, and that intensity gets conveyed to us, the audience. We also see lifts in which a woman is held flat and floating like a table top, and a couple of allegro movements: a series of three jumps with legs in parallel and arms swung back into pre-dive position, and dramatic backwards falls to the floor ending with the body in a plain straight line. Sometimes several moves together repeat as clusters. Transitions from one place to another are simple walks, on the toes, which 'gives a tension'. They become jaunty, even a trifle sneering, during what has come to be called the 'Wild Dance' (at [46], a quick staccato episode leading to a climax at [54-56]),[85] and once or twice they seem to go with the music.

The opening of *Frisson* is striking and energetic, a woman somersaulted forwards down centre stage to the audience, backwards, then forwards again, her four porteurs gradually dropping down to one man, on his back and hoisting her up on his feet. She sits, legs apart, with her feet flexed, iconic, all right angles—one of the motif second position *plié* positions in the air. This final image returns fleetingly at the very end of *Frisson*, but without the same spatial symmetry, off centre, against one of the floating flat-body lifts, and with an extra man jumping on the outside, still moving as the lights go down. Perhaps it is a tease about closure that does not quite happen, just as some musicologists have proposed about the score.[86] It makes us contemplate the larger structure of the piece. So does the point two-thirds of the way through the dance, at [56], the one major stasis, fully committed punctuation, with four of the dancers lying flat and just one facing away to an upstage corner, sitting, tilted forwards, her arms stretched above her. The ensemble stays like that for all of ten bars. Morris says that the stillness was intentionally cued, as a time for 'listening'.

With that major stasis, Morris imposes his own clear large shape, two parts. But his point of division is not the one at [65], when what is generally referred to as the Chorale, the closing section of the *Symphonies*, begins. Nor is it the one at [42], the first of the two premonitions of the Chorale.[87] Morris's moment of punctuation is instead the second premonition at [56]. His choice is to maintain pace, increasing it for the climax of the 'Wild Dance', where there is more action than at any other point in *Frisson*. Events happen in rapid succession and keep our attention over the full width of the stage. Three of the dancers do the 'three jumps' and all but one

Frisson. © Lois Greenfield, 1985

ends up falling flat, a couple, a third, a fourth. Then the big halt happens, unequivocal shift of gear, enhanced by lighting, white/blue, the coldest yet in the piece: in the video of the 1988 performance at the Théâtre Royal de la Monnaie, there is a steady cooling towards this point in the dance. After a kind of breather that has all five in unison in a strange animalian rolling and circling with necks as fulcra, the concentration of the main Chorale begins, and we are calmed by its new cosmic resonance. We see a dance canon bathed in a golden glow, when many of the notes of the melody seem to be dispersed across the ensemble (perhaps a passage of detailed musical articulation at last). Then there are fleeting unisons or almost unisons, a sense of easy communion and a glimpse of wholeness, before the teasing final asymmetry.

Morris takes up the musical suggestions of living in the 'moment' of a particular block of material, and of change as disturbance or point of recognition: he adds further disturbances and points of recognition. His tactics evoke the practice of looking at a sheet of paper overlaid by a transparency and contemplating their marks both separately and in combination through each other. This means that, although Morris's large two-part division is clearer than in the music alone, he seems to have increased the jangles and jolts at a more detailed level. But most of the connections between musical cues and changes of movement speed are not exaggerated. More of these are apparent in the Monnaie film than in the earlier one shot at Dance Theater Workshop, but sometimes we cannot be sure that these connections are engineered to exist at all.

There is another kind of cross-media connection in *Frisson* that is fundamental, creating shape and meaning within the composite work. Just as in *The Death of Socrates*, there is poetic content. What I call here 'feeling moments' pierce the frame of the piece from time to time, like darts, surprising and especially strong in emotional impact, and there are more of them towards the end of the dance. If we agree with Morris that the main tone of the choreography is 'dry...sober...sciency', he is still, like Stravinsky, telling us only half the story. The musicologist Arnold Whittall is convinced of the allusions in the score to 'song, dance, celebration, lament—whose presence, far from the accidental results of the composer's failure to enforce his own logic of abstraction, are essential aspects of the music's integration of form and content'.[88]

Returning to Morris's choreography, one such 'feeling moment' is the big halt, a desolate moment like a death symbol, with so many floored bodies, plus the withdrawal of the woman who sits turned away from us. Another, spectacular in its brevity and the coincidence of our aural/visual intake, occurs during the Chorale, when a man puts his arms around the waists of two women on either side of him and stretches forward between them, a big effort of striving to straighten into a line, at a perilous angle. In the 1988 Monnaie performance, he makes contact with the most poignant harmony in the whole score, the moment of expanded pitch band reached by melodic ascent to E against bass line descent to C (four bars after [70]).

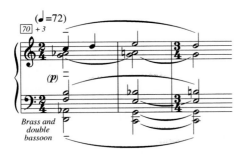

Ex. 5.5 *Frisson*, Stravinsky, *Symphonies of Wind Instruments*.

The effort sets off a flurry of activity, his torso contraction and the women's panic arm gestures, then another contraction, and ricochet reactions from the other dancers, crossing music that has already returned to calm. At the end, it is the same man who is exposed, jumping, the lone mover.[89] During the 1985 and 2011 performances at Dance Theater Workshop and Tanglewood, this musical moment happens at a later stage in relation to the movement. Here, and especially in the Tanglewood performance, where it happens latest of all, the striking harmony stresses the loneliness of the single dancer still dancing. In both 'versions', image and sound combined signal a surprising humanity, and the cosmic becomes earthly. Serenity is close cousin to sorrow in this final Chorale.

Let us now go back to 1984, to *Forty Arms, Twenty Necks, One Wreathing*, Morris's first collaboration with a composer, and the first of two works with Herschel Garfein. It pushed Morris into the high end of musical modernism, a place that he has rarely visited during his career, working with highly complex tonal and rhythmic structures. Created on, and with, the students at the American Dance Festival, it also provided him with an important live music experience. ADF was the occasion when Morris saw Cunningham's *Quartet*, on June 30, a short while before his own premiere on July 10.

The starting point for the new work was an erotic Elizabethan madrigal by Thomas Weelkes, with the following text:

Four arms, two necks, one wreathing
Two pairs of lips, one breathing.
Fa la la la la la,
Two hearts that multiply sighs interchangeably,
Fa la la la la la.

While the madrigal provided the title for Garfein's score ('One Wreathing'), the choreography expanded the numbers tenfold: 20 dancers (four MMDG dancers and a student 'corps' of 16) means 40 arms and 20 necks. The score was for a chamber ensemble (6 players) including a wide range of percussion.

Not only on account of the resources required, this was a highly ambitious project, about thirty minutes long and rushed into performance within about three weeks. Morris created the choreography while the music was being written and taped, right up to the last minute. The four musical movements were: 1. Chacony 2. Return 3. Echo Song (which included a quotation from the Weelkes refrain), and 4. Dance. In the third movement, the clarinettist and harmonica moved to play from behind the audience while, for one section, the ensemble as a whole was divided into two sub-groups playing out of synchronisation in different tempos.

In an interview two days before the premiere, Morris explained his own contribution:

This dance is nothing but rules, very, very strict rules. Penny [Hutchinson], the only woman, can use only circles in her movement, curves. Dee Dee [Guillermo Resto] only uses undercurves. Instead of circles, he does curves on a diagonal. And Erin [Mathiesson] only uses straight lines. My part, which doesn't exist yet, is all diagonals. Also when we travel, we can only travel in those ways. I just made up so many rules on this, that I can only make up a dance with what's left.[90]

The manner of the choreography was plain and 'analytical', the vocabulary geometrical (as in *Marble Halls* and *Frisson*), with many simple leg and arm lifts, all presented in a task-like manner. The audience also had ample opportunity to grasp the development of the choreographic structure, to register the pattern of the crowd copying the soloists and the four occasions when the soloists work in canon in a line, but hold their bodies at different levels, high and low. Sections of simple runs and hops here look straight out of Cunningham. Yet, apart from the casting, Morris's choreography bore little relation to the theme of the madrigal or other references in the score. *Forty Arms* looks about as abstract as a dance can be. In parts of it, Morris also seems more independent from musical structure than anywhere else in his output. He worked between what he calls 'landmarks' (musical cues, some of which are private, not noticed by the audience). This was most probably because of force of circumstances: so little time and having to develop some of the choreography before the music was available. But a hallmark of the Morris-Garfein collaboration was for the participants to allow each other freedom, to talk very little once they got down to work.[91] There were extended blocks of silent choreography (which might have encouraged Morris's all-silent work *Behemoth* of 1990) and the opposite, music only and stage blackout.

The *Forty Arms* project seemed to experiment with as many different variables as possible between media: between the respective forces on stage and off, the choreographic and musical divisions, as well as dynamics and rhythmic detail. Plainly-stated movement found itself alongside a furious ensemble assault, a melancholy flute, the acidic sound of a prepared-piano arpeggio, a plodding baroquish cello, or nothing at all. Cunningham (although using music with less assertive personality) had already shown Morris that such an approach was possible and could be interesting.

On the occasions when the score introduced a regular beat, the dancers found themselves locking into it. Garfein was impressed by Morris's meticulous manner when he dealt with the specifics of the score. He recalls:

In the later rehearsals I saw, I could see that he worked precisely with musical 'landmarks' in the score, and he demanded that all the dancers

know these very well, whether by counting or by listening to melodies....
the last movement was a kind of crazy loud, pulsed thing, inspired by
a blind Boston street musician who used to sit bashing on a drum kit
and blowing in and out on a harmonica harnessed to his neck. The
music of that movement was pulsed and repetitive, but with measures
where a fraction of a beat was dropped by the whole musical ensemble,
who would still come together on the following downbeat and carry on
with the pulse. I remember Mark demanding that the whole company
(including the student 'corps') count that sequence of pulses and frac-
tional pulses correctly, and his dance did articulate those very unusual
phrase lengths. (If memory serves, he may have built in some safety for
the 'corps' by having the most important moments first articulated by
his principals.)[92]

The pieces just discussed, and many of those based on rules and systems,
seem relatively innocent of any postmodern discursiveness. They hardly
represent ironic commentary on, or self-reflexive distancing from, a
reference or source. Most seem open programmatically too, like the music.
In the case of *Forty Arms*, the choreography simply accepts the pressures of
the music in the manner of co-existence.

The next collaboration with Garfein was quite different. The trilogy
Mythologies (1986) began with *Championship Wrestling After Roland Barthes*
in 1984, made soon after *Forty Arms*. It was Garfein's idea to use a political
essay published in 1957 by the French philosopher Roland Barthes,
deconstructions of daily life activities, revealing how institutional powers
encourage prejudices while simultaneously denying their existence.[93]
Together, Morris and Garfein chose three essays, on soap-powders,
striptease and wrestling. 'Soap-Powders and Detergents', for instance, dealt
with the aura surrounding advertising products and how the media feeds
on our fears of dirt and blackness—just as Garfein's musical source, Bach's
Coffee Cantata, played on the coffee cult of the eighteenth century. Morris
explained his view of the trilogy:

> It's not just the three subjects I'm working with, but how they are perceived,
> what they mean. You know: the good and evil aspects of wrestling, the
> good and evil aspects of detergents and striptease, the extremes of what
> those phenomena mean. This concert will be about the viewers too. It's
> a projected thing, 'Mythologies', because it's based on subjects that are
> public, things that you've known about and have thoughts about and
> have thoughts about before you come in and see what Barthes or I say
> about them.[94]

The Morris/Garfein trilogy is a reflection on the essays, with clear narrative content, but fundamentally humanist, at least for Morris, rather than following the political motivations of Barthes.[95]

Although the trilogy is obviously quite a different sort of endeavour from *Forty Arms*, the relation to musical detail was similar, and again, the two artists went their own ways once they started making work. Fehlandt recalls that the music for *Striptease* was finished at the last minute—one reason for the particular freedom of contact there.[96]

For *Soap-Powders*, the first piece in the trilogy, Garfein wrote the libretto (about a Mrs. Michaels of Joliet, Illinois, who is obsessed with getting her wash clean) and scored his cantata for instrumental ensemble and four solo vocalists. When there was a regular pulse, it was natural (and relevant) for Morris to make use of it: Busby Berkeley was a source for the choreography. *Striptease* mixed taped synthesiser music (using the Synclavier II computer music system) and club-style music for live instrumental ensemble. During this piece, a group of dancer-characters strip naked—types such as a bride, cowboy, construction worker and girl in leather. Before he heard the music for *Championship Wrestling*, Morris began developing movement ideas in silence in a duet *Slugfest* (1984). Meanwhile Garfein finished his tape score before giving any of it to Morris. He introduced synthesised music with sounds recorded from live and TV wrestling matches (*musique concrète*). Perhaps the most successful part of the trilogy, showing the excesses of wrestling as spectacle, the choreography was devised as a series of episodes playing out different situations and drawn from 'games'. Garfein recalls Morris challenging several dancers to 'wrestle themselves' as if they were two people:

> Then he would adjust what he saw by changing the way they were using certain parts of their bodies—in effect changing some of the 'rules' of that particular 'game'. Dee Dee [Guillermo] Resto was absolutely brilliant at this self-wrestling, and of course his solo became the final moment of the dance.[97]

One especially interesting passage musically illustrates Morris's 'landmark' approach, tuning in to the large structural features in the score. It is the shared climax of *Wrestling*—though never discussed as such by the two artists—the culmination of a Bunraku-like bout between Hutchinson and Weksler, each with her own group of supporters. Garfein explains:

> The music here is a fifteen-second 'phrase' created by white noise that is being ring-modulated and passed through a filter that is slowly opening up [a big crescendo]. So the spectrum of the white noise is changing very dynamically over the course of the fifteen seconds... [but functioning] like an impossibly vast brass section doing an impossibly perfect crescendo to bring in a different choir of the orchestra.

The two confront each other in big, lifted, slow-motion strides, when suddenly Hutchinson kicks Weksler back into one long, long somersault, during which she is passed down her row of supporters. A barrage of shouts is heard, and their fight now pushes forward under different conditions. Garfein remembers vividly: 'Held like a battering ram [Hutchinson] is carried slowly across the stage to collide with her opponent [Weksler], who is being held aloft with her whole body flexed like a bow.' Hutchinson's fist meets Weksler's abdomen and then there is a real break in the flow, the dénouement ushered in, 'a completely new musical world full of fitful percussive attacks and rather plaintive tones....I'm still amazed,' Garfein continues, 'by how a moment like that in the dance is not just brilliant, but inevitable. As if Mark had come up with the idea and then asked me to write something for it that would time out exactly for the effect he wanted. But I'm not sure it could ever have happened that way.'

This is one of Morris's most inspired examples of extended dance continuity. Not driven by any pulse, it is rather a meeting of forces arising from the shards of a comedic situation, a great tidal wave of movement stretched out by sheer pressure of sound. The smallest of all his dancers becomes the most heroic, her massive recoiling enabling still greater grandeur—she turns into 'an acrobat of God'.[98] Then there is the cut-off, and she and her combatant share their exhaustion. As Barthes put it, wrestling is about 'rhetorical amplification: the emotional magniloquence, the repeated paroxysms, the exasperation of the retorts can only find their natural outcome in the most baroque confusion'.[99]

Mythologies is far from typical of Morris's musical approach—is there such a thing as 'typical'?—but it remains important within the range of experience from which he still draws today. Even in this early period, the range is considerable. But it is often hard to pin Morris down. His work is not simply music visualisation, nor is it simply *not* music visualisation. He moves between categories with the deftness of a chameleon, always ready to try something new and jump back and forth swiftly between tactics. Let us take the year 1981 as an example. It began with a 'real' visualisation *Ten Suggestions* and ended with an exercise in metrical and phrase counterpoint *I Love You Dearly*, which was followed by a substantial work employing mixed strategies—*Gloria*. In 1982, on the same programme, Morris premiered *New Love Song Waltzes*, carefully harmonised with Brahms, and the Tahitian *Not Goodbye*, with its arbitrary 'postmodern' time structure. Then, in December, 1985, again on the same programme, the new *Frisson* sat lightly next to Stravinsky while the angry *One Charming Night* was positively intrusive, fighting the connotations of Purcell's music and its text. 1985 was also the year of *Marble Halls*, another 'real' visualisation, and the time when Morris prepared the *Mythologies* trilogy for premiere in early 1986.

It is at this broad level that Damsholt's idea of Morris's work as choreomusical polemic (see p. 140) makes best sense. Choreomusical tactics shift, sometimes even within individual pieces, but Morris's dances usually have their own, pressing over-arching agendas and are, in any case, partly driven by traditional aesthetic attitudes towards form and expression. The idea, however, that these shifts open up a discourse, a commentary on choreomusical behaviour—the concept of postmodernism looms—becomes much more compelling when we look *across* works and observe their full variety, not forgetting those innocent, non-discursive pieces where irony and distancing seem hardly an issue at all.

Whether the case is so strong when we consider Morris's later work and repertory as a whole is another matter, but here, already in his career, Morris was telling us that any musical approach is possible and right for different circumstances. He absorbs from history as he needs, carrying the ghosts of previous choreomusical styles and their ideological foundations with him. Sometimes, he might even be joking about his own virtuosity with choreomusical style. He is a choreomusical pluralist: if there are rules, he recognises that they are provisional, and he will break them.

Period 2 (Brussels): 1988-1991

If Morris's early experimental period demonstrated that all choreomusical styles are possible, his three years in Brussels, which offered him much enlarged resources, provided robust confirmation of such versatility. Of the eleven dances from this period, all but one was set with live musical performance in mind. Several were of a scale far larger than anything he had created to date (including musical resources), especially the full-evening *L'Allegro, Il Penseroso ed il Moderato* (1988), *Dido and Aeneas* (1989) and *The Hard Nut* (1991).

The first two of these works are the most acclaimed of Morris's entire career. Partly for this reason, I have chosen to analyse both in their entirety within separate chapters. This is also an opportune moment to consider how choreomusical practices shape a work as a whole at the same time as in its detail.

First, in Chapter 6, I embark on *L'Allegro*, set to the Handel oratorio inspired by Milton. Signalling Morris's arrival in Brussels, it represents huge ambition and creative energy. Today, its spell remains as powerful as ever. Unsurprisingly, the London *South Bank Show* documentary (1990) about Morris's work in Brussels used *L'Allegro* as cornerstone piece[1] and in 2001, a beautiful illustrated book dedicated to it was published.[2] In 2014, it was filmed, for broadcast and publication as a DVD the following year.[3] Few, if any, other works of modern dance have ever sustained themselves to that extent around the world—*L'Allegro* is now performed somewhere virtually every year, and it has been taken to Australia, Canada, France, Hong Kong, Israel, New Zealand, Spain, all over the US and three times to the UK.

In Chapter 7, I move on to Morris's *Dido and Aeneas*, which is also exceptionally well-travelled, set to Purcell's opera, and premiered only a few months after *L'Allegro*. Choreomusically it is distinct in many ways from *L'Allegro*. But there are similar advantages with *Dido* for analytical purposes: the work has been broadcast and is commercially available on DVD.[4] With *Dido*, Morris made for himself one of the greatest and most challenging dancing roles of his career, distinguished by his dancing the two leading female roles, Dido and the Sorceress. So we have a chance to witness the choreographer in a second role: as dancer.

Both *Dido* and *L'Allegro* deal with words and recitative as well as with airs (arias) and dances. While they support detailed analysis of choreomusical structures, they give rise to a complex web of meanings, and *Dido* is a fascinating example of conceptual blending involving music, dance and text.

After the analysis of *Dido*, in Chapter 8, I range across the other dances of the Brussels period, paying particular attention to *The Hard Nut*, Morris's commentary on the Tchaikovsky *Nutcracker* ballet (again commercially available on DVD[5]), and *Wonderland*, his detour into a choreomusical approach influenced by narrative film/music techniques.

Selected clips of dances analysed can be found on the MMDG website: http://markmorrisdancegroup.org/jordanbookclips.

6

L'Allegro, il Penseroso ed il Moderato: From Milton to Morris, via Handel and Blake

Gérard Mortier's invitation to Morris was as generous as they come: 'Think of the biggest thing you want to do, the very biggest thing— then do it!'[1] Morris had first heard Handel's choral work in 1985 and was immediately captivated. Now was his chance to realise his dream, and indeed, L'Allegro seems like the most ambitious dance ever, fast-moving, all-encompassing, grand in scale but full of memorable detail—picture images, gestures, events or, as Acocella put it, 'things'.[2] What other choreographic work of any kind demonstrates such range, persuading us that we have encountered in just two hours the whole world of human feeling and experience? There is also a directness of manner: it is one of Morris's least ironic works.

Handel's L'Allegro was already a multi-vocal, pan-historical artwork, an eighteenth-century score (1740) stemming from a seventeenth-century John Milton poem (1631) which, in the nineteenth century inspired a series of water-colour illustrations by William Blake (c. 1816-20). Morris drew eagerly upon all this material.

The Milton poem (or rather, two poems in succession) contains a powerful binary within it, Allegro, followed by Penseroso, representing the poet's conceptions of the active (extrovert) and contemplative (introvert) aspects of the human mind. It is Allegro who goes out into the world, visiting the countryside and the city and engaging with his fellow citizens. Penseroso's pleasures are quieter. He is more solitary, an onlooker and reader. Both speakers inhabit intense worlds of reference: to antiquity—gods and goddesses, graces and nymphs—and literature—plays by Shakespeare and Jonson, writings by Aeschylus and Plato, all situated within the longstanding classical allegorical and pastoral traditions. Countryside and the joys of nature are an especially strong component. Acocella aptly summarises Milton's Renaissance confidence in packing his poems with 'psychology, cosmology, astronomy, meteorology—the whole world, and the history of the world, with the human mind at its centre'.[3]

Handel's librettist Charles Jennens pursued the idea of interweaving Milton's two poems, in the manner of a continuous debate, even contest, between Allegro and Penseroso. For instance, the work begins with reverse invocations,[4] each speaker exaggerating, in order to denounce, the other's state of mind. Allegro (and his music) berates 'loathèd Melancholy/Of Cerberus and blackest Midnight born/In Stygian cave forlorn/'Mongst horrid shapes, and shrieks,/and sights unholy!' Then Penseroso dismisses 'vain deluding joys' to 'dwell in some idle brain'. Still, it is important that this is no oratorio: there is no drama between stable characters. Rather, the structure is episodic, a series of distinct scenes, which Jennens grouped into two Parts. He also modified the text, changing the words occasionally and omitting about one hundred lines: about a third of the original text. Jennens was responsible for one other key intervention. He wrote his own third Part, a short, compromise statement of reason, called Moderato.

Handel's score divides into forty-five distinct sections across the three Parts, comprising recitatives, airs (arias, for male and female soloists) and choruses. Through various means, in accordance with the baroque procedure of word painting and theory of 'affections', Handel illustrates the broad distinctions between the two speakers. Allegro has the simpler melodies and harmonies and the clearer (often dancey) rhythms. Penseroso is associated with arioso and greater dissonance. He listens to the flute as nightingale in Part 1 and to the sacred organ in Part 2, while horns, carillon, trumpet and timpani are occasionally added to Allegro's orchestral colour.[5] But the two are not simply polarised as opposites. Closer relationships between them are also explored, suggesting that the overall statement of the work is about multiple possibilities for mood and temperament. In accordance with this open approach, the solo singers overlap 'roles' rather than adhering consistently to one or other of the speakers. Handel also took special pleasure in depicting the pastoral component within the poems. Literally, we are led upwards towards the moon and heavens. Literally, we hear the bees and birds, the curfew bells and the hunting horn.

Add Morris, responding to both words and music:

> Because of the way Handel already dealt with the contrast within the text—he makes happy music to melancholic text and vice versa—it's already mixed up and answering itself. So dancewise, I always have the option of ignoring or completely literalising the text or rhythm or melodic motifs.[6]

Now, the resonances multiply further and the process of enlargement continues. The whole dance suggests more than is immediately in view. Behind scrims, for instance, in the dim distance, something else goes on, literally, or in the imagination. People enter the stage and quickly disappear again into the wings. They are also hardly ever seen alone. Doubling, multiplication of dancers is an important theme of the piece.[7] As much as in any Morris choreography, they are a community: twenty-four in number, in 1988, his biggest crowd to date, and here, personifying abundance. At the end, a nest of rotating circles conjures up the 'cosmological vision' that Milton understood.[8] Morris says on the *South Bank Show* dedicated to *L'Allegro* and his Brussels work[9] that he incorporated many movement styles, encouraged by the variety that he heard in the music and text. So there is folk dance, Martha Graham modern, ballet, and perhaps most obvious, the pliant barefoot 'Greek' style of Isadora Duncan and the American visualisers of music, Ruth St Denis and Doris Humphrey. The look of the stage shifts constantly, twenty-one different scrims and drops (Adrianne Lobel), lighting changes (James F. Ingalls) and abstract accounts of different vistas—skies, landscapes, the pillars of a building, the grid of a city. Costumes (Christine Van Loon) already distinguish individual dancers, but all of them change boldly between Parts 1 and 2, from rich autumnal hues to an array of bright pastels. Nothing is stable.

At the same time, Morris turns to the past in the postmodern manner of the 1980s, interested in allegory and the static surfaces of symbolic feelings or 'affections' rather than sucking us into the illusion of interior psychological development. His contribution is rather like a series of pictures brought to life, the world captured in a miniature, magic box-set: the pictorial component, the held image, is stronger than usual in his work. Nor are dancers firmly associated with specific characters. Whether they be personifications of abstractions like mirth or melancholy or real presences mentioned in the text, a long list—farmworkers, drunks, lovers, holidaymakers, a city crowd, nymphs, Graces, birds, animals, insects, trees, flowers—they slip from old roles into new, sometimes even within one short section.

Morris's imagination is perhaps more volcanic than Milton's, closer to Handel's, given the terrifying pathos of some of this composer's melodic content and his many heart-wrenching harmonic insertions. The choreography is a representation of the Baroque's darkest passions as well as its bright grace and raunchy humour. Yet frequent devices of wipe-out or cancellation between 'numbers' maintain our distance. To be moved, yet not to be moved...

Finally, we must not forget the visionary Blake whose twelve watercolour illustrations of Milton's poem prompted several of Morris's images, like the moon wandering aloft, the youthful poet dreaming, the holidaymakers in a circle dance, and the strange forms seen curled up on the ground. From Blake there is also the sheer energy and exultation of flying figures streaking across our vision.

Such richness of reference, such interdisciplinarity, has made Morris's

L'Allegro an obvious topic for stimulating critical debate. First, there is the *South Bank Show* and detailed 2001 book of photographs, commentary and essays devoted to it.[10] But there have also been two important symposia involving eminent speakers from across the arts: in Berkeley in 1994 at the time of the US West Coast premiere (the papers documented in Wendy Lesser's *Threepenny Review*[11]), and in Seattle in 2008 to mark the work's twentieth birthday (film footage of which is on the MMDG website).[12] Yet the marked tendency of all these spin-off events and publications has been to focus on the relationship between dance and text. Armed with the full libretto included in every programme, writers have had a field day responding to the leadership of Milton and Jennens. Unsurprisingly, with little video material readily available until 2015, relations with music have proved far more elusive. A notable exception to this is an article by dance scholar Rachel Duerden which focuses on the baroque/postmodern aspects of poetry, music and dance in *L'Allegro* and includes some detailed choreomusical analysis.[13] While acknowledging that text has to remain part of the discussion (as with *Dido*), my own analysis seeks to embed this within a more developed choreomusical discussion.

Some musical preliminaries are addressed first, especially about Morris's own arrangement of the score (the result of a collaboration with Craig Smith, who conducted the premiere). That in itself was a creative act with profound consequences. Then, I travel through several opening numbers of the work, in order to illustrate the particular journey style of *L'Allegro*. Writing in the mode of a guide to the events that the listener-viewer 'happens upon' along the way, I point out salient choreomusical features that differentiate separate numbers. After this, still trying to maintain that sense of an abundance of 'things', I turn to a range of other choreomusical tactics, other surprises and pleasures, that the piece offers. My main sources for analysis were MMDG recordings of performances from 1988, 1994, 2001, as well as the *South Bank Show* rehearsal and performance clips. For the reader, the 2015 DVD is now available.[14]

The following summary outlines Morris's *L'Allegro*, including a brief description of the music and choreography (in italics) of each section and a summary of key information from the score: indications of speaker (Allegro or Penseroso), tempo, casting and notable instrumentation, especially the use of solo instruments. (Morris used the 1965 edition by James S. Hall and Martin V. Hall.[15]) The musical titles come from the score's libretto. The dance titles, which are used for headings in the analyses that follow, come from the 2001 book on Morris's *L'Allegro*. Many of these are derived from the libretto, while others are descriptive, or nicknames adopted by Morris and his dancers. The section numbers are my own, although those in Morris's score (which does not number the recitatives) have been included in square brackets.

L'Allegro: A Summary

Orchestra: two flutes, two oboes, bassoon, two trumpets, two horns, timpani, carillon (celesta), strings, continuo (including harpsichord and organ).
Singers: 3 sopranos, tenor, baritone, plus SATB chorus (according to the premiere programme), but today there are usually two rather than three sopranos (totalling four singers).

Dancers: 12 women, 12 men

Part 1

Overture—Concerto Grosso in G major, Op. 6, No. 1 A tempo giusto—Allegro

1. **L'Allegro** Largo Accompagnato for tenor 'Hence, loathed Melancholy' [1]
Mad Crossing—Towards the end, dancers can be seen racing across the stage in the gloom.

2. **Il Penseroso** Allegro Accompagnato for soprano 'Hence, vain deluding joys' [2]
Mad Scene—Mixed group
Introducing some of the images and gestures that recur throughout the choreography.

3. **L'Allegro** Allegro moderato Air for soprano 'Come, thou Goddess fair and free' plus two oboes [3]
Three Graces—Three women
Involving one, two, then three women in unison and canon.

4. **Il Penseroso** Largo e piano per tutto Air for soprano 'Come, rather, goddess, sage and holy' [4]
Sage and Holy—Three women and two men
Images of shielding the eyes from brightness and seeing (high above) contrasting with lying, legs apart, as if in labour (down on the ground).

5. **L'Allegro** Allegro Air for tenor and chorus 'Haste thee, nymph' [5]
Haste Thee Nymph—Three men and group of women (all twelve)
Images of 'jest' and 'jollity', introduced by three men during the tenor solo, followed in expanded form by the women during the chorus.

6. **L'Allegro** Menuet Air for soprano 'Come, and trip it as you go' [6]
Come and Trip It—Two women and group of nine men
The two women are followed by the men, matching the words consistently, e.g. 'come' is always

shown as beckoning with both arms and 'on the light fantastic toe' attends to the feet.

7. **Il Penseroso** Largo e piano Accompagnato for soprano 'Come, pensive nun' [7]
Pensive Nun—Solo man followed by a woman

8. **Il Penseroso** Andante Larghetto Arioso for soprano 'Come, but keep thy wonted state' [8]
Come, Come—A solo man and woman, and mixed group
The soloists reach towards each other separated by two scrims, while the others walk across the stage in front of, and behind, them (four pathways).

9. **Il Penseroso** Largo Accompagnato for soprano, Arioso for soprano, and Chorus 'There held in holy passion still' [9]
The Diet Dances—Group of women followed by men (full cast of twenty-four)
A women's duet (a shadowed solo) becomes four trios forming circles, followed by the men in two lines of six (to the chorus). The plucking of hands sharply from mouths opening wide refers to the diet of the gods.

10. **L'Allegro** Recitative for tenor, then soprano 'Hence, loathed Melancholy'
Birding—A man and mixed group
The man as bird and group as a flock, a transition into the next section, introducing a series of dances referring to birds.

11. **L'Allegro** Air for soprano 'Mirth, admit me of thy crew' [10]
Male Bird Solo—Male soloist and mixed group
A hopping lark and a flock of birds filling the sky above.

12. **Il Penseroso** Accompagnato for soprano 'First, and chief, on golden wing' [11]
Bird Duet—A man and woman
A meeting between two birds, overlapping into the opening of 'Sweet Bird'.

13. **Il Penseroso** Andante/Larghetto e piano Air for soprano 'Sweet bird, that shun'st the noise of folly' plus one flute [12]
Sweet Bird—The couple from 12 as two birds, then two women and mixed group
One of the women as a nightingale dancing to the flute, later both women together, separated by a scrim, the second woman associated with the soprano. The group interrupt, crossing the stage several times, showing a series of vivacious flying lifts. A few dancers cross back holding the high 'wand'ring moon' (two women) in another high lift, a slow passage, while the watching nightingale attempts several times to reach the moon.

14. **L'Allegro** Recitative for bass 'If I give thee honour due'
The Hunt—Entrance of mixed group setting up the scene in preparation for 15.

15. **L'Allegro** Allegro Air for bass 'Mirth, admit me of thy crew!' plus solo horn [13]
The Hunt (continued)—Mixed group

To a song about the noise of the hounds and horn, a developed story about the chase, with dancers depicting trees, hedges, dogs (and a handler), horses and aristocrats in a carriage, and two terrified vixens (or lesbians) who are finally left hiding.

16. **Il Penseroso** Largo e piano Air for soprano 'Oft, on a plat of rising ground' [14]
Fireplace—Mixed group
Two symmetrical groups visualising the narrator's song about hearing the curfew, the swinging of a bell (one dancer hoisted aloft) and then, in contrast, a cosy indoor scene around the fire.

17. **Il Penseroso** Larghetto Air for tenor 'Far from all resort of Mirth' [15]
Crickets—Mixed group
Couples progress through the landscape and 'crickets' scamper in and out. Male dancers lurch drunkenly across the stage to 'the bellman's drowsy charm'.

18. **L'Allegro** Recitative for tenor 'If I give thee honour due'
Hansel and Gretel—A man and woman
A couple enter hand in hand and exit to 'wander' in the country in 19.

19. **L'Allegro** Siciliana Air for tenor 'Let me wander not unseen' [16]
Hansel and Gretel (continued)—Mixed group
A country scene, visualising the narrator's song, the activities that the visiting couple come across: ploughmen, milkmaids and mowers at work, and a shepherd telling a story to a group of girls.

20. **Il Moderato** Larghetto Air for soprano 'Each action will derive new grace' [38]
Each Action—Mixed group (full cast of twenty-four)
In groups of six or four, depicting the four elements: earth, water, fire and air—although these are not driven here by the text.

21. **L'Allegro** Accompagnato for bass 'Mountains, on whose barren breast' [18]
Mountains—solo woman
Allusions to the might of mountains, resting clouds, daisies, wide rivers, towers and battlements, the act of seeing and the trees mentioned in the text.

22. **L'Allegro** Andante Allegro Air and Chorus 'Or let the merry bells ring round' plus carillon [19]
Merry Bells—Mixed group (full cast of twenty-four)
A communal celebration, after which the tempo slows and the group prepares for bed and sleep.

Part 2

23. **Il Penseroso** Larghetto e piano Accompagnato for soprano 'Hence, vain deluding Joys' [20]
Gorgeous Tragedy—Towards the end, the solo woman of 24 is revealed standing with her back to us.

24. **Il Penseroso** Larghetto e piano Air for soprano 'Sometimes let gorgeous Tragedy' [21]
Gorgeous Tragedy (continued)—Solo woman and mixed group
The solo woman is followed by the group, the numbers growing gradually. Her wide gestural range is a metaphor for the challenging pleasures of the mind. There are parallels with the structure of 6.

25. **Il Penseroso** Recitative for soprano 'Thus, Night, oft see me in thy pale career'
Gorgeous Tragedy (coda)—A solo man introduces 26.

26. **L'Allegro** Allegro Solo and chorus 'Populous cities please me then' plus trumpets and timpani [23]
Populous Cities—Solo man and mixed group
Dancing the cityscape, a noisy, chaotic, excited crowd, enjoying one central moment of respite. This is a rare example of exact ABA, to a Da Capo musical structure.

27. **L'Allegro** Allegro Air for tenor 'There let Hymen oft appear' [24]
Hymen—Mixed group
Called 'Gymnastic Lovers' by the dancers, several couples engage in a long, sweeping phrase and its retrograde (like a rewind), a poet dreams and the familiar 'horse and carriage' image passes through.

28. **Il Penseroso** Accompagnato for soprano 'Me, when the sun begins to fling' [25]
Day's Garish Eye—Three men introduce 29, which follows without a break, their moves illustrating the twilight rays of the sun, and the groves and brook mentioned in the text.

29. **Il Penseroso** Largo e pianissimo Air for soprano 'Hide me from day's garish eye' [26]
Day's Garish Eye (continued)—Two women joining the three men
Still reflecting the inner thoughts and observations of the poet at evening time—referring, for instance, to the busy bee, the murmuring waters, then falling asleep, a nightmare and awakening.

30. **L'Allegro** Pomposo Air for tenor 'I'll to the well-trod stage anon' [27]
The Men's Dance—All twelve men
A jolly folk-style circle dance as metaphor for silliness and nonsense behaviour: the men embrace, punch and slap each other, kiss and make up.

31. **L'Allegro** Andante Air for soprano 'And ever against eating cares' [28]
The Ladies' Dance (also called the Kleenex Dance)—All twelve women
Another circle dance, of the heavenly kind, suggesting wreathes and chains. Later, the women shift into four trios, out of which one of them breaks like a flower opening: 'the hidden soul of harmony' revealed.

32. **Il Moderato** Andante Larghetto Duet for soprano and tenor 'As steals the morn upon the night' plus oboes and bassoon [39]
The Walking Duet—Full cast of twenty-four

The awakening to 'intellectual day'. Drawn from a Thracian line dance, a simple limping step constantly repeats, tracing an abundance of interweaving floor patterns and groupings melting one into another. A feverish central passage is contained within this frame of Reason.

33. **Il Penseroso** Recitative for soprano 'But let my due feet never fail' plus organ
Basilica—A curtain descends, its vertical lines ('pillars') referring to the sacred building of the text. A man enters and moves far upstage gazing towards the ceiling.

34. **Il Penseroso** Grave Chorus and solo for soprano 'There let the pealing organ blow' plus double bassoon and organ [31]
Basilica (continued)—Full cast of twenty-four
The other dancers follow the first man's pathway, spreading across the back, looking upwards likewise, halting during the organ solos, and then reversing (as in a rewinding film) back out again.

35. **Il Penseroso** Largo Air for soprano 'May at last my weary age' plus cello solo and organ [32]
Weary Age—Two women and two men
The reflections of age, a comment on experience, this section recapitulates many images laden with resonance from earlier in the piece.

36. **Il Penseroso** A tempo ordinario Solo for soprano followed by chorus 'These pleasures, Melancholy, give' plus organ added to continuo [33]
Melancholy Octet—Four couples and a solo woman
After the soloist's short introduction (to the soprano), each couple takes one of the four choral voices (SATB) and reflects the organisation of material (the patterns of fugue subject and counter-subject). All progress towards a major climax.

37. **L'Allegro** Allegro Air for bass 'Orpheus' self may heave its head' [29]
Orpheus—Solo man and group of women
Three couplets referring to Orpheus awakening to hear music are exactly repeated, but the music and choreography move on. Eurydice's name is mentioned, prompting the full tragic tale of Orpheus seeking to rejoin his lover (a man here, and the mode is comic) and 'her' second 'death'.

38. **L'Allegro** Allegro Air for tenor followed by chorus 'These delights if thou canst give' plus trumpets and timpani [30]
Finale—Full cast of twenty-four
A stately march accelerates into joyous hopping, skipping and leaping entries, in small groups, the dancers racing down the space to exit. At the end they all join into a nest of three concentric circles moving in alternating directions.

Immediately apparent are the adjustments in Morris's own edition of the written score (in collaboration with Smith), for he dispenses entirely with a

Part 3 Moderato section (most of which music he did not particularly like) and changes the order at the end of Part 2, concluding with the last two Allegro (instead of Penseroso) numbers. Because this choral work is not a drama with a linear narrative, such changes can be more easily made. The final chorus 'These delights if thou canst give', with additional trumpets and timpani, makes for a very lively, public conclusion. 'It's a long night—you have to end *up*', Morris says. 'It has to have a happy ending. It makes sense structurally, emotionally, musically.'[16]

Yet it is interesting that Handel himself had already been in two minds about the structure of his oratorio. By 1741, he too had come up with a two-Part version, removing the Moderato Jennens settings entirely (generally agreed to be less inspired in any case), and replacing them with the Ode for St Cecilia's Day. In 1743, he changed his mind about who should have the last word and ended with the same Allegro chorus as Morris (before the Ode). He also radically cut the Penseroso material just before this, including the very powerful fugue 'These pleasures, Melancholy, give'. Thus, Handel, to all intents and purposes, re-interpreted Milton's text.[17]

Morris did not share Handel's re-ordering (re-reading) exactly. Re-interpreting yet again, he kept all the Penseroso material, but cut two other musical numbers (17 and 22 in his score): 'Straight mine eye' and 'But O, sad virgin'. He also interpolated his two favourite Moderato numbers, 'Each action will derive new grace' in Part 1 (20), and 'As steals the morn upon the night' in Part 2 (32). He wanted to use both these numbers as 'neutral' occasions within the otherwise dialogical arrangement of the text, 'machine' dances he calls them,[18] with all twenty-four performers in white light on a full stage for both, forming 'rational' geometrical patterns.[19] The overall result is thirty-eight numbers in total: recitatives, airs, one duet ('As steals the morn', which is also a duet for oboe and bassoon) and eight choruses, all but one of which is introduced with a solo, and two of which provide the conclusions to each Part. Morris's Part 2 lasts about as long as Part 1 (separated from it by an interval), but, containing fewer lines of poetry, relies more heavily than Part 1 on textual repetition. As we shall see later, like Handel before him, Morris's 'edition' has fresh implications for the reading of Milton's poems.

Morris's score contains a number of other minor adjustments. He introduced an overture before Part 1, the first two movements of Handel's Concerto Grosso Op. 6, No. 1. (At the 1988 premiere, the whole Concerto was performed, the first four movements before Part 1 and the last, fifth movement before Part 2, but Morris later decided to be more economical with overture material.[20]) Within the main part of the score, Morris decided to boost the unison start of 'Merry Bells' with celesta (as the carillon). The score has the carillon starting after the vocal introduction 'Or let the merry bells ring round', but Morris preferred to establish the topic of this chorus immediately. He recalls having arguments with musician colleagues over this. In one especially lengthy, and supposedly, Da Capo (ABA) air 'Sweet bird, that shun'st the noise of folly', Morris dissects the already repetitive A section, so we hear the first half of it before, and the second half after, section B.[21]

On rare occasions when a counter-tenor/alto or mezzo-soprano is available as a fifth singer, Morris has used an alternative version of the air 'Sometimes let Gorgeous Tragedy' in F-sharp minor as opposed to B minor. The same is the case with the solo introduction to the fugal chorus 'These pleasures Melancholy give', where again, the alternative results in a difference in key, here necessitating a full stop, between the two sections.[22] Beyond key, there are other minor differences between these alternative versions. Modifications in the choreography are involved, some in accordance with changes in the text underlay, so that movements continue to synchronise precisely with specific words, a standard device in this piece.

Before embarking on choreomusical analysis, some points about the kinds of musical form that Morris encountered in L'Allegro are useful. 'Populous cities' and 'Sweet bird' are the only two Da Capo numbers. Most other numbers are in some version of vocal ritornello form (see p. 136), mixing orchestral refrains or interpolations with sung verses, and Handel approaches this framework in countless different ways. 'Sweet bird' has especially lengthy framing ritornellos. 'Sage and holy' starts with just one chord and then the voice breaks in, but there are occasional orchestral echoes along the way and a longer final summary. Orchestral material can be more, or less, similar to or distinct from, sung material. When there is previous solo material, choruses tend to match, but slightly elaborate upon, it. Other numbers are more about verse form, like 'Hide me from Day's garish eye', which is a verse followed by two variations. 'Come, but keep thy wonted state' is unusual in L'Allegro in being structured by a ground (repeating) bass; it embarks in A-flat major but ends in the relative minor (F). 'There let the pealing organ blow' (with choreography called 'Basilica') is like a chorale. 'These pleasures, Melancholy, give' is a choral fugue. Morris has often said that Handel taught him structure (see p. 30), and within L'Allegro lie many different challenges.

Performing the Analysis

We begin with the first eight numbers of the score. The opening Allegro recitative ('Mad Crossing', No. 1) happens in near total darkness;

towards the end, we see figures racing across our vision. During the invocation from Penseroso ('Mad Scene', No. 2), there are images of rest and dreaming, and a sinister moment when the dancers mask their faces with their hands. Overlapping with the first air 'Three Graces', as the orchestral ritornello starts up, a man leads a group, including one woman carried as if asleep, across the stage.

3. Three Graces (Allegro)

The libretto refers to Venus and her 'two sister graces', recalling the first Blake illustration of 'heart-easing Mirth' and two dancing figures on either side of her. To the vocal line, in come the three women, one by one, with flying skirts and arms, Isadora style, together with a hint of ballet in the toe steps and joyous leaps. There are six lines of poetry (three couplets):

Come, thou Goddess fair and free,
In Heav'n yclept Euphrosyne,
And by men heart-easing Mirth;
Whom lovely Venus, at a birth,
With two sister-Graces more,
To ivy-crownèd Bacchus bore.

In Handel's setting, music, text and dance are in two-part form, A (all three couplets) followed by A1, a variation with extension (except line 2 of the text is now omitted). Morris responds by repeating the same dance moves (in different directions) to the same text and similar music, and then, to repetition of the last line, there is the extension: different music, different movement.

As the voice begins (with the same melody as the orchestral ritornello), the first entry is by the lead dancer, with a preparation and, on beat 2, a step forwards and up on to the toes in *attitude*. Her arms fly up as she goes. We see this three times, making a phrase.

Ex. 6.1 Handel, 'Come, come, thou goddess fair and free' (*Three Graces*).

This opening dance phrase is repeated again at the start of A1, now two outer dancers in a line in canon with their leader in the centre. Finally, in the closing orchestral ritornello, it is made yet more complex in a canon across all three (the *attitudes* cheekily starting with the woman downstage, then going to the one upstage before moving back down the line).[23] As usual in *L'Allegro*, Morris choreographs freely across orchestral and sung passages of music.

From the opening step into *attitude* on count 2 mapping the rise in pitch, the main emphasis in both dance and music is 'up'. Later, when the dancers are in a line, they reverse this move, stepping back and bringing the other leg up front on '*ivy-crown*-èd', with a more emphatic downbeat emphasis. The final canon builds to a climax, with articulation of 'up' on every beat of the bar, and is literally breath-taking. A canon such as this also creates the semblance of a 3/4 metre (across the musical 4/4) as you might see the three pulses of a single move passing up and down the line of three, and then immediately catch another series of three pulses.

At one point in A1, we hear 'Come, come,' suddenly all by itself. Morris chose this moment to introduce his 'come' gesture, drawn from American Sign Language (ASL).[24] In a sturdy, wide-legged position, the dancers hold their arms in a rounded shape and circle them fast, as if round a small ball out in front of them, but like a command. Morris wants us to remember 'come' for later. Then, each time we hear 'crown-èd', three times in all, they take their hands to their heads and bounce them sharply, down-down-up (short-short-long), again reflecting rise in pitch (the same musical motif that began this number), to make the point. These moments stand out, as a totally different kind of vocabulary, a shift of register, tightly attached to their musical gestures.

4. Sage and Holy (Penseroso)

This is the Penseroso trio to counter-balance 'Three Graces' (three women, here accompanied by two men), and much more solemn, about difficulty rather than ease. There are two contrasting sections, covering the poetry as follows:

A: Come, rather, goddess, sage and holy;
Hail, divinest Melancholy,
Whose saintly visage is too bright
To hit the sense of human sight;

B: Thee bright-hair'd Vesta long of yore,
To solitary Saturn bore.

Acocella provides a good example of the dancers shifting roles here: the three women represent the goddess Melancholy when they enter, then they become the mortals straining to look at her (their hands over their eyes as if holding their 'eyeballs on stalks'), and then her mother (in the act of giving birth).[25]

Morris makes us understand up and down in pitch as an extreme polarity in this dance. Section A emphasises the upward motion of the melody, as follows:

1. striking high 'picture' lifts towards stage left on '*god*-dess', 'di-*vin*-est', '*vis*-age', for each woman in turn, here the lifts repeating in accordance with the musical phrasing, while the text changes;
2. to '*bright*', all three women lifted in a row, the furthest upstage lifted the highest;
3. to '*sight*', the first time we hear it, the men bouncing on their heels as they raise their arms, and arching to look heavenwards. Then they make an uncomfortable, strong, marcato 'eyeball' gesture on the third, unaccented beat of the bar. (The women echo this passage.)

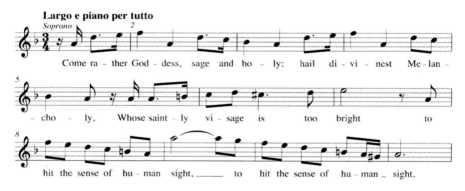

Ex. 6.2 'Come rather, goddess, sage and holy' (*Sage and Holy*).

When Section A repeats, the women come back for more of the same lifts, following the same melodic rise and fall patterns, the first two leaving the stage to return and get lifted yet again (and there were additional smaller lifts just before they left the stage).

Section B, which refers to the birth of Vesta to solitary Saturn, emphasises the downward motion of the melody, and again, movement repeats as text repeats. The pain of labour becomes the focus of both Handel (who repeats the words several times) and Morris (who introduces anguished floorwork out of early modern dance tradition). The sense of pain increases when, to the word 'bore', usually the lowest note of the melodic phrase, the women throw themselves on to their backs and open their legs sharply towards the audience. Your ear is also drawn downwards to the bass during this passage, especially to its gruff punctuating chords.

'Sage and Holy' is a very odd number in several respects. To the earthy opening chord, the two men somersault on to the stage from opposite wings, like jesters. But this will not be a funny dance and soon, you may be worrying about when the series of lifts will end. There is a sense of loss when two of the women leave. Later, when they return, we might well ask: are they the *same* two women? The third time we hear 'To solitary...', while the melody struggles to rise from the depths, the harmonies darken. The women turn awkwardly on to their stomachs like grounded seals and the men stab the 'earth' viciously with invisible instruments, forcing these gestures against the musical legato (just as the marcato 'eyeball' gesture did).

Perhaps the oddest moment of all is when the men take over the women's lifts during the final ritornello. Here, Handel brings back ideas from both A and B, as if to forge a resolution between them. But the act of a man high-lifting another signals an awkward shift of register, especially when one of the lifts goes the 'wrong' way, to the right. (This is definitely not funny.) Morris delays resolution; he holds on to the idea of a terrible birth for longer, the women continue to throw themselves into labour, one by one, and we see the 'eye-ball' gesture once again. Just as Morris enhances the distinction between high and low in pitch in this dance, he expands upon the discomfort suggested in the text and music, an example of expansion as resistance within a conceptual blend (see pp. 97-8).

5. *Haste Thee Nymph (Allegro)*

Laughter and jollity prevail in this number, which contains quotations from a 'jumping up and down' Croatian dance and a 'heel-clicking' dance from the Vlach country of Yugoslavia and Romania.[26] Here, sung and orchestral statements are strongly differentiated, with two men to the tenor solo joined by a third as orchestral 'echo' between them, then, to the related chorus that follows, two bands of women, each forming two lines of three, the second band as 'echo' to the first. The framing orchestral ritornellos are themed with running on the spot, or exiting and entering.

Again, Handel repeats lines of text or parts of lines but, for the chorus, he only uses the first and last couplets of the text, those most insistent about the positive mood:

Haste thee, nymph, and bring with thee
Jest and youthful Jollity,
Quips and cranks, and wanton wiles,
Nods, and becks, and wreathed smiles,

Such as hang on Hebe's cheek,
And love to live in dimple sleek;
Sport that wrinkled Care derides,
And Laughter, holding both his sides.

For the list of ideas in lines 3 and 4, there are six distinctive mimetic arm and head gestures, and later, over 4/4, as line 6 is repeated, there is a repeating on-the-spot step, seen five times, in 3/4: 'Step forward, hop, spring back'.[27] Duerden aptly describes the impression of this passage, music and dance together, as one of 'being frozen in time, unable to move forwards... weaving around'.[28]

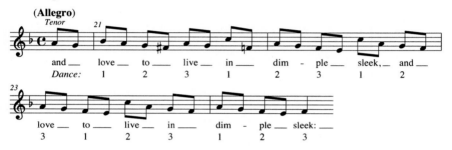

Ex. 6.3 'Haste thee, nymph' (*Haste Thee Nymph*).

Laughter is then depicted by Handel's staccato word-painting—'ho-ho-ho-ho-holding'—and by Morris's dancers rolling around themselves on the floor, spread-legged, holding *their* sides. Duerden points out Handel's typically irregular musical phrase lengths here, with the same words repeated to form units of 2, 7 and 4 bars that are shared by Morris's choreography. The sense of tonic or 'home' note remains strong, there is a 'centredness', she says, and again, 'the music teases us by its doodling, its refusal to settle down and make a full stop'.[29] Morris does much the same, but soon adds to the dottiness by introducing another on-the-spot 3/4—'heel-clicking'—step.

The women follow roughly the same order of dance events as the men, but are freed from the original textual associations. In any case, they do not get so many words to dance to. They also take their cue from the occasional canonic vocal entries, to introduce more counterpoint of their own, a series of canons, sometimes the middle against the outer lines, sometimes between alternate lines, sometimes a canon across all four lines in turn. The 'heel-clicking' step was choreographed with 'do-what-you-want' arms. The twelve dancers now look almost totally out of control. Mayhem and joy.

Let us summarise what has happened choreomusically up to this point.

In following Handel's reading and elaboration of the text, Morris sometimes exaggerates the musical affect or expressive suggestions, and sometimes he nudges us into a new direction. Handel's irregular phrase lengths and rhythms are also assumed choreographically, but occasional short spurts of metrical counterpoint introduced by Morris's choreography contribute additional complexity. Across these few numbers, there are already several different kinds of association between dance and voice or orchestra, and different degrees of attachment to words. There are also varied responses to the rise and fall of melody, sometimes detailed, sometimes referring to larger contour. Overall, you get the impression of an unusually thorough and richly diverse response to music: its rhythms, melodies, harmonies and textures.

According to the dancer Tina Fehlandt, 'Haste Thee Nymph' was choreographed early on, in the US, and was one of the numbers that provided Morris with a kind of template for the whole of L'Allegro.[30] So were the next two numbers.

6. Come and Trip It (Allegro)

During his school years, Morris had encountered 'Come and trip it' in a singing training book[31]—he played the piano, while sister Maureen sang—but only later did he realise its origins. Complementing the solo-chorus arrangement of 'Haste Thee Nymph' (No. 5), the dance starts with two women (6/8, labelled 'Menuet' in the score edition used by Morris and in the most recent edition by Donald Burrows[32]). They mirror each other and are followed by similar choreography for nine men, to a slight abbreviation of the earlier text and music. At one point, the women in the chorus sing in counterpoint with the men, which, as in No. 5, becomes a cue for counterpoint within the dance.

Yet this dance is much simpler than 'Haste Thee Nymph'. For a start, there is much more unison. The scheme is for the movement to map almost totally consistently upon the words of the text, a single couplet, sometimes fragmented, heard several times during each half of the number. The choreography can be divided (as shown in italics) into four moves:

Come, and *trip it* as you *go*,
On the light fantastic toe.

1. *Come*: the circular arm movement introduced in Three Graces. At the end of each half of the score, this movement is shown twice, with a break in between, then three times in quick succession, approximating Handel's repeat in the text.
2. *Trip it*: a sideways step and hop, with the upper body swinging low, drawing attention down towards the feet.

3. *Go*: both arms extended diagonally forward and upwards, with pointing index fingers.

4. *On the light fantastic toe*: a slow sideways trotting-hopping step, lifting the feet, and containing a perky syncopation in the second half of the bar. This syncopated rhythm already lies in the music.

During the short orchestral interpolations, the dancers simply walk to the dotted-crotchet beat. Later, there are short passages of running at quaver rate. So far, this is the least complicated dance of all, as if Morris had applied a formula, it is so firmly attached to its already very repetitive words.[33]

The opening movement phrase emphasises the larger contour of its winding melody—a rise of one tone overall, C to D, but the choreography gives the illusion of a much wider interval:

Ex. 6.4a 'Come, and trip it as you go' (*Come and Trip It*).

L'Allegro, Il Penseroso ed il Moderato, 'Come and Trip It', the 'go' gesture, Tina Fehlandt and Mireille Radwan-Dana. © Leslie E. Spatt, 1997

Ex. 6.4b 'Come, and trip it as you go' (*Come and Trip It*), including indication of the 'trotting-hopping step'.

Later, the sideways, 'horizontal', trotting-hopping step connects with notes repeating at the same pitch, 'trip it' now matches a rising two-note figure, with a hop marking the top note, and the dancers drive forward and upwards again and again with the rising melisma on 'go'. Once such clarity (through connection) has been established, when the music changes for these same words, Morris continues to match them, not the music.

Why does Morris keep this dance so simple? Does it seem a little too predictable? He takes simple repetition a stage further by underlining it. Such faux-naïveté, however, seems appropriate after the complexities of the preceding two numbers. Morris rests our minds and lets us feel particularly secure at this point. He might even make us smile.

7. Pensive Nun (Penseroso)

Near the end, the lonely man of this dissonant recitative embarks on a strange concentrated walk, termed the 'Penseroso walk' by Macaulay.[34] One of his hands is extended forward low, palm facing the floor, pursued by his intent gaze. This becomes the ground motif for the next number.

8. Come, Come [but keep thy wonted state] (Penseroso)

Inspired by the textual image of an 'even step and musing gait', this dance, once described by Morris as the 'Some Enchanted Evening' number,[35] is a kind of love story, with a couple moving back and forth, looking at and yearning for each other, but divided forever by a scrim (a gauze curtain). At the same time, two continuous lines of dancers do the Penseroso walk across the stage, one in a corridor out front, the other behind in the far distance. The soprano air is underwritten throughout by a plodding two-bar ground bass, a non-stop series of quavers.

Except for the framing orchestral ritornellos, when everyone walks to the bass, crossing the stage, the dancers in the two lines map out precisely the rhythm of the vocal line, stopping and starting with the singer's phrasing and sometimes having to walk very fast to keep up with her. When they halt, they convey the touching simplicity and honesty of a woodcut. Sometimes we may think that they are walking the plodding bass too, because the singer's melody line itself contains many regular quavers, and because walking is, after all, a kind of equivalent to a plodding bass.

Meanwhile, the couple mirroring each other through the gauze bring to our ears the words but, instead of the soprano voice, the sporadic orchestral interpolations. A most striking additional feature, however, is when the pair twice intrude into the group's musical 'space', the vocal line, thus enhancing the melodic climaxes. To 'thy won-ted state', they raise their arms up their sides, in the manner of a large intake of breath, then, straight afterwards, with the orchestra again, they sharply fold over forwards, just before the voice descends.

When the music shifts from A-flat major to F minor, the voice rises to 'Thy wrapt soul sitting in thine eyes', a second melodic climax: here, the couple bounce on their heels in excitement and extend their arm gesture into the now-familiar, heavenward-looking 'eyeball' gesture, followed by its release. These moments of climax are compelling examples of conflation, briefly linking all onstage in a hiatus. But, for the couple, they are moments of rapture mixed with pain, 'shocking', as Morris would say, a shift to a totally different plane of experience, a major statement.

'Come, Come' is another example of Morris making much bigger—in terms of both dynamic and emotional stress—what is already a moment of emphasis in text and music. Most surprisingly too, the number stems from an utterly schematic basis, the consistent visualisation of musical rhythm and part-writing, before eruption at two key moments into something of quite another order. You might marvel at how something so apparently pedantic can suddenly take such a poetic turn.[36]

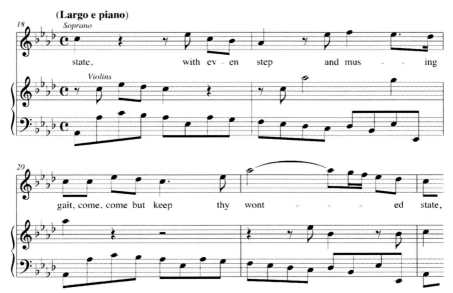

Ex. 6.5 'Come, but keep thy wonted state' (*Come, Come*).

Words

Both 'Pensive Nun' and 'Come, Come' raise an issue about words and word painting in *L'Allegro*, how at different times, text, music and dance compete for our attention. Perhaps the textual layer, which increases the sense of dancers being vessels through which pass many symbolic representations (see p. 185), takes the most time to reveal itself. Unusually, in 'Come and Trip It', the text is so repetitive, you will probably grasp it, then forget about it and attend to one of the other two layers. On the other hand, in 'Come, Come', you may just register specific words: like 'come' itself, because it is repeated and has been heard/seen on several occasions before, and 'even step' and 'musing gait' because the movement here is simple and the descriptions clearly relate to what you see. You may also work to catch the words behind the climaxes that are such obvious representations of strong feeling. There are many different degrees of word power. A number of writers have complained about how hard it is actually to hear the words in the theatre. Inevitably, in such circumstances, they had to resort to their programme libretto.[37] Morris himself insists that the text lies behind everything, except

Sometimes, I go exactly word by word with what's going on, sometimes just the sense of it, sometimes just what's happening musically and not so much the text.[38]

Let us look at further examples. 'Day's Garish Eye' (Part 2, 28), which is thick with words, 14 lines (7 couplets), contains hardly any verbal repetition. (Probably its verbal emphasis was the reason why it was selected for analysis during the *South Bank Show* programme.) Identifying with the woman who is taken on a journey by another with more experience of life, we hear about, and see enacted, bees and streams at evening-time, sleeping, and a nightmare, represented by the upturned gesticulating figure of the woman with experience—it was taken from Blake's eleventh illustration, of Milton dreaming, at this point in the text. Milton and Handel also provide re-assurance of calm wakefulness into day. We see that on stage too. The air begins without any orchestral introduction, and progresses through three musical verses, each a variation on the last, with 'wavering tonality' (between F minor and A-flat major) and a different style of accompaniment appropriate to each stage of the narrative.[39] The choreography pays barely any attention to musical beat. As we concentrate on unpacking the rapid flow of information, listening hard to the text, we may not even be aware of the musical verse form.

In the quartet 'Weary Age' (Part 2, 35), we also encounter many words, but they are used by Morris in quite a different way. Again, some are directly connected with what you see, but often what you see are dance words from the past, recycled within the new verbal and affective context. As well as carrying memories and multiple resonances, the dance words are a metaphor for the wealth of knowledge that comes with age. The music is Largo, with cello and organ continuo strongly featured, and several big fermatas (moments of sustainment) along the way. The various media layers invite us to roam between them in leisurely fashion. The dance is also a metaphor for 'prophetic attainment', the ability to look to the future through the lens of experience and spiritual maturity. The frequent gesturing and gazing upstage, at the start and at the two melodic climaxes (both on a high A), uses the vertical conceptual paradigm: 'up' equated with distance and heaven and 'down' the opposite (see pp. 96-7). As in 'Sage and Holy' (No. 4), pitch is an important parameter for visualisation. There is also striking enhancement of a passage of alternating wide intervals, down-up-down-up-down, to 'Till old Experience do attain'. Developing from a movement pattern introduced in 'Three Graces', the two women fold forwards with the soprano's descent while the two men step back and up on to their toes, raising the front leg (see p. 195), and then vice versa, exchanging roles. All together they create a powerful effect of simultaneous matching and opposition, a favourite Morris device (see p. 130).

Just as Morris has suggested, other dances, those more formal in orientation, treat words in a more general sense. Such is the often-discussed

'Ladies' Dance' (Part 2, 31; to 'And ever against eating cares'), which emphasises the geometries of lines, circles and mazes. The affirming image of circles and individuals emerging from circles eloquently reflects the final couplet:

> Untwisting all the chains that tie
> The hidden soul of harmony.

This is a slow, quiet number, one of the occasions when Allegro's temperamental position seems remarkably ambiguous (see p. 184, and similarly 'Let me wander not unseen', Part 1, 19). The Finale to 'These delights if thou canst give', on the other hand, is quite simply about joy and again, in its closing nest of circles, harmony. Beyond that, it seems entirely formal.

Images of social dance lead to meaning of another sort. 'The Ladies' Dance' is an example, made in heaven. There are others of the more earthly sort in *L'Allegro*, prompted and supported by music with clear dance rhythms. 'Merry Bells' (Part 1, 22) starts off as an ebullient skipping and running square dance, with the full cast arranged in foursomes—the text refers to dancing and to a sunshine holiday, the basis of another Blake illustration. Later, Morris largely ignores Allegro's account of a visit to the theatre in 'The Men's Dance' to 'I'll to the well-trod stage anon' (Part 2, 30). Instead, he responds to its bouncy music and turns the number into a delightfully daft men's round dance.[40]

There is just one, exceptional instance when Morris choreographs to a 'voice' without words, to an instrumental voice. This is 'Sweet Bird' (Part 1, 13), when a female soloist clings with increasing fervour to a flute obbligato, rather than to the soprano who symbolises the poet praising the musical, melancholic nightingale. It is as if the dancer becomes the nightingale itself, embodying, as if possessing, its voice during a series of ornamentations and cadenza-like passages: trilling and warbling translated into fluttering and hopping, a brand new timbral simplicity suggesting special innocence. Later, the woman is joined by another behind a scrim who does assume the soprano voice, with words, becoming both the poet and the nightingale's double, and delighting in close musical exchange with her opposite number.

There is no question as to who leads and who is alter-ego here, and in the end only a long flute cadenza remains and a solo for the flute-nightingale dancer. I suggest that, with the flute woman out front and much the stronger visually, we listen even less than usual to what is actually said. Music and movement say it all.

Morris set up this unique wordless voice-body relationship with great

'Sweet Bird', Julie Worden and Peter Kyle (in foreground) watched by June Omura.
© Ken Friedman, 2000

care. From the start of the opening ritornello to 'Sweet Bird', a man-lark and the woman who will become the nightingale's double twitch their heads in conversation, then exit leaving an empty stage (for nine bars). The flute enters *pianissimo*, and we have time to focus on the purity of its sound. Next, the strings take over, a remarkable ecstatic refrain as other dancers fly in, lifted way overhead. Only then does the flute dancer appear.

In the centre of 'Sweet Bird', when the music changes to a gently chugging Larghetto, the poet speaks of an alternative preoccupation, watching the 'wand'ring moon', represented here by two women carried aloft behind the scrim. Poet and first nightingale now conflate, as the woman out front tries four times to reach the moon, climbing higher each time, into her own flying lifts. This emphasises the melodic ascents, leading to a climax on the soprano's long, high A—'*high*-est noon'.

Side by Side

Naturally, we tend to remember most vividly the tightest connections between music and dance, but there are many other kinds of relationship in *L'Allegro*. Some stand out for the opposite reason, because they are unusually casual choreomusically. There is even one number, 'Basilica' (Part 2, 34; to 'There let the pealing organ blow') in which virtually nothing happens on stage: the dancers enter to the chorale, as if into a high-roofed church, and then exit, simply walking during the singing and stopping to listen during the three organ interludes.

Suddenly, in Part 1, Morris decides to tell us a straight story that is barely hinted at in the text and music. There is 'The Hunt' (14 and 15). The text refers to the early morning racket of hounds and horn, but Morris adds a good deal to this. You imagine that the two running women might be vixens—although he prefers to think of them as escaping lesbians[41]—pursued onstage and off by a pack of dogs, a huntsman plus horn (there is a solo horn in the score), and a couple of pompous aristocrats in a horse-drawn carriage. There is much hilarious rushing about, and at one point a dog pees on a bush, a human bush, because a number of dancers have been recruited as rocks, trees, shrubbery in the manner of baroque scenery and tableau vivant. (They will sidle back in later during 'Hansel and Gretel' (18).) Narrative takes its own time. Although the dancers work with musical cues, they otherwise work independently within specified durations. Look more closely, and you will see that the aristocrats and huntsman (but, notably, not the horses) have been astutely choreographed to match musical beat and articulation. Here, this relation to music makes them seem all the more mannered and ridiculous.

In Part 2, 'Hymen' (Part 2, 27), also nicknamed 'Gymnastic Lovers', the dancers again work with musical cues. But the main impression from the outside is of total freedom from music and text, although Hymen's name is mentioned and the 'youthful poet's dream' (another Blake illustration) is captured by a man centre stage. The pairs of dancers who travel across the stage in this number are its most distinctive feature. They show us surely the longest, most seamless dance phrase in the whole of *L'Allegro*—lifts, somersaults, sexual gymnastics, revelry of many kinds that can be halted at any stage and, once completed, retrograded like rewinding a film.

Whereas 'Come and Trip It' and 'Come, Come' were systems led by words and musical structure, 'Hymen' suggests a dance system imposed upon the music, determined by the length of this movement phrase. On a couple of other occasions, Morris imposes more obvious dance systems. In 'Each Action' (Part 1, 20), there is the orderly transference of gestures representing earth, water, fire and air across four lines of dancers, the entire community.

(There is no mention of these elements within the text.) This is one of the two Moderato sections in Morris's *L'Allegro*, characterised by neutral expression and white lighting, uniformity of motion and geometrical formations.

The other Moderato number, 'The Walking Duet' (Part 2, 32; to 'As steals the morn'), is widely regarded as one of the finest in the work, for both its music and choreography. The text celebrates rationality and proportion over troubled emotions:

> As steals the morn upon the night,
> And melts the shades away:
> So truth doth Fancy's charms dissolve,
> And rising Reason puts to flight
> The fumes that did the mind involve,
> Restoring intellectual day.

Handel's score has great beauty and poignancy while also exuding a firm confidence. It consists of two dialogues, one between soprano and tenor, the other between oboe and bassoon. Morris lets the music speak very plainly and, in its broader aspects, quite independently: his choreography has nothing to do with duets and dialogues (despite his dance title)—the twenty-four dancers work as a solid community for much of the time—and the larger patterns of dance and music often flow seamlessly over each other's boundaries.[42] It is at the detailed level of beat in the outer sections of ABA form that the correspondence between media is exact. Unusually, Morris has provided a detailed description:

> In the A section everyone walks in lines that form patterns. Two lines of 12, alternating men and women, trace radially symmetrical patterns. It's based on a step-drop, step-drop, Thracian-Bulgarian harvest dance. [In the original] the leaders carry a huge sheaf of wheat...

> The B section creates circle groupings and fountains; two lines become four lines; they come from four corners. It's a very straightforward strict canon, with entrances at varying lengths, so that you see the whole phrase. It features swirling, incensey moves...

> At the reprise...the big secret is that the accent in the walking changes. It was step-drop, step-drop. When they come back, it's drop-step, drop-step, so that the downbeat is emphasised—oh, we're back! The point of 'da capo' is that you've learned something in between.[43]

Morris is right that rhythm makes an important contribution to meaning in this number. In the central B section, the musical beat is still the basis (unlike in 'Hymen'), but not articulated so that it stands out. This affords a contrasting lack of clarity, a fluidity, representing the mind under the influence of dangerous 'fumes'. And, a nice touch, when 'intellectual day' is about to be reached and there is an anticipation of reprise in the music, the choreography is still far from calm. Morris's incense remains pervasive, still burning, until the actual moment of musical reprise.

The movement in the outer sections, on the other hand, attends to the beat of the music at the expense of all else. Rather than Morris's reading of a more emphatic downbeat during the reprise, however, I suggest that there is marked change of tone here: from the positive, bold stepping out (and up) into the world during the opening A section, reinforced occasionally by a raised leading arm, to a more relaxed giving into weight at the point of downbeat. The first way connects with the rising tendencies in the melody line, the second takes the ear downwards to the more stable repeating motifs in the accompaniment. Whichever way you look at it, the dance demonstrates Morris's intention: to 'trick people into hearing music better'.[44] Keeping the movement so simple helps make the point.

Counter Points

In just six numbers, Morris introduces brief rhythmic counterpoint between music and dance, which usually lightens the mood. The two instances in 'Haste Thee Nymph', 3s in the dance over 4s in the music, have already been discussed.[45] But the counterpoint in 'Crickets' (Part 1, 17) is an especially sophisticated and witty example and operates in the cause of narrative. This number is surely an instance of Penseroso approaching Allegro in spirit.

While some dancers, in couples, strut around perkily to the continuo beat, others interject from the wings and disappear again, like crickets criss-crossing their legs, to the dotted rhythms in the violins. Mention the 'bellman's drowsy charm', and a series of tipsy men topple with irregular gait across the stage, obviously struggling when they have to fit a series of fussy triplet steps (6/8 time) across the musical metre (3/4). At the same time, a declamatory repeating-note motif makes its appearance, marked by people whizzing in and out of the wings, like anxious intruders.

Ex. 6.6a 'Far from all resort of Mirth' (*Crickets*). The example indicates the beginning of the triplets in the dance, while the brackets show the declamatory repeating-note motif in the music.

When others engage in the triplets against one of the tenor's craziest melismas, it is even more devilishly hard for them to fit the steps between the bar-lines. During the singer's cadenza, one man is left behind a scrim kicking back and forth in desperation, oblivious of the music.

Suddenly, near the end of the final ritornello, for just three bars, the triplets suddenly make new sense. Handel releases the violins from the jerky dotted rhythms into the same continuous quavers as the dancers. The new rhythmic unison, quaver to quaver (although the music is still written in 3/4), lifts the spirits wonderfully, as if the sun had suddenly come out. Again, such changing tactics make you hear the music better. They also tell the story of a country community, a landscape of prancing couples and chirping insects.

Ex. 6.6b 'Far from all resort of Mirth' (*Crickets*). The dancers divide into two rhythmic lines in bar 107.

'Melancholy Octet' (Part 2, 36) is unique in *L'Allegro* both for its music, a choral, SATB double fugue with subject and counter-subject, and Morris's treatment of it: a choreographic fugue locked into the SATB arrangement and its text—another system. It also proves to be one of the most remarkable numbers in the work. A preview dance for a solo woman to a soprano solo introduces the gestural content, equivalent to the words within a single couplet:

These pleasures, Melancholy, give,
And we with thee will choose to live.

Thus, we see:

1. *pleasures*: a stirring gesture of the arms followed by a circling motion of the knee.
2. *give*: kneeling with palms pressed together in front of the body—which represented 'crickets' and warming hands at the 'hearth' in Part 1, and is now more like a gesture of prayer.
3. *choose*: an arm extended with palm displayed, while the body heaves and plunges up and down. June Omura, for whom the solo was choreographed, explains her private image—as if her hand was 'dripping blood'.[46]
4. *live*: a heroic punch skywards, like a manifesto, a position that she will hold upstage throughout the fugue that follows.

It is important to consider these gestures because, although they are not coded—some carried different associations earlier in the work—they still read like mime here and embody struggle and determination. They contribute to what Macaulay has described as *L'Allegro*'s larger qualities of 'tribulation, heroism, pain, and endurance'.[47]

The choral section is driven by pairs of matched dancers, side by side, stapling their material on to the SATB lines. There is an element of gender correspondence between the music and the designated leaders within each couple:

Soprano: a woman leading a woman
Alto: a woman leading a man
Tenor: a man leading a woman
Bass: a man leading a man

The pairs also operate with specified bodily symmetries and asymmetries: each dancer in a pair starting a phrase with the outside leg and arm, or the inside leg and arm, or on the same side of the body (left or right).[48] The leaders are responsible for slight changes in the 'traffic' between performances, always the same number of steps, but a measure of spatial freedom, in terms of how far you get along a pathway, guarantees additional anxiety: 'and it makes you conscious of what's going on around you'.[49] As a stage picture, the dancers seem like isolated couples journeying determinedly through life together, up against the whole world.

Morris explains:

> The dance is done as a steady crescendo. It starts out gentle, and gets more emphatic. It gets bigger. Walking turns into running, and it gets wilder as it goes along. The dancers start out very gently embracing, and by the end they're smashed together. At the very end everybody embraces at the same time because there's a full bar of rest. It's the only time that all voices are rested at the same time. That's the reason that it looks like a fabulous passionate climax.[50]

It is significant that a point of rest in the music turns into a high point of tension in the choreography: Morris is adamant that musical rests are not empty occasions.

Near the end of 'Melancholy Octet', the runs gather power, getting bigger and longer, and, when the music becomes homophonic, they achieve strict unison, articulating the quavers between the notes and creating an effect of tremendous allargando. At the final climax, a woman in the centre is flung round her partner into the air—'like an ejaculation', says Morris, after which she somersaults and kneels defiantly before him. 'Julie Worden [MMDG member from 1994-2011] really stretches it out, which is great', adds Morris.[51] Then we see the desperate tragic embrace across the full cast. Finally, as we hear the adagio descent towards cadential resolution, the implacable Omura accelerates downstage to select one couple (the two bass men), who crumple at her command, as if in death. This is yet another example of complementary motion from 'up' to 'down'.

In their article on Handel's *L'Allegro*, Michael O'Connell and John Powell read this great Penseroso fugue as an expression of learning (fugues are conventionally considered intellectual enterprises) and religious feeling (suggested by the organ scoring).[52] But Morris takes a different view: his vision is one of excruciating passion and the fierce presence of flesh and blood. 'Melancholy Octet' is an exceptionally dark number, strictly systematised, yet with the ingredients to convey huge emotional disturbance. It forges the biggest climax in this work so far.

The next big occasion is the Finale (Part 2, 38), which comes soon afterwards, and in between, is a single Allegro number that Morris turned into a tragi-comedy about *Orpheus* and the (second) loss of Eurydice. (Here, she is a man.) A fundamentally formal dance, the Finale derives from the sheer pleasure indicated in its couplet text:

'Melancholy Octet', with June Omura upstage in the 'live' position. © Elaine Mayson, 2010

These delights if thou canst give,
Mirth, with thee I mean to live.

Once more, rhythmic counterpoint *between* music and dance is a powerful ingredient amongst other wizardries of structural irregularity. The excitement starts during the tenor soloist's introduction, before the chorus joins in. Although you are unlikely to spot this, Morris planned an irregular series of entries here, partly through system, deciding to cast his dancers according to Handel's orchestration. When the tenor sings, more dancers come on stage than when he drops out and the trumpet emerges loud and clear. At first, this is the difference between two dancers and one appearing, later between four and two.[53] Even if the trumpet is a bombastic instrument, we are so used to the human voice-dancer relationship by now that suddenly hearing a trumpet-as-dancer relationship refreshes the sense of personal voice. (The flute(s) did this earlier in 'Sweet bird', and the trumpet in the 'Cum Sancto Spiritu' of *Gloria*, see p. 144.) Otherwise, the sheer size of the orchestra here, bigger than anywhere else except 'Populous Cities' (Part 2, 26), enlarges the dimensions of the work.

As for these entries and passages across the stage, wave upon wave, some are simple runs and skips, arranged to travel in different directions and seen on different dancing groups (threes, fours, twos, and once, just one person). Others, which always happen to the second line of the text, are rhythmically

Ex. 6.7 'These delights if thou canst give' (*Finale*). Men and women are indicated as 'm' and 'w'.

The first set of dancers perform the basic step pattern twice, 3+3+2, followed by two runs, and then exit. The next time this full pattern is performed, by the second set, it starts in the middle of a bar, in accordance with the altered musical phrasing. The musical cadence overlaps with the start of a new phrase in the orchestra, a typical baroque procedure that delights Morris, at which point, the dancers leave and a third set arrive.

The third set of dancers start again with 3+3+2, then on the repeat end with two step-hops (2 counts each), finishing on 'thee': 3+3+2 | 3+3+2 | 2. The impression is quite different on this repeat because of new syncopations in the music. Now 'Mirth...' is heard on beat 2 rather than 1, and again on beat 4, weighting these beats rather than the strong beats of the bar. We are unsettled into thinking that the step itself might have changed, it feels so different, but it has not.

The material of the fourth and fifth sets is the basic step pattern again, displaced one beat from the bar-line, following the musical phrasing.

The sixth time we see this step pattern, its second bar is quite different, with step-hops taking just 2 counts and two additional runs in the middle. It ends on 'live' with the slower version of the step-hop, so the counts in full are 3+3+2 | 2+2+2+2 | 2. Morris diverts us from the simple repetition here of the melodic phrase, which he usually matches choreographically. We have grown to expect 3+3+2 | 3+3+2 and we do not get it.

After the chorus replaces the tenor soloist and a contrasting passage brings all the dancers together in the space, we see the same pattern again, for the seventh time. After the initial 3+3 (which starts on beat 2), there are now six runs, so we are left waiting... until two quick 2-count versions of the step-hop patterns, ending on 'live'. Again, Morris finds a way of defeating expectations: 3+3 | 6+2 | 2.

Finally, for the eighth set, the pattern returns in its simplest form 3+3+2 four times, as the dance group pass through each other centre stage.

---

more complex, at the same time based on a surprisingly economical amount of material. Morris simply varies one basic step combination—a couple of step-hops, one rocking the body down and forward over the raised leg (counted 1-3 at quaver rate), the other up and back towards the leg raised behind (1-3), and a couple of runs (1-2): 3+3+2. The second hop hangs in the air, and creates syncopation, crossing the accentuation within the 4/4 bar of the music. This is a variant of the original steps of the three Graces (see p. 194), while using the same rhythm pattern as the step that crosses the music in *Gloria*'s 'Cum Sancto Spiritu'. The result is that Morris constantly tries out different relationships with musical accentuation, defeating expectations. Ex. 6.7 is an account of how the patterns evolve.

So these passages across the stage change constantly, keeping us on the edge of our seats. Will the dancers leap? When? How? With whom? You can never predict who is going to race towards us next and in what way. Exuberance is greatly increased by the simplest means, movement choices with which we can all easily empathise. Once the singing has finished, the entire cast enter to form three concentric circles, travelling in alternate directions with steps familiar from earlier circle dances. Like the critic Deborah Jowitt,[54] I am inclined to enjoy the memory of those earlier waves more than their resolution. Ultimately, this final glimpse of harmony moves us by contrast with what went before.

Towards a Conclusion

Early on, I mentioned the journey style of *L'Allegro*. It is not a piece that foregrounds large shape and progressive, logical continuity. You accept vistas and events as if out on a stroll, ready to absorb what you come across without pressure of expectation. The way Morris uses the music has been a journey too, the variety of choreomusical relations and effects making a major contribution to the bigger picture of this work, and you never know what might happen next.

As a whole, however, the work tends towards more abstraction, more unsettled reference as it progresses, with more dances about form and fewer about individual words. Indeed, there are literally fewer words and narratives to grasp later on. The clarity and punctuating force that comes from marked, articulated visualisation of words or musical detail eases up considerably in Part 2, from 29 (after 'Day's Garish Eye'). Yet hearing and understanding the words as best we can makes us more aware of the sea-change when they become less prominent. We have seen that, even though Morris has set up equivalences, mime to words or dance rhythm to musical rhythm, he also breaks these apart, and we notice, both when these equivalences emerge and when they are abandoned. The break causes a registral shift, one that opens up wider vistas, contributing to the sense of an expanded world. If Part 1 is more plodding, Part 2 suggests transformation and transfiguration.

Just as he claims today, Morris said on the 1990 *South Bank Show* that he simply had to end the work with Allegro having the last word. There is another claim in the 2001 book on *L'Allegro* that he wanted to resolve the dramatic and musical tension of the entire work.[55] Perhaps he also wanted to convey his initial excitement about being in Brussels. But it is worth bearing in mind that, across his career, he has tended towards positive, wrap-up endings. I am now in two minds about the strength of that resolution in this context. Do people simply go home remembering the joyful, extrovert ending to *L'Allegro*? Or is it possible not to conclude, like Acocella, that seeing the piece was like having 'a day in the sun'?[56] Increasingly, after greater acquaintance with the piece, I respect the weight of Penseroso towards the end of Morris's work, from the ambiguously contemplative 'Ladies' Dance' and 'Walking Duet', then four Penseroso sections in a row through to the huge climactic fugue 'Melancholy Octet'. (Oddly, only Macaulay seems to have spent much time writing about that fugue, and he does so eloquently.) Interestingly, the fugue was once an ending, and a strong one, both of Milton's second poem and of a 1741 version of the score (see p. 192). It was also set in a minor key and, according to convention, conveyed spiritual and learned overtones, that is, until Morris got his hands on it and transformed it into a colossal physical experience. The anxiety element within it is alarming.

We might also question the emotional weight of what follows 'Melancholy Octet'. There is the joyful conclusion, but only after the single, bitterly humorous Orpheus number. Morris made a choice about the large structure of his work, his own, just as Milton and Handel had done, only Morris decided to maintain the strength of Penseroso, while, in 1743, Handel lessened it (and got rid of the fugue). As for what we are left with at the end, in hindsight, what Dr Johnson originally said of Milton's L'Allegro makes sense: 'I always meet some melancholy in his mirth.'[57]

Of the many critics who have written about Morris's L'Allegro, Wendy Lesser is perhaps the one who stands out the most strongly for the Janus-faced inconclusiveness, the provisional nature, of his contribution:

> Morris has simply chosen—arbitrarily, personally, and whimsically—to end on a note of happiness. Nothing in either the world or this work of art leads you to conclude that happiness is a necessary or permanent outcome; and yet the moment feels right, and final, and true.[58]

True, principally perhaps because this is how it ends. Just how persuasive are those final circles? The fundamental conceit of Morris's L'Allegro is that it does not have to end 'up'. It does not drive logically or conclusively towards a particular vision. It just happens. It could end anywhere. But, as the weight of words lessens during the progress of the work, giving fuller rein to the ambiguities of meaning possible within the music, the pressures of dangerous, darker feelings continue to haunt us to the end, through the sun and the joy, and into the future.

7

Dido and Aeneas as Danced Opera[1]

Morris's second work for Brussels was to a sung score actually written for the stage, Purcell's opera *Dido and Aeneas* (1989). His challenge this time, however, was to remove all the singers from the stage and have his dancers take over. By doing so, and drawing immediate international critical attention, he put firmly on the map an alternative possibility for this work.[2] Yet he has always been clear:

> I consider it an opera. We're obviously dancing, but every single part is a coupling of music and dance. I wanted the sound and dancing to be the same thing.[3]

Dido reflects both his love of vocal music and his lasting belief that opera and dance are never far apart: sound and motion are inextricably intertwined. But Morris also understood the particular problem with this opera score:

> I couldn't imagine motivating singers to tell that compressed a story without its becoming a laugh riot...The scenes are so brief, it shifts so fast, and you don't want it to stop and start—that kills it... I wanted to do it as simply and clearly as I could, and my dancers could change characters in a second, instead of having a chorus trudging on and off all the time.[4]

With *Dido*, Morris also made for himself one of the greatest and most challenging dancing roles of his career, distinguished by him dancing the two leading female roles, Dido and the Sorceress, which merge—a good example of character change 'in a second'—into a single role.

Unsurprisingly, the gender issues have already been a major focus of attention, controversial for audiences and critics at the time of its premiere, while appealing to one of the most urgent concerns of dance scholars today (Morris; Burt; Schwartz[5]). The work's postmodern, multi-layered meanings have also been examined (Preston; Martin; Duerden and Rowell[6]), given that it is home for multiple intertexts crossing history and cultures—including intertexts from other dances and other dance styles. Both these perspectives are relevant and, from a broader standpoint, Acocella has illuminated the work brilliantly in her 1993 biography of Morris. Yet it is timely now to open up musical issues for detailed debate.

The following analysis also takes into account the effect of casting changes in *Dido* in recent years. Having relinquished the dual role himself in 2000, Morris divided it in 2006, testing a woman—Amber Star Merkens—as Dido, and a man—Bradon McDonald—as the Sorceress. Then, in 2007, he gave both these dancers and, in 2013, Laurel Lynch, the opportunity to take on the dual role. A woman dancing the female characters throughout implies that the 'text' now exists with much less of the original gender complication.[7] So *Dido* becomes even more of a 'choreomusical' text.

Two existing publications provide valuable background to choreomusical analysis. The article by Rachel Duerden and Bonnie Rowell that demonstrates the critical postmodern sensibility embedded within the work refers to examples of music and dance structure. There is also a conference paper by Sophia Preston that discusses the narrative echoes and flashbacks in both score and setting.[8] My own research has included examination of a series of recordings of the work as well as live performances: Morris insists that his pieces are nothing less than a series of performances, of music as well as dance, each different. McDonald told me that he saw as many of Morris's own performances as he could and they were very clearly never the same twice.[9] Besides, the most accessible commercial recording, as we shall see, is in several respects very different from the theatre piece. I will refer as well to interviews with Morris, McDonald, Merkens and other dancers, taking the opportunity to develop a more thorough documentation of the creative process behind such a key work.

Background 1: Sources and Sexuality

First, to set the scene, Morris's *Dido* was created in Brussels for the Monnaie Dance Group/Mark Morris (during his three-year contract at the Théâtre de la Monnaie), and premiered in the Théâtre Varia, a non-proscenium space, smaller and more spartan than the Monnaie opera house. The musical component was provided by Emmanuel Music of Boston, where Morris had first toyed with the idea of setting the work, conducted by Artistic Director Craig Smith. The intention in 1989 was to mark the 300th anniversary of the opera.[10] Morris told me that his preparation as choreographer involved looking at several editions of the Purcell, reading the opera history, as well as checking the sources of the libretto. He studied, for instance, Curtis Price's valuable, recent Norton Critical Score of the opera (1986), which contains a number of essays, including one by Wilfred Mellers that he decided to include in the premiere programme. Morris encouraged Merkens and McDonald to research likewise.[11]

The libretto is by the poet and playwright Nahum Tate, based on Book IV of Virgil's *Aeneid* (a highly influential text within English literary culture of the late seventeenth century[12]). It tells of the love of Dido, Queen of Carthage for Aeneas, the Trojan hero, and her despair when he abandons her. (Thus, after *L'Allegro*, Morris moved away from a statement about a diverse community of individuals within which soloists and roles constantly shift—ultimately about the world—to one that is essentially about a single individual set against a group.) In Virgil, Aeneas has already been told that he should seek the site of a new Trojan empire (which will be Rome) and Juno sends Mercury to remind him of his destiny when he appears ready to stay in Carthage with Dido. She urges him to stay but, when unsuccessful, she builds a funeral pyre, upon which she stabs herself and dies. The major change introduced by Tate and Purcell is that they centre attention even more on Dido and her inner turmoil than on Aeneas, who is the only soloist without an air (aria). There is no mention of Rome or the imperial project. But there are other differences. Dido dies of a broken heart without thought of revenge or need of a pyre. Rather than divine providence disturbing Aeneas, a Sorceress and coven of witches are responsible for tricking him to leave Carthage (the Sorceress enacts the Spirit of Mercury).

As Alastair Macaulay has pointed out, a Sorceress already lurks within Virgil's story (referred to as a priestess of magic arts).[13] According to Dido, this priestess has advised her on how to deal with Aeneas' intended departure, but she could be merely a 'figment of the self-destructive Dido's brain', a pretence to cover up that she intends to kill herself. Here, perhaps, is the root of Morris's dual characterisation. Virgil also provides the powerful image of a kind of madness from 'love's wound', Dido's profound, body-consuming neurosis—she is her own victim—which supports the dualism of Morris's Dido/anti-Dido[14] as well as the dangerous sexuality that drives his entire vision. Even if my focus here is on choreomusical issues, we cannot ignore this vision. Indeed, as we shall see, it is directly connected with those issues.

Tate leaves the sexuality aside, yet certainly encourages us to think of parallels between the court and the witches' coven, and therefore between Dido and the Sorceress—they are the two leading female protagonists (with hair pinned back and loose respectively), and both have two attendants and an accompanying retinue. Morris was not the first to note this conceit of parallelism: the scholars Curtis Price and Roger Savage both do so for a start,[15] and Savage even proposes that the witch scenes are 'black parody from which the sentiments and rituals of the court can be grotesquely guyed...'[16]

Morris makes us understand Dido's early anxiety and sense of foreboding at least partly in terms of guilt: her awareness of the power of sex/love to lead her into trouble and to over-rule her rationality. At this early stage, her courtiers make her feel better about her feelings by persuading her that marriage would be good for her country.

Acocella goes straight to the point describing Morris's *Dido* as a

profoundly sexual dance....When Purcell's Dido, in her first air, sings of
being 'press'd with torment', Morris's Dido places one hand on her breast
and one on her abdomen, both pointing downward, and slowly opens
her legs. She tells us where it hurts—not just in the heart. Later in Act I
[Scene 1, according to Morris's programme], when she accepts Aeneas'
love suit, she again opens her legs. We know what is coming.[17]

Although it is absent in Tate's libretto, Morris's choreography shows the
consummation, brief and stylised (Scene 3). We also see the link between
sex and death for, soon after the consummation, when Aeneas sings of his
success in the hunt: 'Behold, upon my bending spear/A monster's head
stands bleeding', he holds open his sarong (his back to us) and Dido 'stares
with stony dignity, as if she were gazing at her death, which she is'.[18] (Morris
was originally moved by the sense of loss and terror caused by the AIDS
epidemic when he thought of choreographing *Dido*—another example of
dangerous needs and, at that point, he intended the work to be a solo for
himself alone.[19])

By this later stage of the work, we realise that movement ideas for love,
sex and death are all related, in various ways describing the deep, vertical
line through the body, the 'guts' (as Acocella puts it), linking genitalia to
heart and beyond to head. The Sorceress and her Witches manifest as 'black
joke' the destructive, violent aspects of sexuality, depicting the evil, Acocella
suggests, that is within as well as outside all of us.[20] We find them hilarious,
at the same time as we are horrified. Or, as the critic Deborah Jowitt puts it, the
Sorceress 'epitomises the lust and unreasoning vengefulness that Dido may
experience only as fleeting thoughts, quickly suppressed'.[21] It is the Sorceress
who invents the move of slitting herself from crotch to throat in anticipation
of what she wants for Dido, and it is she who will later simulate masturbation
in gleeful celebration centre stage. It is noteworthy too that, when we first see
the Sorceress, she is hanging over the downstage bench with outspread arms,
which is the pose in which Dido dies at the end of the work.

The fact that a man dances a woman (whether dignified as Dido or
depraved as the Sorceress) has a vital effect on how we read Morris's
work (leaving aside the exceptional casting of Merkens and Lynch). The
Tate/Purcell Dido/Sorceress has been read by some in accordance with
conventional ideological patterns of distressed women: as irrational and
out of control, or malevolent witch (which Susan Foster says, has haunted
the feminine for centuries).[22] But, even if we sympathise with these
readings, they do not work for Morris's *Dido*, which lays stress very clearly on

the nobility and dignity of Dido, and the Sorceress' oppositional behaviour only underlines this. His being a man in the role introduces crucial distance. As Macaulay suggests, his height and weight give him 'the dimensions of classical drama'.[23] Morris himself has often cited the long tradition of men playing women's parts in both Western and Eastern theatre and claimed that the gender of the dancer in the Dido/Sorceress roles simply did not matter. But possibly he was impatient with the over-emphasis on that point at the expense of other aspects of his dance. In 2008, once Merkens and McDonald had each independently assumed the dual role, he explained: 'It has to do with who is great at it. I choreographed Dido on a woman [Ruth Davidson] and the Sorceress on a man [Jon Mensinger]. The poor things never got to do it. I learned the parts from that, me looking at it and deciding what should happen.'[24] (It is Morris's usual practice to choreograph solos for himself on other dancers.) Earlier, he had told a journalist: 'If I'm injured, the person who does the part is a woman.'[25] (But he always got to perform the work because he never was injured.) Studying the role from recordings prior to rehearsals with Morris, both Merkens and McDonald insisted that he taught 'text'—he never directed them how to play gender (or, indeed characterisation or emotion of any kind). But it is interesting that Morris recalls Penny Hutchinson (the first Belinda, Dido's confidante) advising him against 'over-feminising' Dido and acting too 'drag-queeny', so he 'pulled it back'.

At the same time, the matter of gender and sexuality is complex. It is hardly surprising that people were likely to focus on the gender issue given its prominence within current public debate and Morris's very public admission that he is gay. His Dido also opens up intriguing possibilities for masculinity, a fact that remains obvious in most aspects of his physical appearance. And why should his equally obvious voluptuousness be considered primarily feminine? But the Sorceress surely is a 'drag queen', the epitome of 'hyperbole' and 'parody' and thoroughly self-aware. As Gay Morris suggests, this accords with the feminist theorist Judith Butler's understanding of 'drag'—that it is about imitating already imitative gender structures, the performer colluding with the audience as he plays his identity games.[26] It is significant, I suggest, that this, not Dido, was the role that Morris choreographed on a man and when he decided to split the role in 2006, he had the man dance the Sorceress. It is also interesting that, in 1989, contributing to the ambiguity, while at the same time undermining the conceit of a dual personality, the Dido and Sorceress musical casting was split, with a man singing the Sorceress. Then, when, Merkens began her explorations of the Sorceress role and felt that it was not working for her, Morris suggested that she 'play it as a man'. Suddenly, she felt that this made sense. Being 'butch' clearly separated the Sorceress from the Dido character and introduced 'an interesting twist on the gender reversal that existed all along when Mark (and Brady) danced it'.[27]

For my purposes, perhaps Morris's approach to gender, at least in casting himself in the dual role, is most important for renewing a well-worn story. Thus, we can still be moved in an age of lost innocence, and confrontation with the extreme and dangerously horrible (by virtue of the Sorceress and her entourage) allows Dido's tragedy once more to hold deep meaning.

There is one more important Tate/Purcell addition to Virgil that Morris uses, the episode when, as entertainment during a hunt (Scene 3), the lovers are told the story of the goddess Diana and hunter Actaeon. He comes upon her bathing naked, whereupon, in a fury, she turns him into a stag and sets his own hounds on him to kill him. The story is like a warning to the two lovers: Dido can be likened to Actaeon meeting his fate. This is one of the most remarkable sections in Morris's work.

In summary, Morris diverges from both Tate and Virgil in important ways, as much as he draws from them, but, as we shall see, in ways supported by Purcell's music, with its more open capacity for meaning.

Background 2: Structure, Style and Process

As the following summary of his danced opera indicates, Morris turned Purcell's three Acts and their divisions into five Scenes. (The full scenario that Morris wrote for the programme can be found at the end of this chapter.)

1 The Palace	Act I	Dido is anxious about her relationship with Aeneas but decides to give herself to him.
2 The Cave	Act II Scene 1	The Sorceress and Witches plot to bring about Dido's downfall.
3 The Grove	Act II Scene 2	Hunt scene, followed by the Sorceress tricking Aeneas.
4 The Ships	Act III [Scene 1]	Aeneas and his fellow sailors plan to leave and the Witches celebrate.
5 The Palace	Act III [Scene 2]	Aeneas leaves and Dido is resigned to die.

The Cast—Music and Dance (in order of programme):

Belinda (First Woman) [Belinda's sister *qua* confidante]

Dido/Sorceress
Aeneas
First Witch
Second Witch
Second Woman
Spirit [of Mercury—danced by the Sorceress]
Sailor
Courtiers Witches Spirits Sailors Conscience

Orchestration: 4-part string orchestra and continuo

The score is just fifty minutes long, without interval, and thus unusually compact for an opera. Dido's famous Lament in Scene 5, prior to her death, is given special weighting, allocated one twelfth of the opera's time-span. There is an overture, orchestral interludes, solo airs, duets, choruses, recitatives (with some overlap between vocal styles), and the following dances, identified as such within the score:

—The Triumphing Dance (celebrating the union of Dido and Aeneas at the end of Scene 1);
—Echo Dance of Furies (the Witches at the end of Scene 2);
—The Sailors' Dance (Scene 4);
—The Witches' Dance (Scene 4).[28]

A good deal of the music contains the rhythms of dance within it anyway, which undoubtedly encouraged Morris in his ambitious choreographic enterprise. But he acknowledges recitative as such, with a distinction between the styles of dance and mime, even if there is, as in the music, some blurring between these styles. Over half the sections of the work are, or include, choruses,[29] and it was these that Morris choreographed first, then the solos, finally his own role of Dido and Sorceress.

Since 1989, Morris's rule has been to have just one singer for both roles, matching his own dual role dance treatment, and he prefers a mezzo-soprano to soprano, the vocal range shared by both Dido and Sorceress. Lorraine Hunt (later Hunt-Lieberson) was always Morris's favourite singer in this dual role. The critic Richard Dyer wrote that with her, 'his passions devoured the stage, and it was as if a great fire had stripped the atmosphere of oxygen'.[30] In order for the solo singers to be adequately heard and clearly connected to the theatrical event, Morris prefers them to be visible, high in a box or raised at the side of the orchestra pit. At the Tanglewood Music Center performances in 2007, the singers were especially prominent, placed high with the orchestra in a balcony, towering over the characters on stage.

This doubling of visible (particularly solo) singers and dancers creates its own striking effect (see p. 121). Singing already has an intensely visceral edge, emanating from inside the body. Even though there is a sense of visual separation—a voice literally perceived as outside, as well as speaking through, a dancer—there is quite the opposite, a powerful connection. The bond between 'twin' protagonists deepens the sense of physicality and its erotic potential, and presence is enlarged (literally doubled). And what of a woman voicing a man's body, and him embodying her voice? Depending how you look at it, she makes him both more man and more woman.[31]

Other aspects of *Dido* stress theatrical distance, for instance the explicit device of role-shifting, not only for Dido but also the chorus of ten, who are at various times courtiers, witches, spirits, sailors and conscience. Costumes are highly economical and unisex: black sarongs (hitched up for the sailor scene) and sleeveless tops (except Aeneas is bare-chested—'from elsewhere and more vulgar'.[32]) These are supplemented by ear-rings and red nail varnish, except for Aeneas and Dido who wear black and gold polish respectively. Robert Bordo's set comprises a map image of blue sea and islands which spreads from the backcloth on to the dance floor, a balustrade across the back and a bench downstage centre, which is covered with a black cloth like a bier for the Sorceress scenes. For the original Brussels performances at the Théâtre Varia, Morris stressed the ascetic and ceremonial (South-Asian style) aspect of the event more than at any other time. The dancers were seated at the sides of the stage when not dancing (never leaving the space), and they all shared in the extreme preparation of dyeing their hair black. (Morris perhaps looked more slender than at any other time). At the Théâtre Varia too, Bordo's red and white check border evoked the frame of an ancient map, more specific than any mere proscenium: the audience looked through it as through a 'window' on to a sealed-off world beyond. (Again, this is not at all the expansive world of *L'Allegro*. It is confined, economical to the extreme, the world on a small island.) *Dido* was shown alone in the early years. Since 1998, it has sometimes been accompanied by another work on the programme.

Morris's movement vocabulary is pan-cultural and trans-historical, both in terms of gesture and larger body movement, suggesting that the stage community represents both everyone who has ever lived and no one in particular. As Morris puts it, the references are 'fake'. He has also described the style as 'torso-and hand-active'.[33] The following are the sources that have been most frequently documented:

—Greek—'antiquey'—two-dimensional with torqued bodies and angular movement, in the manner of friezes and vase patterning;

—ballet mime;
—American Sign Language (ASL);
—baroque rhetorical gesture;
—Indian (Morris refers to the style of 'mudras'—mime gestures with the hands);
—Indonesian, in the angular hip action in walking, an occasional tilt of the head and the sarongs;
—Irish step dance for the sailors;
—a grotesque vocabulary particular to the Sorceress and Witches, as they squat, upturn themselves, or shudder in spasm, with gnarled arms and sickled feet.

The vamp free-hip and -shoulder style of the Sorceress was based partly on the Cruella De Vil villainess of Disney's *101 Dalmations*.[34] In order to achieve what Morris calls the 'low-slung posture' of the work, which he believes is typical of the dance of hot climates, Morris gave a modern class (never ballet) while he was creating *Dido*. Still today, he asks his dancers to wear sarongs in rehearsal.

Referring both to Bordo's designs and to the frieze-style movement vocabulary, Jowitt has noted a disparity between *Dido*'s visual picture and its music, a severity that 'plays against the lyrical flourishes of Purcell's music'.[35] The point about disparity, disconnection, or, to put it another way, Morris's choreography cutting across Purcell's music, is important, and one that I will refer back to many times later. It becomes a theme. Suffice to say at this point that Purcell's music does have lyrical flourishes, but often speaks of darker things, with its sudden dissonances, harmonic swerves, and distorted stress of words as 'false accents'.[36] So, in a sense, the music already works against itself. Morris's choreography adds to, and enlarges, the component of fracture, in both his own movement style and its relation to the music.

As usual, Morris played an integral role in the musical aspects of his production. He studied the Purcell score assiduously. Originally, he told me when discussing his creative process, he worked with his conductor Craig Smith, deciding on a few points about the score construction and enjoying some freedom, given that the score we know today may not be a complete or definitive source. For instance, Morris and Smith chose the instrumental, rather than choral, recapitulation of 'With drooping wings' at the end of the score and repeated the Grove Scene introduction to Scene 3 (that accompanies the lovers' consummation) at the end of the same Scene, but now as a 'quieter, sadder' account of the music. Today, Morris makes many musical decisions himself, in the manner of any baroque music conductor, regularly coaching and advising instrumentalists and singers and, since

2007, even conducting the work himself. Decisions go well beyond the usual issues of tempo. Depending on the size of the orchestra (whether 30 or 15, he suggests), the style of theatre in which *Dido* is being performed, and the players available, he will decide on which instruments to use for the continuo, for instance, harpsichord or theorbo. Dido's 'Ah! Belinda!' air (Scene 1), for instance, he prefers to have played on cello alone with no other instrument. He also makes decisions about ornamentation and recitative practice.

Back in 1989, Morris's frequent use of baroque music situated him in the midst of the growing early music movement. But the later history of *Dido* has coincided with a general loosening up of purist musical views. Morris is now equally happy whether using 'original' or contemporary instruments and performance styles. Indeed, he welcomes change as a refreshing opportunity and is ready to shift the mood, as the occasion suggests, 'warming it up' or 'cooling it down' (see pp. 30-1, 54).

Before embarking on the choreomusical analysis, some points about film sources are useful. The MMDG recordings that I have accessed cover the full stage activity—that is their aim—and often show the dancers at a distance in long-shot, the camera zooming in when only one or a few dancers are moving. They include an intensely moving film shot at the time of the 1989 premiere. On the other hand, the film by Barbara Willis Sweete (1995, shown on Channel 4 the same year), which is commercially available and therefore most familiar to the general public, is a version of *Dido* in its own right, and contains impressive shots of a raised performance space like an 'island' approached from all four sides (rather than two) by steps. (Bordo designed the set, but did not include his backdrop in the film.)

Close-ups make up for loss of detail and dynamic engagement—not showing the whole body is fine for work that tends not to focus on legs and feet. Close shots of the singers—on high risers as if 'in heaven...on top of the world'[37]—strengthen the effect of vocal power and its connection with the moving body. Some of these shots diminish and, in a few cases, obliterate the choreography. In most cases, however, because movement material in *Dido* usually repeats to the same words and music, the viewer can work out by inference a lot of what is missing. As the camera shifts to capture the dance from different angles, placement of the balustrade and bench also clarifies where 'stage front' would normally be. On the other hand, the film makes very clear the moment of Dido's death, as the camera draws away from an overhead close-up. In live performance, the moment is hidden by the group choreography in front. Time limitations during filming meant that uncomfortably few shots were available for the final cut. Morris says that he was unhappy at first with the result, but now enjoys and recommends the film as an independent version of his work. It is useful to look at this film in conjunction with the following analysis. Crucially, it shows Morris in the role that he created for himself.

Performing the Analysis

Words

The attachment to words as a basis for choreography is an outstanding feature of *Dido*, a much more pronounced and consistent feature than in *L'Allegro*. This is at least partly for reasons of clarity because, Morris explains, the narrative is 'very wordy' and the singers who speak them are not the focus of our visual concentration.

Virtually every word is treated, and Morris built a lexicon equivalent in dance, using invented moves, codes (ASL and ballet mime), pictorial signs and everyday, automatically understood gestures. Many of the words repeat, and the system is such that, when he was near completion of the chorus choreography, the dancers could predict what would come next. (A list of words can be found at the end of this chapter.) This language, already idiosyncratic and rich in terms of individual moves, becomes the language of virtually the entire piece. It infuses both recitatives and dances—where it is stylised within dance, as opposed to speech, structures—as well as songs and textless orchestral sections that serve as postludes to songs.

The language also varies in density, from the slow, deliberate 'declamation' of the recitatives (where Morris might go for shorthand, using one 'dance word' to cover several spoken words) to perhaps the highest rate of events of all in 'Oft she visits' (Scene 3). This 'urgent' story of Diana and Actaeon (the warning to Dido), which Morris calls his 'homage to Bharata Natyam', rushes along at the rate of an allegro dance, the Second Woman's feet printing out every quaver, while her upper body and arms tell the tale through a swift succession of colourful images. Here could be a hint of what dancer June Omura describes as her 'divided body' in Morris's *Dido*,[38] as if two different 'voices' were speaking through her. It is also as if Morris stresses the separation, rather than fusion, of voices in the musical texture by associating melody with the upper body and arms and bass with the feet. As we shall see, the fact that words took precedence during Morris's construction of the dance material has strong implications for the particular choreomusicality of the piece.

Significantly, dance words objectify meaning and have formal value as we see them repeat: they register as moments differently from individual spoken words, which are usually registered as part of, and absorbed within, a phrase of several words. But they also have special impact because they are fewer in number than the actual words, for instance, when they cover a spoken phrase, and sometimes one move stands for several different words. The frequent gesture for 'love', for instance, also serves for 'one night enjoyed' (sex), the 'cure' that is most desired, 'gentle' as Dido's heart, and 'lover', the person loving and loved. Thus, with these relatively stable visual points of recognition, we can appreciate the resonances and tensions that arise as dance words become associated with the different dramatic situations and musical contexts in which they are used. This mapping of text on to dance words can also work the other way round, emphasising or 'capturing' points in the text.

But dance words also have their own autonomous value. Take, for instance, the 'fate' motif, like a mudra, and perhaps the most iconic, most often repeated dance word of all: it entails unfolding the arms overhead to stretch them sideways, with twisted wrists and splayed fingers, and often too with upper body and head counter-rotations (a kind of *épaulement*). Acocella explains the expressive nature of the gesture, which it communicates of its own accord, without you necessarily hearing the real word:

> The long outward stretch of the arms (fate controls the whole world), the raising of the arms (fate is directed by heaven), the muscular tension in the shoulders (fate is powerful), the spidery splay of the fingers (fate is terrible, or will be for Dido).[39]

This gesture is first seen in Belinda's opening dance—'fate your wishes does allow'—when we might well miss the connection between gesture and word, especially if we are not familiar with the work. She spreads her arms into it in a sprightly passing gesture. In her next dance with the Second Woman, it flashes past again, but this time they do it while jumping on to one leg and extending the other in a twisted *arabesque*. That is the version shared during the following courtiers' chorus of encouragement 'When monarchs unite', at which point it becomes a more formal statement, the culminating cadential full-stop: a held pose in strong diagonal alignment multiplied across the unison group, with the hands now as spiky protrusions—'They triumph at once o'er their foes and their fate'. By the time of the recitative when Dido dances 'Fate forbids what you pursue' and Aeneas immediately answers (ironically) 'Aeneas has no fate but you', we are most likely to have assimilated the connection between gesture and word. Here, in any case, the motif is presented much more slowly. Now, it is a serious matter.

In later dances particularly, for instance, during the Diana and Actaeon story, it could be the formal flashback to earlier appearances of the striking 'fate' movement that registers more strongly than any meaning. In the

Dido and Aeneas, Scene 1, the entrance of Aeneas, Amber Merkens as Dido and Craig Biesecker as Aeneas (with his hands in the 'fate' position). © Beatriz Schiller, 2006

orchestral postlude, the 'fate' motif (in the *arabesque* version with raised leg, now applied to Actaeon) again becomes a punctuating moment at a musical cadence (a sudden, surprising shift into F major out of the prevailing D minor). In this dance too, as for much of *Dido*, the series of separate mime moves sometimes turns into a fragmenting force that works against, or cuts into, the flow of the singing voice. The viewer is as likely to 'read' the moves individually, bumping up against each other in quick succession, as to experience their continuity alongside the full text or enjoy them simply as a movement sequence to music. As for the 'fate' motif, we see it in its boldest, most magisterial version at the end of Dido's Lament and in its ensuing orchestral postlude. Finally it is seen flat on to the audience and now utterly symmetrical, her arms gradually descending as she walks backwards towards her death and to a quiet cadence of resignation.

While sharing the same coded vocabulary, the examples described express a range of situation, character and feeling. Add the particular subversive quality of the Sorceress, who assimilates the vocabulary entirely on her own terms: snaky and supple in her rendering of 'love' and 'Carthage'; mocking the court 'chase' as she shoots an arrow and stands on one leg, grotesquely bent and quivering to a flourish of strings; then domineering as the spirit of Mercury, stamping to demand Aeneas not to 'stay', and crowding him with taut arms on 'Jove's command'.[40]

Recitatives

In all the recitative sections, there is rubato, a stretching or quickening of time, alternating with more strict pulse-based sections. Procedures shift according to what is being expressed. The extended recitatives involving Dido are the most dance-like and perhaps the most musically sophisticated. Dido's speech in Scene 1 'Whence could so much virtue spring?' is extremely volatile both harmonically and in tempo. She veers between admiration for Aeneas' public prowess and anxiety about where these feelings might lead her. She is both mad for him and ready to melt with love. There are weighty shoulder shimmies for 'storms' (twice, to gusts of semiquavers, but meaning different things—his experience and hers), 'soft' curves and arm sways to sweet appoggiaturas and, at one point, prompted by a firm musical pulse, the odd stop-start circling of a rigid arm suggesting courage in battle. Enhancing the contrasts within score and text, this is the dancing Dido's response to the man she sees as 'Anchises' valour mixed with Venus' charms' (referring to Aeneas' parents).

Dido's second, much longer recitative (Scene 5) turns into a dialogue with Aeneas and also shifts mood abruptly, but now the moods are sustained for longer and involve greater extremes, even the virtual disappearance of dance. There is particularly remarkable and distinctive imagery after he arrives (bar 15), when she pours scorn upon him and charges him with crocodile tears. (In the Sweete film, Jennifer Lane's voice turns nastily nasal at this point.) Dido's hands turn from a waterfall of tears into fangs (to a dangerous chromatic swerve), then into jaws, as her straight arms snap together—Morris adds extra irony by borrowing what was originally the sign for the hounds who killed Actaeon. 'By all that's good' he remonstrates, slapping both hands together before her, and she parrots his action, while borrowing his F-B-flat-D rising motif. But when she repeats this a third time, the cross-relation between the B-flat and the B-natural in the bass line is, Price says, 'stabbingly cynical'.[41] At this point, Dido proceeds to retract her 'claws', then to release them into fingers that walk away from her towards him: 'All that's good you have foreswore'.

Such mutual enhancement, the combination of movement, music and text, also contributes to the dancerly shape through time of the recitative as a whole. First, there are Dido's three opening appeals upstage to courtiers, earth and heaven, her gestures rising steadily as she pulls herself skywards with the melody line (from D to three climaxes on high G—each note harmonised differently), and finally a collapse (with the drop in the voice) to 'fall' flat. Here, four musical phrases, forming one large arch, mark the stages of Dido's devastating progress from aloft on the balustrade to downstage. Striking too is the moment later on when, with great dignity, she accuses Aeneas quietly and most bitterly: 'For 'tis enough whate'er you now decree/That you had once a thought of leaving me'. At first, the melody line moves relatively little, and the look of the score may have guided Morris here.[42] She stands virtually motionless, but for an unusually modest raising of her arms—and our attention is consequently driven more towards her words. Then she approaches him, literally brushing him aside before stretching into the wide second position of legs and arms at shoulder level that means parting or leaving. The final, accelerating repartee ensues, to fragmented up-and-down arpeggios. Dido directs Aeneas to leave, 'Away! No, no, away!' His mind apparently changed, but unconvincingly, he can only repeat lamely, 'No, no, I'll stay, and Love obey', a somewhat fearful and ridiculous figure bouncing stiffly alongside her. Here is a small man (literally, next to Morris) with a big, low voice. Then the culmination: she rushes into the awful gesture of ripping her guts out, the killing motif—not in the text at this point—and slaps him farewell. Now, all has been said in movement. Dido simply walks forwards, reflecting privately—again our attention driven to words as thoughts, and to the music: 'But Death, alas! I cannot shun/ Death must come when he is gone.'

Within these two recitatives, the dance movement has been largely complementary with, even if an enhanced account of, the score recitative and its dynamic shifts. But there is one striking example of opposition, in Scene 2, when the Sorceress exhorts her fellow Enchantresses to join her in bringing about Dido's downfall. She does this to what has been described as 'some of the most remarkable accompanimental work in baroque opera'.[43] In Morris's setting there is also a kind of contest involving music, dance, and the text, which reads as follows:

The Queen of Carthage, whom we hate,
As we do all in prosperous state.
Ere sun-set shall most wretched prove,
Deprived of fame, of life and love.

As the Sorceress sings 'hate' at the end of line 1, the second violins and violas ornament and problematise the fundamental F minor harmony: 'by moving out of phase and driving a stressed A-natural against violin II's D-flat'.[44] In the dance, 'hate' is juxtaposed with the opposite concept, 'love' (also equated with 'sex'), designated by hand gestures hollowing out the core of the body and twisting into a vertical circle. The Sorceress also raises one foot before her and, most clearly in the Sweete film, ends with her gaze projecting firmly upwards. Then, after turning into bright major for 'prosperous state', there is a reversal back into menacing minor for 'sun-set', when the Sorceress closes one fisted arm flat across the other (the horizon). Later (line 4), 'life' is juxtaposed with 'death', the gesture of ripping out the guts and slitting the throat.[45] Again, this unpredictable gesture-to-word response tends to make narrative continuity take a back seat. We are more likely to read a series of distinct 'word moments', and as an unsettling succession of oppositions within and across text and movement.

Here, using the understood 'up' and 'down' spatial metaphor within music, formal relations with the music also demonstrate opposition. As we naturally try to 'blend' information, the movement for 'love', so ambiguous in its spatial message and so precariously balanced, seems to 'question' or work against the melodic descent to 'hate'. It works against melodic descent, even when it matches the word 'love' at the end of line 4. Thus too, Morris chooses to emphasise and preserve a sense of dubious triumph at the end of the recitative (the rapid move to cadential resolution, and modulation from F minor to C major), rather than rise to the earlier melodic climax at 'life/death'. Morris uses the textual narrative 'voice' in conjunction with musical structure as springboard for telling us more about the Sorceress in this early encounter with her. He tells us about how dangerous and slippery she is, duplicitous, constantly contradicting herself, yet inviting us into the fun of her cabal and, by making us 'work' through the oppositions, into her (his) irony.

The Dances 1: Musical Structure as Template

Such intense opposition between music, dance and text as in the previous example is rare in Morris's *Dido* (and most often, it is associated with the Sorceress and Witches). It feels more extreme than the differences in the affective qualities of visual picture and music that Jowitt observed (see p. 227) or other temporary devices of fracture. As in the recitatives, there is most often a general, underlying sense of complement, in terms of both formal concerns, like metre or phrase structure, and meaning. Recall that Morris stressed in interview: 'Every single part is a coupling of music and dance. I wanted the sound and dancing to be the same thing'. Sometimes, indeed, Morris's response to musical structure is highly analytical and very

Scene 2, Amber Merkens as the Sorceress, in the 'love' gesture. © Susana Millman, 2011

detailed. Yet the constant shifting between structural tactics and devices, and their various effects, is startling, also the fact that nothing lasts long before something else takes over.

Often, we see responses to change in pitch with change in level of movement, although, rather than every detail, Morris likes to match larger melodic contours and points of emphasis. (Still, as words repeat, the same gestures repeat: words always take precedence over musical organisation.) A good example is the opening of Dido's first air 'Ah! Belinda'. The air is set over a 4-bar ground bass, a stable, constantly repeating theme, one of Purcell's favourite devices, over which vocal phrasing, melody and harmony operate with considerable irregularity. Forming Part 1, the opening two vocal phrases are respectively 7 and 9 bars long. The second phrase, which is a musical variation, repeats the words but completes the second line:

Phrase 1:
Ah! Ah! Ah! Belinda, I am press'd
With torment...

Phrase 2:
Ah! Ah! Ah! Belinda, I am press'd
With torment not to be confess'd.
I take the first phrase as my example. Following the general rise and fall

of the melody, from C, up to E-flat, down to G, the seated Dido raises her arms to the side, palms upwards, the code gesture for 'Ah!' (three times), as if breathing with the voice, then she turns and takes her right arm up and over to greet 'Belinda' who stands behind her bench. 'Press'd with torment', now facing front again, continues the direction of movement downwards in a version of the 'guts' motif—'Morris's Dido places one hand on her breast and one on her abdomen, both pointing downward',[46] and the melody falls from A-flat to middle C. A poignant moment (noted by Duerden and Rowell) is the shifting of the usual verbal emphasis here from 'tor-' to 'ment', whereupon Dido, who has turned again to Belinda, 'sinks forward on the bench, softly placing her hands in front of her—one then the other—precisely on each of these melodic notes.'[47] The detailed treatment here emphasises Dido's anguish. She also seems permeable, physically (with distinctly erotic overtones) and emotionally, once more carried, inhabited by the voice.

Ex. 7.1 Dido's first air, 'Ah! Belinda', Part 1, Phrase 1.

Ex. 7.2 Dido's first air, 'Ah! Belinda', beginning of Part 2.

In Part 2 of the air, the response to melody is less regular. We see the initial fall during the words 'Peace and I...'. It complements the melodic shape C-B-C-G (beats 1-3 and 1; bars 20-21), which echoes the start of the ground bass (bars 17-18) and is in turn echoed by Belinda, who enters in canon with Dido when the ground bass itself restarts in bar 21.

But now the bass itself comes to prominence. The rising-falling and falling-rising patterns (the shapes between the bar-lines) on several occasions in bars 21-27 are brought to our attention by Dido, who maps them out with her steps, her arms swinging up and down, or reaching down and back up again. This kind of selective 'matching' enhances moments in such a way that their sound and physical manifestation haunts us beyond their immediate occurrence and during our experience of later, different music and dance material. We seem to carry the memory of shape and weight within us. Later, there are several occasions where Morris casts hard arm accents unequivocally across the legato vocal melody, sharp gestures creating stark syncopations of their own (on beats 2 or 3; bars 30, 35, 42, 43, 65) (see p. 113). In the orchestral ritornello (refrain) that concludes the air, the chorus enter two by two, again following the contour of each of the instrumental entries. But when they dissolve into unison, they briefly bring new attention to the rising-falling motif with a double-time (3/8) version of their earlier movement, which we now experience (bars 62-63) as crossing the 3/4 version of the same motif in the bass.

Perhaps texture is the most obvious feature for complementation by Morris, where you are most likely to think in terms of music 'visualisation'. Like many choreographers would, he follows consistently the solo-chorus alternations that are so prevalent in the score. But he also creates marked contrast between treatments of homophony (using unison as the closest equivalent to this in dance) and polyphony (where individual dancers or groups match individual musical 'voices', including the most striking voice 'entries'). In this respect *Dido* is much more like *Gloria* than *L'Allegro* (which has relatively few choruses offering polyphonic opportunities). Morris's polyphony includes sections that are precisely choreographed as equivalent to SATB (soprano, alto, tenor and bass[48]), and sometimes his approach is highly systematic for an extended passage. Nevertheless, because of his choice of dance material, arrangement of dancers in space and relations with words, his textures and their blend with music are surprisingly varied.

Most choruses in Purcell's score contain elements of both homophony and polyphony. Morris embarks with a remarkably economical setting of the first chorus 'Banish sorrow'. The first two lines are homophonic, with ten dancers in unison in four lines (3,2,3,2): 'Banish sorrow, banish care/ Grief should ne'er approach the fair.' And to nearly every word there is a gesture from the code:

Banish—a crossing of the arms held down in front of the body
Sorrow—the hands raised to the eyes and descending in the manner of tears
Care—a spreading of the arms wide accompanied by a lowering of the body,
after the repeated arm movement on 'banish'
Grief—a turn with one arm circling over head
Ne'er—a semi-circle and then straight line carved with the hand, downwards
beside the body
Approach—one arm is stretched to the side, and the opposite hand touches it
at the wrist and then 'approaches' the shoulder
Fair—the same hand circles the face in the mime gesture for beauty.

Ex. 7.3 Chorus, 'Banish sorrow'.

At the same time, Morris's material follows the general contour of the
soprano melody line, starting low, rising, falling, rising highest with the
arm in the turn (and here emphasising the accented high F rather than
the unaccented, but higher, G of the bar before) and settling down into
middle level at the end. The only example of inverted relationship between
dance and music happens on the word 'ne'er', where the gesture is directed
decisively downward while the soprano line turns upwards.

Now, the polyphony begins, with simultaneous entries from sopranos and
tenors, then from alto and bass two counts later. These are shown in order
of pitch, highest to lowest, as left to right—from the audience—across the
four lines of dancers. But very soon, the individual vocal/dance lines start to
go their own separate ways, as indicated in the following word diagram (for
bars 20-23):

S Ban-ish sor-row, ban-ish care,   Grief   should
A   Ban-ish, ban-ish care,   ban-ish   sor - row
T Ban-ish sor-row, ban-ish, ban-ish   care   Grief should
B   Ban-ish sor-row, ban-ish, ban-ish   care

Apart from some of the vocal entries, this polyphonic treatment changes
the relationships between words and melodic contour. Morris chooses
to map lines of dancers only on to the SATB pattern and the words of its
individual lines, no longer on to the melodic organisation.

The effect of this strict organisation in 'Banish sorrow' is surprisingly
lively, despite the totally systematic approach to texture. Because of his

variety of movement and the visual counterpoint between the clear levels to which the eye is drawn—low, middle and high—Morris gives us an image of gathering tumult, surging waves with unexpected peaks and troughs, which gradually subside as the texture returns to unison. Thus, he expresses in dance the shift expressed in the text from the unsettled emotions of grief and anxiety to hoped-for calm and optimism. Morris has sometimes been criticised for being too systematic, but here he proves (as composers have known for years) just how liberating systems can be.

The expressive value of polyphonic textures is also strong in several duets. 'Pursue thy conquest, Love', for instance (Scene 1), proceeds canonically, the soprano voice answered (with a good deal of freedom) by the continuo bass, and matched by Belinda and the Second Woman dancing in exact canon. Only half a bar apart and in as close spatial proximity as possible, the Second Woman chases in hot pursuit of Belinda. And there are some crazy moves—their arms 'pursue' each other over their heads, hands flicker as a 'flame' and fingers wag to 'her tongue denies'.

Sometimes, there is no longer a precise SATB equivalence in the dance texture. An example of this is 'Haste, haste' (Scene 3), a solo that becomes a contrapuntal group dance. This dance is a metaphor for eccentric crowd behaviour—the courtiers out at the hunt—both funny and disturbing. Belinda has already wound them all up with the movement that the First and Second Witches did earlier (Scene 2), 'driving 'em back to court' with a storm. Now, this is the storm and they must 'haste to town'. Belinda mixes little sideways shunts with frantic double-arm circles, sometimes hitting a melismatic flourish with a circle, sometimes not. Later, she becomes increasingly frantic, rocking back and forth to build up steam for the climax of the dance. There is no predictable pattern. The effect is even wilder when the group takes over in 2-part counterpoint, but here there are two voices against four in the music. The two lines of dancers shunt and circle at different times—and just once, they circle altogether, when melismas in soprano and tenor parts match up.

Nor is there SATB equivalence in 'Thanks to these lonesome vales' in Scene 3, when Morris picks up on a mere hint of polyphony in the score and makes much more of this in his choreography. In the music, a few polyphonic passages emerge after a while, lasting no more than four bars each—simple canonic entries set one bar apart: 'So fair the game, so rich the sport'. The choreography is deceptively complex in several respects. Morris told me that the dance is directed to an imaginary audience stage left, so it is as if we, the real audience, watch from the side. Purcell begins with a solo for Belinda, consisting of two Parts (bars 1-8, 9-24), each repeated, and then he repeats all of this again for chorus (96 bars in total). Morris follows the casting pattern (adding the Second Woman as an alternating soloist), but chooses to cut the music to half its length by replacing the solo repeats with chorus repeats. He introduces just two dance phrases, 1 and 2. These are similar in material, with running steps and pauses to raise an arm in greeting or to let it fall. But they differ in terms of the placement of the running and the pauses.

Ex. 7.4 Belinda (solo) and chorus, 'Thanks to these lonesome vales': Part 1 (music), phrases 1 and 2 (dance–notated from the 1995 Sweete film).

These relaxed but speedy runs (so typical of Morris style, so hard to perform without looking rushed) are at quaver rate, faster than the pulse you hear in the music, and so the two dance phrases create their own independent rhythm patterns.[49] Crucially, Morris does not wait for the brief patches of musical counterpoint in Part 2: he starts his own counterpoint during the repeat of Part 1 with a canon (dance Phrase 2), three dancers, one bar apart, crossing the stage and back again, and three others matching them further downstage. In the space between, three more dancers take up one of the arm motifs at half speed, stepping at crotchet rate. Later (Part 2), for the chorus repeat of 'So fair the game', Belinda and the Second Woman take over the half-time motif and the other eight dancers enter in canon in pairs between them (returning to Phrase 1), crossing, and folding back across, the stage to create a very complex texture:

Dancers 1 and 2 start at bar 9
Dancers 3 and 4 start at bar 10
Dancers 5 and 6 start at bar 13
Dancers 7 and 8 start at bar 14

The dancers finally gather stage left and merge into unison for the last three bars (22-24). During this last passage, as if to cap it all, Dido and Aeneas, who have been seated on the balustrade upstage, walk right through the busy group, greeted by passing members of the ensemble until they emerge in front. The whole dance is a miraculous example of elegant, mobile spatial and rhythmic tracery. A sense of sophisticated conversation emerges between people and between music and dance, from what is in fact very little material and the working out of an essentially simple system of canons.

Purcell's irregular phrasing offers Morris many lively opportunities, particularly in the sections with ground bass. Here again is a response to texture, to what is essentially two 'voices': the literal singing voice and the rhythmically independent instrumental ground. As we have seen, 'Ah! Belinda' has a 4-bar ground but opens with two vocal phrases 7 and 9 bars long respectively, following the composer's common procedure of extending a phrase when it repeats. The first phrase starts one bar into the ground; the second consequently coincides with its third opening. The Lament, on the other hand, opening with phrases of 6 and 4 bars, starts at the point of cadential resolution in bar 5 of a 5-bar ground (see p. 252, Ex. 7.10).

But 'Oft she visits' (Scene 3)—the Diana and Actaeon story—is the most virtuoso example of vocal phrases shifting freely over a ground bass. We hear a 4-bar ground 13 times, during a song and its orchestral postlude.

Ex. 7.5 Second Woman, 'Oft she visits', ground bass.

The vocal phrasing starts in synchrony with the ground, and then diverges from it, getting shorter, then longer, as repetition is added within the text. The song, which also hints at different keys, ends with a refrain of line 3. The libretto text (without the added repetitions) is as follows:

> Oft she visits this lone mountain,
> Oft she bathes her in this fountain,
>   Here, Actaeon met his fate,
> Pursued by his own hounds,
> And after mortal wounds,
>   Discovered, discovered too late.

The following diagram shows the shifting bar-lengths of individual vocal phrases, all of which Morris adheres to and which, after the orchestral introduction (the first ground), encompass seven more grounds:

4 [bars]	Orchestral introduction
2	Line 1 [of the libretto]
2	Line 2
2	Line 1
2	Line 2
3	Line 3
2½	Line 3
2½	Line 4
2	Line 5
4½	Lines 5 and 6 [forming one phrase in terms of sense and without a separating comma in the score]
4	Lines 5 and 6
2	Line 3

The orchestral postlude that follows the song encompasses five more grounds, to make the total of thirteen. Morris retimes his dance material (retaining the order precisely), packing the whole story into these grounds, but with no refrain at the end and to entirely different writing above the bass. The dancers are no longer rooted to the spot, but rather run to and fro on the bass quavers with, occasionally, a hopping step or pause. 'Oft she visits' proves to be a remarkable assembly of layered phrasing, verbal phrases in and out of phase with the ground, and then Morris's new, more compact phrasing of the story in dance alone, this time synchronising with the ground.

[Ground]	1.	Lines 1 and 2
	2.	Lines 1 and 2
	3.	Line 3
	4.	Line 4
	5.	Line 5

Morris's decision was perfect for this final section because, at the same time as the material becomes more like formal dance, it makes a story that is already urgent even more so.

In some sections of *Dido*, there is virtually no dancer-to-voice correspondence at all. In the chorus 'Cupid only throws the dart' (Scene 1), with its 'rather painfully dissonant texture',[50] Morris marks the entries of musical voices by having one dancer at a time merge into a long, weaving crocodile. But then the main choreographic conceit proves to be a gradual accelerando with the dancers randomly throwing little (painful) darts at Aeneas, stepping first to every minim, next to every crotchet, then finally running at quaver rate.

The opera's final chorus 'With drooping wings' represents yet another approach to texture. Here, Purcell introduces polyphony that resolves into homophony at phrase endings and concludes with a section of sustained homophony. Morris's approach is unison, or near unison, or to pass simple single gestures across the dancing group, angular drooping 'wings' softened by their placement on the weak beats of the bar. Again we see a system unfold and work itself out to include everyone present, engendering a sense of calm and inevitability appropriate to this final stage of the drama. We also enjoy the warm gesture of 'love' the final time we hear the word 'gentle' ('as her heart')—Morris suddenly brings all ten dancers into unison.

The Dances 2: Counter Points

Even if he is led to a large degree by textual phrasing, Morris's rhythmic tactics range widely. To different degrees, they evoke a sense of disconnection, disruption or even irony. Earlier, we saw how the dance patterns take off with their own logic in 'Thanks to these lonesome vales', although they still fit the 3/4 musical metre very neatly. Yet it is worth pointing out that the music here itself demonstrates baroque hemiola characteristics with three bars of 2/4 breaking across the equivalent of two bars of 3/4 on several occasions. Purcell's own disruptions, hemiola and syncopations, here and elsewhere, may well have encouraged Morris to take this aspect of style a stage further in other sections of *Dido*. Such rhythmic disruptions are much more prominent in this work than in *L'Allegro* (in both Handel's music and the choreography).

A number of times, Morris injects his own spicy syncopation in the form of brief metrical crossings. There is the gentle, lilting down-up-down 3/8 over 3/4 (just done twice) in the early 'Ah! Belinda' chorus (see p. 237). You barely notice it, except for the hint of faster tempo. Then, in the unison chorus 'When monarchs unite', Morris introduces his own hemiola pattern, here 2/8 against the musical 3/8 (a counterpoint that resolves itself within two bars of music). The device occurs within a simple two-step pattern backwards, and here is another example of phrase extension (by one bar— 'They triumph') on repeat.

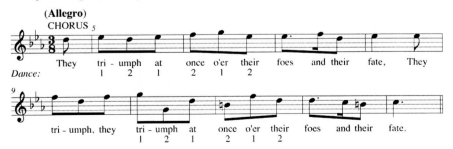

Ex. 7.6 Chorus, 'When monarchs unite'.

The 'Fear no danger' chorus (Scene 1) contains three more examples of hemiola from Morris, all strikingly different in effect, and countering the regular 3/4 metre in the music (see pp. 114-15, Ex. 4.8). For Belinda and Second Woman and then the whole chorus there is:

> 1. a little jumping pattern that we see many times as the opening music repeats: from flat foot on to heels, down-up, 3 times 2/4 over 2 bars of 3/4 (bars 3-4). It contrasts smartly with the very definite matching of bold musical syncopation elsewhere in this passage, and it is thrilling to hear as well as watch the feet.
> 2. a more lightly accented 2/4 rocking step and hop, to one side and then the other (bars 15-16).
> 3. three slow, lilting steps—down-up-down—over 2 bars of 3/4 (making a 3/2 dance bar), soft and sensual with arms moving out-in-out and swaying hips and shoulders (bars 29-30). Here, the vocal line refers to the flowers that have been 'gather'd from Elysian bowers' to strew Dido's path. So the verbal image is soft and sensual too. We are drawn to the silky quality of body and arms rather than to the impulse of steps.

Additional irony is suggested by the Sailors' hemiolas in 'Come away' (Scene 4), to the phrase 'But never intending to visit them more [meaning the nymphs on the shore]' (bars 53-56). Their 2/4 dance pattern across 3/4 in the music (from bar 54) is very sharp: confined to two dimensions as in a frieze. There is a step-hop three times driving backwards, full of angles at ankles and knees, with taut arms pumping forwards and back. On repeat, the 'Never' slice of the arm (the half-circle and line 'word') becomes additionally acidic with the false accent on the second syllable. As Preston has pointed out, there were similar false accents at the ends of words in 'Fear no danger', characterising the 'ever smiling' Aeneas, 'who is, after all, planning exactly the same betrayal'.[51] The deceit of 'Come away' is especially pronounced given the cynical passage immediately preceding: the Sailors hold fingers to their lips for 'And silence their mourning/With vows of returning', at the precise moment where there is an ominous anticipation in the bass of the chromatic descending ground in Dido's Lament.

In 'To the hills and the vales' (Scene 1), the dynamics of rhythmic crossing are different yet again, but once more tinged with discomfort—the very light staccato prick of toes on the floor seems heartless, and it is literally as far as possible from the heart. In a tight group, the chorus embark across the stage with a 4-count step, 4/4 over 3/4 in the music, three times:

> Step forwards 1, toe prick in front and bend the head forwards 2, step on the front foot and arch back 3, two double-time steps 4

Scene 1, 'To the Hills and the Vales', Mark Morris as Dido and Guillermo Resto as Aeneas.
© Cylla von Tiedmann, 1995

This particular crossing is harder to register, and probably to perform, than plain hemiola, but you still 'feel' that something odd is going on. The discomfort continues. Soon, after a sudden disturbing side-step to the chord of G minor,[52] the dancers descend to the floor and land with a bump—'cool shady *foun*tains'. The landing moment is another surprise, with the false relation (a searing chromatic clash between voices) introduced in a G major chord.[53] A dotted rhythm counterpoint passage follows: 'Let the triumphs of love...'. There is a semblance of following SATB voices with the 'stop-start circling' of hard piston arms (the battle arms of Dido's earlier recitative, see p. 232). This is soon resolved into 'triumphant' unison 'love'—but, by now, that gesture reads as distinctly questionable.

The dances written as such by Purcell are relatively square in terms of phraseology, 2-, 4- and 8-bar units, according to the tradition of the time, and, at the same time, these create a sense of regular 2- or 4-bar hypermetre. But again, their rhythmic structures become less regular in Morris's hands. The Sailors' Dance following 'Come away', which is musically like a hornpipe, carries on the rhythmic jokes and camaraderie in the manner of folk dance (Irish step dance with lots of kicking up of legs, and arms held firmly down the sides.) Again, we hear the dance. First there is the footfall in syncopations and decorative steps between the notes. There is also a strange clapping passage as the lead Sailor and group take turns to traverse the stage, up and down and crossways: the first clap as syncopation on beat 2 (bar 5, the group), then another clap on the downbeat that follows (bar 6, the Sailor who is up in the air from a jump—and accents in the air are relatively unusual in dance), and a third (the group again, now accompanying the Sailor up in the air) on the downbeat of bar 7. Second time round, the jumping and clapping roles are reversed. (Morris conceived of this originally as an accumulative structure, the claps marking the ends of units on counts 2, 3 and 4 across three bars.)

Ex. 7.7 The Sailors' Dance.

If this does not sound like much to write home about, consider the slight jarring that we feel as we see/hear the passage: the unusual airborne downbeats, the asymmetry of the first clap, the unexpected passing of claps from group to soloist and back and the change in volume as they do so. It is all good fun. True to form, Morris does not do anything like this ever again.

Perhaps, however, the most intricate, sophisticated rhythmic play lies in the Triumphing Dance that breaks in immediately after 'To the hills and the vales', to end Scene 1. Dido and Aeneas celebrate their union with the courtiers and, after dancing with them, set off round the periphery to enjoy their intimacy alone, escorting each other on and off the balustrade. But is the opening of the music in 3/4 or 2/4? That is the first question. Morris notes that, even if written in 3/4, it sounds like both. Bars 1-2 of the outer parts—and the bass is the 4-bar ground that permeates the whole section—clearly move in 2/4 (the top line reads as C G, C A, D B, in contrary motion to the bass). So the pattern is 'always reversible,' he says. 'I love it when music starts and you can't tell what metre it is, whether a note is pick-up or downbeat'.

Morris's choreographic solution is to make a unison phrase for the arms on 5s, one gesture for every crotchet, broken down as 2 counts (the arms go out on 1 and return to centre on 2) plus 3 counts (the arms go up on 3, out on 4, and return to centre on 5). Halfway through the dance there is a single irregularity in the musical phrasing which, up until now, has been arranged

Ex. 7.8 The Triumphing Dance.

in 4- and 8-bar segments. The violins and violas take over alone for two bars with an inversion of the opening tune. At this point, at the side, Dido and Aeneas repeat the 5-count arm phrase, but now walk with it in saucy, hip-swinging fashion.[54] Meanwhile, the chorus accompany with the arm phrase at half speed, one gesture for every minim, further defining 2/4 (as 'augmentation'—to use the musical term). This is witty and exhilarating. Yet the musicologist Wilfred Mellers has observed the underlying current of danger:

> The final dance, though still in the major, has become a little uneasy, with sharply accented dissonant passing notes that hint that all may not, after all, be for the best in the best of all possible worlds.[55]

Indeed, Dido seems to be turning into the Sorceress as she flirts with Aeneas, and shortly afterwards, the courtiers, too, metamorphose into Witches, all in wide second position, rattling their heels against the floor, ready for the next scene...

The Dances 3: Choreomusical Relations and Forces of Evil

The Sorceress and her Witches operate in a totally different world of musicality, or rather the Witches do, for it is they who undertake most of the 'dancing', prompted by her recitatives. Morris gives them considerable flexibility, asking them to improvise within rules for much of the time and to make every performance as different as possible. In such instances, they show blatant disregard for musical detail. 'The dance has to have no relation to the rhythm,' Morris says, 'only to the duration.' For example, in the Echo chorus 'In our deep-vaulted cell' (Scene 2), when the Sorceress 'conducts' the witches from her bench, their own calls and echo responses simply occupy the same brief time-spans as those in the music. Lack of control is strategically managed. Morris explains that the witches stand round a circular, opaque curtain (in the stage *Dido*, not in Sweete's film) and, on the echoes, copy as best they can what they see their neighbour do, perhaps a whole phrase, or just the end of it. Taking turns as team-leaders doing the calls, they copy whatever the movement is as it gets passed down the line, and it changes along the way. The choral writing is strictly homophonic here; if the dancers try to match up to this effect, they fail.

For the Echo Dance that follows, Purcell has scored a rush of semiquavers, forming another series of short phrases with echoes. Now, the First and Second Witches take turns to lead the whole group in improvisation as question and answer, going somewhere on stage and doing just anything that comes to mind, a cartwheel, a fall, or a tiny movement. Again, the others follow as best they can. 'Think of something to do and do the opposite of that,' instructs Morris. 'It's fun and dangerous!'

In Scene 4, all hell lets loose. First, in 'Destruction's our delight', there are totally improvised murders, electrocutions and suicides – any manner of death can be simulated. The final Witches' Dance begins with set material, two couples in turn enacting the Dido and Aeneas story, meeting, kissing, and one killing the other. Then the Sorceress can be seen simulating masturbation downstage, while, behind her, Witch couples embrace and 'explode' off each other. 'It has to be chaos', Morris points out. Dancer David Leventhal perceives this as one of the most extreme examples of opposition between music and dance in the whole work. The score here is mock grand and ceremonial; the 'bawdy and rough' choreography 'rubs against it'. The result is a layer of irony, although it is important that the audience experience this while the dancers themselves play straight.[56]

In these big group dances, relations with music seem to double the damage of the Witches' violence and depravity. Their literal assault on the score, forcing us to hear their falling, stamping and slapping as part of the aural event, is an effect in itself. Gross fleshly spillage projects itself between us and the music. Morris does not simply make us hear the music differently, he makes it harder to hear, celebrating a culture of bad behaviour that goes well beyond baroque self-mockery.

In complete contrast, the Witches are responsible for some of the most overt 'mickey-mousing'/musical mimicry in the entire work, shaking and shivering to laughter and storm music, stumbling endlessly to and fro to the counterpoint as they play at courtiers being driven home when the weather turns bad. (The Sorceress is visibly irritated and bored by them: Scene 2, 'But ere we this perform'.) In their duets, the two witch leaders punch out their beats and repeat their absurd gesticulations with unnatural force and predictability. If they mock the behaviour of Belinda and the Second Woman, perhaps the Witches do here represent Morris performing a little stylistic self-mockery, acting up to his reputation as outstanding music visualiser of his time.

But there is one thing that the Sorceress and Witches cannot do: proper 'conversation' with music. Having no relaxed, civilised connection with beat means that they cannot engineer clean counterpoint. At one point, however, Morris shows what they do when they get somewhere near to this. Naturally, we make comparisons with the real thing. In the trio 'Our next motion/ Must be to storm her lover on the ocean' (Scene 4), they start out galloping gleefully to the 3/4 'ceremonial dotted rhythm',[57] but, for the storming (bars 5-7), they shift gear into a noisy run with shoulder shimmy that blatantly crosses the music. Morris has clarified this as another 'two-against-three'. And so it is. The running makes a regular pulse, with right foot stamps, two stamps (four steps), per bar of 3/4 (halting in bar 7). But there is nothing like the precision *effect* of the earlier hemiola examples. Why? Because only the first of every four steps hits an actual beat in the music, on the downbeat of each 3/4 bar.

Ex. 7.9 Sorceress, 'Our next motion'.

So, although Morris's mathematics here are typically strict, the effect is definitely not. That way is preferable: in character, apparently messy, certainly crazy, ready yet again to degenerate into witch chaos.

After this account of an astonishing variety of choreomusical techniques and interactions, let us turn back to Dido, the most thoroughly drawn character in Morris's work, and to her final Lament. There will be an especially detailed analysis of this air because it represents an important registral shift as well as an especially complex, subtle blending of the forces of music and dance in the Morris/Purcell dance opera. It is also one of the most powerful sections of the work.

Dido's Lament

In embracing an air that involves several arts media and more than one strand within the medium of music itself, I will combine structural analysis with analysis using the principles of conceptual blending and voice/persona. Discussion of conceptual blending (from CIN theory, see pp. 97-8) opens up spatial concerns that become especially significant at this point in Dido. It includes, but is not restricted to, reference to interactions based on the verticality schema. My choreomusical analysis works from a shared 'generic space' that 'contains' the concept of Dido preparing to die, her heart broken by Aeneas.

Purcell's Lament begins with the words 'When I am laid in earth' and is preceded by a recitative/mime section. Tate's text is as follows:

Thy hand, Belinda, darkness shades me,
On thy bosom let me rest.
More I would but death invades me,
Death is now a welcome guest. [end of recitative]

When I am laid in earth [may—added by Purcell] my wrongs create
No trouble in thy breast,
Remember me, but ah! forget my fate.

Morris's Lament begins on and around the downstage bench, which is by now a well-established focus for intimacy. It is where we first saw Dido and Belinda (Scene 1), and there are many other links between Dido's two airs, in terms of slow tempo, form and movement content.[58] But it is now Belinda who is seated on the bench for the dance (in Scene 1 it was Dido), and there is also a new emphasis on spatial symmetry, more than at any earlier point in Morris's choreography.

The music is slow, in a minor key, with a 5-bar ground bass that is heard eleven times. Ellen Rosand has traced the descending tetrachord ostinato back to lament in earlier seventeenth-century Italian opera, noting its 'intrinsic affective implications'.[59] The chromatic descent of the ground, a feature anticipated by the long descent within Dido's preceding recitative, symbolises death and the grave. Janet Schmalfeldt points out that 'the short-long rhythm of the ground establishes new metric stability while at the same time creating a halting effect; conversely, the new rhythm within the [final] cadential segment seems to impel the ground to its cadential goal.'[60] Led by the ground bass, for strings and continuo only, and presumed to have been written out by the composer himself, the accompaniment is relatively independent of the vocal line. For instance, first heard alone as an introduction, the completion of the ground marks the beginning of the vocal line. The vocal line itself creates a series of arches within a two-part form, and each Part is repeated, the first two lines of the text from 'When I am laid' forming Part 1, and the third, from 'Remember me', containing the climax, in Part 2. Morris follows (with some adjustments) the musical pattern of two repeated Parts.

I refer now to Adam Ockelford's useful application of CIN theory to the music and text,[61] establishing blended content and structure, and, resulting from this, blended aesthetic response. In summary, he stresses the enhancement from music of the feelings of sadness and anguish suggested in the text through:

1. several temporal devices: the slow enunciation of words, their repetition, and sometimes separation, in time, and the 'reminders' from violins as they imitate Dido's vocal line;
2. chromaticism and appoggiaturas that symbolise sobs, sighs or death;
3. the development of the 'pre-verbal expressions of raw emotion— "Ahs!"' into melismas.

There is also the stillness of 'remember me' on a repeating note D, playing *against* the relentless motion in the bass, and, furthermore, Ockelford proposes, 'music adds an additional narrative line to the words—Dido dies in the music, not the text'. He also looks at details within the Lament, and suggests yet another enhancement device within the first appoggiatura (bars 6-7):

The first denotation of Dido's fate is supported musically with the use of a powerful dissonance and only partial resolution, and reinforced through delayed imitation of the descending bass and use of the 'weeping' motif... However, the music adds subtle depths to the verbal message by dragging its heels in relation to the bass line and thereby grinding against it harmonically—an indication that although Dido speaks of her impending doom, psychologically she is still partly resisting it.

Ex. 7.10 Dido's Lament.

Repetition (or varied repetition) contributes significantly to meaning in the Purcell score in several ways. Through selective verbal repetition, there is a particular emphasis on Belinda not being 'troubled', and on 'remembering', stressing Dido's wish to live on in the mind if not in the body, as if overcoming her death through remembrance.[62] The repeat of Part 2 is not exact. The vocal line starts one bar later in relation to the ground bass than the first time round and then has to catch up (bar 32). So Dido is hurried into 'but ah! forget my fate', perhaps a suggestion of an impatience to move into the future (her own anguished impatience or the result of some outside pressure upon her). In any case, repetition in the score does not necessarily mean that singers perform the same music twice in exactly the same manner. I have heard performances by Lorraine Hunt and Emma Kirkby that stress change between the repeats in Part 2, but in contrasting ways, either by increasing volume (Hunt, in a performance with MMDG in 1994) or by slowing and quietening (Kirkby, 2000) for the climactic account of 'remember me'. In their respective interpretations, both make the climax register more strongly on the repeat.[63]

Ockelford refers to 'resistance', as if there are two forces, Dido and, perhaps, her 'doom', as suggested by the accompanying bass. But he is not the only writer to have drawn attention to the ground bass (and its harmonic implications) as a separate 'domain' within the music itself, often in opposition to the vocal line. Rosand and Schmalfeldt do so, for instance. We could apply CIN theory to this aspect as well, that is, drawing into a blend two input spaces from the music by itself. Thus, in the Lament, vocal line/melody and accompaniment are seen to conflict and ultimately find resolution in emphasising descent.[64] But when blending dance with music/ text, we can read Morris's Dido as dancing 'against' a rather more complex concept of voice in the bass. This could still be perceived as the voice of 'doom' or the 'world outside' but, embodied by the dancing chorus, it could also represent Dido's courtiers, the cupids with 'drooping wings' who will 'scatter roses on her tomb' (referred to in the final chorus that follows the Lament) or her conscience (another chorus representation listed in the programme, the 'outside' within Dido herself). So, in the danced *Dido*, the ground bass line has become a much enriched 'voice', carrying a variety of human traits. By using the chorus in this way, Morris further emphasises the duality between ground and melody, or bottom and top of the musical texture. Here is a variation on the 'divided body' concept (see p. 229)— upper body and arms (Dido's emphasis) against bass (the chorus).

During the introductory ground, before Dido begins her song, the chorus move upstage to exit the space. In 'becoming' the ground, they trace its short-long pattern, while also highlighting the halting effect of the appoggiaturas, the chromatic notes on beat 1 of bars 2 and 3, F-sharp resolving to F, E to E-flat on the third beat of each bar:[65]

1. transfer weight to the front foot on beat 3 (like an upbeat);
2. step forward again 1;
3. hold back by reversing direction and sinking on to the back foot 2;
4. repeat the pattern on the other leg, stressing counts 3 and 1 with the steps forward.

When the ground pushes forward in plain crotchets before the cadence, the chorus walk forward continuously in correspondence with each note. I will now describe the solo dance as it unfolds alongside the music, before returning to further discussion of the blending of inputs from both dance and music/text.

When the singer's vocal line begins (bar 6), Dido, who has been crouching on the floor, clasps Belinda's hand and starts to move anti-clockwise around the bench in slow, smooth, deliberate rising-sinking steps. In one phrase, without a break, her steps mark the downbeats—beat 1 of each bar of 3/4 time—later quickening to a step every two beats as the melody gathers momentum, with steps on beats 1, 3 and 2 ('When I am laid, am laid in earth' (bars 6-9)). She holds the other hand to her breast in the 'fate' position.

Ex. 7.11 Dido's Lament.

All the while, Dido pulls upwards and away from Belinda in opposition both to the text which refers to being 'laid in earth' and to the descending contour of the second part of the melody (bars 8-9). But there are some 'partial resolutions' in this passage, as in the music: Dido sinks with each slowly delivered footfall, occasionally coinciding with a falling interval in the melody. Then, at the end of a brief run to one side of the bench—'May my wrongs'—she suspends briefly on her toes (on the B-flat) and falls into a more hasty run on the word 'create' (six runs over the first two beats of bar 11), all the way round to the back of the bench. This is a rare occasion of full cadence at the end of the ground (bar 11), yet not an occasion for showing a gap between words, or taking a breath—and the movement presses on accordingly. Schmalfeldt describes the progress of the air from this point:

> As Dido now rises to her E-flat, it is as if she must will herself to overcome the inertia of the ground's cadence, and, in doing so, to cancel its effect. Coinciding as it must with the F-sharp in the ground's third chromatic descent, her E-flat on the word 'trouble' at measure 11 [numbered 12 in some score editions] gains indescribable poignancy.

At this poignant moment, tracing the singer's sobs (the falling intervals of fifths), Dido's circular motion gives way to strong, gestural impulses on the spot behind Belinda. Specific reference to the words begins. Like a knife, Dido's hand carves in the air the curve and line of the mime word 'ne'er' (see p. 238), to the words 'No trouble...'. (Morris explained that he meant

'Never trouble in thy breast'.) Outlining Belinda's body on one side and then the other, the gesture could also imply comfort, concern, affection, pleading or simply Dido's need to be close to her sister. Belinda responds by sharply averting her head on beat 2 of bars 12 and 13, as if she cannot face the future, accentuating the drop in pitch on 'trouble'.[66]

Now comes a minor shock—on 'breast', the final word of Part 1. The physical connection with the meaning of the word is suddenly direct, not the result of any code, and therefore especially strong. Dido presses one flat palm down onto Belinda's chest ('breast') while raising the other, palm facing us, over her head, extended fingers pointing down and up respectively. Belinda throws her head up and back and opens her knees sharply, pressing against them with her arms. Her palms are turned to us in the vulnerable 'forsaken' gesture. This is also a sudden signal, and an accent of angularity (glittering finger nails too). The women create the taut image together, Dido's vertical line slashing through Belinda's V-shape from feet to knees and an inverted V from knees to head. Belinda adds further stress by holding her position like an after-image for five beats, long after Dido has moved away. This moment seems like the 'centre', the peak of tension and precision that the circle and 'never' gestures have been driving towards. But it is also an accent of recognition, as a version of the deeply sexual 'guts' motif (see p. 222), perhaps the most obvious reference back to the movement in Dido's opening air and, as we shall see, a link with the vertical spatial emphasis of Part 2 of the Lament. There seems to be no clear match in tension and counter-pull within the music here, even though there is a complimentary curve upwards and avoidance of harmonic closure at the end of the vocal line. So, already in the Lament, we have seen a shifting pattern of compliance and resistance, with the emphasis on resistance, as well as a marked shift from relatively level dynamics to a burst of high energy activity.

With the repeat of the Part 1 music, there is a modification in the choreography rather than a straight repeat, which is highly unusual for Morris in this work. Dido's hand of 'fate' is now extended skywards, exaggerating the pull upwards and away from Belinda and from gravity, indicating her determination not to end up 'laid in earth' and her struggle to express her feelings. (Here, Merkens lingers high for longer and more desperately than does Morris on film.)

In Part 2, the singing Dido pleads 'Remember me!' twice, holding on to a high D, then leaping up a fourth to G for a third utterance, the climactic moment in the Lament. The whole sequence is repeated. The dancing Dido's moves now begin to invade the larger stage space. She first runs to plead with the chorus on each side of the stage, repeating her movement with the musical repetition, plucking one hand from the other, then extending the arm overhead and arching into a fall backwards. (Morris told me that this movement—which is seen for the first time in the Lament—derives from the ASL word for 'learning', as if 'taking information from a book,' so there is an additional edge here to the textual meaning.) From both sides, the chorus take three steps in towards Dido, hinting at their previous relationship to the ground bass. The line of Dido's upper body and her pathway side to side across the stage also reflects the level pitch and corresponding look of the score. At the G climax, in contrast, she hastens close to Belinda centre stage, facing the audience, so we see the same 'remember me' arm gesture primarily as a pull upwards. This works against a counter-pull down through the other hand stretched towards Belinda's bowed head. Here is a clear 'visualisation' of the rise in pitch and an assertion of the vertical, but the image is also like the opening of jaws in a scream, or a painful extension from the depths of Belinda's brain. Again, like Part 1, Part 2 contains shifts between relatively level dynamics and bursts of high energy. The rest of the dance phrase responds to the text with familiar movements: the wordless 'ah!' (the one occasion when the harmonic progression over the ground bass does not keep to the established pattern); 'forget' (touching the forehead with the heel of each hand in turn as in 'thinking', a hint of staccato against the legato melody); and 'fate' (yet again).

The Part 2 choreography is more varied on repeat than it was in Part 1. The first two accounts of 'Remember me' are contracted, Dido's body and arms appear crumpled, and our eyes are suddenly drawn in towards physical detail. She is yet more anguished. She traverses less of the stage now that the chorus have started to move in towards her, and reveals a new, halting progress that, while not articulating the vocal rhythm, suddenly draws our attention to the separation of notes and their pattern. Merkens and McDonald remember Morris's image of 'giving up' at this point.[67]

Now there is a twist. The final 'Remember me' is a colossal moment, much larger than anything we have seen before. Dido reverses her movement, rushing upstage and on to the balustrade (the fourth and last point of the compass[68]), now primarily reaching *up* to the 'gods' with her *front* arm, her *back* arm pulling *down* behind her as the counter-force. This is a major shock. The whole space has suddenly re-opened, and the gap, or rather stretch, between the extremes of 'up' and 'down' (and across the two women) is unprecedented. S/he is huge and heroic aloft, definitely a woman-man. The effect, however, is especially devastating because in this, her supreme resistance to earth, Dido is also vulnerable—there are the clear 'death' implications of arching and falling backwards into the dancing space. (Sweete's film treats the moment very effectively but quite differently, cutting to a shot from above and behind the balustrade, so we see Dido reaching up to us, the audience.) This moment on the balustrade also shows concepts relating to size (large), distancing with acceleration, and height all working together towards the same powerful end.

Finally, Dido's song ended, the violins rise as if to enfold her. The dancing chorus return with the ground bass as they escort Dido upstage to her death, although now, the sinking back in their step pattern also reflects the falling semitones in the upper strings. She walks in a reverse version of their step pattern, facing them—McDonald told me that her step forward (up and over) to their sinking backwards is like 'Dido's weight pushing them back'.[69] Still there is a small resistance. Meanwhile, her 'fate' arms slowly descend, marking her readiness for death.

I now return to conceptual blending theory and to summarise how this informs analysis of the Lament. Incorporating Morris's dance component, the discussion develops from Ockelford's application of the theory to the music and text.

First, the choreography 'fleshes out' the music (and especially the vocal and bass lines) as a conduit for human subjectivity. Not only does Dido now become a moving human being, but the bass line is the speech of courtiers, cupids and conscience. Then, by reflecting melodic contour and phrasing, the choreography increases the pressure for Belinda not to be troubled and the emphasis on remembrance as an alternative to the finality of Dido's physical death.

Meanwhile, Morris illustrates choreographically the metaphorical connection between pitch relationships and vertical space. The up-down/ascending-descending paradigm is especially strong in the Lament, stronger than anywhere else in Morris's *Dido*. In this context, the connection between dance and music stresses the tension between living and dying (for which vertical space is yet another metaphor). Furthermore, the highlighting of pitch relationships through choreography plays back on itself, even to the degree that dance itself might suggest sound. You imagine Dido speaking with tension in the throat from her crumpled body on the quieter utterances of 'Remember me' (the repeat of Part 2) and screaming to the climactic account of these words.

At the end of the Lament, Dido and the group illustrate the resolution between voice and accompaniment, completing the blend as it were. As her song concludes, Dido's vocal line parallels the descending bass. The violins continue the theme of descent during the postlude, now reflecting the falling semitones in the bass, finally echoing, appropriately, the diatonic conclusion of her song. From the choreographic point of view, Morris uses the integrated musical structures to underscore Dido's resignation and the group's agreement to support her (which the choreography makes clear):

in other words *their* integration. As Dido's arms descend throughout the postlude, connecting most obviously with the violins, she and the chorus also begin to step in tandem with each other here, and in harmony with both upper and bass lines. To elaborate upon the blend, we might ask: what will happen next? Dido goes to her death with immense dignity, having demonstrated maximum nobility and stoicism during struggle. It is entirely appropriate that Morris minimises the moment of actual death, symbolised when, during the chorus, Dido lies across the balustrade.

Yet there is still a compelling, pervasive element of resistance within this blend that I have already touched on, even during the postlude. While Ockelford stresses musical enhancement of the feelings of sadness and anguish suggested in the text, I propose that the choreography takes this further in the form of a double resistance, not only to the bass ground, but also, on some noteworthy occasions, to the voice of the singing Dido. This is immediately clear from the choreographic enlargements, which are not matched musically, during the repeats of Parts 1 and 2. There are also the bursts of movement that work against the fundamentally slow tempo of the music, in the turns and quick 'Never' gestures, and in the running, round the bench, to the chorus on each side of the stage, and finally up on to the balustrade.

As for the up-down/ascending-descending paradigm, the dance movement not only draws attention to pitch change (or lack of it), it is also influenced by that change. In Part 1, there is sometimes a resistance to the downward pull of the music. Then, as Dido's song descends towards completion, she holds her arms upwards with determination—they reach their downward completion later, with the orchestra.

But I return to the point about enlargement, that other kind of resistance. The tension within the image at the end of Part 1, which suddenly introduces vertical linearity, seems to enlarge upon the tension in the music at this point. In the remarkable image on the balustrade in Part 2, yet one more expression of the 'extreme' in this work, there is even a momentary sense of triumph after the mighty effort to achieve this image—the movement at one with the upward direction of the voice, but now expanding upon it, and upon what we saw previously. We feel a sense of utter transformation, something that no singer, however much she modifies her own repeat, is likely to achieve (although perhaps Hunt was aiming for this in her 1994 Adelaide performance). The effect is so powerful, we may be under the illusion that the musical interval has expanded as well. Of course, different choreography could have brought out (or counterpointed) different features in the music, but that only highlights the aptness of Morris's decisions in this particular dramatic situation. Morris's choreography confirms not only that pitch relationships are relationships in vertical space but here, they are literally a matter of life and death.

So we find in this single dance-song an extraordinary complexity of congruence and opposition, and of meanings assembled from both the music/text and dance and their interaction. There is also a clear shift of style in the Lament, a focus on spatial concerns rather than on the rhythmic content that seemed more important earlier, marking the importance of this song and its pivotal place within the drama of Dido. Analysis of this dance-song has demonstrated especially vividly the usefulness of applying frameworks from cognitive science and linguistics, specifically metaphor theory, alongside methods used for other parts of *Dido* that derive from more traditional music theory.

Yet, while Morris draws on our basic cognitive capacities, whether consciously or not, perhaps what is most remarkable is that we may not notice any 'system' or 'scheme' in *Dido*, either in the Lament or earlier in the work. Prior to the Lament, this sense of freedom is undoubtedly due to the particular nature of the techniques that he uses: an intensity of rhythmic disruption rare in Morris's dances, sometime spicy and sharp, sometimes rough in kind; choreographic polyphony frequently enlivening, and challenging the fundamental homogeneity of, a series of compact choral groups; and finally, a hectic pace of delivery.

Morris responded enthusiastically to the opera's 'compressed' story not only by removing the singers from the stage, but through dramatic pressures of his own. Furthermore, the choreomusical component of his *Dido* is definitely not an 'extra' layer, rather, it is thoroughly integrated with other aspects of the piece. Above all, it reveals the potential within Purcell's score for the dancing body to speak through it—passionately and eloquently.

Mark Morris's Programme Note for *Dido and Aeneas*–as used since the premiere

1. The Palace

The Trojan war is over. Aeneas and his people have found themselves in Carthage after a treacherous sea voyage. His destiny, as decreed by the Gods, is to found Rome, but he has become obsessed with Dido, Queen of Carthage. Her sister and confidante, Belinda, and other optimistic courtiers urge her to enjoy her good fortune, but the young widow Dido is anxious. Aeneas arrives to ask the Queen, again, to give herself to him. Belinda notices, with relief, that Dido seems to be capitulating. Dido and Aeneas leave together. Love triumphs.

2. The Cave

The evil Sorceress summons her colleagues to make big trouble in Carthage. Dido must be destroyed before sunset. Knowing of Aeneas' destiny to sail to Italy, the Sorceress decides to send a Spirit disguised as Mercury to tell him he must depart immediately. Since Dido and Aeneas and the rest are out on a hunt, the witches plan to make a storm to spoil the lovers' fun and send everyone back home. The witches cast their spell.

3. The Grove

Dido and Aeneas make love. Another triumph for the hero. The royal party enters and tells a story for Aeneas' benefit. Dido senses the approaching storm. Belinda, ever practical, organises the trip back to the palace. Aeneas is accosted by the false Mercury with this command: 'Leave Carthage now.' He accepts his orders, then wonders how to break the news to Dido. He is worried.

4. The Ships

Aeneas and the Trojans prepare for the journey. The Sorceress and her witches are quite pleased to see that their plot is working. Once Aeneas has sailed they will conjure an ocean storm. They are proud of themselves.

5. The Palace

Dido sees the Trojans preparing their ships. Aeneas tries to explain his predicament and offers to break his vow in order to stay with her. Dido is appalled by his hypocrisy. She sends him away and contemplates the inevitability of death. 'Remember me but forget my fate.' Dido dies.

Dance 'Words'

The guide here is Sophia Preston's excellent list (2000) of regularly used dance 'words', with words sharing the same dance gesture grouped together. In 2013, she made additions to this list.[70] Preston assumes further directly related concepts, e.g. your/my/his could be supplemented by you/her:

> shake; brow; fate; allow; empire/Italian ground/Hesperian shore; pleasures flowing/ Elysian bowers; smiles; you; banish; sorrow; care; grief; never/no trouble; fair/Queen/ Dido/royal fair; Ah!; Belinda; press'd/heart/breast; torment/oppress'd/distress'd; confess'd; languish; guess'd/know/known/forget/sensible; Trojan guest/Royal guest/ Aeneas/hero; Carthage/state/this land; revive; monarchs/Troy; foes; storm; soft; strong/wretches/wretched; woe/bless'd; see; piety/pity; loves/lover; strew; pursue; fire/flame; flight; your/my/his; fall; conquest/fact/resolv'd; triumph; raven; appear; Jove/god-like/gods/the Almighty powers; commands; tonight/here/this night/this place; drive/haste/away; vaulted cell; Diana/Actaeon/Cupid/in chase; hounds; after; mortal wounds; obey/decree; anchors weighed; part; forsook; heaven; bereft; die/death; deceitful streams/ocean/fatal Nile; good; touch; shelter; more; hard; drooping wings.

I add the following to Preston's list: crocodiles (added to hounds), desire (to fire/flame), counsel (to obey), earth (to soft), leaving (to part), give (to woe), shun (to drive/haste); scatter (to strew (referring to flowers)). The following are new words added by Preston in 2013: remember, stay, fleet, sunset/sunrise, mountain, and kill. In 2013, she also suggested one amendment: decree is the same as command and will (with the arms extended horizontally and palms facing forward), but not the same as obey (where the elbows are lifted, wrists flexed and palms face downwards).

8

Still Abroad: *The Hard Nut* and Other Dances

Morris's last work of the Brussels years, *The Hard Nut*, is more obviously a commentary on, or re-vision of, another existing dance than any other piece he has ever made.[1] This places it firmly within the genre of postmodern dances that look at the past through the lens of the present, both questioning and celebrating the source, while the two periods inevitably clash. Not for nothing has the piece been likened to the work in opera of the theatre director Peter Sellars.[2] *The Hard Nut* is unusual because of the peculiar power of the concept upon which it is based, that is, *The Nutcracker*, source of the well-known traditional nineteenth-century ballet, which is about children, a family Christmas, and the dreams of a young girl—usually Marie or Clara, depending on the version—being taken to the magical Kingdom of Sweets.

The original *Nutcracker* was conceived for the Mariinsky Ballet by Marius Petipa, who fell ill when staging began, after which Lev Ivanov carried out the choreography for the 1892 premiere. Since then, there have been countless productions all over the world, almost half of these in the US.[3] We simply cannot forget the 'old' *Nutcracker* when we watch Morris's retitled version. This is partly because Morris's re-vision is shot through with allusions to the original scenario and choreographic ideas: there is indeed a good deal of dancing in classical ballet style, including a wonderful white-ballet Snow scene, even though clearly performed by modern dancers with a modern dance attitude. Tchaikovsky's great score bears prime responsibility for keeping all the memories alive and *The Hard Nut* offers a fascinating opportunity for comparative study.

The following analysis is informed by comparison with a few of these other versions. First is Peter Wright's 1984 Royal Ballet production that looks back to the original Ivanov, using whatever choreography could be gleaned from the Russian Stepanov notations, including the Snowflakes scene and Act 2 Grand pas de deux. Then, there is the most celebrated US production, by Balanchine (1954), and various others of Soviet lineage—the Kirov (Vassili I. Vainonen, 1934); two that incorporate Vainonen's Snowflakes choreography, those of the Royal Ballet (Rudolf Nureyev, 1968, prior to Wright's production and later in the repertoire of Paris Opera Ballet) and of American Ballet Theatre (Baryshnikov, 1976); and the Bolshoi production (Yuri Grigorovich, 1966). Another postmodern re-vision was examined (again, not a classical ballet as such), the 1992 *Nutcracker!* by Matthew Bourne, which opens in a Dickensian orphanage.[4]

Morris's ideas were stimulated in collaboration with the American horror-comics artist Charles Burns. His re-vision is a 'psycho-sexual drama' for adults, he told everyone in the original publicity. No children are seen dancing in it—although children can still enjoy watching it. He returns to the disturbing tone of Hoffmann's original tale 'The Nutcracker and the Mouse King', which was edited and sweetened for the original ballet. The new setting is a TV-obsessed American suburban family, treated in hilarious cartoon style, their Christmas party a riot of indecorous behaviour. Most of those present are drunk and sexually obsessed. The costumes are loud, in clashing colours, the younger participants in bell-bottoms and headbands of a bygone Carnaby Street. Out of all this kitsch and vulgarity Morris's Marie stands as a serious idealist, and the work shows her in the process of growing from childhood into womanhood. She it is who makes the offer of love to her 'Prince', the nephew of the enigmatic family friend Drosselmeier.

In Act 2, Morris returns to Hoffmann's sub-plot story, the Krakatuk tale, told to Marie by Drosselmeier, about a Princess Pirlipat who is cursed to be ugly by a rat queen. The only way to remove the curse is to find a magic nut and the young man who can crack it with his teeth. Drosselmeier travels all over the world to the divertissement music of the old ballet's Kingdom of Sweets—Spain, Arabia, China, Russia and France—but eventually finds the nut at home and his own nephew able to crack it. When Young Drosselmeier then steps on the rat queen and kills her, and the ugliness curse falls on him, Marie stops the story. She makes the big decision. If the Princess will not now have him as prize, she will, and he becomes handsome once more. As Morris writes in his programme note:

> This is a love story between two people but it's also about the love that's already in the world. In other words, you can search for the thing you want, and then you find it waiting for you back home. You just didn't recognise it before. You had to grow up.

This sub-plot is set to music originally intended for other purposes, mostly the music for the Nutcracker Prince's narrative at the start of Act 2, while the dénouement occupies the introduction to the Waltz of the Flowers. Although it is a way of making the original, very weak, ballet story more coherent, this whole section remains the least successful part of Morris's work—most of the divertissement dances are not very interesting, and the Pirlipat story is too rushed to be convincing. Morris once admitted ending up having to 'smash' his story into the music, which says a lot.[5] Yet the

Pirlipat story fits the music as if made for it: the mime gestures and timing seem to have been determined to a considerable extent by what the music already suggested.

Morris draws upon the basic themes of learning and sensual exploration that permeate the traditional ballet. In a fascinating essay using Judith Butler's theories of gendered identity, scholar Sarah Cohen suggests that, through the use of stereotypes, Morris's work emphasises physical identity as a construction. At the same time, she suggests that this can be destabilised:

> Morris' ballet, through a tangible deployment of constructed physicality, advances in its own way the debate over how the body performs—and potentially reconfigures—its troublesome materiality...

> Most importantly, the performance of identity no longer serves as the ballet's invisible assumption, but advances to the forefront of the drama itself.[6]

The emphasis on trying things out at the raucous party, through many different kinds of pairing, is an instance of this de-stabilisation, and the ballet reinforces this playfulness through an exceptionally large number of *en travesti* opportunities. Later, there is stress on Young Drosselmeier learning from his uncle in an unusual duet for two men, then on Marie from her mother Mrs Stahlbaum, whose early step combination she borrows. It is her mother, symbol of fecundity, who leads the plant world in the Waltz of the Flowers, just when the new partnership between her daughter and Young Drosselmeier has been announced.

Turning now to Morris's use of Tchaikovsky's score, his purist approach may well seem surprising after such alarming re-visioning: the score is all there, and in the right order. In this, he is unusual.[7] Balanchine himself cut some pages, altering the order of the Act 2 pas de deux by moving the Sugar Plum Fairy variation to the beginning of the Act and cutting her Cavalier's variation. The score was still, as so often, Morris's starting point. He had long wanted to use it and to make people hear it in a new way. The musicologist in him spoke loudly. Morris has never been more adamant about tempo than in *The Hard Nut*. Most notably, bracing written tempos must remain bracing in performance. He told an interviewer:

> ...most people do the tempos completely wrong. Tchaikovsky wrote very specific tempi and of course in the Russian tradition, you just speed up and slow down for whoever's doing it that night. For something like the Tarantella [the cavalier's Variation in the Grand pas de deux], which is written [*Morris hums the upbeat melody*] at that speed, it's usually done [*the melody becomes slow and bombastic*] for the big jump. It's not a big

jump. It's a *Tarantella* [see p. 107, Ex. 4.4]. And something like Arabian, which is [usually] done slow-motion—it's a gorgeous barcarole, and it's done slow-motion so you can pull your foot over your head. It's insane. I think it's ghastly what's happened to the music, and the extrapolations and the edits are just idiotic for me.[8]

Morris handles the various kinds of music with aplomb. Take the action music of Act 1 first, which he keeps for action—many choreographers do not. Morris considers that the quality of the music in this scene is often obscured in traditional productions:

...The music from Act I, which everyone just sleeps through because it's the most boring fucking thing in the world—that music is incredible. And that's the hard music to play and to conduct. It changes tempo and metre constantly; it interrupts itself all the time. It's wonderful, wonderful music. [9]

The score here is full of gesture and changes of mood, some startling, some more gradual: party emotions let rip or come to the boil more slowly. Asking him to write music of feeling, Petipa's instruction words to Tchaikovsky—like 'jubilant', 'furious', 'serious', 'sinister', 'droll', 'bright', 'merry'[10]—all make sense to us in *The Hard Nut*. Morris's party originally developed from improvisation, but it has always remained open to change and re-invigoration between performances, and is therefore to some degree unfixed choreomusically. (A recent addition is an episode of 'Gangnam style', the recent dance craze from South Korea.) When it comes to the social dances, Tchaikovsky's beat is clear and the rhythms simple—as befits dances created for young children and the daft anyone-can-get-up-and-do-it dances of the 60s and 70s: like the stroll, the hip-jerking frug, the hokey-pokey and the dirty bump. Waltzing fits waltz music, as was intended.

As for ballet style, Morris understands that it is the style of dreams and other worlds, and he includes pointe work. (There was far more of this in Morris's 1991 *Hard Nut* than nowadays: it was also used for the Spain, China and France divertissement dances.) To what is clearly music written for women, scored according to convention, for instance, for flutes or violins, he had both men and women dance on pointe. Tottering around thus is simply the way the black maid walks: it is a drag role (nearly always taken by Kraig Patterson). In the original Snow Waltz, some dancers chose to try out pointe work and some not. After an interview prior to the New York premiere, Jennifer Dunning tells us that this 'evoked and underscored for him [Morris] the chill sharpness of snow'.[11] There is something both refreshing and poignant about non-ballet dancers performing ballet style (including modern dancers who have had a lot of ballet training): they betray the effort, determination and joy of doing it, and an intriguing dichotomy between ballet lightness and their natural, weighty style. But the choreography must be strong in such circumstances and the dancers as secure with the musical rhythms as Morris's are. In other less confident hands (or rather bodies), ballet style might simply look embarrassing.

There is also something refreshing and innocent about barefoot ballet, for instance, when we hear the famous celesta of the Sugar Plum Fairy variation (its first use in Russian music) while watching Marie's pliant feet and, as if in our own bodies, 'feeling' their pads caress the floor. Petipa asked for staccato music 'as if drops of water shooting out of fountains are heard'.[12] We remember through the music the sharp pointes and *petite batterie* (small beats of the feet) of the traditional Fairy. But it is good to be faced with alternatives: water can also be soft.

Critics have complained that Morris's Act 2 pas de deux choreography fails to rise to the swell of Tchaikovsky's score. Among them, David Vaughan was also unhappy that the Finale intended for a big ensemble had been turned into the main pas de deux opportunity, later than originally intended.[13] It is worth mentioning that Morris disliked this music intensely. 'That's where the Chinese people usually come out and wave', he once said.[14] Perhaps he hated most of all what it had come to mean within the old ballet. But, by this point in *The Hard Nut*, the music intended for the main pas de deux has already broken free of its original, formulaic associations. To this music, no longer is there an Adagio duet, two separate solo Variations and a fast Coda. Instead, during the opening Adagio music—where Petipa had instructed Tchaikovsky 'to produce a colossal impression'[15]—the couple are kept apart and lifted, in turn, by a crowd of people from their past. With every section of the ballet represented, the lifts get bigger and higher to meet the enlargement within the score. After this, there are two, far from traditional, solo variations, for the man, then the woman, and finally the Coda, which, in *The Hard Nut*, again becomes the sole property of the crowd, before the couple are finally united.[16]

In the concluding section of her article, 'The Inventive Body', Cohen argues for the new assertiveness of the crowd members and Marie by the end of the ballet. Yet confronting the work's most radical suggestion, that identity can be destabilised, she can only agree that there is a problem at this point:

> One might well wonder what one could ever do with one's body that forges something completely original...Morris's aesthetic problem is, in the end, our social problem: if the performance of social identity, fully acknowledged and compellingly probed, can subvert our expectations through its own, resourceful process, can the process itself ever be

surmounted? It is precisely at the moment of emotional contact between lovers that Morris draws back, as if recognising that 'true' feeling cannot so easily be reinvented.[17]

From one point of view, the couple's steps to the Finale are bland, and the allusions back to what Drosselmeier taught his nephew are drearily rational, Marie confirming the rightness of the love between her and Young Drosselmeier or some kind of bonding with all the other lovers in the world. But perhaps there is something else going on here. Considering relations with the music, and in particular, the treatment of its triumphant repeating theme, opens up another interpretation.

The principal image of this duet is of kissing, long, long, passionate kisses, one mouth clamped to the other, the real thing, and no dancing to accompany it. When Lauren Grant and David Leventhal dance Marie and Young Drosselmeier (a married couple offstage), this is the boldest kissing you are likely to see in performance, especially as they are totally isolated on a bare stage, with nobody watching...except us. They start with the triumphant theme: one kiss, then two, three, even four! 'When will they stop this exclusive behaviour?' you might ask yourself. Audiences often gasp with pleasure, or anxiety, or both. Then the dancing starts up again. Led by the music, when you hear the big theme again and see the happy pair press close together, you are likely to ask: 'will they do it again, or won't they?' Delay increases the tension. Finally, they *do* do it again, now spinning round and round as if into eternity. This links literally and metaphorically with their final walk side by side into the hypnotic spiral 'spinning' on the backdrop. Memories of the crowd who usually dance this music only underscore (by contrast) the privacy of the lone couple.

In the epilogue of *Hard Nut*, when Marie's brother and sister see them on the television, they are still kissing... So this is the final discovery (or learning), and surely a radical move on Morris's part towards an inventive body that we are hardly likely to imagine within a dance performance. He shows us love as both physical and emotional experience, with all the dancing and public performing of identity disappeared, instead giving way to an ideal of intimacy and an overhearing of powerful music as it throbs through us all. Just as we will find later in Morris's *Romeo and Juliet*, this is not at all the usual happy ending.

Again, much of the strength of Morris's version lies in its constant dialogue with a very different kind of *Nutcracker* and with how that used the same music. So, to the burning question: why bring in the crowd to the old Adagio duet music? one answer is that 'they all helped' bring about the happy conclusion in this production.[18] But as a consequence, when the merry clutter of friends from 'reality' and 'story' leave the stage, the central pair seem all the more free and direct in their behaviour. Then, why no crowd at all during the Finale when it *should* be there? With some irony, that very loss, a positive absence, intensifies the focus upon what is most important about the *Hard Nut* story, a relationship between lovers.

There are many other occasions when *The Hard Nut* lets us hear the music anew. Let us examine further sections of the piece, first, the dance for the mechanical life-size dolls brought in as presents for the children in Act 1. Ivanov introduced a sutler (a seller of army provisions), soldier, Harlequin and Columbine who have survived into some current productions.[19] In Morris's production, they are a long-legged Barbie Doll and a metallic Robot. Petipa asked Tchaikovsky for 'a sharp, disjunct waltz with clear rhythm'.[20] None of the productions I know captures that disjunction as cleverly as Morris: he heard the distinctions between the rhythms of melody and bass and took advantage of them. Barbie adopts the 3/2 hemiola in the melody— across two written bars of 3/4, she does three steps and then casually lops a leg up high, showing the swoop upward of the melody. (Some versions of *Nutcracker* stab rather unkindly at that top note rather than showing the process of getting there.) Meanwhile, Robot takes over the 3/4 bass line with a silly stuttering little walk precisely on each note—on beats 1 and 2, later on every other beat:

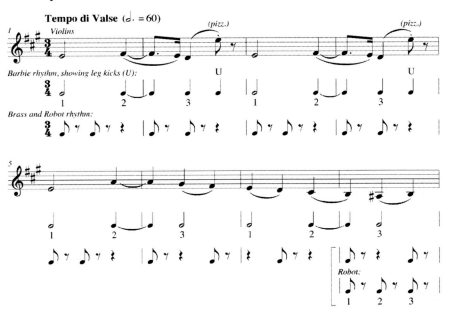

Ex. 8.1 *The Hard Nut*, Tchaikovsky [*The Nutcracker*], Waltz of Barbie Doll and Robot. The brass and Robot divide into two rhythmic lines in bar 8.

The Hard Nut, Act 1, Billy Smith as Robot and Elisa Clark as Barbie Doll (showing her leg lift). © Susana Millman, 2009

Later, he totters around Barbie in response to a series of continuous quavers. So, just like any mechanical dolls, their motion is strictly prescribed, and they are constantly, literally, out of phase with each other.

To take another example, in her solo in the Act 2 pas de deux, Marie alludes to the toe-steps of Ivanov's Sugar Plum Fairy, but her solo has a more clearly etched shape. Her first step, 'learnt' from her mother, a *glissade* followed by a *sous-sus*, grows into two *glissades* and a *sous-sus*, then into three, an accumulation, varying the relationship to musical phrasing and bar-lines and at the same time becoming more expansive.

Ex. 8.2 [Dance of the Sugar-plum Fairy], Marie's solo. Accumulating numbers, 1, 1 2, 1 2 3 indicate *glissades* to the right; U and D indicate *sous-sus* (a spring up on to the toes in 5th position, followed by a spring down again in *plié*, notated from a 2002 MMDG recording).

On the other hand, her final rush down the diagonal, with circling runs and little *jetés*, gets tighter. The runs are gradually eliminated and more and more *jetés* gather momentum and urgency, until she falls into Young Drosselmeier's arms and kisses him smack on the mouth. It is in the middle of this solo that their kissing 'motif' begins, as if Morris heard what film people refer to as 'stingers' in the music—sudden sforzandos that can be used to illustrate sudden dramatic tension.[21] First, Young Drosselmeier kisses her, chastely, on the cheek, then on one hand, again and again, and then she offers her other hand. There are seven stingers in all, so seven kisses, each on the final quaver of the bar and in increasingly rapid succession.

Ex. 8.3 [Dance of the Sugar-plum Fairy], Marie's solo, showing the seven 'stingers'.

Aaron Mattocks, once MMDG company manager, describes the passage particularly well, after seeing Grant and Leventhal:

> It's as though this zing of vibration is actually felt in her heart, or, perhaps with Morris, even lower. And there's a joke at the end—but it's also serious and we all know the feeling—she eventually sticks out the other hand: she likes the way this feels, adulthood, love, and she wants more.[22]

Rooting out these stingers, absorbing them into the dance and making them significant choreomusical moments, Morris enlarges the expressive range of the dance and prevents the solo from being as saccharine as the original. Other more conventionally and regularly phrased choreography uses these accents to far less effect.

One of the most admired sections of Morris's *Hard Nut* is the Snow Scene. Roland John Wiley, the Ivanov/Tchaikovsky authority who advised Peter Wright at the Royal Ballet, believes that it is in the Snowflakes Scene, a Waltz, that 'Tchaikovsky carries rhythmic disjunction to the furthest point of any of his ballets.'[23] The main theme itself, which is repeated several times, crosses the 3/4 bar-lines. At a detailed level, it is heard in 2/4, while, at a higher level, it creates 3/2 hypermeasures (see p. 114) across every two bars of the written score. This is further complicated by the little syncopated semiquaver figures on the flutes that begin one quaver after each 2/4 downbeat.

Ex. 8.4 [Waltz of the Snowflakes], Snow, showing the musical rhythm and two different dance rhythmic lines.

In these circumstances, there is considerable ambiguity: is the semiquaver figure rather than the preceding bass note heard as the 2/4 downbeat? By contrast, other material in the Waltz is clearly in 3/4 metre, the prime example being the striking wordless melody ('Ah!') introduced by a boy's choir (bar 117). But we also hear this as the dominant metre when Tchaikovsky starts to blend 3/4 thematic material with further syncopated 2/4 semiquaver figuration (from bars 85 and 165).

Ex. 8.5 [Waltz of the Snowflakes], Snow, the added 3/4 thematic material.

Later, continuing into the 2/4 Presto Coda, there are many big accents, often including the crash of cymbals, still more 'stingers', but they are irregularly timed, unpredictable, and choreographers have to decide how, or whether, to confront such forceful musical information. Petipa's instructions to the composer were brief and simple: 'A whirling waltz. In the third quarter of the waltz a furious burst of wind causes all the dancers to spin around.'[24] Petipa and Ivanov must have been surprised by what Tchaikovsky came up with.

Morris proves more than ready for the challenge, constantly shifting his tactics and surprising us. The handling of the snow (fistsful of confetti picked up in the wings) by the 'Snow' dancers helps him make his point. (Morris's band of twenty-two men and women are dressed identically in bikini tutus and Dairy Queen cone head-dresses, so we are chuckling from the start.) Most other productions have the snow simply drifting down from the rafters throughout the Waltz, but Morris gets his dancers to throw the snow in careful coordination with musical structure. He treats the main musical theme in several different ways. At first, he uses the 3/4 *barring* of the score in a *balancé* (counts 1-3) followed by a *piqué* step into a sturdy tilted *attitude* with a strong outburst of snow (count 1, hold 2, 3): the combination as a whole occupies what is *heard* as a 3/2 bar in the music (see Ex. 8.4, dance rhythm 1). This opening step is strangely earthy and energetic, while the snow falls very gently after it, softening the effect of the throw. Later, Morris devises steps across the stage (without snow) reaching out into second position, then closing (with arms to the side, then overhead), now pushing directly towards those edgy flute semiquavers. These steps and gestures mark the 2/4 metre (see Ex. 8.4, dance rhythm 2). When 3/4 becomes more prominent in the music, Morris respects the change. Always there is tautness and attack: the dancers even run exactly *on* the quick beats.

Other settings of the main musical theme conform blandly to the 3/4 written bar-line (Wright, Kirov), or with the 3/2 hypermetre (Bourne), or just show the syncopations (Grigorovich). In his highly effective, urgent setting, Balanchine stages *coupés-chassés en tournant* as the fundamental step to the main theme, showing the downbeat with the preparatory step, then the moment in the air on each syncopation. But no other choreographer gets so deeply into the musical machinery as Morris. We do indeed hear the music afresh and awaken to its complexity and constant instability.

Elsewhere in the Snow Waltz, Morris underlines the music with 'up' accents, catching the moment of suspension (the peak of a leap—a *pas de chat* or *grand jeté*—plus snow) and keeping us on the edge of our seats. On one occasion, when the music is consistently in 3/4, the dancers pop up in an erratic canon, whenever they feel like it, trying not to match any of their companions, so that your eye darts all over the place. But later, they pop up regularly to match each semiquaver-figure syncopation (attached to beat 2 of each bar: bars 165-96), at which point your eye moves steadily down the line crossing the stage.

Most spectacular of all is Morris's treatment of the big cymbal-crash sforzandos, when he has the dancers leaping in long diagonals across the stage, throwing snow on each 'up' accent. (Most other choreographers match these accents with the step before take-off into the leap or with the landing afterwards, which has much less thrilling effect.) As these big accents occur with increasing frequency towards the end of the dance, we are left—a hiatus point—looking at a thick cloud of snow hanging in the air, then falling softly before the dancers return for a quiet Poco meno conclusion. No other version I know provides such an extraordinary and literally brilliant climax. This Snow Waltz gradually opens to the heavens, a tremendous expression of joyful achievement from so many 'everybodies', and to which choreomusical relations make a central contribution. In the Poco meno section, as the snow storm abates— with rhythmless *bourrées* to shimmering harp and strings—the dancers, now dribbling snow from their fingers, watch the older Drosselmeier on his journey home. In turn, they drop to their heels to stand still as he passes by, and we are amazed by their humanness, reminded that they are, after all, like us.[25]

All the Brussels premieres so far discussed involved analytical musical strategies. Morris, however, continued to experiment more freely with structure, using music to different ends (or none at all). *Wonderland* (1989) and *Behemoth* (1990) pursue the direction initiated during earlier collaborations with the composer Herschel Garfein—especially *Forty Arms* and *Championship Wrestling* (see pp. 172-6).

For *Wonderland*, Morris turned to Schoenberg's *Accompaniment—Music for a Motion Picture*, Op. 34 (*Begleitungsmusik zu einer Lichtspielszene*, 1930), followed by his *Five Pieces for Orchestra*, Op. 16 (1909). He was interested in using these scores 'atmospherically' in the manner of film music, relying primarily on their emotional and expressive capacities. The Op. 34 piece had been commissioned by Heinrichshofen, a Magdeburg publisher specialising in music for use with silent film, although with no specific example in mind.

Finding Schoenberg's music 'extremely romantic, extremely violent and extremely tender', Morris decided to make a piece that evoked Hitchcock, a 'perfect companion' to this composer,[26] and the darkly-lit *film noir* genre of the 1940s. He constructed the choreography for five individuals, all stereotypes of gangland culture. There was Baryshnikov as the Private Eye (the 'little detective', he called himself), memorably set against Rob Besserer, the Big Boss—a 'giant beauty Cary Grant',[27] Ruth Davidson as a Blonde Floozie, Olivia Maridjan-Koop a kind of Younger Sister or Secretary, and Keith Sabado the lurking Punk.[28] Morris's private joke was that, for this tiny cast, he would require from La Monnaie an orchestra of almost one-hundred players.[29] The piece was performed on only one other occasion after the premiere season, to tape, in New York in 1990. Practically-speaking, revivals of *Wonderland* with live music are unlikely.

Schoenberg is closely linked to expressionism, the art movement that exposed the subconscious and extremes of feeling. The *Five Pieces* were created at a time of great turbulence in his life. His wife had left him temporarily for another man, and, as a composer, he struggled to find a way out of the historically-established tonal system (based on major and minor key structures) into total chromaticism and then the highly influential twelve-note, serial system of pitch organisation. Although the composer was reluctant to pin himself down to titles,[30] he came up with the following for publication: 'Premonitions', 'Yesteryears', 'Colours (Summer Morning by a Lake)'—inspired by a dawn visit to Traunsee—'Peripatia' and 'The Obligatory Recitative'. *Accompaniment—Music for a Motion Picture* is a fully-fledged serial work, with telling subtitles—'Threatening Danger', 'Fear' and 'Catastrophe'—although here Schoenberg did not specify to which parts of his score these belong.

In both scores, the incorporation of short, fragmented motifs within a highly complex texture is the structural tool—a technique Schoenberg termed 'developing variation'. This replaces tonal drive and the sense of expectation and fulfilment from tonality (see pp. 109-10). From this too, there is the sense of a series of emotional 'states' with no apparent logic behind them and of compressed time. There are none of the solid blocks of material and themes that are confident and, to some extent, predictable structural signposts in the music that Morris usually chooses. Most Hollywood film music of the time was of quite a different order too: tonally-based and far less volatile. The quiet, haunting third movement, 'Colours' ['Farben'], is exceptional within the *Five Pieces*, without any traditional motivic associations, instead, a single harmony as generating device, 'coloured' by constantly shifting orchestration. It becomes a still centre within the work.

Crucially, Morris borrows several key musical features for his choreography, although his methods are not characteristic of him. He is led by shifting timbre/sound quality and dynamics far more than usual. Thus, the moves tend to be short, fragmented and forced into a high octane collage: stamps, spasms, fierce double *pirouettes*, a gesture like frantically rubbing a hand on a skirt as if to remove evidence, covering a mouth wide open in terror, looking at the palm of a hand as if it bears blood, or putting a hand into a pocket to get a handkerchief. Or will it be a gun? Any single move might trigger another and lead to a physical confrontation, violent assault, rushed escape, or chase behind a scrim upstage. Sometimes, there is what Morris calls 'empty time' in the choreography, when a character stops still, but this remains occasion for vigilance. Whenever we see a body on the ground, we feel compelled to ask: who did the deed? Hearing the music, as we often do subliminally when watching films, we sense that something terrible is going to happen. Yet, although there is always the urge to make something coherent from the intensity of information, we are inevitably defeated. There are, after all, clues, but no over-riding narrative, no solutions, instead, inexplicable changes of behaviour. Dead people always get up and rejoin the action.

Wonderland is like a meta-narrative of *film noir* and its music, a condensed reflection on hundreds of instances of the genre, their style and form. The tensions of horror, threat, and convoluted human entanglements become far more important than any individual plot. It is as if Morris pulled to the surface the deep veins of the genre.

Sometimes, Morris drives us to become detectives ourselves, standing outside the frame of the 'film'. As Deborah Jowitt remarked,

> Watching it, you feel as if someone were running and re-running frag-ments of footage from a 30s film whose scenario was lost long ago. Every action seems cut off before its end ...[When it ends], I immediately want to see the whole thing again and play detective among the dark, spare film clips.[31]

As we struggle to fathom what is going on, the device of forward and rewind, most often enacted as simply walking forwards and then back, pretends to help us.

Set in silence between the two Schoenberg pieces, one section, inspired by Akira Kurosawa's film *Rashomon* (1950), maximises the formality of Morris's work. He lets us see a crime scene from four different angles, then a fifth time in slow motion, each occasion under a single overhead spotlight and separated by a blackout. Each shot plays upon our memory of the event as we saw it previously.[32] Baryshnikov stands over a dead woman (Davidson), picks something up from the ground and, as if it could be incriminating,

Wonderland, Mikhail Baryshnikov and Rob Besserer. © Klaus Lefebvre, 1990

puts it in his pocket; Besserer hurries past, avoiding the scene; the other two characters approach and look down in horror. As Alastair Macaulay wrote in his review:

> You see more each time this 'simple' episode is reprised, and then you wonder: was what you noticed the fifth time there before? (It's like the title scene from Antonioni's *Blow-Up*.) When the couple of passers-by pause, there's something in his hand. You may not notice the first two times, because you're still attending to Baryshnikov and the corpse centre-stage. But then you do. Is it a gun he's pointing? Then, as you see it in slow motion, you find it was only his glasses. But what was it the previous four times?[33]

The silence of this whole passage is especially compelling after musical presence: it encourages us to become more intensely analytical, to look more closely. The music seems doubly sinister when it returns.

Morris's working method here was closer to theatre direction than usual: he provided instructions and imagery for improvisation. As an example, the *South Bank Show* shot during this period captures Morris instructing Sabado: 'You're going to kill her and you're shot accidentally, from behind. The gun Rob is trying to return to Ruth accidentally goes off...your front explodes.'[34] Working backwards and forwards, Morris built, moulded and assembled material to fit the music, but never in the cause of linear narrative. Besserer recalls a passage when Morris simply directed him to stay on one leg while wildly flailing his other leg and arms, freely, as he wished. 'The world is changing' was, Morris recalls, the image behind this.[35]

The larger structure of *Wonderland* was clearly defined by the main musical sections, which determined distinct scenes divided by blackouts and lighting changes. The final section, to 'The Obligatory Recitative', last of the *Five Pieces*, has a systematic dance structure. It is a series of five episodes between which the dancers switch from one type of activity to another. During each episode, we see simultaneously a solo, a dancer walking forwards and then in retrograde, two others frozen—one standing, one on the floor—while the remaining dancer is offstage. Once created, the choreography was fixed to landmarks in the score, some of these obvious points of connection, most, however, only for the benefit of the dancers inside the piece. The overriding impression is of a loose fit: there was never any counting. But Morris insists that the dancers felt, and engaged with, the expressive qualities of what they heard, despite the independent nature of the creative process.[36]

Examples of obvious choreomusical connections can be found in the terse fourth of the *Five Pieces*. On three occasions when huge crescendos start to emerge and the music shrieks and screams, we expect brutality. Baryshnikov, then Maridjan-Koop, then Davidson, are hurled towards us across the floor, trapped within the central spotlight. Baryshnikov is hauled up again, a survivor, but the two women remain grounded, as if dying or dead. Other moments of connection are much quieter. Suddenly, during the mesmerising third movement, 'Colours', there is an upward leaping motif. Schoenberg likened it to one of the 'jumping fish'[37] that he saw at Traunsee. Within *Wonderland*, it meets Maridjan-Koop's sudden collapse flat to the floor and close by, Baryshnikov turning sharply to the side. Then, an answering motif marks the arrival of Sabado, who startles Baryshnikov by grabbing him by the arms from behind. Later 'moments' like this in the music and dance do not coincide, but the clarity of articulation from that initial contact remains with us as we continue to watch and listen.

At other times, an instrumental utterance attaches itself to a character: like the deceptively sweet celesta used ironically to mark the occasion in 'Yesteryears' when Davidson walks back and forth obsessed with the palm of her hand.[38] Towards the end of the film score, a regular tolling starts up, and all five characters in a line fling their heads back in throbbing anguish (another repeating movement motif). This is a rare instance when Morris picks up a musical beat in *Wonderland*.

Schoenberg's music can be overwhelming, carrying the characters along with its turbulence, or virtually stopping them, as if rendering them powerless. It can also be so quiet that we hear the dancers' feet and breath fighting to be strong against it, or that we feel the loneliness and vulnerability of a single body. Choreomusical relations, even if highly unusual for Morris within this piece, are still of central importance.

The next step for Morris was to dispense with music entirely, taking the plunge after the big silent dance episodes in *Forty Arms, Twenty Necks, One Wreathing* and *Wonderland* to make a full, large-scale work without accompaniment. Morris cites *Behemoth* as his main tribute to Merce Cunningham (following *Frisson*, see p. 167), borrowing from the older choreographer the principles of autonomy for dance movement, non-linear time and decentralised stage space. Sometimes, Morris told interviewers that his new piece was silent because he could not find music suitable for what he wanted to express, at other times, that he simply wanted to find out what silence would be like. The vocabulary was 'abstract' and geometrical, continuing the style of *Forty Arms* and *Frisson*.[39]

Ironically, removing what Morris loved the most, and what was most expected of him, somehow made it hugely *present*. The silence was deafening, especially on a programme entitled 'Loud Music', with the noises of Brussels city audible yet dissociated from the action trapped on stage.

The title *Behemoth* refers to a large or monstrous beast: Morris admitted that what he had come up with was 'giant' and 'scary'.[40] The scene is toil and struggle, frozen bodies erupting into deliberate, angular allegro and dislocated coordination—tics, shudders, quivers, a trail of non-sequiturs. On two occasions, a lone man lying with his feet towards us laboriously pushes himself upstage, his face out of view, the friction of his body against the floor making a moaning sound. We also hear the sounds of dancers' stamps and claps and, near the end, the banging of their heels against the floor. But these are not like the organic sounds from folk dance. They are definitely not music, rather arbitrary, clumsy shocks that can trigger reaction at a distant point on stage. There are ten sections, each demarcated—again—by blackouts, like brutal erasures. (The piece was very tightly structured, incorporating systems. Morris describes one part of *Behemoth* as 'a beautiful machine'.[41])

Most critics found *Behemoth* intensely disturbing, as if it spoke of some terrible loss. Macaulay read it as the symbol of the incoherent physicality associated with neurological disorders. He was reminded of Oliver Sacks's 1973 book *Awakenings*—very much in the air at the time, and the film of the book premiered just after *Behemoth* in 1990—in which a patient suffering from Parkinson's disease describes her condition as 'wooden, mechanical... unmusicked'.[42] Macaulay found the piece stifling:

> Whereas Cunningham without music roams free through the world, Morris without music is a house without windows—almost air without oxygen.[43]

Meanwhile, as Morris worked on *Wonderland* and *Behemoth*, he also created pieces that used sound/music in more characteristic ways. To the cowboy romp *Going Away Party* (1990) he brought his full flair with texted music, this time country-western style. In *Motorcade* (1990), he continued to explore delicious rhythmic detail and employed the trumpet in Saint-Saëns' *Septet* to spectacular effect as an instrument of announcement. For this was White Oak's debut piece and, at one point, the trumpet heralded big Besserer transporting Baryshnikov like a champion in a high lift across the stage. In *A Lake* (1991), set to Haydn's horn concerto, the interaction with scoring was less convincing. Concerto instruments speak strongly and independently from the orchestra as a 'voice' or subjectivity (see p. 103). Here, except for the cadenzas when it is attached to individual dancers, the horn seems to have an uncertain relationship with the stage. Once again, Morris was experimenting with a freer approach to form and told an interviewer that he chose not to work with a score:

> That was fun, and interesting, and easy—but it wasn't as easy as if I'd

used the score just to check out symmetries and stuff. So I just started at the beginning and went through to the end, and made it up as I went along—wherever I finished one day in rehearsal, I would start at the next bar the next day. So there were irregularities in it that I really liked, that I didn't adjust, whereas I usually even those things out.[44]

One of those irregularities seems to have been *not* to support the musical dialogue between soloist and group, a staple feature of most concerto choreography. A curious result of this evasion is that our ears range around more than usual, trying to forge connections between movement and musical under-parts or memories. Again, in *Ein Herz*, made for the Paris Opera Ballet in 1990 and set to Bach's eponymous cantata (BWV 134, 1724), there are wonderfully buoyant rhythms, but unfortunately, this dance is an instance when Morris seems to have been led by musical structure at the expense of all else.

The outstanding music visualisation of this period is the short, nonsense trio *Pas de Poisson* (1990), for Baryshnikov, Penny Hutchinson and Morris himself. It is another choreomusical joke, using Satie's Entr'acte music for what was originally the surrealist René Clair's film within the ballet *Relâche* (Ballets Suédois, 1924). Morris choreographed to Darius Milhaud's desiccated piano reduction. The score itself is as mechanical and inexpressive as Satie could devise, with autonomous cells as ostinatos, each usually one-bar in length (2/4 or 4/4), and grouped into units of 8 or 4 bars. To visualise music like this means machine choreography, and so Morris sets the dancers in ridiculously repetitive motion, respecting meticulously the abrupt divisions between units as well as most of the recurrences of material. When the music gets stuck in a groove, which it often does, shunting forward and back between a pair of notes or chords, so does the choreography. The music encouraged Morris to exploit this device to an absurd degree. The score contains a quote from Chopin's Funeral March, originally intended to accompany a mock funeral on Clair's film—which prompts a stiff halting procession across the stage, each dancer in turn. When the music is reduced to the simplest series of oscillations, this is occasion for a series of silly walks. At one point, Morris breaks free to perform his own surrealism. To one rendition of the loud main theme, all three dancers commence a relay, passing rubber fish (as in *poisson*) from one to the other and out into the wings. If you want to visualise Satie, this is the way.

The Brahms setting of *Love Song Waltzes* (1989), sequel to *New Love Song Waltzes* (1982), also premiered during this period, alongside the *Wonderland* premiere. Together, opening with the earlier choreography, these two works framed the Schoenberg piece. (After *Wonderland* disappeared from the repertory, they have been programmed alone and, within the same performance, one after another.) The two Brahms pieces are quite different in spirit. *Love Song Waltzes* acknowledges a community with a more severe, formal style than the one inhabiting the earlier work. At the end of the dance, there are images of separation, a man compelled repeatedly to leave his circle of friends, and finally one who walks out, alone, a kind of death, Acocella suggests, while 'dance and the group are the image of life'.[45] But movement motifs and choreomusical procedures form a strong link between the two pieces, as if telling the story of a single community, except that it has grown less innocent. From one piece to the other, memories are carried of rhythm, accentuation, and a particular attitude to gravity conveying aspiration, tenderness and breathless excitement. There is again the lightness of feet, easing into waltz rhythm, flying in double time, or simply darting through the beat. We also see the accent 'up' a great deal, in simple *jetés*, sometimes creating hemiolas, sometimes supported in lifts, also in the striking airborne completion of a defiant jumping phrase. Exactly the same jumping phrase is introduced in both pieces, and in the same position, Waltz No. 11 (see p. 154). One of the main distinctions is the prevalence of waltz steps during the later work, the presence of the formal dance itself adhering to the familiar down, up, up bass accompaniment. No one has ever complained about this kind of music visualisation.

Perhaps, although Morris remained prolific during the Brussels period, the difficulties of working in that city prompted several dark pieces and extreme musical tactics in two of them: that is, not to celebrate pleasure in music. *Behemoth* was not like the vigorously angry dances of his earlier period; it was far more desolate. Although Morris revives it from time to time, as if willing us to view a difficult but essential part of his experience, he has never since made a piece in silence. As Macaulay put it:

> Surely not even Morris could make such a work again; it would be like recrossing the Styx for a second helping.[46]

Instead, and ever since his return to the US, music has remained central to Morris's practice, big, live, complex music that he has intensely interrogated and, far more often than in the past, without the help of words.

Period 3: 1992-2014

The period since 1992, when Morris returned to the USA from Brussels, occupies more than half his career, but I have chosen to concentrate here on the key developments in his approach to music, in other words, what is new choreomusically.

In Chapter 9, I explore the branch of Morris's work that is led by relatively conventional narrative, that is, pieces with plots and characters, his work in opera, and his treatment of two full-length ballet scores, *Sylvia* (2004) and *Romeo and Juliet* (2008). Much of this has taken Morris beyond the institutional boundaries of his own company into other organisations, although sometimes incorporating MMDG dancers. The work in opera leads naturally from the important series of earlier dances set to vocal music, culminating in the 'operatic' dimensions of *L'Allegro* and *Dido*. Morris directs opera more frequently during this period, playing a more dominant role in productions, sometimes without involvement of any dancers or specific development of choreography. But there are also several pieces for MMDG that are decidedly unconventional narrative treatments incorporating text. I cover these in Chapter 10: *Four Saints in Three Acts* (Thomson, 2000), *Bedtime* (Schubert, 1992) and *Socrates* (Satie, 2010).

Taking an overview of this period, it is noteworthy that the proportion of MMDG dances using text-based music has diminished, even more so since the millennium. Perhaps work in opera satisfies this need. Perhaps, with Morris now more insistent about working with live music, this is also because of the expense of including singers in the MMDG repertory, particularly touring with them. Yet there are still pieces that drive against the tide: Morris remains fearless in pushing hard against the style and spirit of dances that he has just made, even working on very different pieces simultaneously. For instance, surely no one would ever have expected him to come up with his wacky *A Wooden Tree* (2012), set to the recordings (not even live music this time) of the idiosyncratic Scottish poet-singer Ivor Cutler.

In Chapter 11, I progress to Morris's collaboration with the composer Lou Harrison and to a survey of the series of eight pieces to his music. These began with the 1987 *Strict Songs*, but were otherwise all created during the post-Brussels period and explored non-programmatic instrumental scores. The Harrison pieces include the one 'collaboration' from scratch *Rhymes with Silver* (1997) and the 'symphonic' *Grand Duo* (1993), one of Morris's most celebrated and popular works. I place the Harrison pieces within the context of other Morris work that synthesises sources beyond western culture.

Morris's use of large-scale, non-programmatic (and often multi-movement) 'symphonic' instrumental scores is characteristic of this later period. At this point, he engages in a more intense conversation with structure than ever before, in scores, for instance, by Bach, Beethoven, Ives, Mozart, Schumann and Villa-Lobos. Chapter 12 covers this other kind of work, while Chapter 13 focuses on an evening-length programme of multi-movement scores, two piano concertos framing a piano sonata, *Mozart Dances* (2006).

Selection means leaving out of discussion many important pieces from this period. It is essential to emphasise that Morris still frequently works with 'small' scores, including those that combine short numbers into a series or suite, sometimes formed by the composer (as in *Three Preludes* (1992), composed as a group by Gershwin), sometimes re-assembled by the choreographer (as in *Three Russian Preludes* (1995), selections by Morris from Preludes and Fugues by Shostakovich). Some of the smaller-scale scores, including those mentioned, follow in the piano ballet tradition, and two have the piano on stage next to the dancers: *Candleflowerdance* (Stravinsky, 2005) and *Peccadillos* (Satie, 2000, using toy piano). In *Sang-Froid* (2000), the Chopin ballet tradition inevitably springs to mind—for instance, of Michel Fokine's *Les Sylphides* (1908) and Jerome Robbins' *Dances at a Gathering* (1969) and *The Concert* (1956). But Morris favours an exceptionally rugged interpretation of Chopin and prefers to think of 'restoring, rescuing' him[1] rather than commenting on existing ballets.

As usual, it is not possible to divide Morris's work into neat compartments. There is always both tension and flow between narrative and structure, meaning and abstract values, in his work, and most of the analyses that follow address both, while trying to show the particular play between polarities that exists within each individual piece.

As before, selected clips of dances analysed can be found on the MMDG website: http://markmorrisdancegroup.org/jordanbookclips.

9

Big Stories: Operas and 'Ballets'

Glance at reviews of Morris's early opera direction and the word 'conservative' crops up on several occasions. To Morris, by the time of his 1996 setting of Gluck's *Orfeo ed Euridice* a choreographer with an international reputation, that was no bad thing. He assured an interviewer prior to the West Coast premiere of this opera:

> I don't think conservative means evil...I think it means that there aren't a lot of guns or waterfalls in this show or a helicopter landing... The piece is not very funny. It's very clear and simple. If that's what conservative means, hurrah.[1]

Once again, Morris was led by music, the large-scale opportunities of opera scores, not the lure of production values. Here too, as in his *Dido*, doing opera usually meant borrowing (without distortion) an existing, straight narrative of the kind that he had not hitherto used in his dance repertory. Yet, examining his work in opera, increasingly direction as well as choreography, we soon find him exploring the forces of both singers and dancers, particularly their integration on stage, in a distinctive manner. The works that I look at in most detail are *Orfeo*—Morris was involved in three different productions of it (1988, 1996 and 2007), and the score holds a particularly important position within the history of danced opera—followed by *Platée* (1997, Rameau), then *King Arthur* (2006, Purcell).

I also discuss his two 'straight-narrative' dances to ballet scores, following the precedent of *The Hard Nut* (1991). These are the three-act ballet *Sylvia* (2004) to the familiar score by the nineteenth-century composer Léo Delibes, created for San Francisco Ballet, and a modern dance setting (for MMDG) of the full-length *Romeo & Juliet, On Motifs of Shakespeare* (2008), which was partly a musicological enterprise, using the original, happy ending of Prokofiev's score.

The following list of Morris's opera work across his career sets his later productions within the context of his earlier work in the USA and Brussels. The list also indicates the involvement of MMDG within initial performances of these opera productions.

Salome (Richard Strauss), Choreographer (1986), Seattle Opera, Seattle (Morris choreographed Salome's Dance of the Seven Veils for Josephine Barstow)

Nixon in China (John Adams), Choreographer (1987), directed by Peter Sellars, Houston Grand Opera, Houston (Morris choreographed two pieces as parodies of the Chinese communist ballet *The Red Detachment of Women*, the Act 2 agitprop ballet and the Act 3 dream ballet for the hero and heroine)

Orpheus & Eurydice (Gluck), Choreographer (1988), directed by Stephen Wadsworth, Seattle Opera, with MMDG

Die Fledermaus (Johann Strauss), Director (1988), Seattle Opera (all dancing done by the singers)

Le Nozze di Figaro (Mozart), Choreographer (1988), directed by Peter Sellars, PepsiCo Summerfare, SUNY, Purchase (Morris choreographed the Act 3 fandango, in rock 'n' roll style)

Dido and Aeneas (Purcell), Director and Choreographer (1989), Théâtre Royal de la Monnaie, Brussels, with MMDG

The Death of Klinghoffer (John Adams), Choreographer (1991), directed by Peter Sellars, Théâtre Royal de la Monnaie, Brussels, with MMDG

Le Nozze di Figaro (Mozart), Director (1991), Théâtre Royal de la Monnaie, Brussels (including Spanish-style choreography for Penny Hutchinson in the Act 3 fandango)

Orfeo ed Euridice (Gluck), Director and Choreographer (1996), Handel and Haydn Society, Hancher Auditorium, Iowa City, with MMDG

Platée (Rameau), Director and Choreographer (1997), Royal Opera, Edinburgh Festival, with MMDG

The Capeman (Paul Simon), Choreographer (1998) [Broadway musical]

Four Saints in Three Acts (Virgil Thomson), Director and Choreographer (2000), English National Opera, London Coliseum, with MMDG

Idomeneo (Mozart), Choreographer (2003), Glyndebourne Festival Opera, with dancers Sonja Kostich and Hans-Georg Lenhart (Morris choreographed the Act III ballet)

King Arthur (Purcell), Director and Choreographer (2006), English National Opera, London Coliseum, with MMDG

Orfeo ed Euridice (Gluck), Director and Choreographer (2007), Metropolitan Opera, New York, with MMDG and additional dancers from the Metropolitan Opera Ballet

L'isola disabitata (Haydn), Director, Gotham Chamber Opera (2009), Morris's first opera without choreography, Gerald W. Lynch Theater, John Jay College

Rosencrantz & Guildenstern Are Dead (Herschel Garfein), Director (2009), excerpts from a new opera, James and Martha Duffy Performance Space, Mark Morris Dance Center

Opéras-minutes: La délivrance de Thesée, L'enlèvement d'Europe, L'abandon d'Ariane (Darius Milhaud), Director (2011), Tanglewood Music Center

Curlew River (Benjamin Britten), Director (2013), Tanglewood Music Center

Acis and Galatea (Handel, arr. Mozart), Director and Choreographer (2014), Cal Performances, Berkeley, with MMDG

Morris's career in opera began when he asked soprano Josephine Barstow to dance stripped down to a G-string in Seattle Opera's production of *Salome*

(1986). His first experience of direction came two years later with Johann Strauss's *Die Fledermaus,* which he staged in realist style. Then there was his choreography for Peter Sellars' two operas to new scores by John Adams. *Nixon in China,* the first, included a hilarious gun-toting parody of an agit-prop point-shoe ballet (*The Red Detachment of Women* (1964)). *Death of Klinghoffer* was about the hijacking of a passenger liner by the Palestine Liberation Front in 1985 and the resulting murder of a Jewish-American passenger. Here, the process was more collaborative, Morris being consulted on specifications before the musical score was completed:

> The piece is built like an oratorio, and Alice Goodman, the librettist, wrote the choruses specifically in the sort of mythical, monumental style that she, in her way, was basing on my treatment of *Dido and Aeneas.* She would check the writing for the choruses with me before she gave it to John, and then John would write them. The dances are big, block choruses...[2]

Then, after choreographing the fandango for Sellars' *Le Nozze di Figaro* in 1988, Morris went on to direct the whole opera himself, again in realist style. It was his final work in Brussels.

Morris was one of the first in a group of American modern dance choreographers to move into opera direction in recent years—among these Trisha Brown, Lucinda Childs, Martha Clarke and Joe Goode. Their opera settings have often been co-productions, the costs shared between American and European companies. To some extent, this move went hand in hand with the burgeoning interest in seventeenth- and eighteenth-century opera, in which a dance component was composed into the scores, and, in the case of the French operas of Lully or Rameau, present in almost every act or prologue.

Gluck's *Orfeo,* composed with a significant choreographic component in mind, has perhaps attracted the largest number of choreographer-directors over the years. They range from Gasparo Angiolini in the 1762 original, to Emile Jaques-Dalcroze (1913), George Balanchine (1936, a highly controversial production that closed after two performances), Frederick Ashton (1953), Pina Bausch (1975, revived Paris Opera, 2005), Martha Clarke (1997), Lucinda Childs (2002 and 2003), and Ashley Page (2015). Then there is Morris himself, twice (1996 and 2007), after choreographing the dances in a 1988 Seattle Opera production by Stephen Wadsworth.

Morris has often talked about the intimate connection between singers and dancers, all of them relying on their own bodies without any intervening instrument: 'They're both very, very vulnerable', he says (see p. 19).[3] Yet the handling of singers in opera raises a number of questions. Sometimes, choreographers choose to put all the singers in the pit, as did

Morris himself in *Dido* and *Four Saints*. The reasons may sometimes be to do with theatrical timing—it takes too long 'having a chorus trudging on and off all the time',[4] Morris once said. At other times, they are to do with getting singers to move with ease and fluency, although today's movement training for singers is better than it once was. Morris once claimed that too many of them are ruled by fear:

> They feel embarrassed physically around dancers. They're thrilled and intimidated by what my dancers can do, and suddenly they don't even know how to walk anymore.[5]

Also, singers, unlike dancers, have trouble with basic rhythm:

> ...they become so self-conscious on the stage that their rhythm goes away. You have to train them to walk on the beat. So, I focus on physical tempo and breathing. I have found that, with most of the mammals I work with, if they breathe, they can relax. [6]

Above all, he wants dancers and singers to do what they do best, and be comfortable:

> They sing, we dance...[7]

> With the dancers you can choose whether or not to do something, or to do it on whatever leg or whatever arm. The timing's usually prescribed.

> With the singers I make very specific moves and paths and then everything else is open. I set down milestones, musically, spatially, gesturally... But really what I want for them is to sing fabulously. Stand-and-sing never bothers me. I have no problem with that. You don't have to be lying on your face so I'll believe the situation. You don't believe the situation, you *understand* it.[8]

Morris also recognises that 'singers hate being given blockings in short bursts. They need to keep the musical line going, the text logical.'[9]

Given Morris's principal aesthetic aim of many years—to give full power to music, this 'conservative' approach is entirely logical. Yet, explaining Morris's methods for the 1996 *Orfeo*, the counter-tenor Michael Chance, who took the title role, observed that he still had to come to terms with an unusually dominant movement component:

> Mark's musical awareness is extraordinary. He choreographed certain aspects of the production very precisely; at other times he surprised me by saying, 'I want you here for this bit, there for that bit, and the rest is up to you.' He prescribed certain gestures, then I had to find a way of

performing that wasn't at odds with what the dancers were doing. The point was to find a synthesis that served the piece, while allowing dance to be the principal form, rather than merely bringing in a choreographer for the dance bits...I learnt a lot about freeing the body; I felt myself not being afraid to hold my arms in a dancery way.[10]

This manner of integration, while 'allowing dance to be the principal form' in the case of *Orfeo*, is unusual, if not entirely Morris's own. It was with the 1996 *Orfeo* that Morris moved away from a realist style of direction.

Orfeo ed Euridice

It is significant that the eighteenth-century *Orfeo* project was already steeped in the concept of integration. This is clear both from the aesthetic aims of the score and the history of the original Vienna production involving the librettist Ranieri de' Calzabigi and choreographer Gasparo Angiolini. *Orfeo* was an early example of reform opera, a radical shift away from the standard baroque formulae, especially the da Capo (ABA) aria—with its expectation of florid, virtuoso vocal decoration during the repeat—away from the unimaginative use of the orchestra, the continuo-only dry recitative, and the subjugation of drama and emotion to the whims of showy performers. (Yet *Orfeo* was still in Italian, the language of the dominant *opera seria* of the time.)

Musical sections in *Orfeo* are also far less clearly differentiated than they were previously, their forms less predictable, and all recitatives are accompanied over and above the continuo. In the words of the contemporary theorist Joachim Winckelmann, the late eighteenth-century ideal was that of 'a noble simplicity and a calm grandeur'.[11] Consider the striking and startling manner in which Orfeo is introduced during the first chorus: with merely three 'stony exclamations'[12] of his wife Euridice's name, like elemental screams.

One of the most notable features of the original 1762 production, and especially important for dance, was the role of the moving chorus, its frequent presence integral to *Orfeo* as a whole. Behind this, lay the principles of the ancient Greeks and their concept of dancing, gesturing choruses.[13] The *Orfeo* chorus gestured alongside their singing counterpart as well as performing several straight orchestral dances marked 'Ballo', including a group of these (in succession) when the happy ending of the story is celebrated. (As the opera's premiere was scheduled for the birthday of Emperor Francis I, the *Orfeo* collaborators felt compelled to have Amor return Euridice to her husband after her second death.)

There are two versions of Gluck's *Orfeo* score, and Morris had direct experience of both. A second version was made for Paris, premiered in 1774, with additional dances and many different textual details: it was for this version that Morris choreographed the dances in Seattle in 1988. At the time, Acocella described this Seattle production as postmodern:

> one of those up-to-date productions where Orpheus and Eurydice have a nice apartment with Danish modern furniture, and Orpheus goes down to the underworld in a Burberry raincoat. At the same time it is, in the postmodern way, a historically learned production, with Cupid descending from the flies on a magnificent cloud machine just such as might have flown him to the stage in Gluck's original, 1774 production: fluffy cumuli supporting a white silk chaise on which the love god reclines serenely.[14]

She also applied this opposition to the dancers in the concluding chaconne, with its prescribed patterns and manners, alluding to both past and present again and, by drawing attention to representation ('arthood' and 'madeness'), refreshing our perceptions of both periods.

> By comparison with *vernacular* modernity (the T-shirts, the hop-kicks), we see its [the chaconne] high tone, its artificiality. And so we have the postmodern experience: the retrieval, the juxtaposition, the irony, the experience of distance, the meditation on representation.[15]

Morris, however, preferred the leaner original Gluck *Orfeo*, happily dispensing with some of the most well-known music from the later score, the long Dance of the Furies (which occurs between the two underworlds) and The Dance of the Blessed Spirits. He once described the Paris version of the Blessed Spirits as 'padded and simpering'.[16]

The 1996 *Orfeo* was a collaboration with the Boston-based Handel and Haydn Society, conducted by Christopher Hogwood. It used early instruments such as cornets and chalumeaux (which have been replaced today by oboes and clarinets), but no harpsichord continuo, and as far as is known, matched the number of performers (singers and instrumentalists) who took part in 1762.[17] It was performed with two intervals, all three Acts separated. In 2007, at the Metropolitan Opera, modern-day instruments were used, and Morris and his conductor James Levine, Music Director at the Met, decided to play the entire ninety-minute opera without any interval. Lorraine Hunt-Lieberson had been cast as Orfeo in this production, following the practice of using female singers in the part (originally sung by a castrato), but she died before the production was created. So David Daniels took the role of Orfeo and subsequently Stephanie Blythe, who featured in the Live from Lincoln Center broadcast of 2009.

Morris created the 1996 version in what he called his 'Arcadian' manner, the choreography similar to the barefoot Duncan-balletic movement in *L'Allegro*, but incorporating a kind of Ausdruckstanz (German modern dance) style for the Furies. The performers were dressed accordingly in soft, flowing robes and tunics, while the set consisted of mobile, see-through curtains. Morris's design team, by now regular collaborators, were Martin Pakledinaz (costumes), Adrianne Lobel (sets), and Michael Chybowski (lighting).[18] The Handel and Haydn chorus, in black evening dress, stood on banks of steps, or risers, on either side of the stage, operating in the manner of 'modern-day witnesses'.[19]

In 2007, the singing chorus played a far more dominant role than in 1996, often arranged centrally to face the audience directly, 100-strong and consequently able to produce very high volume. They sat or stood on two three-storey high constructions (designed by Allen Moyer) that could swing to different angles, turn around to reveal a rocky staircase from hell, or, set side by side, form a kind of amphitheatre behind an intimate stage area below. They now took on the role of witnesses to history, in period costume, as opposed to the three soloists and dancing chorus in modern dress (and shoes). (Costumes were by the fashion designer Isaac Mizrahi.) You could spot any number of characters from the past: like Truman Capote, Hiawatha, Louis XIV, Marie Curie, Liberace, the two Queen Elizabeths, Mahatma Gandhi, Abraham Lincoln, Jimi Hendrix, Benjamin Franklin, and Princess Diana. Morris explains that the idea of historical figures came from the 'heaven' figures in the 1946 Michael Powell and Emeric Pressburger film *A Matter of Life and Death* (*Stairway to Heaven*).[20]

Again, in both productions, Morris demonstrated a penchant for crossing historical periods and cultural forms. In 1996, this was relatively easy-going, not as obvious or combative as in many other narrative works. Morris tells us that his choreographic style was 'Greek in the way that early modern dance was Greek...but also relates to the neoclassicism of the 18th century that this opera typifies, and to Greco-Roman numbers in movies, like the water-nymph ballet in *Goldwyn Follies* [1938] with Vera Zorina [wife of its choreographer Balanchine].' Pakledinaz adds that the curtains were 'like the big white sets from 1930s movies, where a drape can become a column'.[21]

Morris explains that

> the dance numbers are always in the context of what's being sung. It's not 'and now, time for another dance number'. The choreography comes in and out of the singing naturally.[22]

A continuum of movement style is evident across different types of music—

accompanied recitative, aria, chorus, ballo—edging more or less towards formality and symmetry at one end, at the other, towards asymmetry and individual moments of improvisation. A number of reviewers at the time noted the special mobility within the big duet between Orfeo and Euridice in Act 3, using the space behind and in front of the curtain, pulling both protagonists close together and separating them across the full width of the stage. (This section, covering their journey up from the underworld, is especially weak in the 2007 production, when they spend almost half an hour barely moving and masked by the set from the waist downwards.) Also memorable, in Act 2, when Orfeo starts his process of placating the Furies, asking for their mercy, Morris got Chance to move with them, on the beat: swaying in determined big strides from side to side—playing his lyre, in mime, at the same time.

It is the gestural behaviour of the singers, developing from Morris's earlier work, which is most telling. In Act 1, with no dancers on stage, Morris cleverly extended the narrative within Amor's aria of warning and advice 'Gli sguardi trattieni'. This aria, as the translation demonstrates, is constructed from alternating slow and fast sections—A B A B A1 B1 (the final repeats abbreviated):

Gli sguardi trattieni, affrena gli accenti, rammenta, se peni, che pochi momenti hai più da penar.
Non sai che talora smarriti, tremanti con chi gl'innamora son ciechi gli amanti, non sanno parlar.
Slow (A):
Deny her your glances without explanation.
But let this console you.
In only a moment your torment will end.
Fast (B):
Remember, a lover in his confusion often seems blind and unable to speak.[23]

To the slow music, he set sign (or mime) language with the hands, which we read as speech. The quick tempo sections are freer from the words, an opportunity for Amor to show her impatience as she shifts around Orfeo, mocking, pushing and pinching him. (She is a jolly, vaudevillian character, perhaps the only touch of irony in this production, although her intrusive presence helps to make more sense of the absurd happy ending.) Most intriguing, however, Morris turned this highly repetitive aria into a narrative of progressive learning, Amor first miming while Orfeo watches her, then teaching Orfeo to perform her gestures, until finally he does them on his own. At this point, Orfeo is on his way, ready to claim his wife. In the 2007 production, Amor and Orfeo are far less active.

The section of the 1996 *Orfeo* singled out for most praise was the 'Echo' aria in Act 1—'Chiamo il mio ben così'—when Orfeo stands on the risers upstage right and a dancer (Joe Bowie) echoes his gestures opposite him, from the left. The twinning of singer and dancer onstage may have been prompted by Peter Sellars' earlier directorial practice in *The Death of Klinghoffer*,[24] but here, the score prompts the echo structure, its haunting feature being the quiet repetition throughout of short vocal fragments by an offstage orchestra (strings and chalumeaux). There are three song verses, all referring to Orfeo's mourning for Euridice and need for her response: first, there is none, then, in the second verse, the Echo responds, and finally, so does the river, murmuring as it passes by. Each verse closes with a series of repeated phrases ending with the word '*risponde*', and between each verse is a recitative. Chance likened the dancer's choreography to an 'extended riff' on his own singing, showing the two sides of Orfeo, 'the public and the private'.[25]

At the start, Chance and Bowie work in unison, Chance offering a rather freer account as he allows his vocal expression to nuance his movement. The words are:

Chiamo il mio ben così, Quando si mostra il dì, Quando s'asconde.
Ma oh vano mio dolor! L'idolo del mio cor, Non mi risponde.
Thus do I call my love when day reveals itself and when it disappears.
And yet I mourn in vain the idol of my heart who gives me no answer.

Several of the words are treated like mime, such as 'call'—one arm raised; 'my heart'—holding the hands at the heart; 'day reveals' and later 'hides its face'—an arm opened upwards, an arm lowered. Other dance words are understood through association, like 'my love' and 'Euridice', which are always visualised by one arm extended sideways, the other bent across the front of the body. Her name and image are invoked so frequently, you very quickly learn the meaning of this position.

Soon Bowie starts to go his own way, and to the '*risponde*' phrases, turns around, circling his arms vigorously over his head, finally drawing his clasped hands downwards. Soon too, he starts to face different directions, introducing his own full-body movement, varying speed, bursting into the central stage space, and descending to the floor. Some of his echoes are literal, his movement repeating what Chance did to the same music, but not all, and he is totally absent during one echo, having swept out like the wind mentioned in the text. During this aria, he constantly passes in and

Orfeo ed Euridice, Echo aria, Joe Bowie. © Dan Rest, 1996

out of vision, sometimes like a sympathetic, comforting companion, yet also magical, untamed—uncontainable.

Occasionally, Bowie illustrates Chance's text—and understanding the Italian enriches your experience—the flat expanse of a seashore, a tree in a forest, carving a message to Euridice on the bark of a tree, Orfeo playing the lyre at the mention of his name, and finally, the murmuring river. The song concludes with both in unison again, arms outstretched, as if recognising the positive response of the river. Finally, however, the Echo has to leave for good, and Orfeo gazes after him in dismay.

The twinning structure in the Echo aria relates to Morris's previous practice of linking singer and dancer in *Dido* (see p. 121). Now, with the presence on stage of both singer and dancer, both choreographed to underline musical and textual detail, you might sense an even greater pressure and urgency of bonding forces, even something of the oppressive effect of the early 'angry dances' (pp. 154-60).

By contrast, Morris's treatment of the Echo aria in 2007 seems more reined in, restrained by the strophic structures and musical repetition. On the tiers behind, to each echo, it is the chorus here who make small hand gestures, in unison, the same gestures for each verse. Indeed, the ownership of gesture is one of the main distinctions between the 1996 and 2007 productions. In the later one, the solo singers gesture very little, instead, matching arm movements indicate sympathetic connections between the singing chorus and those who dance. And the chorus are sometimes fearsome, shouting Furies, looming over those below, reaching out to them with big, sharp arm gestures, even slamming their hands noisily on to the hand-rails. Always, stylised gestures happen precisely *on* the musical rhythm.

In the 2007 production, unlike in 1996, the final group of celebratory dances represent major transformation, the monochrome range of costume colour from black to grey to white suddenly exploding into every bright colour imaginable. These dances are amongst the most beautiful, musically-interesting group dances of a social, celebratory kind that Morris ever made.[26] The choreography is essentially the same as in 1996, but modified to emphasise the reality of social dance, in couples, foursomes and circles. Morris adds a series of chair lifts at one point, when one dancer suddenly emerges aloft between two colleagues: a surprising, brilliant introduction of the vertical dimension.

Although the Gluck score only carries tempo indications, the music of the dances clearly represents French archetypes: minuet, contredanse en rondeau, musette and chaconne.[27] Morris introduces any number of rhythmic gems: displaced accents; selected musical motifs pulled out for emphasis; unaccented, easy leg lifts on accented downbeats; two against three (in metre). Especially impressive are the vigorous gestures of arms and legs—filled with air—on the characteristic double-upbeat of the final chaconne, not to mention how Morris develops a dance from very little material (the contredanse especially), varying his deployment of dancers with effortless virtuosity when the music is impossibly repetitive.

There are also many dances in Morris's productions of Rameau's *Platée* (1745) and Purcell's *King Arthur* (1691). Here, MMDG joined forces with the Royal Opera, Covent Garden and English National Opera, in 1997 and 2006 respectively. For both too, Morris choreographed to sung as well as orchestral numbers. Yet these productions are very different from *Orfeo*, each, in its own way, far more anarchic. They also take the device of integration of singers and dancers even further. *Platée* is a comédie-lyrique (subtitled 'ballet bouffon') about an ugly, vain and desperately ambitious swamp nymph who believes mistakenly that the god Jupiter wants to marry her. *King Arthur* is a semi-opera about English mythology and patriotism.

As for the rampant misbehaviour, perhaps it is significant that both these operas involved collaboration with Mizrahi. (Lobel was the set designer again.) Morris was clearly stimulated by Mizrahi's appetite for making giddy, sometimes wildly clashing, associations between the baroque opera project and the popular culture of films, musicals and fashion ('Neo-baroque' aesthetics (see p. 160) crossing with postmodernism). So these pieces find Morris at his most ambitious referentially. His working procedure was to get his collaborators to listen to the music, then develop ideas of their own for sharing, and he was persuaded by wild ideas. When, for instance, in *King Arthur*, after the storm scene, Mizrahi suggested having a parade of pantomime animals—a giraffe, duck, bear, flamingo and cheetah (after all, animals do come out from shelter after storms)—Morris's immediate thought was to scrap the idea. Nothing in the score or text suggested it. But somehow, the animals never went away.[28]

In the UK, modern instruments accompanied both the *Platée* and *King Arthur* productions, but when they reached Berkeley, California, conductor Nicholas McGegan brought to them the period sound of the Philharmonia Baroque Orchestra.

Platée

The 1997 production of the little-known *Platée* proved an immediate success. It begins with a Prologue, a Bacchanale within a big-city bar, mixing characters you might just expect to find—a secretary, painter, dyke (in a man's suit), baroness, sailor, showgirl (in full silver regalia) and policeman—and some you would not—like Bacchus the god of wine, Thespis and Thalie, the inventor and muse of comedy, Momus, personification of sarcasm, L'Amour, god of love, and a mere satyr. But, Morris suggests: 'Nothing surprises you at three o'clock in the morning in Hell's Kitchen in New York.'[29] Nor, therefore, should the mix of movement vocabulary, as the various characters show what they do best, fragments of Charleston, hornpipe, rock 'n' roll, high kicking, shimmying, while a loose ballet style eventually brings them all together. After a discussion about marital infidelities, including the story of Junon's jealousy of Jupiter, the drunken party ends up, as Morris puts it in his programme synopsis, singing about 'putting on a new kind of show'. Cue a spot-light on the bar's terrarium, which then expands into a full stage set: a swamp lush with dank vegetation and a water dish as pond feature. Now, the story proper begins, the first of three Acts.

The nymph Platée is clearly self-deluded, awaiting kings and gods to fall in love with her. Meanwhile, arriving at her swamp from the heavens (in a 'baroque-ist' flying-machine), Mercury hatches a plot to teach the jealous Junon a lesson, by getting Jupiter to pretend to fall in love with Platée. Just as their marriage is about to take place, Junon arrives on the scene, realises the joke, reunites with Jupiter, whereupon Platée is banished back to her swamp. Extraordinary as it may seem, the original score was written to honour the marriage of the Dauphin Louis of France to the homely Princess Maria Teresa of Spain. For Rameau was clearly writing a satire, a cruel story about an ugly woman, while at the same time ridiculing an assortment of other characters—satyrs, gods, mortals, Graces, philosophers and babies who dance—*fous gais* and *fous tristes*—as well as royalty, and perhaps even us too.

In Morris's production at least, it is the creatures who probably fare best, those that inhabit the swamp and observe from it what goes on. It literally throbs with life—listed in the programme as Cockatiel, Lizard, Alligator, Peacock, Frog, Toad, Blue Jay, Duck, Firebird, pair of Snakes, Robin, Tortoises, and four Feathered Birds. (Morris and dancers had all watched, as preparation, *Microcosmos*, the 1996 documentary about insect behaviour.[30]) Most of the time, these creatures function within character, lurching, crawling, twitching or beating their arms like wings. Morris explains how they arrived at the detail:

> I would choreograph a basic sort of thing and each person, based on his or her animal, would dance it in a different way. The duck person moves like a duck and the turtles move like turtles... Even if it's all the same material, everybody does it in a different way.[31]

Character distinctions are also highlighted by the many changes of role, creatures in unitards transformed by masks and carapaces, Thespis (originally Mark Padmore) becoming Mercury after the Prologue, and all the dancers of the Prologue demoted (or promoted, depending how you look at it) to swamp kingdom. This goes hand in hand with a huge diversity of costume and image. First, there is the extraordinary, powerful presence of Platée herself, played by the literally tiny high tenor (*haute-contre*) Jean-Paul Fouchécourt. Mizrahi makes her a slimy green, web-footed dowager, kitted out with pearls and a lorgnette (inspired by Margaret Dumont of the Marx Brothers' films), with pendulous breasts, protruding paunch and long, long, knob-ended fingers that wag at unsuspecting males. Further examples of clash of reference and colour are Padmore (as Mercury), dressed in yachting blazer and slacks, Junon and Jupiter in Christmas-red velvet and cheap gilt crowns—as 'Eurotrash royalty', suggests Mizrahi,[32] L'Amour in a pink dressing-gown and Iris the rainbow goddess (who appears after a storm) as a human disco-ball in a hooded unitard covered in mirrors. (*Platée* takes the cacophony of characters in *The Hard Nut* into a new dimension.)

The choreography (segueing into opera direction) continues this theme of misrule, for even though dancers sometimes match each other within groups or sub-groups, the *Platée* style is predominantly asymmetrical and unpredictable, with dancers clustering into odd formations, facing different directions, or splintering off to interrupt your vision from the sidelines. Nothing lasts for long, nor does it in Rameau's score: the construction is fragmentary, like a raw mosaic. Wendy Lesser writes persuasively on the theme of a 'show' with rough edges and open seams:

> There is an endearing kind of amateurishness...a purposeful, rehearsed, precision-designed, spectacularly skilled, but nonethess effective tone of artlessness. It is the 'Let's put on a show' quality of old Judy Garland-Mickey Rooney movies...and it is also the elegant amateurishness of a palace production done for a coterie of friends and relatives.[33]

Most important of all, the participants form 'a whole world'.[34] Out of so much difference, whatever they wear or however they move, everyone begins to look as odd—or not odd—as everyone else, and consequently equally acceptable. Singers and dancers alike, they all muddle along together. 'This is a show about inter-species dating', says Morris.[35] The style is very different from Morris's 1996 and 2007 *Orfeo* productions where, despite occasional matching gestures, dancers and singers tend to keep within their own spaces. In *Platée*, where such gestural duplication only operates in the Prologue, and much more informally, the protagonists spill over into each other's territories, mingling freely, often illegibly, and spreading further still into the

Platée, Act 2. showing Graces, satyrs. La Folie, King Cithéron, Platée (Jean-Paul Fouchécourt) and birds. © Bill Cooper, 1997

encroaching swamp. The treatment by Morris and his collaborators widens the referential base of the satirical score. In the Prologue, we recognise immediately that the production speaks of our own urban culture as much as of the eighteenth century and Greek mythology, and then, within the main body of the opera, we are introduced to an exotic fantasy world.

Morris affirms the score's own wacky modernity. In Act 2, when Platée meets Jupiter disguised as an owl, four masked birds, each carrying a pair of giant feathers, clap them together in furious self-defence. They make five big accents, to the most extraordinary wall of dissonance. Graham Sadler describes this 'charivari' of frightened birds in the score as 'a Messiaen-like realism'.[36] Earlier, in Act 1, we hear the strange rumbling of strings as 'croaking' (visualised by the frog, toad, lizard and alligator) pitted against the two-note exclamations of cuckoos (danced by the blue jay, peacock, robin and, flitting independently, the firebird, but no cuckoo). Here is an example of different species sharing the same move—a pattern of three steps—but treating it differently, taking it into a spread-legged waddle or high on to the toes. To the cuckoo call, the dancers lower their arms and cross their wrists (as in *Swan Lake*) or replicate the beating of wings (as in *The Firebird*). Sometimes this coincides with what you hear, sometimes it appears as anticipation or echo.

Visualisation of music introduces temporary clarity to such wild proceedings. In Act 1, the creatures identify with the clipped phrases of the first passepied (a baroque dance form). This is the closest to mickey-mousing that Morris gets in this opera. The birds tend to show the beat immaculately with their feet, while the heads and torsos of other creatures swing to the musical gestures. Sudden moments of visualisation also turn into points of emphasis. In the Prologue, the showgirl does a flirtatious shoulder shimmy, and then the others join in with their hips too. This stands out to the chattering repeating notes in Rameau's second rigaudon, another of his devices for humour, and especially silly within this competitive, drunken 'cabaret'. A further device is the exaggeratedly wide melodic skip: up, then down, an octave regularly 'catching' a galumphing jump.

But the funniest visualisation is when the two turtles copulate to the four thick, sustained chords that open the second half of a minuet (No. 2 in Act 2). They show you each chord, but alternate with and against the stepwise rising pitch: up (in), down (out), up (in), down (out).

Naturally, the absurdity of their motion—their shells negotiated with difficulty—and the accuracy of their timing with the score, draws our attention away from the two snakes (trailing long tails of wire-framed cloth behind them) out front. This is the moment you remember most. Nearly all the critics wrote about it.

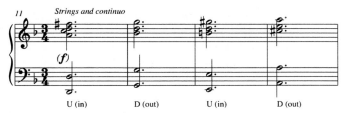

Ex. 9.1 *Platée*, Rameau, Act 2, Minuet 2.

As at the end of *Orfeo*, Morris knows how to handle a heavy dose of musical repetition, and no better than in the big chaconne in Act 3, intended to delay Jupiter's wedding to Platée. 'Mercury and Jupiter make a long dance longer', writes Morris in his programme synopsis. It lasts 232 bars, more than a third of which is sheer repetition, and most of it blocked in steady 8-bar units. Morris divides the dance into three sections. First, there is a series of entries, six in all, across the stage—starting with two frogs, including three Graces, four satyrs, and ending with the four feathered birds. Then the whole group appears all over again, in rather less orderly fashion, descending from a hillock upstage. Finally, everyone, including Jupiter and Mercury, joins in a big circle dance.

But that is not all. In the same chaconne, Morris has devised different steps with different 3/4 rhythms for each set of characters. The first two entries are an example. The frogs start arm in arm on the chaconne upbeat (beat 3), but then weight the musical downbeat with a marked step on the heel, as if they have started a kind of 3-beat, down-up-up *balancé*, but shifted the accent from first to second step to match the musical accentuation. We are immediately surprised. But when the three 'Greek' Graces give us the normal, waltz-rhythm down (accent)-up-up, we can relax. Bringing up the rear and moving in separate directions, the four feathered friends surprise us again with a high-stepping pattern that includes a syncopation and halt on the second beat of the bar. (You might also notice a delinquent at the back dropping out at one point to do his own thing.) During this tedious dance, another Rameau joke, Morris keeps our attention by showing us different personalities organised differently within the stage space, varying their material, getting them to share their steps in the big circle, *and* keeping us rhythmically alert.

Platée too engages physically with the music—Fouchécourt is wonderfully curious and lively in the role. So, when Jupiter plays the joke on her (the pretend marriage proposal), arriving first in the form of an ass, she prances alongside him with considerable agility. When he turns into an owl, she literally leads him a merry dance, gliding, galloping and bobbing in time. As an onlooker, she likes to tap or smack her flippers on the floor. Typically, critics found her light and dancerly and, largely because of her movement skill, both dignified and fun. By the end, they inevitably felt sorry to see her downfall: Lesser calls the dénouement 'horrifying'.[37] It is also a musical moment, ironically through absence: a rest that is a signal of abandonment, the only absolute silence in the entire production. Here, Platée leaps from the water dish, lands on the floor with a heavy thud, and rushes offstage. When the jolly wedding music picks up again, she returns, naked, and to the swamp. But this is also sport. Indeed, as Lesser points out, Platée is a major source of ambiguity in this production. We recognise how easily our feelings are buffeted about, even to the extent that we accept cruelty, while not taking the story, or ourselves, too seriously.

When the British critic Jann Parry asked Morris whether singers or dancers would dominate his production—he simply replied: 'Platée—it's her show'.[38] It is—and she is both. Yet, as the score itself indicates, there is an unusual degree of integration and slippage between performance modes in this opera. As well as Platée, the other singers enjoy an easy, ranging mobility, and no one more than the drunken Thespis (Padmore) in the Prologue. Meanwhile, Morris's dancers, who are used to singing in rehearsal as a matter of course (see p. 73), find themselves lip-synching during the chorus that ends the bar-scene. When they become creatures, they continue to have a voice. Rameau's orchestra deftly paints the kinds of sounds they should make, while sometimes they seem actually to be 'sung' by the chorus in the pit. Indeed, such is the catch-all style of the production that, as animals and birds, they soon seem no less strange to us than their human colleagues.

King Arthur

In some respects, *King Arthur*, another collaboration with Mizrahi and Lobel, is even more messy and wayward than *Platée*. Again, it appears to be about 'putting on a show', but here, in the postmodern manner of distancing, we see the act behind the show—the rehearsal and scene backstage. A dancer (dressed as a technician) walks towards a semi-circle of chairs downstage at the start, removes a standard lamp and walks off. Then we are in a working studio, the set looking a little like a school auditorium, a little like castle walls (Arthur's castle) and the props like *objets trouvés*. 'What would be around if you were putting on a show', Morris says. 'When you rehearse, you use chairs and apple crates.'[39] The costumes—and there are many changes—juxtapose contemporary shorts, jeans and military camouflage with period plumed helmets, breast plates and ruff collars. They include odd concoctions like a gold lamé jacket topped by aviator goggles. As well as the animals after the storm, a ballerina strays in as if from *Giselle*—

or, Morris says, like 'a visiting artist'—in pointe shoes, long tutu and ballet jumper, later joining up with her cavalier in tights.[40]

Morris's programme note as director was very simple:

King Arthur is here presented as a pageant—a sort of vaudeville—a sequence of production numbers sacred and profane, small and large, sad and happy, sung and danced.
I chose to discard the spoken text (which I don't like) and keep all of the music (which I do).
The setting is the stage. The time is now. The performers are themselves.

The layout of Acts in terms of 'story' information, including Morris's own programme subtitles (in italics) is as follows:

—Act 1 (*Scene 1: Ritual Sacrifice; Scene 2: Off-stage Battle*): a call to battle, between Arthur's Britons and the Saxons.

—Acts 2, 3 and 4 (*Act 2, Scene 1: The Chase; Scene 2: A Pastoral; Act 3, What Love Does; Act 4, Scene 1: Double Seduction; Scene 2: Love's Lesson*): pastoral in kind, while celebrating love and sex, featuring shepherds and shepherdesses, Cupid awakening the Cold Genius of winter, and two seductive river sprites.

—Act 5 (*Fairest Isle*): the storm and menagerie, Venus singing the famous 'Fairest Isle' from an 'island' (a rostrum centre stage), and all kinds of jollity including a maypole dance and rousing verses:
We'll toss off our ale till we cannot stand...
And heigh for the honour of old England.

The director's note indicates a significant difference in procedure from *Platée*. For Morris created his own large form or score for *King Arthur*, just as he had in *L'Allegro*, except that here, in this semi-opera mixing speech with music, he simply got rid of all the speech. He ejected the central Dryden story about the many exploits of Arthur struggling against the Saxon Oswald to regain his blind beloved Emmeline and reunite the British kingdom. Morris's *Arthur* is merely a crown moved around on stage between different scenes. So we have the non-linear narrative of a pageant, a series of discrete Acts, lots of different things going on within each Act, and non-stop music. Reducing the time-length from over four hours to just under two, this was a very bold re-shaping, and it is likely that some people were disturbed to see Dryden (and Arthur) treated so ignominiously. It was also the outcome of over a decade of struggle to set *King Arthur*, during which time Morris had toyed with, and rejected, various options, such as including speaking actors for a portion of the text, and introducing film.

Once Morris had made his decision to drop Dryden, he asked the conductor Jane Glover to assist him with musical matters. 'Jane and I auditioned all of the principal singers and assigned the orchestral lines together,' says Morris, 'which instruments play treble, which play which wind parts'.[41] They also made decisions about repeat schemes and re-locating certain sections of music. Sometimes decisions were based on practicality, the need, for instance, to add music for scene or costume changes. Or, in order to end with a song in praise of the English patron St George, they placed the traditional chaconne finale (for the maypole dance) just in front of it.[42]

Morris continued his close work with singers on their movement, sometimes borrowing their own ideas, sometimes choreographing them alongside the dancers. A passage mentioned in nearly every review was the 'Frost Scene' involving the Cold Genius (Act 4), a role for the bass-baritone Andrew Foster-Williams, in which he emerges, grey-suited, from a domestic refrigerator. First, Cupid opens the top compartment and we see his head and staring eyes, next she opens the bottom part and we see only his frozen crumpled body. Then to a faltering, shivering, ascending chromatic line charged with dissonant harmonies, he complains:

What power art thou, who from below
Hast made me rise unwillingly and slow
From beds of everlasting snow?

Cold Genius slides out of his prison and embarks on a creaky walk, but it is his hands in white gloves that now become the focus of attention: fingers spread awkwardly, the third protruding. Foster-Williams came up with the idea: 'And the reason it looks the way it does is because I'm double-jointed.'[43] His unforgettable image enlarges the conflict between humour and pathos already embedded in the music.

Who too can forget the men's trio 'For folded flocks' (Act 5)? Morris turned the number into a play on words: a ritual of methodically folding woollen blankets (the flocks) from out of a laundry basket, by collar-and-tie stockbroker types who would not normally be seen doing this kind of housework. The understated absurdity and gentle, un-phrased movement of the task are compelling. Morris's great punch-line is when all three proclaim 'The British wool is growing gold', and stand proudly before us, with plaid blankets flung Scottish-style over their shoulders.

Elsewhere, Morris frequently gets soloists to mime sung words, while their gestures are duplicated simultaneously by a group of dancers. The air 'Fairest Isle' (Act 5) is an example, where Venus is aloft upon a central rostrum surrounded by the female dancers. During one number, the

King Arthur, Act 5, 'Fairest Isle', Mhairi Lawson as Venus. © Peter Da Silva, 2006

passacaglia 'How happy the lover' (Act 4), all seven soloists sing and gesture from the rostrum while a big circle of dancers augment their movement. (Dancers also embody the words of the singing chorus in the pit.) This device takes us back to *Orfeo*, particularly the Echo aria (a visual duet), but here it has a much larger formal presence. Unusually, too, the dancers join in with real singing, during the morris dance 'Your hay it is mow'd' and, in full SATB, the final 'Saint George'.

Amongst the formal dances, some are especially memorable because of what Morris does with rhythm. One is the dance that starts Act 2 with two women, adding more couples as it progresses. This is set to a parallel additive musical arrangement, an orchestral ritornello moving into the solo and then chorus 'How blest are shepherds'. The choreography is striking in showing rhythm through the hands, which creates a rare quality of rhythmic event: partners touching, pushing off each other gently, or simply using hands to initiate a phrase. Morris uses both the basic 3/4 metre and the occasional counter-suggestions of 2/4 (in the melody line of the opening bar, for instance (see pp. 246-7)). But he also introduces subtle dialogue, with gentle stresses occurring at different times, the slightest hint of music and dance syncopating against each other. This is definitely not blatant music visualisation.

In the 3/4 maypole dance of Act 5, an outer circle of men step out the rhythm '3 and 1' while an inner circle of women do '1 and 2'. This is followed by jumping runs in 2/4 metre with the accent of landing on every other beat, and sometimes adjacent dancers operating in canon at one beat, creating alternating accents. Always, you can enjoy the ease with which the dancers swing up and down and around each other. Maypole dances always look good—observing the ribbon patterns emerging and transforming into others, the scheme working itself out, is already directly appealing—and this example is one of the best. Audiences always roar with approval at the end.

In *King Arthur* as a whole, however, the progress of ideas, both staging and choreography, is relatively slow for Morris, and the dances far more repetitious, far less adventurous, than when he is at his best. A lot of the time too, we cannot be sure what is going on and why. You might decide, however, that with the programme and surtitles, a pageant-style theatrical event like this makes a virtue of its confusion. You can after all make up your own story or stories. Themes of love and tenderness become more important by the end, for instance, even through the lens of silly patriotism and Merrie England. Double-sidedness is evident yet again. 'As always with Morris's irony,' wrote Lesser, 'there is a kind of longing for those naïve feelings lying side-by-side with the criticism and mockery.'[44]

On several occasions since *King Arthur*, Morris has directed straight narrative opera without incorporating dance or dancers. This is a logical step, for a constant throughout his work has been to allow power to music, even to show that it does not always need choreography. He is also interested in people on stage looking like people. Given the right material, singers without the overlay of dance training can move very well. So Morris did not hesitate when Herschel Garfein asked him to workshop sample sections from his new opera *Rosencrantz & Guildenstern Are Dead* (2009), based on the play by Tom Stoppard. Involving five singers/characters, the excerpts were shown at Morris's own James and Martha Duffy Performance Space at the top of the Mark Morris Dance Center. For New York's Gotham Chamber Opera he chose Haydn's *L'isola disabitata* (2009), a tale of two women lost on a desert island and eventually united with their lovers. This was a very physical production in any case—with running, falling, rolling and simulation of sex—all the action taking place on a bare-rock island. The movement component became increasingly prominent, so that by the end, Morris introduced his favourite big-gesture style, a signal of happiness and extroversion, with choreographed phrases specific to each character presented, then shared when they all sing together.

During this post-Brussels period, Morris also undertook two full-length settings of ballet scores, *Sylvia* (2004) and *Romeo and Juliet* (2008).[45] Of these, *Sylvia* was set as an actual ballet, for San Francisco Ballet, the classical company with which Morris has worked most regularly.

Sylvia

The score by Léo Delibes is regarded as one of the finest written for ballet during the nineteenth century, and fellow ballet composer Tchaikovsky was a big fan. 'It is the first ballet', he enthused:

> in which the music constitutes not just the main but the only interest. What charm and elegance, what riches in the melody, the rhythm, the harmony. I was ashamed. If I had known this music before, I would not have written *Swan Lake*.[46]

Yet it is often considered that the 1876 score suffers from problems of dramatic drive and a rather silly plot. As was typical in the nineteenth century, Delibes constructed it (for premiere at the Paris Opera) according to the instructions of the original choreographer Louis Mérante. He followed his plan of three acts, each divided into mime sections alternating with dance and with time lengths mapped out. The plot was based on a sixteenth-century mythologically-inspired pastoral play by Torquato Tasso. Sylvia, a nymph of the goddess Diana, is sworn to chastity, so when she is pursued by Aminta, a shepherd in love with her, she kills him with her hunting arrow. The god Eros then pierces her heart with an arrow, prompting her to fall in love with Aminta. Eros then brings him back to life. Meanwhile, the evil hunter Orion has abducted Sylvia. Eros intervenes again, helping her to escape and bringing the lovers together. There is one final hurdle: Diana tries to prevent the marriage, but is reconciled once Eros has reminded her of her own earlier affair with the shepherd Endymion. General rejoicing.

Convinced that the love theme was still relevant in the twenty-first century, Morris also spotted feminist and community values in the story.

> It's not that Sylvia's tamed, it's that she falls in love with somebody who's in love with her...[47]
>
> Act I is about an all-female society, Act II is an all-male society, and Act III is a fully realised community. The humans win.[48]

His Sylvia is also feisty and modern: she literally steps outside of the classical mould, with feet turned parallel and firmly on the ground when she is not dancing.

Morris had never seen any other *Sylvia* production when he embarked upon his own, but, by chance, 2004 was also the year when Frederick Ashton's 1952 production, one of the most acclaimed of recent times, was reconstructed (by Christopher Newton), a co-production for the Royal Ballet and American Ballet Theatre. Much to the surprise of some viewers, Morris's version was an untroubled embrace of the past, the choreographer treating the story seriously, with none of his usual irony and ambiguity. But, while reception of his ballet was mixed—some welcomed his new approach to the story and characters, others found awkward his response to the classical ballet model and vocabulary—little critical consideration has been given to how Morris wove his choreography into the mesh of Delibes' score. Morris was passionate about the music from the start, its brilliant orchestration, leitmotif approach and 'the multitude of infectious tunes and rhythms that add up to a compulsively dance-worthy sound world.'[49]

Here, and perhaps surprisingly, given the dramatic weaknesses of the score and story, Morris undertook no editing: he took the whole score in the original order and also found the stage directions in it a useful resource. For instance, as David Vaughan has pointed out, the score prompted the idea of Sylvia sitting on a swing at the beginning of the Act 1 Valse Lente,[50] while an attendant nymph pushes her to and fro:

> *Sylvia s'élançe sur les lianes qui unissent les arbres d'un bord a l'autre et, s'en servant comme une escarpolette, elle s'y balance en effleurant l'eau du bout de son pied.*
> Sylvia races towards the creepers suspended between the trees, and making use of them as a swing, rocks to and fro, skimming the water with the tip of her foot.

Also, the original 1876 Sylvia (Rita Sangalli) is seen on a swing in both a frontispiece to the score and the ballet programme, while there is a photograph of the Russian ballerina Olga Preobrajenska seated likewise during a later Russian production.[51]

It is significant that Morris avoids stereotypical footwork for female ballet dancers, even when the music suggests vocabulary of this kind. For instance, he does not make the Valse Lente a dance about pointe work as much as Ashton. To the striking long upbeat (four quavers in 2/4 time), where Ashton tends towards *bourrées* or *piqués*, Morris sets sweeping preparatory movements of the body or legs. To the crowning accents at the end of each phrase (featuring woodwinds in octaves and the ring of a triangle), Ashton's dancers always hold a conventional balance on one leg on pointe. Morris, on the other hand, introduces a range of alternatives that are not typical of classical ballet, including a bold lunge and a sturdy wide second position of the legs.

As usual, Morris draws our ears towards musical structure and detail in *Sylvia*. One unusual feature is the leitmotif principle (from Wagner) that he mentioned in interview. Repeating musical ideas are associated with particular characters, whether they be on stage or alluded to as offstage presences: Sylvia's horn call, for instance, Eros's powerful theme featuring descending fourths, and Orion's fanfare, which includes the tritone (augmented fourth) nicknamed the 'devil's' interval. The significance of these leitmotifs is noted in the score.

Perhaps the most telling example of leitmotif, however, is the theme associated with Aminta (from his first appearance in Act 1): it becomes the love theme that binds him to Sylvia. In other words, it becomes more than the signal of his presence (or absence, when in the mind of someone else on stage), and has particular steps associated with it. It is characterised by an opening rise of a fourth, a short series of repeated notes followed by a decorative semiquaver figure, and, in the first instance, by light orchestration, a flute solo accompanied by clarinets.

Ex. 9.2 *Sylvia*, Delibes, Act 1, Le Berger (Pastorale).

The theme establishes itself firmly as the opening of Aminta's Act 1 solo. He performs a slow turn in *attitude*, then *plié* on the same supporting leg, followed by steps and gentle *brisés* (beaten jumps) that relate loosely to the decorative figure and reach down the diagonal of the stage. His approach is thoughtful and quiet—he presses gently through the musical pulse and seems to fill the *attitude* turn with longing—and perhaps the difficulty of phrasing it smoothly encourages inner concentration. After this the theme undergoes transformation, as in Wagner's operas, unlike the simple motivic repetitions characteristic of Adolphe Adam's earlier score for *Giselle*. When, on being discovered hiding by Sylvia's huntresses, Aminta admits his love, she dismisses him angrily—and we hear the motif again, in a more dissonant harmonic context, on noisy strings.

Significantly, when Sylvia has been pierced by Eros's arrow and starts to fall in love with Aminta, she assumes his original steps—except she turns the *brisés* into a *posé* and *arabesque*. We hear the theme to the gentle flute once more, now tentative and suspended over a dominant pedal note. Later occurrences of this leitmotif are cut short. Its appearance in Act 2 on the low clarinet suggests that something is wrong. Awakening from sleep, Sylvia curls her arm around Orion's neck, believing that he is Aminta, and then recoils in horror; Morris draws a movement parallel here with the moment when Aminta is brought back to life by Eros in Act 1 (except it happened then without the musical motif). Finally, in Act 3, cut down to just the first bar, and played quietly on the oboe, the leitmotif conveys Aminta's longing as he searches for Sylvia (we see the *attitude* turn again). This is only to be rudely interrupted by *forte* string exclamations, perhaps suggesting the crowd presence around him, or his own impatience. Thus, Morris gives this leitmotif special attention as the one associated with the main narrative theme of the ballet. He acknowledges the significance of its harmonic transformations and re-orchestration and the flute's symbolisation of the private, central relationship between the two lovers.

From a narrative point of view, Morris's treatment of solos is especially interesting. Score directions for Aminta's first solo are already mime-laden. They refer to his reverie, putting aside his crook, his more impassioned thoughts to a surging cello theme, and to begging the statue of Eros for an opportunity to see Sylvia again. All this becomes a dance in Morris's hands, one that suggests emergent thought process, Aminta searching into the world beyond, and finally turning back into himself. Morris uses classical moves, but arranges them in long developing phrases that constantly change direction. The lack of straight repetition and spatial symmetry tells a story in itself.

While following the conventional framework of nineteenth-century variations, the Act 3 solos are similarly off-centre, but the effect seems doubly strange here, so strongly are we haunted by historical precedent. Morris follows the lead of Balanchine in re-working classical models, but most unusually, gets Sylvia to *start* in counterpoint with the musical rhythm, three different step patterns, each beginning with 3-count units against 4 in the music (one bar of 2/4=4 counts). Such crossings normally happen *during* a dance (in Balanchine's work too), not when it starts. (Morris introduces this early crossing on at least one other occasion, the opening of 'Twenty-Seven' in *Mozart Dances* (2006), see pp. 463-4). So there is a touch of insecurity at the outset of Sylvia's variation. She is an explorer, however, with an independent imagination, ready to try out many different qualities of movement—sharp, languorous, hasty, expansive. Later, she meets the musical metre exactly: the outcome of the solo is directly triumphant. Notably, Morris ignores the traditional implications of pizzicato for a woman's solo, just as he did when setting the Sugar Plum Fairy's variation in *The Hard Nut* (see p. 267). This is another female solo that is not primarily about pointe work.

The lively music for Aminta's solo was originally written for Sylvia, but works well for a man, especially as it eschews conventional virtuosity. It is especially striking that several big, plain *pirouettes*, including one at the start, are used as upbeats to phrases rather than flamboyant, cliché endings. (Morris refreshed *pirouettes* by timing them idiosyncratically in his earlier ballet *Drink to Me Only*, see pp. 148-9) There are hints of Aminta's earlier vocabulary, the *brisés*, for instance, but their placement within this new context highlights his change of heart. Longing is now a thing of the past— the man is the same, but he has a different outlook on life—instead, he demonstrates a new exuberance and confidence. Thus, Morris confirms the role of both Act 3 solos within the larger narrative of the ballet: they are not merely opportunities for display. He makes a point about both using the conventions of the past *and* undermining them.

Romeo & Juliet

Morris's *Romeo & Juliet, On Motifs of Shakespeare* (2008) was created for MMDG and, once more, he made a point about not cutting any of the music. In every other respect, this work posed a very different, indeed unique, series of choreomusical questions. As musicologist Simon Morrison put it in his programme summary, *Romeo & Juliet* 'is arguably the most popular ballet of the twentieth century, but the composer never saw it performed as he intended'. In 2006, Morrison had visited the Russian State Archive of Literature and Art in Moscow and discovered an earlier version of the score than the one from the 1940 Soviet premiere that we know well today. Dating from 1935, the most striking feature of the earlier version is the non-Shakespearian happy ending. Before becoming resident scholar in the summer of 2008 at Bard College, upstate New York, Morrison suggested to Leon Botstein, the conductor and President of the College, that the original score be revived, with its orchestration completed. Botstein subsequently brought Morrison into contact with Morris. Virtually all settings of Prokofiev's score up to that point had been ballets: exceptionally, Angelin Preljocaj created a version mixing modern dance and ballet for the Lyon Opera Ballet in 1990 and, in 2003, theatre director Declan Donnellan took the unusual step of asking the dancers to dispense with pointe shoes for his Bolshoi Ballet production. (Especially well-known ballet settings are by Leonid Lavrovsky (the Soviet premiere, Kirov Ballet, 1940), then Frederick Ashton (Royal Danish Ballet, 1955), John Cranko (Stuttgart Ballet, 1962) and Kenneth MacMillan (1965)). The collaboration between Morris and Morrison established, Botstein agreed that the 2008 premiere should take place at Bard, with he himself directing the American Symphony Orchestra.[52]

So Morris, in this unique instance, was prompted to choreograph by an ambitious musicological, historical enterprise. He says that he would never have wanted to choreograph the familiar version of the score. With the happy ending too, he was drawn back into asking questions about narrative and dance, although he was to be haunted by earlier productions more than he envisaged. His *Romeo & Juliet* (as opposed to his *Sylvia* and *Hard Nut)* answers to a particular tradition of romantic realist production, dominated today by MacMillan's setting and the 1968 Franco Zeffirelli film of the play. This was one reason why his *Romeo & Juliet* turned out to be less well-received critically than his other full-length works. Crucially, it did not focus on the expected high emotional drama between the lovers as did earlier productions, which was soon understood to be *the* correct interpretation of the score. Quite apart from this was the question of whether critics found the new dramatic conception convincing or the choreography interesting. A number did not. Morris's *Romeo & Juliet* was a risk: a costly, lengthy, labour-intensive enterprise, although unsurprisingly, the discovery of more music and a new, positive ending attracted considerable publicity. The production toured several US cities after Bard. It also went to London, where it was accompanied by the London Symphony Orchestra. Stefan Asbury conducted all the performances after Bard.

Originally, Prokofiev's score had been commissioned by the Bolshoi Theatre in Moscow and the scenario was a collaboration with the experimental theatre director Sergei Radlov. Composer and director both thought that their happy ending was a politically correct solution, in accordance with Stalin's communist authority at the time, about the struggle between the old feudal order and the young progressives, with the latter triumphing. Radlov claimed that this made *Romeo and Juliet* 'the most Komsomol-like [Communist-Youth-League-like] of all of Shakespeare's plays'.[53] It was decided, however, because of the altered ending, to call the ballet *Romeo & Juliet, On Motifs of Shakespeare*, which was the title that Morris chose for his production.

Morris's programme synopsis ends thus:

Elsewhere. Love triumphs. Juliet and Romeo live in love forever.

But what exactly is this place to which the couple go at the end? The 1935 script simply indicates that Romeo takes Juliet into a grove. In Morris's version, the lovers express their joy in a special star-lit arena. Morrison believes this space expresses the 'infinite' concept of love deriving from Christian Science, the faith that Prokofiev had espoused since 1924. It refers to a particular death-denying symbolic life within a greater reality. Later, in 1941, Prokofiev himself suggested choreographic reasons for the change of ending: 'Living people can dance, the dying cannot.'[54]

In any case, the authorities were dismayed by (after initially being supportive of) the tampering with Shakespeare's tale, and Prokofiev was forced to write a tragic ending. He left the old ending behind in a piano score with notes on orchestration in the margins. The rest of the score was orchestrated according to the composer's instructions by his assistant Pavel Lamm. Meanwhile, several of the ballet's promoters at the Bolshoi had been executed during a political purge, and the ballet was dropped. Instead, it received its premiere in Brno, Czechoslovakia in 1938,[55] which was the moment when the Kirov Theatre in Leningrad began to show interest, with Lavrovsky billed as choreographer. There were now further changes afoot.

Right up to the time of the premiere in 1940, Prokofiev was required to make a number of alterations, some of them without any initial consultation. New solos had to be composed for the lovers in Act 1, the music for the big group dances (the Folk dance—Tarantella and 2/4 celebration dance in Act 2) was re-ordered, edited and simplified, and a new group number, the 'Morning Dance', was added to Act I. Further repeats within numbers were inserted as well. Even the musical style changed. The modernist impulse that the composer had acquired from his experiences with Diaghilev's Ballets Russes in Western Europe was considerably toned down. As Morrison explained to Acocella: 'All the great melodies were there, but in the 1940 version they were reharmonised, re-rhythmicised...The original score was lean and mean.' As for the orchestration: 'They padded it, monumentalised it, laid on the violins.'[56] An orchestra of fifty-nine musicians became seventy (four French horns, for instance, became six). In the reconstructed original, certain instruments can be heard more clearly than in the 1940 version, the saxophone, percussion, cor anglais and clarinet (the *arabesques* in the final dance), and some bravura passages were brought back after the Kirov dancers had supposedly found them too hard to dance. Morrison reports that certain other sounds, for instance, when pitches were re-assigned to the bass clarinet and contrabassoon as rhythmic cues for the Kirov dancers, were removed in the restoration of the original. In general, the restoration relied on the orchestration of the 1936 and 1938 *Romeo and Juliet* orchestral suites, which predate the thickening of the orchestration by the Kirov, and which have faster tempo indications and a lighter but more percussive sound. The suites have Prokofiev's approved orchestrations.[57]

Still, out of a score lasting almost three hours, just twenty minutes of music was added to what is already well-known, much of this based on familiar themes: there was only eight minutes of entirely new material. Given the publicity, some critics were surprised by this. On the pages that follow is a diagram of the early version of the score as used by Morris, with reference to the changes that appeared in the 1940 score.[58]

Outline of the original, intended *Romeo and Juliet* (1935), with notes on changes made for the 1940 Leonid Lavrovsky version

The section numbers below have been taken from Simon Morrison's scenario in Appendix A of his book *The People's Artist: Prokofiev's Soviet Years*.[59] The scene titles come from Morris's programme, in order to clarify relations with his *Romeo and Juliet* production. Numbers given in brackets refer to those in the published scores and reflect the 1940 version of the ballet. Only a broad outline of the changes made in 1940 is provided.

1.Introduction

ACT 1

Scene 1 The Street
2. Romeo
3. The street awakens
4. The quarrel   [In the Lavrovsky version, a group number Morning Dance [4] was inserted before the quarrel]
5. The fight
6. The Prince gives his order
7. The Prince departs. Interlude   [7 and 8 in Lavrovsky version]

Scene 2 House of the Capulets
8. Preparing for the ball   [9]
9. Juliet as a young girl   [10]
10. Arrival of the guests   [11]
11. Entrance of Romeo, Benvolio, and Mercutio   [12]
12. Dance of the Knights   [13]
13. Mercutio's dance   [15]   [In the Lavrovsky version, a new solo for Juliet [14] was inserted before Mercutio's dance]
14. Romeo and Juliet's madrigal   [16]
15. Tybalt recognises Romeo   [17]
16. Gavotte (followed by departure of the guests)   [18]
17. The half-dark, empty hall   [19]   [This became the balcony scene in the Lavrovsky version]
18. Romeo and Juliet duet   [21]   [In the Lavrovsky version, a new solo for Romeo [20], derived from the abandoned happy ending, was inserted before the duet.]

ACT 2

Scene 1 The Square. A Festival
19. Folk dance—Tarantella 6/8   [22]
20. Romeo and Mercutio   [23]
21. The celebration continues 2/4 (including a Procession)   [24]
22. The Nurse   [26]   [In the Lavrovsky version, the Dance with mandolins [25] was inserted immediately before this dance]
23. Mercutio teases the Nurse   [omitted from the Lavrovsky version]
24. The Nurse gives Romeo Juliet's ring   [27]
25. General dance based on the 6/8 folk dance—Tarantella and 2/4 celebration   [omitted from the Lavrovsky version]

Scene 2 At Friar Laurence's
26. Romeo with Friar Laurence   [28]

27. Romeo and Juliet—the marriage   [29]

Scene 3   The Square
28. The general dance based on the 2/4 celebration and 6/8 folk dance—Tarantella continues   [30 and 31]
29. Tybalt meets Mercutio Tybalt   [32]
30. Tybalt's duel with Mercutio   [33]
31. The duel continues   [33 continued]
32. Mercutio's death   [34]
33. Romeo decides to avenge Mercutio's death and kills Tybalt   [35]
34. The stage fills, Romeo flees, and the Capulets promise vengeance on Tybalt's death   [36]

ACT 3

Scene 1   Juliet's Bedroom
35. Introduction   [37]
36. Romeo and Juliet (Juliet's bedroom)   [38]
37. Farewell before parting   [39]
38. The Nurse   [40]
39. Juliet refuses to marry Paris   [41]
40. Juliet alone   [42]
41. Interlude   [43]

Scene 2   At Friar Laurence's
42. Friar Laurence gives Juliet the sleeping potion   [44]
43. Interlude   [45]

Scene 3 Juliet's Bedroom
44. Juliet tells her parents that she will marry Paris   [46]
45. Juliet alone   [47]
46. Entrance of Paris and others with gifts   [48]
47. Dance—the gift of jewels [called Dance of the four Antilles girls in the original scenario]   [49]
48. Dance—the gift of carpets [called Dance of the three Moors in the original scenario, omitted from the Lavrovsky version]
49. Dance—the gift of liquor [called Dance of the two Pirates in the original scenario, used as the Dance with Mandolins [25] in the Lavrovsky version]
50. At Juliet's bedside   [50]

ACT 4

Scene 1 Juliet's Bedroom   [most of this using the original scenario and piano score that were abandoned after the tragic ending was written]
51. Romeo enters, discovering Juliet as if dead, tries to stab himself, but Friar Laurence stops him   [51]
52. Juliet begins to breathe
53. Friar Laurence strikes a gong. Romeo carries Juliet offstage into a grove.
54. The stage begins to fill.

Scene 2   Elsewhere
55. Entrance of Romeo and Juliet
56. Romeo and Juliet duet   [unscripted in the original scenario]

As for Morris, he enjoyed the fact that the original was 'more through-composed, less stop and start'.[60] In preparation, he read the original script, reread the Shakespeare, and watched three films: directed by George Cukor (1936), Franco Zeffirelli (1968) and Baz Luhrmann (1996). He deliberately avoided looking at recordings of other choreographic settings.

Morris's *Romeo & Juliet* was to be a chamber-size modern dance, not a ballet,[61] for a cast of twenty-four, featuring everyone as strong individuals (all dressed differently), and including four older dancers from MMDG history as the Capulet and Montague parents: 'the antiques road-show', Morris called them.[62] They form a thrilling, disturbing and hot-headed crew, as nobles mix with the lower echelons of society, always on the verge of swelling into a vicious clash or breaking apart in fury. This is not the choreography of stylised steps. Mostly, the protagonists walk and run, segueing with ease into and out of social dances, or gesture their conversations. Amongst his many sources, Morris used a book by Andrea de Jorio on Italian mime.[63] We can spot the ballet mime of clenched crossed fists for 'death'; Morris's invention for the concept of marriage, hands folded over each other, then turned 180 degrees; the two lovers meeting palm to palm (taken from the play); the old vernacular 'do you bite your thumb at us, sir?'; today's 'Fuck you!'; and many a lewd comment.

Morris also developed some of Shakespeare's characters. The nurse, often portrayed as a padded-out, possibly absurd old woman, is as young as Lady Capulet—as she is in the play—or younger still, trim, bustling and no-nonsense (Lauren Grant). Deborah Jowitt aptly describes the new vision of Paris (Bradon McDonald), who 'isn't the usual entitled wimp, but an arrogant suitor who might well become a wife-beater'. Two of the main male characters are played by women, both of whom have singular personalities: Mercutio, she describes as a 'raunchy tease' and Tybalt, as having an air of 'soul-twisted bravado'.[64]

This gender-switching, which forces us to double-take, is but one example of Morris's anti-realist vision for *Romeo & Juliet*. As Paul Parish has noted, there are 'frequent reminders that we are looking at a representation'.[65] (Or, Morrison adds, as Morris never fails to note, 'It's PRE-TEND.') Not only is there the crossover between contemporary and Renaissance attitudes, but the design is like a wood kit. The walls are like marquetry and the protagonists wield wooden swords. Scattered around the stage are wooden models of fifteenth-century Italian villas and a church—small enough to sit on—and boxes as furniture, all of which can be moved on and offstage to delineate piazza or interior. The stage lights are visible up above, part of a stage-set unit with built-in lighting and speakers. Morris and his collaborators (Moyer, Pakledinaz and Ingalls) are 'putting on a show' again (see p. 300), and he himself styles the production 'postmodern'. Most significant of all, the final twist in the story creates a major sense of artifice, placed against the unreality of a star-studded firmament, the background bluer than blue, as if the lovers no longer have their feet on the earth.

Of course, Prokofiev fought against far less history than Morris when he composed the music, even when he conceded the tragic ending. Today's choreographers have the burden of a big ballet past to contend with, and so do many in the audience. All this only exaggerates the anti-realist sense of Morris's production. By 2008, Prokofiev's original intentions offered a postmodern opportunity, and Morris grasped it.

It is the music that is primarily responsible for the over-familiarity. The few new additions to the Lavrovsky score now seem shocking. If some were originally rejected because their rhythms and harmonies were deemed too difficult, too modernist for comfort in the 1930s, today, they are shocking because they burst out unexpectedly from musical surroundings that we know so well. On the other hand, choreographing familiar music in a new way can also be unsettling, especially when we know what it meant in previous stagings. Here, for dancegoers, that experience is unusually close to home.

Perhaps the most striking example of 'original' music from the 1935 score is the 'Grand Fight' section, like an intrusion in the centre of Act 2. Using the anti-realist device of time stopping, it occurs during the celebratory group dances that block the course of the drama. There are two strands of these group dances, a folkish Tarantella in 6/8 and a dance in 2/4 broken by a striking Procession—Verona's Prince Escalus takes the lead around the stage, while his cohorts punch the air constructivist-style with arms like pistons (Nos. 19 and 21). There is a great deal of repetition of material across these dance passages, although, with increasing frequency, Prokofiev shifts his harmonies and cuts back and forth almost cinematically between ideas. Morris proves himself more than capable of meeting the composer at his game by varying his crowd formations, as well as their facing directions and mime gestures. It is during the last 2/4 section, Scene 3 (No. 28), that the 'Grand Fight' occurs, an 8-bar transition (from [230]) followed by 32 bars in a brand new dotted rhythm, a bold shift out of frame.

Twenty dancers have gathered on stage, lining up along the three 'walls' of the stage, and the lights dim. In 'free' timing, they break out into a chaotic stage picture, in heated gestural confrontations—including some glimpses of earlier behaviour—while the Prince and his flag-bearer process before them. The theatrical and musical treatments suggest a tension without precedent, a premonition of matters about to get much worse. Lights up again, the crowd disperses, as if nothing odd has happened, and we are launched straight back into the jolly Tarantella.

Some productions leave out this final Tarantella section (although it is in the published score), directors preferring at this point, with good reason, to drive straight on with the central drama of the marriage of the lovers and the duels and deaths that follow. But the musical intrusion is strange, even suggesting *entfremdungseffekt*.[66] Although the authorities probably wanted nothing to do with it, Morris understands brilliantly its potential. In his hands, it is like a turning point, the essence of paranoia, one of the most tantalising passages in his entire production. Oddly the Yuri Grigorovich/Lavrovsky production for the Bolshoi Ballet includes this passage in Act 2, Scene 1, to fit an earlier account of the Tarantella music. Here, there is no apparent recognition of its strangeness, nor any good theatrical reason for it.[67]

Another striking example of time stopping comes earlier in Act 2. When, in No. 20, Romeo enters dreaming of Juliet and meets up with Mercutio and Benvolio, the small groups of townspeople scattered around the 'houses' at the periphery freeze mid-motion. This is a moment of particular concentration: to the big tune from the 'madrigal' (No. 14), supported on either side by Mercutio and Benvolio, Romeo continues with his reverie.

The end of Prokofiev's score, which features the longest section of 'new' music, draws a great deal from familiar musical themes. No. 51 of the 1935 score (the return of Romeo) matches No. 51 of the 1940 version, after which the score moves into new territory. First, there is a long pause, full of mystery, as Romeo hovers expectantly over Juliet's lifeless body in bed. Then, we hear the pulse of silvery sound-drops from the celesta and a tentative piccolo melody from No. 27 (when Juliet arrived for marriage). Juliet awakens, and warm strings add encouragement. In complete contrast, Nos. 53-54 are raucous and bustling, complete with Friar Laurence ringing a bell at the side of the stage to call the crowds (diegetically, it is taken out of the pit).[68] Morrison tells us that the jubilant theme here cannot be found anywhere else in the score: Prokofiev found a home for it in the scherzo of his Fifth Symphony (1944).[69] Meanwhile, the lovers have left for the stars. Perhaps here there is just too much musical time spent on the excited people of Verona.

Morrison reminds us that the happy arrival of the lovers in 'Elsewhere' is marked by the theme associated with Juliet's death in the more familiar ballet score. It comes from 'Juliet as a young girl' (Act 1, No. 9) and, by the end of the work, represents mature feeling. So we understand it not only as a motif within the story, but also as a theme that has acquired new meaning, its joyful effect enhanced precisely because it has escaped its usual dark associations at this point in the ballet. Such layering of meaning recalls the theory of conceptual blending (see pp. 97-8).

Another example of layered meaning is Juliet's moment of resolve to re-visit the Friar after her parents' second attempt to force marriage with Paris (Nos. 40-41). Desperate, she sinks on to her bed as the music builds to a climax and then, to a thunderous tumult of arpeggios, in most productions, she runs, sometimes right across and around the stage, with her cloak flying melodramatically behind. (In the MacMillan version, in one of the ballet's most powerful, extreme moments, she starts by sitting motionless on the bed for what seems like ages.) In Morris's dance, Juliet gets up calmly, simply walks to pick up a modest wrap, and leaves thoughtfully, purposefully, briskly—no fuss. For most of the orchestral tumult, the stage curtain is down, and we have time for private thoughts. Morris took his cue from the words 'preparedness' and 'calmness' in the original scenario.[70] His strong Juliet does not dare to give in to her feelings. So are we doing the feeling on her behalf? Is this a musical voice from outside the stage character? Again, from a historical point of view, is there a sense of loss here, even irony? 'No, I won't give you what you expect,' could be Morris's playful suggestion.

It is not surprising that the authorities got rid of the Act 3 divertissement in its entirety. It does, after all, halt the central drama at a crucial point. Prokofiev clearly appreciated irony. Without anyone knowing, neither Capulet parents, the Nurse, nor Paris and his entourage, Juliet lies 'dead' in bed throughout! The divertissement hails from the tradition of exotic dances, a set of trios arriving with gifts: girls from the West Indian Antilles (jewels), Moors (carpets) and Pirates (booze). Two numbers, 46 and 49, feature mandolins, the second of these (for the Pirates) moved to an earlier point (Act 2) in the 1940 ballet, as the Dance with Mandolins (part of the crowd celebrations). MacMillan moved the first, the entrance of Paris and company, back to Act 1, where Juliet is seen playing (diegetically) an accompaniment to one of the dances at the ball. The Antilles number, on the other hand, became a pleasant dance (with lilies) for Juliet's female friends, who arrive to awaken her before her wedding to Paris. The Moor's dance, an uneasily gruff, dissonant number, completely disappeared.

In the context of Morris's setting, the mandolin sounds especially spiky, even nasty, and the violin solo that supplements it, even more devilishly bravura than usual. For the unlikeable Paris shows off, playing, in mime, the mandolin on stage. (Once more, music sops up external information and is perceived differently in different contexts.) Paris misreads the situation seriously with a presentation that is tawdry, daft, even insulting. The Antilles girls circle their hips sensually, but for whose pleasure? In the ballets, they are well-behaved friends on pointe. To all accounts, dancing while throwing carpets around looks ridiculous. The Pirates are awkward, brutish, the irregular rhythms of their elbow-shoving emphasising this. Even here, however, the lighter orchestration, bracing tempos and jesting cross-rhythms contribute to an impulsive liveliness that goes well beyond most other versions of *Romeo and Juliet* (Ashton's is an exception). But Paris and company outstay their welcome.

This is not the only longueur in Morris's production. With *Romeo & Juliet*, Morris came closer to the performance of musicology as archaeology than at any other point in his career. Perhaps then, in the interest of musicological purity, in the attempt to present the score as Prokofiev originally intended, Morris did not undertake the kind of editorial cutting that he might well have done on other occasions. We might also ask whether the composer himself, had he seen his original score visualised, would not have pressed for some editing, as often happens when composers are faced with the reality of theatre. Acocella recalls Morris working on the piece in his studio and muttering things like 'Everything happens a thousand times.'[71] With so much in favour of the enterprise, revisions would undoubtedly be worthwhile.

So what does all this add up to as a version of 'arguably the most popular ballet of the twentieth century'? The idea of devoting more attention to the society that the famous lovers inhabit proved its promise. The treatment of the star-crossed lovers who, after all, are still central to the activity on stage, turns out to be the least interesting aspect of the work. Marked with the 'real choreography', a kind of semi-balletic, motif-ridden vocabulary, they come across strangely wan.

They do, however, allow room for what is especially Morrisian about the piece: his sideways glance at the lovers' tale and critique of its dance and musical history, his profound lack of interest in the grand, over-blown and over-certain. Eric Griffiths has suggested of the lovers that 'we don't believe their story as they believed in it', although, to some degree, we would like to believe that 'love is a salve for the world's woes'.[72] Thus, Morris asks us to approach it via the twinkle in his eye and to trust in his nerve to break with Shakespearian orthodoxy, to be ready for a fresh Prokofiev/Shakespeare experience. Yet, with Morris being no Christian Scientist, there is also a tinge of regret at the very end, introducing an ambiguity that is typical of him, both troubling and moving. The 1935 instructions read: 'The music is bright, but it does not attain a *forte*.'[73] Morrison understands that the happy ending, being impossible, is sadder than the tragic ending, which is supported by Prokofiev's tonal logic. The composer moves from major to minor to major again, which, as Schubert and Schumann both teach us, is not a progression from 'Happy' to 'Sad' to 'Happy', but a progression from 'Happy' to 'Sad' to 'Sadder'.[74] So there is no triumph here, just as, Morris points out, there is none at the end of *The Hard Nut*.[75] Wendy Lesser notes how the lovers end up circling further and further away from each other as the lights dim—'we may be able to see a reference to the version of the play that is not here, an implied allegiance to that original plot in which the two lovers were separated by death and joined forever in memory'. Shakespeare and Prokofiev are, she says, 'not, in the end, so very different after all'.[76] The further irony is that Morris's dance proved troubled in reception, just like the Prokofiev score that had opened the door for him.

The big story pieces discussed in this chapter uncover a surprising range of choreomusical strategies. We find Morris changing his tactics to suit many different contexts, from opera that invites lean, neoclassically-informed treatment, to opera that prompts a messier style of Neo-baroque, from the formal twinning of dancers and singers through shared gesture to freer relationships of difference, and then a nineteenth-century ballet score that brings for re-vision its own conventions. Meanwhile, there is Morris's own construction of a large pageant-style event, and finally his staging of new historical research into a renowned twentieth-century ballet score. Yet looking across Morris's entire repertoire, by far the majority of his 'big story' pieces are opera-led: very few come directly out of dance. Telling stories straight is not his most natural idiom.

Morris worked with just one other 'big story' score during this later period, another opera, the Virgil Thomson/Gertrude Stein collaboration *Four Saints in Three Acts* (2000). But, as one of Morris's most exploratory approaches to text, this is a subject for the chapter that follows. Here, he we find him breaking away from the model of linear story, even more radically than he did in the pageant *King Arthur*, injecting his own alternative conceptions into the musical and textual material that he inherited and questioning the very nature of dance narrative and its relations with music.

10

Forms of Narrative: Three Experiments

Most of Morris's 'big story' pieces have a clear, linear plot running through them. The group of dances discussed in this chapter, however, are experiments developing from a narrative starting point, but that are prompted by Morris's fascination with musical structure and its potential either to reinforce or pull against narrative impulse. The formal component is quite as intense, if not more so, than the specifics of a human situation or story line. All three pieces incorporate text, and the term 'narrative' here is used in a broad sense, referring to programmatic information in general.

In her 1993 book, Joan Acocella makes a case for all Morris's dances being 'half-narrative'. Broadly speaking, she suggests two ways of achieving this, either from the abstract, 'musical' treatment of narrative movement material (as in *Gloria*), or the narrative treatment of abstract movement material (as in *One Charming Night* and its use of ballet vocabulary).[1] She also proposes that, while Morris treats his music analytically, in other words, as structure, at the same time, he uses it as an emotional or dramatic basis that can temporarily come to the fore and take over from purely musical demands. So music and narrative feed back and forth from each other.[2]

Morris is not the only choreographer to have worked like this. Yet his manner is distinctive, perhaps most of all for the way that he operates at the macro-level, questioning the boundaries (within music, text and choreography) between larger structures driven either by narrative or by form (see Chapters 12 and 13), even by having these apparently oppositional approaches represented within a single dance. Once this binary is exposed, it can become subject matter.

The first piece analysed is the Virgil Thomson/Gertrude Stein opera *Four Saints in Three Acts* (2000). Then, we look back to *Bedtime* (1992), settings of three separate Schubert songs, and forwards to a setting of Satie's *Socrates* (2010), the last section of which, telling the story of the philosopher's death, Morris had choreographed once before, in 1983.

Four Saints in Three Acts

The *Four Saints* opera is a MMDG repertory piece that has been revived twice since its premiere. It is worth special consideration as one of his most testing settings of words. Indeed, the result suggests a shifting of media balance towards words, at least to begin with, partly because the choreography often emphasises the text, partly because the peculiar density of Stein's text commands our attention. The work also demonstrates Morris's re-shaping of a big score and scenario again—just as he had done for *L'Allegro* and *King Arthur*. At the same time, far more than in either of these works, the score of *Four Saints* drives towards abstraction, undoubtedly determined by the particular nature of Stein's text, which, in turn, allowed Morris freer rein than usual to devise his own structures. But the re-shaping process had begun even earlier, when Thomson set Stein's text.

Premiered in 1934, *Four Saints* (produced by John Houseman) is the opera that became a notorious theatrical landmark within American modernism. Considered of rare beauty and certainly unusual in having an all-black cast of singers and dancers, after its first performances in Hartford, Connecticut, it enjoyed the longest ever Broadway run up to that time. There was already an important movement component: this original production was staged, as well as choreographed, by the young Frederick Ashton. As Thomson explained to Stein during rehearsals in December, 1933, he wanted Ashton to be in charge of the whole show, 'so that all the movements will be regulated to the music, measure by measure, and all our complicated stage-action made into a controllable spectacle'.[3]

Stein and Thomson

Typical of Stein here are her radical, repetitive verbal assemblages, often humorous non-sequiturs and sudden conceptual interpolations, and a brand new kind of sense that pops out of non-sense. The very title is a misnomer: there are four acts, not three (including a Prologue), and many saints mentioned in her play, not just four.[4]

Stein's writing here has a kind of divine illogicality. The work centres on two sixteenth-century Spanish saints who never actually met, but do here—Teresa of Avila, the contemplative poet-nun, and Ignatius Loyola, the erstwhile knight turned missionary. There is also a community of companion saints. In Thomson's imagination, these characters should evoke the 'childlike gaiety and mystical strength of lives devoted in common to a non-materialistic end'.[5] Logically-speaking, they are all in heaven already, where nothing happens. Instead, there is permanent rapture. 'A real saint never does anything,' wrote Stein.[6] As if to confirm this, time jumps forwards and backwards playfully between memory and present. When the text includes directions like 'Act 1' or 'Scene 7', tugging us outside the theatrical frame, they are often out of chronological order. Logic does not matter. Stein does not set them apart as directions, nor does she give precise indications as to speaker, or whether a name means a speaker or not.

The opening is immediately absurd. It appears like this:

> To know to know to love her so.
> Four saints prepare for saints.
> It makes it well fish.
> Four saints it makes it well fish.

But the realist end completely shatters the theatrical frame, even Stein's new non-sense frame:

> Last Act
> Which is a fact.

Bringing us sharply down to earth, it is both funny and disturbing, ironic confirmation of the spiritual doubt at the root of this enterprise.

As Daniel Albright suggests, Stein thought of a play 'as a literary act that is not a story', and her prose is an 'open, denarrativised field of words'.[7] She described her plays instead in terms of 'landscape',[8] a structure of present reality rather than one that progresses through time. Discussing the distanced nature of the *Four Saints* text, Jane Bowers proposes that the 'language represents, not speech, but thought'.[9] Even Thomson reflected on completion of his work that it was 'less like an opera than an oratorio *about* an opera.'[10]

Four Saints is indeed an extreme statement, which is perhaps right for an opera about the vacuum and inaction of heaven. Here, it is important that words become objects which, through repetition, lose some of their denotative power—as if part of their meaning has been drained out of them—and where denotation is often so fragile that concepts of similarity and difference merge. It is also important that words generate rhythm— Albright observes how 'nounless strings of words tend to move quickly, since there's little to detain the mind'[11]—and can at the same time be valued as sound in a musical sense. This is the formalist Stein, suggesting an alternative way of hearing and understanding. Leonard Bernstein once suggested that Stein came 'closer than any other writer except Joyce to the medium of music'.[12] Take the rhyming shouts of 'All the Saints' in Act 2, which begin:

> When. Then. When. Then. Then. Men. When Ten.

Such tactics also cause us, as audience, to turn in on ourselves and examine our own mental operations as we struggle to make sense out of what we hear. Stein means work. It pays off to look at, and listen to, Morris's *Four Saints* several times.

Albright analyses vividly an especially 'oversaturated, loopy, verbal field' intersecting meaning and sound near the end of Act 3:

> Letting pin in letting let in let in in in in let in wet in wed in dead in dead wed led in led wed dead in dead in led in wed in said in said led wed dead wed dead said led led said wed dead wed dead led in led...

He explains the process of change:

> At first Stein seems to be playing with a pun on *let in* and *inlet*; but when the *l* of *let* metamorphoses into a *w*, the *let-wet* rhyme suddenly opens up some new potentials: change the *t*'s to *d*'s, and a wedding procession starts to wend its way: *led-wed*. With one more mutation of the syllable the wedding procession becomes a funeral march, or some heavenly ceremony that might be imagined indifferently as wedding or funeral, since the categories of life and death no longer apply: *dead-wed*. And then the light iambs turn into heavy spondees, for a while, though the unstressed syllable *in* doesn't stray far and returns to leaven the texture and to provide a ghost of prepositional force. It is as if rhyming can generate new sorts of sentence structures, on an axis at right angles to the axis of normal subject-predicate formations. The opera seems to explore dimensions of syntax little known in earth.[13]

I add to Albright's observations the gentle shifts between the vowels *i* and *e*, shifts that contribute to the music of this passage.

In contrast with such extended and elaborate metamorphoses, Stein sometimes inserts a complete non sequitur, without following it up. Some of these test our brains, like the alarming question:

> If it were possible to kill five thousand chinamen by pressing a button would it be done. Saint Teresa not interested.

And another question that is impossible to answer:

> How many saints can remember a house which was built before they can remember.

Or the interpolation of a popular ditty:

> One two three four five six seven all good children go to heaven...

Is this a different kind of thinking? Soon a surprise is no longer a surprise, and even what Albright would call a dissonance is recognised as just part of a greater consonance.[14]

Stein completed her text in 1927, and the following year Thomson's process of re-shaping began as he built his piano score. Out of the odd text she presented, he felt he had to forge a real libretto, something that would work in the theatre. He explains how he worked with her style of text:

> For with meanings jumbled and syntax violated, but *with the words themselves all the more shockingly present*, I could put those texts to music with a minimum of temptation toward the emotional conventions [and] spend my whole effort on the rhythm of the language and its specific Anglo-American sound, adding shape, where it seemed to be needed— and it usually was—from music's own devices.[15]

Of course, the addition of another medium was bound to alter matters, but Thomson actively pushed for change. Providing contours, a range of moments from large to small, was central to his task of making Stein's text intelligible, at least according to his terms, so much so that the writer Wiliam Carlos Williams referred to Thomson's work as interference. It 'swallowed the words and froze them into forms that they themselves never rigidly hold'. I will return to this point later.[16] Yet Thomson already had much in common with Stein in terms of aesthetic stance, a profound interest in objectivity—rather than psychology or emotion—and a commitment to clarity of materials.

In *Four Saints*, Thomson introduced a more distinctly American tone to the proceedings—against Stein's obsession with Spain—as well as his own kind of assemblage. Removing himself from the harmonic dissonance and stylistic complexity of the dominant contemporary musical avant-garde, he turned to the commonplace for materials—such as folk-dance tunes, ragtime, patriotic marches, gospel-singing, Protestant and Catholic chants and hymns—although he tantalises us by leaving his sources on the brink of recognisability. The orchestration for approximately twenty players includes the unusual feature of accordion and harmonium, instruments that were probably familiar to Thomson from French and American popular culture.

The style is unashamedly simple, melody and rhythm always allowing the words to be easily heard, and the style declamatory with few melismas. (Thomson has been widely acclaimed for his word setting.) The harmonies are frequently restricted to simple alternations, for instance, between tonic and dominant, so much so that tonality seems de-naturalised, tensionless. The textures are likewise plain, while formulae-like repeating oom-pah basses are characteristic.

Thomson is, however, a modernist in terms of his syntax. There is, for instance, an absence of closed forms, and he often introduces uncomfortable juxtapositions of material. Sometimes these shifts underline Stein's mosaic structures, even if they do not identify with all the verbal detail and its meanings. But many are Thomson's own, a kind of resistance to Stein. Listen to the opening chorus of the Prologue, featuring an accordion, which is heard again as the hymn of communion in the heavens in the final act. An *oom*-pah-pah, tonic-dominant waltz becomes accompaniment to a song in 4/4 time (with the odd 5/4 or 3/2 bar): the relationship between stresses in voice and accompaniment constantly shifts.[17] (When the 3/4 *oom*-pah-pah bass returns in the Prologue, after a break—'Saint saint a saint. Forgotten saint...', Morris shows the dancers trudging right-left, right-left, in 2/4, which underlines Thomson's earlier rhythmic point.)

Thomson was clear about his independent approach when he set to work, once Stein and he had established common boundaries. This enabled his own structural processes:

> You don't try to match collaborators, you try to complement them. A bumpy, troublesome text [like Stein's, he implied] is better communicated to listeners by a smooth and untroublesome setting. If you match each other, you just throw more grit in the wheels... You are not under any obligation, and I hope not even temptation perhaps, to match in one art with an approach which is characteristic of another.[18]

A further link with Morris's interests years later, Thomson took his cue from Satie, whose work, especially *Socrate*, he much admired:

> Satie warned Debussy against going all Wagnerian. He said, 'Look out for this business of developing leitmotifs. Music should stay where it is, not follow the play. It should be like a décor. A property tree doesn't go into convulsion because an actor crosses the stage.'[19]

He took Stein's ideas for two set dances (the Dance of Angels and Tango in Act 2), also her proposals that Saint Ignatius' aria 'Pigeons on the Grass' (Act 3) should represent a vision of the Holy Ghost and that 'Letting pin in' should be set as a religious procession. Then he had to divide the text into parts for characters to sing (the score names eighteen original singing saints), elected to have two Teresas (soprano and alto) and two choruses, small and large, and introduced a couple of commentators called Compère and Commère.[20] He also decided to include the stage directions and act/scene announcements within the sung text (following Stein's precedent within her text layout).

Two other developments are highly significant and represent still further, radical shaping of Stein's work. At a later stage of composition, and after initial minor editing of her text, he undertook more extensive cutting. Stein gave way to him. She also approved, after completion of the score, an imposed, detailed scenario by Thomson's life partner Morris Grosser, one that introduced another, more concrete theatrical sense to Stein's prose, a series of tableaux staging imagined earthly meetings of saints at the cathedral of Avila, in Spanish gardens and in the country, finally in communion back in heaven. (Designed by Florine Stettheimer, the original production was lavish and highly original, with cellophane canopies, feathered trees, ecclesiastical robes and materials such as lace, glass, and gold paper.) But, as Albright suggests, according to Stein's 'landscape' aesthetic and her 'open, denarrativised field of words', both no stories and all stories are appropriate for setting alongside her text.[21]

The Third Voice: Morris

When Morris entered the fray preparing for his 2000 premiere at the London Coliseum, the re-shaping process began all over again. His was a very different vision of the piece. Unlike most other directors of *Four Saints*, he paid limited attention to Grosser's contribution, and instead went straight to the words and music, to create a theatricality of his own. (But he did use the wonderful stage direction, 'St Teresa II in ecstasy, seated, with angel hovering', when, in Act 1, to a low chime, a 'statue' saint is carried high across the stage with St Teresa in front.[22]) Crucially, he chose to work with the version of the score that Thomson had

> painfully but realistically abbreviated for RCA Victor Records; they had allowed him five disks (ten sides) at 78 rpm (about forty-five minutes' worth of the ninety-minute opera).[23]

This version, a further re-structuring by Thomson, was recorded by Leopold Stokowski in 1947.[24] As always, Morris maintains that he was led primarily by the music but, in this instance, he felt it would be boring (theatrically) to use the whole score.[25] Employing the 1947 recording as his basis meant omitting one of the specified dances, for angels, in Act 2, although it is important that the recording preserves most of the original instrumental interludes (Thomson's longest cuts occur in the opening Prologue and Acts 2 and 3).

Morris added some material back from the full-length version, and it is interesting to consider the implications of what he chose to reinstate. He generates a greater sense of expectancy in the Prologue by repeating the references to preparing for saints, the words 'for' or 'four' saints allowing him to introduce a quartet of dancers as a pun. He also keeps the joyous return of 'oom-pah' music before the saints enter heaven. The 1947 Prologue was breathlessly brief. Generally, because of such a non-linear text, Morris's 'additions' seem to be far less about the meaning of what is said and far more about enhancing the contour of theatrical energy, creating a clearer dynamic form. It helps that this kind of text is already less resistant to editing than traditional scenarios.

In Act 2, shouting 'Once in a while' many times (not just once), which leads into the 'When. Then...' series of shouts (see p. 327), supports the entry of the dancing group one by one, and builds tremendous energy. Morris decided to give St Ignatius an expanded solo opportunity (the only one) in Act 3, by bringing back his speech: 'Once in a while and where and where around is around is as a sound and around is a sound'. Grosser had taken this to be a reference to Gabriel's trumpet and prediction of the Last Judgement,[26] and Morris's setting is a powerful, urgent statement that contrasts impressively with the slow unravelling of the ensuing procession 'Letting pin in...' The final Morris work lasts about 55 minutes.[27]

Meanwhile, Morris emptied out a lot of the clutter of characters and situations, thereby immediately increasing the level of abstraction, although still allowing strong feeling content to emerge. Just five named saints other than the St Teresas have sung parts, but only two appear as stable characters amongst the group of saints on stage, one St Teresa and St Ignatius (at the premiere danced by Michelle Yard and John Heginbotham). Morris moved all the singers from the stage and into the pit (as he had done in his 1989 setting of Purcell's opera *Dido and Aeneas*), and where feasible, the soloists into side boxes. The stage he gave to fourteen dancers, a relatively small number for a Coliseum-size stage and much smaller than the 1934 cast. They are active nearly all the time, whether they do mime (a lot of the time), or gesticulate in mime-style, or perform more generalised meditations through dance movement. In tune with Thomson's aesthetic, Morris keeps the outline of the choreography simple, often introducing line-ups and circle formations and creating material out of short repeating units of movement.

The cultural reference is, appropriately, Spanish-American, costumes (Elizabeth Kurtzman) in vibrant reds and yellows, while each of the four acts is dominated by a different backdrop (Maira Kalman) hovering above the action, showing a procession with garlands, then flowers, birds and finally stars. Together these demonstrate a heavenwards progress. Continuing the theme of unrealism, the dancers symbolise a lively miniature world-heaven beneath. Emphasising the importance of words as material, as well as aiding audience comprehension, a front-cloth opens and closes on several occasions crammed from top to bottom with a summary of Stein's text.

Morris once said that he wanted the religion in *Four Saints* 'to be fun'.

He decided to cast the leading pair (in white) in a kind of marriage, largely of a spiritual kind, but always on the verge of sensuality. In knickers and billowing shirt, St Teresa thrills to the occasion, leaving contemplation behind to host this merry party and expanding into free ballet style, with generous swinging leg gestures and luscious *arabesques*. In contrast, St Ignatius rushes about with missionary zeal, in his more extreme moments of piety shuttling himself sideways on his toes, with one arm aloft in a gesture of blessing.

The group has a composite character, men/women at labour/play/ devotion. We see them in social dances—a series of Spanish numbers, a jota, sevillana (the number called tango in the score, and featuring castanets), sardana and farruca, and there is even a suggestion of getting a little drunk—'how much of it is finished'. But they seem above all serenely happy in their belief, sometimes inflecting this with African-Americanisms, speaking in tongues (as mime), hands shaking hallelujah-style, occasionally approximating ancient staring icons. Morris extends Stein's original premise by showing the entry of multiple saints into heaven through the break in the front-cloth, not just once—in the Prologue—but twice, again in Act 4, ready for the final heavenly communion (which is now in accordance with Grosser's scenario). Except for the long string of saints names in the Prologue, the text itself barely suggests such activity. It does not matter.

Otherwise, Morris's setting of *Four Saints* tends to emphasise individual words. For *Dido*, he had invented a bigger, more consistent lexicon of movement words to express the libretto's couplets. He had also introduced a more consistent sense of dance phrase and more actual dance episodes . But the meanings in *Four Saints* cannot develop from Stein's word play in any such straightforward narrative manner.

First, although voices and dancers tend to match in gender, there is otherwise no clear relationship between Morris's cast and individual singers. But you hardly need to know that it is St Settlement or St Chavez who speaks—it is simply someone who is a saint. Morris is selective too. We attend most easily to the words when he keeps the movement simple. Sometimes, words leap out at us because he choreographs a connection with their meaning, creating an especially emphatic frozen moment that draws you closer into his miniature heaven. Perhaps such faux-naif underlining speaks of belief (or rather a yearning to believe) in goodness, magic and innocence. This small-scale 'shaping' is what the writer Williams would have considered radical interference. But changing tactics create anxiety: how can we catch all this information, and what might we be missing, when certain things are stressed but others ignored? Sometimes, we have to make a choice: to listen or to watch. Morris encourages an active response. As suggested earlier, he makes us work, just as Stein does.

An example of obvious mime, St Teresa acquires a movement motif as soon as she arrives: she curtseys to her name, spreading her arms. When we hear that she is 'seated', her companions bob down, bending their knees. Later, as a piece of mime non-sense formalised into continuous choreography, the chorus race to match references to her (the curtsey), to her being 'seated' (the sit), then to her not 'standing' (arms flung overhead) and to her not being 'surrounded' (arms thrown up one side and down the other). But the process is fundamentally static, the same few words, gestures and tonic/dominant musical harmonies recurring again and again. We also register alternating motions—side to side mapping on to 'inside' and 'outside', 'left' and 'right' shown by the feet, and much of the time this kind of pattern imitates the sway between two harmonies.

Soon, in a rare celebration of chronological order, from one to ten, the men and women illustrate the text antiphonally, to the single-note chant of Commère and Compère:

Commère: One a window [*the men's arms outline the shape*].
Compère: Two a shutter [*the women open their arms*].
Commère: Three a palace [*together the men form the outline of a building*].

up to

Commère: Nine a seat [*the men sit against each other's backs*].
Compère: Ten a retirement [*the women sink to the floor*].

The most musical passages of text are treated more freely. 'When then', for instance, is a series of gunshot leaps as the singers take turns with each word, accompanied by military percussion. 'Letting pin in...said led wed dead...' becomes a slow travelling frieze: a continuously unfolding pattern of dancers shifting from one position to another traverses the stage, while St Teresa walks in front, like a visual monotone. As the words suggest, this procession carries funereal overtones, and Thomson responded by casting a continuous series of E minor (dark) chords over a scalewise descending bass (see Ex. 10.1).

As Albright notes, the vocal line (Compère and Commère alternating again) starts locking into place, an effect of slowing the momentum still further, at the point where the four key words are reached 'said led wed dead': E, F-sharp, G repeat again and again until, for the first time, at the very end, in retrograde—G, F-sharp, E signals dubious closure.[28] There is a corresponding sense of closure, visual loss, as the dancers disappear into the wings.

In some parts of *Four Saints*, we search with difficulty for equivalence between what we see and the words that we hear. The famous 'Pigeons on the grass alas' passage in Act 3 (when St Ignatius is supposed to have a vision of the Holy Spirit) shows all the men striding heavily with swinging

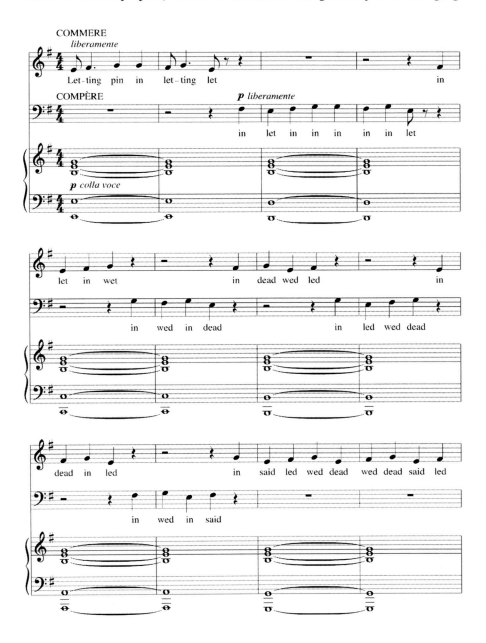

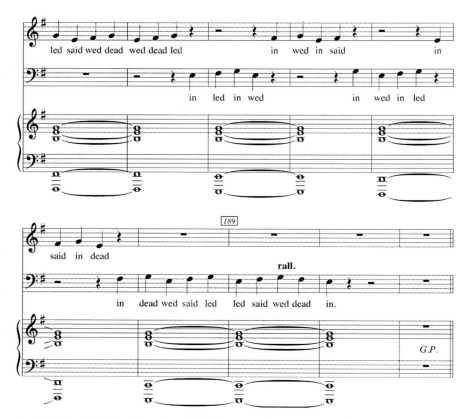

Ex. 10.1 *Four Saints in Three Acts*, Virgil Thomson, 'Letting pin in...'

arms, straight out of vaudeville. (The stride had already been introduced in the Prologue, from 'In narrative prepare for saints...'). To 'short longer grass', there is a nice pun: St Ignatius steps out a short-long rhythm. 'If they were not pigeons what were they' is the question. The chorus answer 'It was a magpie in the sky'—and the connection now becomes clear. Leading the group, the bird images created by St Ignatius' raised arms nicely resonate with those on the backcloth above.

There is a wonderful, quietly mysterious duet in Act 2 (in Grosser's scenario a love scene between Compère and Commère), like a counterpoint to the merry activities of Morris's lead pair: minimal gestures to the most skeletal utterances—simply intoned falling intervals set against a pedal chord punctuated by the sound of a glockenspiel. During this uneasy meeting, the relationships between verbal and physical seem at their most oblique, most taunting. Every statement and response, said or done, prompts further enquiry, but the direction is never entirely clear. Here are examples:

[*Commère sings and the woman moves*]   [*Compère sings and the man responds*]
Scene Eight.   To wait.
[He reaches up toward her. Does it mean 'When will she let him love her?']
Scene One.   And begun.
[He puts his arms about her. Does this suggest 'Is this the beginning?']
Scene Four.   Attached or.
[He embraces her more closely, sinking to grasp her waist. 'Will she respond?']
Scene Eight.   To wait.
[She leaves the stage and he watches her go. 'Will this ever continue? How long will he have to wait?']

Another aspect of this work, however, is not at all about words in any sense, neither their meaning, nor the manner in which they are structured. Indeed, thanks to Thomson's vivid imagination, there are many times when words are suddenly forgotten and the unsayable takes over: catchy dance rhythms, high chanting, bell-like vocalisations, bursts of melody that you could take home singing, an astonishing combination of poignancy and raw energy. 'Shocking', Morris would say. Little spots of dance emerge from early in the piece, to the tiniest breath of melody or musical impetus, and the weight that they accrue is surprising, given the minimal real time that they occupy. Perhaps it is significant that the sheer weight of words decreases as *Four Saints* progresses and just as Morris's dance episodes (some with, some without, words) increase and expand. Three of the four dances composed as dance music—and without words—occur in Act 3 (before the very brief Act 4), and, of these, the Tango is the longest (all of one and a half minutes).

When Morris choreographs full-body movement—big lifts and grand, enthusiastic arm gestures—to bloom with the music, it speaks volumes. This is often the case in the choreography for St Teresa and St Ignatius. Early on, we find St Teresa leaping up and down an avenue formed by her saintly colleagues and reaching out in extended *arabesque*. There is an increase in sound volume, and the emotional temperature soars. Contrast her sweet solo of repeating, expansive gestures near the end of Act 1, which occurs to a relaxed melody and quietly repeating words: 'There can be no peace on earth with calm with calm...' Later, there are loving little duets with St Ignatius. In the one near the end of Act 2—without words and again 'extended' (just over a minute)—a sudden burst from the orchestra prompts the pair to step side by side in smiling ecstasy.

The briefest moments can represent peaks of emotion. There are several examples already in Act 1: the 'Ah!' s that erupt out of nowhere from a female voice—on a high A, A-flat or G; St Teresa's outburst of feminist conviction, set against 'Can women have wishes'; Thomson's passionate musician's

Four Saints in Three Acts, Act 2, 'In the morning to be changed...', Michelle Yard and John Heginbotham. © Bill Cooper, 2005

voice speaking across, resisting, words that are emphatically ordinary of meaning (high As mark the words shown here in italics):

How many are there *halving*.
Saint Teresa having *known* that no snow in vain as snow is not vain.

Morris relishes all these emotional musical opportunities, despite his move away from specific characters and situations. I wonder whether his inclination would have been to expand further in this direction, to have an even freer hand for dance, but the whole style of Thomson's *Four Saints* is to take you somewhere fast and then hastily shift you somewhere else. Still today, the work challenges familiar norms of construction and meaning.

Albright's brilliant analysis of the opera stresses nothingness, emptiness, even a perversity on Thomson's part: 'dismembered, deliberately incompetent euphony is the final sophistication', he proposes.[29] For a while, it was logical to parade Thomson against the overwrought background of nineteenth-century romanticism as well as the new cerebral modernism. Notably, Albright avoids all mention of choreographic possibilities, of the opportunity for dance to add yet another voice. Writing about the original

1934 production, he does not even mention Ashton's name, surprising, given the centrality of the choreographer's contribution. Yet Morris, re-shaping the score/text in his own way as the culmination of so much previous re-shaping, clearly digs out and cherishes the emotional potential in Thomson's music, in other words, its dynamic form—even if, like Stein's text, it may be heard as ultimately so much non-sense. As usual, he is firmly ambiguous: he believes and he un-believes, both with fervour.

Finally, in Morris's setting, St Ignatius pushes St Teresa higher and higher on a celestial swing, so that she can join the stars. 'When this you see remember me' is the accompanying hymn of communion. Choreography, text, music and design bond together most powerfully, or so it seems. Or is it a sham? 'Last Act,' says the Compère. 'Which is a fact', all shout from the stage. We are left to decide. Or perhaps, as Morris's work suggests, we don't need to decide, and the very act of deciding would be false. End.

Yet Morris's *Four Saints* is also a highly controlled, formal work. Thomson provided momentous closure before the final question mark—a return of the opening, memorable music, the hymn that he had already reinforced through repetition in the Prologue. (A reminder of its pronounced oom-pah also comes with the Intermezzo music preceding the last Act.) Here, in Morris's production, the various saints enter heaven through the opening between the front curtains, an expanded version of their Prologue entry, his own confirmation of closure. Thomson and Morris were responsible for this rounding off, not Stein, and Morris added his own kind of formal impact by staging a clear development away from the territory of words (mime) into the territory of no words (dance). (This is a heightening of his procedure in *L'Allegro*, see p. 217.) All three artists here, in their various ways, play at the very edge of narrative reason and, encouraged by Thomson, Morris introduces architectural force as rescue device in such a precarious situation. We now turn to two other Morris works that tantalise us by exploring that same edge.

Bedtime

For *Bedtime* (1992), Morris shaped his own score and 'narrative' out of three unrelated Schubert songs. It is not unusual for choreographers to select a series of short pieces and 'compose' them into an order that suits their purposes: like Morris's own plotless dances to miniatures, for example, *Sang-Froid* (2000) to piano music by Chopin and *Sandpaper Ballet* (1999) to orchestral numbers by Leroy Anderson. Other plotless dances, especially to songs, reflect a variety of moods and emotions, for instance, Morris's *I Don't Want to Love* (1996), to a series of Monteverdi madrigals alternating recitative and aria and speaking in various ways about love. The method of musical selection has also proved useful to choreographers who want to introduce an element of plot without commissioning a new score tailored to fit. Morris did this in *One Charming Night* (1985), a story about a young girl's seduction by a Vampire-devil (see p. 157) that develops across several Purcell songs. *Bedtime,* however, is perhaps Morris's oddest construction of a score from a group of short compositions, because of its unique juxtaposition between tale and manner of telling. Here, the dialogue between formal and narrative concerns could be construed as a primary purpose.

Each of the songs is well-known, *Wiegenlied* (Cradle Song: D 498, 1816), a lullaby, *Ständchen* (Serenade: D 920, 1827), the song of a lover outside the beloved's bed chamber, and, most familiar of all, *Erlkönig*, the story of the mythical Erlking's power over a young boy (D 328, 1815). All are night songs, concerned with sleep and dreams that turn into nightmares and death, while exposing the thin line between reality and fantasy. Morris chose a woman singer to provide a link across all three songs, originally his favourite mezzo-soprano, Lorraine Hunt, speaking to the baby rocked by its mother in the cradle, then as the lover addressing the beloved, and finally as the narrator of (and characters within) the Erlking story. In *Ständchen,* she is accompanied by a small chorus of tenors and baritones. As the 'narrative' across the three songs moves towards darker regions, the songs themselves become less cold form, more through-composed, and Morris's choreography becomes more complex and turbulent. *Bedtime* is dressed in satin pyjamas, and set for a group of eight women (in blue) and four soloists (in different colours).

Schubert's *Wiegenlied* is the setting of a simple strophic poem, each verse beginning 'Schlafe, schlafe' ('Sleep'). The message is static, as becomes a lullaby, in different ways encouraging sleep and offering the comfort of the mother's protection and love. The three verses are musically identical. In the dance, we find three prone male figures in a line downstage (who will turn out to be three of the work's soloists) and three women in blue, opposite them upstage. A woman in gold as a kind of guardian angel (the fourth soloist—a mother figure?) dances a long, slow phrase up and down between each pair in turn, drawing each of the women downstage towards her charge (a child?). The angel starts with the pair stage left and leaves stage right. As each verse ends, the figures downstage switch to a new position, the last being the most angular and strained—here, they shift on to their bellies, raising a flexed foot behind them.

Morris parallels the varied repetition within each verse of the poem, and there are a number of 'rocking' movements, like a leg swinging forward and back, or alternating arm gestures, up-down, open-close. But he also creates an entirely symmetrical structure, with the movement of the first verse transferred exactly to the opposite side of the body in the third verse. That of the central verse is similar again, although there is clearly an attempt to show the body in symmetry as far as possible, like a halfway point between verses 1 and 3. We are unlikely to notice this level of detail at first viewing, but there is probably some sense of déja-vu as the dance develops, while the large spatial structure is entirely predictable, systematic. We see it working itself out, another comforting experience absolutely appropriate to the tone of the poem. Form contains meaning. Of course, the verse structure is also a kind of poetic/musical system, but, unlike the choreography, we cannot predict when what we hear will end.

For *Ständchen*, the three women in blue expand to the full eight (roughly a counterpart to the male singing group accompanying the mezzo-soprano), and are set against the quartet of soloists, all of whom are now up on their feet and mobile. The main structural premise of the choreography is of waves and canons that take your eye all over the place, up and down a line, and back again, or crossing through a group. The stage picture is wonderfully lively and playful, although it is impossible for your eye to keep up with the patterns. That seems to be the point: a certain tension, yet a sense of fun and, like the poem and its music, essentially untroubled experience.

The dance organisation follows the phrasing and device of recapitulation in the music, but, as in *Wiegenlied*, remains largely independent of individual words. Morris simply picks up on a few images from the poem, such as 'knocking' at the door—at the start, each soloist knocks on the back of the one standing immediately before him, and later, pairs of dancers knock fists; hushing or calling for attention to speak—a cautionary finger raised, or the blue group 'swelling' up from the floor on the word 'schwellend'.

A couple of motifs clearly echo the first song, so a link with the past is established. Early on, for instance, we see the group in the three sleeping positions of the 'children' who lay downstage in *Wiegenlied*. Similarly, a number of movements from *both* songs go into the final *Erlkönig*. The boy, for instance, in this song, lies dead in the opening position of the 'children'. From *Ständchen* comes a striking hopping and toe-tapping step, and sometimes the manner in which the blue group raise their arms or drop to the floor is familiar. But the context of these movements has radically changed, bringing to them new quality and meaning: from the start, *Erlkönig* signals alarm.

Schubert's story is linear, and thus of quite a different order from the other two songs. Based on a ballad by Goethe, a man and his son are riding home at night in a storm. A spirit, the Erlking, tempts the boy to come away with him. The father does not see the Erlking and ignores the frightened boy, but when he arrives home, he finds the boy dead in his arms. Goethe's poem, which is a series of verses, features a framing narrator as well as the three characters, whom he gets to speak directly by putting their words in quotation marks.

It is useful first to consider a range of critical interpretations of Schubert's song. Richard Capell (1928) and Donald Tovey (1937)[30] claim that Schubert makes us empathise with the terrified child, getting out of the real world and into his world of fantasy. Theirs is a child-centred interpretation. Later, Lawrence Kramer (1984) argues for a more father-centred interpretation, about 'the failure of paternal power',[31] with the son 'as a middle term between the natural and the fantastic', and suggests that what destroys the son is 'the psychic stress of living between the two realms.' Christopher Gibbs (1995) prefers to cast the Erlking himself as the central figure and as a representation of the uncanny—'the combination of sweetness and terror...both human and supernatural, sweetly alluring and threatening, intimate and profoundly alien'.[32] The more seductive characteristics of the music were precisely those that had alarmed many nineteenth-century critics about Schubert's setting. Often, he has been perceived to resist the voice of Goethe in some way—not simply serving the text, but taking it into new affective areas and veiling the straightforward verse structure of his poem. It could be, as Carolyn Abbate proposes, one of those

> so-called 'through-composed' settings of narrative ballads [which], by breaking free of repetition in order to create musical representations of action-sequences, overwhelm their texts by burying them in musical matter with its own fascinations.[33]

Indeed, the song drives forward rapidly across its eight verses, to the moment of climax in verse 7—the seizure of the child, followed by the chilling announcement of death by the narrator. There are many changes of key, clear stepwise rising sequences established for both the Erlking and the Son screaming 'Mein Vater, mein Vater' (see pp. 348-9) from verse 4 to the climax. There is also clear demarcation of register between characters: the Narrator using middle range voice, the Father, low, the Son high, and the Erlking very mobile, also the only character to be presented predominantly in major tonality. The singer's vocal line varies a great deal in style, but the accompaniment is obsessive, repeated-note triplets hammering away from the start (usually read as the sound of the horse's hooves), with an occasional rumbling bass interjection, relieved only by the lighter triplet figures for the Erlking and the very bare final three bars.

Although no dancers are named as specific characters in the programme, Morris follows the tale in detail. He also matches the steady trajectory towards the climax. This is one of the most remarkable moments in the song, the vocal line reaching G, its highest note. Now, the terrified boy, lifted overhead for the third time by the Father, remains hanging there, motionless, his descent dramatically delayed during the vocal descent, until the point when it ends cadentially, an octave lower. We might at this point consider how Morris's use of characters as 'voices' interacts with what Goethe and Schubert came up with before him (see pp. 101-4).

Morris encourages us to identify dancers with roles, in a relatively stable sense: the three characters in the story, a narrator and a chorus. The children of the first song (and perhaps the second too) are now grown-up. Morris himself, the soloist of the quartet dressed in grey, turns out to be the Erlking in the last song (he danced the role for many years). The guardian angel in gold is the Narrator, the Father is in rust, and the Son in green. The chorus of eight women in blue, on the other hand, represent all kinds of things: the wind, mist (or fog), trees, the Erlking's games and daughters (also mentioned in the text), as well as the galloping horse. Sometimes, they connect with the words, sometimes with the piano accompaniment. As Acocella suggests, any of their activities can also represent doom and terror.[34]

Morris adds to the pressure of the song by keeping his characters active when they, themselves, are not 'speaking' and embodying the vocal line. When not speaking, characters work alongside those who do, enlarging or counterpointing their movement. Most of the time, the Narrator, Father and Son occupy stage left, while the Erlking and chorus rush in and out threateningly from stage right—the Erlking stays around and invades the others' territory increasingly as the song progresses. You can only begin to understand the rich interplay of information after a number of viewings; everything happens extremely quickly.

Morris's take on character is very much his own. His Erlking is without doubt the central figure here: he is literally bigger physically than the others and inevitably projects the commanding voice of the choreographer. To some degree, his Erlking is like Gibbs's interpretation, a conflation of the 'human and supernatural, sweetly alluring and threatening, intimate and profoundly alien'. He also brings 'the maternal promise of comfort and the siren's enticement to pleasure'.[35] More than just about any other male dancer, Morris brings to his dancing the soft, pliant voluptuousness that is often considered primarily feminine (although exactly why is highly debatable, see p. 223). But it is important in this particular choreographic situation that we carry the memory of what he was in the past, in the second of the songs, into *Erlkönig*. It is there that he danced most softly and pliantly, and we do not forget this image.

Here, in *Erlkönig*, while Schubert's character sings seductively, Morris's dancing emphasises strength and power. Or, to entice the Son, he turns away from the vocal line to burrow into the piano accompaniment, dabbing spitefully at its lighter staccato beat—the pounding octaves let up during the Erlking's main statements (verses 3 and 5). As a result, the beat commands our attention more than at other comparable points in the song, countering the feminine wiles sounded by the singer and, as the dancing Erlking 'blends' with this accompaniment, he seems to detach it, using it to say something in addition to, and quite different from, the singing siren. (The Son is clearly drawn by the Erlking's rhythm and, during verse 5, uses his beat to dance a neat 3/4 step that crosses the music's 4/4.) Crucially, Morris's Erlking plays the joker. Audiences laugh during his verses, when he plays his games (verse 3, intended to amuse the child), or when he bounces down an avenue of 'daughters' as if counting them or playing a xylophone (verse 5). They laugh again, as we will see later, at the very end. Neither Goethe nor Schubert suggests anything like this. Adding information and assembling it in new ways, Morris shows the double- or even multi-sidedness of his Erlking.

The Narrator is to some extent rather like the singer, framing the proceedings and, at different times, 'becoming' each of the other three characters. She too pulls at different strands of information, including the music, and jams them together. Acocella charts vividly the complication of her persona:

> If you tried to chart the planes of her action, you would end up with something like a cubist sculpture. She begins by miming the story—pointing to the father, the son. But soon she is part of their dance. Then, she is on the floor (the coming death), drumming her feet (the horse, the music, the doom). Then she is in league with the Erlking, playing in his games, dancing with his daughters, being held up by him on the words 'golden gowns' [referring to the Erlking mother's attire]. (She is wearing gold-coloured pyjamas.) Then she is twirling again (the music), then jumping (the vocal line shooting up). As the terror mounts, she becomes scared of her own story. When the boy leaps into the father's arms, she too leaps—into the Erlking's arms. When the boy dies, she throws her head back (the audience's emotion).[36]

Then there is the father—just how loving and consoling is he in Morris's choreography? Not as the words suggest, he is rather a brute, sometimes a bit like the Erlking, wrestling with his Son, forcing him to calm down, even threatening.

Thus, Morris continues to open up meanings and questions beyond those suggested by Goethe and Schubert, as his characters occasionally blur into others, or into other phenomena such as the wind, the mist, and the horse. The fresh humour too, of the nasty, ridiculous kind, only makes us squirm the more, given the awfulness of the circumstances—especially at the end. Here, the music veers towards A-flat major, at which point the four characters are lined up before us on stage:

Erlking   Son   Father   Narrator

Schubert decided to halt the obsessive accompaniment at this point, and to leave the singer isolated for the chilling announcement of death—'In seinen Armen das Kind' ('In his arms, the child...'), faltering before declaiming the last two words, 'war tot' ('was dead'). (Goethe's approach was straight, no break, no emotion and, according to Kramer, in the mode of Romantic irony.) Schubert's harmonies then shift far away from conventional logical sequence, so, although the recitative 'In seinen Armen das Kind' does nothing to disturb the sense of A-flat tonality, the following diminished-seventh chord and the C-sharp to D 'war tot' certainly do (see Ex. 10.2). As Kramer says:

> The D points to the dominant of G, but its proximity to A-flat gives it a dissonant aura that is at once shocking, frightening and poignant.

He continues:

> The song then comes to an abrupt end with a ritualistic cadence formula, V7-I [dominant seventh to tonic harmony, based on D, then G], that carries little conviction. The tonic has been dissociated, largely depleted of its closural power, in order to enact a tragic recognition. Like the father, the listener is confronted with the blank arbitrariness of final things.[37]

Morris notes a relationship here between the 'ritualistic cadence' and the conventional completion of a baroque recitative.[38]

But Morris pushes anguish still further. In his staging, the Son falls to the ground (into the opening position of *Bedtime*) during 'In seinen Armen das Kind'. Then Morris compounds the bitterness behind the musical comment that follows. On the final chord, his Erlking, now replacing the Son and leaning against the Father, looms over him, having turned sharply to look him straight in the eye. Acocella suggests the following possibilities for meaning: 'Now, perhaps, you believe in me...[or] *I'm* his father now... [or] You're next'.[39] He could also be mocking the father by identifying with his son. Indeterminacy of meaning continues to the end. Our giggles ring hollow as we recognise the true bleakness of the situation.

Morris enhances certain features of *Erlkönig* by underlining selected words, musical notes and parts of the musical texture, but his choreography

Bedtime, 'Erlkönig', near the end, Mark Morris, Kraig Patterson, and Guillermo Resto.
© Tom Brazil, 1992

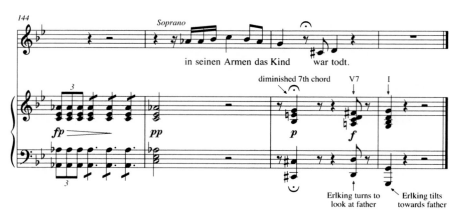

Ex. 10.2 *Erlkönig*, Schubert, the ending.

adds extra complexities, disrupting what may previously have seemed like coherent voices and erupting out of the safety and formal constraints of the previous two songs. Sometimes, as with the humour, the choreography seems to overwhelm the meanings of text and music (recall Abbate on the music), although we might experience this resistance to text and music most strongly if we have already experienced the songs without dance.

Meanwhile, the singer's struggle to hold together in her imagination the characters of her story seems far more intense and urgent than in concert, such is their enlargement through visual presence and the proliferation of information fighting both to hold the characters apart and to play games with their identity. Morris and Craig Smith coached Lorraine Hunt for the premiere (accompanied by Linda Dowdell). The choreographer was clear that he did not want word-painting, rather the singing should be

> more 'character-y', to sound 'ugly', with the dramatic tension so often missing from today's opera...like a radio show—you can tell who sings by the sound.[40]

Acocella recalls Hunt declaiming *Erlkönig* as if it were 'a national emergency'.[41]

Looking at *Bedtime* as a whole, it is important that this third song is understood in relation to the previous two, for the re-contextualisation of dancers and their movement within this over-arching 'story' and setting tells us that good and bad dreams, life and death are disturbingly close to each other. As a trio of songs, *Bedtime* also exposes an extreme opposition between form and narrative, while, starting as one kind of piece and ending as another, it emphasises that these binaries are inextricably bound together. This is a primary topic of *Bedtime*, and it is musical structure that led Morris in this direction. His first song setting is emphatically systematic and, in this respect, related to recent minimalist choreography, while the last is an emotionally overwrought narrative. We feel a rare pressure to resolve the unusually extreme distinction here. We look forward, and have our expectations disrupted. We look back and remember—the system, the channels etched up and down the stage, the uncompromising severity of the outlines of the opening lullaby. The pressure to come to terms with the opposition makes us more than usually reflexive.

Indeed, we are primed from the start of *Bedtime* (by the system itself) to consider our perceptual and cognitive processes (what the eye and ear can absorb and how our minds make sense of information), only to be aware of the complexity confronting us as meanings and cross-references proliferate towards the end of the piece. This too, an act of distancing, becomes subject matter. So the nightmare of *Erlkönig* becomes our nightmare too.

**Erlkönig: outline of the story and speakers
across the eight verses, including selected details of tonality**

1. Introduction G minor

Narrator

Setting the scene of the father riding home with his child

2. Father

Son

Father

About the anxious son seeing the Erlking and the Father saying that what he sees is just a wisp of fog

3. Erlking B-flat major

The Erlking trying to entice the child with talk of games, flowers and the mother's golden robes

4. Son's first appeal 'Mein Vater, mein Vater', D to E-flat, in G minor

Father

The anxious son seeing the Erlking again, and the Father saying that what he sees is just the wind

5. Erlking C major

The Erlking trying to entice the child by saying that his daughters will wait on and dance for him, and help him to sleep

6. Son's second appeal 'Mein Vater, mein Vater', E to F, in A minor

Father

The anxious Son seeing the daughters in the gloom, but the Father says that he sees the shimmer of willow trees

7. Erlking E-flat major

Son's third appeal 'Mein Vater, mein Vater', F to G-flat, in B-flat minor

The Erlking professing love, threatening that he will force the child to be with him, and the Son shouts that he has been seized

8. Postlude   G minor (with shifts towards C minor and A-flat major)

Narrator

The Father takes the child home, whereupon he discovers that he is dead

---

Socrates

Like *Bedtime*, the style of Morris's *Socrates* (2010) 'moves' towards more detailed narrative, but the manner of doing so and style of narrative are totally different. Set to Satie's score of 1918, everything about this work seems extraordinarily original, as if it sprang out of nowhere. Morris took over a year making it, a painstaking process, much longer than usual, and, for nearly thirty years had been haunted by the score, as if setting it was his 'life's work'.[42] Quiet, reflective, like a meditation, utterly reduced in its materials—'white music' is how Roger Shattuck described the score—*Socrates* is in three Parts:

> Part 1: Pairs of dancers in antique tunics tow each other across the stage, each pair linked by a short rope—strange games to sturdy piano accompaniment, while a tenor voice intones.
> Part 2: Gentle undulating waves and after-waves, music and text speak of the progress of a river, while dancers pass from right to left across our vision. The surtitles[43] take us in the opposite direction.
> Part 3: Pictures emerge as groups assemble around a series of individual figures—all of them might be Socrates, as the singer suggests? Stories are told, about conversations, attentiveness, death, love...and the groups dissolve. Blocks of repeating motifs, as visual and aural underlay, comfort our eyes and ears.

Socrates is a fundamentally homogeneous statement, although moments of emphasis arise out of nowhere, some loud, others quieter. Sudden changes constitute high drama in such restrained circumstances, and their poignancy grows with acquaintance (as with the music of Thomson, a great admirer of Satie). Moments like these pass swiftly. *Socrates* retains its mystery.

Such elusive qualities put a strain on the kind of analysis that breaks a piece down into component parts. The business of tracing the intricacy of construction and points of story here is compelling, also the tracking of moments of musical and textual visualisation and intermediate punctuation. Yet it seems unusually important to preserve the particular sense of continuity and liveness through which *Socrates* casts its spell. Methodologically, from time to time, it seemed necessary to leave the piece alone for a while, and to forget, and then watch the piece again straight through, savouring it as performance.

Very late during this Morris book project, in 2014, a highly insightful article by Alice Miller Cotter was published that made me re-think *Socrates* yet again. A student on Morris's 2010 seminar for music graduates at Princeton University (see p. 62), she argues that Morris had responded to the 'intentional spiritual discourse' within Plato's meditations on Socrates and in Satie's music. This had previously been noted by the Russian theorist Vladimir Jankélévitch as springing from an aesthetic of detachment and reticence.[44] But Cotter takes this a step further, linking Socrates' philosophy with Buddhism, both ways of thinking leading to calm, composed understanding of death, the great, inevitable *absence*, knowledge of which frees the human soul. Morris, in turn, had told her that he was challenged to 'get at *nothing* without boring the audience'.[45]

Many Satie structural features mentioned during discussion of Morris's 1983 *Death of Socrates* (to Part 3 of the score, see pp. 164-7) are relevant here for the whole work (with its three Parts): the mosaic of repeating motifs—one of these the four rising triads spanning a tetrachord that has been labelled the 'Socrates motif' (in Part 3, see Ex. 10.3);[46] the scales like 'wipes', as transitions within each Part; the modal basis and consequent lack of harmonic drive and firm cadential completion; the independence between the non-repetitive, melodious vocal line delivered plainly, 'en lisant'—'like reading out of a phone book' says Morris[47]—and the brief accompanying ostinatos.

Ex. 10.3 *Socrates*, Satie, Part 3.

Satie subtitled the score 'symphonic drama'. This may seem strange, given that there is barely any symphonic development of material, that he scored it for a chamber ensemble, and that the style of drama is distinctly odd. Of the three totally distinct Parts, two bear hardly any story, and a narrator replaces speaking characters in the third. Francis Poulenc more aptly described *Socrates* as 'the beginning of horizontal music which will succeed perpendicular music. It is essentially to this that *Socrate* owes its limpidity, which is like running water.'[48]

All three Parts use text drawn from Plato's 'Dialogues' in the translation by Victor Cousin.

> Part 1, 'Portrait of Socrates': the disciple Alcibiades' eulogy of Socrates at a banquet, comparing his eloquence favourably against the flute-playing of the satyr Marsyas.
> Part 2, 'The Banks of the Ilissus': a conversation between Socrates and Phaedrus while they stroll beside a river and eventually find a resting place beneath a plane tree.
> Part 3, 'The Death of Socrates': related by his pupil Phaedo, who was present with other friends at the time. He recalls Socrates speaking of the immortality of the soul, liberated from the body and in union with the gods, his rebirth into a better world.

As in *Bedtime*, there is no single coherent narrative, rather three different styles of writing. Furthermore, these selected texts distance us from Socrates the thinker, speaking first through Alcibiades, then presenting him in an informal pastoral conversation, finally remembering him through the poignant account of someone who was present at, and deeply moved by, his death.

All this contributes to the particular enigma of *Socrates*, its standing as perhaps Satie's most elusive and fascinating work. To Pietro Dossena, who has undertaken intriguing 'genetic' research into the compositional process, it seemed to be about

> a private matter between Satie, Plato and Socrates: a match between Satie and Socrates—two rounds and the decider—with Plato as referee.

Dossena provides a map of its plentiful cultural and biographical references, most importantly:

> cubism; esprit nouveau, the 'cult of restraint' and Guillaume Apollinaire; identification between Satie and Socrates; an exercise in Atticism; neoclassicism and 'rappel à l'ordre'.[49]

Originally, Satie intended the music for four sopranos and chamber orchestra, although it has most frequently been performed by one soprano, as in the recording that Morris used in 1983 for his setting of Part 3. Returning to *Socrates* in 2010, however, Morris decided to work with Satie's piano score and to use a tenor solo: the recording by the Swiss tenor Hugues Cuénod had inspired him.[50] (This choice was also more logical, given that Plato's text was about male speakers and characters and that touring the work with the piano was a far less expensive option.) The piano sound is cooler than the orchestra—and Morris felt that it made the score's rhythmic content more interesting[51]—yet his movement here is more pliant, and softer, with less pressure to hold angular shapes in the body than in his 1983 work. Freed from one strict system across a large musical canvas, the driving force behind the earlier setting, Morris turned more poetic. The singer at Morris's premiere was Jean-Paul Fouchécourt (who had taken the title role in *Platée*) and, at most later performances, Zach Finkelstein.[52]

In the meantime, Morris took ideas from the 1787 painting 'The Death of Socrates' by Jacques-Louis David, which is housed in the Metropolitan Museum of Art in New York. There is, for instance, the position of Socrates' arms as he sits on his bed, one extended sideways to grasp the cup of hemlock, the other with the index finger pointing up towards the gods. On several occasions in Part 3, one or more dancers strike this arm and finger motif. Sometimes this happens when Socrates' name is mentioned: the combined effect is an impressive theatrical moment and striking example of conceptual blending (see pp. 97-8). Morris borrowed the principles of depth and interior/exterior from David. Figures are seen leaving on a distant stairway outside Socrates' cell; Morris's up- and down-stage groups and Michael Chybowski's black screens raised and lowered to open up or close off imaginary space recall these features of the painting. The weeping in the picture also finds its way into the choreography. Perhaps most important of all, the colours in the painting, soft russets, brown and blues were adopted by Martin Pakledinaz for the dancers' Grecian tunics.

Returning to the full score and its text, it is significant that Morris is led to a considerable degree by musical construction. He does not highlight the dialogue structure between speakers in Parts 1 and 2. Their speeches are not identified with particular dancers, and the fifteen dancers are deployed relatively evenly across the text. The same follows for Part 3, where several dancers take turns to 'be' Socrates.

With all the dancers too, Morris responds to the large form of each Part. There is a 'settling' towards the ends of Parts 2 and 3. Here, individual musical ostinatos continue for much longer than in Part 1 and at the same pitch, and Morris brings all his dancers together in shared activity. The 'settling' at the end of Part 2 makes literal textual sense. Here, for a while, the dance follows the overriding textual image, of a river, always moving onwards and downstream. Satie regularly introduces fresh musical ideas, so Morris does too, although 'fresh' can only be seen as relative within such a homogeneous style. All the dance statements (groups) move from stage left to right. (They can choose which 'corridor' to use, up- or down-stage, and whether or not to wear a cloak as they pass through.) Finally, just as a sustained musical ostinato suggests, the dancers find rest, as do Socrates and Phaedrus under a plane tree. We leave them all sitting quietly.

At the end of Part 1, on the other hand, there is a kind of coda as Socrates responds to Alcibiades, the only occasion when he speaks:

> *Tu viens de faire mon éloge: c'est maintenant à moi de faire celui de mon voisin de droite.*
> So much for your kind words about me. Now it is my turn to praise the companion on my right.[53]

A lone dancer, originally Maile Okamura, undertakes a fourth zig-zag crossing during the response, and this time, exceptionally, she appears to identify with the philosopher.

In other respects, the 2010 *Socrates* is still one of Morris's most schematic dances, a fact that, on this occasion, did not seem to worry the critics. Regularly, throughout the work, somewhere on stage, you will see a group of dancers 'doing' the piano accompaniment (often an ostinato) and repeating the same visualisation when the same accompaniment pattern comes back. See, for instance, the opening rope movement in Part 1, when pairs of dancers tug each other across the stage, following the long-short-long pattern in the score as they go.[54] Then, in Part 2, they dance the pervasive skipping rhythm, as if reflecting the undulations on the surface of the river.[55]

In Part 3, Morris defines the activity of his dancing groups (three groups of five, dressed respectively in blue/gold, yellow/russet and beige) in terms of just three possibilities—'rhythm', 'narrative' and 'offstage'. Let us consider rhythm first. The walking to the opening 'Socrates motif' (see Ex. 10.3) consists of patterns of four steps that mainly project forwards to the four rising crotchet triads (bars 1-4), but the dancers recognise change of pitch and walk backwards as the triads reverse direction (downwards) in bars 5-6.

One of the most pervasive movement ostinatos in Part 3 is to a 4-note melodic motif. Once again, the musical rhythm is walked, but here the curve down and up is shown too, with the head, in arm gestures, and in complementary bending and straightening of the legs.

Ex. 10.4 *Socrates*, Part 3.

Occasionally, dancers walk to the quick, quaver beat, which means that they have doubled the speed, while the music does not necessarily give this impression.

Morris treasures musical detail and presses for it not to be missed, for the simple and seemingly insignificant to become more tangible. So, on several occasions in Part 3, the dancers show us the patter of triplets emerging briefly out of 4/4 time, while an arm circling up and over traces their pitch contour. These passages are like sudden gusts of wind. On a few occasions in Part 2, when the voice strikes out in duple time across the primary 6/8 metre, the dancers take off in small buoyant leaps (bars 84, 148-50 and 152). Such changes are enlivening. In Part 3, there are two passages of material (bars 52-59; 237-44) where quavers in the right hand piano line are grouped into units of 3/4. The voice above and bass below continue in 4/4. Morris clearly wants us to register the metrical change, so he introduces slow, smooth triplet steps that pick out the middle line.

Sometimes the musical information brought to our attention is yet more secretive. In three striking passages in Part 2, the dancers embark on a series of jazzy, jaunty *tendus*, tapping a foot forwards and backwards several times, and swinging their arms in opposition (see Ex. 10.5). This happens exactly where crotchet beats in one part of the music cross the 6/8—twice in the accompaniment, the last time in the vocal line—but this crotchet beat (which the dancers follow) is not the one that stands out. The dynamics lower to *pp* or *ppp*. Morris makes us hear what we are inclined to miss, offering us a sudden, magical close-up for our ears.

Towards the end of Part 3, a low tolling bass commences (repeating the note A), and the singer describes the moment of Socrates' death—plain declamation, solemn intoning mainly on the note E: '*Un peu de temps après il fit un movement convulsif.*' ('A short while afterwards, there is a convulsion.') The dancers glide across the stage to the exact rhythm of the voice, with a correspondingly level walk. But look back to bars 191-94 and 201 and we find anticipations—the same level style of vocal line, the same gliding. The vocal line, however, is so undistinguished here, and the passage so brief, that it would hardly be possible to remember it. Perhaps this is the most secret connection of all. But it does signal the arrival of the poison that will kill Socrates.

Morris emphasises points of visualisation through unisons, anything from simple doubling to all fifteen dancers doing the same thing, sometimes in compact groups, sometimes spread across the stage, and with increased intensity towards the end of the piece. But the movement dynamics are highly unusual, an unforgettable combination of delicacy, quirkiness (like the jazzy steps) and sturdy precision. Visualisation does not normally look

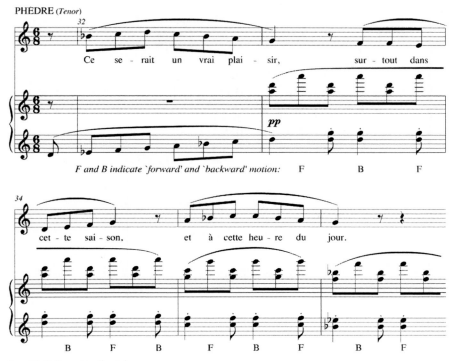

Ex. 10.5 *Socrates*, Part 2.

(or feel) like this. On the other hand, unison both formalises and enlarges the impression of a movement sequence. It freezes images in the mind and provides a comforting ground, or solidity, against complication elsewhere. It is important that these structural devices of music visualisation and unison are entirely appropriate to the expressive and spiritual statement of *Socrates*, which is about the avoidance of excess and the clarity of simplicity.

Yet, in both music and dance, repetition is frequently inexact, containing a modest element of change. As Cotter points out, Satie's repeating motifs, like the opening triads, contain a component of fluctuation at the same time as implying stasis, transposed, set against a different vocal line, or subject to new dynamic treatment.[56] Likewise, as is characteristic of him, Morris frequently changes the context of dance material when repeating it, giving it a different place in space, a different facing, or setting it against other movement material.[57] Meanwhile, the text winds on inexorably, visually in the surtitles (which distract us from the stage) as well as aurally, with no repetition whatsoever.

Let us turn now to the narrative aspect of *Socrates*. As so frequently in Morris's work, words provide another layer for visualisation and emphasis

Socrates, Part 3, Domingo Estrada, taking his turn as 'Socrates'. © Gene Schiavone, 2010

and, in the case of *Socrates*, increasingly so as it develops. In Part 1, there is little, if any, connection of this kind. In Part 2, the movement links with the mention of objects and simple actions, not yet human situations or interactions: lying down, grass, cicadas rubbing their wings, the movement of the river. Statues seen by Socrates and Phaedrus on a nearby altar prompted an elongated steeple image, a group of dancers seen with stretched arms and palms meeting overhead. This is one of several images that carry over into Part 3, and here, the surtitles really come into their own. Not only does the name 'Socrates' itself carry with it a motif—the raised index finger. Socrates' situation and conversations in the gaol are also recalled. Several dancers in turn embody him, the focal figure within their 'narrative' clusters: Socrates showing his leg (imaginary fetters around it), sitting on his bed, taking a bath, while others in groups demonstrate increasing pressure of reference to the cup, the poison, and the drinking of the poison. At one point, there is a quote from dance history. A line of dancers sit and fold over their front leg in a 'Dying Swan' pose, as Socrates is recalled saying:

> *Les cygnes, quand ils sentent qu'ils vont mourir chantent encore mieux ce jour-là qu'ils n'ont jamais fait, dans la joie d'aller trouver le dieu qu'ils servent.*
> Swans, when they know they are about to die, sing better than they have ever done, from joy at going to join the god they serve.[58]

Just after the jailer has handed the cup of poison to Socrates, the statue/ steeple pose from Part 2 turns into a climax: in unison, across the entire cast. This is one of the few, but outstanding, *forte/fortissimo* moments in the whole work.

On the other hand, even though there is progression towards greater narrative content in Morris's *Socrates*, this happens at a considerable psychological distance (far more than in *Erlkönig*), in the manner of allusion, illustration as suggestion. There are no stable characters, no trains of action or thought, just moments visualised, the occasional marks of conceptual blending, a constant process of evolution and dissolution. In turn, the three groups of dancers form chains and rush like waves through the space, assembling and re-assembling imagery from Phaedo's tale. At the same time, these narrative occasions show us the longer continuities of musical organisation, while the 'rhythm' dancers show us the detail of individual beats and bars. Sometimes, it seems that Morris chooses to emphasise the ritual aspect of Plato's discourse, the formal impulse behind the spoken ideas rather than the ideas themselves and their story.

It is through his musical and textural approach that Morris creates his own composite contour of energy through the piece, enlarging the large moments in the score, and quietening those that are already quiet. I have already noted how the mention of Socrates' name and appearance of the Socrates arm and finger motif reinforce each other. We both hear and see more acutely under these conditions. The motif registers most forcefully of all when Socrates asks for the offering of a rooster to Aesculapius, god of healing—all fifteen dancers stand with an index finger pointing up to the gods, a better place, and the lights gradually dim. Morris makes a great deal of this point in the text.

Moments of f and ff become more visually prominent towards the end of the piece, with the unison steeple, and soon afterwards when, after drinking the poison, the full ensemble rise from the floor as if to question the oppressor: us. The biggest moment of all is when Socrates says that he can no longer feel his foot—'*Il dit que non!*' The poison is working. The three groups, banked in three lines, strike angular positions, those lying on the floor (all of them Socrates?) flinging their arms over their eyes, blinding themselves in their distress.

At the other extreme, there are profoundly restful occasions—hiatus points with a rallentando or apostrophe marked in the score—sometimes complete stillness, when the dancers appear to be simply remembering, or meditating. It is by working with these extremes that Morris's big moments, suddenly achieved and as suddenly removed, fill us with fierce emotion. The more architectural the choreography—with hard body designs and mass unisons—and the greater the distance from the 'real' death of Socrates, the more forceful the effect.

By the end, a central theme emerges of individuals subsumed within their community, and it is crucial here that, as if deeply touched by the story of Socrates, the whole group shares in embodying his experience. This is another of Morris's pieces about community. As Alastair Macaulay suggests, things have changed: 'Socrates' very particular story moves on to become a story that's experienced by others—by, indeed, the world'.[59]

The bass begins to toll, the fifteen dancers support the singer's declamation, and one by one drop to the floor in a 'death', each differently, marking the text—the convulsion, the closing of the eyes, then of the mouth, until one remains to glide offstage, who will not die...yet? For the last two bars, Satie stops the tolling and strikes a pedal B over an E-sharp/F-sharp oscillation; he leaves us hovering on the F-sharp. Meanwhile, all those lying spread across the stage raise an arm, a leg, the head, as if levitating in harmony with the ascent in the oscillation. Is this the spirit rising, released from the body, a sharing in the new knowledge of Socrates? Or, as Cotter suggests, is this a signal that they are all about 'to begin again—a new cycle, a new series of movements that could continue on endlessly'?[60] Yet, with all the dancers joining in unison again, it is as if narrative and form finally dissolve quietly into each other, both, in this instance, having come to represent absence. Morris's ending is, in the end, ambiguous, as his best endings always are and, as is so often the case, music is his strongest guide.[61]

11

Going West: Morris Meets Lou Harrison

To this day, Morris draws upon a range of cultural sources that extends beyond the traditions of Western high art. Since his period in Brussels, several dances have addressed European and American folk traditions: *Home* (1993), for MMDG, which includes step-dancing to the singer-songwriter Michelle Shocked and rock 'n' roll bassist Rob Wasserman; *The Office* (1994) to Dvořak Bagatelles, for the Ohio-based group Živili—Dances and Music of the Southern Slavic Nations;[1] and, in 2012, *Carnival* (Saint-Saëns), for the Philadelphia-based Voloshky Ukrainian Dance Ensemble.

In other work, however, Morris has looked West across the Pacific to Asia. He has done so ever since his youth in Seattle, where consciousness of this cultural range was an integral part of life (see p. 21). Early dances used recordings picked up in 1982 when touring India and Indonesia with Laura Dean: Indian, classical (for *O Rangasayee*, Sri Tyagaraja, 1984) and popular (*The "Tamil Film Songs in Stereo" Pas de Deux*, 1983). Morris also used traditional Tahitian (*Not Goodbye*, 1982) and popular Thai (*Celestial Greetings*, 1983). Then, in 2002, continuing his explorations of Indian culture, he made *Kolam*, a collaboration with Zakir Hussain and Ethan Iverson, based on the idea of drawings (Kolams) as prayers to the gods. The piece crossed Indian and jazz genres, incorporating yoga-influenced movement style, and had a backdrop by the distinguished British artist and Indophile Howard Hodgkin. Morris still today makes regular visits to India.

The most significant branch of Morris's work since the 1990s, however, has used scores that synthesise elements of Indonesian gamelan music with western genres, most of these by the West Coast composer Lou Harrison (b. 1917). Partly because of their shared cross-cultural interests, Harrison became the contemporary composer with whom Morris developed the strongest rapport. In fact, he used Harrison more often than any other composer, of any period,[2] staging eight pieces in all to his music, although only one of these was made together from scratch, *Rhymes with Silver* (1997).[3] Another, for Morris's own company, *Grand Duo*, turned out to be one of his most popular ever, in the repertory every year since its 1993 premiere. Harrison died in 2003, at which point Morris stopped making dances to his music. Looking to the future, however, he has indicated interest in choreographing Harrison's concerto for organ and percussion.

The full list of Morris's dances to Harrison scores is as follows:

1987 *Strict Songs*: 1955 *Strict Songs*, for 120 male chorus (in version for Morris), chamber orchestra (2 trombones, piano, harp, percussion, strings)   10 dancers

1992 *Polka*: 1988 *Grand Duo* (last movement), for violin and piano   16 dancers

1993 *Grand Duo*: 1988 *Grand Duo*, for violin and piano[4] (the longest, fourth, slow movement, Air, omitted)   14 dancers

1995 *Pacific*: 1990 *Trio for Violin, Cello and Piano* (3rd and 4th movements)   9 dancers
Commissioned and premiered by San Francisco Ballet

1995 *World Power*: 1991 *Homage to Pacifica* (two movements selected: 'In Honor of the Divine Mr. Handel' and 'In Honor of Mark Twain'), for chorus, Javanese gamelan (slendro and pelog) and harp; and 1976 *Bubaran Robert* (music for Kyai Hudan Mas), for Javanese gamelan (slendro and pelog) and piccolo trumpet   14 dancers

1997 *Rhymes with Silver*: 1996 *Rhymes with Silver*, for violin, viola, cello, piano, percussion (the Gigue and Musette written in 1943 and arranged for *Rhymes*). 16 dancers   Commissioned by MMDG[5]

1997 *Waltz in C*: 1945 *Waltz in C*, for piano, Morris dancing with three fluffy puppets, in Sesame Street programme (Children's Television Workshop)   Solo

2003 *Serenade*: 1952 *Serenade for Guitar* (with optional percussion)   Solo

Both Morris and Harrison were inspired by the timbres and scales offered by Asian music and by alternatives to western equal temperament, especially the more 'natural' and 'pure' intervals of just intonation (see p. 55). In this respect, it is significant that both welcomed the interval theories of Harry Partch, a friend of Harrison's who was particularly impatient with Western tradition. Morris had set some of Partch's music in his early career (see pp. 25-6), returning to him once more in 1998 for the solo *Greek to Me*. This was a setting of the 1946 *Studies on Ancient Greek Scales*, played in recording on one of Partch's home-made instruments (the harmonic canon—a horizontal, plucked, stringed instrument). The traditional-Greek style of Morris's costume eased the viewer into thinking ethnographically. Also in common between Morris and Harrison was their commitment to live performance. They were both gay as well, which some, as we will see later, consider important to an examination of their work.

Harrison had more dance background than most of Morris's composers. He not only had some training and performing experience as a child (onstage and socially), but also considerable experience since the 1930s of working with American modern dancers on West and East Coasts, long before Morris turned to his work. Harrison soon became central to this dance world, as class pianist, composer, and performer in their dance concerts, and he also taught courses in composition for dance.[6] Perhaps too because of his own powerful kinetic sensibility, he naturally thought of the two arts as

Grand Duo, 'Polka'. © Katsuyoshi Tanaka, 2010

inseparable. 'Music is basically a song and a dance' was his often-quoted manifesto.[7]

Examples of Harrison's collaboration with celebrated modern dancer/choreographers are his work in the 1930s and 1940s with the Los Angeles-based choreographer Lester Horton, Jean Erdman in New York (Harrison lived on the East Coast 1943-53), and, in the early 1950s, Katherine Litz at the artistically radical Black Mountain College, North Carolina. Back in California, he worked with Eva Soltes (recently director of a documentary film on Harrison[8]) and Remy Charlip. Harrison also became a close colleague of Merce Cunningham and John Cage, another erstwhile dance composer and accompanist, and, in 1947, wrote the score for Cunningham's *Open Road.*

A seminal influence upon Harrison's musical development was Henry Cowell, the 'central information booth'[9] for many American composers, he called him, immensely important for encouraging an experimental attitude towards composition and an openness towards cultural practices beyond the European legacy. Cowell too was a dance composer. Later, Harrison studied with Arnold Schoenberg in Los Angeles, and then, in New York, to which he followed Horton and his company, he was invited by Virgil Thomson to write regular music criticism for the *New York Herald Tribune.* In the meantime, Harrison was instrumental in bringing the work of Charles Ives into print and public performance. It is noteworthy that Morris has set the music of all the American composers just mentioned. He used Cowell four times, in *Prelude and Prelude* (1984, Set of Two for violin and harpsichord, first movement, see pp. 162-3), *Mosaic and United* (1993), the 'Sesame Street' *Anger Dance* (1997) and *Jenn and Spencer* (2013, Suite for violin and piano).

Harrison became enamoured of the gamelan from recordings that he listened to in the mid-1930s, after which, in 1939, he encountered it live at the Golden Gate International Exposition in San Francisco. But it was in New York that he began to study Asian music seriously. Over the years, after returning to California, Harrison made several extended visits to Asia, researching further the music and culture, and learning to play traditional instruments: first to East Asia—in 1961 to Japan and Korea, in 1962 to Taiwan—and then in 1984 to Java. In 1975, back in California, he began studies of traditional Indonesian practice, with the gamelan master and teacher K.R.T. Wasitodiningrat (aka Pak Cokro). Increasingly absorbed by this music, he built several gamelans himself with his life-partner William Colvig, starting with 'Old Granddad' in 1971, his American gamelan, a concoction of found sounding objects, and moving on to others modelled more precisely upon Indonesian principles. Already, for some years, critics had spotted the 'gamelan timbres' in Harrison's music, whether from established western, or home-made, instruments, but, after working with Cokro, he was ready to compose for, and make hybrids using, traditional Indonesian ensembles.

As regards Harrison being a synthesist, mixing Asian and western compositional practices, some discussion of related political issues is helpful. Much has been written about the appropriation of Asian forms by Westerners and the power imbalance involved. More recently, however, that aura of negativity has itself been brought into question, and there are suggestions instead that the act of borrowing or sharing—although acknowledgement of sources is ethically essential—might be seen as a two-way process of 'exchange and creative response....appropriation generates new meanings for a new context'.[10] Certainly, Harrison demonstrated full awareness of the power issues involved and of the impossibility of dispensing with his own primary background in western culture.[11] Morris describes Harrison's incorporation of diverse musical references as 'an integral element in the composition. It's inclusive music.'[12] His own take, which is essentially similar, has been described by Beth Genné in an article on *Gong*, his 2001 setting of the gamelan-influenced symphonic score *Tabuh-Tabuhan* by the Canadian composer Colin McPhee, commissioned by American Ballet Theatre.[13] Genné says that Morris's ballet is

> not an ethno-choreographical exercise in mimicking Balinese dance, nor is it his attempt to graft Balinese gestures onto classical dance as a kind of decorative accent.[14]

There are 'no "direct quotes"'. Instead, there is assimilation at a deep level, in order to create a new language or style for a new dance.

Examining cultural appropriation from another point of view, in line with recent queer scholarship, Alessandra Lopez y Royo has suggested that the gamelan plays its part in the negotiation of sexuality, as a 'gay marker' linking Harrison, for instance, with the Benjamin Britten of *The Prince of the Pagodas* (1957), the McPhee of *Tabuh-Tabuhan* (1936) and Morris. The gamelan, the music of the 'other' Asian culture, Lopez claims, would serve to mark what came to be regarded in the late twentieth century, and by Harrison himself,[15] as the gay 'other'. Thus, writes Lopez:

> In Mark Morris' use of McPhee's music [or Harrison's] there is a coded acknowledgement by a queer choreographer of the legacy of McPhee, a gay man, responsible for introducing the gamelan in American music, and for the impact this had on the twentieth-century American musical landscape. The gamelan was taken up by a community of gay composers... In contemporary American art music the gamelan sound is queer.[16]

Lopez then situates her view of the 'gay marker' within the scholarly debate about appropriation, as having the potential to generate 'new meanings for a new context':

> Queering the gamelan is also culturally appropriative, but it is an appropriation which affords a decentring and destabilising of hetero-sexuality and its normativity. Through a staging of sexuality, it acts as a corrective to the perception of a projected neutrality of music and dance, normally upheld as a basis for the exercise of power.[17]

Such cultural appropriation might be conscious or unconscious, intended or subliminal. But this can be seen as an extreme interpretation. It seems important here to point out that neither Harrison nor Morris claim to make 'gay' music or dance,[18] indeed Harrison used consistently to deny this. Nevertheless, he was one of the first to acknowledge that, as a gay 'outsider', he was likely to be attracted to other 'outsiders', including non-western cultures and societies in which gays are more readily accepted.[19]

It is significant that Harrison learnt his craft as a composer for dance at a relatively early stage in American modern dance history, a time when exceptional agendas for collaboration operated. Beginning in the 1920s, there was a strong reaction against the application of musically-based form to dance, as in music visualisation or interpretation. Instead, there was a call for autonomy for dance, or, at least, for dance to take precedence in the creative process. Influenced by German modern dance, and particularly Mary Wigman's working processes, the new theory was that dance music should be functional, not necessarily suitable for independent concert performance: its chief role was to support or frame the dance. The result was a number of silent dances and dances for which the music was composed to counts after the choreography had been completed, the opposite way round to usual procedures (see p. 81). Responding to the realities of dance studio economy, common characteristics developed within the new dance music, the use of piano and percussion particularly favoured (sometimes too, found, sounding objects), and stylistically, the kind of dissonance and rhythmic irregularity that spelt modern, urban anxiety.

No sooner had this shift in practice taken place, but Cowell led the way in pressing for freer relationships that would allow autonomy for both artforms, and that included contrapuntal opportunities. Between 1934 and 1941, he penned a series of writings on alternative modes of music-dance interaction. In 1937, he put forward his theory of 'elastic form', as summarised here by the scholar Leta E. Miller:

> ...containing units that dancers could expand, contract, repeat, omit, transpose, invert, or interchange in various ways—allowing the sound to respond to the choreography without disturbing its own validity. Cowell recommended writing sections or sentences as 'block-units' whose order could be shuffled; composing melodic phrases with the potential for extension or curtailment; authorising the repetition or omission of entire sections; and varying the instrumentation.[20]

Cowell adds to this:

> The whole work may, then, be short...or as long as is desired...It may be performed with percussion alone, with piano alone, with orchestral instruments, or with one orchestral instrument, or with any combination of these... The whole work will, in any of its ways or presentation, have form; but it may be easily adapted to the changes and freedoms so essential to the dancer's creation.[21]

Morris himself came across such 'elasticity' when setting two Cowell string quartets in his 1993 *Mosaic and United*: the *Mosaic Quartet*, No. 3 (1935) and *United Quartet*, No. 4 (1936). With mosaic form in mind, Cowell had stipulated that the five movements of No. 3 could be played in any order and repeated at will. Morris chose an abbreviated palindrome pattern: 1 2 3 4 5 3 1. The final 3 and 1 are clear variants on the earlier, corresponding movements. The number 'five' also found its way into the casting.

Cowell's *United Quartet* already demonstrates the kind of systematic structural approach that intrigues Morris—once set up, there is a built-in lack of human control, here an edifice constructed entirely from patterns of 'five':

1. in rhythm: long, long, short, long, short, at various levels, in every bar, in phrases of 5 bars, phrases clustering together into 5s within each movement, and five movements within the whole quartet;
2. dynamics: loud, loud, soft, loud, soft;
3. tonal structure: C, C, G, C, G.

Then Morris cast the three men and two women to reflect Cowell's pattern, which is most obvious in the series of five solos in the first movement.

Systems apart, 'Mosaic' and 'United' are quite different from each other, the first full of strong moods—expressionist at times—pressed into rigorous forms, the second foregrounding structure and simplicity, more unison, less human. Both are harshly economical in vocabulary. To repeat movements 3 and 1 of 'Mosaic' is to repeat the most disturbing material. The work as a whole is like *Bedtime* in reverse, a progress from more to less story. Re-purposing some of the 'Mosaic' motifs in 'United' only reinforces the point.[22]

Harrison's own procedures for dance were influenced by both Cowell's flexibility and his systematic mind. He also shared Cowell's theory that music and dance should operate as partners, neither art form subordinate to the other. In assembling his composer colleague's *Ritual of Wonder* (1939), he gained direct experience of working 'elastically'. Cowell provided the basic materials that Harrison formed into a dance score.[23] About half a dozen works by Harrison used what he called his 'kit' principle, which was another way of allowing choreographers to create their own compositional structure, assembling phrases or sections, repeating, juxtaposing, and omitting them as they wished. Examples are *Io and Prometheus* (1985) for Jean Erdman and *Ariadne* (1987) for Eva Soltes. *Rhymes with Silver*, for Morris, will be discussed in more detail later. Although the genesis of this work through a kit has often been discussed, its situation within the context of composition for American modern dance is far less familiar.[24]

Both Cowell and Harrison enjoyed creative lives outside, as well as within, the dance studio, but the position of house dance composer solidified during this period, this kind of work seen by many as a valuable source of exposure and income. (Some composers, like Louis Horst, Martha Graham's associate, and Norman Lloyd, are known almost exclusively for their work with dance.) At the same time, something of a stigma was attached to the label 'dance composer'. In 1940, after Cowell had moved to New York, Harrison wrote to him: 'I never imagined this damned dance-curse I have would pop up in N.Y.!...This is one reason I am giving up dancers—critics and musicians are trying to make a new Delibes of me!'[25]

Maintaining a foot in the dance studio throughout his career, Harrison also had an open, business-like approach to collaboration. Always with strong views of his own about music, on several occasions, Morris chose not to use all the movements of an existing Harrison score. He began choreographing and presenting just the last movement, the Polka of *Grand Duo* by itself, then later, when he went further back into the score, left out its longest, fourth movement, the slow Air.[26] *Pacific* (for San Francisco Ballet) was choreographed to just the last two movements of the Piano Trio: 1. a. Dance b. Rhapsody c. Song; 2. Allegro.

For *World Power*, he elected to use just two movements out of the eight that make up *Homage to Pacifica* ('In Honor of the Divine Mr. Handel' and 'In Honor of Mr. Mark Twain'), choosing another short piece *Bubaran Robert* to complete his dance. In all these cases, the full scores are longer than what he normally uses in a triple bill, but it is also clear that he favoured the rhythmically more robust, dance-friendly movements: in the Trio, for instance, the section actually called 'Dance', and the last movement with its catchy syncopations.[27] The flexible Harrison was willing to make revisions to suit Morris. At the choreographer's request, he re-worked the original *Strict Songs* (for eight baritones) to accommodate the 120-strong Seattle Men's Chorus.

Before detailed examination of selected dances, it is useful to make some general observations about the Harrison scores that Morris has used. Most striking are the particular sound qualities resonating from Asian tradition and 'exotic' to western ears: the 'gamelan timbres' long associated with Harrison's music, even before he studied Indonesian music in detail, both pitched gongs and un-pitched percussion. Then there are the modal melodic structures, often expressed through limited intervallic collections, a small group of pitches, which he called 'melodicles', using just intonation.

Strict Songs is a good example of these structures. Inspired by Navaho ritual songs, the poems, written by Harrison himself, express a profusion of nature imagery, some of which Morris illustrated in his choreography. The four untitled sections of text begin as follows: 1. Here is Holiness... 2. Here is Nourishment... 3. Here is Tenderness... 4. Here is Splendor... For this score, the fixed-pitch harp and piano had to be specially retuned for just intonation, while the string and trombone players could match these pitches by ear. Mixing bowls containing different levels of water in order to represent different pitches also contributed their own idiosyncratic sound. While each movement featured a different pentatonic mode, the tuning accorded with the two different types of pentatonic scale, which Harrison prefers to describe using Indonesian terminology: slendro (without any semitones, for movements 1 and 3) and pelog (with semitones, for movements 2 and 4).[28] In his programme note for the Piano Trio (used in *Pacific*), Harrison simply specified that the particular movements Morris chose were 'modal in character', and that 'the entire work is melodic'.[29]

The composer was also interested in experimenting with new piano sounds, borrowing Cowell's idea of using cluster chords of adjacent notes. He extended this principle to produce a peculiarly aggressive, concentrated sound in *Grand Duo* and *Rhymes with Silver*, introducing the 'octave bar', a wooden device that can strike all the black or white keys within the span of an octave.

We turn now to more detailed analysis based on four of Morris's dances to Harrison's music. Together, these offer a range of perspectives on creative process (including a particularly strong musical contribution from Morris), structure and expressive statement.

World Power

World Power is the Morris work that uses a traditional Javanese gamelan, comprising both slendro and pelog instruments, which, in keeping with his commitment to liveness in performance, he imported for every performance of the piece. These instruments constitute bronze hanging and pot gongs (of different pitches marking out and subdividing the cyclical structures of the music), metallophones (bronze-keyed instruments with bamboo resonators), bamboo flutes and drums. Padded and unpadded sticks are used for striking instruments. Harrison, a pacifist, had introduced a strong political message against American imperialism into his composition. The second movement, which was selected by Morris, includes a sung version (by a chorus) of a famous statement by Mark Twain, referring to the 1899-1902 Philippine-American war:

> We have pacified some thousands of the islanders and buried them; destroyed their fields; burned their villages, and turned their widows and orphans out-of-doors; furnished heartbreak by exile to some dozens of disagreeable patriots; subjugated the remaining ten millions by Benevolent Assimilation, which is the pious new name of the musket; we have acquired property in the three hundred concubines and other slaves of our business partner, the Sultan of Sulu, and hoisted our protecting flag over that swag.

> And so, by these Providences of God—and the phrase is the government's, not mine—we are a World Power.[30]

In Morris's choreography, two men illustrate the text through a loose version of arm signing, while an accompanying group of dancers delivers images of suffering and violence. Morris's decision to end his piece with the earlier score *Bubaran Robert* opens up a fascinating dialogue with Twain's barbed writings. *Bubaran* is a specific form defined by time lengths marked out by gongs and other instruments and by a drumming pattern. But in this particular score, Harrison superimposed repeating statements on a piccolo trumpet, a western instrument that can be read as both military and celebratory.[31] The movement vocabulary in Morris's formal dance complements the irony created by his juxtaposition of scores. His formal, patterned, 'celebratory' finale contains images of distinct unease: an impatient stamping motif and 'verses' ending with a retreat into the wings, heads tilting backwards, hands shielding faces, as if in horror.

In *World Power*, as in other Morris choreography to Harrison, there are hints of Asian sources in the movement, the turned-out bent-legged walking and emphasis on hand gestures. But the ethnic accent is nearly always unspecific and integrated within a language much more varied in resonance than such brief description would suggest. Certainly, in the ballets, the Asian sources have enriched what is often seen as restrictive classical behaviour, in *Pacific*, for instance, a surprisingly free use of upper body and arms. The men here wear similar sarong-style skirts to the women. In *Gong*, the palms are joined—the conventional gesture of respectful greeting in Asia—although held overhead in this context, and always ready to slip into other, asymmetrical arm positions as part of a new geometrical language.

Other features of Harrison's style are important to his work with Morris. The Horton dancer and choreographer Bella Lewitsky once said of Harrison's texture that it is 'not dense, not overpopulated by multiple things happening at once... all the spaces aren't clamped into multiple sounds.'[32] Morris seems to have been attracted by such economy. Frequently, and certainly in the music that he chose to choreograph, textures consist of just two lines, a melody and an accompaniment, sometimes made bolder through duplication at the octave. Harrison made rhythm and melody his compositional focus, rather than harmony. He also enjoyed the kinetic buoyancy of metrical irregularity and crossing patterns and welcomed choreographers adding more rhythmic trickery of their own. On the other hand, long, winding and expressive cantilenas become the predominant feature in several sections of *Pacific*, *Strict Songs*, *Grand Duo* and *Rhymes*.

There is little place in Harrison's music for progressive harmonic structures, instead a more relaxed attitude to time, a privileging of sonic beauty, and power growing through repetition and accumulation of forces. In interview, Morris expressed the challenge that he faced in *World Power*:

The music is Asian and quite horizontal so there isn't an apotheosis or anything. There's not a Western-style climax to this music. There aren't modulations. It starts and goes on for a while and then it's over. It's like, 'Oh, OK'. That's why this music is hard for me because it is sort of stress-free. It's beautiful and dark but The Big Thing doesn't happen, which is why I was drawn to the music in the first place.[33]

The first movement of *World Power* (entitled 'In Honor of the Divine Mr. Handel') is constructed out of simple phrase repetition and elaboration in music and dance. The dance material maps precisely on to the changes from one repeating pattern to another in the music, but adds its own accents, sometimes countering what you hear. Then, at the end, when Harrison repeats his main 'theme' with additional orchestral forces, Morris introduces a further seven dancers to add to the unison, doubling his numbers. But he has a curious response to Harrison's firm ending, a perfect cadence, dominant to tonic, an outright reference to western convention.[34] It is as if Morris undermines the closure, by introducing a new thrusting gesture from the newcomers. They push out into space, speaking of confrontation, unfinished business, while the first seven dancers retreat upstage, arms billowing. Both moves lead us into the future of *World Power*. The title of this first movement indicates Harrison's particular fondness for Handel's music as well as the fact that he identified with him: 'an immensely imaginative composer with a cosmopolitan outlook too'.[35] Handel was also one of Morris's favourite composers.

The *Bubaran Robert* choreography is equally interesting for not following the entirely flat structure of the music: a series of verses, AB or BA, many repeating statements by the piccolo trumpet accompanied by gamelan and constructed according to the following plan:

A Accompaniment (gamelan) only (8 bars)

B Trumpet and B Accompaniment (8 bars)

A Trumpet and A Accompaniment (8 bars)

A Accompaniment only (8 bars)

A Trumpet and A Accompaniment (8 bars)

B Trumpet and B Accompaniment (8 bars)

The whole of the above pattern then repeats from the beginning.

Finally, the music just slows down and stops. While the choreography is equally repetitive, the dance energy swells and subsides, several times, as the number of dancers waxes and wanes, suggesting that Morris was not inclined towards the degree of Asian 'horizontality' that he heard in the music. (The same issue arose later, in 2010, in his setting of Satie's 'horizontal' music in *Socrates*, see p. 351.) *World Power* was originally shorter than it is now. After *New Yorker* critic Arlene Croce lamented that the work 'dies just as we need a clincher...[but it is] potentially a great piece', he added a final repetition to *Bubaran Robert*.[36]

The 'flat' approach to musical structure relates to Harrison's penchant for simple repetition forms, without sophisticated tonal evolution through modulation: binary (with both halves repeated and the possibility of moving easily to dominant tonality at the end of the first half); the medieval estampie with its couplets (e.g. aa)—each line of a couplet having a different ending (e.g. a—x—a—y); ternary (ABA); and rondo (e.g. ABACADA). It is significant in terms of harmonic principles that Harrison claimed to be most fond of the French rondo, 'not the Viennese rondo with its transposition [modulation] of the subject, as in Mozart and Haydn'.[37]

Serenade

Dedicated by Morris to 'the Divine Mr. Harrison', *Serenade* exemplifies the composer's use of simple repetition forms:

1. Round A A1 B B A
2. Air A B A C B A
3. Infinite Canon 'At least three times, please'
4. Usul A A B (closing with the first eight bars of A)
5. Sonata A A B B

Morris tells us that he was interested here in working with guitar for the first time, so the piece was partly led by the desire to explore a new timbre. These five little dances also turned out to be 'prop' dances, incorporating a box, a copper pipe, a fan, followed by sounding percussion, finger cymbals, then castanets.

Like many of Morris's solos from the later period of his performing career, *Serenade* is an exploratory dance. Acocella described it as 'aggressively simple', suggesting that it harked back to Morris's transformative experiments as a child. 'In a sense, he is still doing that—showing us how a copper pipe, carried in a certain way, can be a sceptre, a torch, Excalibur.'[38] It is not so distant either from *Ten Suggestions* (see p. 128). There is indeed a sense of childlike wonderment as Morris, always the charismatic performer, demonstrates that something small and mundane can be intriguing and worth showing (and hearing) several times. His enjoyment in the moment of performance is infectious. Yet, the miracle is that, while, once again, Morris dances the musical repetition forms precisely, you would hardly spot this—so intricate is the mosaic of dance and musical information, and so rarely does the dance settle and allow our attention to rest.

Morris had the idea of playing the castanets during the final 'Sonata' movement, drawing upon his early Spanish dance experience and the fact that the music was modelled on the Spanish baroque keyboard sonatas of Domenico Scarlatti. He was intending to ask Harrison's permission, but learnt of his death before he was able to do this:

> I imagined him giving me a long-distance eye-roll over the line from his home in Aptos, Calif., a sigh and a 'Go ahead if you must, you'll do it anyway.' I did it anyway, Lou.

So, for the 'Sonata', a brief invasion of the composer's territory, Morris wrote his own, independent castanet line and concluded the dance with an exuberant clattering exit. But it was a 'non-Spanish' dance.

Serenade provided Morris with a rare opportunity to describe his working process publicly, writing about the piece for *The New York Times* (quoted above) as if he were encouraging readers to choreograph themselves: 'Now you can make up a dance of your own.'[39]

Rhymes with Silver

Morris describes the conversation he had with Harrison when the collaboration *Rhymes with Silver* began:

Lou, I would like you to write a piece for me.
How long?
It doesn't matter—twenty minutes maybe. I don't care.
What's the instrumentation?
That's up to you. You're the composer.
Is there text?
I don't know. I only want it to include a piano part and a cello part.
But on tour, you can't take much with you.
Don't worry about it. That's my problem. Whatever you want.
I'm used to writing a piece after something is choreographed.
I've never done that before. I can't imagine it. If you want, I'll start making some stuff up and send tapes to you.
No, you don't work that way.
Okay, fine. So let's do it my way.
All right; I'll write a piece for you but never ask me about it again. It might be done in a week; it might be five years. I'll send it to you when it's done.
That's great, whenever it's done.[40]

Morris also asked Harrison for some 'limping' rhythms.[41] Then, Harrison just wrote the music:

> Mark is a trained musician, and whatever he does is so wonderfully in accord with music. And I have the feeling of Mark's kinesis, and know the

kind of feeling his body and his soul give. So I felt that instead of writing for his counts, which is what I used to do with all my ballets—write music to the counts that the choreographer had already down—I'd just write.[42]

The piece was also to feature the cellist Yo-Yo Ma.

Oddly, this single 'collaboration' demanded even more of Morris as a 'composer' than *Serenade*. He recalls that Harrison was peeved about his removal of the Air from *Grand Duo*[43] (and possibly other instances of editing too), so the resulting kit, which made Morris do the structural work himself, suggests that the composer was being deliberately playful. On the other hand, as we have seen, these kits were already integral to Harrison's work with dance. Here too was the surrender of creative control that had interested Morris in Cowell's instructions for the *Mosaic Quartet* and that was built into his own choreographic systems procedures. Furthermore, Sophia Preston suggests that, unlike in Asian cultures where music and dance are considered indivisible, working with Harrison 'altered neither Morris's usual practice of making dance to a set piece of music nor the separation of the roles of each artist'.[44]

Harrison sent his score packaged as follows:

I   Allegro (piano and percussion)
II   Ductia
III Six Songs: 1.Gigue and Musette. 2. Romantic Waltz. 3. Fox Trot 4. Threnody
     5. Prince Kantemir. 6. Round-Dance
Four Solos for Yo-Yo Ma: 1.Prelude 2. Scherzo 3. Chromatic Rhapsody 4. 5-tone Kit

The composer added a note that the 5-tone [5-note] Kit had an optional percussion accompaniment and that different lengths of score were possible, for instance, you could choose to use just the six small Dances (labelled 'Songs'), which would total about fifteen minutes, or the piece could last two days. Morris elected to use all the material, in a version that lasted about forty-five minutes. The percussion ensemble comprised a variety of drums, tambourines, chimes, vibraphone, sleigh bells and antique cymbals. Assisted by pianist Linda Dowdell (see pp. 36, 39–40), Morris realised the overall structure: they decided on the 'arc' of the piece—which suggests anything but a 'flat' structure, as well as the repeat schemes and tempos. 'I made the dance as I put the music together', Morris said.[45] He ended up spacing out the cello numbers, interleaving them with the small dances and other items, beginning with the cello 'Prelude' and ending with the 'Round Dance', a sure-fire positive ending. The final order of movements is as follows:

Prelude	Cello solo
Allegro	
Scherzo	Cello solo
Ductia	
Gigue and Musette	
Chromatic Rhapsody	Cello solo
Romantic Waltz	
Fox Trot	
Threnody	
In Honor of Prince Kantemir	
5-tone Kit	Cello solo and percussion
Round Dance	

Turning first to the two kits, the sequence chosen by Morris for the eight lines of the '5-tone Kit' (each seven bars long) is documented as

A B B C G B D F D F E F G H B D F H

The section title here refers to the 5-note limitation, a pentatonic scale, applied throughout: using the notes D E G A C. All the lines match in metrical structure, the seven bars organised as follows:

4/4 3/4 3/4 4/4 3/4 3/4 3/4

Regarding the earlier 'Allegro' kit, the sequence chosen by Morris for its ten lines of music (each eight bars long) is presented in the score as follows, using Roman numerals:

PIANO	PERCUSSION	PIANO	PERCUSSION
1. rest	VI	10. II	II
2. I	II	11. III	VI
3. II	II	12. IV	III
4. V	III	13. VIII	VIII
5. IV	IV	14. VI	I
6. VIII	V	15. IX	V
7. IX	VI	16. X	V
8. VI	IX	17. II	II
9. V	IV	18. I	I

Again, all ten lines match in metrical structure, the eight bars organised as follows:

4/4 4/4 3/4 3/4 2/4 2/4 2/4 2/4

Ex. 11.1 *Rhymes with Silver*, Harrison, original '5-tone Kit' for solo cello, facsimile from published score. Percussion was added later to the solo cello part.

For the 'Allegro', Morris created a rounded overall structure: after a chimes-only fanfare (No. 1, VI), lines I and II in the piano part (as Nos. 2 and 3, containing marked similarities and therefore suggesting a longer continuity across the pair), which reappear in reverse as Nos. 17 and 18. There is also a reminder of II in the centre of the dance. Morris chose not to use line VII at all, either for piano or percussion. He put piano lines IV and VIII together twice—they are outstanding for their continuous run of semiquavers, again creating continuity as a pair, and now too a long ascent, followed by descent, in pitch. The percussion lines in the Allegro movement are generally very fragmented, darting from one timbre to another, but Morris wrapped up the whole movement with I (No. 18) played loudly, supplementing the confirmation afforded by the piano recapitulation. Nos. 15 and 16 he made especially quiet (for both piano and percussion), so that the conclusion seems even more affirmative by contrast.

Like *Rhymes* as a whole, Morris could have constructed this 'Allegro' movement quite differently, and to very different effect. He might have provided fewer signposts by keeping similar lines of material apart, or progressed towards a quiet, open ending, or concluded the dance with the spare haunting chimes of No. 1. But this was his opportunity to 'compose' a musical structure and, as with his choreography, there is a clear logic and contour behind it.

The '5-tone Kit' also reveals Morris's clear sculpting. Each of the lines B, D and F is a continuum of quavers and it seems therefore that, by using them more than the others, he wanted to emphasise perpetuum mobile and encourage identification with the return of key material. On this occasion, however, he opted for a quiet, restful ending (H), using longer note values.

In one of the 'Songs/Dances', the 'Waltz', Morris felt bold enough to ask Harrison to make a slight adjustment: he sensed incompletion. 'I was scared to tell him,' said Morris. The composer responded, not by adding but by cutting six bars. It lost Morris a rhythm 'hook' that he was especially fond of (a touch of 6/8 within the 3/4 main metre) but he recognised that Harrison had resolved the problem: 'It came back perfectly balanced.'[46] The 6/8 rhythm, however, remains in the choreography (in bar 15).

Harrison's titles betray an assortment of reference and style: besides the kit sections and cello solos, there are also medieval ('Ductia'), baroque ('Gigue' and 'Musette') and contemporary ('Fox Trot' and 'Waltz') dance forms. Once more, *Rhymes* contains Asian traces, but far less obviously than in *World Power*. Morris's response is similarly eclectic, although, as usual, he built a coherent language across the piece and within its individual numbers. This means that the same moves are seen many times under different musical conditions and transformed in the process. During the

'Allegro' kit, for instance, a limited number of moves are seen in different spatial and contrapuntal arrangements, at different speeds, against different music. During the '5-tone Kit', the dance vocabulary is even more limited, apart from occasional solo motivic interpolations stage right, just two phrases crossing the space, one slow, one fast, both fitting the musical metre immaculately, almost like a stable ground to the variety that you hear.

Elsewhere, we find a range of choreomusical tactics, like mapping on to the alternating thematic material and timbres of the cello ('Scherzo'), associating a woman with the cello as a private instrument and three men with the more public piano ('Ductia'), and casting lines of three in rhythmic counterpoint with each other and with the music ('Prince Kantemir'— which refers to a Moldavian Prince, and is an example of Balkan style, see p. 117). Even more than usual, rhythmic counterpoint is a major style feature. At the same time, there is close association of dance with musical material and its repetitions, within the constantly changing contexts of spatial organisation and casting. Consequently, not only the binary forms of 'Gigue' and 'Waltz' are matched choreographically, but also the much more unruly structures of the Chromatic Rhapsody—the outstanding central dance in *Rhymes*, the one that attracted most critical attention.

For the 'Chromatic Rhapsody', the backdrop (another by Howard Hodgkin) turns an angry red. Morris (who premiered the solo) catapults himself across the stage to the cello's surging and tumbling arpeggios, up and down like the dark wave-lines across the drop, his long hair flying and head wobbling. He tries desperately to make contact with a 'statue' figure in the middle of the stage, who is motionless but for one splay of the hands when Morris flicks his fingers at him (or is the man part-paralysed?). Morris stands near him, explores the space around him, and the cello's low isolated pizzicato notes generate from Morris a dangerous tic. Acocella asks: 'What is he? A dybbuk? A Hindu vengeance god?'[47] But could he also be some unrequited lover? Is he trying to rid himself of his own demons? He seems to speak in several voices, like the cello. At the end he stumbles and crawls painfully out into the wings. It is an appalling outcome, the reverse of the disturbing entry of a man in the earlier Musette who started on all fours and ended upright on stage. Morris mixes extreme vigour with characteristically soft touches, like his seductive Erlking (see p. 343). He seems set apart from the rest of the cast as the older figure, like Merce Cunningham in later years, but much bigger, more dominant than him, in build. Bradon McDonald, who took on the role in later performances, flung himself into the imagery with more violence. 'Chromatic Rhapsody' bursts out of the frame of *Rhymes*. There is nothing else like it in the dance repertory.

However flexible and fascinating the original creative process, *Rhymes*'s kit sections seem comparatively academic, in the manner of old-style modern dance classes with bracing percussion accompaniment and a driving beat. The dancers here seem like abstract figures, representations, pattern-makers, even puppet-like. In the freer cello cantilenas, like the 'Chromatic Rhapsody', they become individuals, speaking the same language of moves, but in a very different way, more human, vulnerable and exposed. Thus, the lonely woman in the 'Ductia' spreads her arms wide, showing the stretch across their underside and her chest, as if yearning to embrace and be embraced. When the same move turns up later as the plain opening of phrases in the '5-Tone Kit', it seems much reduced. Variation in *Rhymes* is not decoration. It is a change of circumstances, and a metaphor for the private voice struggling to emerge from the public, stylised body— breaking out, and turning inwards again. Within the long, uneven chain of events that constitutes *Rhymes*, that expressive point is most potent, and most mysterious, at its centre, the 'Rhapsody'. The importance of a central focus in Morris's work will be discussed in more detail in the chapters that follow.

Grand Duo

Grand Duo could hardly be more different in construction and tone, consisting of four movements, in the order slow-fast- slow-fast. Not for nothing has this piece often been referred to as Morris's *Rite of Spring*.[48] It, too, could be read as a stark portrayal of a pre-historic community struggling for survival, and the motoric, machine element that constitutes the trajectory of power through Stravinsky's score is likewise present in Harrison's fast movements.

Criticism of the original Nijinsky *Rite* in 1913 by the French critic Jacques Rivière establishes intriguing links with Morris's dance. Rivière expanded upon Nijinsky's radical sociological and biological statement with a compelling account of its lack of moral purpose or compassion, describing a vision of man dominated by something 'more inert, more opaque, more fettered than himself,' a larger society representing a 'terrible indifference', a sea of faces bearing no trace of individuality.[49] Morris's *Grand Duo* starts with isolated gestures across the fourteen dancers, their arms taut, fingers pointing skywards and circling, like tendrils of vegetation snaking towards the light—back to nature again with Harrison. Gradually, the stage brightens, the dancers link into small groups, and a 'human' community is born, but more willed than willing, and always on the verge of crisis. In the second movement, a ferocious fight breaks out, the community explodes, while, in the third, there is temporary respite, but always with a subterranean tension, a stiffness in sharply designed bodies and arms piercing the space.

Then, there is the 'Polka' finale. The Russian ballet critic André Levinson summed up the Nijinsky ballet as 'an icy comedy of primeval hysteria'.[50] So too we imagine an uncomfortable smirk lurking behind the groin-slapping and stamping in Morris's finale. Alastair Macaulay called it 'a nearly comic war-dance'.[51] This was choreographed in 1992—'I immediately fell in love with "Polka",' Morris said, 'and had to make up a dance that second.' But soon he moved backwards into the rest of the score leading up to the 'Polka', which he now hoped would come across as 'desperate and exhausted[52]…. like a last gasp'.[53]

The following is the layout of the musical score with additional notes on choreomusical features.

1. Prelude: ABA form, Moderato 4/4—A, violin cantilena with steady quaver figuration on the piano and low register bass in octaves; Lento—B, *liberamente*, violin cadenza with piano interruptions; exact repeat of A. The dance movement evolves relatively independently, often appearing to fight against the searing violin and commanding piano, and the choreography continues to develop—it does not follow the ABA form.

2. Stampede: Allegro, 3/4—a series of couplets as in the medieval estampie. The choreography follows the couplet structure, and in the centre is the most striking extended visualisation of musical rhythm of the entire piece (more detailed analysis follows below).

3. A Round (Annabel & April's): Molto moderato, Generally Tender, 2/4—a series of variations based on a 17-bar theme (the piano responding as in a round to the violin, but in inversion). A long strand of movement attaches itself to selected notes, and is shown in various ways across the dancing group, for instance, antiphonally, in canon and in unison.

4. Polka: 2/4—following the rondo form of the music. Like a ritual dance, the choreography uses the music's motor rhythms and cross-rhythms to generate power.

Harrison's 'flat' repetition forms and open textures (often just two lines) are key features, also his racing rhythms and the abundance of patterns of 2 against 3 in the fast movements. It is likely that dance audiences are hardly aware of the intricacy of forms in this meeting between Harrison and Morris—they do not need to be. Some detail is worth revealing, however, given the deftness with which Morris's choreography flows over musical seams, disguising them and thereby increasing the sense of momentum. Again, he does not think as 'horizontally' as Harrison.

The 'Stampede' is especially interesting: it approaches chaos. The title term is a cognate of the medieval French term 'estampie',[54] one of Harrison's favourite forms. The couplets are repeating lines with 'open' and 'closed' endings. Fourteen bars long, these endings act like refrains, and are

Grand Duo, 'Stampede', the 'dance fight'. © Ani Collier, 2013

common across all the couplets. In the following structural diagram, two couplets (A and B) are shown as examples, the primary material of each, a and b, and the two endings x and y common to both:

A = a—x—a—y
B = b—x—b—y

Harrison maintains the same tonal centre across all the couplets. The form of the 'Stampede' as a whole is as follows:

A B C D (incorporating octave clusters on the piano. This is the 'dance fight' between two groups, and their vicious gestures—like throwing knives—accent each cluster chord precisely.) E A1 D1

Each couplet has a distinctive texture, which continues underneath the refrain endings.

Morris's 'Stampede' recognises the fundamental couplet structure every time we hear it. This, as we already know, is his common method with large structure—associating dance with musical material—but here, you may barely notice this. The most immediate impression is of a seething dancing group—that 'larger society'—constantly bursting its boundaries, like an unruly organism shaping and re-shaping itself. So the arrangement of dancers always changes for the second half of a couplet (when the movement and musical material repeats), and Morris does not match all the detail of refrain repetition—he pushes on into new territory. Towards the end, he carries Harrison's hint of variation (A1 and D1) much further, jamming together a plethora of motifs from earlier in the dance, and getting the dancers to blast from the wings group by group, shooting out their arms as they did in the fight, then retreating, only to return re-charged. Rhythm is the key, and one frequent move is like a 'talisman', when the dancers lift their feet gleefully, leaping from one leg to the other (or its variant, the wagging of one leg from under the knee). It marks a lively syncopated passage in the piano line, in 6/8, thereby crossing the established 3/4 metre (see Ex. 11.2). Morris clearly found that syncopation compelling and took delight in it. It haunts the choreography, a highlight nearly every time you hear it in the score.

Macaulay saw the Polka by itself at the 1992 Edinburgh Festival. Later, in the context of the whole *Grand Duo*, he observed that it 'still has something of its original Keystone quality, but every time I want to smile at its antics I am appalled at the human furnace before me'. By itself, it is a party piece. Sometimes, today, it can still seem tacked on at the end of the larger work, but it can also be read as typical of Morris, leaving us with the danger of ambiguity. Macaulay again:

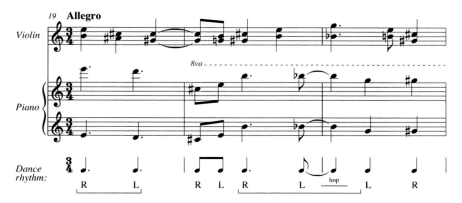

Ex. 11.2 *Grand Duo*, Harrison, 'Stampede', the 'talisman' bars. The brackets highlight the repeating 'talisman' motif.

> Here is society, says *Grand Duo*, compulsively militaristic even in this primitive form, not without absurdities, but certainly not without mesmerising and awesome force.[55]

Just like the original *Rite*, I would add, the message is mixed, both thrilling and appalling.

There is much more sense of a whole in *Grand Duo* than in *Rhymes*, partly because the score is so consistently powerful and exhilarating. It is also the strongest of Morris's dances to Harrison's music. Ironically, it might have evoked from Morris its especially powerful response *because* the score already existed in its own right, *because* Harrison was not role-playing as a 'dance composer'. Given that this plotless work is so strongly driven by musical form (and, significantly, borrows the music's title), it leads us neatly towards the principle of symphonism and those works, using large-scale musical form, that are the subject of the next two chapters.

12

Big Forms

Released from both text and text-less plot, the most significant development of the last two decades of Morris's career has been his embrace of symphonic-scale 'big forms'. These are often multi-movement scores, occasionally substantial single movements, and virtually without exception, situations where the spotlight is on the music alone, without any programme, or even any programmatic title, to contend with. This was not entirely new, rather Morris's recent attention to this kind of score has been far more concentrated than in his earlier career. The scores span from the baroque period to the present, but Morris's principal focus during this period is on classical models and their legacy and it is to these that we first turn.

Whether realised as sonata, symphony, concerto or as works bearing generic labels like quartet and trio, classical 'big form' came into its own during the late eighteenth century, most notably through the work of Haydn and Mozart, but it has been adapted and extended for different purposes by composers ever since. Traditionally, although there are variants, it occupies a standard pattern of fast, slow, fast movements, sometimes with one more movement of moderate/fast tempo in penultimate position. It is also endowed with a hallowed first movement structure, called sonata form, governed by principles of tonal and thematic drama. To some, such a model might seem a hopelessly abstract, dance-unfriendly proposition or, at the least, a challenge, as it means taking on a part of musical tradition that has, over the years, acquired particular gravitas and the authority of classical roots. It might also have been tainted by the countless dry-as-dust, 'meaning-less' formalist accounts by music analysts. But how can choreography engage with such musical structures, in other words, visualising (or not) the broad layout of a score, as opposed to its detail? Morris has proved ambitious in trying out many possibilities.

There was already a considerable history of work of this kind within both twentieth-century modern dance and ballet. It ranged from Isadora Duncan and the duo Ruth St Denis and Ted Shawn and their early realisations of mainly nineteenth-century sonatas and symphonies (see p. 80), to the genre known as 'symphonic ballet' in the hands of Fedor Lopukhov and Leonid Massine, and then to George Balanchine and his exploration of an unprecedented breadth of large musical forms, instrumental ensembles and historical periods. As much as many choreographers sought the seriousness and depth that good music could offer dance, some, prior to mid-century, had to ride the storm of criticism—that dance should not take on the most revered, 'absolute' music, especially symphonies. Since then, many choreographers have worked these scores without exciting comment. The Balanchine example is undoubtedly closest to Morris's experience, and perhaps these two choreographers have done more work of this kind than any other. In terms of Morris's own career, it was a sign of his maturity and acquired skills that he could now explore larger timespans and, indeed, expand the possibilities of choreography to such big musical forms.

The list of composers used since 1992 by Morris for dances in this genre (some of them ballets), is as follows, in chronological order:

> Born in the late eighteenth or nineteenth centuries: Mozart, Beethoven, Schubert, Hummel, Weber, Donizetti, Schumann, Glazunov.

> Born in the late nineteenth and twentieth centuries and demonstrating freer accounts of the classical forms, sometimes a radical departure from them: Ives, Bartók, Stravinsky, Martinů, Villa-Lobos, Harrison (whose *Grand Duo* was discussed at the end of the last chapter), John Harbison.

The John Adams commission *Joyride* (2008) is another work of this kind. Most of the big classical forms that Morris uses contain three or four movements. Just a few are single movement scores: *Rondo* (Mozart, 1994), *Rock of Ages* (Schubert, 2004)—both in rondo form, with repeating refrain material—and *A Choral Fantasy* (Beethoven, 2012)). On the other hand, *Mozart Dances* (2006), analysed in the next chapter, is an assemblage of three three-movement scores back to back, forming a complete programme. A variety of instrumental ensembles is represented across Morris's repertory of big-form scores. Unsurprisingly, none of his choreography to these scores has anything as specific as a plot. Stories are not, in any case, Morris's natural inclination. Besides, as other choreographers have found,[1] the timing of this kind of music does not readily suit specific, developed narratives, although, in his symphonic ballets, Leonid Massine found ways of exploring generalised themes of Man and Destiny, the drama between good and evil, and with identifiable characters or human representations.

In some cases, Morris has simply adopted a musical title for his dance, like *Rondo, Italian Concerto* (Bach, 2007) and *Kammermusik No. 3* (Hindemith, 2012). On other occasions, titles refer more obliquely to the musical score, as in *Mozart Dances*, naming the composer, while the individual scores are given titles referring to the chronological number of the particular concerto (Eleven or Twenty-Seven) or to the use of two pianos in the central sonata

(Double). *V* (Schumann, 2001) refers to the quintet ensemble, but also to a recurring spatial organisation of dancers, *All Fours* (2003) to the use of Bartók's fourth string quartet, but also to the four solo dancers (and chorus of eight—two times four). Other titles are more poetic and elusive, even, which is not unusual for Morris, downright perplexing: like *Maelstrom* (Beethoven, 1994), *Quincunx* (Donizetti, 1995), *Empire Garden* (Ives, 2009), *Visitation* (Beethoven, 2009), *Petrichor* (Villa-Lobos, 2010), *Beaux* (Martinů, 2012) and *Crosswalk* (Weber, 2013).

The works selected for discussion here demonstrate a range of large forms, including the freer forms of the twentieth century, as well as several different manners of dealing with musical detail. There are examples of 'music visualisation', in the old, strict sense of the term (the kind of dance that consistently 'duplicates' musical detail), of boldly independent layers of dance, of conceptual, reflexive explorations, and of different degrees and kinds of narrative content. One piece, *Italian Concerto*, is out of line historically, set to Bach (an earlier eighteenth-century composition) and using three-movement baroque concerto form, its outer movements structured thematically according to ritornello principles of block repetition (see p. 136). It is included as a further, important example of Morris's independent layering of dance over big musical form. At the opposite end of the spectrum, *Empire Garden* stands out: as an idiosyncratic, modernist construction. But the last analysis is a tease, Morris's setting of a ballet score: Stravinsky's *The Rite of Spring*. The reason it has its place in this chapter is that Morris saw it as a big form (two Parts) rather than a story. He got rid of narrative as far as possible, and instead celebrated the barely programmatic nature of the musical writing, which is re-worked here by the contemporary jazz trio The Bad Plus.

Let us now consider in more detail the various models of classical form in the scores selected by Morris, taking as the main example first movement sonata form. More than any other, this is the paradigmatic formal type of the late eighteenth century, although it is important that, underpinned by drama, it was always a mobile concept, never fixed in stone. It consists of divisions that are normally termed as follows:

—exposition (a section that is often repeated and that contains a first group of ideas in the tonic and a second group in another key, usually the dominant—sometimes referred to as first and second 'subjects');
—development, working through material from the exposition;
—recapitulation, or return, a closing section that often matches the thematic plan of the exposition, sometimes, from the nineteenth century, followed by a more developed coda.

Most important in terms of the drama of sonata form—more so than thematic organisation into subjects—is the contribution of its tonal scheme. There is a move away from, and back to, stability, the shift from a first home (tonic) key area to a second (dominant), after which the project is to regain the tonic through reversal of the harmonic trajectory. Further tonal digressions taking the listener a greater distance from home are likely along the way, especially within the development section, while the recapitulation both begins and ends in the tonic key. Thus, a three-part design based on the layout of material fits into a two-part, polarised, tonal structure.

Diagram of Sonata Form Structure

Exposition		Development		Recapitulation
major AI	BV	to other keys	AI	BI
minor Ai	BIII	to other keys	Ai	Bi

KEY:
Major: I = tonic   V = dominant
Minor: i = tonic   III= mediant (relative major)

A and B: two groups of thematic ideas, as first and second subjects

Sonata form, regularly equated with the first movement of a multi-movement work, can also be found in a work's other movements, although there are alternatives for these. 'Slow movement form' is sonata form minus the development section, or with only a brief transition between exposition and recapitulation. Slow movements can also follow a simple ternary, ABA form. Finales of multi-movement classical works are often in sonata rondo form, a cross between simple rondo form, with its refrain repeating in the same key and episodes in between, and sonata form, with its tonal shift to the dominant and central development section.

Diagram of Sonata Rondo Structure (major key example)

Exposition			Development	Recapitulation		
AI	BV	AI	to other keys (C)	AI	BI	AI

The above forms are modified within the context of a concerto, which deals with interactions between soloist and orchestra and retains some elements of the baroque ritornello principle for the orchestra. This will be discussed during the analysis of *Mozart Dances* in the next chapter. In four-movement works, the penultimate position is typically taken by a triple time movement, such as a minuet (or more often a scherzo, in the nineteenth century), with a trio forming its centre. The structure here is usually compound ternary, with each of the three parts in a binary form of some kind (AB, or AA, which reflects similarity between the two halves).

All these musical forms vary under different circumstances and at different times. Consider some of the developments in sonata form during the nineteenth century: the exposition repeat often removed; no longer the simple polarisation between tonic and dominant, rather, more complex key patterns; the climax displaced from the moment of recapitulation, of tonal resolution, until later, often in the coda; and growth in the duration of individual movements. Now too, thematic personality and development takes on more formal responsibility, the duality felt between theme groups, or 'subjects', defined more often as 'masculine' and 'feminine'. In the light of this, sonata form was theorised in the nineteenth century less often as 'binary' (according to the tonal plan, as generally viewed in the eighteenth century) and more frequently as 'ternary' (privileging thematic material and its development).[2] Twentieth-century big forms often use the same three- or four-movement plans, but apply the classical models more loosely with, for instance, a freer notion of return or recapitulation. In atonal examples, the once central forces of tonal polarity and resolution have disappeared.

In Morris's work, however, it is revealing to assess the drama of these forms in more detail, in addition to consideration of abstract models and tonality. This involves acknowledging a change from the balance of power in much twentieth-century musical analysis, as well as looking at drama from the opposite point of view to previous chapters, from the base line of form. It is useful, for instance, to consider historical practices of the time when the music was written.

Significantly, during the eighteenth and nineteenth centuries, instrumental music was frequently discussed in terms of meaning and affect (rather than structure, the twentieth-century bias). An extreme example that uses Mozart and the *Dido* story as its basis (thereby linking nicely with Morris) demonstrates the point forcefully. Early in the nineteenth century, the little known French composer and theorist Jérôme-Joseph de Momigny went so far as to attach his own text for Dido's Lament to the first movement of Mozart's String Quartet in D minor K. 421. Nearly every phrase of the first violin part was thus underpinned. This was in effect an attempt at translation of the music, and Momigny, extraordinary as it may seem to us, felt totally justified. To him, it was as if Dido's 'voice' sings through Mozart's quartet. The music was operatic:

> I have tried to make it clear that the feelings expressed by the composer were those of a woman in love who is about to be abandoned by the hero

she adores: Dido, who had a similar misfortune to lament, came immediately to mind. The elevation of her station, the ardour of her love, the
celebrity of her misfortune—all of these made me decide to make her the
heroine of the plot.[3]

Opera specialist Roger Parker adds that, although Momigny does not
claim that these words are the *only* ones that could clarify the music, he
nevertheless feels that detailed words are entirely appropriate to this aim. In
Parker's words, Momigny seems to assume that 'wherever there is music...
words will lurk beneath the surface, ready to voice specific dramas when
invoked for the purpose of critical understanding.'[4] But it is the fact that
Momigny could seriously think in this way that we, today, should take
seriously. Despite the tendency in the twentieth century to think in terms of
abstraction, it is not wrong to hear music as narrative, although the manner
in which we might consider it as narrative, notions of acceptability, may
change from one historical period to another.

The musicologist Anthony Newcomb contends that, in the nineteenth
century, the symphony was viewed predominantly in narrative terms,
conceived indeed as a sort of 'composed novel'.[5] (We are talking here in
terms far less specific than those of Momigny.) Newcomb uses the term
'plot' in a particular way, claiming that a number of what he calls 'plot
archetypes' were understood during this period, such as suffering followed
by redemption, or struggle followed by victory. His example is Schumann's
Second Symphony, widely believed at the time to convey the suffering-
redemption story (like Beethoven's Fifth Symphony, and sometimes his
Ninth). His analysis, which focuses on the most weighty last movement (a
sonata form), signifies too the growing superiority of thematic evolution
and interaction (here to convey reconciliation) over tonal drama during this
period (see analysis of *V*).[6]

Newcomb maintains that, even if certain codes are no longer understood,
music is still heard narratively by many listeners: 'as a mimetic and
referential metaphor, the mimesis involved is of modes of continuation, of
change and potential.' Borrowing from narratological theory, including
the work of Jonathan Culler and Paul Ricoeur,[7] Newcomb's thesis is that,
as in reading literature, we process musical events in relation to paradigm
plots (like sonata form), shifting back and forth, recollecting, developing
expectations and so on.

Another recent theoretical trend is to read the meaning within classical
forms according to the terms of social critique. Sonata form, for instance,
has been interpreted as a vehicle for showing conflict between masculine
identity and the feminine Other, or a metaphor for the stance of the author,
demonstrating power and domination or rebellion against social repression.[8]

Such readings are less clearly contextualised historically.

But the main point here is that Morris sensed a narrative component within the big musical forms that he chose, and felt free to engage with that narrative. It was his own reading, of course, which might be quite different from anyone else's. As we will see, he prefers to keep things unspecific (not to go down the Momigny route, not to suggest anything as concrete as plot). Sometimes, we might even feel that the musical narrative has prompted from him a counter-narrative.

One other general practice needs to be reviewed briefly in relation to Morris's big-form dances, the managed coherence through deployment of motifs. This is an aspect of his earlier work, including *L'Allegro* and *Dido*, but it becomes especially important when he deals with large, textless musical canvasses (particularly the huge *Mozart Dances*, making a whole out of several parts never intended to go together). In the 1980s, Morris had read about Haydn's economy and logic of thematic/motivic development in Charles Rosen's book *The Classical Style*[9] and enthusiastically took note of this musical aesthetic principle for his own choreography. Now, embracing nineteenth- and twentieth- as well as eighteenth-century classical forms, he could enjoy the trajectory of development within musical tradition itself, the extending of thematic/motivic coherence across all the movements of a multi-movement work, and sometimes the drawing together of the threads of an entire work as it nears conclusion. Music history supported both Morris's thematic inclinations and his drive to be expressive.

Rondo

A couple of big-form pieces betray Morris's past, that he had not finished with the good old music visualisations of the mothers of modern dance and still wanted to embed himself in musical structure, in all its glorious detail. In 1994, he choreographed a single-movement solo for himself, a *Rondo* to Mozart (the Rondo in A minor for piano, K. 511, 1787) reminiscent of his other solos in its shifting moods, for instance, the 1981 *Ten Suggestions*. But here,[10] he was no longer a youth: there was a different intensity within the detail, a demonstration that ornamentation, changing with every repeat of the rondo refrain, was an integral part of the content and expression of the piece. The feelings conveyed also seemed bigger, stranger, more urgent. Now, Morris seems exposed, in silk shorts, while at the same time extravagantly human, a big, big dancer and personality. (The solo he choreographed, as usual, on someone else—Teri Weksler—one of the smallest, lightest dancers he has ever worked with. Then, in 2006, he gave it to Lauren Grant and Amber Star Merkens to perform.)

The *Rondo* comprises two returns of a refrain (A), which is initially introduced as a three part-form in itself: aba. The overall form is as follows:

A   B (Episode 1)   A   C (Episode 2)   A   Coda based on A

Morris follows the musical outline fervently. It is a substantial solo, about twelve minutes long, Andante, in siciliano rhythm.

To a musical 'turn', Morris twists curled hands in towards each other and out again, then to a dotted rhythm, he eases them apart and back together. After this, he stiffly points his index fingers, a sharply defined position that recurs many times later and sometimes looks like aiming a gun. As the melody line climbs chromatically, he presses both hands upwards (four times, once per beat), as if pleading, or wishing for something, pushing them much higher when the melody eventually leaps upwards.

Ex. 12.1 *Rondo*, Mozart.

He closes the musical phrase, ungracefully bent over, but in a kind of 'old classical' position, his front foot on three-quarter pointe. (Later, bent forwards in the same way, he bluntly steps out chugging quavers in the accompaniment.)

The solo continues, stuffed with seemingly illogical juxtapositions, yet with each move stapled tightly to the music. As the score opens out, the dance refrain develops, one hand and then the other raised quietly, again four times—now reflecting the appoggiaturas and their resolution (the pattern of dissonance to consonance)—while shoulder shimmies pursue Mozart's increasing embellishment. Then there is a version of the refrain that is barely there, minimal, on the spot, only to become huge (from bar 151), when Morris thrashes his arms desperately, as if fighting off demons.

Various other emotional swells happen along the way, as he races, swirling across the stage to fast figuration, while, on other occasions, like the music dancers of history, he calls attention to his listening in operatic manner, a self-conscious hand to his ear or chin. Such behaviour enlarges the music and solidifies its affect. There are further memorable images: Morris circling his lower arm to a trill; running forward and back as the music swings up and down, a move later decorated (like the music) with a hop on each run; suddenly lopping a leg skywards, creating a giant upbeat to a new phrase, whereas Mozart's upbeat is much more modest; his back turned, dropping his shoulders in stages, one, two, three, four times, enlarging our perception of each simple stepwise descent in pitch.

It is important that some aspects of this dance are not at all like early twentieth-century visualisations, but of a quite different, objective order. First, there is what Morris calls a 'mathy' component within the piece, a couple of sections 'divided by time':[11] he takes up a series of poses on the floor (three the first time—one per beat, bars 46-48, five the second time, bars 69-73), after which he reverses the order of events back to the beginning. Dividing time in such a way makes for a relatively arbitrary relationship to the score, certainly one that is not about response to musical detail. But Morris explains that he was creating a miniature palindrome (or 'chevron' form) within the big, approximate palindrome of Mozart's entire rondo. There is another suggestion of palindrome when the lights go out, just before the final cadential chord: he lowers his arms and body to the first bent-over, three-quarter pointe position, just as he did slowly and deliberately before the music began. During the 'mathy' section, Morris seems to move outside of the emotional frame, to adopt a composed, task-like attitude, as if to counteract the dangers of strong feeling. But this may also seem ironic. It reminds us that music visualisation is merely a convention, one of many, and that it can be easily dismissed.

Still other activity was inspired by Balinese dance, be it a wide-legged stance, a flexed foot, or fingers spread across the chest: the solid kind of movement used for depicting 'male monster characters'.[12] Such radical shifts of activity indicate that, while Morris operates along the continuum between high emotion and restraint, *Rondo* is a reflexive intellectual and cultural exploration as well. It was also a memory test for the choreographer, his task being to make something deliberately hard to remember. This too creates tension in performance, and he nuanced the piece differently each time he danced it.

As much as it points backwards to the music visualisations of Morris's early career, the *Rondo* solo points forwards, in two directions, to *V*, a strict visualisation and more aesthetically straightforward celebration of music, and to other dances that lay more independent structures over the music— like the quartet *Rock of Ages* and, in *Italian Concerto*, another exploratory solo for himself with deliberately planned non-sequiturs.

V

Using Schumann's Piano Quintet (Op. 44, 1842), the first example of a work written for that ensemble (at least by a major composer), *V* (2001) is one of the most positive, jubilant pieces that Morris has ever made, and a particular favourite with audiences and musicians. Morris arrays his dancers in V formations at various points in the piece, the upright V (its point towards the audience), the V upturned, or both versions simultaneously. (Although later, after the 9/11, September 11, 2001 attack on New York, Morris dedicated the work to the city of New York, the idea of V for 'victory' over evil was never an intention.) It could be significant that Morris chose to make such a positive statement through one of his most detailed visualisations of a score, as if confirming his faith in the visualisation method. This was the piece that inspired Emanuel Ax to ask Morris for a collaboration, and that was described by another musician as a wonderful example of musical analysis (see pp. 52, 85). The dancers look like angels, seven of them dressed in blue satin loose tops and knickers, and another seven in light green tops and trousers.

Morris borrows from Schumann his economy of ideas and the device of linking his four movements thematically. In 2010, he reminisced enthusiastically:

> In choreographing it I learned that there's nearly nothing there except the tiniest bit of musical material that is just unbelievably imaginatively structured. It's really a few four-note themes.[13]

Schumann's Allegro brillante first movement opens thus, two striking upward leaps followed by a circuitous descent:

Ex. 12.2 *V*, Schumann, Piano Quintet, first movement.

Later on in this movement, Schumann selects for 'development' the descent bars 3-4. A variation on these bars becomes part of the opening theme of the Allegro ma non troppo finale, with a new introduction that betrays its origin in one of the upward leaps:

Ex. 12.3 *V*, Finale.

Then, in the coda of the finale, these two opening themes are the subjects of a double fugue,[14] the one from the first movement now especially emphatic, with augmented note values:

Ex. 12.4 *V*, Finale.

Throughout the score, we find other examples of motifs and variations on motifs—truncations, inversions and so on. Morris does not necessarily match all these variations choreographically but, as usual, devises his own motifs for crossing musical movements. Sometimes, these are anticipatory glimpses before later, full exposure, sometimes they are confirmations of what is already well-known. But it is especially important that Morris regularly repeats dance material to the most obvious musical repetitions. When the opening musical theme of the first movement returns in the coda of the finale, for instance, a big moment, so does Morris's original arm phrase.

Let us examine how this arm phrase visualises musical detail at the start of *V*:

The dancers commence tilted to the right, with their arms stretched sideways.
1. On the first chord, they centre the torso, step down and forwards towards the audience, bringing their arms together in front (move 1).

V, the ending. © Robbie Jack, 2001

2. On the leap upwards in pitch, they step up, open their arms and tilt to the left (move 2).
3. As the melody line lowers in preparation for the next leap, they repeat move 1, and hold (they do not visualise the second upward leap in the music).
The whole pattern progresses forwards: in/down, out/up, in/down.

We see the trace of a V shape in the movement. Just as the music reverses motion in descent, the dancers retreat in preparation for a repeat. When the music repeats (a variation), their gestural alternations happen the other way round: out/up, in/down, out/up, in/down, in opposition to musical pitch, another favourite Morris device (see p. 130). In both instances, Morris makes us hear musical detail better.

In the coda of the finale, these alternating movements of arms find their logical conclusion, both versions presented simultaneously, as pairs of dancers, one after another, meet centre stage and wrap their arms about each other, first one partner doing the wrapping, then the other. In this manner, they sway back and forward ecstatically as a unit, until the logic of the pattern determines that they end together in a total embrace. Driven by musical patterning, the moves become both a dance pattern and a statement of joy.

Morris used the same procedure of thematic linkage for other works of this later period, reflecting existing links between musical movements: in *Visitation* (2009, to Beethoven's Sonata No. 4 for piano and cello, Op. 102, No. 1), about a group and an outsider, where a block of movement material from the Andante introduction (prior to the Allegro vivace sonata form) comes back to related music before the finale; in *Petrichor* (2010, to Villa-Lobos' String Quartet, No. 2, W100), an all-women dance to a four-movement structure that is relatively free from classical models, where specific choreography is attached to the arpeggio theme that recurs across the piece; and in *All Fours* (2003, to Bartók's Fourth String Quartet, see pp. 411-19).

Morris delights too in the large repetitions within individual movements of Schumann's quintet, a 'perfect sonata form'.[15] He follows the plan of each movement's material exactly. In the opening Allegro brillante, this means following not only a repeat of the musical exposition and a virtually literal recapitulation, but also a large block repeat (moved down one tone) within the development. The two expositions are danced first by the blues, then by the greens. There are choreographic modifications: their opening pair of arm phrases are in reverse order, elsewhere, they operate in mirror form (on the other side of the body), and often too, the material is spatially inverted, so downstage becomes upstage and vice versa. For the recapitulation, Morris puts these two expositions on top of each other, everything doubled, and sometimes with the patterns spatially overlapping and interlocking. Yet such is the over-riding symmetry and regular association of dance with music, similarity wins easily over difference. In the sonata rondo slow movement (indicated In modo d'una marcia—'in the manner of a march'), Morris alters the spatial patterns more radically as well as the number of dancers on repeats. A Scherzo and two different Trios (Molto vivace) follows. The Scherzo sections are all the same and build from long diagonals, although these are formed first by all the men (blues and greens now mixed), next—the opposite diagonal—by the women, then—back to the first diagonal—by the men again, until they all assemble together for a final line-up.

The Allegro non Troppo finale is another sonata rondo, but an especially complex, free-form example, with some very short refrains, and a huge coda, almost as long as the 'main' form, if, indeed, you can speak of a main form in this context. It is Schumann at his most expansive and weighty, overflowing with what seem like brand new ideas as well as new versions of what we already know, a fugato using the main theme, a hiatus point containing massive energy, released into the big, celebratory double fugue. Here, Morris relishes the opportunity to summarise his past and to develop still further variations on familiar material. The blues and greens start out divided again, but cross-colour partnerships are thoroughly reinstated during the coda.

Let us look again at how Morris borrows from musical structure at the more detailed levels within the piece. Especially striking is the opening of the Scherzo when the men in a line take turns with a two-bar scale progression that ends (or begins, whichever way you look at it) with a chord accent. Each dancer curves a raised arm down, then upwards, to complement the rising scales, with a raised position held to mark the chord and to start off the next man in line. The music shifts into different syncopated material in bars 11-12 and 15-16, when our eyes turn towards the freshly rhythmed feet of dancer 6, then (after dancer 7 with the scale again, now descending, bars 13-14) to all of their feet in unison. So the men dance perfectly the smaller phrase structure. The women do exactly the same when the same music returns.

Ex. 12.5 *V*, Scherzo, third movement.

In similar fashion, the striking opening of the finale forms a phrase structure aabaa, each unit four bars long, and a quartet of greens can be seen dancing that too. They also show the sustained peak of the melody in their first move with a jump skywards on to the toes or into the air, into the strong picture of a cross, with their arms held horizontal. After this, still following pitch contour, our eyes are taken downwards to watch the flick of a lower leg gesture, then upwards again to finish (bars 4-5, see Ex. 12.3).

Although the big-hearted dancing in *V* to joyful music seems at first to be very stirring, and probably like a call for courage after the atrocities of 9/11, the work does not stand up to multiple viewings. (This is a personal opinion, despite the fact that *V* is the Morris work most frequently requested by presenters, often for programming in consecutive years.[16]) There is simply not enough choreographic stimulation. It is as if Morris's delight in Schumann's economy of ideas had stifled him (Beethoven's did in *Visitation* too). Soon, confirmed by the over-riding symmetry of spatial organisation, distinctive ideas come to look more and more like one thing, a single statement many times reiterated, and the patterns likewise too tidy, too neat—even wrapping limbs as pattern-making objects—too logical to be interesting. After a while, goodness and bounty no longer ring true. Morris deals with large form issues more successfully, with greater impact of surprise, in many other pieces.

The slow March in *V*, however, is of quite a different order, undercutting the goodness and inserting an extraordinary, alien image. 'I like slow...I'm very good at slow', Morris says. He also notes that his slow movements within big forms often turn out to be centres, or keystones, from which a whole piece 'radiates outwards'.[17]

Two dancers are left behind at the end of the Allegro brillante, a blue woman, lifted by a green man, reaching an arm ecstatically heavenwards (a motif). When the music commences, both slip down on to all fours, crawl away from each other and exit on opposite sides of the stage. Soon, they are joined by their respective teams of blues and greens crawling in lines across the stage, described variously by critics as looking like geckos, insects, lizards, in other words, not human. During a Q and A session after a 2002 performance, one audience member said that he saw them as rock-climbers moved through 90 degrees, to which Morris wholeheartedly agreed: they all started walking upright and then he dropped them down, 'to look like climbing and a lot of work...not much progress.' Is this Morris's version of a paradigm plot about suffering before redemption? It is thus that they slow-march on and on, for extended periods of time, during each March refrain. Always too, they rise to their feet when they meet another line of dancers, then march gently to the 2/2 beat. Morris claimed that his choreography here 'looked exactly to me what the music is uttering.'[18]

In formal terms, those on all fours do not march to a beat: they crawl precisely to the halting rhythm of the refrain melody, but share its notes, alternating between the two colours, one dancer or line of dancers moving roughly one note after the other. The pattern starts like this in relation to the music notation:

Ex. 12.6 *V*, March, second movement.

The effect of this unusual organisation is to break up the melodic flow, to make us feel each note as more staccato and separate from its neighbours than it really is. This creates a tension, and both the jerky moves forwards and the in-between watchful suspensions of these strange creatures contribute to this. (Morris is ˙adamant that the beat is maintained accurately, against the tendency of musicians to shorten the suspended moment of a rest.) The contrast with the joyous airborne Allegro brillante is overwhelming, and similarly the more human, upward-striving episodes between the March refrains.

Originally I found this crawling quite disturbing—ungainly, too blunt, unmusical. Was it a joke? But the music did not seem to be a joke. Morris's setting became increasingly intriguing. For a start, the intense degree of repetition, the simplicity of the movement and its fierce attachment to the notes exudes a confidence, a confirmation, which composer Barbara White refers to as a kind of 'overhearing', a particular 'loudness and intensity when sound and movement join together in glorious excess'.[19] Yet at the same time, the movement goes against the grain. Perhaps the butts-up style is rather embarrassing, and we resist it a little? Morris has frequently used old, noble music in this way, music that we expect to be treated gracefully, even today, from the tradition of Balanchine and Paul Taylor, and this March shares the intensity of connection of his early 'angry dances' (see pp. 154-60). But perhaps this crude, rude approach, danced with eminent objectivity, is a way of waking us up once more to being emotionally moved, and the dual action of 'visualising' the music's structural detail, while setting movement that goes against its likely connotations, opens up fresh perspectives. There is a sense of renewal.

Further questions arise. Is the 'ungraceful' movement really ungraceful? After a while, do we begin to see it differently? Don't those lizards become noble? Deborah Jowitt writes of this passage:

> Instead of repetition seeming arid, it sucks you deeper and deeper into beauty...Repetition tames surprising ideas into harmony.[20]

It is these creatures who leave behind the most important memory in V, a private, compelling statement.

The ending of the March is decidedly asymmetrical. A few bars before the end, to a sudden dissonance, a musical digression, one of the crawling dancers is lifted aloft and backwards, forced to recommence the stage crossing all over again. It is like an act of torture met with silly, but magnificently courageous, determination.

Rock of Ages

Morris describes Schubert's Nocturne ('night piece') for piano in E-flat (Op. 148, D 897, 1825) as 'so weird, it belongs nowhere—very, very poignant...and saddish...'[21] Another Rondo (ABABA), its two sections diminish in length as it progresses. The 2/2 refrain (A) is predominantly quiet and contemplative, rhythmically regular, with a stable opening, single bars repeated over tonic harmony, moving simply to the dominant, then back to the tonic. The style of accompaniment changes as it repeats, and the final appearance of the refrain is in the nature of a coda, both abbreviation and diversion. In contrast, the 3/4 episodes (B) are turbulent, underpinned by semiquaver triplets suggesting allegro tempo, while exploring more distant keys.

Morris took his title from the hymn tune (the American version of the hymn) suggested at one point in the melody line. He asks for a very slow musical interpretation with stretched fourth beats (reading 2/2 as 4/4).[22] This means that any established pulse is constantly derailed and near-immobility implied. It also means that the four dancers regulate their rhythm by 'breathing' with the music and with each other, as opposed to being motor-driven. Visualising the melody, they articulate just the first long note of each bar as a sustained breath gesture, and the fourth beat of the bar as a second, brief gesture (actually delayed in the choreography by one quaver).

Ex. 12.7 *Rock of Ages*, Schubert, Nocturne in E-flat major. Arrows above the score indicate the timing of arm gestures.

It is in the episodes that motor becomes forceful and persistent. Here, the dancers demonstrate the metre, a slow pulse (three beats in a bar of 3/4) or a faster one (six beats in a bar).

The movement Morris gives his dancers is objectively announced, clearly carved out in space, and organised in a highly schematic manner (as was the 'mathy' section in *Rondo*). Each dancer has her/his own phrase during the refrain, or rather, they each introduce a different response to the action topics or textual sub-structure provided by Morris, such as 'drape, twist, scan, move an arm or leg (front or back) up or down, hold your hands behind your back, and then release them'.[23] One of the moves is common across all four: arms to the side, head resting on a neighbour's arm. The dancers perform their phrases in couples, their gestures spatially overlapping:

1. dancer a with dancer b, then c with d;
2. after the first episode, a with c, b with d;
3. after the second episode, all four together, simultaneously, but now starting out spatially separated.

So the phrases interlock differently when the permutations of dancers change. The structural process is rather like a Lou Harrison or Henry Cowell kit (see p. 365).[24]

Seeing the piece for the first time, we may well stand back, adopt an analytical stance and question our perceptions. Did we really see that move before? (It looks so different in a new context.) Do the dancers relate to each other beyond rhythm? Why did one person release her hands and not her partner? The straightforward, plain performance of moves provokes curiosity. Morris also changes the permutations of dancers between performances, for instance, using just men, or two women and two men, or one woman and three men, and so on, which prompts still further questions about conventional readings of gendered partnerships. There are twenty-four possible permutations and, in a sense, knowing the dance is about knowing all its permutations. (Morris loves the fact that he did not engineer the effects of casting changes—'it happened'.[25]) Occasionally, during transitions, the subject of personal relationships is raised, with eye contact from a distance or actual touch. Or a fall to the floor is upsetting—an alternative to emotional passivity. But the shared phrasing itself introduces a striking intensity of feeling.

The most startling emotional moment comes near the end, when all four dancers perform their separate phrases simultaneously. Suddenly, entirely logically according to the scheme, they find themselves close together in a line and in unison, with their single shared move, now three heads supported, then gently lifted, by the arm of each neighbour. Morris calls

Rock of Ages, the 'line', Joe Bowie, David Leventhal, Bradon McDonald, and Craig
Biesecker. © Susana Millman, 2004

this sudden exposure of the dancers coming together the 'pay-off' or 'pure
theme', doing the opposite to the music here, which, he claims, 'falls apart'.[26]
(It is also opposite to the additive, summary procedure, the move towards
greater complexity, that we find at the end of so many of his other works,
like *V*.) Now suddenly enlarged across the group, we see this coalescence as
a sign of deep intimacy and communal caring.[27] The moment is shockingly
ephemeral. No sooner does it happen, but the dancers start to move out
of synchronisation again. Choreomusical relations are crucial. Morris sets
up this formation to happen at the quietest point in the piece, marked *ppp*,
corresponding with a devastating harmonic shift (to the submediant, the
chord on the sixth note of the scale), followed by a scalewise descent pitched
so high and staccato that it seems to pluck at your brain. He makes this
moment the emotional climax of his piece: the *fortissimo* that follows is
simply the signal for the group to split and leave the stage.

Thus, as in *Rondo*, there is an intriguing irony within this piece. Here, it
arises as Morris simultaneously works closely with, and at a distance from,
the music, in dialogue with both its large structure—reversing it, while
clearly reflecting its phraseology—and its emotional implications. Certainly,
the perfect formal system that he sets up is a bizarre way of dealing with
poignancy and sadness, constantly cooling any feeling into ritualised
response, while the two modes, form and feeling, never cease to tug against
each other.

Italian Concerto

Another compelling slow movement is the last solo that Morris made for himself (in 2007), to the central movement of Bach's keyboard work *Italian Concerto* (1735), a solo that plays a unique role within my Morris experience. I had the opportunity to learn it in 2011 from the dancer John Heginbotham, and this not only provided further useful information about the dance, but also led to additional thoughts of my own about its structure and meanings.[28] The solo reveals other kinds of choreomusical interaction, its own special journey through relations of complementation and co-existence, and invites application of concepts from cognitive science (see pp. 105-8).

At the end of Chapter 4, I touched upon some methodological issues, explaining how, in attempting to rationalise its structure as a composite of music and dance, I tried to remind myself of the intended experience of *Italian Concerto*: as in the theatre, for the first time, fresh, all the way through without a break, allowing certain moments to be forgotten, and others to be emphasised and remembered. From time to time, it seemed important to avoid sampling moments, as analysts often do, outside the context of an evolving whole. I also delayed reading the musical score until late on during research.

Morris's solo is situated between two quick movements, each featuring a pair of other dancers from his company. The choreographer is on stage at the start, standing next to another man, only to exit and be replaced by a woman as soon as the music begins. At the conclusion, all five join up on stage—Morris the last to return—showing us their distinctive dance motifs in a flurry of counterpoint, sharing some of these across the group and ending up in a smart unison line. So there is clearly a distance between the outside and inside of the piece: Morris at the 2007 premiere, 51 years of age and in black, set apart from his much younger dancers in their brightly-coloured costumes; jubilant extroversion versus a more thoughtful, introverted statement about a single personality; bright daytime lighting contrasting with nocturnal evocation; lightness versus weight, literally and metaphorically. The central solo is intensely moving, whether danced by Morris or by another dancer, such as Samuel Black, who learnt the solo for some of the UK performances, or John Heginbotham, who appears on the best quality recording of *Italian Concerto*.[29] The duets are less intriguing, but they are full of jokes and little shocks, superbly crafted and convincing as a foil for the heart of the piece.

Of course, the central, Andante movement of Bach's concerto is already very different from the other two, with a very different continuity from the cheerful motor rhythms and block ritornello repetitions that are typical of baroque concerto outer movements. The concerto was originally intended

Italian Concerto, second movement, Mark Morris. © Stephanie Berger, 2007

for a two-manual harpsichord with melody and accompaniment separated between the manuals, although it is now often played on the piano, the 'richer', more 'expressive'[30] instrument that Morris chose to use. The melody line, a long cantilena, starts at bar 4, highly complex and embellished further with ornaments (Morris likens it to a 'fantasia'). The accompaniment consists of a one-bar rhythmic motif, repeating in the manner of an ostinato or ground bass, strict in tempo (Morris's image is of a 'machine'), though varying in pitch pattern.

The large structure of the slow movement is two Parts, with a modulation at the centre from D minor to F major (bar 27), then an abrupt switch back to D minor, with long dominant pedals towards the end of each Part, and finally (at bar 45) a coda. Although we sense that both Parts have much in common, the general impression is of a free fantasy, movement forwards into new territory in contrast to the déjà vu from the blocks of repeated material that characterise the outer movements of the concerto. The ground in the bass is the only real motif, shown by itself as foreground at the beginning of each Part.

Not at all to be expected, Morris sets to this cantilena a series of distinct movement images, nearly all of them focusing attention on the hands or arms. Many of these have appeared in the opening Allegro, some of them several times, so we have had a chance to register them. (Others, introduced for the first time in the solo, reappear later in the Presto finale.) Here, in the solo, we ask: why now is Morris, a very different personality, making these same moves? What is his relationship to the first young couple that he should borrow from what they did? Pulling the hand into a fist seems to be the primary motif of the whole work, although it can be both exultant, like taking up a challenge, and the opposite, slow and gentle, as the hand uncurls from, or curls into, the position. Striking reminiscences from the opening Allegro are a full-on, deep-level step, with arms swinging from side to side in big arcs, and a loose *pas de bourrée* and hop, with arms linked above the head when this repeats, facing, or with back to, the audience. But these moves look very different in the solo, especially on Morris, who experiments with the timing, freely working his way around the notes in the *pas de bourrée* step (performed here without the hop), and invests the deep-level step and arm-swing with a kind of forced impatience.

Some ideas read simply, like searching, reaching out (as if Morris 'speaks' directly to us, the audience) or surprise. Other ideas, detailed hand movements especially, are mysterious, secret, but very precious, so much so that the idea of asking Morris in interview what prompted them felt like an impertinence or intrusion.[31] Morris originally worked with verbal images when he created the solo. (He created it on Dallas McMurray.) For example, this is how Heginbotham instructed me in the opening move: 'As you walk forward, get bigger and fatter like Kathakali dancers—the effect of their movement is large. It's a gradual transformation. You've been in pencil pants and now you're in this wide skirt.' I learnt that there are also passages of 'speed skating'—the deep-level step and arm swing—and 'milking'—hands alternating as if working a cow's udder—and making the sudden, firm gesture of 'unsheathing a sword.'

One especially memorable moment occurs during a dissonant musical suspension in the coda, before final resolution on to the tonic chord: the fingers of his left hand press towards his eye sockets, masking his face, a tragic, deeply upsetting image (bar 44, beats 2-3). Morris told me that this image came from Shakespeare's Hamlet holding the skull of his childhood inspiration, the jester Yorick. (Being party to this kind of information revealed Morris's interesting working process, yet curiously, at the same time, it solidified meaning and reduced the power and fascination of semantic uncertainty and ambiguity. This confirms the point that movement can speak in ways that words cannot, and with great clarity of another kind.[32]) From the exceptional 'language' of the solo emerges a distilled representation of the protagonist's eloquence and knowledge, and the sheer wealth of movement ideas speaks of an ambitious ranging imagination—always questioning, unable to rest for long in the same mental or physical place. The solo can be seen, at least partly, as a metaphor for a thought process shadowed by a mercurial subconscious. I will return to this point later. I also appreciate the physical presence of Morris, with an older body, quite different from the youthful stereotype of the dancer. Let us now consider how this choreography works alongside Bach's music.

Morris understands the underlying two-part structure of the music and clarifies it, but on his own formal terms. His Part 2 is a telescoped version of Part 1, demonstrating a clearer symmetry than in the music alone. There are omissions, but also additions and occasional reversals of direction, upstage to downstage and vice versa. Thus, he creates his own 'choreomusical' form, which is not an entirely choreographic matter: it stems from the *interaction* between the music and his choreography. Choreomusical engagement is further exemplified at a more detailed level, but quite differently from the pieces discussed earlier in this chapter. There are several noteworthy instances of visual capture or of the music 'sopping up' visual information.[33] On several occasions, common accents turn into structural signposts, moments in the score pulled out of their cantilena surroundings by dance movement, as if 'frozen' out of their context (see p. 106), and thus allocated additional impact.

At the beginning, Morris touches his chest lightly with his right hand, marking each low bass note D (the second and third quavers of bar 2; repeated bar 27 as the introduction to Part 2), the first with a touch, the second with a move forward from the chest extending towards the audience. (Morris told me that he derived this from the Muslim gesture of greeting: 'I'm your friend.') Then, with the ornamented entering pitch of the melody (bar 4; repeated bar 28 as the beginning of Part 2), he throws an arm upwards and forwards as if casting an object across water (a chain with a rock attached was Morris's image, but the move also suggests casting a fishing line).

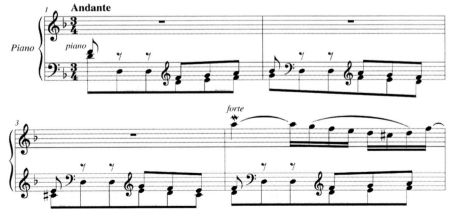

Ex. 12.8a *Italian Concerto*, Bach, second movement, opening of Part 1.

Ex. 12.8b *Italian Concerto*, second movement, opening of Part 2.

The entire solo maintains a pathway 'up and down', just off stage centre, and Morris inhabits this line several times with a distinctive lunge and swing out backwards with an arm. He first pulls towards upstage, away from the direction of travel, later in the reverse direction, pulling back towards the audience as he moves upstage. Each time, he draws upon a syncopated leaping interval in the melody line (at the beginning of bars 11, 19, 20, 38 and 39) and the leaps become larger and more urgent. He also shows us that 'up' in music can connote distance (away from place or goal), not simply height in the vertical dimension (see p. 97).

Ex. 12.9a *Italian Concerto*, second movement.

Ex. 12.9b *Italian Concerto*, second movement.

Ex. 12.9c *Italian Concerto*, second movement.

There are two other moments when he appears to pull an imaginary rope taut (which Heginbotham refers to as 'unsheathing an imaginary sword'), drawing attention to another syncopation. This time, it happens on a descending interval: he pulls forward and down, to one side, and then to the other (at the beginning of bars 23 and 25), lowering further with the interval when it repeats without a break (in bar 41).

Ex. 12.10a *Italian Concerto*, second movement.

Ex. 12.10b *Italian Concerto*, second movement.

When I learnt the solo, I discovered yet another moment when raised hands and eyes turn round towards the audience and 'blink' (bar 15, both eyes and hands closing and opening).

As suggested in Chapter 4, when this phenomenon was discussed theoretically, there is an argument here for visual capture, in that the physical movements at these particular points are especially powerful within their context. The syncopated moves, especially, stand out from their context, as major accents, more so than the 'accompanying' musical syncopations, which are part of the regular style of the unfolding cantilena. Perhaps too these 'common accent' moments can be read metaphorically, as moments of sudden realisation or crystallisation emerging from thought process and the murmuring subconscious.[34]

The continuity of Morris's solo is also striking. This is partly due to the independent rhythms and dynamics within the choreography. In terms of movement ideas, Morris stages one for each bar of music more or less (each slow bar lasts quite a long time). But we are never encouraged to think in this schematic way, because of the liberated timing and lack of predictable, conventional match between the movement and the regular musical beat. Yet Heginbotham taught me the solo using counts as a guide, and in a way that proved revealing. These counts were not of the kind that drive the body, rather they articulated the movement rhythm and dynamics. For instance, occasionally, after a long, slow dance bar, time suddenly breaks up into more rapid articulations—and when you try out the movement, the quickening from adagio feels like high drama. 'One two.....': Heginbotham stressed the 'two', a moment of tension when you suddenly stand upright and hold still. On counts 4-6, you waver, 'unstable as if on a raft'. Then 'one, two, three', a vocal crescendo—you lift an arm, a leg, swing the leg sideways—and end up balancing precariously on the toes.

Furthermore, the assemblage of movement ideas is mosaic-like and fragmentary. Although these make contact with the music at key points, they maintain their own autonomy and distinction, never becoming a consistent part of the musical flow. As in the 1994 Rondo, Morris deliberately made the movements hard to perform and remember as a sequence, 'awkward...anti-intuitive...anti-organic', and a particular quality of inner concentration emerges from the dancer. This was his way of dealing with what he perceived as a 'tension in the music'.

Interestingly, this suggests another way of considering his performance persona, less as a person within a role communicating, through monologue, an imaginary character's inner state, more as the 'real' Morris, or the real Morris as dancer, working through a series of tasks (as in the 'mathy' section of Rondo). It is quite possible that such a tricky cacophony of images leads to this kind of persona, which is more like that of early American postmodern choreographers such as Yvonne Rainer. Now I know this from the inside, having performed the tasks myself, except that, unlike most pedestrian dance, Morris's 'performance' happens to engage with the detail of musical structure at the same time.

Here, it is worth digressing to consider the performance theorist André Lepecki's critique of the modernist project of choreography. He refers to it as a 'necessary technology for an agitated subjectivity' and of the 'entrapment of subjectivity in spectacular compulsive mobility'.[35] Perhaps there is, after all, a dark underside to the cheerful, motor-driven outer movements of *Italian Concerto*, to the performance of 'agitated subjectivity' in these movements? Perhaps Morris demonstrates an attitude of resistance in his central solo, showing the body here with agency, *not* motorised by music? At this stage, given the flexibility of performance frame, perhaps we might begin to understand the whole *Italian Concerto* as a conceptual, reflexive choreomusical exploration.

Turning now to the outer movements, not only does the musical motor appear to drive the bodies in the outer movements, but the musical repetitions also determine the movement patterns of the dancers. The opening Allegro starts with one dancer, then a second (bar 5), shooting a fist into the air on the downbeat, racing the music to emphasise the high note a quaver later.

Ex. 12.11 *Italian Concerto*, First movement.

This is a motif that we see each time we hear the opening music, five times in all which, as we have already seen, is typical of Morris's repetition procedures. Both dancers perform it in unison and hold the raised-fist position for a surprisingly long time (almost five bars) the last time round. An assortment of distinctive, quick, light steps, turns, and arm or hand gestures forms the material between the recurrences of this striking fist motif. Nearly all these movement ideas are associated with particular musical patterns—mostly repeating one- or two-bar units that form longer stretches of four or six bars. Many of them respond to other aspects of musical detail, such as pitch, accentuation and, of course, hectic motor pulse. Morris's choreographic procedure in the finale is much the same, until the dancers from earlier movements return with their motifs and complicate the choreographic texture. Again, hear the music a second or third time and you are bound to see the moves that were set to it when you first heard it. Yet Lepecki's critique seems absurdly severe given Morris's numberless ways of nuancing the dance repetitions, in both outer movements, asking the dancers to change facings, to swap roles, to match then not match, to separate into question and answer, 'will you? won't you?' or into hot-on-the-heels canons, or to join in happy unison. Things are always a little different, even though the movement is clearly familiar. Morris's choreography is both a marvel of structural economy and a virtuoso staging of wit and surprise, features that the dancers fully reinforce within their performance. Furthermore, the rare snippets of material that never become familiar and are experienced once only during *Italian Concerto* (whether in the movement or the music) retain a particular freshness after repeated viewings of the piece.

Perhaps it is significant that I only noticed the genesis of the opening motif of the finale after many viewings. This motif starts with the 'rope-tautening' movement (discussed earlier as it appears within Morris's solo, bars 23, 35 and 41). It continues with the fist of the back arm pushing down, forward and up to draw three quarters of a circle. This clearly matches the contour of the finale melody (a dramatic downward leap followed by a scale-wise progression upwards):

Ex. 12.12 *Italian Concerto*, third movement.

The woman in the opening Allegro performs these moves as a fleeting, barely visible, transition across bars 120-21. Later, Morris performs them adagio. In both these cases, although there is far more ambiguity than in the finale, the movement encourages us to hear features of complementary contour in the music. In other words, Morris highlights motivic similarities in the music and potential thematic relationships across the three musical movements—and he does this with far greater subtlety than in *V.* For instance, with the fist pushing straight upwards at the start of the first movement, then down before up in the third, he makes us feel more keenly the relationship of inversion between the main musical (ritornello) themes of the outer movements: first, a low chord in the bass leading to a high note (meeting the fist) in the melody, later, a high note leading to an accented octave descent.

Relations between music and dance in *Italian Concerto* contain meaning and play a crucial role in revealing the distinction between its outer and inner movements. But *Italian Concerto* can also be seen as a reflexive piece, yet another in this line of Morris's work, and this one fundamentally *about* such relations.

All Fours

We now progress to twentieth-century scores, to two examples that do not use conventional tonality and models of big form: *All Fours* to Béla Bartók (2003) and *Empire Garden* to Charles Ives (2009). Both dances contain a stronger narrative component than the others discussed so far in this chapter. Ives's score already contains programmatic reference.

Bartók's five-movement Fourth String Quartet (1928) is one of his most celebrated scores. The composer's synthesis of Hungarian folk sources and western modernism appealed readily to Morris; this was especially clear when he heard it played by the Takács String Quartet in concert alongside an actual folk ensemble, Muzsikás, devoted to the preservation and performance of Hungarian folk music. Morris says that, unlike so many other listeners who find the quartet 'scary modernist', he felt it resonated naturally with his folk dance background and eagerly researched Bartók's own folk recordings as part of his preparation.

The main reason why listeners might find Bartók's music difficult is his orientation away from conventional tonality. The use of triads and 'logical' progressions, such as between dominant and tonic, is rare, although there is sometimes a sense of key, a focus on a particular note, that is occasionally simply the result of 'brute assertion'.[36] According to Bartók himself, this quartet is 'on', not 'in', C.[37] His idiosyncratic approach to pitch structures (which is also part of his technique of motivic transformation) has been the focus of many Bartók theorists, and the cause for many a formal analysis. But Morris, although deeply committed to structural detail, felt deeply the passion, vigour and violence in the music, pressing this point during his 2012 Princeton seminar (see p. 62). Finding a choreographic equivalent to Bartók's musical extremes brought him closer to the expressionist early modern dance choreographers. These qualities also led him towards a layer of narrative that is a personal addition, not taken from any specified musical programme.

The percussiveness and uncomfortable asymmetries of Bartók's rhythms also contribute to Morris's expressionist approach. He has described passages as 'shards of sound stacked up and re-arranged in many ways...a figure and a short rest, a figure and a longer rest, almost the same figure and a shorter rest...It's like taking an extra step at the end of a stairway... jarring.'[38] Rhythmic continuity is further broken by violent lighting changes (and scrim colours) in all but the central movement, ranging from fiery red, to blue, white and blackout, highlighting the dancers' skin or grey costume material—apparently irrational shifts, happening when you least expect them. There are also novel, highly evocative timbres, spectral glissandos, eerie nature noises, and Bartók's invention, the snapped pizzicato where a string rebounds against the fingerboard, and which Morris believes reflects the sound of the Hungarian *gardon* (or folk cello).

So how, if at all, do Bartók's forms relate to the eighteenth- and nineteenth-century models already discussed? The composer prefaced his score with his own analysis, which Morris used (alongside writings by the Hungarian scholar János Kárpáti).[39]

In his analysis, Bartók explains first that the five movements of the quartet create one of his characteristic *Bogen* forms, in other words, a palindrome, or arch form:

> The slow movement is the nucleus of the piece, the other movements are, as it were, bedded around it: the fourth movement is a free variation of the second one, and the first and fifth movement are of the identical thematic material. Metaphorically speaking, the third movement is the kernel, the movements I and V the outer shell, and the movements II and IV, as it were, the inner shell.

Morris describes this form in more motional and emotional terms in the thorough, insightful Labanotation score of *All Fours* (by Sandra Aberkalns).[40] The central movement is the focus again:

> the soul of *All Fours*. All of the other movements radiate outwards from this movement.[41]

For him, this is clearly another example of a keystone slow movement (as in *V* and *Mozart Dances*).

Beyond the arch form, Bartók's analysis demonstrates a commitment to classical, closed forms, with several designated 'recapitulations', be several of them 'free' in kind. The first movement he sees as a full sonata form, with exposition, development and recapitulation. But this terminology is misleading, both thematically and tonally, and denies the composer's own innovations. The force of constant development and growth through motivic transformation works against the old models, and Morris's choreography follows Bartók's lead. Stephen Walsh, unusual amongst music scholars in celebrating the composer's expressive qualities alongside analysis of structure, notes a largely continuous development from the beginning of the first movement through to bar 60 (while Bartók indicates a formal development starting at bar 49). What the composer identifies as the moment of recapitulation (bars 92-3) is more obvious: Morris choreographed a free recapitulation accordingly, and confirms that his dancers readily heard the moment of return as such. The Finale is similarly developmental, and again, the choreography follows suit. Walsh suggests that: 'In the end the sense of return vies with the classical idea of resolution for *domination* [my italics] of the Quartet's closing pages'.[42] The last page is trump card, an exact repeat of the end of the first movement. Using the same dance material, but in new spatial organisation, Morris's choreography joins the fray with fierce enthusiasm.

Indeed, form, for both composer and choreographer, is a harsh restraining device, with points of emphasis made especially powerful, working to counteract the spillage of energy. This is an aesthetic approach that we have seen before in Morris's work, in, for instance, 'Mosaic' (from *Mosaic and United*), *Bedtime* and *Grand Duo* (see Chapters 10 and 11). It is just more up front, the oppositional encounter between form and content being more aggressive than usual, in *All Fours*.

The symmetries between musical movements manifest themselves in various ways. All are fundamentally contrapuntal, while the central slow movement is homophonic and harmonically distinct, strongly featuring the whole tone interval. Important thematic material is shared between movements 1 and 5, and between movements 2 and 4, which are both scherzos with trios, marked by rapid scales.[43] But there are also distinctions within these pairings. The first scherzo is chromatic and uses muted strings throughout, the second more diatonic, encompassing a larger pitch range, and consistently pizzicato. There is also a notable progression between the outer pairs of movements, once more betraying Bartók's urge for development. Walsh perceives a more 'open' view towards material in movements 4 and 5, 'as if the arch were being looked at not face on but at an angle, with one pillar nearer the eye than the other'.[44] Morris says that he wanted his last movement 'simpler, easier...even if it's still edgy, violent music'.[45] After furious strikes up and down with alternating arms, it turns into a sprung-rhythm folk dance. In the choreography, parallel symmetries are demonstrated in casting and costuming. A crowd of eight dressed in black and brown dance the outer movements. Two men, then two women, in grey, perform the two scherzos, forming a quartet for the central movement; all four re-appear briefly in the finale. Morris also demonstrates symmetry in mapping material on to the thematic structure of the music, both across and within the five movements.

Morris's narrative layer developed as he worked on the piece. The quartet in movement 3 became a family, parents and two children, at which point he began also to see the duet pairs as family members. (This completely changed his earlier vision of the second of these duets, which already existed, first as a solo (1975), and later with a second dancer added (1980).) The eight dancers in black and brown, operating as a group with its own, very different vocabulary, represent the violent extreme within the music and are anonymous, like a Greek chorus. They jump, spreading their arms wide behind them like a big bird's wings, then, on landing, raise their hands overhead, palms pressed hard against each other, in the manner of desperate pleading (the two movements combined as a motif are sometimes nicknamed the 'Eagle' and are referred to thus in the Laban score). Later, they walk with feet and hands like claws, or bend forwards, hovering on their toes like insects, or hold a tense hand cupped around one ear, as if alert to messages (nicknamed 'Telephone' in the Laban score).[46] Always they contract, jerk or jump, some kind of spasmic activity to every whiplash or accented gesture in the music, but always with deadpan faces. In an earlier choreomusical discussion of *All Fours*, musicologist Hamish Robb refers to the insistent repetition of their movement as less-than-human, automatic, robotic behaviour.[47]

For this choreomusical analysis, we will begin with the keystone of the arch form, the slow movement. This is characterised by a unique quality of suspension and stillness, brought about musically through static, relatively relaxed harmonic blocks with melodies unfolding above, below or between them. As Walsh observes, the context of this movement is all-important, occurring after two swift movements with complex chromatic textures.[48]

The opening chord is a compressed form of interrelated fifths on the note A, which at the end are opened out to span a larger pitch range, with an additional D at the top. 'Tension grows,' writes Kárpáti, 'in proportion to the disintegration of the fifth-structure and the enrichment of the melodic elements.'[49] As well as this, the slow movement introduces at its centre (and briefly in the coda) the most idiosyncratic timbres and modes of articulation of the entire quartet (including non-vibrato alternating with vibrato), examples of Bartókian 'Night Music', the sounds of birds chirping and twittering, or (Morris adds) of insects buzzing. Analysing the articulation markings and performance indications, Amanda Bayley proposes the presence of a particular speech-like quality in this movement, which is confirmed by the rhapsodic solo lines given to each instrument.[50]

This central movement gave rise to Morris's strongest narrative contribution. In the score is the following instruction:

> This quartet should have a time lapse of about twenty years. It begins at a certain point in a person's life and every 'episode' is a few years later.[51]

Just before the coda (bars 55-63), Morris signals to the 'parents': 'Now you're old'.[52]

There is clear familial tension, a sense of menace or watchfulness growing from the start: the two 'children' in chase, the girl caught several times, frozen, by her father, mid-flight; the same girl later tilting at her brother as if in 'a desperate escape through the man's stomach';[53] passionless finger kisses passed between the protagonists. At another point, to the aphoristic bird twitters, all four stand in a line jerking one foot forwards into a wide deep *plié*, then dragging the other one in to join it. This later turns into the hobbled, stuttering walk of the aged parents in the coda, each of them led across the stage by a now grown-up offspring—the power balance reversed. As Robb suggests, Bartók's naked, sustained final chord is illustrated by the spacing-out of the dancers and their final dispersal, leaving only one behind, a bleak end—bleaker perhaps than the music alone suggests—the family members far from mutual understanding.[54] It is significant, however, that performance attitude and facial expression here are plain, not in any sense impassioned or tragic. Morris is quoted in the Laban score: 'Regular, matter of fact. That's what makes this a mystery.'[55]

The story here is, however, partly choreomusical, drawing from interactions that are unique to this central movement. No longer is there consistent response to musical detail. For much of the time, the protagonists seem to fight against musical detail, not driven by what they hear, but driving themselves in short bursts, testing their own agency even if, in the end, they seem to get nowhere. Just occasionally, each of them bonds with a single instrument, the boy and girl 'speaking' with the viola and second violin (bars 42-49), and then, most strongly of all, as if deeply internalising an individual musical voice, the father with the cello and the mother with the first violin, in canon (bars 55-63). Here, it is as if the parents achieve a temporary reconciliation. The music is a rough mirror canon at first (up/down symmetry), turning into a straight canon in bar 59, with instrumental lines marked by intervals of a fourth or fifth. The parents follow the same pattern, in mirror canon (right/left symmetry) then straight canon. The structure means that oppositions of up and down between their movements, and between them and musical pitch, gradually disappear (see p. 104, Ex. 4.2). At the same time, they gradually rise from lying on the floor, finally to stand in unison side by side, the point of maximum calm. Notes in the Laban score reflect the undulating spatial scheme: 'As one thing goes down another floats up',[56] until the point of resolution.

We will return to the grey dancers later, but at this stage it is useful to consider the motivic coherence and transformations across Bartók's other quartet movements and Morris's response to this musical organisation.

The short, compact motifs that Bartók favours—often just a few notes—eminently suit Morris's structural style. Likewise, the composer's device of recapitulating earlier material in his finale is very much in tune with his own practice, in this case, musical ideas from the first movement, including the almost literal repeat on the final page. As we have already seen in *V* and *Italian Concerto*, Morris likes to summarise previous material at the end of his long dances.

Consistent use is made of the first movement's intervallically-compressed 'proto-motif' (Kárpáti's term[57]): Morris fixes his own 'Eagle' motif to it. We first hear this proto-motif in the cello part in bar 7, covering just a minor third, B-flat to D-flat—although it is prefigured in bar 1 (the notes shared between the two violin parts).

Ex. 12.13 *All Fours*, Bartók, Fourth String Quartet, first movement. The bracket indicates the proto-motif.

Morris fits his 'Eagle' jump with spread arms to the second quaver, note C, part of a rising sequence, and the landing with palms pressed into 'pleading' on to the next C, with the descent. The sheer size of movement might well make us hear pitch changes as larger than they actually are. In bars 11-12, we find the proto-motif within overlapping counterpoint, as just described and in inverted form. Morris matches this development in his choreography: he reverses the order of his two big moves to correspond with the musical inversion. Furthermore, when the music tells him, he fragments his movement. To the first three notes of the proto-motif, the dancers do the bird wings alone (bars 28-29). To the last three notes, they do the 'pleading' gesture (bar 143). They do this even to a single note prefaced by a grace note (bars 155-56). To a brusque note or chord, Morris typically introduces the 'Telephone' motif first seen in bar 25. As a variation, this is tacked on to the end of the 'Eagle' (bars 135-44, and on several occasions during movement 5). In the matching closing bars of movements 1 and 5, Bartók introduces an extended version of his proto-motif, repeating it in canon between first violin/viola and second violin/cello. Accordingly, Morris's 'Eagle' is extended, followed by a turn that ends again with another 'pleading', a combination repeated several times, and he scores his eight-strong black and brown group in canons that match precisely the organisation of those in the music.

But Morris takes the principle of obvious links across movements further than Bartók, enticing us to believe that there is closer musical connection

All Fours, first movement, the black and brown dancers, including the 'monumental sculpture'. © Stephanie Berger, 2004

than there actually is. He brings back the grey quartet twice in movement 5. They first appear very briefly (bars 149-60), during a rest followed by muted, sustained notes on second violin and cello. We see the parents as we did near the start of movement 3, their arms around each other's waists; then all four leave rapidly. We see them all again during bars 341-65 (another passage of sustained notes and chords, including fifths, set up as an accompaniment), but this time the siblings walk behind and, significantly, do the big arm swings hitherto associated with the dark group: they start to borrow from that other community. Morris saw these occasions as opportunities to link back to the central movement. Although there are tenuous links within the music alone, they are much more obvious when choreography is added (as in *Italian Concerto*, see p. 410). The quartet exit yet again, but return straightaway for the conclusion, alongside the dark group canon. The final tableau shows the parents stopped in their tracks, about to leave the stage, while the girl stands high on the boy's thighs, a monumental sculpture, yet another moment usurped from the dark group. This is the only occasion when Bartók's proto-motif is not matched by the 'Eagle'. Now we might ask: to what purpose is this borrowing, and on what terms? Have the two communities joined? Are the greys triumphant? Or have they been brainwashed? Morris's ending is characteristically ambiguous.

Similarly, the first scherzo borrows dance movement from the previous

Allegro, forging another choreomusical link. There are, for instance, the 'lazy turns', initiated by the swing of a leg around the body, seen during the Allegro to rising and falling glissandos (bars 75-92), then to single notes developing into rising arpeggios (bars 135-44). In the scherzo, the context is totally different. The turns are performed in pairs on two occasions (bars 95-97 and 142-5), the second time as the culmination of a sequence of rising-only glissandos, their effect more like a whiplash than before. When the turns recur for the last time, in movement 5, we can literally hear the motion of the dancers, because the turns are now accompanied by eerie *pianissimo* rising scales. So music that could hardly, by itself, be registered as motivic, or as motivic development, becomes so through Morris's choreography. In movements 2 (bars 155-60) and 4 (bars 63-64), dancers jump from one leg to the other, a particularly accented style of *jeté* to musical accents: this jump too came from movement 1 (in most extended form during bars 82-91). Again, we perceive connections across the music that we might not otherwise think of as such.

If these are rarified examples of music visualisation, there is an interesting point to be made about the more obvious kind that saturates all but the central movement: the kind that is accent to accent, motif to motif, voice to voice as Morris digs deep into the musical texture. The point here is about history and breaking the rules of history. Recall that the dance critic Edwin Denby denounced the early expressionist modern dancers for matching their music too closely, or for being matched too closely by their composers after completing their choreography (see p. 81):

> It is no fun seeing a dancer dance smack on his *Gebrauchsmusik*, and he looks as dramatic doing it as a man riding an electric camel.[58]

It sounds as if Denby would have loathed Morris's expressionist response to the Bartók. But I suggest that Denby never encountered such a challenge to his theory, the powerful rhythmic tension of such a score only increasing when choreography meets it with such ferocious precision. Indeed, it is pertinent to recall music critic Alex Ross's description of Morris's Bartók setting, as like having 'the lights switched on': the choreography inspired in him a greater understanding of the music (see pp. 85-6). In the outer movements, as much as the contrapuntal detail drives Morris and provides him with useful limitations, it fires his imagination prismatically, to splinter and re-group his dark group spatially in a multitude of ways, severely testing the eye and nerve of the audience, an entirely appropriate tactic in these circumstances.

All Fours does not feel remotely like one of the old music visualisations. It is difficult and alarming. One after another, the Morris dancers told me how hard the dance was for them musically. It stands out in their experience. But what other company has been trained up for the accuracy to meet such rhythmic irregularity and complication, and thus to be so fiercely effective?

Empire Garden

If Morris and Bartók fight for, and finally assert, firm control amidst violence and fracture, Morris and Charles Ives test the limits of legibility and turn that into an expressive force. The amount of information contained within *Empire Garden* (2009) is all but overwhelming.

Ives's Trio for Violin, Cello and Piano S.86 (written and revised between c. 1896 and 1915[59]) is one of the most rhythmically and texturally complex scores that Morris has ever used and, like *Socrates*, it took much longer than usual to create a dance. For Ives, the trio was an experiment in finding his own solution to large form within the context of a multi-movement work. There are three movements, but that is about the only gesture towards a classical past. They do not correspond to a fast-slow-fast model: the first movement is Moderato, the second a Scherzo, and the third, by far the longest (about 15 out of a total of 27 minutes), in several sections, predominantly slow, but with an Allegro centre. The Scherzo is the most curious of the movements, titled 'TSIAJ' (which stands for 'This Scherzo is a Joke'), Ives's biggest-ever quodlibet. Here is the kind of adventurous collage for which the composer became famous, with clashing, borrowed tunes operating both vertically (in simultaneous layers) and horizontally (consecutively).

Ives introduces his sources thus:

> ...The Trio was, in a general way, a kind of reflection or impression of his college days on the Campus now 50 years ago. The 1st movement recalled a rather short but serious talk, to those on the Yale fence, by an old professor of Philosophy—the 2nd, the games and antics by the Students on the Campus, on a Holiday afternoon, and some of the tunes and songs of those days were partly suggested in this movement, sometimes in a rough way. The last movement was partly a remembrance of a Sunday service on the campus—Dwight Hall—which ended near the 'Rock of Ages'.[60]

Others have worked out the detail of Ives's sources, over twenty-five borrowed melodies (although some are yet to be identified), regimental songs, popular songs associated with the Civil War or with southern slavery and work in the fields, dance tunes, and hymns, of which Thomas Hastings' 'Rock of Ages' (the American version of the hymn, see p. 399) is one.[61] So there are both secular and spiritual allusions. Today, many of these melodies and their (unheard) texts are no longer familiar, even to Americans, but we can easily sense their presence from their style. Morris makes much of these sources, sometimes, as we shall see, with references to their textual content.

The title *Empire Garden* refers to a Chinese restaurant, Morris confirms, although it touches the choreography only lightly and obliquely—as usual, he works against any single strand of allusion. Jowitt noted the likeness to 'a Szechuan feast with samplings of many dishes running into one another on your plate'.[62] The electric colours of the costumes (yellow, red, green, blue, by Elizabeth Kurtzman) might also resonate with things Chinese, but they are more obviously the colours of national flags, which reinforce other, choreographic images, of jingoistic soldiers, or imperialist dictators speech-making from atop a pulpit of bodies. Dancer Julie Worden describes how she felt inside the piece: 'There are moments of pure communism, where we are part of a political concept that feels so real, I get chills.'[63] Could the dancers also be bell-hops, cheerleaders, or workers in the field? And the dictators—could they also be evangelical preachers, while their pulpits morph into fountains decorated with open-mouthed gargoyles that could be read as human screams? Or perhaps Morris critiques all kinds of tyranny in this piece. References abound, but more certain is that the work acquires increasingly sinister overtones: dance critic Sarah Kaufman called it 'part carnival, part shattered kaleidoscope'.[64]

The Scherzo is the carnival, a riot of fun, racing from one song to another, but there are premonitions of dangers to come, several orators aloft in turn interrupting the mayhem. The costumes already distance the dancers from us: we know them not as real people, rather as ciphers, even toys, enacting broken experience while, at the same time, behaving as if programmed. Emotional contact between them is withdrawn. During the long, last movement, there are images of terrifying awkwardness and loneliness, crab crawls—one body upturned on all fours, supporting another on top, the pair eying each other suspiciously—or one partner framing the face of another, as if wanting to touch, until the other's face drops out, leaving the frame empty. The shattered 'Rock of Ages' Coda ends up with memories of the carnage of war, a slow motion image of soldiers mown down on the battlefield,[65] then just a few left, still straining to live.

An examination of each movement in turn reveals how particular choreomusical relations contribute to *Empire Garden*'s idiosyncratic 'story'. MMDG's rehearsal director Matthew Rose told me that the piece 'looks like what Morris thinks it sounds like',[66] but it looks like the music in a very different way from his other dances.

Movement 1. Moderato

The large musical form is nothing like first-movement 'sonata form'. There are three sections of approximately equal length—1. A; 2. B; 3. A and B played simultaneously—matched by Morris as follows:

A: Bars 1-27 Piano (treble clef)	Cello	Two lines of music Two lines of dance on two pairs of dancers (in unison within pairs), relating to each line of music
B: Bars 28-51 Piano (bass clef)	Violin	Two lines of music Two lines of dance, on three dancers in unison and one separate dancer, relating to each line of music
A and B: Bars 52-80 Cello, violin and piano (both clefs)		The music and dance material of A and B superimposed, four lines in both music and dance—seven dancers as two trios (in unison across, but not within, trios) and one separate dancer

One musical feature that drove Morris is the un-phrased continuity of each musical line in the first half of each section. At the same time, Ives builds up a complex polyrhythmic texture, including triplets at different speeds: quavers, crotchets and minims, surging across the 4/4 written metre. Similarly, and un-typically, Morris spins long skeins of unpunctuated movement, with little built-in repetition, just here and there a brief oscillating movement from up to down or right to left, all performed factually in the manner of callisthenics.

About halfway through each of the three sections, the tempo indication changes from Moderato to Più mosso and the polyrhythms disappear, giving way to a string melody with block chord piano accompaniment and later, quaver figuration. Again, Morris's choreography reflects these changes. During the Più mosso, he simplifies: one or more dancers always drop out of the action. In bar 15, for instance, three dancers stand still and leave one other performing a solo of hieratic right arm gestures (seen later as the movement of the dictators/preachers). Otherwise, music and dance operate remarkably independently. If you think that a dancer simply visualises one particular musical line, you are soon proved wrong: she or he segues temporarily into the other line or functions detached from both.

The opening beat is a rest in the dance—not in the music, and not because the dancers are late—it is choreographed as such. After that, Morris's choreography is responsible for showing us the regular pulse, before we hear it in the music. (He is particularly pleased with that point.)[67] So here, in *Empire Garden*, you experience the calm, steady motor drive because you see it physically enacted. Then, in bar 5, you see a staccato triplet twice, on each occasion before we hear it echoed by the cello. The dance anticipates the music. Ex. 12.14 shows the two dance rhythmic lines alongside the opening eight bars of the music.

Ex. 12.14 *Empire Garden*, Charles Ives, Trio, first movement.

The result of plain performance manner and independent movement detail is that rhythm acquires a life of its own in *Empire Garden*, almost like a motor force beyond the dancing body. This force continues through later passages when music and dance share motor rhythm, during the steady quavers that end each section and carrying on into the Scherzo.

During this first movement, Morris also confirms the rhythmic outline at moments of special musical clarity, as in bars 7-8, when the cello and piano already achieve rhythmic union. To each musical triplet, three times in all, the dancers circle their heads and arms. They make circles again, and their hips too, at the corresponding point in the other two sections and walk or run to the continuous quavers. Such passages stand out. Otherwise, Morris adds further trouble to the interplay between musical lines. Introducing passages that do not ground the dancers in the music helps keep their identities unsettled, unemotional, removed.

Movement 2. Scherzo

The second movement could hardly be more of a contrast. Morris presents us with perceptual difficulties, making our eyes chase round the stage for the various dance layers that identify with the popular tunes and polyrhythms. It is rather like watching a fairground (or carnival) overfilled with delights and always on the verge of chaos. The stage picture constantly dissolves and re-assembles, the mood mainly bracing and jolly, although it is interrupted twice by the ominous speeches of high-standing orators (now doing the hieratic arm gestures with two arms in canon), ironic responses to a fragment of the gospel hymn 'In the Sweet Bye and Bye'.

Morris has by now returned to his more familiar style of short repeating dance units, responding to the skeletal rhythms and metres of the music and introducing an occasional touch of mime. As a sample, the following diagram lists events during the first part of the movement.

Bars 1-15 Presto 6/8 Irregular accents in both music and dance (random occurrence in the dance). All fifteen dancers on stage.

Bars 16-42 Allegro moderato (march time), strings 6/8 ('A band of brothers in DKE',[68] a fraternity song), piano (3/4) with hemiola effect. The choreography is split between dancers moving to the 6/8 of the strings and others to the piano 3/4.

Bars 43-64 Più mosso Shifting metres, beginning with 2/4 'Marching through Georgia' leading into 'Few days'. Three groups of dancers: a central trio dance to the violin, another trio follow a repeating stepwise falling pattern in the cellos, and two lines cross upstage marching in canon to the piano vamp (articulating a crotchet beat). The two lines own their own patterns of counts, one group a de-accumulation—11-, 10-, 9-, 8-,

7-count units followed by another group as an accumulation—starting from a 7-count unit, and ending with one of 11 counts.

Bars 65-67 2/4 shifting to 3/4 The tune 'Freshmen in Park' accompanied by quaver triplets with strong accents on every other quaver. The dancers wave their arms up and down on the accents.

Bars 68-83 4/4 Cadenza-like waves in the violin and piano (right hand) surround song melodies 'My Old Kentucky Home' and 'That Old Cabin Home upon the Hill'. The dancers, in free rhythm, do the 'vomit move', as if spilling out their guts, which overlaps with others miming cotton-picking and throwing the cotton into baskets on their backs. Then they all roll across the floor, mouths wide open, and finally get up to mime firing rifles.

Bars 84-87 Adagio Piano melody 4/4 ('In the Sweet Bye and Bye'). An orator 'speaks' and others crowd around or fall to the ground.

A hornpipe breaks in (bar 89) for a few bars...

The pay-off is at bar 178, when all fifteen dancers coalesce into a single line, arranged for the first time according to costume colour, from stage right to left, red, blue, yellow and green. 'There is a Fountain Filled with Blood' is the hymn tune here, loud and boldly accompanied by block chords. All march in unison towards the audience, spreading their arms like fountains and picking up imaginary buckets of blood.

Movement 3

This is the slow movement of *Empire Garden*, dominated by lyrical Andante/Adagio and Maestoso, but introduced by a vigorous fanfare and interspersed with faster passages, including an Allegro central section. The form is ternary, ABA, and the layout, indicated by tempo changes for different material, is as follows:

Section A:
Moderato con moto bars 1-9
Andante sostenuto bars 10-14
Maestoso bars 15-45
Con moto (quasi allegro) bars 46-57
Meno mosso (or Tempo 1—variation on earlier Maestoso) bars 58-67
Andante con moto (marked Adagio for later repeat) bars 68-82

Section B:
Più mosso (related to the Con moto) bars 83-90
Allegro moderato bars 91-129, leading into

Section A: repetition from bar 6 to bar 76

Coda:
Adagio cantabile using 'Rock of Ages' tune and extending, in the piano part, from the
earlier Andante con moto/Adagio bars 130-43

Although slow pace allows us to absorb information more easily, there
is a different kind of complexity here from that in the earlier movements
of *Empire Garden*. Each of the three main sections ABA is itself like a quilt,
which lessens the clarity of the larger ternary structure. Each section
contains sub-sections of different tempi, but there are also material overlaps
across parts of, and between, sections A and B. Morris introduces long skeins
of material again (without repeats) for the core slow passages. As usual, he
emphasises the main recapitulation of musical material through repetition,
but here with a number of choreographic additions and significant ideas
summarised from movements 1 and 2. There are some re-workings: the
dictators/preachers have been replaced by mass symmetrical sculptural
groups, the first called by Morris 'a giant sunrise'.[69] A jaunty polyrhythm
within the Con moto sections reminds us of the Scherzo, and Morris
choreographs it—a 5/8 piano vamp (as 3/8+2/8) under 6/4 antiphony
between the right hand of the piano part and the strings.

The slow passages make movement 3 the emotional centre of gravity of
Empire Garden. Heartrending cello lines are pervasive, seeping in the coda
into 'Rock of Ages', where the rock 'cleft for me' (words by Augustus M.
Toplady) is a metaphor for the Christ figure whose blood (water) cleanses the
sinner singer. (The dancers mime being cleansed.) A single duet emerges,
the least dense casting so far in the piece. In the recapitulation, this becomes
a crowd of duets in layers of counterpoint. The extreme difference in
numbers has the effect of making the musical recapitulation seem more like
a dramatic development than any formal resolution. This is also because the
duets, which often descend to the floor, suggest for the first time a longing for
personal contact, beyond the representation of human types or toys.

Ives's music suggests a mystical transcendence that begins with the
hymned Adagios and cadenza-like passage at the end of movement 2.[70]
With its lines left unfinished, broken, however, 'Rock of Ages' evokes deep
sadness. Morris adds his own profoundly bitter twist, employing strategies
that maintain distance between partners and finally, introducing individual,
improvised timing, separating them into a ragged stream of recollections
of the past. He keeps at bay the musical lyricism. The dancers do not ease
themselves into the score. Often, they fight against its rhythms and spirit
with sustained force, moments of sudden attack, and angular body designs.
Ultimately, the struggle to communicate, to unleash trapped humanity, fails.

Slow-motion leads to a final desolate tableau, and Ives's score ends with a dissonance.

Choreomusically different, yet again, from *Rondo* and *Rock of Ages*, *V* and *Italian Concerto*, interlocking with Ives in other ways, the strategies of *Empire Garden* range from matching polyrhythmic intricacies to working with considerable freedom from musical detail, ultimately breaking with its form. It is one of Morris's most curious pieces, both disturbing and moving. It is also the example in this chapter furthest removed from the classical models of big form. Instead, here, Morris celebrates the new idiosyncratic proposals with which Ives marked the arrival of the twentieth century.

Spring, Spring, Spring

Morris's setting of Stravinsky's *Rite of Spring* in 2013[71] comes as a surprise, and not only because he tends to avoid music written for dance. It did not seem like Morris to take on such a heavily-used score, indeed the most used ever—already over two hundred settings recorded—and the most notorious, burdened by a dangerous mythology. Furthermore, he choreographed it in its centenary year, alongside still more *Rite* premieres, although he claimed that no connection was ever intended.

Far less surprising, Morris, so often the unconventional musician, used neither the orchestral nor four-hand piano originals, nor, he says, would he have ever done so. Instead, he choreographed a treatment by the jazz trio The Bad Plus, created in 2011 for a multimedia show entitled *On Sacred Ground: Stravinsky's Rite of Spring*. (*Rite* is sufficiently iconic to have been subject to various arrangements in recent years, like those of Hubert Laws (1971), Larry Coryell (1983) and The Butchershop Quartet (2004)). The new dance was premiered at the Ojai North! Festival in Berkeley in 2013. It brought Morris back into collaboration with pianist Ethan Iverson, his former Music Director, and author of a highly insightful, finely researched blog article on Stravinsky performance practice, including that of his *Rite*.[72] Stravinsky was 'the original prog-rock kind of guy' Iverson once said in interview,[73] and Morris says that he likes this version because 'it's interesting, alive, exciting...it swings...and it's rhythmically precise without being robotic'.[74] The choreographer made the work quickly: a couple of trial sessions to test out initial ideas, a three-week block, then completion the evening before the premiere.

Iverson summarises the Bad Plus version as 'an anthology of the crucial elements of both [the orchestral and piano originals] plus stuff that's not in the scores at all'.[75] But the trio (piano, bass and percussion) base their work most closely on the piano score (which Morris used in rehearsals), bringing out its rhythms, ornamenting it melodically and with syncopations, and sometimes clarifying individual parts of the musical texture. Big accents are often made bigger, and unworldly sounds are produced as Reid Anderson plucks a melody from the strings of his bass, or David King's drumstick caresses the surface of a cymbal to sound a shiveringly high squeak. Iverson's hands fly wildly, often to independent purpose.

The beginning and end of the Bad Plus *Rite* are, however, exceptional. Taking their cue from Stravinsky, who never intended his prologue to be danced, Iverson and Anderson pre-recorded it (and we hear it in blackout), enhancing it technologically—overdubbing four tracks to register all the notes of an impossible-to-play score, hugely elongating the unforgettable first long (bassoon) note, and at one point inputting a brief soundscape from Stravinsky's 1927 orchestral recording, a touch of history. But Morris stepped in and asked the group to get rid of the heartbeat 'ba-bum, ba-bum' and human sigh that they had introduced in 2011: by now, these ill-suited his different, developing conception.[76] At the end, perhaps reminding us that the conclusion of Stravinsky's *Rite* is often considered an anti-climax, The Bad Plus perform a raucous signing-off riff, freed from the composer, something only they can do: they quote from their own composition *Physical Cities* (2006).

There are a couple of other minor structural changes by The Bad Plus, as in the Spring Rounds, when repeating accompaniment chords are given a lift on three occasions with modified harmony and miniature suggestions of melodic movement, or there is an extension at the end of Procession of the Sage, when repeating material repeats for longer (eight bars become thirty-six, with a page of the score played three times). 'The Bad Plus often sits on things for a while', says Iverson.[77] It is important that these changes are startling for those, and there are many, who know the Stravinsky originals well. They invite comparison.

To this new version of the *Rite* score, Morris created a dance called *Spring, Spring, Spring*, with no evident plot, and no victim, nor does the choreography use the score's sub-titles. Once more, however, there is the inevitable weight of *Rite* tradition: it is virtually impossible not to read each new setting against history. Morris's own title comes from the celebratory song in the film musical 'Seven Brides for Seven Brothers' (1954), although this has no further implications for the dance, other than for mood. (Again, Morris departs from the original Bad Plus conception, which was darker.) Otherwise, there are three teams of dancers (four men, five women, and three male-female couples), and Morris treats the music like a symphonic, architectural concert enterprise not so far from the composer's own wicked re-vision of his work. Famously, by the 1920s, Stravinsky was already erasing the devastating theatrical past of his score, proclaiming that it was primarily 'an architectonic rather than anecdotal work'; later, he was categorical: 'I prefer *Le Sacre* as a concert piece.'[78] (But Morris is not the first choreographer to take this alternative approach—a string of others have done so since 1960.)

Morris spins from this score a highly complicated dance, with his usual motivic network of steps and gestures, and—a pun on the title—literally a lot of springing. Morris's dance, as critic Alastair Macaulay suggested in *The New York Times*, could also refer to 'Californian devotees of alternative cultures',[79] with the women in Grecian-nymph dresses, the men in bright jeans and everyone with garlands in their hair. Several other critics saw the presence of pregnant Amber Star Merkens as significant: resonant of abundance and regeneration (the reason for the original Chosen One's demise). To the final assault of The Bad Plus, the crowd, women and men raggedly intermeshed, plunge to the floor in a squat, an inconclusive kind of death.

Stravinsky's famous motor rhythms remain powerful in this treatment, but are of a different, jazz kind, with the essential component of 'swing', the juice that acquires its power from pulse. Indeed, Morris's choreography here is largely *about* rhythm. Immediately, he locks into the quaver pulse of Augurs of Spring (one twice as fast as in the classic *Rites* by Maurice Béjart and Pina Bausch), and only later sets against this a firm crotchet pulse. But there is no obvious music visualisation here of the famous irregular syncopated bumps, rather Morris sets up conflicting metrical systems (3s against 4s at quaver rate) that here look fresh and dotty. Yet Morris still picks up on basic principles that guide the score. During the Procession of the Sage, he sets in motion his three teams, one by one crossing the stage, again and again, to the excessive musical repetition of The Bad Plus, each group changing the metre and rhythm pattern of the last and, as in the music, creating the effect of accumulating layers. There is too an extraordinary play between accenting the beat and the 'backbeat' (to use the jazz term), alternating in and out of rapid-fire syncopations in several sections: Augurs of Spring, Glorification of the Chosen One and the Sacrificial Dance. Thus, the prime example, driving to the climax at the end of Augurs, groups of dancers shift between accenting quavers 1 and 3 of each bar and those on 2 and 4, sometimes countering each other simultaneously across groups.

In the Sacrificial Dance, Morris starts off with his own motor rhythm, perhaps the only choreographer ever to do so, because Stravinsky virtually denies this at this point. In chains, the dancers simply walk regularly at quaver rate, immediately, striding vehemently across the famously irregular surface of the signature material. (Admittedly, The Bad Plus do bring out the motor here more than usual.) To take an example, this works out as six walks across the first musical motif (bars 2-5: 2/16+3/16+3/16+2/8), fifty-four walks and heel-pulses across the entire opening section. When the dancers stand beating their heels, Morris says that it should look like 'marking time'.[80] Just a few times they look like zombies—for instance, the line of four men tilting stiffly right and left to the viciously irregular accents that follow the opening of the Sacrificial Dance. The next moment, they are back in the 'groove', enjoying the hippy, playful sensuality of a jazzy *Rite*.

Possibly no other choreographer has investigated *Rite*'s rhythms in such detail and with such vitality. Morris even keeps edgy the repetitive opening of the score's second part (Largo and Andante con moto), articulating lyrical, legato melody notes with hard, sharp gestures. Some of the choreography here is allegro, using the short sub-beats of the music, no mean feat. This, he feels, with justification, is the point where the score sags, in danger of losing its momentum. It is as if Morris took the opportunity with the iconic *Rite* to show off his virtuoso musicality, all that is, by now, a matter of course in his technical toolbox, revealed here in extreme form. The renewed physicality of stage rhythms, not only from the dancers, but also the musicians bobbing at the side, transfers powerfully to us, in the audience, twitching and toe-tapping from our seats.

Ultimately, *Spring, Spring, Spring* is not one of Morris's finest works, but it is nevertheless an imaginative take on the ingenious internal workings of the *Rite* score. Despite the considerable burden of its history, and certainly inspired by the re-visioning of The Bad Plus, he asks interesting questions. He even pays ironic tribute to the composer's own re-conception of the score as an 'architectonic', abstract entity.

Coda

Morris's shifting responses to big form are naturally determined by the changing nature of the musical forms themselves, from the baroque and classical of Bach and Mozart in the eighteenth century to the stretched models and breakout experiments of Bartók and Ives in the twentieth. Yet Morris's works, virtually without exception, respect the large outlines of the score by associating dance material with major musical thematic material and recapitulations, even when musical themes lead him across the boundaries of individual musical movements to create long-distance relationships. The choreography of *V* stands out as the most direct, straightforward response to repetition structures, from the larger outline of Schumann's score to its detailed ingredients. But Morris nearly always experiments more radically than in *V* with the manner of dance repetition, by introducing very different spatial arrangements and casting, or by adding layers of counterpoint. Thus, he disguises the original relationship in some way, often seriously testing our seeing, hearing and memory. More often than not, too, Morris likes to manage his own motivic coherence and summaries, a clutch of motifs often revealed in compressed form towards the end of a work.

Perhaps this urge to embellish, to tease, not to do the obvious, betrays Morris's inclination towards drama, developing an idea about human relations that emerges during his creative process or, at least, unsettling our expectations. To take an example, what is new about a restatement is often dramatically significant, no more so than in the very recent *Crosswalk* (2013) set to Weber's *Grand Duo Concertant* for clarinet and piano. Here, a boisterous, athletic opening reveals several dancers dashing in different directions across the stage. To the clarinet's high entry note (bar 3), a woman in the centre rushes straight at us, reaches upwards, then falls backwards to the descending arpeggio, hitting the floor flat on the final, lowest note. When she repeats the move to the same music, she turns around ninety degrees, her head towards us. At the point of recapitulation, she crosses the stage left to right between two other women, and we expect her to fall yet again. Instead, it is her companions who fall, to the same note, while she rushes on into the wings. The change of tactics is a delicious surprise. Audiences laugh.

In the Andante con moto that follows, which is yet one more centre-of-gravity slow movement, there is much less to smile about. Morris, as he so often does in slow movements, darkens further the musical tone. Jowitt describes vividly the activity of two women on either side of Noah Vinson in the central section of this movement:

> close together, walking on their hands and feet, as ungainly and out of step with each other as two straggling cows being urged along... Vinson's the momentary herder.

But Morris undermines any sense of resolution or, at least, confirmation at Weber's point of recapitulation. He summarises in telescoped and more pressured form the choreography up to this point, reintroducing the early walking steps of the accompanying community, but forcing the trio straight back into its oppressively close, nagging material, which does *not* start off this Andante movement. The power relationship between Vinson and the two women changes too. Jowitt:

> Pretty soon you can't tell for sure who's controlling whom, let alone why. I think he dies.[81]

Vinson is left lying abandoned onstage. The ending is open, uncertain, no resolution there, either. Drama momentarily controls form.

Contrast the very different approach to Hummel's sonata form in the first movement of *Festival Dance* (to the Piano Trio No. 5 in E major). While the recapitulation here is another of Morris's varied exposition repeats, the opening musical theme (sixteen bars) is now singled out more emphatically than in probably any of his other dances. It is always allocated the same choreography, and always danced by a single couple upstage left. The couple start in an embrace, then one by one dance a statement and response, and finally join together in unison. Only the couple casting changes each time you see it. Redundancy forces us to look more closely at the movement and its nuancing by different dancers, just as the musical theme is refreshed each time we hear it: in E major (at the exposition opening—Morris cuts the repeat of the exposition here), in A major (during the development, orchestrated differently), in E major again (at the point of recapitulation) and finally in the coda, again in E major. Now, for this last occurrence, we hear only the first eight bars: the music moves on differently, while the steps continue as before. So much exact choreographic repetition becomes a joke. At the end of the entire work is the punch-line: the opening embrace on the couple who introduced *Festival Dance*, yet again upstage left, a point of maximum closure, form as dramatic confirmation. Or is the piece about to begin all over again? These inextricably linked duets/themes become structural markers, foundational ingredients within a dance that has couples as its subject matter.

It is useful at this point to compare the procedures of Balanchine, the other leading exponent of big-form choreography. Far more often than Morris, he goes out of his way to mask musical return in favour of evolution and openness (as in *Serenade* (1934) and the first movement of *Ballet Imperial* (1941)—both to 'romantic' Tchaikovsky). On the other hand, when he foregrounds musical return in 'classical' or baroque scores (in parts of *Symphony in C* (Bizet, 1947), *Symphonie Concertante* (Mozart, 1945) and *Concerto Barocco* (Bach, 1941), Balanchine is far more likely to show the repetition straight, without the transformations that delight Morris.[82]

Pursuing this point further, I suggest that Morris's fascination with form restrains his urge towards narrative and emotion. Musical recapitulation nearly always curbs narrative flow—there is usually no reason for a repeat within a story, although, in an ABA da capo aria, especially if ornamented, it can signify a singer's re-affirmation of the primary statement.[83] Recapitulation might even disturb the performance frame of story, removing any illusion of role playing and suddenly shifting our attention to formal device. In several Morris pieces, that sudden turn to schematism and, with it, to another performance frame, is very striking. Morris is rare amongst choreographers in mixing such conventionally incompatible aesthetic points of view and introducing to us the particular jarring effect of doing so. On the other hand, he is possibly at his best setting sharply-etched musical structures, because they give him the most to work against.[84]

We have also seen that, within his big forms, Morris introduces various degrees and intensities of mirroring or visualising musical detail. When such mirroring is at its most intense, it proves its effectiveness in radically different ways, from joyous confirmation in the fast movements of *V* (which in the end exhausts itself), to an utterly surprising (and far more interesting) taut doggedness during this work's slow movement, to an oppressive, vicious re-affirmation that conjures up a terrifying vista during the outer movements of *All Fours*.

In the next chapter, we consider an even bigger form and long-range relationships that extend across a whole evening's performance.

13

Mozart Dances: An Evening of Big Forms

Morris's decision to make *Mozart Dances* (2006), a full-evening setting of three large-scale piano pieces that were never intended for dance, was immediately controversial. There was the challenge of size—he had never before attempted anything so big without a programme attached to the music: choreography to two concertos and a sonata, each with three movements. Nor had he ever foregrounded a single sonority so extensively, although several choreographers had already used the concerto form and the antithesis between soloist and group that it offered: for instance, Balanchine—on several occasions, Bronislava Nijinska, Jerome Robbins and Kenneth MacMillan.[1] Morris was seen as audacious too in setting the most light-footed, sparkling and iconic of 'classical' composers, Mozart, never one to be associated with earthy, bare-foot dance style.

The international network of co-producers was un-phased by the ambition of Morris's project: New Crowned Hope in Vienna (a festival celebrating Mozart's 250th birthday and the venue of the premiere), Lincoln Center for the Performing Arts (the Mostly Mozart Festival, New York) and the Barbican Centre (London). In 2007, the US television station PBS undertook to broadcast *Mozart Dances* live during its second season at Lincoln Center. The work has maintained its place in the repertoire every season since, as well as in further foreign programming (to Canada, New Zealand, France, Israel, China and Spain).

Mozart Dances also demonstrates an unusual complexity of form and meaning, within its three separate parts and across the whole, with its exceptionally long-range choreomusical relationships. It invites discussion of tonal procedures and of how these might be reflected choreographically, of Morris's added layers of meaning and of how he negotiates a range of textures and narrative potential prompted by concerto and two-piano instrumentation. My analysis is informed by having seen the work live several times, in London and Madrid, as well as in several recordings.

At one time, Morris had reservations about the composer. 'I love Mozart', he told Joan Acocella in 1993, 'but I find that the structure of his work is often too fragile, too sophisticated for dancing.'[2] It is interesting then, because the point was raised in 2006 by several American dance critics, that, late in his career, Balanchine had also had reservations. Oddly, he seems to have changed his mind after having already created six ballets to his music.[3] Prior to his *Mozart Dances* (2006), Morris had already set two Mozart piano pieces: the tongue-in-cheek *Fugue and Fantasy* (1987) and, more recently, the *Rondo* discussed in Chapter 12. He had also choreographed for the operas *The Marriage of Figaro* (1988) and *Idomeneo* (2003) and directed his own production of *Figaro* at the Monnaie in 1991. Yet none of this should be surprising, given that so much of Mozart's music is based on the rhythms and metres of social dances. An influential 1983 book on Mozart's music (by Wye Allanbrook) focuses on just this point: it covers the dance element permeating *Figaro* and *Don Giovanni*, with references to other, instrumental music.[4]

By 2006, Morris was telling interviewers that he was thrilled by the huge impact of the smallest adjustments in Mozart's scores. A repeat is often not an exact repeat, he explained: 'It almost is—it's just that the chord is slightly different or there's an extra bar, or an appoggiatural dissonance. It's like *Woooow*. Where did this come from?' He was also overwhelmed by the distressing and jarring qualities of the composer's music:

> Why is this tiny melody, this tiny little nothing *killing* me? What is it? It's nothing. And I've never heard it before—*and* I have always known it. It's that change, that shift or that revelation of complete love and confusion. It's astounding music, every single inch of it. Maybe I am finally smart enough to recognise it.[5]

This reading of Mozart's music as dark and troubled has been around for a long time, alongside that of him as delicate, sentimental salon composer. It stems from the nineteenth-century cult of Mozart as violent and subversive composer, although, famously, Schumann read his Symphony No. 40 as nothing but lightness and grace.[6] During Morris's time, the sentimental view of Mozart was challenged vociferously again from within the academy, writers since the mid-1980s, such as Rose Subotnik, Susan McClary and Neal Zaslaw, updating the nineteenth-century portrait and claiming signs of rebellion against social repression within his music.[7] But, as we shall see, even if Morris often emphasises the 'killing' properties of Mozart in interviews, it is clear that the composer speaks to him of a myriad of things, including the bright and joyous.

The director of New Crowned Hope was Peter Sellars, Morris's colleague from his early career and for whom he had first choreographed the wedding scene in *Figaro* in 1988. (New Crowned Hope was the name of the Masonic Lodge to which Mozart belonged.) According to the premiere programme note, Sellars wanted to acknowledge Mozart's leanings as 'one of the most intensely political artists in history'. Another of his ideas was to celebrate the work of 1791, the last year of Mozart's life. Immediately fired by the prospect of choreographing concertos, Morris selected the last one for piano, No. 27 in B-flat major, K. 595. Its finale used Mozart's recent children's song 'Longing for Spring', which, beginning with the words: 'Come, dear May, and clothe the trees in green once more', was a Masonic statement about the hope for political thaw and an alternative Europe beyond autocracy and monarchy.

Initially, Morris thought of complementing that last piano concerto with horn and clarinet concertos, but he had met the pianist Emanuel Ax, and they were keen to embark on an ambitious collaboration. To open his work, he chose the little-known Piano Concerto No. 11 in F major, K. 413 (1783), which was partly a practical choice: it also existed in a string quartet version suitable for later MMDG touring. At one point, he had in mind the Concerto for Two Pianos, K. 365 as a centre piece (involving Ax's wife Yoko Nozaki), but finally selected instead the two-piano Sonata in D major, K. 448 (1781), the slow movement of which he found especially inspiring. Here, once again, was his centre (see pp. 397, 412), or, in this case, within a triptych of three-movement works, the centre of centres. Using his by now favourite image, 'The intention was for the evening to radiate out symmetrically from the sonata in both directions', said Morris.[8] The outer parts of *Mozart Dances* are designated according to their position in Mozart's concerto output, 'Eleven' (referring to the Eleventh concerto) and 'Twenty-Seven' (referring to the Twenty-Seventh). The title 'Double' refers to the two pianos of the central sonata. (In the analysis that follows, when individual musical movements are referred to, these three parts are numbered in the order of *Mozart Dances* as, for instance, I/3, II/1 or III/2.)

Other pianists have sometimes played for *Mozart Dances*, including members of the MMDG Music Ensemble. Using smaller instrumental resources, 'Eleven' (the string quartet version) and 'Double' have also been presented separately from 'Twenty-Seven', with *Grand Duo* (to Lou Harrison's music) or *V* as the third, closing item on the programme. The first conductor was Louis Langrée (in Vienna and New York); later performances have all been conducted by Jane Glover. The backdrops are by the British painter Howard Hodgkin (who had previously collaborated with Morris on *Rhymes with Silver* and *Kolam*); other designs are by Morris's regulars, costumes by Martin Pakledinaz and lighting by James F. Ingalls.

Preliminaries

Some general observations by the choreographer are useful prior to choreomusical discussion of the three parts in turn of *Mozart Dances*.

Before the Vienna premiere, Morris discussed his gender politics for the piece in an interview with Joan Acocella in the printed programme. At the outset, he decided that his work would include a dance for the women (to 'Eleven'), and another for the men (to 'Double').[9] He wanted to expand his dancers' range of expression but, especially relevant to us here, also planned to work against received views of what Mozart's music might mean for dance:

> It's no accident that in the slow movement of the women's dance, 'Eleven', the women are all standing apart from one another on the stage. They do this sort of tortured, beautiful stuff [he gesticulates], but they're always alone because I didn't want it to become a group hug, which can happen with women, dancing to music like that. And their movement is extremely angular and powerful. Also, in the closing section of their dance, the action is all lateral and linear—thrust, drive, line. The women had a hard time with this. I had to push them to be stern, to sharpen their attack. The women, when they put on those pretty dresses and hear Mozart, tend to go soft and pastel, and to me that's dead.

Morris sought an unusually robust dance treatment of Mozart. As for the men:

> I've had to push them in the opposite direction. Just as the women, in their slow movement, are all strong and singular and isolated, the men, in their slow section, are all together, co-operating. They dance in circles, nourishing, nesting...They had a hard time, too, just like the women.

Opera and Gesture

Choreomusically, Morris was keen to confront for the first time a distinctive characteristic of the music that he had chosen. 'I think that every one of the three Mozart pieces we used is like an opera,' he said in the programme interview, and even mentioned one by name, *Così fan tutte* (1790), an opera buffa, the type that invokes characters drawn from everyday life. What this really means deserves investigation. Certainly, the numerical titles carry no hint of this. Musicologists have for a long time recognised a mutual relationship between Mozart's concertos and operas, arguing about the precise nature of this relationship in terms of formal, gestural and thematic parallels. But more important here is the general agreement about a fundamentally dramatic conception. Significantly, the issue of concerto as drama had been discussed by Charles Rosen in *The Classical Style*, the book that Morris had studied assiduously.[10]

Most obviously, drama stems from the dialogue between a soloist and orchestra in a concerto—sometimes involving individual instruments selected from the orchestra—a dialogue that might at different times be conversational, confrontational, or collaborative. This is an example of musical 'voices' speaking from a musical texture, with the soloist especially likely to suggest a human persona (see pp. 101-3). The musicologist Donald Francis Tovey likened the protagonists directly to human experience:

> Nothing in human life and history is much more thrilling or of more ancient and universal experience than the antithesis of the individual and the crowd; an antithesis which is familiar in every degree, from flat opposition to harmonious reconciliation, and with every contrast and blending of emotion, and which has been of no less universal prominence in works of art than in life.[11]

Interpretations from the eighteenth century describe the interaction of these voices in terms of a kind of co-participatory relationship. This is helpful to an understanding of Morris's approach to Mozart's instrumentation, which uses the musical dialogue as a source for direct human interaction on stage. In 1793, Heinrich Christoph Koch, a leading music theorist and critic of his time, wrote:

> To it [the orchestra], he [the soloist] displays his feelings, while it now beckons approval to him with short interspersed phrases, now affirms, as it were, his expression; now it tries in the Allegro to stir up his exalted feelings still more; now it pities him in the Adagio, now it consoles him... I imagine the concerto to be somewhat like the tragedy of the ancients, where the actor expressed his feelings not to the audience but to the chorus, which was involved most sparingly in the action, and at the same time was entitled to participate in the expression of the feelings....[12]

As Jane R. Stevens, Koch's translator points out, 'instead of antagonists or simply cooperating partners, the solo and tutti are semi-independent, interacting elements in a sort of dramatic intercourse'.[13]

At the same time, just as the concerto is not about linear plot and characters with agency, but is rather metaphorically 'dramatic', so is Morris's dance. It is in this way that he references from a distance both opera and perhaps too, the narrative tradition within dance, especially ballet.

In keeping with different theoretical concerns, the drama has also been explained with reference to formal models that apply to sonatas, quartets, symphonies as well as concertos. Let us take as our example first movement sonata form, the paradigmatic formal type of the late eighteenth century (see pp. 385-6), although this was always a mobile concept, never set in stone. But there are important distinctions when it comes to concertos.

Here, the initial exposition is orchestral (otherwise known as a tutti or ritornello, referring to the history of concerto form and its links with aria, see pp. 136, 193). Then there is a repeat of the exposition, but with material redistributed between the soloist and orchestra. In Mozart's case, there is often additional, even totally new, material for the soloist—he is renowned for the remarkable abundance of ideas that tumble out one after another through his work. A development section follows the exposition, as is customary in sonata form, then a recapitulation (a return) leading to a cadenza for the soloist, and finally a coda.

One other key distinguishing feature of concerto first movement form should be mentioned. It is only during the second exposition, which includes the soloist, that the modulation from a first key area to a second takes place. As Richard Taruskin remarks, the over-arching tonal scheme is essential in dramatising the relationship between soloist and group, 'individual' and 'crowd', in Mozart's concertos.[14] And Mozart's dramatic ambitions drove him hard. He played with the model forms in multiple ways, resisting, as well as conforming to, established tonal and thematic expectations and setting himself different problems with every new work. All three of Morris's chosen Mozart works have different structural stories to tell, and he responds to their differences.

It is also relevant to a discussion of Morris's contribution to introduce the 'topic' (topos)-based analytical approach that probes expressive (dramatic) content alongside formal process. This again was partly prompted by Mozart. Topics are codes of reference, another kind of 'voice', understood by composer and audience, drawing upon associations with opera and the manner in which the behaviour of characters is depicted in opera, but often, too, the precedents of popular musical and dance culture. Mozart was especially brilliant at assembling sharply-defined topic-based material in a manner that was dramatically exciting, cogent, and with an urgent sense of motion overriding flux and interruption. In her article 'Comic Issues in Mozart's Piano Concertos', Allanbrook explains the procedures absorbed from opera buffa into the concerto:

> ...powerful and repeated cadential thrusts and a clear articulation of topics or expressive stances, facilitating the quicksilver shift from one to the next—in short, the ability to embed references to many musical styles in the continuous context of a piece, to construct a cosmos in a sonata allegro movement.[15]

Allanbrook sometimes calls these topics 'gestures', because they refer to the imitation of kinds of music written to accompany human action (not only gesture in the narrow sense of arm or hand movement). In her earlier study of Mozart operas, she includes dance metres in this category. Morris's Mozart selections provide examples in their respective finales: marked Tempo di Menuetto in K. 413, while the last movement in the sonata K. 448 starts out as a fast, strident march and the 'song' 'Longing for Spring' in K. 595 masquerades as a jig. Drawing again from Allanbrook, from her studies of both Mozart's operas and instrumental music (piano sonatas and concertos), examples of other topical 'gestures' that appear in these scores are 'singing allegro' (the right hand of the piano like the voice of a soprano); brilliant, bravura style; the hunt call; and the affective style of 'Sturm und Drang' (the high-emotion eighteenth-century 'Storm and Stress' movement). One or more of these topics can sometimes be overlaid, integrated to create further, nuanced effects. The result of this Allanbrook describes as 'theatre', even though (unlike for Momigny, see pp. 387-8) the references are subliminal and not spelt out in words.[16]

Morris's *Mozart Dances* choreography turns out to have a particular affinity with Allanbrook's approach to the music. Let us consider as an example the entrance of the piano solo in the K. 413 concerto. (This was originally choreographed for Lauren Grant,[17] who dances the whole of the piano part during the first movement of this concerto.) The first phrase is a new theme, a tactic that Mozart often adopted for the introduction of the soloist in his larger concertos, prior to the repeat of the first subject of the exposition (see Ex. 13.1a). It starts (bar 56) with a kind of fanfare, three high repeated notes (C), that immediately shift into something more like personal, singing allegro, made expressive through the use of appoggiaturas in the melody line (in typical Mozart style, strong beat dissonances that need to be resolved—here, upwards). Meanwhile an Alberti bass, a simple, mechanical style of accompaniment of Mozart's time, provides a demure accompaniment. After a leap upwards in the melody, a decorated falling interval of a seventh introduces a sudden touch of bravura before the cadential closure. The first subject itself refers to the same topics. Later, in bar 82, Mozart turns to brilliant figuration, a rush of semiquaver arpeggios, while gruff, thick chords in the bass hint at 'Sturm und Drang'(see Ex. 13.1b). The parallels here to Allanbrook's lexicon are not always exact, but her underlying principles are nonetheless very useful.

Ex. 13.1a *Mozart Dances*, Piano Concerto No. 11 in F major, first movement (I/1).

Ex. 13.1b *Mozart Dances*, Piano Concerto No. 11 in F major, first movement (I/1).

Morris grasps the highly volatile musical surface as an opportunity although, as we will see later (in the slow movement of the same concerto), he does not always underline musical topics or affect, he can also ignore, or work against, them. Here, he exaggerates the volatility as Grant's solo begins. The complete sequence of dance events to the first phrase is as follows:

—bars 56-58: Grant rushes forward to the fanfare as if alerted by something out in the audience, but stops sharply in her tracks on the third high C, staring at us.
—bars 59-62: She becomes more pensive, turning right, then left, more 'into herself', gathering composure.

—bars 63-64: She performs an expansive turn, then halt, to the high G and decorated seventh interval that follows—her own touch of bravura style. When the musical gesture cuts off, she stops dead again, staring out at the audience.

—bars 65-67: She quickly turns her back and exits.

Later, to the semiquaver arpeggios, the image of Grant as brilliant soloist returns for longer. She relishes her power in more turning and running, and, as if on the rampage—slightly mocking 'Sturm und Drang'?—pounding from one foot to the other, raising her legs sharply to the bass chords.

At the same time as Morris confirms Allanbrook's musical topics during the passages described, he also responds to the more literally motional, physical qualities (another kind of topic) in the music. From the choreography, we enjoy a heightened experience of both rhythmic motion and motion within the vertical dimension. Morris uses for arm gestures what 'sound' like these as much as like vocal cantabile. The frequent, phrased two-note melodic patterns are characteristically visualised by single, big gestures, some of which also match rise and fall in pitch. When the 'hiccup' of the decorated seventh interval re-appears a fifth higher (bar 116), Grant exaggerates it with a cat-like spring.

The variety and prominence of arm gestures is already a very familiar aspect of Morris's work, but here in *Mozart Dances*, these are not coded mime or sign language. Many have something of the quality of gestures that go hand in hand with vocal utterance, whether pre-verbal gasps or sighs, or deliberate communication, the actual speaking of words. The presence of human bodies brings these 'utterances' closer to consciousness than music does alone. Morris said in his programme interview that situations arise in dance simply because people are centrally involved and visible. Yet he teases us in *Mozart Dances* with a context that supports the idea of gesture as vocal utterance: looks between individuals, intrusions, disappearances, meetings and abandonments, just as you would find in a Mozart opera buffa, and suggestions of the stage as a room with doors and an outdoors.

One gesture appears throughout *Mozart Dances*, a raised index finger that itself could say many things: 'What was that? Did I hear something? Wait a minute! Be careful!' This was actually choreographed for 'Double' (see p. 456), but on some occasions, Morris lets his dancers choose when to introduce it. Crucially, it always suggests urgency and enquiry, with the hope of resolution, and it commands our attention.

Morris, however, avoided fixing and clarifying through words during the rehearsal process; he provided very few verbal images to his dancers that relate to human feeling, communication and situation. 'I know what the situation is, but it's not a word situation,' says Morris in the programme interview. 'It's not a play; it's music.'

Grant, on the other hand, offers many verbal images from her experience as a dancer. She remembers feeling, at various times, 'tentative, bold, fearful, curious, exuberant'. She also refers to movement quality: 'floating, stopping on a dime, soaring, darting, spinning, balancing softly'. 'I have a very rich inner life', she recalls Morris joking with her. 'Sometimes I have to be toned down...Mark trains us out of story.' So these images (even of feelings) emerge from the movement and music in the process of creation and performance, rather than being the product of motivation, and the expressive qualities of that opening solo were, Grant observed, simply 'built in...the sudden stops and darts...are what they are'. She remembers Morris regularly shouting, 'Do something new...different...fresh',[18] in other words, asking her not to fix an interpretation, not to think ahead.

Perhaps Morris chose Grant for this particular role precisely because she had such a 'rich inner life'. 'I love all those changes,' she adds enthusiastically. Mozart's 'topic' style suits her perfectly. In her 2013 Madrid performances, Grant looked and felt freer than before, bolder, luxuriating in her movement, confident about doing every performance differently, making decisions on the spur of the moment, whether, for instance, to storm off stage or to leave more quietly.

Explaining further his intentions for *Mozart Dances*, Morris recommends the article 'Variations on the Right to Remain Silent' by the poet and translator Anne Carson.[19] In it, she discusses the concept of the untranslatable, for instance, the case of Joan of Arc who refused to explain the 'voices' she heard, for fear that they would lose their force and identity if she did. Another of her examples is the painter Francis Bacon, who, rather than 'explaining' by using the conventional relationship between figure and ground, wanted to remove the traditional 'screens' and represent 'the brutality of fact'. 'I want to paint the scream more than the horror,' he said about his series of portraits of a screaming pope (variations on the famous picture of Pope Innocent X by Velasquez).[20] As Carson puts it, Bacon wanted to 'create a sensible form that will translate directly to your nervous system the same sensation as the subject. He wants to paint the sensation of a jet of water, that very jar on the nerves....to grant sensation without the boredom of its conveyance.'[21]

Morris aims to do much the same thing. The raised finger creates a sensation too, a potent 'silence' whenever it appears. So do the palms pushing skywards as if shielding a person from 'a falling building',[22] and the extending of hands or pressing them to the breast, which may, or may not, convey important feeling towards another person. Another compelling movement example involves a pair of gestures. First, a straight arm strikes diagonally upwards. It can look like a forceful command and, a couple of times, other dancers respond to it by falling flat. Then, the raised hand waves lightly side to side on a downward trajectory—'like a falling leaf' was the image (not a feeling).[23] It seems to wipe away all anxiety. In another context, the same moves might read quite differently. During the silence before the 'Eleven' finale, Grant's raised arm might be a lively greeting. Then she does the falling hand as rhythmic cue (two bars for nothing) to the orchestra. You sense deeply the difference in quality between the two moves. All these gestures, while defying secure verbal explanation, and without the ground of full-blown plot-driven narrative, seem to resonate sensually and emotionally as utterly precise and clear.

There is also a discursive aspect to reckon with as we observe these gestures. Alongside the immediate gut experience, faced with a context that encourages us to interpret, yet constantly holds back from fixing sense, we might well find ourselves considering what they add up to, all these mysterious signals and odd juxtapositions. Morris's withholding of the literal offers freedom. His dancers are invited to make these gestures 'authentic' for themselves. We, as audience, ask our own questions about their meaning at the same time as engaging with them as direct, pre-verbal experience. The interpretations in the analysis that follows are therefore my own. I am certain too that they varied from one performance to the next.

Motifs

Gestures form one part of the motivic mosaic of *Mozart Dances,* alongside movement that calls much less upon us to consider meaning and social relations. Such motivic organisation is more dense and complex in this work than in perhaps any other by Morris, partly because of his decision to bind together three very substantial musical scores. Surprisingly few moves occur only once. Again, Morris was driven by the principle of thematic economy and coherence, 'logical' thematic development through motivic variation, the legacy of Haydn (not so much Mozart) that he learned from his reading of Rosen (see p. 389).

Motifs change their tone when they cross the major boundaries within and between Mozart's scores. An example is the staccato, angular closing and opening of the arms originally created for the men in the third movement of 'Double' (II/3, from bar 85).[24] There, it takes two bars of 3/4, one move per bar; it looks fun, even jubilant. Later, it found its way into the choreography for the women in I/1, performed by Grant within a single bar of 3/4 in the rhythm short-long (crotchet-minim), here like a smart call to attention (bars 110-13). The female group lined up behind her reinforces all her open positions, on the minims, every other move, matching the reinforcement of

Mozart Dances, 'Eleven', first movement, the 'angular arms', Lauren Grant as soloist, with Maile Okamura, Julie Worden and Elisa Clark. © Susana Millman, 2007

the piano by the strings.[25]

Another travelling motif, introduced by Grant in I/1 (bars 172-79), is later utterly transformed. The music is in 3/4 time, and, on count 2 of the bar, meeting the opening of the melody, she opens into a sturdy second position *plié*, led by the right hand, with palm flat and facing downwards. On count 1 of the next bar, she twists to the right and quickly extends her other arm diagonally upwards. The rhythm is long-short (minim-crotchet), counted as 2 3 1, with the main accent, a syncopation (as in the music), on the initial *plié* (often with lower melodic pitch too), and then the motif is repeated in sequence. Soon afterwards, she turns the motif into 4/4 metre, crossing the musical rhythmic structure for seven bars, again starting on count 2, now in very long—short rhythm (dotted minim-crotchet) (bars 185-91). Her upward reach appears more throwaway than before, while the sturdiness of the *plié* is further stressed. Now without the accentuation shared or regular across music and dance, the overall effect is unstable. (Interestingly, Grant chooses to count this 4/4 motif musically, in 3s, which suggests that she might inflect each repetition of it slightly differently. MMDG dancers, Grant explains, have the option to count either way in circumstances like this.[26])

Ex. 13.2a Piano Concerto No. 11 in F major, first movement (I/1).

Ex. 13.2b Piano Concerto No. 11 in F major, first movement (I/1).

In 'Double' (II/1), where the music as well as choreography is in 4/4 metre, Joe Bowie dances this travelling motif, but begins it on the downbeat, although first, his rhythm is even (minim-minim, bars 9-11), and then very long—short and throwaway on the upward reach (dotted minim-crotchet) (bars 13-15). The effect of beginning on the downbeat count 1 and sharing the music's 4/4 metre is different yet again.

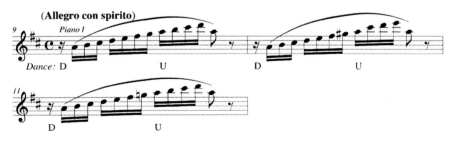

Ex. 13.2c Sonata in D major for Two Pianos, first movement (II/1).

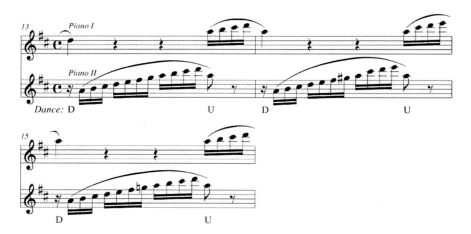

Ex. 13.2d Sonata in D major for Two Pianos, first movement (II/1).

It is telling that it took several viewings even to notice this motivic connection across 'Eleven' and 'Double', such was the transformation via rhythmic means.

In 'Twenty-Seven', Morris summarises his material across the entire work (see p. 416), recalling motifs from both 'Eleven' and 'Double', the gathering of familiar, 'old friends', alongside new ideas to new music—by the end of a full programme, a sense of plenty. In *Mozart Dances*, solo dancers, in other words, people, become motifs too, like main 'characters'—at the premiere, Grant, Bowie, Noah Vinson and Julie Worden. Watching them when they return later in the work, we remember their earlier appearances, and sometimes they repeat actual movement from their past.

Occasionally, Morris introduces the device of anticipation—a brief glimpse of material that is for a while left unrepeated, like a loose end, only to be confirmed through repetition some time later. The doubtful recognition, the sense that you barely grasp a fresh idea, often keeps you on edge in this thematically complex piece. The question: what is going on here? is closely related to the question: was it there at all? Insecurity itself becomes a precise sensation. An example is the women's simple, gentle breathing of the arms, marked by unison, after a pause, near the end of the cadenza in I/1. This becomes a key motif in III, performed by the whole cast on several occasions, a calm statement of their unity.

Another motif example, first seen in I/3 three times in succession, is an upward flick of the hands and one foot, then, after stepping backwards, a halt in an 'old ballet', baroque-style position, up, then down, in both movement and music (bars 72-75). At the end, the foot rests on the toes behind the standing leg, arms extended sideways, thumbs and third fingers pressed together.

Ex. 13.3a Piano Concerto No. 11 in F major, third movement (I/3). R (halt) means placement of the right foot on the toes behind the left foot.

We see the move just once again, near the end of 'Eleven' (I/3, bar 214), unexpectedly, to an interruption of the main musical theme. It stands out stylistically as if from another era—that of Mozart. But it acquires much greater definition in the first movement of 'Double', within a considerably strengthened context of eighteenth-century reference and, as an anticipation, relating to a striking new musical pattern, a much enlarged up-down pathway covering the interval of a seventh. Here it is a declamatory wake-up call.[27]

Ex. 13.3b Sonata in D major for two pianos, first movement (II/1).

Mozart Dances is like a detective story that you enjoy returning to in order to trace how its events fit together. All dances are about memory, seeing what is happening in the light of what has happened (and what will happen, if you know the dance well enough). But here, premonition acquires especially prominent force.

Performing the Analysis

Separate analyses follow of the three parts of *Mozart Dances*, and in the order of their individual movements. This allows the reader to understand how Morris responds in different ways to the large forms of eighteenth-century music, forms that were already moulded and subverted in various ways by Mozart himself. The analyses also enable other comparisons to be made across the work as a whole and highlight striking choreomusical detail. Some readers may find it most useful to skim-read and concentrate first on the introductions to each part and the final chapter summary, before engaging with the detailed analysis.

Structural diagrams of the whole work explain some of these formal features, in line with Morris's own fascination with the visual devices of scores and charts. Readers are encouraged to listen first in detail to the three Mozart works by themselves, without the dance, as Morris himself did, and then, if they can, to follow their scores.

Mozart Dances: summary diagram of musical structure*
I = tonic V = dominant; A, B and C = subject or theme groups

Eleven: Piano Concerto No. 11 in F major K413
Cast: Female soloist and seven women

1. Allegro F major: 3/4 sonata form

Exposition 1 (orchestra and 6 men)		Exposition 2		Development	Recapitulation	Cadenza	Coda
AI	BI	AI	BV	V to other keys	AI	BI	I

2. Larghetto B-flat major: 4/4 slow movement form

	Part 1				Part 2		
AI (orchestra)	AI	V Transition		AI	AI	Cadenza	Coda I

3. Tempo di Menuetto F major: 3/4 sonata rondo form

Exposition		Development		Recapitulation	Coda
AI	BV	AI	CIV (sub-dominant)	AI	I

Double: Sonata for Two Pianos in D major K448
Cast: Male soloist and seven men

1. Allegro con spirito D major: 4/4 sonata form

Exposition			Development	Recapitulation		Coda
‖: AI	BV	:‖	to other keys	AI	BI	I

2. Andante G major: 3/4 sonata form

Exposition (and second soloist)			Development	Recapitulation (and 8 women)		Coda
‖: AI	BV	:‖	V to other keys	AI	BI	I

3. Allegro molto D major: 2/4 sonata rondo form

Exposition			Development	Recapitulation		Coda
AI	BV	AI	CIV (sub-dominant)	BI	AI	I

Twenty-Seven: Piano Concerto No. 27 in B-flat major K595
Cast: Eight women and eight men

1. Allegro B-flat major: 4/4 sonata form

Exposition 1 (orchestra)		Exposition 2		Development	Recapitulation		Cadenza	Coda
AI	BI	AI	BV	V to other keys	AI	BI		I

2. Larghetto cantabile E-flat major: 4/4 ternary form

Part 1		Part 2	Part 3	
AI	Codetta I	BI to other keys	AI	Coda I

3. Allegro scherzando B-flat major: 6/8 sonata rondo form

Exposition				Development	Recapitulation				Coda
AI	BV	Cadenza	AI	C to other keys	AI	BI	Cadenza	AI	I

* This is a summary diagram of structure, a simplification of Mozart's sophisticated diversions from formal models. It is not drawn to scale.

'Eleven' (I)

Mozart's Piano Concerto No. 11 in F major is orchestrated for strings, oboes and horns. A group of men dance the initial orchestral tutti exposition, and then exit, leaving the remainder of the concerto to a group of seven—described by Morris as tall, 'giant Easter Island women'[28]— plus Grant in the piano role, the smallest dancer in MMDG. Dancing to the string quartet version of this concerto, Grant says that she missed the contrast between the 'tiny little piano sound and the great big colour of the orchestra', but admitted that the small chamber ensemble suited the 'spare' choreography and her 'lonely' track through the piece.[29]

The designs are black, both the women's dresses and Hodgkin's giant brushstrokes on the backdrop.

1. Allegro

In accordance with the sonata form of the first movement of a concerto, there are two musical expositions, the second with the piano moving to the dominant key of B-flat major and featuring greater abundance of thematic material. The development introduces further, minor keys, progressing to the recapitulation in the tonic, which then incorporates a cadenza and final orchestral tutti as coda.

Immediately when the solo piano enters, so does Grant, establishing her own solo status, and taking us through a range of movement content and mood that maps on to the great variety of event within Mozart's score. At different times, she might be any of the following: personal and quiet, confident, brilliant, confrontational, as if there are forces out in the audience and on stage with which she has to contend—self-sufficient, strict, but occasionally voluptuous, even fun. The development section introduces an element of anxiety: obsessive repeating patterns (including the diagonal arm and second position *plié* motif in 3/4 and 4/4, see Exs. 13.2c and d) and, towards the end, rather manic, beckoning gestures.

The first movements of the concertos in *Mozart Dances* tend to show the clearest distinction between piano/solo dancer and orchestra/group, especially here in 'Eleven'. Grant possesses the most extended solo work of all, and her small size seems to make her power and presence all the more compelling. She nearly always rushes offstage left when the piano is not playing, emphasising its absence while leaving a trail of memories behind her. For just two orchestral bars in the development, the group emerge briefly out of the wings only to retreat back again. There is no time for Grant to leave: the impression is that she has the entire development section to herself, including her own musical theme as introduction. Morris further sets off the variety and volatility of her piano exposition material by keeping the men in simple unison and stable spatial arrangement throughout the initial orchestral exposition.

In 'Eleven', Morris is especially strict about musical return or long-distance repetition. In the recapitulation, there is an exact repeat of the piano exposition content (except for maintaining the tonic key area instead of moving to the dominant), and Morris reinforces this in the choreography in the strongest terms, repeating it in exactly the same spatial arrangement.

It is perhaps surprising to find Morris visualising the solo/group distinction and thematic organisation so literally, but this helps to make complex material legible. Choreomusical relations loosen after this. As we have already seen in other pieces, associating movement with music (most of all when repetition is exact) makes us more aware of the material identity of both; mutual reinforcement helps us grasp information more quickly.

The duplication in movement of musical rhythms, dynamics and pitch detail further supports this. All in all, most of this first movement is textbook 'music visualisation'.

As the music drives towards the cadenza, Grant enters downstage and falls to the ground. (Later, this fall becomes an important motif.) Suddenly, all civilised behaviour flies to the winds. Grant appears to be writhing on the floor. (Rolling is a move that Morris gave her as a basis for improvisation at this point—she needed a rest.) Meanwhile, the group of tall women erupt into solos all over the stage, doing anything they choose in any direction, whether borrowing from Grant, or anticipating things to come: Morris told them that they could work freely with his material between musical landmarks. It is a crazy scene. There could be trouble brewing.

2. Larghetto

This is in slow-movement form, binary, moving to the dominant F of B-flat major, with a short transition between each of the two parts. The main theme is first presented by the orchestra and then repeated, varied, on the piano. The second part is extended to include a cadenza and much embellished with expressive ornamentation. According to Emanuel Ax, Morris asks for this movement, like all the other slow movements in *Mozart Dances*, to be played more slowly than usual (see p. 70). The phrase structure is especially irregular, and Morris follows its lead. For instance, the orchestra's opening eight bars break down into:

1½ + 1½ (each unit, for strings, ending with a wind echo, for which there is no equivalent in the string quartet version of the score)
1 + 1
3

Ex. 13.4 Piano Concerto No. 11 in F major, second movement (I/2).

Then, from bar 9, the piano varies this construction. 7 bars break down into:

1½ + 1½
2 + 2

The next reiteration of the theme on the piano, further varied and moving towards the dominant, is more extended. From bar 16, its twelve bars break down into:

1½ + 10

First, in the silence, a lone woman positions herself upstage, her head bowed, the fingers of both her hands directed to her breast bone, an image of humility and pain. (She is the sub-soloist of the first part, originally Julie Worden.) During the orchestral introduction, the group walk in, then start to dance when the piano enters. They drop their heads and arms to the first orchestral echo and jab their arms out to the side on the second, a stiff position reaching from a contorted shoulder line with head uncomfortably angled. They continue with hard attitudes, bodies in torsion, pressing their hands to their heads and faces and fiercely splaying their fingers. The image of suffering intensifies, still more so when Worden dances her private agony (from bar 16).

Grant arrives at the point of musical transition (bar 27), continuing to operate separately from the group, but now as leader, heading up a line traversing the stage. During the piano cadenza, however, after running through a forest of standing bodies, she blends with them, replacing one of their members (originally Elisa Clark, sub-soloist for the second part), who exits. (Earlier, Grant had raised her finger and held it up for a long time—the motif, a curious intrusion—when the same woman stood before her.[30]) The group depart at the end, leaving her alone.

In this second part, there is no longer any clear association between dancers and specific orchestration. Indeed, Grant's initial entry is to orchestral material after the group had danced to the piano supported by the orchestra. Here, their music is a repetition in varied form of the opening orchestral material, and Morris responds with variation himself. He adopts his familiar tactic of changing the spatial arrangement of dancers. He also adds to the number and asymmetry of those performing and, by speeding up their rate of event, heightens the anxiety conveyed by the new, expressive piano ornamentation. On the other hand, as major contrast, the dancers hold a twisted, unison stillness on the floor for much longer than before, the whole of bar 46.

Morris's choreography in the Larghetto seems to be led primarily by harmony and the melodic construction of harmony. The rhythmic impulse is far less clear than in I/1. Instead, his handling of the extended theme from bar 16 demonstrates his understanding of the long-range harmonic motion and drama that is key to large musical constructions. Now, for the first time, the harmony becomes very unsettled, moving towards the dominant key of F major, with digressions, a touch of G minor along the way, several dissonant appoggiaturas, the promise of, but delaying of, resolution. Worden opens her solo with a version of the group's first phrase, embroidered with more turns (1½ bars). Like them, she drops her head and arm during the first musical echo and moves into the stiff arm position when the second is expected—although it is withheld on this occasion, leaving her stranded.

Soon, however, during the 10-bar musical unit that follows, she takes that arm position to the floor, turning herself from one side to the other—a painful manoeuvre, especially as we cannot see her face. Then, at the most painful moment of all, when the dominant seventh of F major is reached, not giving in to the promise of musical release, Morris makes her twist around on the floor to face the audience directly, raising both her arms behind her into a frightening suspended V. (It is impossible to imagine how she got herself into such a position.) A little later, two women raise her to standing, and push her backwards on her toes right across the stage—still twisted—struggling against her resistance. Together, the trio heighten the tension of the dominant pedal, with the extra frisson of a *bourrée* during the cadential trill, before final resolution in F major.

Another response to harmonic change that is especially noteworthy is in the cadenza, within a much briefer timescale. Mozart refers back to an earlier descending cadential figure (bars 52-53) but now repeats this with several notes flattened, and immediately, the mood turns darker. Then, by way of contrast, he interpolates a series of quiet falling broken chords. Morris accents the high opening notes of each chord with a simple, wide, opening of the arms, passed between the dancers: it is like a sudden message of exposure (the breast opening to communion) in striving for resolution.[31]

As he hinted in his programme note interview, Morris adopts a generally robust approach to Mozart's music in this movement. For much of the time, the dancers resist musical lyricism and legato. The effect is deeply disturbing.

After such intensity, the mood lightens.

3. Tempo di menuetto

The music of the finale is in 3/4 metre, as in a minuet, and in sonata rondo form. As so often with Mozart, this is not the standard form because the normal repeat of the first episode material (B) is omitted, to form the following structure:

A B A C A Coda

Typical here are the clarity and simplicity of the rhythm and phrasing and the tonal stability of the main theme, befitting the role of this finale as a resolution of earlier tensions.[32] Completed by a full cadence on the tonic, this main theme lasts for 32 bars, which can be broken down into component parts, each 8 bars long, aaba. The tone of the finale is moderate, without major landmarks along the way, and the material is both integrated and mobile, a constant spinning of variations—the main theme never re-appearing in quite the same way, and the episodes building from main theme material. The movement ends *pianissimo*.

Again, Morris's finale choreography does not forge a particular link between piano and solo dancer or between group and orchestra. Here, Grant is an integral part of the group, so there is a kind of resolution of forces. All the same, she finds herself alone at the end and walks off straight past a woman lying on the floor, holding the tortured stiff V arms from the Larghetto. Trouble is certainly brewing now.

The musical material suggested to Morris a series of small groups and individuals crossing and re-crossing the stage, reinforcing every plain statement of the main musical theme, and sometimes stopping off en route. He also responded to the tempo indication by coming up with his own minuet step, modest in scale, as was the academic style of Mozart's times, 6 counts long, and, like the original eighteenth-century minuet step, palindromic (see pp. 391, 412). For a while, drama gives way to social dance reference, although Morris makes a great deal of the striking sideward fall with which Grant ended the first movement, shared here by the other women. There is now a hiccup after the landing, a small heave that shifts the body further across the floor; its awkwardness is surprising. It could read as a gentle joke, or just a heave.

'Double' (II)

The score for the Sonata in D major for two pianos indicates exact exposition repeats in the first two, sonata-form, movements. Morris chooses to include the musical repeats on both occasions, while, from now on, in both 'Double' and 'Twenty-Seven', he treats all major musical repetition (including recapitulations) as a challenge to make changes in his choreography and, in some instances, to make us hear the same music very differently. His 'story' needs this development. Fundamentally the same movement material recurs in 'Double' while, as usual, altered in terms of number and spatial organisation of dancers, but a new, possibly unique feature is the incorporation of additional lines of choreography, only for textures to thin out again later on. The choreography seems strikingly different, unlike the music.

In concert, seeing the two pianists in the sonata might well contribute an element of drama, as they often pass material between them and take turns with the main melody and accompaniment. Here, within *Mozart Dances*, we have to check the score, as Morris himself did, for information about their dialogue.

Morris choreographed the sonata for seven men and one male soloist, originally Joe Bowie. A group of women join them for the conclusion of the second movement, a kind of balance to the brief statement by the men at the start of 'Eleven', but the women's role here is much more prominent.

Historical reference asserts itself most strongly of all in 'Double' (the first and third movements). Bowie stands out from the group in a dark eighteenth-century-style frock coat. Some have read him as a Mozart figure—but not Morris. At various times, he seems to be leader, mentor, shadow, even perhaps dream figure. The title 'Double' also means 'doubling'—the concept of alter-ego is especially resonant here as Bowie finds himself attached to a series of individuals, and most strongly in the central movement (to Noah Vinson). The single piano sonority binds the cast together. By the same token, 'Double' can also seem claustrophobic.

Hodgkin's black brushstrokes on the backcloth are now more plentiful and more urgent.

1. *Allegro con spirito*

Morris theatricalises the music's large repetition structure—the repeated exposition and its recapitulation—by changing the casting in a highly significant manner. First, Bowie performs the exposition entirely alone (entering after a 4-bar introduction), then, when it repeats, he performs the same dance material again, while a series of different men (at one point all of them together) run in to join and then leave him along the way. It is as if he is their teacher. Then, in the recapitulation, as he drops out, they take charge, one by one, repeating what they have 'learnt' without his guidance. The first man to join Bowie, on the repeat of a 2-bar musical unit, now looks as if he missed his entry. Should he have entered with the music the first time round? *Was* he late? Simply maintaining the integrity of structural device or system and doing nothing else—the late entry just happened automatically—becomes a stroke of wit. Meanwhile, Bowie's absence, to the same music, gives him a special kind of presence. By now, we know his contribution so well that he haunts the recapitulation as a 'missing person'. The device of loss here, as we will see, anticipates something much bigger, much more profound, in the second movement. But Bowie makes one brief entry from the wings, only to leave immediately. There is a reason: Morris draws attention to a musical transition, the point where the recapitulation starts to differ from the exposition, here without its modulation to the dominant key. Only if you are fast enough do you catch this secret moment.

Often, Morris draws attention to distinctions between the two piano parts. The shift in Bowie's step with the arm extending upwards on the fourth beat of the bar (instead of the third, see Ex. 13.2d) highlights the new echo, in the part of piano I (Ax's role), of the end of the rising scale of piano II (Nozaki's role, bars 13-15).

Morris's treatment of the second subject is especially noteworthy. This is the place where he specifically choreographed the finger motif. He totally ignores piano II at first and turns to piano I alone. Here, nothing happens during the first six bars, except for three isolated high notes E, one every two bars (on the fourth beat of the bar), each preceded by a grace note as decoration. They are like after-thoughts, and Morris choreographs their isolation at the same time as he lets them add definition to his key gesture. Bowie turns upstage on the first, with finger raised: 'What was that?' then, to us, on the second: 'Did *you* hear that?' (a knowing collusion with the audience that suddenly stands outside the established theatrical frame, see pp. 104-5).

The musical theme repeats as counterpoint between the two pianos (and without the repeated Es), but Bowie does exactly the same moves again, revealing what is now an absence—he helps us hear the Es, but now as memory, again to experience absence as presence. When the exposition repeats, other men enter to visualise the counterpoint (as piano I and II), but the absent Es are still danced, by Bowie and his shadow—now made more complicated as the shadow follows exactly one bar in canon after Bowie. In the recapitulation, two shadows dance the isolated high notes, which are now As instead of Es, because the passage has reverted to the tonic key. Finally, to the contrapuntal repeat in the recapitulation, the original shadow dances all the absent notes by himself, again one bar late. But by this point, the beginning of the dance canon (originally Bowie a bar before him), has also disappeared. The layers of memory increase as this Allegro movement progresses.

The group have responsibility for the development section: to a new musical theme, both new and familiar movements freshly assembled. The same musical theme returns, like an insertion, at the end of the recapitulation. Bowie now takes over the group material, the previous direction of distribution reversed.

2. Andante

The slow movement of the sonata captured the imaginations of critics more than any other part of *Music Dances*. Approaching half the

Ex. 13.5 Sonata in D major for two pianos, first movement (II/1), second subject. B refers to Bowie performing the 'finger' motif, while S indicates a shadow figure.

'Double', first movement, Joe Bowie, the 'finger' motif. © Susana Millman, 2007

length of the entire sonata, it is also Morris's favourite movement.

The outer sections of this sonata form are especially substantial and leisurely in delivery. The second part of the exposition (from bar 13) is built upon a succession of overlapping cadences, delaying convincing closure in the dominant key (D major) of the new home key of G major, and it contains a lot of repetition (a statement on one piano immediately copied by the other). From bar 13, ornamented cantabile phrases descending from a high, sustained note (usually D) are pervasive, first as one- and two-bar units, later extended, interspersed with chordal passages and rounded off at the 'double' bar line by a couple of brief staccato utterances.

Ex. 13.6 Sonata in D major for two pianos, second movement (II/2), an example of melodic phrases starting on D.

Especially surprising is the late 'start-up' of a melody unfolding into a 4-bar timespan (again from a high D, bar 36), cutting into the cadence that concludes the previous material. Once again, the development section is short and introduces new thematic ideas; towards the end, it suddenly moves into minor keys, and the mood darkens.

Morris set the slow movement in such a manner that it leads logically from the slow centre of 'Eleven', the women's equivalent. It develops upon the gravity of the earlier dance, to become the centre of *Mozart Dances* as a whole. The choreography here is all about circles, beginning with one for six men holding hands and simply walking, with remarkable tenderness. Then, as Morris explained in the programme interview:

> Noah [Vinson] does a solo inside the circle [to the exposition repeat]. Then he does it alone [to the recapitulation], which to me is the most tragic thing I've ever seen. But that's also because of the context. First we saw

the circle, then we saw a filled circle—filled with Noah's solo—and then we see Noah's solo alone. We've learnt how to see it.

The absent 'presence' of the circle during the recapitulation emphasises Vinson's loneliness. (The lighting throughout is dark, as it was in I/2). Later, he is re-joined by the other men, then momentously, by a group of eight women in grey gauze skirts, like wilis or sylphides out of early romantic ballets such as *La Sylphide* and *Giselle*. Weightless and noiseless, they seem to be barely there, even as they envelop the stage like a dangerous mist.

During both expositions and the recapitulation, the circle re-invents itself in various guises. It is first taken to and fro across the stage as the men walk, one step per crotchet beat, with occasional short bursts of 'double'-time walking at quaver rate, or as one man, then his opposite number on the far side of the circle, are lowered towards the ground. Later, it is released into a running chain, and finally it is divided into miniature circles of two or three men.

Each musical phrase starting from a high note (usually D)—nine in all during each exposition—is strongly marked with a step into high *attitude* by one man at a time, then a couple, eventually the whole group. Finally, the *attitude* is taken into a lift. The men come across as both supportive and peaceful in what seems like a timeless ritual, but which might also convey inability to escape their attachment. Vinson himself seems profoundly troubled, falling to the floor within the circle, racing upstage to seek solace, clutching his chest and looking heavenwards, then re-assuming introversion as his companions' arms urge him across the stage.

I discussed earlier the unusual quality of the walking that starts this movement (see pp. 119-20). The men are between steps on the musical beat—'It's a leap rather than a walk. There's a lift...the beat is suspended,' says Morris.[33] So there is a tiny moment of tension during the super-legato of a single step. Later, running chains smooth over larger musical divisions, each one starting by piercing an archway of arms and then working freely, not marking beats, between fixed musical cue points. Morris times each of these differently, starting fast and decelerating (in the first exposition), starting slowly and accelerating (in the repeat exposition), and keeping even tempo (in the recapitulation: involving both men and women). The pressure of crossing the musical rhythm adds to their tension. They also make the 'start-up' *attitude* (bar 36) look even more startling, like a gasp, even more a point of fissure.

As for the *attitudes*, whether on the toes or lifted, and the final, cutting unison arm gesture of the exposition, these moves seem surprisingly hard and staccato, stressing the corresponding musical moment (and the high D is already a melodic accent). Some would probably consider this bluntness most un-Mozartean. Others might be dismayed by the apparent break in melodic flow when a single moment is 'frozen' out of context (see p. 106).

On rehearsal videos, however, Morris can be heard clicking his fingers at such points, an urgent reminder to dancers who do not find this emphasis 'natural'. Such moments refocus our attention during the leisurely musical progress and pull against any inclination towards sentimentality.[34]

For the development section, Bowie arrives to teach and comfort Vinson (they share movement material), but when the music suddenly veers into the minor, they strike angular poses borrowed from the women's slow dance. At the culmination of their duet, each stretches an arm vertically upwards, palm to palm, into the sharp image of a steeple, anticipation of a motif explored later (and used again by Morris in *Socrates* (see p. 356)). Bowie disappears and the recapitulation begins.

Here, with the return of the high Ds, Vinson rushes to support the women, who now step into *attitude* from the wings, while the men continue as before, stage centre. Soon these women become part of that centre, adding to the protective circle and chains. The 'story' in Morris's choreography, unspecific as it is, increases dramatic pressure for longer than sonata form suggests. There is no sense of impending resolution at the point of his recapitulation— Vinson's solo is a 'tragic thing' and questions remain. Is this Vinson's dream: of Bowie, who returns during the final bars, or of the women, or of the other men too? Does Vinson have premonitions of death? Are the women dangerous ghosts—like the wilis were in *Giselle?*[35]

At the end of the Andante, rather than matching the end of his exposition, Mozart's recapitulation veers off into different coda material. Many of Mozart's sonatas (far less the concertos) contain near-literal repeats of all their exposition material within the recapitulation, but not here. It is as if the composer 'opened up' his writing during the latter part of the recapitulation, or rather stopped short and replaced it with a highly ambitious digression as coda. Morris makes full use of this opportunity.

Suddenly, there are two disturbing sforzandos (on chords of the seventh), upon which two women arrive, in lifts, out of the wings, their skirts billowing like sails driven by the wind. This is a new image. To a rush of cadenza figuration, Vinson is taken by another two women down to the floor and up into a lift; and then there is calm. It was at this point that Morris persuaded Ax to break the musical phrasing and to stress a new beginning as the women glide quietly across the stage (a step pattern seen in I/3 and during Vinson's solo, see p. 71). Eventually, the women are left, in a closer, more pressured version of the circle, after which they silently disperse, leaving Vinson and Bowie in the centre side by side, facing opposite directions. Morris's resolution is far less certain than Mozart's, if it is one at all.

3. Allegro molto

The last movement of Mozart's sonata is another sonata rondo, like the finale of Concerto No. 11, but this time, in the composer's 'delayed return' version. In the sonata, the main theme A (16 bars long) re-appears only after the other 'exposition' material (B) has been recapitulated, before the rounding-off Coda. The layout is as follows:

A B A C B A Coda

There are much bigger shifts in style and mood in the music here than in the rondo finale of 'Eleven', and the choreography reflects this as an occasion for showing the high spirits of a boisterous band of men. Morris treats the repetitions as opportunities for renewal. The core material of section B, for instance, which is fast and 'baroque-ish' then slow and declamatory, is presented by two consecutive trios first time round, then, when it returns, by a quintet followed by one man. Bowie is no longer a central figure, instead he joins in from time to time, as one of the band, finishing at the far end of a line-up across the stage. He has done his job, but remains a supporter.

As for the fun of the finale, it depends greatly upon the match between choreography and music. The men waddle upstage to semiquaver figuration (an eccentric version of ballet *emboîtés*). The commanding arm of one man (see pp. 442-3) results in others falling 'dead' to a series of accented chords followed by a pause, the first time Bowie, the second, everyone but him. The central section (C), a sudden turn into bright G major, is wonderfully fresh. Again and again, to a repeating phrase, one man is thrown from one end of a line of three to the other. Then Bowie enters downstage left, gesticulating to the three men in turn. They can choose how to respond, hands extended or pressed to the breast and, as usual, we race to interpret what they might be saying. 'What is it you want? How can I help? Do you mean me?' Bowie marches off again. The special delight is when he returns to the same music with three henchmen on his back, urging even more impatiently for answers.

The finale is a merry interlude. 'Double' shows the worlds of men and women getting closer, but not without an element of tension and mystery. 'Twenty-Seven' takes this 'story' a stage further.

'Twenty-seven' (III)

The orchestration for Mozart's final piano concerto in B-flat major K. 595 is richer than for the F major K. 413—flute, oboes, bassoons, horns and strings—and the wind play a prominent part. For example, just a few bars into the first movement, unison wind calls interrupt the opening string melody and, during the development section of the same movement, a significant conversation emerges between wind and strings. There is a closer relationship than before between the piano and specific instruments of the orchestra, a 'chamber' style,[36] contrasting with the dominant virtuoso presence of the piano in much of the earlier concerto.

Morris seizes the richer, subtler orchestration as an opportunity: to make his concluding statement about community, bringing the men and women together, sixteen in all—eight plus eight—while also treating them as a group of individuals. For Morris, everyone appears to be a soloist in 'Twenty-Seven', with one dancer, Worden, occasionally emerging as a special 'character' during cadenza passages.

The scenography here is radically different too, reflecting the change in spirit. Although individually designed, the costumes are all white and, now, Hodgkin's red brush gestures dominate: a single black one remains.

1. Allegro

Morris treats the first movement drama between piano solo and orchestra radically differently from that in 'Eleven'. A series of solos by different cast members replaces the single figure of Grant.[37] But let us consider the progress of the piece from the beginning.

The movement begins with the lower strings introducing a quiet oscillating figure. When the melody starts in bar 2, the full cast of men and women are seen dancing 3/8 triplet patterns, swaying to one side and then the other, all of them holding up one arm in a manner of their own choice. The triplets may well appear rhythmically arbitrary. Although they add up to three musical quavers very neatly, the quaver beat division feels awkward and uncertain against the 4/4 metre of the score. Nine triplets later, there is the first unison wind call. All the dancers stop sharply in their tracks and look overhead, again, as they choose, some as if shielding themselves—the 'falling building' idea is back. It is a decidedly quirky way of starting a dance. Already we see a community of individuals. The dancers resume the triplets once, twice, more.

Ex. 13.7 Piano Concerto No. 27 in B-flat major, first movement (III/1), first subject.

This opening leads into a much lengthier, and more complex, orchestral and big group section than in 'Eleven', a 'cosmos' of 'topics' (see p. 438), with carefully articulated musical seams. Take the first twenty-five bars as an example of the diversity of choreographic content: the triplets to singing allegro and anxious gestures to each wind interruption; a fall to the ground on descending quavers—'Sturm und Drang'; more singing allegro as the dancers twist their hands slowly upwards, like 'beautiful flowers growing towards the sun';[38] the dancers dropping their hands and freezing for three bars (doing nothing on the floor, with their faces averted, looks shocking)— more 'Sturm und Drang'. Then they rise quietly to their feet and prepare for the second musical subject.

Allanbrook describes what happens to such patchwork material in Mozart's piano concertos:

The parts are not developmentally fused, one to another, but detachable: they almost never appear in the same arrangement in the ritornello [orchestral opening], exposition, and return [recapitulation].[39]

In K. 595, for example, the order of events towards the end of the orchestral exposition changes during the recapitulation. The material of bars 47-53 is extracted and linked with the original tutti ending (bars 76-80) to complete the movement, after the cadenza. The intervening bars 54-75 (which are absent from the solo exposition) now happen before the cadenza, starting with piano material choreographed as the final solo, a decorated version of what the full group did originally to the orchestra. Morris's choreography honours Mozart's thematic re-distribution.

The heart-rending beauty of the second subject melody has often been mentioned by music scholars, a scalewise descending progression that is emotionally transformed on repeat when several notes are chromatically flattened. Morris sets to this the run, fall and 'hiccup' from I/3, with the land after the hiccup happening after the melody ends, to a chord in the bass. Falling with the music in this way, the hiccup that seemed like a joke or heave in I/3 now seems like a sob. During the orchestral exposition, we see it first done by the group. They start to repeat it, to the musical repeat, but omit the fall.

Ex. 13.8 Piano Concerto No. 27 in B-flat major, first movement (III/1), second subject.

During the solo exposition, one woman does it with the fall (to the orchestra), followed by the group with the chromatic version (the piano added) and with the fall again, seeming to follow in consolation as if sharing her sorrow.

With such a large cast involved in this concerto, Morris can visualise a range of orchestral forces, both large and small. Thus, he turns significant orchestral tuttis into landmarks: his biggest groups are seen at the opening, at the end of the solo exposition (before the development), at the start of the recapitulation, a couple more times before the cadenza, and finally in the Coda. Again, the groups dance the same material when the same tutti material comes back. Meanwhile, on several occasions during orchestral interpolations, the danced solos that cover the piano part are commented upon by individuals or small groups emerging close to the wings.

The solos, which have varying degrees of personality and shift between men and women, treat familiar musical material in a new way. Often they reflect the ornamentation that the piano introduces. They continue right through the development and into the recapitulation, at which point the exposition solos are repeated in mirror form (on the opposite side of the body and stage). Because of the gender shifts and mirroring, you may not realise at first that the choreography is familiar. In any case, just as there are minor modifications within the music in this section to suit the adjusted tonal plan, there are subtle choreographic alterations. At one point, for instance, a woman ends her solo throwing herself dramatically to the floor on to her back (an idea first seen in I/2). So Morris seems to relax a little here from his usual highlighting of major thematic repetition/variation across a large structure.

The two solos during the development section are the most dramatic and substantial, appropriately so. To the violently jagged modulations that open the section (from F major, to B minor, C major/minor, E-flat major/minor), a man gestures impatiently and obsessively (the beckoning move from Grant's development in 'Eleven'). Then a woman takes over with more of the same gestures, followed by bold turns, leaps and rolls, circling the stage to waves of semiquaver piano figuration. Morris introduces further brief solo interpolations during these two solos to match Mozart's interjections. To each fragment of the opening theme by a wind instrument (flute, oboe or bassoon), a dancer emerges briefly from the wings with the triplet steps that opened 'Twenty-Seven'.

Thus, Morris's emphasis on solos draws out not only the piano, but also selected orchestral instruments. He enhances Mozart's 'chamber style', enlarging the democratic statement so that 'Twenty-Seven' becomes an overtly multi-vocal experience (see pp. 142-4). Furthermore, running the solos across the piano exposition, development and recapitulation and complicating this with cast changes and mirroring has structural implications: the demarcations and hierarchies of large musical structure are blurred, while the impression of a through-composed series of short episodes is considerably strengthened.

The cadenza introduces Worden as 'special' soloist, in an intricate, 'baroque-ish' step sequence first danced by the men in 'Double', now powerfully surging towards us in free rhythm between staging posts within the music. She is like a storm cloud passing through. Soon, however, a quartet based on the circle choreography of II/2 takes over, and the mood lightens again.

2. Larghetto

Mozart's slow movement is in ternary form, ABA with a Coda. The piano is an almost constant presence, as in the slow movement of K. 413, although here it also opens the movement. (Once again, there is no special association between the piano and any solo on stage.) The main theme A forms a clear aaba structure and gives rise to rather stiff, formal movement led by the quartet from the Allegro cadenza. On the other hand, the two most substantial orchestral interludes, the codettas after theme A material, are occasions for stage drama. Powerful seventh chords, a rising melody and a crescendo prompt a return of the 'steeple arms' and sailing lifts from II/2.

Section B opens with the same quartet and a return to formality. As groups decompose into male/female couples, however, several other mini-dramas start to emerge, a theatrical line eased gently over the score. Four couples cross the stage, the men lifting their partners high overhead to mark the peak points of the melody (clear positions held, like the men's *attitudes* on the Ds in II/2). Worden, the last to rise aloft, lingers longest, before suddenly dropping to the ground, pensive, her head lowered. Then she gets up and hops in *arabesque*, supported by her partner, rather stiffly and uncomfortably, to a chugging bass line. She seems fixed within her own private world. These are striking, new images in *Mozart Dances*, and more follow.

Soon, our attention shifts to two other couples in turn, the women (originally Maile Okamura, then Michelle Yard) throwing themselves front-on at their partners, once, twice, as if in desperate need. But in need of what? A loving relationship? Yard moves away, confused, uncertain, followed at first by her partner, before she exits. Later, both are simply absorbed into the formal dance for the repeat of section A. Here, before long, we see variations on the same dramas, some to different music: more supported hopping in *arabesque*, more descents to the floor, and finally, one couple, enhanced by new, poignant, descant phrases, broken apart decisively when the woman leaves the stage.

Could this movement be a reflection upon the goings-on in Mozart's *Così fan tutte*, that story of infidelity, departures and abandonments, two pairs of lovers, and the men testing their partner's constancy?[40] Drawing on key threads from 'Eleven' (I/1: Grant gets to dance a fragment of her solo choreography again) and from 'Double' (II/2), the Larghetto could be the closest we ever get to an actual opera buffa story in *Mozart Dances*. The work turns out after all to be a story about couples.

3. *Allegro*

The last movement of K. 595 is again a sonata rondo, but in yet another variation of the standard form. It is useful to compare it with both the finales of the Concerto No. 11 and of the Sonata for two pianos. The layout here, together with cadenzas, is as follows:

A B Cadenza A C (containing a short cadenza) A B Cadenza A Coda

As the musicologist Cuthbert Girdlestone has pointed out, ideas from the A refrain constantly re-appear during this movement, for instance, as the foundation of the whole of the central, development episode (C).[41]

This Allegro also demonstrates a continuous collaboration between the piano and individual instruments of the orchestra, more than at any other time in either Concerto No. 11 or indeed this one. Morris responds with choreography for couples and groups, in other words, another way of stressing community: now, there are barely any solo passages. Regularly, he accompanies A material with skipping, leaping, galloping steps; there is not the intensity of event that we experience elsewhere in *Mozart Dances*. Morris pared down his original ensemble for the final recapitulation of A—to just one couple—to be in sympathy with Ax's soft dynamics at this point, a nice touch.[42]

Three cadenza passages break up the flow. The first, at the end of the B episode, is the most fun. Down a long avenue of dancers, put in place during a crescendo, rushes a lone man (Vinson), who leaps into the arms of another waiting at the far end. Everyone holds still for several long seconds as the cadenza commences. The leap and catch seem desperate, but also make audiences laugh. Serious passages in the other two cadenzas recall the troubled slow movements of 'Eleven' and 'Twenty-Seven'. The second passage is a very brief entry and exit of couples from the wings to form 'steeple arms', while the last, at the end of the second B episode, is a much longer affair. Here, after the formation of another avenue leading to a hiatus, the group leave one by one and, as the rhythms become more erratic and the harmonies more chromatic, Okamura is seen once again, throwing herself at her partner, then departing with him. Finally, only Worden is left behind, doing the same, but dropping out of the lift to the floor, just as she did in the Larghetto, then hopping in *arabesque* towards the wings. She is still stiff, slightly absurd, regardless of her supporting partner, presumably inconsolable. There are many whimsical and volatile accounts of the end

'Twenty-Seven', third movement. © Stephanie Berger, 2006

of this piano cadenza, but Ax's interpretation in *Mozart Dances* is relatively straightforward, bold and clear, an appropriate ground for the dancers to convey an anxiety that is left unresolved.

A kind of 'happy ending' comes soon after this. The couples break into separate groups of men and women facing each other across the stage and choosing how to gesture to each other. 'That's the end of *Così fan tutte*,' says Morris, describing this moment:

> Some of the dancers place their hands on their hearts, but the others put their arms out as if they were asking a question. So it's like, 'Huh?' Or 'Just a minute, I'm not finished with you.' Or 'I love you'. Or 'What's wrong?' That, to me, is *Così*. The reason the end of *Così* is so confusing and distressing is that the switched lovers got too close. There was too much duplicity for the problem just to be solved by an amnesty. So the opera ends in chaos. And the end of *Mozart Dances*, I think, has that same irresolution.[43]

Acocella in *The New Yorker* said she was uncertain that you catch this point without Morris's explanation. She only saw jollity.[44] When I interviewed him in 2012, Morris declared that the final statement was positive after all.[45] He seems to have changed his mind.

Mozart's opera endings have been read at various times as merely following convention or, according to Allanbrook, affirmation of a particular world view, the social ideals of the Enlightenment, the comic choice: 'The happy ending of comedy celebrates the restoration of the proper orders, no matter what the difficulties in reaffirming them...a celebration of the social man, of reconciliation, and of accommodation to the way things are'.[46] Significantly, she argues the same case for the ending of Mozart's concertos.

Understanding the tradition of Morris's work of the twentieth and twenty-first centuries, I would read his *Mozart Dances* (the work as a whole) as fundamentally ambiguous. His ideal of harmonious community remains strong, the endeavour to reach it, as is perhaps the case with Mozart, and yet memories linger of those disturbed slow movements, darker applications of the music than many might expect, and of the cadenzas that never relinquish their mystery, stressed by the concreteness of bodies evoking painful experience. But can we really sense complete resolution at this point, any more than in *Così*? Does the happy ending come too soon for us to believe in it? A similar ambiguity confronts me at the end of *L'Allegro* (see pp. 217-8). As for the final separation of men and women into two bands, do they stand before, or rather against, each other?

Coda

Mozart Dances confirms for us that Mozart's music is operatic, even if it was not written as opera. After he had set K. 595, Morris himself realised that the deeply mysterious encounters between men and women, so poorly served by verbal description, reminded him of *Così fan tutte*. His settings are a distillation of opera. He also confirms that Mozart's scores are dance music, just as Allanbrook observed about Mozart's operas: dance is embedded within the foundations of both concertos and the sonata in between.

Morris, however, refuses to give us a pretty, easy account of the composer. The range of moods he suggests is broad, encompassing both pleasure and pain, and he makes use of Mozart's rare capacity to cover a 'cosmos' of attitudes or 'topics' within a short space of time, to dart impatiently from one to another, not to assert for any single state any special privilege. Like Mozart, Morris underlines the fact that sadness and joy are close cousins. Yet, like Sellars, who commissioned him to create *Mozart Dances*, he also views Mozart as a robust figure, no fragile personality—committed to the idealistic, social, community values that are especially important to him as a choreographer.

Morris's different treatments of big forms illustrate this commitment—

Mozart Dances grows towards a fuller expression of community. If we compare his settings of the K. 413 and K. 595 piano concertos, we find him starting out with a brazen binary of leader versus group which, no sooner than it is established, begins to unravel. In making everyone a soloist in the K. 595 concerto, he also makes the work multi-vocal, taking his cue from Mozart, but making more of this opportunity than the music alone suggests. He develops upon the composer's increasing integration of orchestral forces, breaking down the barrier between individual and group (or rather groups, of varying sizes and gender balance) and exploring collaboration more often than confrontation. This also reveals itself in the heightening of interpersonal relationships within couples in the second and last movement of K. 595.

Again, encouraged by Mozart's innovations, Morris sets about interrogating the well-established models of classical musical form, their hierarchies and certainties. A process of development across *Mozart Dances* is especially clear because he is unusually affirmative of musical structure at the start of the evening programme. Here, big blocks of material repeat more exactly than anywhere else in Morris's entire output, including *V*, and the visualisation of musical detail is at its most intense. Later, while he works with tensions in tonal progression, long-range musical processes, more obviously than elsewhere in his work, on several occasions, he refuses to wrap up tidily, or resolve, situations: he is especially resistant to tonal resolution in his slow, central movements. Thus, Morris also blurs hallowed sonata form structure, in 'Double', by introducing progressive, unsettling narratives of gain and loss across two movements of its score, and in 'Twenty-Seven', by casting a string of solos over much of its first movement.

Finally, returning to the composer himself, Morris's *Mozart Dances* also represents an historical progression, from a 1783 concerto to the last that Mozart wrote for piano, completed in 1791, the final year of his life. This vision of progress drives across the three multi-movement works to culminate in the last, extending Morris's familiar devices for thematic coherence, and introducing appropriately the song 'Longing for Spring', an impassioned call for democratic values, a better world in the future. Once again, choreomusical tactics contribute significantly to meta-narrative.

Present into Future

In the autumn of 2014, as I finish work on this book, Morris is making a new piece called *Words*. Meanwhile, the MMDG is about to operate more globally than ever before, splitting in two for tours covering Europe and the Far East as well as the US. An alternative version of *Words* will work for the full ensemble when it re-unites in Beijing. Morris's appetite for challenge remains insatiable.

How then to end this book? Is there a logical reason for stopping at this point? Only that I have to stop somewhere, and in the true spirit of liveness, a concept central to Morris's thinking, somewhere is now.

Yet endings can be misleading. If you read the book from start to finish—and there are many other options—you might feel that such a huge 'abstract' dance as *Mozart Dances* (settings of three large scores, two with orchestra) is the culmination of a straightforward linear progress. That is definitely not the case.

Of course, it is impossible that Morris could have come up with recent works like *Socrates* and *Mozart Dances* at the beginning of his career. Today, he mixes creative tactics with consummate ease, drawing upon a huge body of choreomusical experience, sometimes even within a single dance. His work is no less robust, but it is far more nuanced, less angry: there is no more fighting against noble music, and he is more consistently committed to getting deep into the mesh of a score. An exceptionally musically astute team of dancers enables Morris to achieve this.

So too, Morris shows us that a wide range of choreomusical techniques have their place, context is all-important—and that the 'old' and 'simple' ways can still be valuable. Even music visualisation, for which Morris was once so frequently castigated, has proved to be an asset in particular circumstances. Experience has also brought subtlety to his choreomusical approach—no technique leads to just one kind of result.

If there has to be a meta-narrative across Morris's career, it must be that he constantly tricks himself with opposing methods, jumping from the very large-scale to the very small, going more literary after a more formal experiment, trying out a new style of popular music after steeping himself in the classical canon, getting entangled in music's detail after working with its larger contours. Or he will simply grasp an opportunity—after all, *Mozart Dances* was a unique style of commission, and *Words* is the result of a unique practical situation.

Morris's story, however, extends beyond his development as a choreographer. We have seen that it now embraces his work as a musician, coaching, conducting and teaching musical interpretation and performance practice. It is also about how he represents himself through MMDG programmes, which means revisiting his past and presenting it to audiences as context for his new work (as well as for the sake of variety). Choreomusically, this means that audiences are exposed to his broad range of experiment. But this takes different forms. Looking, for instance, at the repertory of 2013-14, we find two of Morris's favourite full-evening orchestral works: the 1988 *L'Allegro, il Penseroso ed il Moderato* and the 2006 *Mozart Dances*. (2013 was the twenty-fifth anniversary of *L'Allegro*, which was filmed for broadcast and commercial distribution in Madrid in 2014.) Meanwhile, the touring repertory each year comprised about twenty-five smaller dances, engaging the very fine MMDG Music Ensemble. These smaller dances cross Morris's entire career, and include a few from the early 1980s: *Ten Suggestions, The "Tamil Film Songs in Stereo" Pas de Deux, Canonic 3/4 Variations,* and *New Love Song Waltzes*. Here, choreomusical approaches are especially clearly defined, and Morris likes to remember that. The first two are straight music visualisations; the other two foreground counterpoint (and canons).

On the other hand, for London, to which MMDG made a triumphant return in 2013 after an unusually long three-year gap, the theme was total renewal: seven very recent dances. No sooner had I identified a trend in Morris's work away from using words than three of these dances did just that: the decidedly wacky *A Wooden Tree,* a setting of Ivor Cutler songs; the great *Socrates* to Satie (widely acclaimed as the high point of recent years); *The Muir,* to Beethoven settings of English, Irish and Scottish folk songs. All three carry an element of mime or enactment relating closely to the words. And now, at the end of 2014, there is a piece actually titled *Words...* although there aren't any! Set to ten of Mendelssohn's *Songs Without Words,* this gestural dance is about their absence, and the alternative: speaking through movement.

In the meantime, Morris has directed two more operas. For the Tanglewood Music Fellows in 2013, he undertook Benjamin Britten's *Curlew River,* here joining together singers and instrumentalists, but no dancers, on stage. The 2014 *Acis and Galatea* Morris calls a 'through-danced' opera. It is a totally integrated production with dancing happening almost all the time—MMDG and the singers amidst them. Both opera productions have been enthusiastically received, Alastair Macaulay of *The New York Times* describing *Acis* as 'a large-spirited drama of innocence, pathos, metamorphosis and transcendence.'[1]

As for the future, one thing is most certain, that Morris will continue to surprise us, just as I have been continually surprised while researching and writing this book. He urges us to listen and watch anew, in ways that we might never have thought possible. For him, working closely with music remains a field for experiment. At the same time, he forces us to encounter our own deep-seated prejudices about how dance should respond to music, which can be highly unnerving, yet ultimately, illuminating. Morris has enlarged our conceptual apparatus, while confirming that the detail of a work's construction informs our understanding of its humanity and expressive potential. Most powerfully, his dances answer back to existing theories of music and dance, and we adjust our frameworks for thinking accordingly. Listening and watching in the future will never be the same.

Chronology of Works by Mark Morris 1971-2014

The following chronology focuses on Morris's musical choices. It is derived from the 2014 MMDG website listings and the chronology in Joan Acocella's book *Mark Morris*. More detailed information on individual works can be found in the MMDG website listings and, in many instances, within the main text of this book. Chapter 9 (p. 288) includes further details of the operas with which Morris has been involved. Unless otherwise indicated (under 'Title'), all dances were originally choreographed for MMDG. The chronology indicates when a few works not originally made for MMDG were later performed by the group.

Title	Date of Premiere	Music
Boxcar Boogie *(Piece by Piece)* Verla Flowers Dance Arts	June 18, 1971	Four pieces, by Jacques Lasry, Conlon Nancarrow, Harry Partch, Steve Reich
Cape Dance Verla Flowers Dance Arts	June 18, 1971	Traditional Spanish
The Wizard's Gift Christmas Musical-Seattle Youth Theatre	December, 1971	Jonathon Field, David Kiesel, Gary Lanz
Renaissance Northwest Ballet Ensemble, Dance Theatre Seattle	April 29, 1972	Sixteenth-century French traditional music
Mourning Without Clouds Verla Flowers Dance Art	June 15, 1972	Mark Morris (Score for 7-piece chamber orchestra and 6-person chorus)
U.S.A. *(Tango, Charleston)* Show based on John Dos Passos's *U.S.A.*- Franklin High School, Seattle	Nov/Dec, 1972	Popular songs 1900-1929
It's Almost Like Being Alive Dances for a musical comedy- One-Reel Vaudeville Show	April, 1973 (?)	Phil Shallat and adaptations of popular songs
Celebration *(Dances)*	Spring, 1973	Harvey Schmidt
[Spanish Dances] Verla Flowers Dance Arts	July 19, 1973	Traditional Spanish
Barstow Summer Dance Laboratory, Port Townsend, Washington	August 1, 1973 (MMDG Premiere: November 28, 1980)	Harry Partch (*Barstow: Ten Hitchhiker Inscriptions*)
In Pruning My Roses Verla Flowers Dance Arts	June 20, 1974	Mark Morris (Composition for Cello and Piano), Dmitri Shostakovich (Sonata in D, Op.40, 2nd movement)
Jota de Alcañiz Verla Flowers Dance Arts	June 20, 1974	Traditional Spanish

Ženska First Chamber Junior Company, Seattle	May 28, 1975 (MMDG Premiere: November 28, 1980)	Béla Bartók (String Quartet No. 4, 4th movement)
Farruca Jerezana Verla Flowers Dance Arts	June 19, 1975	Traditional Spanish
Spanish Verla Flowers Dance Arts	June 19, 1975	Traditional Spanish
Saint George and the Dragon (Dragon's Solo) Christmas Entertainment-Northwest Chamber Orchestra Young People's Concerts	December 20, 1975	John David Lamb
Brummagem Pacific Northwest Ballet	July 22, 1978 (MMDG Premiere: November 28, 1980)	Ludwig van Beethoven (Trio in B-flat major, for Piano, Cello and Clarinet, Op.11, 2nd and 3rd movements)
Rattlesnake Song Steffi Nossen Dance Company	April 19, 1980	Four songs performed by Jimmy Driftwood
Castor and Pollux	November 28, 1980	Harry Partch ('Castor and Pollux' from Plectra and Percussion Dances)
Dad's Charts	November 28, 1980	Charles Thompson and Illinois Jacquet ('Robbins Nest')
Études Modernes	February 13, 1981	Conlon Nancarrow (five items from Studies for Player Piano)
Ten Suggestions	February 13, 1981	Alexander Tcherepnin (Bagatelles, Op.5)
Schön Rosmarin	August 21, 1981	Fritz Kreisler (from Alt Wiener Tanzweisen)
I Love You Dearly Kinetics Company	November 20, 1981 (MMDG Premiere: December 12, 1981)	Three traditional Romanian songs
Gloria	December 12, 1981	Antonio Vivaldi (Gloria in D, RV 589)
Canonic 3/4 Studies	July 29, 1982	Carl Czerny and others (Short piano pieces in 3/4 time, arr. Harriet Cavalli)
Jr. High	July 29, 1982	Conlon Nancarrow (Studies for Player Piano, Nos.10 and 7)
Songs That Tell a Story Kinetics Company	September 4, 1982 (?) (MMDG Premiere: November 4, 1982)	Four songs by the Louvin Brothers
New Love Song Waltzes	November 4, 1982	Johannes Brahms (Neue Liebeslieder, Op.65)
Not Goodbye	November 4, 1982	Three traditional Tahitian songs

Ponchielliana	July 19, 1983	Amilcare Ponchielli (Quartet in B-flat major for Wind Quartet and Piano)
Caryatids	September 29, 1983	Harold Budd (*Madrigals of the Rose Angel*)
Celestial Greetings	September 29, 1983	Thai popular music
Deck of Cards	September 29, 1983	Jimmy Logsdon ('Gear Jammer'), Dallas Frazier ('Say It's Not You'), T. Texas Tyler ('Deck of Cards')
Dogtown	September 29, 1983	Four songs by Yoko Ono
Bijoux	December 8, 1983	Erik Satie (*Quatre petites mélodies, Ludions*)
The Death of Socrates	December 15, 1983	Erik Satie ('The Death of Socrates' from *Socrate*)
Minuet and Allegro in G	December 15, 1983	Ludwig van Beethoven (Allegro and Minuet in G, WoO 26)
The "Tamil Film Songs in Stereo" Pas de Deux	December 15, 1983	Contemporary Indian
Vestige Spokane Ballet	February 4, 1984 (MMDG Premiere: May 9, 1985)	Dmitri Shostakovich (Sonata in D, Op.40 (1st movement omitted))
O Rangasayee	March 15, 1984	Sri Tyagaraja ('O Rangasayee')
Love, You Have Won	June 7, 1984	Antonio Vivaldi (Solo cantata *Amor hai vinto*, RV 651)
My Party	June 7, 1984	Jean Françaix (Trio in C)
Prelude and Prelude	June 7, 1984	Henry Cowell (*Set of Two*, 1st movement)
She Came from There	June 7, 1984	Ernst von Dohnányi (Serenade in C, Op.10)
Forty Arms, Twenty Necks, One Wreathing	July 10, 1984	Herschel Garfein (*One Wreathing*)
Come on Home	August 21, 1984	Six songs, by Horace Silver, Dennis Lambert, Jon Hendricks, George Gershwin, Leroy Kirkland
Slugfest	October 3, 1984	[In silence]
The Vacant Chair	October 3, 1984	George Frederick Root ('The Vacant Chair'), Oscar Rasbach ('Trees'), Carrie Jacobs-Bond ('A Perfect Day')
Championship Wrestling After Roland Barthes	November 28, 1984	Herschel Garfein

[Capri Sun Television Commercial (non MMDG performers)*]*	1984	
Marble Halls Batsheva Dance Company	March 14, 1985 (MMDG Premiere: May 9, 1985)	Johann Sebastian Bach (Concerto in C minor, BWV 1060)
Lovey	May 9, 1985	Five songs by Gordon Gano
Jealousy	September 6, 1985	George Frideric Handel (*Hercules*, No. 36, chorus: 'Jealousy')
Retreat from Madrid	October 9, 1985	Luigi Boccherini (Quintet No. 9 'La Ritirata di Madrid', 4th movement)
Handel Choruses	December 6, 1985	Four choruses by George Frideric Handel
Frisson	December 7, 1985	Igor Stravinsky (*Symphonies of Wind Instruments*)
One Charming Night	December 7, 1985	Four songs by Henry Purcell
Mort Subite Boston Ballet	February 5, 1986	Francis Poulenc (Concerto in G minor)
Mythologies	February 27, 1986	Herschel Garfein (*Championship Wrestling After Roland Barthes, Soap-Powders and Detergents, Striptease*)
Salome (*Dance of the Seven Veils*) Opera (choreog.)-Seattle Opera	March 22, 1986	Richard Strauss
Ballabili	June 10, 1986	Giuseppe Verdi (*Aida*, Act II, Scene 2-'Triumphal Scene', Nos.20-22)
The Shepherd on the Rock	July 11, 1986	Franz Schubert (*Der Hirt auf dem Felsen*, D 965)
Esteemed Guests Joffrey Ballet	September 24, 1986	Carl Philipp Emanuel Bach (Concerto in A, W 172)
Pièces en Concert	November 12, 1986	François Couperin (five items from *Pièces en Concert*)
Stabat Mater	November 12, 1986	Giovanni Battista Pergolesi (*Stabat Mater*)
Sonata for Clarinet and Piano University of Washington School of Music and Division of Dance	March 6, 1987 (MMDG Premiere: October 30, 1987)	Francis Poulenc (Sonata for Clarinet and Piano)
Strict Songs	March 19, 1987	Lou Harrison (*Four Strict Songs*)
La Folia Cornish Dance Theater	April 10, 1987	Antonio Vivaldi (Trio Sonata in D minor, RV 63: 'Variations on *La Folia*')

Fantasy	July 23, 1987	Wolfgang Amadeus Mozart (Fantasia in C minor, K. 475)
Nixon in China (Act 2 agitprop ballet and Act 3 dream ballet) Opera (choreog.)-Houston Grand Opera	October 22, 1987	John Adams
(Scarlatti Solos) *	October 27, 1987	Domenico Scarlatti (Sonata in D, K. 491)
Fugue and Fantasy	October 30, 1987	Wolfgang Amadeus Mozart (Fugue in C minor for 2 pianos, K. 426; Fantasia in C minor for piano, K. 475)
Orpheus & Eurydice Opera (choreog.)-Seattle Opera, with MMDG	January 16, 1988	Christoph Willibald Gluck
Offertorium	February 4, 1988	Franz Schubert (*Salve Regina (Offertorium)*)
Die Fledermaus Opera(dir.)-Seattle Opera	May 7, 1988	Johann Strauss II
Drink to Me Only with Thine Eyes American Ballet Theatre	May 31, 1988	Virgil Thomson (thirteen Etudes for Piano)
Le Nozze di Figaro (Act III wedding scene) Opera (choreog.)-PepsiCo Summerfare	July 13, 1988	Wolfgang Amadeus Mozart
L'Allegro, il Penseroso ed il Moderato	November 23, 1988	George Frideric Handel (*L'Allegro, il Penseroso ed il Moderato*)
Dido and Aeneas Opera (choreog. and dir.)-Théâtre Royal de la Monnaie, with MMDG	March 11, 1989	Henry Purcell
Footprints in the Snow	June 24, 1989	Bill Monroe
Love Song Waltzes	November 4, 1989	Johannes Brahms (*Liebeslieder*, Op.52)
Wonderland	November 4, 1989	Arnold Schoenberg (*Accompaniment-Music for a Motion Picture*, Op.34; Five Orchestral Pieces, Op.16)
Behemoth	April 14, 1990	[In silence]
Going Away Party	April 14, 1990	Eight songs, by Thomas Dorsey, Benny Davis, Bob Wills, Cindy Walker, Kokomo Arnold, Hoyle Nix (arr.)

* This unofficial title refers to a series of solos performed by Morris to Scarlatti's Sonata in D over the course of a year. Joan Acocella writes (p.279), 'This solo was completely improvised, different at every performance, and differently titled at every performance. At its premiere it was *Lies*. Later it was *More Lies; Big Lies; Utter Lies; Fraud; Run, Children, Run; Copperhead; Always*; and *Never*.'

Ein Herz Paris Opera Ballet	June 6, 1990	Johann Sebastian Bach (Cantata, BWV 134, *Ein Herz, das seinen Jesum lebend weiss*)
Pas de Poisson	October 7, 1990	Erik Satie ('Cinéma' symphonic interlude from *Relâche*, piano reduction for four hands by Darius Milhaud)
Motorcade White Oak Dance Project	October 24, 1990	Camille Saint-Saëns (Septet in E-flat major, Op.65)
The Hard Nut	January 12, 1991	Pyotr Illyich Tchaikovsky (*Nutcracker*, Op.71)
The Death of Klinghoffer Opera (choreog.)-Théâtre Royal de la Monnaie, with MMDG	March 19, 1991	John Adams
A Lake White Oak Dance Project	July 30, 1991 (MMDG Premiere: March 17, 1992)	Franz Joseph Haydn (Horn Concerto No. 2 in D)
Le Nozze di Figaro Opera (dir.)-Théâtre Royal de la Monnaie, Brussels, with MMDG	December 17, 1991	Wolfgang Amadeus Mozart
Paukenschlag Les Grands Ballets Canadiens	March 14, 1992	Franz Joseph Haydn (Symphony No. 94)
Beautiful Day	April 7, 1992	Attrib. to Johann Sebastian Bach (Cantata, BWV 53, *Schlage doch, gewünschte Stunde*)
Polka	April 7, 1992	Lou Harrison (*Grand Duo for Violin and Piano*, 5th movement)
Bedtime	June 2, 1992	Franz Schubert (*Wiegenlied*, D 498; *Ständchen*, D 920; *Erlkönig*, D 328)
Three Preludes	June 2, 1992	George Gershwin (Preludes)
Excursion to Grenada: A Calypso Ballet	July 7, 1992	Four pieces, by Lionel Belasco and His Orchestra, The Growler, Lord Executor, Sam Manning
Grand Duo	February 16, 1993	Lou Harrison (*Grand Duo for Violin and Piano*)
Mosaic and United MMDG and White Oak Dance Project	April 29, 1993	Henry Cowell (String Quartet No. 3, *Mosaic*, I-II-III-IV-V-III-I; String Quartet No. 4, *United*, I-II-III-IV-V)
Home	April 29, 1993	Three songs by Michelle Shocked and instrumental music by Rob Wasserman

Jesu, Meine Freude	June 8, 1993	Johann Sebastian Bach (*Jesu, meine Freude*, BWV 227)
A Spell	August 17, 1993	Four mid-seventeenth century songs by John Wilson
Maelstrom San Francisco Ballet	February 8, 1994	Ludwig van Beethoven (Trio in D major for Violin, Cello and Piano, Op.70, No. 1, *Ghost*)
The Office Živili - Dances and Music of Southern Slavic Nations	April 22, 1994 (MMDG Premiere: July 5, 1994)	Antonín Dvořák (Five Bagatelles for two Violins, Cello and Harmonium, Op.47)
Lucky Charms	June 7, 1994	Jacques Ibert (*Divertissement*)
Rondo	July 14, 1994	Wolfgang Amadeus Mozart (Rondo in A minor, K. 511)
Quincunx Les Grands Ballets Canadiens	March 16, 1995	Gaetano Donizetti (String Quartet No. 3)
Pacific San Francisco Ballet	May 9, 1995 (MMDG Premiere: February 25, 2015)	Lou Harrison (Trio for Violin, Cello & Piano, 3rd and 4th movements)
Somebody's Coming To See Me Tonight	June 6, 1995	Nine songs by Stephen Foster
Three Russian Preludes White Oak Dance Project	June 24, 1995 (MMDG Premiere: February 21, 2006)	Dmitri Shostakovich (Preludes from 24 Preludes and Fugues, Op.87: No. 17 in A-flat major; No. 22 in G minor; No. 15 in D-flat major)
World Power	October 27, 1995	Lou Harrison ('In Honor of the Divine Mr. Handel' and 'In Honor of Mr. Mark Twain' from *Homage to Pacifica*; *Bubaran Robert)*
Orfeo ed Euridice Opera (choreog. and dir.)-Handel & Haydn Society, with MMDG	April 8, 1996	Christoph Willibald Gluck
I Don't Want to Love	August 12, 1996	Seven madrigals by Claudio Monteverdi
Falling Down Stairs	March 6, 1997	Johann Sebastian Bach (Suite No. 3 in C for solo cello, BWV 1009)
Rhymes With Silver	March 6, 1997	Lou Harrison (commissioned score)
Waltz in C Sesame Street (Children's Television Workshop)	March 13, 1997	Lou Harrison (*Waltz in C*)
Anger Dance Sesame Street (Children's Television Workshop)	March 13, 1997	Henry Cowell (*Anger Dance*)

Platée Opera (choreog. and dir.)-The Royal Opera, with MMDG	August 11, 1997	Jean-Philippe Rameau
The Capeman Broadway musical (choreog.)	January 29, 1998	Paul Simon
Medium	February 13, 1998	John Harbison (*November 19, 1828*)
Greek to Me Peter Wing Healey, American Repertory Dance Company	August 15, 1998 (MMDG Premiere: August 3, 1999)	Harry Partch ('Studies on Ancient Greek Scales' from *Eleven Intrusions: Olympos' Pentatonic, Archytas' Enharmonic, Olympos' Pentatonic*)
Dancing Honeymoon	October 22, 1998	Fifteen songs by various composers (including 'Limehouse Blues', 'You Were Meant for Me', and 'Do Do Do')
The Argument	February 26, 1999	Robert Schumann (*Fünf Stücke im Volkston*, Op.102)
Dixit Dominus	March 18, 1999	George Frideric Handel (*Dixit Dominus*, HWV232)
Sandpaper Ballet San Francisco Ballet	April 27, 1999	Ten pieces by Leroy Anderson
Flight	June 2, 1999	Dion McGregor (text only (somniloquist))
Zwei Harveytänze	June 3, 1999	Ethan Iverson ('Laura' (Raskin arr. Iverson); 'Flatbush Stomp')
Silhouettes Maximum Dance Company	June 10, 1999 (MMDG Premiere: August 2, 1999)	Richard Cumming (*Five Pieces for Piano*)
Biblical Pieces De Nederlandse Opera	June 14, 1999	Seven pieces by Igor Stravinsky
Four Saints in Three Acts Opera (choreog. and dir.)-English National Opera, with MMDG	June 28, 2000	Virgil Thomson
Sang-Froid	July 13, 2000	Nine pieces by Frédéric Chopin
Peccadillos	August 1, 2000	Erik Satie (*Menus propos enfantins; Enfantillages pittoresques; Peccadilles importunes*)
From Old Seville	January 20, 2001	Manuel Requiebros (*A Esa Mujer*)
A Garden San Francisco Ballet	February 23, 2001	Richard Strauss (*Tanzsuite für Orchester*, after keyboard pieces by Francois Couperin)

Gong American Ballet Theatre	May 1, 2001	Colin McPhee (*Tabu-Tabuhan*)
V	October 16, 2001	Robert Schumann (Quintet in E-flat for Piano and Strings, Op.44)
Piper Piece	October 30, 2001	Traditional Scottish (bagpipes)
Later San Francisco Ballet	January 30, 2002	Franz Schubert (Impromptu Op.3, No. 3 in B-flat major)
Foursome	February 27, 2002	Erik Satie (*Gnossiennes* Nos.1, 2, 3) and Johann Nepomuk Hummel (Seven Hungarian Dances)
Kolam	April 19, 2002	Three pieces by Zakir Hussain (arr. George Brooks) and two by Ethan Iverson
Resurrection	July 18, 2002	Richard Rodgers (*Slaughter on 10th Avenue*)
Something Lies Beyond the Scene	October 3, 2002	William Walton (*Façade: An Entertainment, with poems by Edith Sitwell*)
Non Troppo American Ballet Theatre, Channel 13 WNET, *Dance in America*	February 3, 2003	Robert Schumann (Quintet in E-flat for Piano and Strings, Op.44, 4th movement)
Serenade	March 8, 2003	Lou Harrison (*Serenade for Guitar*)
Idomeneo *(Act III ballet)* Opera (choreog.)-Glyndebourne Festival Opera	June 10, 2003	Wolfgang Amadeus Mozart
All Fours	September 12, 2003	Béla Bartók (String Quartet No. 4)
Sylvia San Francisco Ballet	April 30, 2004	Léo Delibes
Violet Cavern	June 8, 2004	The Bad Plus (*Violet Cavern*)
Rock of Ages	October 28, 2004	Franz Schubert (Piano Trio in E-flat, Adagio, D 897)
Cargo	June 26, 2005	Darius Milhaud (*La Création du Monde*, Op.58)
Candleflowerdance	September 22, 2005	Igor Stravinsky (*Serenade in A*)
Up and Down Boston Ballet	March 16, 2006	Alexander Glazunov (Quartet for 4 saxophones in B-flat major, Op.109)
King Arthur Opera (choreog. and dir.)-English National Opera, with MMDG	June 26, 2006	Henry Purcell

Mozart Dances (comprising 'Eleven', 'Double' and 'Twenty-Seven')	August 17, 2006	Wolfgang Amadeus Mozart (Piano Concerto No. 11 in F major, K. 413; Sonata in D major for two Pianos, K. 448; Piano Concerto No. 27 in B-flat major, K. 595)
Italian Concerto	January 17, 2007	Johann Sebastian Bach (Italian Concerto in F major, BWV 971)
Orfeo ed Euridice Opera (choreog. and dir.)-The Metropolitan Opera, with MMDG	May 2, 2007	Christoph Willibald Gluck
Looky	May 15, 2007	Kyle Gann (six *Studies for Disklavier*)
Joyride San Francisco Ballet	April 23, 2008	John Adams (*Son of Chamber Symphony*)
Excursions	June 26, 2008	Samuel Barber (*Excursions for the Piano*, Op.20 (IV, III, II, I))
Romeo & Juliet, On Motifs of Shakespeare	July 4, 2008	Sergey Prokofiev (*Romeo & Juliet, On Motifs of Shakespeare*, Op.64)
L'isola disabitata Opera (dir.)-Gotham Chamber Opera	February 18, 2009	Franz Joseph Haydn
Empire Garden	August 5, 2009	Charles Ives (Trio for violin, violoncello, and piano, S.86)
Visitation	August 5, 2009	Ludwig van Beethoven (Cello Sonata No. 4 in C major, Op.102, No. 1)
Rosencrantz & Guildenstern Are Dead Opera (dir.)-American Opera Projects	November 20, 2009	Herschel Garfein
Cease Your Funning	December 29, 2009	Five Irish and Scottish folk songs arr. Ludwig van Beethoven
Socrates	February 23, 2010	Erik Satie ('Portrait de Socrate', 'Bords de L'Ilissus', 'Mort de Socrate', from *Socrate*)
The Muir (development from *Cease Your Funning*)	June 27, 2010	Nine Irish and Scottish folk songs arr. Ludwig van Beethoven
Petrichor	October 14, 2010	Heitor Villa-Lobos (String Quartet No. 2, Op.56)
Festival Dance	March 17, 2011	Johann Nepomuk Hummel (Piano Trio No. 5 in E major, Op.83)
Renard	June 28, 2011	Igor Stravinsky (*Renard*)

Opéras-Minutes: La délivrance de Thesée, ***L'enlèvement d'Europe, L'abandon d'Ariane*** Opera (dir.)-Tanglewood Music Center Fellows	July 10, 2011	Vocal compositions: operas by Darius Milhaud; interlude songs by Claudio Monteverdi, Georg Philipp Telemann and Giacomo Carissimi
Beaux San Francisco Ballet	February 14, 2012	Bohuslav Martinů (Concerto for Harpsichord and Small Orchestra; No. 1 (Lento) from Two Pieces for Harpsichord)
A Choral Fantasy	March 1, 2012	Ludwig van Beethoven (Fantasia in C minor for Piano, Chorus and Orchestra, Op.80)
Carnival Voloshky Ukrainian Dance Ensemble	September 14, 2012	Camille Saint-Saëns (*Le Carnaval des animaux*)
A Wooden Tree	October 4, 2012	Fourteen songs by Ivor Cutler
Kammermusik No. 3 Pacific Northwest Ballet	November 2, 2012	Paul Hindemith (*Kammermusik Nr.3*, Op.36, No. 2)
Jenn and Spencer	April 3, 2013	Henry Cowell (Suite for Violin and Piano, HC 397)
Crosswalk	April 3, 2013	Carl Maria von Weber (*Grand Duo Concertant*, for clarinet and piano, Op.48)
Spring, Spring, Spring	June 12, 2013	Igor Stravinsky (*The Rite of Spring* arr. The Bad Plus)
Curlew River Opera (dir.)-Tanglewood Music Center Fellows	July 31, 2013	Benjamin Britten (*Curlew River: A Parable for Church Performance*)
Acis and Galatea Opera (choreog. and dir.)-Cal Performances, with MMDG	April 25, 2014	George Frideric Handel, arr. Wolfgang Amadeus Mozart
Words	October 8, 2014	Felix Mendelssohn (*Ten Songs Without Words*, for piano and violin)

·

Notes

Endnotes are formatted to provide each reference in full on first appearance within a chapter, thereafter in abbreviated form. In endnotes, unless otherwise indicated, 'Interview with Morris' refers to the author's own interviews with the choreographer, documented in the list below.

2005: February 14, November 18 (on *Frisson* and *Candleflower Dance*, for *Stravinsky Dances: Re-Visions Across a Century*, 2007, but also useful to the current volume)

Interviews undertaken for *Mark Morris: Musician-Choreographer*:

2009: October 8, October 10, October 30
2010: April 15, July 23, October 8
2011: June 29, July 10, November 14, November 15
2012: March 2, July 10, November 1, December 30
2013: April 4, June 12, November 30, December 3

Similarly, unless otherwise indicated, interviews with other individuals were carried out by the author.

INTRODUCTION

1 Helen Wallace, Letter from the Editor, *BBC Music Magazine*, July, 2000, p.2.

2 Paul Hodgins, 'Making Sense of the Dance-Music Partnership: A Paradigm for Choreomusical Analysis,' *Journal of the International Guild of Musicians in Dance*, 1 (1991), pp. 38-41. Hodgins' ideas were greatly expanded in his book, *Relationships between Score and Choreography in 20th Century Dance: Music, Movement and Metaphor* (Lewiston, New York: Edwin Mellen Press, 1992).

3 Jordan, *Moving Music: Dialogues with Music in Twentieth-Century Ballet* (London: Dance Books, 2000).

4 Jordan, *Stravinsky Dances: Re-Visions across a Century* (Alton, Hants.: Dance Books, 2007).

5 Jordan, *Striding Out: Aspects of Contemporary and New Dance in Britain* (London: Dance Books, 1992).

6 The London Dance Umbrella programmes included Morris's *Slugfest* (a study for the later *Championship Wrestling* section of *Mythologies*), *The Vacant Chair*, *Deck of Cards*, *Lovey* and *Jealousy*.

7 Joan Acocella, *Mark Morris* (New York: Farrar, Straus and Giroux, 1993), p. 248.

8 Jeffrey Escoffier and Matthew Lore, eds., *Mark Morris' 'L'Allegro, il Penseroso ed il Moderato: A Celebration'* (New York: Marlow & Company, 2001).

9 For a list up to 2013, see Jordan, 'Moving "Choreomusically": Between Theory and Practice', *Les Cahiers de la société québécoise de recherches en musique*, 13/1-2 (September, 2012), pp. 11-19.

10 John Heginbotham was an MMDG company member from 1998 to 2012.

11 In the same session, Heginbotham also taught me a phrase from *Rhymes with Silver* (1997).

CHAPTER 1

1   Morris quoted in Jennifer Kapuscik, 'Mark Morris: Something Happens', *Gaylife*, October 31, 1985, p. 18.

2   Morris quoted in 'Hear it Now: Mark Morris at BAM', The Leonard Lopate Show, WNYC, February 19, 2010, *http://www.wnyc.org/shows/lopate/2010/feb/19/ mark-morris-at-bam*, accessed July 6, 2013.

3   Morris quoted in Joe Hansen, 'Mark My Words, Mark My Moves', *Santa Barbara News Press Scene Magazine*, May 16-22, 2008.

4   Morris quoted in Toby Tobias, 'The New York Interview: Mark Morris', *New York Magazine*, December 11, 1995, p. 58.

5   Walter Pater, 'The School of Giorgione,' *Fortnightly Review*, 22 (October, 1877), p. 528.

6   Interview with Linda Dowdell, January 20, 2011.

7   David White quoted in Joan Acocella, *Mark Morris* (New York: Farrar, Straus and Giroux, 1993), p. 248.

8   Lincoln Kirstein quoted in Richard Buckle, *George Balanchine: Ballet Master*, in collaboration with John Taras (London: Hamish Hamilton, 1988), p. 80.

9   Nathan Milstein, 'My Friend George Balanchine', *Ballet Review*, 18/3 (Fall, 1990), p. 24; see also Maria Tallchief, *Maria Tallchief: America's Prima Ballerina*, with Larry Kaplan (New York: Henry Holt, 1997), pp. 95, 102.

10   See, for instance, Morris quoted in Alastair Macaulay, 'Umbrellosis', *The Dancing Times* (January, 1986), p. 318; and by Sophie Constanti, 'Dance Umbrella: Dreams and a Diary', *Dance Theatre Journal*, 4/1 (Spring, 1986), p. 31.

11   Virgil Thomson, *An Autobiography* (New York: E. P. Dutton, 1985); Eric Bentley, ed., *Shaw on Music* (New York: Applause Books, 2000); Alex Ross, *The Rest is Noise: Listening to the Twentieth Century* (London, New York: Harper Perennial, 2009); Charles Rosen, *The Classical Style* (New York: Viking Press, 1971), p. 324; Roger Shattuck, *The Banquet Years: The Origins of the Avant-Garde in France–1885 to World War I* (New York: Vintage Books/Random House, 1968).

12   Interview with Emanuel Ax, October 4, 2010.

13   Emanuel Ax quoted in Rebecca Milzoff, 'Let Me Hear You Dance', *New York Magazine*, August 21, 2006, p. 77.

14   Interview with Colin Fowler, November 16, 2010. Later information and quotations from Fowler in this chapter stem from this interview.

15   Interview with Nancy Umanoff, November 23, 2010.

16   Kathryn J Allwine Bacasmot, 'Mark Morris Dance Group and Music Ensemble at Harris Theater', *Chicago Classical Music*, March 4, 2011, http://www. chicagoclassicalmusic.org/review/2011/3/4/mark-morris-dance-group-and-music-ensemble-harris-theater, accessed July 6, 2013.

17   Astrid Stevens, 'Modest Star of Choreography', *East Anglian Daily Times*, March 18, 1995.

18   Tobias, 'The New York Interview', p. 58.

19   Morris quoted in Suzanne Carbonneau, 'Modern Dance Masters', typescript of interview with Morris, November 2008, in the MMDG archive.

20   Morris quoted in Acocella, *Mark Morris*, p. 82.

21   Mark Morris, 'A Symposium on the Piano', *The Threepenny Review*, Fall, 2009, p. 20.

22   Ellen Dunkel, 'A Classic in Comic Book Style', *Hackensack, New Jersey Record*, November 29, 2002.

23 Morris, 'Live Music', in *Mark Morris Dance Group: Celebrating Twenty-Five Years* (New York: Mark Morris Dance Group, 2005), pp. 34-35 [speech at the Midwest Arts Conference, Cleveland, Ohio, September 17, 1998, also published in *The Way*, November 1, 1998].

24 Morris quoted in Laura Collins-Hughes, '*Petrichor*, Step by Step', *The Boston Globe*, October 10, 2010.

25 Doris Humphrey, *The Art of Making Dances* (New York: Grove Press, 1959), p. 134.

26 Barbara White, '"As if they didn't hear the music," Or: How I Learned to Stop Worrying and Love Mickey Mouse,' 'Sound Moves' [issue], *The Opera Quarterly {Performance+Theory+History}*, 22/1 (Winter, 2006), pp. 70-1.

27 Interview with Ethan Iverson, November 24, 2010. Unless otherwise indicated, later information and quotations from Iverson in this chapter stem from this interview.

28 Dowdell is quoted by Acocella as saying: 'Sometimes the most personal thing he gives us is the way he hears,' in *Mark Morris*, p. 182.

29 Information for this section of the chapter owes much to Acocella's Chapter 1, 'Childhood', in *Mark Morris*, supplemented by my own interviews, including those with Morris himself. See also Scott Haas for some of the song titles: typescript of interview with Morris, September 20, 1992, in the MMDG archive. Acocella continues to be a foundation for biographical information up to 1993, supplemented by information from interviews and reviews in the MMDG archive.

30 Interview with Morris.

31 Martha Ullman West, 'Making Dance Sing: Mark Morris's Choreography for Opera', *Chronicle of Higher Education*, April 20, 2007.

32 Acocella, *Mark Morris*, p. 21.

33 David Leventhal, email communication, January 5, 2011.

34 Harriet Cavalli, *Dance and Music: A Guide to Dance Accompaniment for Musicians and Dance Teachers* (Gainesville, Fl.: University Press of Florida, 2001).

35 Interview with Morris.

36 Acocella, *Mark Morris*, p. 159.

37 Carbonneau, 'Modern Dance Masters'.

38 Mikhail Baryshnikov recalls Morris's 'commendable' playing from the *Nutcracker* score in his own New York apartment in the early 1990s, after Morris had returned from Brussels: interview, June 21, 2011.

39 Haas, typescript of interview with Morris.

40 Acocella, *Mark Morris*, p. 35.

41 Morris quoted in Thea Singer, 'Singing the Body Electric', *The Boston Phoenix*, June 1, 1990.

42 Interview with Penny Hutchinson, January 29, 2011.

43 Walter Piston, *Orchestration* (London: Victor Gollancz, 1965); interview with Morris.

44 Acocella, *Mark Morris*, p. 36; interview with Hutchinson.

45 Harry Partch, *Genesis of a Music* [1947] (New York: Da Capo Press, 1974).

46 Partch had intended *Castor and Pollux* (1952) to be choreographed. It was subtitled 'A Dance for the Twin Rhythms of Gemini'.

47 Morris in interview with Barbara Lane, Jewish Community Center, San Francisco, September 26, 2006, DVD in the MMDG archive.

48 Interview with Page Smith, February 10, 2011.

49 Morris quoted in Gia Kourlas, 'Mark His Words...', *Time Out New York*, 144, June

       25-July 2, 1998, clipping, unpaged, in the MMDG archive.

50   Arlene Croce, 'Mark Morris Comes to Town', *The New Yorker*, January 2, 1984, reprinted in Croce, *Sight Lines* (New York: Alfred A. Knopf, 1987), pp. 157-60.

51   Acocella, *Mark Morris*, pp. 54-6.

52   Acocella, *Mark Morris*, p. 65.

53   Alterman's title was initially 'group manager', then 'general manager', then, during and after the Brussels period, 'general director'.

54   'Mark Morris', *Great Performances: Dance in America*, directed by Thomas Grimm, produced by Judy Kinberg and Grimm, PBS, 1986.

55   See, for instance, Morris quoted in Karen Campbell, 'A Moving Masterpiece', *The Boston Herald*, May 27, 1994.

56   Morris in interview with Gigi Yellen, 'On the Boards', Seattle, April 15, 2008, http://markmorrisdancegroup.org/resources/media/3-interviews, accessed July 6, 2013.

57   Interview with Morris.

58   Interview with Morris.

59   Richard Taruskin, 'The Pastness of the Present and the Presence of the Past', in Nicholas Kenyon, ed. *Authenticity and Early Music: A Symposium* (Oxford: Oxford University Press, 1988), pp. 205-6.

60   Kenyon, ed., *Authenticity and Early Music: A Symposium*.

61   Jacob Siskind, 'Hot Young Dancer Saves his Energy for the Stage', *The Ottawa Citizen*, November 24, 1986.

62   Interview with Morris.

63   Morris also mentions the Catalan musician Jordi Savall as a source of inspiration, a major figure in early music since the 1970s: interview with Morris.

64   Acocella, *Mark Morris*, p. 138.

65   See also Morris in interview with Joe McLellan in 'Morris Speaks', www. redludwig.com, May 2, 2003, print-out in the MMDG archive.

66   The title of the piece was originally *Canonic Waltz Studies* but was changed when Morris discovered that not all the musical selections were Waltzes: Acocella, *Mark Morris*, p. 271.

67   Karen Fisher, 'The Morris Experience', *The News and Observer*, Raleigh, North Carolina, July 8, 1984.

68   Interview with Herschel Garfein, November 17, 2010.

69   Interview with Tina Fehlandt, November 18, 2010.

70   Herschel Garfein, email communication, November 9, 2010.

71   Acocella, *Mark Morris*, p. 165.

72   'A Conversation with Mark Morris and Joan Acocella', International Festival of Arts and Ideas, Shubert Theatre, Boston, June 23, 2009 – February 25, 2010, http://www.artidea.org/event.php?id=269, accessed July 6, 2013.

73   Acocella, *Mark Morris*, p. 176.

74   Prior to this, Morris had used inexpensive costumes (often bought from stores), rarely any sets.

75   Nancy Umanoff in interview with Acocella, October 30, 2008, DVD in the MMDG Archive.

76   While *A Lake* was premiered by the White Oak Dance Project, most of it was choreographed on MMDG with the intention that both companies would perform it. Morris completed the work on the White Oak dancers.

77   Baryshnikov was initially supposed to dance the role of Fritz, which was the

reason why he went to Belgium. Then, due to the illness of Jon Mensinger, who was scheduled to perform the role of Young Drosselmeier, Baryshnikov learnt his role and Marianne Moore danced Fritz. Just before opening night, Baryshnikov injured his knee and did not perform at all (Nancy Umanoff, email communication, June 27, 2014).

78 'The Hidden Soul of Harmony', *South Bank Show*, directed by Nigel Wattis, London Weekend Television, 1990.

79 Interview with Morris.

80 The style uses tune books such as *The Sacred Harp* and allows singers to have fun shifting across the usual hierarchy of soprano, alto, tenor and bass. The application of coded shapes to note heads (square for the tonic, for instance) was designed to help singers find pitches without having to read clefs.

81 Dowdell quoted in Acocella, 'Mark Morris: The Body and What It Means', *Dance Now*, 3/2 (Summer, 1994), p. 44.

82 Morris quoted in Alan M. Kriegsman, 'Rocking and Rolling in the Monnaie', *The Washington Post*, October 21, 1990.

83 Morris quoted in *Online NewsHour with Jim Lehrer*, PBS, March 23, 2001, http://www.pbs.org/newshour/bb/entertainment/jan-june01/morris_03-23.html, accessed July 6, 2013.

84 Interview with Morris.

85 Acocella, *Mark Morris*, p. 237.

86 Morris quoted in 'Mark Morris', *New York Magazine*, December 16, 2002, http://nymag.com/nymetro/arts/dance/n_8102/index2.html, accessed July 6, 2013.

87 Elaine Schmidt, 'Choreographer Likes His Music Live', *Journal Sentinel*, April 9, 2011, http://www.jsonline.com/entertainment/arts/119440044.html, accessed July 6, 2013.

88 Interview with Umanoff, June 27, 2011.

89 Leesa Dahl is a second rehearsal pianist (but only for a specific programme), while others cover Colin Fowler when needed.

90 Fowler in Ojai Insight interview with Chris Hailey, June 8, 2013, DVD in the MMDG archive.

91 Ethan Iverson, email communication, April 6, 2011; interview with Iverson, June 13, 2013.

92 Interview with Umanoff, June 27, 2011.

93 Robert Cole quoted in Allan Ulrich, 'Mark Morris: 20 Years of Serious Fun-- Statistical Data Included—Interview', *Dance Magazine* (April, 2001), p. 48.

94 *L'Allegro* was performed in Seattle the second time (2008) under its chief conductor Gerard Schwarz.

95 'Mark Morris Dance Group', *South Bank Show*, directed and produced by Nigel Wattis, London Weekend Television, 2000.

96 Ffm Web, Comments: http://www.latimes.com/entertainment/arts/culture/la-et-cm-ojai-festival-review-20130611,0,342562.story, accessed July 4, 2013.

97 The Tanglewood commissions are *Cargo, Excursions, Visitation, Empire Garden* and *Renard*.

98 Tanglewood is also the venue where Morris met the conductor Stefan Asbury.

99 Morris suggests this in Carbonneau, 'Modern Dance Masters', typescript of interview with Morris.

100 The full list of ballet companies in North America who have performed Morris's ballets is as follows: Joffrey Ballet, American Ballet Theatre, Boston Ballet,

Pacific Northwest Ballet, Les Grands Ballets Canadiens, Ballet British Columbia, Pittsburgh Ballet Theatre, Houston Ballet, and The Washington Ballet. The re-staging on different companies is not something that Morris undertakes with work made for the MMDG, with the exception of student groups, some of whom learn his MMDG pieces as preparation for their own professional careers in modern dance.

101   Ma quoted in Anita Amirrezvani, 'Dancing with Cellos: Yo-Yo Ma Joins Mark Morris Dance Group to premiere "Falling Down Stairs" in Berkeley', *Contra Costa Times*, February 28, 1997.

102   Ma quoted in Timothy Mangan, 'Free Wheeling Journey', *The Orange County Register*, April 6, 1999.

103   Interview with Umanoff, November 23, 2010.

104   Ibid.

105   Morris quoted in 'Hear it Now: Mark Morris at BAM', The Leonard Lopate Show.

106   Morris in interview with Richard Dyer, ICA, Boston, March 7, 2007.

107   Morris quoted in 'Listening to Music—A Conversation with Mark Morris', July 28, 2003, http://markmorrisdancegroup.org/press_releases/15, accessed July 6, 2013. The theremin is an early electronic musical instrument invented in 1920 by a Russian physicist Léon Theremin, used in films for its eerie timbre, but also in pop and avant-garde 20th and 21st century music.

108   Morris, 'Table Talk', *The Threepenny Review* (Spring, 2000), http://www.threepennyreview.com/samples/morris_sp00.html, accessed December 29, 2009.

109   Morris quoted in 'Listening to Music—A Conversation with Mark Morris'.

110   Interview with Morris.

111   Interview with Morris.

112   Robert Cole in interview with Morris, World Arts Alliance (WAA) Conference, Los Angeles Public Library, August 31, 2007, http://calperformances.org/learn/watch_listen/archive/page6.php, accessed January 1, 2012.

113   Nicholas McGegan quoted in Matthew Gurewitsch, 'In Partnering a Ballet, the Orchestra Must Also Dance', *The New York Times*, September 29, 2002.

114   See, for instance, Morris's 2006 programme for *King Arthur*.

115   Morris quoted in Perry Brass, 'Cracked Nut', *Gay City News*, December 13-19, 2002.

116   Morris in interview for *Live at Lincoln Center* broadcast of *Mozart Dances*, PBS, August, 16, 2007, DVD in the MMDG archive.

117   Alex Ross, 'Yo-Yo Ma: The Rest Is Noise Interview', September 20, 2007, http://www.therestisnoise.com/2007/09/yo-yo-ma-the-re.html, accessed July 6, 2013.

118   Morris quoted in Gia Kourlas, 'The Music Man', *Time Out New York*, June 3-10, 2004, p. 89; Morris quoted in 'Dance', *Chicago Sun-Times*, October 8, 2000 [clip in the MMDG archive--no author given]; Morris quoted in Thea Singer, 'Morris Brings Chopin, Satie to Jacob's Pillow', *Boston Sunday Globe*, June 4, 2000.

119   Morris quoted in Acocella, *Mark Morris*, p. 176.

120   Arion Berger, 'One Man Movement', *Washington City Paper*, May 7, 1999.

121   Interview with Iverson, November 24, 2010; see also 'Mark Morris: Dusty Wright Show 036', August 15, 2006, http://culturecatch.com/podcast/mark_morris, accessed July 6, 2013.

122   Interview with Umanoff, November 23, 2010.

123   Morris quoted in Thea Singer, '*Home* Again: Mark Morris is back in residence in

Boston', *The Boston Phoenix*, May 21, 1993.

124   Interview with Iverson, November 24, 2010.
125   Interview with Umanoff, November 23, 2010.
126   Mark Morris quoted in 'Mark Morris', in Joyce Morgenroth, *Speaking of Dance: Twelve Contemporary Choreographers on Their Craft* (London: Routledge, 2004), p. 183.
127   Interview with Umanoff, November 23, 2010.
128   Interview with Morris.
129   Interview with Morris.
130   Interview with Umanoff, November 23, 2010.
131   Ara Guzelimian and Morris in the opening Ojai Festival Talk 'Choreographer as Musician', June 6, 2013, DVD in the MMDG archive.
132   Ellen Highstein, email communication, April 24, 2014.
133   Interview with Highstein, November 24, 2010.
134   Interview with Highstein, February 2, 2011.
135   Morris quoted in Johanna Keller, 'Let's Play the Music (and Dance)', *The New York Times*, July 11, 2004.
136   Morris quoted in Stuart Isacoff, 'Stravinsky Crashes the Party', *The Wall Street Journal*, August 4, 2011.
137   Anne Carolyn Bird quoted in Johanna Keller, 'Let's Play the Music (and Dance)'.
138   José Lemos quoted in Richard Dyer, 'To Perform with Mark Morris, Musicians Learn New Movements', *The Boston Globe*, July 1, 2004.
139   Norman Fischer quoted in Richard Dyer, 'To perform with Mark Morris...' During the 2010 *L'Allegro* season at the London Coliseum, drawing from the Tanglewood model, dancer Bradon McDonald taught a workshop for Jane Glover's post-graduate students at the Royal Academy of Music and Morris coached their physical and verbal presentation.
140   Interview with Simon Morrison, January 8, 2011.

CHAPTER 2

1   Unless otherwise indicated, the sources of information on Morris's methods in this chapter stem from the author's series of interviews with him.
2   Interview with Emanuel Ax, October 4, 2010.
3   Interview with Page Smith, February 11, 2013.
4   Robert Irving in interview with Tobi Tobias, Oral History Project Transcript, New York Public Library Dance Collection, July-December 1976, p. 67. See also Jordan, *Moving Music: Dialogues with Music in Twentieth-Century Ballet* (London: Dance Books, 2000), pp. 90-1.
5   Anthony Twiner in interview with Howard Friend and Stephanie Jordan, 'The Musician's View: Insights into Music and Musicality at the Royal Ballet', *World Ballet and Dance*, 4, 1992-93, ed. Bent Schonberg (London: Dance Books, 1993), p. 16.
6   Bausch chose the recording by Pierre Boulez with the Cleveland Orchestra, CBS Records, 1969.
7   Interview with Colin Fowler, November 16, 2010.
8   Interview with Ethan Iverson, November 24, 2010. Unless otherwise indicated, this interview is the source of all other information and quotations from Iverson in this chapter.

9   Morris quoted in interview with Joe McLellan in 'Morris Speaks', www.redludwig.com, May 2, 2003, print-out in the MMDG archive.

10   Morris quoted in *Online NewsHour with Jim Lehrer*, March 23, 2001, http://www.pbs.org/newshour/bb/entertainment/jan-june01/morris_03-23.html, accessed July 6, 2013.

11   Morris did not, however, attempt to direct cellist Yo-Yo Ma's interpretation when he played for *The Argument*.

12   When other musicians know their music by heart, Henckens provides a music stand with a light and a sheet of white paper in order to reveal their presence (email communication, May 22, 2014): 'It's hard to hear an instrument but not see where the sound comes from, especially when all other musicians are seen.'

13   Interview with Fowler.

14   Interview with Lauren Grant, January 10, 2013.

15   Yo-Yo Ma quoted in Anita Amirrezvani, 'Dancing with Cellos: Yo-Yo Ma Joins Mark Morris Dance Group to Premiere *Falling Down Stairs* in Berkeley', *Contra Costa Times*, February 28, 1997.

16   Ma quoted in Timothy Mangan, 'Free Wheeling Journey', *The Orange County Register*, April 6, 1999.

17   *Falling Down Stairs*, directed by Barbara Willis Sweete, in *Yo-Yo Ma: Inspired by Bach*, Rhombus Media (1997), Sony Music Entertainment (2000). Work on the film commenced in 1992 and it was shot at Tanglewood in 1994.

18   Ma quoted in Mangan.

19   Interview with Lauren Grant, May 25, 2014. In Dresden at the time, Grant also discovered a new connection with cellist Jan Vogler, a feeling of 'opening up' on the penultimate chord of the Sarabande: 'we locked eyes and held the moment together'.

20   Emanuel Ax quoted in Jed Distler, 'Emanuel Ax—Leader of the Dance', *Gramophone*, May 2007, http://markmorrisdancegroup.org/resources/press, accessed July 6, 2013.

21   Interview with Ax, October 4, 2010. Unless otherwise indicated, this interview is the source of all further information and quotations from Ax in this chapter.

22   Emanuel Ax quoted in Distler, 'Emanuel Ax—Leader of the Dance'.

23   Ibid.

24   Ibid.

25   Louis Langrée quoted in Rebecca Milzoff, 'Let Me Hear You Dance', *New York Magazine*, August 21, 2006, p. 77.

26   Interview with Johan Henckens, June 28, 2011, also email communications, May 22 and June 20, 2014. Unless otherwise indicated, Henckens' information stems from these communications.

27   Another extreme situation that Henckens notes is lack of space for a piano: 'We've done shows where the pianist is cued by a dancer in the wings on the opposite side of the stage mimicking an onstage dancer (*Italian Concerto* in Bermuda). Not having space for a piano has been solved by using an electronic keyboard on two occasions (both at Jacob's Pillow, when performing a piece with a piano quintet).'

28   The following is the list of dances where musicians are 'choreographed' to be onstage whenever possible: *The Argument*, *Candleflowerdance*, *Drink to Me Only With Thine Eyes*, *Excursions*, *Falling Down Stairs*, *Peccadillos*, and *Serenade*. *Looky* uses a player piano (when available), which is placed upstage right.

29   Morris quoted in Maura Keefe and Marc Wordworth, 'An Interview with Mark Morris', *Salmagundi*, 104-5 (Fall, 1994-Winter, 1995), pp. 231-2.
30   Morris quoted in 'Mark Morris', in Joyce Morgenroth, *Speaking of Dance: Twelve Contemporary Choreographers on Their Craft* (London: Routledge, 2004), p. 176.
31   Information from MMDG company class given by Morris, September 13, 2010.
32   Morris quoted in Robert Greskovic, 'Not a Member of the Club', *The Wall Street Journal*, February 25, 2010.

CHAPTER 3

1   Morris quoted in 'Mark Morris', *Great Performances: Dance in America*, directed by Thomas Grimm, produced by Judy Kinberg and Grimm, PBS and Danmarks Radio, 1986.
2   See Roger Copeland, 'Mark Morris, Postmodernism, and history recycled,' *Dance Theatre Journal*, 13/4 (1997), pp. 18-23. Noting that postmodernism in dance was originally equated with the founders of New York's Judson Dance Theater in the 1960s, Copeland and some other scholars consider that their work does not have the historical or ironic features that accord with the more generally accepted notions of postmodernism across the arts. For a summary of discussions about postmodernism in dance, an especially popular subject for enquiry in the 1980s, see Jordan, *Striding Out: Aspects of Contemporary and New Dance in Britain* (London: Dance Books, 1992), pp. 3-6; for reference to Morris, see Rachel Duerden and Bonnie Rowell, 'Mark Morris's *Dido and Aeneas* (1989): A Critical Postmodern Sensibility', *Dance Chronicle*, 36 (2013), pp. 143-71.
3   Robert Bordo quoted in Joan Acocella, *Mark Morris*, p. 253.
4   Acocella, 'Morris Dances', *Art in America* (October, 1988), p. 181.
5   Acocella, *Mark Morris*, p. 193.
6   Interview with Morris.
7   Ruth St Denis, 'Music Visualization', *The Denishawn Magazine*, 1/3 (Spring, 1925), pp. 1-7; reprinted in Selma Jeanne Cohen, ed. *Dance as a Theatre Art* (New York: Dodd, Mead & Co., 1974), pp. 129-34.
8   Clive Barnes, 'Mad About the Boy', *Dance & Dancers* (January, 1987), p. 17.
9   Laura Shapiro, 'Cheers for Mark Morris,' *Newsweek*, May 30, 1988, quoted in Acocella, *Mark Morris*, p. 6. See also Anna Kisselgoff, 'Who Does What to Whom, or, A Kinetic Wit at Play,' *The New York Times*, June 29, 1990; Clive Barnes, 'Amazing Grace, Morris Makes His Mark', *The New York Post*, April 16, 1992.
10   Suzanne Carbonneau, 'Modern Dance Masters', typescript of interview with Morris, November 2008, in the MMDG archive. Earlier, in interview with Joyce Morgenroth, Morris hotly denied the possibility of translation: 'It's not automatic that the dance *looks* like the music *sounds*—because there's no such thing. That's a complete fallacy': see Morgenroth, *Speaking of Dance: Twelve Contemporary Choreographers on Their Craft* (London: Routledge, 2004), p. 175.
11   Acocella, *Mark Morris*, p. 177.
12   Karen Campbell, 'Morris Group Knows the Score, and More', *Boston Globe*, online edition, July 30, 2005, http://www.boston.com/ae/theater_arts/articles/2005/07/30/morris_group_knows_the_score_and_more/, accessed August 8, 2014.
13   John Rockwell, 'Stomping, Flexing, and Some Vernal Romps, Too', *The New York Times*, March 10, 2006.

14   Alastair Macaulay, 'Umbrellosis', *The Dancing Times* (January, 1986), p. 318.

15   Acocella, *Mark Morris*, p. 65.

16   Morris quoted in 'Mark Morris', *Ballett-Tanz* (October, 2006), pp. 19-20.

17   Morris, 'Foreword', in Mindy Aloff, *Hippo in a Tutu: Dancing in Disney Animation* (New York: Disney Editions, 2008), p. 9.

18   Yet when they were co- teaching a course on music and dance at Princeton University in 2010, Morris and Morrison elected to show as their animation example the Mickey Mouse short *Steamboat Willie* (1928).

19   This is noted by Macaulay, 'Disney's Dances', *The Dancing Times* (December, 1989), p. 262.

20   Barbara White, '"As if they didn't hear the music," Or: How I Learned to Stop Worrying and Love Mickey Mouse,' 'Sound Moves' [issue], *The Opera Quarterly (Performance+Theory+History}*, 22/1 (Winter, 2006), p. 68.

21   Ibid.

22   Ibid., p. 66.

23   For further discussion of early twentieth-century choreomusical theories and practices, see the survey in Jordan, *Moving Music: Dialogues with Music in Twentieth-Century Ballet* (London: Dance Books, 2000), Chapter 1: 'Liberation Movements', pp. 3-60. See also, Jordan, ed. *Fedor Lopukhov: Selected Writings*, in the series *Studies in Dance History* (Madison, Wisconsin: University of Wisconsin Press, 2003), trans. Dorinda Offord.

24   John Martin, *The Modern Dance* [1933] (New York: Dance Horizons, 1965), Part IV, 'The Dance and the Other Arts', pp. 99-116.

25   Doris Humphrey, *The Art of Making Dances* (New York and Toronto: Rinehart, 1959), p. 137.

26   Ibid., p. 164.

27   Edwin Denby, 'Graham's 'Chronicle'; Uday Shankar' [January-February, 1937], reprinted in Denby, *Dance Writings*, ed. Robert Cornfield and William Mackay (London: Dance Books, 1986), p. 43.

28   Yvonne Rainer, *Work 1961-73* (Halifax: Press of the Nova Scotia College of Art and Design; New York: New York University Press, 1974), pp. 111-12.

29   Selma Jeanne Cohen, 'A Prolegomenon to an Aesthetics of Dance', *The Journal of Aesthetics and Art Criticism*, 21/1 (Autumn, 1962), p. 24.

30   Michael Blackwood, 'Retracing Steps: American Dance Since Postmodernism', 16mm film, directed by Blackwood, New York: Blackwood Productions, 1988.

31   Acocella, *Mark Morris*, p. 177.

32   Carolyn Abbate and Roger Parker, 'Dismembering Mozart', *Cambridge Opera Journal*, 2/2 (July, 1990), p. 187.

33   It is important that the music world did not always approve of translations of music, but the period when music critics denounced on principle choreography to 'abstract' musical forms like sonata and symphony had ended by the 1950s. See Jordan, *Moving Music*, pp. 10-15.

34   Susan Tomes, *Out of Silence: A Pianist's Yearbook* (Rochester, New York: Boydell Press, 2010), p. 235. See also Tomes, 'Mark Morris at the Coliseum', April 19, 2010, http://www.susantomes.com/mark-morris-coliseum, accessed July 12, 2013.

35   Alex Ross, 'Music in Motion: New Scores at New York City Ballet', *The New Yorker*, June 28, 2010, p. 76.

36   Interview with Jane Glover, January 12, 2011.

37   Christopher Hogwood quoted in Karen Campbell, 'Choreographer Mark Morris and Handel & Haydn Society Take Steps to Put Dance and Opera on Equal Footing', *Boston Sunday Herald*, April 7, 1996.

38   Hogwood quoted in Steven Winn, 'Datebook: Opera: A Match Made in Classical Heaven', *San Francisco Chronicle*, April 28-May 4, 1996.

39   Hogwood quoted in Nick Kimberley, 'Not Waving But Dancing', *The Independent*, August 14, 1996. Mark Swed writes that 'Morris' choreography functions as a kind of ear training', in his 'Review: Handel Dances in Mark Morris' "Acis and Galatea"', *Los Angeles Times*, April 28, 2014.

40   Ross, 'Measure for Measure', blog, http://www.therestisnoise.com/2011/08/measure-for-measure.html, accessed September 6, 2014.

41   Ross, email communication, August 23, 2013.

42   Nancy Umanoff, email communication, December 28, 2013.

CHAPTER 4

1   Guillaume Du Manoir, *Le Mariage de la musique avec la danse* [1664] (Bologna: Bibliotheca Musica Bononiensis, 1985).

2   This chapter expands upon an earlier methodology outlined in Jordan, *Moving Music: Dialogues with Music in Twentieth-Century Ballet* (London: Dance Books, 2000), Chapter 2, 'Hearing the Dance, Watching the Music: Issues of Analysis, Identity and Working Process', pp. 63-89.

3   Allen Fogelsanger and Kathleya Afanador, 'Parameters of Perception: Vision, Audition, and Twentieth-Century Music and Dance', *Proceedings of the 38th Annual CORD Conference*, Tempe, Arizona, 2006. The paper is a rare example that brings together audio-visual intermedia theory and theory from cognitive science. See also, 'Fogelsanger and Afanador, 'A Mirror in Which to Dance: Actions and the Audiovisual Correspondences of Music and Movement,' in Stephanie Schroedter, ed., *Bewegungen zwischen Hören und Sehen. Denkbewegungen zu Bewegungskünsten* (Wurzburg: Königshausen & Neumann, 2012), pp. 129-49.

4   See the work of Emile Jaques-Dalcroze, *Rhythm, Music and Education*, trans. Harold F. Rubinstein (London: Chatto & Windus, 1921), p. 150; Ruth St Denis, 'Music Visualization', *The Denishawn Magazine*, 1/3 (Spring, 1925), pp. 1-7. For a discussion of the concept of energy, see Jordan, *Moving Music*, pp. 86-7.

5   Barbara White, '"As if they didn't hear the music," Or: How I Learned to Stop Worrying and Love Mickey Mouse', 'Sound Moves' [issue], *The Opera Quarterly {Performance+Theory+History}*, 22/1 (Winter, 2006), pp. 81-2.

6   Ibid., pp. 73-4. Claudia Gorbman drew attention to the problem of limited vocabulary, querying whether 'the music "resembles" or ... "contradicts" the action or mood of what happens on the screen...Is there no other way to qualify film music which does not lie between these opposites but outside them?...It is debatable that information conveyed by disparate media can justifiably be called *the same* or *different*': 'Narrative Film Music', *Yale French Studies*, 60 (1980), p. 189.

7   Kathryn Kalinak, *Settling the Score: Music and the Classical Hollywood Film* (Madison, Wisconsin: University of Wisconsin Press, 1992), pp. 29-31.

8   Hanns Eisler and Theodor W. Adorno, *Composing for the Films* (London: Dennis Dobson, 1947), p. 70. Note that Adorno's role was uncredited in the original English edition.

9   Gorbman, 'Narrative Film Music', pp. 189-90.

10   Michel Chion, *Audio-Vision: Sound on Screen* [1990], ed. and trans. Claudia
      Gorbman (New York: Columbia University Press, 1994), p. 137.
11   Gilles Deleuze and Félix Guattari, *A Thousand Plateaus* [1980], trans. Brian
      Massumi (Minneapolis: Minnesota University Press, 1987); Michel Bernard, *De la
      création chorégraphique* (Paris: Centre national de la danse, 2001), p. 159.
12   Doris Humphrey, *The Art of Making Dances* (New York & Toronto: Rinehart,
      1959), p. 80.
13   Ibid.
14   Nicholas Cook, *Analysing Musical Multimedia* (Oxford: Oxford University Press,
      1998), p. 70.
15   George Lakoff and Mark Johnson, *Metaphors We Live By* (Chicago: University of
      Chicago Press, 1980), p. 142. Note that Inger Damsholt uses metaphor theory in
      her choreomusical study of Morris (see Chapter 5, pp. 138-45).
16   Cook, *Analysing Musical Multimedia*, p. 98.
17   Ibid., p. 103.
18   Lawrence M. Zbikowski, *Conceptualizing Music: Cognitive Structure, Theory, and
      Analysis* (New York: Oxford University Press, 2002). See Chapters 2 and 6 in
      particular.
19   Zbikowski, *Conceptualizing Music*, p. 66. He points out that it is accepted practice
      to use capitals like this when citing conceptual metaphors. See also Helen Minors,
      'In Collaboration: Toward a Gesture Analysis of Music and Dance', in Stephanie
      Schroedter, ed., *Bewegungen zwischen Hören und Sehen. Denkbewegungen zu
      Bewegungskünsten* (Wurzburg: Königshausen & Neumann, 2012), pp. 163-80.
20   Mark Turner, *The Body in the Mind: The Bodily Basis of Meaning, Imagination, and
      Reason* (Chicago: University of Chicago Press, 1987).
21   Zbikowski, *Conceptualizing Music*, pp. 70-1 and 76; Mark Turner, *The Literary Mind*
      (New York: Oxford University Press, 1996), chapter 3. This theory is similar to
      Nicholas Cook's concept of 'enabling similarity' between domains in *Analysing
      Musical Multimedia*, p. 70.
22   Zbikowski, *Conceptualizing Music*, p. 71.
23   Zbikowski, 'Music and Movement: A View from Cognitive Science,' in Stephanie
      Schroedter, ed., *Bewegungen zwischen Hören und Sehen*, pp. 151-62.
24   Zbikowski, *Conceptualizing Music*, p. 69.
25   Ibid., pp. 67-8.
26   Ibid., p. 71.
27   Zohar Eitan and Roni Y. Granot, 'How Music Moves: Musical Parameters and
      Listeners' Images of Motion', *Music Perception*, 23/3 (2006), pp. 221-47; Zohar
      Eitan and Renee Timmers, 'Beethoven's last piano sonata and those who follow
      crocodiles: cross-domain mappings of auditory pitch in a musical context',
      Proceedings of the 9th International Conference on Music Perception and Cognition,
      Bologna, Italy, 8 (2006), pp. 875-83.
28   Mark Turner and Gilles Fauconnier, 'Conceptual Integration and Formal
      Expression', *Journal of Metaphor and Symbolic Activity*, 10 (1995), pp. 183–203;
      Fauconnier and Turner, *The Way We Think: Conceptual Blending and the Mind's
      Hidden Complexities* (New York: Basic Books, 2002).
29   Zbikowski, *Conceptualizing Music*, p. 80.
30   Zbikowski explains that the topography of a conceptual integration network
      guides three operations, composition (the first stage), completion and elaboration,
      p. 80.

31   Bronislava Nijinska, 'Creation of *Les Noces*', trans. and introduced by Jean M.
      Serafetinides and Irina Nijinska, *Dance Magazine*, 48 (December, 1974), p. 61.
32   Edward T. Cone, *The Composer's Voice* (Berkeley: University of California Press,
      1974).
33   Carolyn Abbate, *Unsung Voices: Opera and Musical Narrative in the Nineteenth
      Century* (Princeton: Princeton University Press, 1991). See also Claire Taylor-
      Jay's comments on recent work that has used the concept of 'voice', in 'The
      Composer's Voice? The Compositional Style and Criteria of Value in Weill, Krenek
      and Stravinsky', *Journal of the Royal Musical Association*, 134/1 (2009), p. 88.
34   Lawrence Kramer, *Music and Poetry: The Nineteenth Century and After* (Berkeley,
      Los Angeles and London: University of California Press, 1984); 'Review: Song
      and Story,' *19th-Century Music*, 15/3 (Spring, 1992), pp. 235-9; *Classical Music
      and Postmodern Knowledge* (Berkeley, Los Angeles and London: University of
      California Press, 1996); *Franz Schubert: Sexuality, Subjectivity, Song* (Cambridge:
      Cambridge University Press, 2003).
35   Cone, *The Composer's Voice*, pp. 17-18.
36   Abbate, *Unsung Voices*, pp. x-xii. See also Lawrence Kramer for a critique of
      Cone, *Classical Music and Postmodern Knowledge* (Berkeley, California and London:
      University of California Press, 1995), p. 119.
37   Kramer, 'Review: Song and Story', p. 239; Kramer, *Music and Poetry: The
      Nineteenth Century and After*, p. 11.
38   Kramer, 'Review: Song and Story', p. 239.
39   Kramer, *Classical Music and Postmodern Knowledge*, p. 119.
40   Cone, *The Composer's Voice*, p. 7.
41   Ibid., p. 16.
42   Ibid., pp. 21, 79.
43   Ibid., p. 35.
44   Ibid., p. 19.
45   Kramer, *Music and Poetry: The Nineteenth Century and After*, p. 127.
46   Cone, *The Composer's Voice*, p. 143.
47   Lawrence E. Marks, *The Unity of the Senses: Interrelations Among the Modalities*
      (New York: Academic Press, 1978), p. 197.
48   Chion, *Audio-Vision*, p. 5.
49   Kathleya Afanador, Ellen Campana, Todd Ingalls, Dilip Swaminathan, Harvey
      Thornburg, Jodi James, Jessica Mumford, Gang Qian, and StJepan Rajko, 'On
      Cross-modal Perception of Musical Tempo and the Speed of Human Movement,'
      *Computer Music Modeling and Retrieval: Sense of Sounds, 4th International
      Symposium, CMMR 2007*, Copenhagen, Denmark, August 27-31, 2007, revised
      papers, ed. Richard Kronland-Martinet, et al. (2008), pp. 235-45.
50   The 'freeze phenomenon' was first noted working in the opposite direction, with
      sound enhancing visual perception, in Jean Vroomen and Beatrice de Gelder,
      'Sound Enhances Visual Perception: Cross-modal Effects of Auditory Organisation
      on Vision', *Journal of Experimental Psychology: Human Perception and Performance*,
      26/5 (2000), pp. 1583-90.
51   Interview with Morris.
52   See, for instance, Bruno H. Repp and Amandine Penel, 'Auditory Dominance in
      Temporal Processing: New Evidence from Synchronisation with Simultaneous
      Visual and Auditory Sequences', *Journal of Experimental Psychology: Human
      Perception and Performance*, 28/5 (2002), pp. 1085-99; 'Rhythmic Movement

is Attracted More Strongly to Auditory than to Visual Rhythms,' *Psychological Research*, 68 (2004), pp. 252-70.

53 Noel Carroll, *Art in Three Dimensions* (Oxford: Oxford University Press, 2010), Chapter 24, co-written with Margaret Moore, 'Feeling Movement: Music and Dance', p. 491, note 4.

54 Raina Katzarova, 'Sur un phénomène concernant le manque de coïncidence entre la figure chorégraphique et la phrase mélodique', *International Folk Music Journal*, 12 (1960), p. 69. There are other Eastern European dance ethnographers who have observed the effects of metrical incongruity, including Felix Hoerburger, 'On Relationships between Music and Movement in Folk Dancing', *International Folk Music Journal*, 12 (1960), p. 70; György Martin, 'Considérations sur l'analyse des relations entre la danse et la musique de danse populaires', *Studia Musicologica*, 7/1-4 (1965), pp. 333-4; Ernó Pésovár, 'Three Round Verbunks', *Dance Studies*, 1 (1976), p. 50. Recently too, Serbian scholar Selena Rakocevic has notated examples of triplet rhythm (three bounces on the supporting leg timed as three minims) crossing two bars of musical 2/4: see *Igre Plesnih Struktura, Tradicionalna igra muzika za igru Srba u Banatu u Svetlu uzajamni uticaja* [Interweaving Dance Structures: Traditional Dance and Dance Music of the Banat Serbs in the Light of their Mutual Relationships] (Belgrade: Fakultet Muzicke Umentnosti, 2011), pp. 338-42.

55 Jordan, *Moving Music*, pp. 78-88.

56 'I like to see people do what they're not expected to do. I like to see how slow things relate to fast things,' Morris once said, quoted in interview with Martha Duffy, 'The Mark and Misha Show', *Time*, September 17, 1990, http://www.time.com/time/magazine/article/0,9171,971166,00.html, accessed July 26, 2013.

57 Terry Teachout, 'A Choreographer Who First Hears the Dance', *The New York Times*, January 9, 2000.

58 Acocella, *Mark Morris*, p. 33.

59 See note 54.

60 For the Macedonian Žensko Berance step, see http://www.youtube.com/watch?v=danVp3WkOxoor, accessed July 19, 2013.

61 Interview with Gergana Panova-Tekath in Berovo, Macedonia, April 18, 2012.

62 See Tellef Kvifte, 'Categories and Timing: On the Perception of Meter', *Ethnomusicology*, 51/1 (Winter, 2007), pp. 64-84.

63 Morris quoted in John Gruen, 'Man/Child in the Promised Land: Mark Morris: He's Here', *Dance Magazine* (September, 1986), p. 50.

64 Interview with Penny Hutchinson, January 29, 2011.

65 Interview with Morris.

66 Interview with Morris.

67 David Leventhal, email communication, April 24, 2014.

68 Interview with Morris.

69 Edwin Denby, 'In the Abstract' [1959-60], in Denby, *Dance Writings*, ed. Robert Cornfield and William Mackay (London: Dance Books, 1986), pp. 465-7.

70 Richard Middleton also refers to musicians choosing between two sides, the 'front side, the music feels urgent and edgy' and 'back side, the groove feels earthier and heavier': in 'Inside Music: 'New Views on Groove' (2001), http://www.richardmiddleton.com/insidemusic/viewsongroove.html, accessed July 20, 2013.

71 Interview with Morris.

72 Nicholas Cook, 'Theorizing Musical Meaning', *Musical Theory Spectrum*, 23/2

(Autumn, 2001), p. 188.

73 Elisabeth Le Guin, *Boccherini's Body: An Essay in Carnal Musicology* (Berkeley, Los Angeles, London: University of California Press, 2006), p. 102.

74 Ibid., p. 5. See also Abbate, 'Music—Drastic or Gnostic?' *Critical Enquiry*, 30 (Spring, 2004), pp. 505-36.

75 Roland Barthes, 'The Grain of the Voice' [1972], in Barthes, *Image-Music-Text*, trans. Stephen Heath (London: Fontana/Collins, 1977), pp. 179-89.

76 Ibid., p. 189.

77 Acocella, *Mark Morris*, p. 82.

78 There is a history behind this practical approach. I incorporated 'sketch learning' regularly within analyses for a variety of Stravinsky projects culminating in *Stravinsky Dances*. During the Morris project, I also shared ideas about Morris's work in practical workshops with students at the University of Roehampton.

79 See John Rink, ed., *The Practice of Performance: Studies in Musical Interpretation* (Cambridge: Cambridge University Press, 1995). Since this publication, Rink has directed the collaborative AHRC Research Centre for Musical Performance as Creative Practice based at the University of Cambridge, 2009-14.

80 Anthony Twiner, *The Muncey Music Book* (London: Dance Books, 1986); Katherine Teck, *Ear Training for the Body: A Dancer's Guide to Music* (Pennington, New Jersey: Princeton Book Company, 1994); Eric Taylor, *AB Guide to Music Theory*, Part 1/2 (London: Associated Board of the Royal Schools of Music, 1989/91).

81 Stephen Walsh [Review of Peter Hill, *Stravinsky: 'The Rite of Spring'*], *Music & Letters*, 83/1 (2002), p. 143.

CHAPTER 5

1 I also watched a variety of company recordings of other performers, as well as of Morris dancing *Ten Suggestions* in 1992 and 1996.

2 John Gruen, 'Mark Morris: He's Here', *Dance Magazine* (September, 1986), p. 50.

3 Ruth St Denis's husband Ted Shawn created a very different style of music visualisation for men.

4 Morris in conversation with Annie Leibowitz in 'Pillow Talk', Jacob's Pillow, Massachusetts, August 25, 2011, DVD in the MMDG archive.

5 Interview with Morris.

6 Acocella, *Mark Morris*, p. 65.

7 Ibid., p. 273; 'Mark Morris', *Great Performances: Dance in America*, directed by Thomas Grimm, produced by Judy Kinberg and Grimm, PBS, WNET/13, 1986. A number of dances discussed in this chapter feature in this film.

8 Tobi Tobias, 'Rites of Passage', *New York Magazine*, June 6, 1988, p. 63.

9 Tina Fehlandt, who took the alto part, made notes on the choreography on her own score, for example: 'head, bounce to neutral; left hand 1 2, right hand 3, left 4; slap [the back of your right hand across the colleague on your right] 1 2, lean 3 4; feet shake; daven 1 2 3 4.' Fehlandt explained the word 'daven'—'as in Jewish prayer when the head bobs up and down': email communication, May 28, 2011.

10 Ruth St Denis, 'Music Visualisation' [1925], in Selma Jeanne Cohen, ed., *Dance as a Theatre Art* (New York: Dodd, Mead & C., 1974), p. 132.

11 Interview with Morris.

12 Christopher Hogwood identified this, quoted in interview with Nick Kimberley, 'Not Waving But Dancing', *The Independent*, August 14, 1996.

13 Alastair Macaulay, 'Umbrellisima', *The Dancing Times* (December, 1984), p. 219.

14 Macaulay, 'Modern Dance to the Baroque', *The Financial Times*, January 6, 1990.

15 The original version of the concerto was lost, but has been reconstructed and published in the *Neue Bach-Ausgabe*. See the list of works by Bach in *The New Grove Dictionary of Music and Musicians*, ed. Stanley Sadie & John Tyrrell, 2nd edition (London: Macmillan, 2001), Vol. 2, p. 374.

16 Interview with Morris.

17 Acocella, *Mark Morris*, p. 251.

18 The opera is *The Bohemian Girl* (1843) by Michael William Balfe, confirmed by Morris in interview.

19 Interview with Tina Fehlandt, October 7, 2010.

20 In bars 50-52, for instance, there is a tierce de picardie cadence, a swerve into G major from G minor. The tonic chord of G major then becomes a dominant 9th, leading to a cadence back into the original key of C minor.

21 The 1984 revisions are minor from a choreomusical point of view, although Morris says that he simplified the choreography.

22 For Acocella's motif descriptions, see her *Mark Morris*, pp. 144-5. See also Inger Damsholt, 'Choreomusical Discourse: The Relationship Between Dance and Music', unpublished PhD dissertation, University of Copenhagen, 1999; Damsholt, 'Mark Morris, Mickey Mouse, and Choreomusical Polemic', 'Sound Moves' [issue], *The Opera Quarterly* {Performance+Theory+History}, 22/1 (Winter, 2006), pp. 4-21; the description of *Gloria* by Laurie Lassiter, 'Mark Morris Dance Group', *The Drama Review: TDR*, 29/2 (Summer, 1985), pp. 119-25.

23 'Mark Morris', *Great Performances: Dance in America*.

24 Mark Morris, 'The Creative Process', *Vantage Point* (September/October, 1984), p. 33. Diagrams accompanying the notes are also printed in *Mark Morris Dance Group: Celebrating Twenty-Five Years* (New York: Mark Morris Dance Group, 2005), p. 26.

25 Acocella, *Mark Morris*, p. 121.

26 Macaulay, 'While the Music Lasts', *The New Yorker*, May 11, 1992, p. 82.

27 Acocella, 'Morris Dances', *Art in America* (October, 1988), p. 65.

28 Damsholt, 'Choreomusical Discourse: The Relationship Between Dance and Music', pp. 188-93.

29 Michel Foucault, *The History of Sexuality: Volume I: An Introduction*, trans. Robert Hurley (London: Penguin Books, 1978), pp. 100-1.

30 Damsholt, 'Mark Morris...', p. 7.

31 Interview with Morris.

32 Damsholt, 'Mark Morris...', p. 11.

33 Ibid., p. 13.

34 Acocella, *Mark Morris*, p. 167.

35 Ibid.

36 Ibid., p. 121.

37 Damsholt, 'Mark Morris...', p. 14.

38 Ibid.

39 Acocella, 'Morris Dances', p. 65.

40 Lassiter, 'Mark Morris Dance Group', p. 120.

41 Interview with Morris.

42   Charles Rosen, *The Classical Style* (New York: Viking Press, 1971).
43   Interview with Morris.
44   Since the mid-1980s, this theory of unity has been broadly questioned within the New Musicology movement.
45   Morris quoted in Charles Siebert, 'Footloose!' *Esquire*, December, 1985, p. 146.
46   Charles Rosen, *Sonata Forms* [1980] (New York, London: W.W. Norton, 1988), pp. 131, 177, 187-8. George Balanchine and Doris Humphrey, amongst others, similarly borrowed from musical principles, but Morris has gone further than most choreographers in this direction. See Humphrey, *The Art of Making Dances* (New York: Grove Press, 1959), pp. 149-56.
47   Morris quoted in John Gruen, 'Mark Morris: He's Here', *Dance Magazine* (September, 1986), p. 50.
48   Tobi Tobias, 'Manchild in the Promised Land: Mark Morris', *Dance Magazine* (December, 1984), p. HC-29.
49   Acocella, *Mark Morris*, p. 52.
50   Interview with Morris.
51   Interview with Harriet Cavalli, January 26, 2011.
52   Interview with Matthew Rose, April 14, 2014.
53   Interview with Penny Hutchinson, January 29, 2011.
54   See also No. 14 of *New Love Song Waltzes*, in which fountains of arms shoot up amongst the two lines of a long-ways 'vertical' set (from upstage to down and back up again): to 'Flammenauge, dunkles Haar' ('Flaming eyes, dark hair').
55   Acocella, 'Morris Dances', *Art in America* (October, 1988), p. 182; Acocella, *Mark Morris*, Chapter entitled 'Heaven and Hell', pp. 117-36.
56   Nancy Vreeland, 'Mark Morris', *Dance Theatre Journal*, 3/3 (Autumn, 1985), p. 2.
57   Sophie Constanti, 'Dance Umbrella: Dreams and a Diary', *Dance Theatre Journal*, 4/1 (Spring, 1986), p. 31.
58   Acocella, *Mark Morris*, pp. 129-30.
59   There is similar irony within the vertical dimension, and in a religious context, in Morris's 1988 *Offertorium* solo, set to Schubert's *Salve Regina* ('Hail, Queen, Mother of Mercy'). At the *high* climax ('*in hac lacrimarum valle*'—'mourning and weeping in this valley of tears'), Morris pitches forwards *down* on to his hands in a kind of *penché*, one leg raised behind him, then he bends his arms and back leg, lowering further as the musical hiatus continues and the melody descends towards a cadence.
60   Deborah Jowitt, 'To Drive Dark Winter Away', *The Village Voice*, January 7, 1986.
61   Macaulay, 'Vivamus Atque Amemus', *The New Yorker*, June 20, 1988, p. 86.
62   Acocella, 'Mark Morris: The Body and What it Means', *Dance Now*, 3/2 (Summer, 1994), p. 41.
63   Macaulay, 'Vivamus Atque Amemus', p. 86.
64   Roslyn Sulcas, 'Man on the Move', *Dance & Dancers* (January/February, 1992), p. 10.
65   Daniel Albright, *Untwisting the Serpent: Modernism, Music, Literature, and Other Arts* (Chicago and London: The University of Chicago Press, 2000), p. 28.
66   Acocella, 'Morris Dances', p. 182.
67   Omar Calabrese, *Neo-Baroque: A Sign of the Times* (Princeton, New Jersey: Princeton University Press, 1992); Angela Ndalianis, *Neo-Baroque Aesthetics and Contemporary Entertainment* (Cambridge, Mass: The MIT Press, 2004). See also Mark Franko, 'The Baroque Body', in Marion Kant, ed., *The Cambridge Companion*

　　　to Ballet (Cambridge: Cambridge University Press, 2007), p. 49.

68　Acocella, *Mark Morris*, p. 164.

69　Sally Banes, *Terpsichore in Sneakers: Postmodern Dance* (Middletown, Conn.: Wesleyan University Press, 1987), pp. xv, xx.

70　Morris quoted in Jennifer Dunning, 'Mark Morris, a Choreographer Who Makes Things Happen', *The New York Times*, November 5, 1982.

71　Interview with Morris.

72　Acocella, *Mark Morris*, p. 11.

73　Edward Said, *Musical Elaborations* (New York: Columbia University Press, 1991), p. 100.

74　Arlene Croce, 'Mark Morris Comes to Town', *The New Yorker*, January 2, 1984.

75　Deborah Jowitt, 'A Giggle for the Postmodern Mind', *The Village Voice*, January 3, 1984.

76　Erik Satie, *Socrate* [and *Mercure*] with Mady Mesplé (soprano), Pierre Dervaux (conductor) [recording], Orchestre de Paris, EMI, 1972.

77　Roger Shattuck, *The Banquet Years: The Origins of the Avant Garde in France: 1885 to World War I* [1955] (New York: Vintage Books, 1968), p. 160.

78　Alan M. Gillmor, *Erik Satie* (Basingstoke and London: Macmillan Press, 1988), p. 223.

79　Interview with Morris.

80　Interview with Morris.

81　Morris quoted in 'Edinburgh Nights', BBC TV, 1994.

82　See further analysis, especially of the music, in Jordan, *Stravinsky Dances: Re-Visions Across the Century* (Alton, Hants: Dance Books, 2007), pp. 149–56. Morris used a recording for the premiere at Dance Theater Workshop, New York, although the full live wind ensemble was available for performances at the Théâtre Royal de la Monnaie, Belgium (1988) and Tanglewood (2003 and 2011).

83　Alexander Rehding, 'Towards a "Logic of Discontinuity"', in Stravinsky's *Symphonies of Wind Instruments*: Hasty, Kramer and Straus Reconsidered', *Music Analysis*, 17/1 (1998), pp. 48, 61.

84　Information on the creative process behind *Frisson* came from interview with Morris.

85　Eric Walter White, *Stravinsky: The Composer and his Works* (London: Faber and Faber, 1979), pp. 293–4.

86　Rehding, 'Towards a "Logic of Discontinuity"', p. 60.

87　Jonathan Kramer, *The Time of Music* (New York: Schirmer Books, 1988), p. 283.

88　Arnold Whittall, 'Stravinsky in Context', in Jonathan Cross, ed., *The Cambridge Companion to Stravinsky* (Cambridge: Cambridge University Press, 2003), p. 50; Richard Taruskin, *Stravinsky and the Russian Traditions: A Biography of the Works through 'Mavra'*, 2 vols. (Oxford: Oxford University Press, 1996), pp. 1488–9, 1493.

89　In assessing different video recordings of *Frisson*, Morris was particularly insistent that the Monnaie performance should be scrutinised.

90　Morris quoted in Karen Fisher, 'The Morris Experience', *The News and Observer* (Raleigh, N.C.), July 8, 1984.

91　Morris told Fisher in 'The Morris Experience' that he and Garfein worked in parallel based on shared ideas, without attempting to match up conventionally.

92　Herschel Garfein, email communication, November 3, 2010.

93　Roland Barthes, *Mythologies* [1957], trans. Annette Lavers (London: Vintage,

1993): 'The World of Wrestling', pp. 15-25; 'Soap-powders and Detergents', pp. 36-38; 'Striptease', pp. 84-87.

94   Morris quoted in Sharon Basco, 'Unusual Themes to Dance Program', *The Boston Herald*, February 26, 1986.

95   Acocella, *Mark Morris*, pp. 194-6.

96   Interview with Fehlandt, November 18, 2010.

97   Herschel Garfein, email communication, November 9, 2010. Other quotations from Garfein on *Championship Wrestling* stem from this email.

98   Mindy Aloff, 'Mark Morris Dance Group', *The Nation*, January 12, 1985.

99   Barthes, 'The World of Wrestling', in *Mythologies*, p. 23.

PERIOD 2 pp. 180-181

1   'The Hidden Soul of Harmony', *South Bank Show*, directed by Nigel Wattis, London Weekend Television, 1990.

2   Jeffrey Escoffier and Matthew Lore, eds., *Mark Morris' 'L'Allegro, il Penseroso ed il Moderato': A Celebration* (New York: Marlow & Company, 2001).

3   Morris, *L'Allegro, il Penseroso ed il Moderato* (DVD), directed by Vincent Bataillon, produced by François Duplat, John Walker and Joan Hershey, Bel Air Media, 2015 (broadcast WNET 13, *Great Performances*, 2015).

4   Morris, *Dido and Aeneas* (DVD), Barbara Willis Sweete (director), Image Entertainment, 2000 (broadcast Channel 4, 1995).

5   Morris, *The Hard Nut* (video/DVD), directed by Matthew Diamond, produced by Judy Kinberg, Nonesuch, video 1992, re-released as DVD, 2007 (broadcast PBS, 1992).

CHAPTER 6

1   Morris quoted in Clement Crisp, 'Mark Morris Dance Company, Coliseum, London', *The Financial Times*, April 17, 2010.

2   Joan Acocella, 'L'Allegro, il Penseroso ed il Moderato', *Ballet Review*, 17/2 (Summer, 1989), p. 9.

3   Acocella, *Mark Morris* (New York: The Noonday Press/Farrar Straus Giroux, 1993), p. 240.

4   Roger Downey, 'Secular Dialogues', note in premiere programme, Théâtre de la Monnaie, Brussels, 1988.

5   Michael O'Connell and John Powell, 'Music and Sense in Handel's Setting of Milton's *L'Allegro and Il Penseroso*', *Eighteenth-Century Studies*, 12/1 (Autumn, 1978), pp. 25-35.

6   Morris quoted in Andrew Gilbert, 'Morris' 'L'Allegro': Setting Poetry in Motion,' *San José Mercury News*, March 2, 2000.

7   Doubling is an especially frequent feature, as in the two dancing Nightingales in 'Sweet Bird', the two foxes in 'Hunt' (see p. 207) and, very briefly, a second woman crossing upstage at the end of the 'Mountains' solo.

8   Acocella, 'L'Allegro, il Penseroso ed il Moderato', p. 17.

9   'The Hidden Soul of Harmony', *South Bank Show*, directed by Nigel Wattis, London Weekend Television, 1990. An edited transcription of Morris's script during the film, 'The Hidden Soul of Harmony', is published in Selma Jeanne

Cohen, ed., *Dance as a Theatre Art: Source Reading in Dance History from 1581 to the Present* [1974] (2nd ed.; Princeton, New Jersey: Princeton Book Company, 1992), pp. 251-6. Morris refers to his movement styles on p. 255.

10 In terms of critical commentary, see in particular the essays by Acocella, 'A Silvered World' (pp. 16-21) and Alastair Macaulay, 'Creation Myth' (pp. 126-33) in Jeffrey Escoffier and Matthew Lore, eds., *Mark Morris' 'L'Allegro, il Penseroso ed il Moderato: A Celebration'* (New York: Marlow & Company, 2001).

11 Wendy Lesser, ed., 'A Mark Morris Symposium', *The Threepenny Review* (1995), pp. 20-3 and, in particular, essays (untitled) by Acocella (pp. 21-3) and Macaulay (p. 23).

12 See http://markmorrisdancegroup.org/allegro, accessed August 1, 2013.

13 Rachel Duerden, 'The Mis-shapen Pearl: Morris, Handel, Milton, and *L'Allegro, il Penseroso ed il Moderato'*, *Dance Research*, 28/2 (Winter, 2010), pp. 200-17.

14 Morris, *L'Allegro, il Penseroso ed il Moderato* (DVD), directed by Vincent Bataillon, produced by François Duplat, John Walker and Joan Hershey, Bel Air Media, 2015 (broadcast WNET 13, *Great Performances*, 2015).

15 Georg Friedrich Handel, *L'Allegro, il Penseroso ed il Moderato*, ed. James S. Hall and Martin V. Hall (Leipzig: VEB Deutscher Verlag für Musik, 1985): separate edition taken from *Hallische Händel Ausgabe*, Series I, Vol.16 (1965).

16 Interview with Morris.

17 For further up to date information about the different versions of Handel's score, see Donald Burrows, *Handel's L'Allegro, il Penseroso ed il Moderato*, programme note, English National Opera, London Coliseum, 1997; and Burrows, 'Reconstructing Handel's Performances of *L'Allegro'*, *The Musical Times* (Spring, 2013), pp. 69-76. There is now a score indicating three different versions of *L'Allegro* (from 1740, 1741 and 1743) edited by Burrows (London: Novello, 2014).

18 Interview with Morris.

19 Acocella in Lesser, ed., 'A Mark Morris Symposium', p. 22.

20 This follows Handel's precedent of performing 'two of his new op. 6 Concerti Grossi at the start of Parts One and Two': Burrows, 'Reconstructing Handel's Performances of *L'Allegro'*, p. 70.

21 There is ambiguity here already. In some editions prior to the new Burrows edition, there is no sign of the return position in the written score that is signalled by the Dal Segno at the end of section B.

22 Interview with Morris.

23 This kind of device Balanchine has used, for instance, near the end of the Coda of the first Pas de Trois in *Agon* (1957): Stephanie Jordan, *Moving Music: Dialogues with Music in Twentieth-Century Ballet* (London: Dance Books, 2000), p. 161. Sometimes, in this dance phrase by Morris, the step on to the toes is replaced by a hop.

24 Morris quoted in 'The Making of *L'Allegro'*, in Escoffier and Lore, eds. *Mark Morris' 'L'Allegro....*, p. 144.

25 Acocella, '*L'Allegro, il Penseroso ed il Moderato'*, p. 14; Mark Morris mentioned the 'eye-balls' gesture in interview.

26 Morris quoted in 'The Making of *L'Allegro'*, in Escoffier and Lore, eds., *Mark Morris' 'L'Allegro....*, p. 147.

27 Duerden, 'The Mis-shapen Pearl...', p. 207.

28 Ibid., pp. 207-8.

29   Ibid., p. 206.
30   Tina Fehlandt quoted in 'The Making of *L'Allegro*', in Escoffier and Lore, eds. *Mark Morris' 'L'Allegro.....*, p. 141.
31   Interview with Morris.
32   See note 17.
33   There are a couple of exceptions, where Morris's choreography deviates slightly from the formula.
34   Macaulay in Lesser, ed., 'A Mark Morris Symposium', p. 23.
35   Acocella, '*L'Allegro, il Penseroso ed il Moderato*', p. 14.
36   It is salutary to consider, in comparison, the visualisations of Bach's Two- and Three-Part Inventions and Mozart's Symphony No. 40 in G minor by Ted Shawn (in 1919 and 1938 respectively), which are equally driven by system (part-writing and detailed rhythm patterns), but never more than that. See Jordan, 'Ted Shawn's Music Visualizations', *Dance Chronicle*, 7/1 (1984), pp. 33-49.
37   There were, for instance, many complaints about words not being heard by critics during the 1997 performances at the London Coliseum.
38   Morris quoted in 'The Making of *L'Allegro*', in Escoffier and Lore, eds., *Mark Morris' 'L'Allegro.....*, p. 142.
39   Winton Dean, *Handel's Dramatic Oratorios and Masques* (London: Oxford University Press, 1959), p. 322.
40   Acocella mentions, however, that Morris does refer to Ben Jonson's 'learned sock' (meaning Jonson's 'comedy') through punning: the dancers sock one another and stick out their feet to show us their socks: '*L'Allegro, il Penseroso ed il Moderato*', p. 15.
41   Macaulay refers to Morris mentioning the lesbians during the Berkeley symposium, in Lesser. ed., 'A Mark Morris Symposium', p. 23.
42   When *L'Allegro* was performed at the London Coliseum in 2000, members of the ENO chorus, singing from the side boxes and thus able to watch the dancers' performance, were so excited by 'Walking Duet' that they asked the dancers to teach it to them. The conductor Jane Glover had pressed for the placement of the singers thus, so that they could see what they were enabling. Interview with Glover, January 12, 2011.
43   Morris quoted in Antony Peattie, 'Morris Dances', *BBC Music Magazine* (July, 2000), p. 32.
44   Morris quoted in Charles Siebert, 'Morris Dances', *Vanity Fair*, 52/4 (April, 1989), p. 221.
45   Other examples are as follows: the swift 5-count curving around on the spot in 'Populous Cities' (Part 2, 26), separate groups to each of the vocal entries on 'the busy hum of men'; the sudden interpolations of jerky 3s against 2s in the middle of the 'The Men's Dance'; and the more limpid 2s against 3s towards the close of the 'The Ladies' Dance'.
46   Interview with June Omura, April 16, 2010.
47   Macaulay, 'Creation Myth', p. 132.
48   Interview with Morris.
49   Ibid.
50   Morris quoted in Escoffier and Lore, eds., *Mark Morris' 'L'Allegro.....*, p. 110.
51   Morris also pointed out in interview that the movement of a woman being flung round her partner comes from 'The Men's Dance'.
52   Michael O'Connell and John Powell, 'Music and Sense in Handel's Setting of

Milton's *L'Allegro and Il Penseroso'*, pp. 35, 41.

53   Morris quoted in 'The Making of *L'Allegro'*, in Escoffier and Lore, eds., *Mark Morris' 'L'Allegro....*, p. 147.

54   Deborah Jowitt, 'Melancholy Hence!' *The Village Voice*, October 23, 1990.

55   Morris, 'The Making of *L'Allegro'*, in Escoffier and Lore, eds., *Mark Morris' 'L'Allegro....*, p. 147.

56   Acocella, '*L'Allegro, il Penseroso ed il Moderato'*, p. 17.

57   Christine Rees, ed., *Johnson's Milton* (Cambridge: Cambridge University Press, 2010), p. 171; *The Works of Samuel Johnson*, Vol. 9, Talboys and Wheeler, 1825: http://www.archive.org/details/workssamueljohn02murpgoog, accessed May 13, 2015.

58   Lesser quoted in Escoffier and Lore, eds., *Mark Morris' 'L'Allegro....*, p. 125.

CHAPTER 7

1   This chapter appeared in an earlier version in Jordan, 'Mark Morris Marks Purcell: *Dido and Aeneas* as Danced Opera', *Dance Research*, 29/2 (Winter, 2011), pp. 167-213.

2   There is at least one earlier, fully danced, setting, by the German choreographer Reinhild Hoffmann (1984), but it has received nowhere near the same level of recognition. Unusually too, Morris's radical re-vision of *Dido* was not the project of an opera company—it has always been part of his own dance company repertoire although, in 2000, the work was performed by MMDG under the auspices of English National Opera. There are many other examples of choreography within *Dido* productions. For other *Didos* with a considerable dance component, see those by Henry Oguike (2003), Sasha Waltz (2005) and Aletta Collins (2007). Catherine Turocy directed and choreographed *Dido*, in period style (1997), and Pina Bausch set the Lament within *Café Muller* (1978).

3   Morris quoted in Robert Greskovic, 'Dido is no Drag', *Interview*, June, 1990.

4   Morris quoted in Terry Teachout, 'Opera and Dance, Siblings Too Often Estranged', *The New York Times, Arts and Leisure*, June 6, 1999.

5   Gay Morris, '"Styles of the Flesh": Gender in the Dances of Mark Morris', in Gay Morris, ed., *Moving Words* (London and New York: Routledge, 1996), pp. 141-58; Ramsay Burt, *The Male Dancer* (2nd ed.; New York and London: Routledge, 2007), pp. 164-67; Selby Wynn Schwartz, 'Bad Language: Transpositions in Mark Morris's *Dido and Aeneas'*, *Dance Research Journal*, 44/2 (Winter, 2012), pp. 71-94.

6   Sophia Preston, 'Iconography and Intertextuality: The Discreet Charm of Meaning', *Proceedings of the Society of Dance History Scholars (SDHS) 21st Annual Conference*, University of Oregon, 1998, pp. 241-52; Preston, 'Mark Morris's *Dido and Aeneas'*, 2013, http://markmorrisdancegroup.org/dido, accessed July 20, 2014; Carol Martin, 'Mark Morris's *Dido and Aeneas'*, in Janet Adshead-Lansdale, ed., *Dancing Texts: Intertextuality in Interpretation* (London: Dance Books, 1999), pp. 130-47; Rachel Duerden and Bonnie Rowell, 'Mark Morris's *Dido and Aeneas* (1989): A Critical Postmodern Sensibility', *Dance Chronicle*, 36 (2013), pp. 143-71.

7   In reviews, Merkens is referred to by her former name Darragh. Morris is now clear that he prefers to see the continuity of one person in the dual role, maintaining the dramatic pressure: 'It's over in a second. I like that whirling activity of one person getting worn out by the end of it': 'Maestro! Interview:

Mark Morris Picks Up the Baton', *The Phoenix*, May 19, 2008.

8   Sophia Preston, 'Echoes and Pre-Echoes: The Displacement of Time in
    Mark Morris's *Dido and Aeneas*', *Proceedings of Dancing in the Millennium: An
    International Conference*, Washington DC, 2000, pp. 344-8. Rachel Riggs-Leyva
    discusses *Dido* in terms of dualism, and of 'visualisation' (in a broader sense
    than Ruth St Denis and Doris Humphrey) as representation of the libretto and
    translation of the musical score, using the Emile Jaques-Dalcroze framework as a
    starting place: 'Reading Music, Gesture, and Narrative in Mark Morris' *Dido and
    Aeneas*', in Melanie Bales and Karen Eliot, eds., *Dance on Its Own Terms: Histories
    and Methodologies* (New York: Oxford University Press, 2013), pp. 389-409.

9   Interviews with Bradon McDonald, April 16 and September 14, 2010. I
    interviewed Morris on *Dido* on several occasions, mainly during 2010. Unless
    otherwise indicated, all information and quotations directly attributed to Morris
    stem from these interviews. See also interview with Amber Merkens, September
    16, 2010. A variety of MMDG film recordings have been used for the analysis,
    also the commercially available 1995 film: *Dido and Aeneas* (DVD), directed by
    Barbara Willis Sweete, Image Entertainment, 2000 (broadcast Channel 4, 1995).

10 Since then, doubt has been cast on the date of the first performance. It was
    definitely performed in 1689 and, as the programme wordbook described, 'at
    Mr Josias Priest's Boarding-School at Chelsey. By Young Gentlewomen'. But
    a considerable body of recent research now suggests that it could have been
    premiered earlier in the 1680s. A recent contribution is Andrew Pinnock, '*Deus
    ex machina*: a royal witness to the court origin of Purcell's *Dido and Aeneas*,' *Early
    Music*, 40/2 (May, 2012), pp. 265-78.

11 Henry Purcell, *Dido and Aeneas An Opera*, The Norton Critical Score, ed. Curtis
    Price (New York: W.W. Norton, 1986); see the essay in this volume by Wilfrid
    Mellers, 'The Tragic Heroine and the Un-Hero', pp. 204-13. McDonald and
    Merkens trawled the Web and researched *A Woman Scorn'd: Responses to the Dido
    Myth*, a collection edited by Michael Burden (London: Faber and Faber, 1999),
    with contributions from the fields of fine art, history, English literature, classics
    and music.

12 Anthony Welch, 'The Cultural Politics of *Dido and Aeneas*,' *Cambridge Opera
    Journal*, 21/1 (March, 2009), p. 2.

13 Alastair Macaulay, 'Dido's Wounds', *The Dancing Times* (June, 2000), p. 816.

14 Ibid (drawing from Macaulay's interview with Morris).

15 Price, '*Dido and Aeneas* in Context', in Purcell, *Dido and Aeneas An Opera*, pp. 9, 27;
    Savage refers in the same volume to Dido's 'destructive anti-self', in 'Producing
    Dido and Aeneas', p. 265.

16 Ibid., p. 265.

17 Acocella, *Mark Morris*, p. 98.

18 Ibid.

19 'A Conversation with Mark Morris and Joan Acocella', International Festival of
    Arts and Ideas, Shubert Theatre, Boston, June 23, 2009 – February 25, 2010,
    online: http://blip.tv/artidea/mark-morris-3325681, accessed August 6, 2014.

20 Acocella, *Mark Morris*, p. 100.

21 Deborah Jowitt, 'Deceitful Crocodile', *The Village Voice*, June 20, 1989.

22 See Foster, 'Dido's Otherness: Choreographing Race and Gender in the Ballet
    d'action', in Susanne Franco and Marina Nordera, eds., *Dance Discourses:
    Keywords in Dance Research* (London: Routledge, 2007), p. 127; Anthony Welch,

'The Cultural Politics of *Dido and Aeneas*', p. 19 (acknowledging the suggestion of Suzanne Aspden); Janet Schmalfeldt, 'In Search of Dido', *The Journal of Musicology*, 18/4 (Autumn, 2001), pp. 587-8.

23   Macaulay, 'Dido's Wounds', p. 816.

24   'Maestro! Interview'. Choreographing his own solos on others, including women, is Morris's normal practice.

25   'Purcell's "Dido" Inspires Daring Dances of Morris', *The Ann Arbor News*, April 14, 1996.

26   Gay Morris, '"Styles of the Flesh"', p. 146. She draws from Judith Butler, *Gender Trouble: Feminism and the Subversion of Identity* (London and New York: Routledge, 1990), p. 139.

27   Merkens, email communication, August 12, 2011. Merkens and McDonald told me (see note 9) that they both performed in a burlesque show in summer 2005, the year before they shared the Dido role together. McDonald noted that this experience, which involved some cross-dressing, proved important preparation for acting the Sorceress.

28   Michael Burden has discussed the possibility of further, missing dances, in 'To Repeat (or not to repeat)? Dance Cures in Restoration English Opera', *Early Music*, 35/3 (August, 2007), pp. 397-417.

29   Carol Martin, 'Mark Morris's *Dido and Aeneas*', p. 130. The weight of chorus choreography has sometimes had an impact on readings of Morris's *Dido*. Morris enjoyed an intense, longstanding personal relationship with Resto, and that intensity was keenly felt by those on stage. However, the dancer Tina Fehlandt has suggested that, watching the work from a distance or above, or with an alternative dancer in the Dido role, has the effect of shifting the balance of power more towards the chorus (in interview, November 18, 2010); see also Thea Singer, 'Reimagining *Dido and Aeneas*', *The Boston Globe*, May 30, 2008.

30   Richard Dyer, 'Listening to Mark Morris' *Dido*', *The Boston Globe*, June 9, 1989.

31   See for further discussion Jordan, 'Choreomusical Conversations: Facing a Double Challenge', *Dance Research Journal*, 43/1 (Summer, 2011), p. 58.

32   'A Conversation with Mark Morris and Joan Acocella'. The costume designs are by Christine Van Loon, the lighting by James F. Ingalls.

33   Morris quoted in Janice Berman, 'Daring Dancing', *New York Newsday*, Part II, June 21, 1990.

34   Acocella, *Mark Morris*, p. 192.

35   Jowitt, 'Back-to-Back Glories: Operas from Two Centuries Assume Vibrant Contemporary Life', *The Village Voice*, March 21, 2006.

36   See Preston, 'Echoes and Pre-Echoes'. I am grateful to Preston for opening up this issue for debate.

37   Interview with Sweete in 'Mark Morris: Dance on Camera', Lincoln Center Dance on Camera Festival, January 13, 2007.

38   Interview with June Omura, April 16, 2010.

39   Acocella, *Mark Morris*, p. 143, which also includes a photograph of the 'fate' pose.

40   The Spirit in the Sweete film is not danced by the Sorceress, but by a chorus 'in the heavens'.

41   Price, '*Dido and Aeneas* in Context', p. 34.

42   Inger Damsholt reflects upon Morris's response to the look of the musical score in: 'Mark Morris, Mickey Mouse, and Choreomusical Polemic', *The Opera Quarterly*,

22/1 (Winter, 2006), pp. 14-15.

43   Martin Adams, *Henry Purcell: The Origins and Development of His Musical Style* (Cambridge: Cambridge University Press, 1995), p. 279.

44   Ibid.

45   We might argue here that the Sorceress is merely enacting the real textual meaning 'deprived of...life', except that, within the same phrases, she matches 'fame' and 'love' 'correctly', and we might easily overlook the word 'deprived'.

46   Acocella, *Mark Morris*, p. 98.

47   Duerden and Rowell, 'Mark Morris's *Dido and Aeneas*', p. 148.

48   Morris first borrowed the SATB model from music in *Gloria* (Vivaldi, 1981) and used it extensively during this early work (see pp. 138-45).

49   Dancer David Leventhal drew attention to the rhythms of this passage as something he had to consider carefully as distinct from his own dance pattern: interview, April 16, 2010 and email communication, August 1, 2011.

50   Wilfrid Mellers, 'The Tragic Heroine and the Un-Hero', in Price, p. 208.

51   Preston, 'Echoes and Pre-Echoes', p. 346.

52   Mellers, 'The Tragic Heroine and the Un-Hero', p. 208.

53   Preston draws attention to the harmonic surprise at this point, 'Echoes and Pre-Echoes', p. 347.

54   This is related stylistically to the 'Gather'd from Elysian bowers' passage in 'Fear no danger' (see p. 24).

55   Mellers, 'The Tragic Heroine and the Un-Hero', p. 208.

56   Interview with Leventhal, April 16, 2010.

57   Mellers, 'The Tragic Heroine and the Un-Hero', p. 211.

58   There are distinct references back to Martha Graham's famous *Lamentation* (1930). Here, Graham sits on a bench enclosed head to toe in a piece of cloth that stretches expressively as she pulls her legs wide and extends her torso through space.

59   Ellen Rosand, 'The Descending Tetrachord: An Emblem of Lament', *The Musical Quarterly*, 65 (1979), p. 356.

60   Schmalfeldt, 'In Search of Dido', p. 608.

61   Adam Ockelford, 'More Than the Sum of its Parts: Conceptual Blending in Dido's Lament', Research Seminar, University of Roehampton, October 14, 2008.

62   I am grateful to Lawrence Zbikowski for highlighting for me this reading of Dido's aria: email communication December 14, 2010.

63   See *Purcell: Dido and Aeneas*, Conductor Andrew Parrott (Emma Kirkby as Dido), Chandos CD, 2000. The 1994 MMDG archive recording of Lorraine Hunt performing with the Morris Group in Adelaide shows a marked increase in volume during the repeat of Part 2. Earlier performances with Hunt in a dress rehearsal prior to the 1989 Brussels premiere (sound recording only) as well as in a 1989 company video show both accounts of Part 2 matching very closely.

64   We could also take into account the role of inner instrumental lines.

65   I am grateful to Kimiko Okamoto for pointing out the harmonic construction that creates the halting effect: email communication, November 19, 2010.

66   In 1989, Morris walks more evenly and slowly in the circle than in later recordings, maintaining the same level with bent knees—there is no suspension at the side, but he holds at centre front for longer. Nor does he raise his outside arm on the repeat of the circle.

67   Interviews with McDonald and Merkens.

68   Macaulay referred to *Dido* directing the same gesture to 'east, west, south and
      north' in his review 'Dido and Aeneas', *The Financial Times*, August 20, 1992.
69   Interview with McDonald, September 14, 2010.
70   Preston, 'Echoes and Pre-Echoes', p. 348. See also the list in Duerden and Rowell,
      'Mark Morris's *Dido and Aeneas* (1989): A Critical Postmodern Sensibility', pp. 150-2.

CHAPTER 8

1   The main film source is *The Hard Nut* (video/DVD), directed by Matthew Diamond,
      produced by Judy Kinberg, Nonesuch, 1992, re-released as DVD, 2007 (broadcast
      PBS, 1992).
2   Joan Acocella, *Mark Morris*, p. 190.
3   See Jennifer Fisher, *'Nutcracker' Nation: How an Old World Ballet Became a
      Christmas Tradition in the New World* (New Haven and London: Yale University
      Press, 2003); Alastair Macaulay, 'The Sugarplum Diet', *The New York Times*,
      November 10, 2010.
4   Details of recordings of *The Nutcracker* viewed in comparison with *The Hard Nut*
      are as follows:
      The Royal Ballet, Rudolf Nureyev [1963], incorporating choreography by Vassily
      I. Vainonen, directed and produced by John Vernon, Kultur, DVD, 2000; The
      Royal Ballet, Lev Ivanov and Peter Wright [1984], directed by John Vernon, The
      National Video Corporation, 1985; New York City Ballet, George Balanchine
      [1954], directed by Emile Ardolino, produced by Robert A.Krasnow and Robert
      Hurwitz, Warner Brothers Entertainment, video, 1993; American Ballet Theatre,
      Mikhail Baryshnikov [1976], incorporating choreography by Vassily I Vainonen,
      directed by Tony Charmoli, produced by Yanna Kroyt Brandt, Kultur, DVD, 2004;
      Kirov Ballet, Vassily I. Vainonen, directed by Yvon Gérault, produced by Michio
      Takemori, Cameras Continentales/NHK, Philips Classics Productions, Amaya
      Distribution, video, 1994; Bolshoi Ballet, Yuri Grigorovich [1989], produced
      by Lothar Bock, Arthaus Musik: Bolshoi Theatre, NHK Enterprises, Videofilm/
      Bolshoi, Japan Arts Corporation, DVD, 2005; Matthew Bourne, *Nutcracker!*
      [1992, a re-vision of the traditional ballet], directors Kieran O'Brien and Ross
      McGibbon, producer Simon Flind, Screen Stage for BBC, DVD and BBC broadcast,
      2003.
5   Morris quoted in Iris Fanger, 'Dancing to a Different Beat', *The Boston Herald*, June
      8, 1990.
6   Sarah H. Cohen, 'Performing Identity in *The Hard Nut*: Stereotype, Modeling and
      the Inventive Body', *The Yale Journal of Criticism*, 11/2 (1998), p. 487; pp. 489-90.
7   Alastair Macaulay suggests that Alexei Ratmansky may be the only other
      choreographer who plays all the music in the right order: 'A Diversity of
      "Nutcrackers"', *The New York Times*, December 18, 2013.
8   Morris quoted in Gia Kourlas, '*The Hard Nut*: Mark Morris Cracks Open his
      Seasonal Classic', *Time Out New York*, December 3, 2010: http://www.timeout.
      com/newyork/art/the-hard-nut, accessed August 10, 2013.
9   Ibid.
10   Roland John Wiley, *Tchaikovsky's Ballets* (Oxford: Oxford University Press, 1985),
      pp. 371-3. Morris did not read this book as part of his preparations for *The Hard
      Nut*.
11   Jennifer Dunning, 'Mark Morris Gives 'The Nutcracker' a Twist', *The New York

Times, December 6, 1992.

12 Wiley, *Tchaikovsky's Ballets*, p. 376.

13 David Vaughan, 'Mark Morris: Here and There—II', *Ballet Review* (Spring, 1991), p. 53.

14 Morris quoted in Acocella, *Mark Morris*, p. 199.

15 Wiley, *Tchaikovsky's Ballets*, p. 376.

16 In terms of references to the nineteenth-century pas de deux, there are a few hints of the vocabulary, from what is considered to be the original Ivanov choreography: a version of the fish dive, the *développé* into second position and turn into *arabesque*, the repeating turns circling the stage, and the *pirouettes* with the leg in second position (performed by twelve dancers in Morris's coda).

17 Cohen, 'Performing Identity in *The Hard Nut...*', p. 501.

18 Acocella, *Mark Morris*, p. 147.

19 Wiley, *Tchaikovsky's Ballets*, p. 334.

20 Ibid., p. 372.

21 This could be called 'mickey-mousing' but the word 'stinger' feels more apt in this context. On the 'stinger' in film, see Claudia Gorbman, *Unheard Melodies: Narrative Film Music* (Bloomington: Indiana University Press, 1987), pp. 88-9.

22 Aaron Mattocks, 'Mark Morris and The Hard Nut', *Culturebot*, December 15, 2010: http://culturebot.net/2010/12/8988/mark-morris-and-the-hard-nut/, accessed August 10, 2013.

23 Wiley, *Tchaikovsky's Ballets*, p. 235.

24 Ibid., p. 374.

25 Accented airborne moments can also be seen in the Adagio that introduces the Act 2 pas de deux and in the duet between Drosselmeier and Young Drosselmeier.

26 Morris quoted in 'The Hidden Soul of Harmony', *South Bank Show*, directed by Nigel Wattis, London Weekend Television, 1990.

27 Interview with Mikhail Baryshnikov, June 21, 2011.

28 Clement Crisp and David Vaughan were both reminded of character play in John Huston's film *The Maltese Falcon* (1941). See Crisp, 'Mark Morris and Baryshnikov', *The Financial Times*, November 7, 1989; Vaughan, 'Two Leaders: Mark Morris and Garth Fagan', *Ballet Review* (Summer, 1990), p. 40.

29 Interview with Morris. Morris's early *Handel Choruses* (1985) were another experiment in using a minimal cast against huge musical scoring.

30 Malcolm MacDonald, *Schoenberg* ('The Master Musicians') (London; J.M. Dent, 1976), p. 115.

31 Deborah Jowitt, 'When Worlds Collide: Mark Morris Meets Maurice Béjart', *The Village Voice*, December 6, 1989.

32 *Rashomon* (1950) is a Japanese film based on a 1915 short story 'In a Grove' by Ryunosuke Akutagawa. It relates the rape of a woman and the murder of her samurai husband from four different angles, through the mutually contradictory accounts of four witnesses, the bandit/rapist, the wife, the dead man (speaking through a medium), and the narrator.

33 Macaulay, 'The Prophet Without Honour', *The Weekend Guardian*, November 25-26, 1989.

34 Morris quoted in 'The Hidden Soul of Harmony', *South Bank Show*.

35 Rob Besserer, email communication, January 18, 2012; interview with Morris.

36 Interview with Morris.

37 MacDonald, *Schoenberg*, p. 116.

38 The celesta is heard again when Davidson repeats this in the fifth of the *Five Pieces*: bars 450-1.
39 Dale Harris, 'Mark Morris Back in U.S., Triumphantly', *The Wall Street Journal*, July 6, 1990; Christine Temin, 'Morris' New Surprise: A Dance to Silence', *The Boston Globe*, June 12, 1990.
40 Temin, Ibid.
41 Acocella, *Mark Morris*, p. 165.
42 Oliver Sacks, *Awakenings* [1973] (London: Picador, 1990), p. 60. Morris, however, denies that he used this source for his dance.
43 Macaulay, 'While the Music Lasts', *The New Yorker*, May 11, 1992, p. 83.
44 Morris quoted in Roslyn Sulcas, 'Man on the Move', *Dance and Dancers* (January/ February, 1992), p. 10.
45 Acocella, *Mark Morris*, p. 114.
46 Macaulay, 'While the Music Lasts', p. 83.

PERIOD 3 pp. 283-285

1 Interview with Morris.

CHAPTER 9

1 Morris quoted in Laura Bleiberg, 'The New Song and Dance Director', *The Orange County Register*, April 21, 1996. In interview with Jordan, Morris explained this as his rejection of the fanciful production style of European 'directors theatre'.
2 ['Mark Morris talks to Lynn Garafola about his offbeat opera career'], *Opera News*, April, 2007, p. 36.
3 John Rockwell, 'A Frigidaire in the Court of King Arthur', *The New York Times*, March 2, 2008.
4 Terry Teachout, 'Opera and Dance, Siblings Too Often Estranged', *The New York Times, Arts and Leisure*, June 6, 1999. There is also the celebrated instance of Michel Fokine's production of *Le Coq d'or* for Diaghilev's Ballets Russes in 1914: its roles were aurally and visually divided between singers ranged up the sides of the stage and dancers miming the action in the space between them.
5 Morris quoted in Terry Teachout, 'Opera and Dance, Siblings Too Often Estranged'.
6 Morris quoted in Allan Ulrich, 'Song and Dance: Choreographers Invade Opera', *Dance Magazine* (January, 2007), p. 76.
7 Morris quoted in Alan Morrison, 'Pushing his Gluck', *The List*, August 16-22, 1996.
8 Morris quoted in Mark Swed, 'On Good Behavior', *The Los Angeles Times Calendar*, April 24, 1996.
9 Morris quoted in Jann Parry, 'Girl Seeks Boy. Good Sense of Humour. Green Skin Preferred', *The Observer Review*, August 3, 1997.
10 Michael Chance quoted in Nick Kimberley, 'Not Waving But Dancing', *The Independent*, August 14, 1996.
11 Richard Taruskin, *Music in the Seventeenth and Eighteenth Centuries* (*The Oxford History of Western Music*, Volume 2), (Oxford, New York: Oxford University Press, 2010), p. 453.
12 Ibid., p. 455.

13   Recent research by Bruce Alan Brown demonstrates that *Orfeo* was directly stimulated by the experimental, reform ballet-pantomime that developed in Vienna at the time, and probably gained considerably from the shared experience of the same three collaborators working on the ballet-pantomime *Don Juan* the year before the *Orfeo* premiere (1761). Brown refers not only to the precedent of this genre in its use of the work of the 'ancients' as aesthetic basis but also to its formal models and new approaches to continuity. See Brown, *Gluck and the French Theatre in Vienna* (Oxford: Clarendon Press, 1991).

14   Joan Acocella, 'Reviews: Eye on Performance—Seattle', *Dance Magazine* (April, 1988), p. 18.

15   Acocella, 'Morris Dances', *Art in America* (October, 1988), p. 181. Acocella adds that Morris's chaconne, traditionally the last dance in a final divertissement (prior to the Minuet here) moves in the rose pattern recorded in Fabritio Caroso's *Nobiltà di Dame* (1600), although Morris does not recall using this source.

16   Morris quoted in Christine Temin, 'Mark Morris Goes for Baroque...Again', *The Boston Globe*, March 31, 1996.

17   Ibid.

18   Morris's other 'Arcadian' pieces are his settings of *Socrates* and *Sylvia*, both of these again dressed by Martin Pakledinaz, and *The Death of Socrates*, with designs by Robert Bordo.

19   Temin, 'Boston', *Ballet Review* (Summer, 1996), p. 4.

20   Interview with Morris.

21   Morris and Pakledinaz quoted in Temin, 'Mark Morris Goes for Baroque...'.

22   Morris quoted in Temin, 'Mark Morris Goes for Baroque...'.

23   The words vary slightly in repetition, but not in meaning. They are taken here from the *Live from Lincoln Center* broadcast, The Metropolitan Opera, January 24, 2009.

24   ['Mark Morris talks to Lynn Garafola about his offbeat opera career'], p. 36.

25   Michael Chance quoted in Scott Duncan, 'Going After the Higher Concept', *The Orange County Register*, April 21, 1996.

26   Also fine is the final group of celebratory dances to different music in the 1988 Seattle *Orpheus & Eurydice*.

27   Brown, *Gluck and the French Theatre in Vienna*, p. 367.

28   Morris in interview with Cori Ellison, January 31, 2008: http://podcast.nycopera. com/pr/nycopera/podcast/podcast-post.aspx?id=692, accessed August 20, 2015.

29   Morris quoted in Michael Pye, 'Do Not Adjust Your Opera Glasses', *Edinburgh Festival (Magazine)*, 1997 [from fax copy sent to MMDG, July 11, 1997]. The names of characters in this analysis here appear as in the Royal Opera House programme.

30   Wendy Lesser, 'Amphibious Pleasures', *The Threepenny Review*, 75 (Autumn, 1998), p. 21.

31   Morris quoted in Georgia Rowe, 'A Full "Platée",' *Contra Costa Times*, June 4, 1998.

32   Mizrahi quoted in Christopher Bowen, 'Swamp Thing Comes A-Courtin', *San Francisco Sunday Examiner and Chronicle*, June 7, 1998.

33   Lesser, 'Amphibious Pleasures', p. 22.

34   Acocella, 'Rameau's World According to Mark Morris', *The Wall Street Journal*, June 16, 1998.

35   Morris quoted in Michael Pye, 'Do Not Adjust Your Opera Glasses'.

36   Graham Sadler, 'A Testament to Comic Genius', The Royal Opera programme [Covent Garden], 1997, p. 16.

37   Lesser, 'Amphibious Pleasures', p. 22.

38   Jann Parry, 'Edinburgh Festival', Dance Now, 6/3 (Autumn, 1997), p. 17.

39   Morris quoted in Nancy Dalva, 'New York City Opera: Something Old, Something New', Playbill, March 4, 2008, www.playbillarts.com/news/article/7576.html, accessed August 20, 2013.

40   Ibid.

41   Ibid.

42   Morris in interview with Cori Ellison. This Chaconne has sometimes been played as the overture to King Arthur.

43   Andrew Foster-Williams quoted in Lesser, 'The Past Recaptured', The Threepenny Review, 75 (Summer, 2007), p. 32.

44   Lesser, Ibid.

45   There is also the one-act Cargo (2005) to Darius Milhaud's La Création du monde, but this contains the mere sketch of a story, the games of a cargo cult resulting in a deadly ending.

46   Tchaikovsky quoted in David Nice, 'Would You Give Up the Ring for Sylvia', The Royal Ballet Sylvia programme, 2004; the quotation is from the composer's letter to Nadezhda von Meck, November 23/December 5, 1877.

47   Gia Kourlas, 'Bows, Arrows and Sylvia,' Time Out New York, July 20-26, 2006, p. 84.

48   Mark Morris, 'Creating Sylvia', Dance Magazine (May, 2004), p. 53.

49   Morris, 'Creating Sylvia', p. 50. Morris also mentions early use of the saxophone in a symphonic context, referring to an alto saxophone, as lyrical instrument, introduced for the Barcarolle of Act 3.

50   David Vaughan, 'Two Choreographers', Ballet Review (Winter, 2006), p. 51. The Valse Lente is the number with a striking harp accompaniment.

51   The photograph of Olga Preobrajenska as Sylvia, St. Petersburg, 1901 appears in: http://en.wikipedia.org/wiki/Sylvia_(ballet), accessed August 20, 2013.

52   The major sources used in researching Morris's Romeo and Juliet were Simon Morrison's book The People's Artist: Prokofiev's Soviet Years (Oxford: Oxford University Press, 2009): it includes the original scenario, pp. 395-402; Morrison's programme notes; the website on the Morris production: Sergey Prokofiev's Romeo and Juliet, On Motifs of Shakespeare http://lovelives.net, accessed August 21, 2013; Serge Prokofiev, Romeo and Juliet [piano score, 1940 version] (Hamburg: Musikverlag Hans Sikorski, 1958).

53   Sergei Radlov quoted in Morrison's programme note.

54   Prokofiev quoted in Morrison, The People's Artist, pp. 37-8.

55   Morrison says that there is no certainty about what ending was premiered in Brno, but it appears, from the evidence of the dancer in the role of Juliet, that Prokofiev's two orchestral suites were danced with a speaking chorus filling in the details of the plot: email communication, August 4, 2012. I am very grateful to Morrison for examining my text and adding further information on the score.

56   Morrison quoted in Acocella, 'Romeo, Romeo', The New Yorker, July 7, 2008.

57   Morrison, email communication.

58   Once Prokofiev's intended structure had been determined, the composer Gregory Spears set about orchestrating the happy ending music, using as his models the composer's original orchestration for the scherzo from the Fifth Symphony (1944) and the 1938 ballet suites (numbers 1 and 2), all of which included

passages of music from the abandoned early ballet score.

59 Morrison, *The People's Artist*, pp. 395-402.

60 Morris in interview with Jeff Spurgeon, WQXR, July, 2008.

61 This distinction was clearly recognised by Deborah Jowitt, 'Star-Crossed Lovers Saved!' *The Village Voice*, July 16, 2008; and by Gia Kourlas, 'Merriment (and Eternal Love) in Both Their Houses', *The New York Times*, May 15, 2009.

62 Morris in interview with Spurgeon.

63 Andrea de Jorio, *Gesture in Naples and Gesture in Classical Antiquity* [La mimica degli antichi investigata nel gestire napoletano, 1832], ed. and trans. Adam Kendon, Bloomington and Indianapolis: Indiana University Press, 2000; Morris also used Edward Muir, *Mad Blood Stirring: Vendetta in Renaissance Italy* (London: John Hopkins University Press, 1998).

64 Jowitt, 'Star-Crossed Lovers Saved!'

65 Paul Parish, 'Never-ending Love', *Bay Area Reporter*, October 2, 2008.

66 Morrison points out in his email communication that the original idea was to interrupt the Renaissance Verona action with a 'Soviet' procession, thus making the allegorical connection between the youthful revolutionaries of the past and present explicit.

67 *Romeo and Juliet*, Lavrovsky [1989], with revised choreography by Yuri Grigorovich, Arthaus Musik: Bolshoi Theatre, NHK Enterprises, DVD, 2004.

68 Morrison points out that Prokofiev's manuscript calls for an onstage bell in Act 1 and gong in Act 4: email communication.

69 Morrison, *The People's Artist*, p. 39; and see note 58 on Fifth Symphony.

70 Morrison, *The People's Artist*, p. 402.

71 Acocella, 'Romeo, Romeo', p. 47.

72 Eric Griffiths, 'Time Together, No Time to Spare', *Times Literary Supplement*, November 21, 2008.

73 Morrison, *The People's Artist*, p. 402.

74 Morrison, email communication.

75 Morris quoted in Acocella, 'Romeo, Romeo', p. 47.

76 Lesser, 'In Fair Verona', *The Threepenny Review*, 117 (Spring, 2009), http://www.threepennyreview.com/samples/lesser_sp09.html, accessed August 19, 2013.

CHAPTER 10

1 Joan Acocella, *Mark Morris*, pp. 137-58, 'The Story'.

2 Acocella, *Mark Morris*, pp. 171-4.

3 Letter from Thomson to Stein (December 6, 1933) in Donald Gallup, ed. *The Flowers of Friendship: Letters Written to Gertrude Stein* (New York: Alfred A. Knopf, 1953), p. 272. Morris researched the original *Four Saints* production thoroughly. One of his key sources was Steven Watson, *Prepare for Saints: Gertrude Stein, Virgil Thomson, and the Mainstreaming of American Modernism* (New York: Random House, 1998). More recently, a new *Four Saints* score has been published with an introductory essay that proved invaluable to analysis: ed. H.Wiley Hitchcock and Charles Fussell (Middleton, Wisconsin: A-R Editions, 2008).

4 In 1927 Stein wrote the *Four Saints* text; Thomson wrote the piano score in 1928.

5 Liner note to RCA Victor DM-1244 (1948) quoting a 1942 radio talk.

6 Gertrude Stein, *Everybody's Autobiography* (New York: Random House, 1937), p. 112.

7   Daniel Albright, *Untwisting the Serpent: Modernism in Music, Literature, and Other Arts* (Chicago and London: The University of Chicago Press, 2000), p. 354.
8   Stein, *Lectures in America* (New York: Vintage Books, 1975), p. 122.
9   Jane Bowers, 'The Writer in the Theater: Gertrude Stein's Four Saints in Three Acts', in Michael J. Hoffmann, ed., *Critical Essays on Gertrude Stein* (Boston: G.K. Hall, 1986), p. 212.
10   Thomson, *Music with Words: A Composer's View* (New Haven, Conn.: Yale University Press, 1989), p. 110.
11   Albright, *Untwisting the Serpent*, p. 322.
12   Leonard Bernstein's review of Stein's *Last Operas and Plays* (1949) in *The New York Times*, quoted by Peter Dickinson, 'Virgil Thomson, Gertrude Stein and "Four Saints"', English National Opera programme, London, 2000.
13   Albright, *Untwisting the Serpent*, p. 331.
14   Ibid., p. 311.
15   Thomson, *Music with Words*, p. 52.
16   Ulla E. Dydo, with William Rice, *Gertrude Stein: The Language That Rises 1923-1934* (Evanston, Illinois: Northwestern University Press, 2003), p. 199; Dydo refers to William Carlos Williams, 'A 1 Pound Stein', *Selected Essays of William Carlos Williams* (New York: Random House, 1954), p. 162.
17   Albright, *Untwisting the Serpent*, pp. 344-6.
18   'Virgil Thomson: The Composer in Conversation with Bruce Duffie' (1985): http://www.bruceduffie.com/vt.html, accessed June 29, 2012.
19   Thomson, *A Virgil Thomson Reader* (New York: E.P. Dutton, 1981), p. 528.
20   Thomson changed Stein's spelling of Thérèse to Teresa.
21   Albright, *Untwisting the Serpent*, p. 354.
22   Interview with Morris.
23   Introductory essay to the 2008 score of *Four Saints*, p. lii.
24   RCA Victor DM-1244 (1948). In the original production there was one intermission; Morris dispenses with this in his shorter version of the score.
25   Interview with Morris.
26   Albright, *Untwisting the Serpent*, p. 355.
27   All text quotations in my analysis draw from the text that Morris selected. Morris seems to have been unusual in returning to the original text for his production, and not to the Grosser scenario, although Robert Wilson did the same for his 1996 production; see Ulla E. Dydo, with William Rice, *Gertrude Stein*, p. 202.
28   Albright, *Untwisting the Serpent*, p. 352.
29   Ibid., p. 343.
30   Richard Capell, *Schubert's Songs* [1928] (New York: Macmillan, 1957 [2nd edition]), p. 109; Donald Francis Tovey, *Essays in Musical Analysis*, Vol. V (London: Oxford University Press, 1937), p. 195.
31   Lawrence Kramer, *Music and Poetry: The Nineteenth Century and After* (Berkeley, Los Angeles and London: University of California Press, 1984), p. 149.
32   Christopher H. Gibbs, "Komm, geh' mit mir': Schubert's Uncanny Erlkönig', *19th-Century Music*, 19/2 (Autumn, 1995), pp. 132-3.
33   Carolyn Abbate, *Unsung Voices: Opera and Musical Narrative in the Nineteenth Century* (Princeton: Princeton University Press, 1991), p. 72. See also Lorraine Byrne, *Schubert's Goethe Settings* (Farnham, Surrey: Ashgate, 2003), p. 233.
34   Acocella, *Mark Morris*, p. 154.
35   Gibbs, "Komm, geh' mit mir", p. 133.

36 Acocella, *Mark Morris*, p. 154.
37 Kramer, *Music and Poetry*, pp. 158-9.
38 Morris, email communication, June 26, 2014.
39 Acocella, *Mark Morris*, p. 154.
40 Interview with Morris.
41 Acocella, 'The Music Man', *The New Yorker*, March 18, 2002, http://www. newyorker.com/archive/2002/03/18/020318crte_television, accessed August 24, 2013.
42 Morris quoted in interview (November 15, 2010) with Alice Miller Cotter, '*Socrates*: Mark Morris on Death and Dying', *Dance Research*, 32/1 (2014), p. 2.
43 *Socrates* was Morris's first dance to use surtitles. He had used them previously in operas, *Platée* (a translation from the French) and *King Arthur* (the original Dryden text).
44 Vladimir Jankélévich, 'Music and the Ineffable', trans. Carolyn Abbate (Princeton: Princeton University Press, 2003), pp. 48, 146-67.
45 Morris quoted in interview with Cotter.
46 Alan Gilmor, *Erik Satie* (Basingstoke and London: Macmillan Press, 1988), p. 223.
47 Unless otherwise indicated, information on the working process behind *Socrates* comes from Jordan's interviews with Morris.
48 Francis Poulenc's May 15, 1920 letter to Paul Collaer quoted in Collaer, 'La fin des Six et de Satie', *La revue générale: perspectives européennes des sciences humaines*, 6-7 (June-July, 1974), p. 2.
49 Pietro Dossena, 'A la recherche du vrai *Socrate*', *Journal of the Royal Musical Association*, 133/1 (2008), p. 4. Satie was deeply moved by the Socrates story, linking it with the sacrifice of Christ, Dossena suggests, and he felt that he too was a victim, facing punishment for responding abusively to negative response to his *Parade* score, pp. 12-13.
50 The recording that had inspired Morris was *Erik Satie: Socrate*, performed by Hugues Cuénod (tenor) and Geoffrey Parsons (piano), recorded 1977 or earlier, Nimbus Records, NI 5027 (1985).
51 Interview with Morris.
52 Morris's initial idea was to work with the British singer Mark Padmore and his Music Director pianist Ethan Iverson.
53 Translation of the *Socrates* text by Roger Nichols, 1985, included in the MMDG programme.
54 Morris found 'not using hands' interesting for a change. He enjoyed the idea of a towing device using a short rope while noting its resonance with the idea of slavery. He was also influenced by Aristophanes' speech from Plato's symposium, claiming that human beings are all 'halves' wanting unity with their other half, and that there are varieties of union: man-woman, woman-woman, man-man. Morris says that he began his working process by staging a symposium discussion in the rehearsal studio, with the dancers seated, eating and drinking.
55 Morris is not pedantic about following such musical patterns: if theatrical need tells him, he quietly breaks out of them, and the spectator may not even notice this.
56 Cotter, '*Socrates*: Mark Morris on Death and Dying', pp. 7-8.
57 When, for instance, in Part 3, Satie's opening eight bars are recapitulated, a key structural pillar within the score, Morris's accompanying 'rhythm' dancers occupy a different part of the stage from before, now stage right, rather than left, and

behind the 'narrative' dancers, who again line up, but more rapidly, downstage right. The dancers were often free to make choices in performance, where to perform something on stage, whether to pick up a cloak for Part 2, although, for reasons of memory, they usually ended up setting the material for performance.

58   Translation of the *Socrates* text by Roger Nichols.

59   Alastair Macaulay, 'Cheekily Defying Expectations', *The New York Times*, February 24, 2010.

60   Cotter, '*Socrates*: Mark Morris on Death and Dying', p. 17.

61   At the very end of each Part of *Socrate*, Satie adds a sideways shift in pitch, disrupting harmonic stability.

CHAPTER 11

1   *The Office* is a very disturbing dance in which a group in captivity are compelled to leave the stage one by one. People immediately linked the dance to the Bosnia conflict, but Morris prefers not to be that specific.

2   I am grateful to the scholar Sophia Preston for alerting me to this comparison with Morris's use of the music of other composers. In relation to this chapter, Preston has published two important articles on Morris and Harrison (including reference to other West Coast American composers): 'Mark Morris and Lou Harrison, 'Trans-ethnicism' and 'Elastic Form', *Choreologica*, 6/1 (Winter, 2013), pp. 57-68 [including analyses of *Strict Songs* and *World Power*]; 'Mark Morris and the American Avant-garde: From Ultra-Modernism to Postmodernism', *Dance Chronicle*, 37/1 (2014), pp. 6-46 [arguing for relations with the work of the American modern dance pioneers, Morris's use of non-progressive form and self-reflexive, postmodern approach, including analyses of *Barstow*, *Castor and Pollux* (to Harry Partch), *Prelude and Prelude* and *Mosaic and United* (to Henry Cowell), *Strict Songs*, *Grand Duo* and *World Power* (to Harrison)].

3   'Silver' was Harrison's middle name; nothing (at least nothing obvious) rhymes with it.

4   In April, 1993, the work was performed at BAM, as part of a programme entitled 'Dances to American Music'.

5   In April, 1997, the work was performed at BAM, as part of a programme entitled 'In Honor of the Divine Lou Harrison'.

6   Leta E. Miller and Fredric Lieberman, *Composing a World: Lou Harrison, Musical Wayfarer* [1998] (Urbana and Chicago: University of Illinois Press, 2ⁿᵈ ed. 2004), p. 86. This is the seminal text on Harrison and has been used extensively here for factual information about his life and work.

7   Harrison quoted in Miller and Lieberman, *Composing a World*, p. 220. In Morris's 2006 programme for *King Arthur*, a similar quotation appears: 'Music is a song and a dance.'

8   *Lou Harrison: A World of Music*, directed and produced by Eva Soltes, 2012.

9   Harrison, 'Asian Music and the United States', in *Third Asian Composers' League Conference/Festival Final Report* (Manila: National Music Council of the Philippines, 1976), p. 87.

10   Kathleen Ashley and Véronique Plesch, 'The Cultural Processes of Appropriation', *Journal of Medieval and Early Modern Studies*, 32/1 (2002), p. 6.

11   Maria Cizmic, 'Composing the Pacific: Interview with Lou Harrison', *Echo* (1999) http://www.echo.ucla.edu/Volume1-Issue1/cizmic/cizmic-interview.html,

accessed August 28, 2013.

12 Morris quoted in Miller and Lieberman, *Composing a World*, p. 98 (from a
    November 6, 1995 interview with the authors).

13 McPhee was one of the earliest Westerners to research Balinese music; both
    Harrison and Morris had read his book *A House in Bali* [1947] (North Clarendon,
    Vt.: Tuttle Publishing, 2000).

14 Beth Genné, '*Gong*: A New Mark Morris Work at the Royal Ballet', *The Dancing
    Times* (October, 2002), p. 47.

15 Alessandra Lopez y Royo, 'The Prince of the Pagodas, Gong and Tabuh-Tabuhan,'
    Indonesia and the Malay World, 35/101 (March, 2007), p. 58. See also Cizmic,
    'Composing the Pacific'; Philip Brett and Elizabeth Wood, 'Lesbian and Gay
    Music', *Electronic Musicological Review*, 7 (2002), p. 19: http://www.rem.ufpr.br/_
    REM/REMv7/Brett_Wood/Brett_and_Wood.html, accessed August 28, 2013.

16 Lopez y Royo, 'The Prince of the Pagodas, Gong and Tabuh-Tabuhan', p. 58.

17 Ibid., p. 59.

18 Morris calls his all-male 2012 ballet *Beaux* exceptional in this respect—'gay', he
    says, because the men actively cooperate rather than fighting or competing with
    each other. It is dressed in pink unitards.

19 Miller and Lieberman, *Composing a World*, Ch. 10 and p. 191.

20 Miller, 'Henry Cowell and Modern Dance: The Genesis of Elastic Form', *American
    Music*, 20/1 (Spring, 2002), p. 4.

21 Henry Cowell, 'Relating Music and Concert Dance: An Idea for Elastic Form',
    from *Dance Observer*, January 1937, abridged and reprinted in Katherine Teck,
    ed., *Making Music for Modern Dance: Collaboration in the Formative Years of a New
    American Art* (Oxford, New York: Oxford University Press, 2011), p. 90.

22 Cowell was also concerned that choreographers should develop their sense of
    form. With that in view, in 1939, he proposed that Indian drumming principles
    could provide a useful model for choreographers, functioning over both long and
    short timespans: Cowell, 'East Indian Tala Music', from *Dance Observer*, December
    1939, reprinted in Teck, *Making Music for Modern Dance*, pp. 208-10.

23 Miller, 'Henry Cowell and Modern Dance...', pp. 12-16.

24 Preston comments on the connection with early American modern dance in both
    her articles, see note 2.

25 Miller, 'Henry Cowell and Modern Dance...' pp. 1-2. Miller's source here was
    Harrison's letter to Cowell, n.d. New York Public Library Cowell papers.

26 The Air is indicated 'Slow and sometimes rhapsodically'. It is about ten and a
    half minutes long—the other four movements already total about twenty-five
    minutes.

27 In *Gong*, Morris felt free to add silent interludes within the score in order to
    alleviate the 'push' of McPhee's 'relentless duple metre': Morris quoted in Genné,
    '*Gong*', p. 48.

28 For further information about *Strict Songs*, see Miller and Lieberman, *Composing a
    World*, pp. 54, 113-14.

29 *Pacific* has also been staged on Washington Ballet, Pacific Northwest Ballet and
    Grand Théâtre de Genève.

30 According to Miller and Lieberman (*Composing a World*, p. 336, note 91),
    Harrison took this text from Howard Zinn, *A People's History of the United States*
    (New York: Farrar, Straus and Giroux, 1993).

31 For many years, Mills College, California, used *Bubaran Robert* for its graduation

processions: Miller and Lieberman, *Composing a World*, p. 68.

32 Miller and Lieberman, *Composing a World*, p. 82: from interview with Bella Lewitsky, June 8, 1995.

33 Morris quoted in Frank Rizzo, 'Morris: A Serious Good Time', *The Hartford Courant*, October 9, 1995 [fax date recorded in the MMDG archive].

34 Henry Spiller, 'Lou Harrison's Music for Western Instruments and Gamelan: Even More Western than It Sounds', *Asian Music*, 40/1 (2009), p. 47. In his article, Spiller also seeks to demonstrate how, in this movement of *World Power*, Harrison's rhythms are often front-weighted, based on Western principles, rather than end-weighted as in Indonesian tradition.

35 Ibid., p. 43.

36 Arlene Croce, 'Musical Offerings', *The New Yorker*, January 8, 1996, p. 75.

37 Geoff Smith, 'SoundCircus: An Interview With Lou Harrison' [1999], www.soundcircus.com/releases/sc005/lou_int.htm, accessed August 28, 2013.

38 Joan Acocella, 'Double Takes', *The New Yorker*, April 14, 2003. Morris said in interview with Jordan that *Serenade* was choreographed as a tribute to Harrison's early partner, Remy Charlip, whom he saw performing a dance with a pole as prop.

39 Morris, 'Mark Morris: The Making of My Dance', *The New York Times*, March 23, 2003.

40 Morris quoted in Miller and Lieberman, *Composing a World*, pp. 99-100.

41 Harrison quoted in Sheryl Flatow, '*Pacific*', *Performing Arts*, 10/2 (February, 1997), pp. 15-16.

42 Thea Singer, 'Mark Morris is a Choreographer Who Knows the Score', *The Boston Sunday Globe*, May 4, 1997.

43 Interview with Morris.

44 Preston, 'Mark Morris and Lou Harrison, "Trans-ethnicism" and "Elastic Form"', *Choreologica*, 6/1 (Winter, 2013), p. 67.

45 Morris quoted in Justin Davidson, 'Maverick In the Mainstream', *Newsday*, April 13, 1997; see Thea Singer, 'Mark Morris is a Choreographer Who Knows the Score', *The Boston Sunday Globe*, May 4, 1997.

46 Morris interviewed by Joe McLellan in 'Morris Speaks', www.redludwig.com, May 2, 2003, print-out in MMDG archive.

47 Acocella, 'Dance: Mark Morris Delivers the Goods', *The Wall Street Journal*, April 24, 1997.

48 Alastair Macaulay, 'The Last Great American Choreographer', *Dance Theatre Journal*, 12/1 (Summer, 1995), p. 10; see also Mary Clarke, who ranks *Grand Duo* similarly, 'Mark Morris Dances', *The Dancing Times* (May, 1995), p. 775.

49 Jacques Rivière, 'Le Sacre du printemps', *Nouvelle revue française* (November, 1913), in François Lesure, ed., *Igor Stravinsky, Le Sacre du printemps: Dossier de Presse* (Geneva: Edition Minkoff, 1980), pp. 47-8 (author's translation).

50 André Levinson quoted in Richard Taruskin, 'Stravinsky and the Subhuman: A Myth of the Twentieth Century: *The Rite of Spring*, the Tradition of the New, and "The Music Itself"', in Taruskin, *Defining Russia Musically: Historical and Hermeneutical Essays* (Princeton: Princeton University Press, 1997), p. 386; translated from André Levinson, 'Russkiy balet v Parizhe', *Rech'*, June 3, 1913.

51 Macaulay, 'The Last Great American Choreographer', p. 10.

52 Morris quoted in Miller and Lieberman, *Composing a World*, p. 99.

53 Morris quoted in Thea Singer, 'Home Again: Mark Morris is Back in Residence in

Boston', *The Boston Phoenix*, May 21, 1993.

54 Miller and Lieberman, *Composing a World*, p. 221.
55 Macaulay, 'The Last Great American Choreographer', p. 10.

CHAPTER 12

1   Story ballets by Antony Tudor are a notable exception in using existing, unedited scores, such as *Jardin aux lilas* (Chausson, 1936) and *Pillar of Fire* (Schoenberg, 1942).
2   James Webster, 'Sonata Form', *Grove Music Online*, http:// www.oxfordmusiconline.com/subscriber/article/grove/ music/26197?q=sonata+form&search=quick&pos=1&_start=1#firsthit, accessed March 10, 2013.
3   Jérôme-Joseph de Momigny, *Cours complet d'harmonie et de composition*, I (Paris: c. 1803-6), translated in Roger Parker, 'On Reading Nineteenth-Century Opera: Verdi Through the Looking-Glass', in Arthur Groos and Parker, eds., *Reading Opera* (Princeton, New Jersey, Princeton University Press, 1988), pp. 288-9.
4   Parker, 'On Reading Nineteenth-Century Opera...', p. 290.
5   Anthony Newcomb, 'Once More "Between Absolute and Program Music"', Schumann's Second Symphony', *19th-Century Music*, 7/3 (April, 1984), pp. 233-50.
6   Newcomb, 'Schumann and Late Eighteenth-Century Narrative Strategies', *19th-Century Music*, 11/2 (Fall, 1987), p. 167.
7   Jonathan Culler, *Structuralist Poetics* [1975] (London: Routledge & Kean Paul, 1994); Paul Ricoeur, 'Narrative Time', *Critical Enquiry*, 7 (1980), pp. 169-90.
8   See Susan McClary, *Feminine Endings: Music, Gender and Sexuality* (Minnesota: Minnesota University Press, 1991); Rose Rosengard Subotnik, 'Evidence of a Critical World View in Mozart's Last Three Symphonies', in *Developing Variations: Style and Ideology in Western Music* (Minneapolis: University of Minnesota Press, 1991), pp. 98-111.
9   Charles Rosen, *The Classical Style* (New York: Viking Press, 1971), p. 324.
10 There is a film of Morris performing *Rondo*, Brooklyn Academy of Music, December 14, 1995.
11 Interview with Morris.
12 Ibid.
13 Morris quoted in Danna Wolfson, 'Interview: Choreographer Mark Morris', *FrontRow*, June 17, 2010, http://frontrow.dmagazine.com/2010/06/interview-choreographer-mark-morris/, accessed March 11, 2013.
14 The opening theme of the Finale begins to change at the end of bar 4.
15 Morris quoted in Danna Wolfson, 'Interview: Choreographer Mark Morris'.
16 Nancy Umanoff, email communication, May 11, 2014.
17 Interview with Morris.
18 Morris in Q and A session, Shubert Theatre, Boston, March 15, 2002, recording in the MMDG archive.
19 Barbara White, '"As if they didn't hear the music," Or: How I Learned to Stop Worrying and Love Mickey Mouse', 'Sound Moves' [issue], *The Opera Quarterly* {*Performance+Theory+History*}, 22/1 (Winter, 2006), p. 66.
20 Deborah Jowitt, 'Spring Vintage', *The Village Voice*, March 12, 2002.
21 Interview with Morris.

22   Interview with Morris. At one point, the stretching was such that the metre felt
      like five beats in the bar, but Morris later tightened this.
23   Interview with Morris.
24   Ibid.
25   Ibid.
26   Ibid.
27   The fourth person stage right cannot do the move in its entirety, without an arm
      to rest upon.
28   The lesson took place November 16, 2011 at the Mark Morris Dance Center, New
      York. Film sources include a video of Morris himself in the solo, made just after
      the premiere, very poor quality and distant, nevertheless a revealing record of
      an extraordinary performance. I also saw *Italian Concerto* live in Northampton
      during the Morris Group's 2009 UK tour. This analysis of the piece is a modified
      version of the analysis published in Jordan, 'Mark Morris Marks Music, Or: What
      Did He Make of Bach's *Italian Concerto?*', in Stephanie Schroedter, ed., *Bewegungen
      zwischen Hören und Sehen. Denkbewegungen zu Bewegungskünsten* (Wurzburg:
      Königshausen & Neumann, 2012), pp. 219-36.
29   A DVD performance of *Italian Concerto*, with John Heginbotham in the solo, was
      shot at Jacob's Pillow Dance Festival, August 9, 2007.
30   Interview with Morris. Morris also explained that he had first worked with Bach's
      Two-Part Inventions before turning to the 'two-part' texture of the *Italian Concerto*.
31   Later, I sometimes regretted that these ideas from interview were no longer secret.
      It was as if they got in the way of the 'real piece'.
32   Morris also explained in interview that he develops gestural content as a means
      of avoiding the conventional codes of arm positions and moves.
33   'Visual capture' is the psychological term for the phenomenon of movement
      exaggerating an event in the music (which may be barely perceptible, in the
      background) and influencing our perceptions of the music (see pp. 105-8). It has
      also been described by psychologist Lawrence E. Marks as one medium 'sopping
      up' attributes from another: *The Unity of the Senses: Interrelations Among the
      Modalities* (New York: Academic Press, 1978), p. 197.
34   This develops from Edward Cone's idea of music in dance theatre usually
      operating as analogous to the dancer's subconscious: *The Composer's Voice*
      (Berkeley: University of California Press, 1974), pp. 141-44 (see my pp. 103-4).
35   André Lepecki, *Exhausting Dance: Performance and the Politics of Movement* (New
      York & London, Routledge, 2006), p. 58.
36   Joseph N. Straus, 'The Pitch Language of the Bartók Quartets', in Evan Jones, ed.,
      Intimate Voices: The Twentieth-Century String Quartet, Vol. 1: Debussy to Villa Lobos
      (Rochester: Rochester University Press, 2009), p. 97.
37   Stephen Walsh, *Bartók Chamber Music* (London: British Broadcasting Corporation,
      1982), p. 55.
38   Morris quoted in 'Making All Fours', BBC Wales, Cardiff, Dec. 4, 2003.
39   Bela Bartók, *Streichquartett IV* [Philharmonia Scores] (Vienna/London: Universal
      Edition, 1929); János Kárpáti, *Bartók's Chamber Music* [1976] (Stuyvesant, New
      York: Pendragon Press, 1994), pp. 339-64.
40   Mark Morris, *All Fours* [Labanotation score by Sandra Aberkalns] (New York:
      Dance Notation Bureau, 2006), p. 110. Since this work, Aberkalns has notated
      Morris's *Crosswalk* and *Spring, Spring, Spring*.
41   Kárpáti may have given Morris the key image of 'radiating outwards from' the

central movement, as in *V: Bartók's Chamber Music*, p. 152.

42   Walsh, *Bartók Chamber Music*, p. 48.

43   In his analysis of *All Fours*, Hamish J. Robb also mentions the key 'centres' of all but the third movement of the work: in 'Looking Beyond Facile Understandings of "Literalness" in Music-Dance Collaborations: Mark Morris's *All Fours*', *Dance Research*, 30/2 (Winter, 2012), p. 145, note 17.

44   Walsh, *Bartók Chamber Music*, p. 54.

45   Morris quoted in 'Making All Fours'.

46   Regarding the variety of intricate hand gestures in this work, Morris told me that this partly stemmed from working alongside the notator Aberkalns, having fun testing her by changing his mind, to see whether the Laban system could cope with such difficulty.

47   I do not, however, share Robb's interpretation that the group morph into 'more social beings' like peasant folk ('Looking Beyond Facile Understandings...', p. 140), or his reading that the forces of good and evil resolve into a clear happy ending.

48   Walsh, *Bartók Chamber Music*, p. 49.

49   See Kárpáti, *Bartók's Chamber Music*, p. 353, and Walsh, *Bartók Chamber Music*, p. 49.

50   Amanda Bayley, 'Bartók's String Quartet No. 4/III: A New Interpretative Approach', *Music Analysis*, 19/3 (2000), pp. 353-82.

51   Mark Morris, *All Fours* [Labanotation score by Sandra Aberkalns], p. 110.

52   Ibid., p. 148, referring to bars 55-63.

53   Ibid., p. 135, referring to bars 38-39.

54   Robb, 'Looking Beyond Facile Understandings...', pp. 138-39.

55   Mark Morris, *All Fours*, p. 110.

56   Ibid., p. 148.

57   Kárpáti, *Bartók's Chamber Music*, p. 343.

58   Edwin Denby, 'Graham's "Chronicle"; Uday Shankar' [1937], in Denby, *Dance Writings*, ed. Robert Cornfield and William Mackay (London: Dance Books, 1986), p. 43.

59   The dates are from James Sinclair's online Ives catalogue<http://drs.library.yale. edu:8083/HLTransformer/HLTransServlet?stylename=yul.ead2002.xhtml.xsl& pid=music:mss.0014.1&query=&clear-stylesheet-cache=yes&hlon=yes&big=y& adv=&filter=&hitPageStart=&sortFields=&view=c01_7#s7>; accessed February 24, 2014. I am grateful to the musicologist Matthew McDonald for drawing my attention to this catalogue.

60   Ives quoted in John Kirkpatrick, 'Critical Commentary' [1984, on Ives's Trio], p. 2. The passage quoted is Ives's sketch for a letter explaining his Trio: http:// www.charlesives.org/critical_commentary/index.htm, accessed September 5, 2013.

61   J. Peter Burkhholder, *All Made of Tunes: Charles Ives and the Uses of Musical Borrowing* (New Haven, Connecticut: Yale University Press, 1995), pp. 373-4; Kirkpatrick, 'Critical Commentary', p. 2.

62   Deborah Jowitt, 'Mark Morris Matches Wits with Beethoven and Ives', *The Village Voice*, August 25, 2009.

63   Julie Worden quoted in Gia Kourlas, 'Julie Worden: The Mark Morris Dancer Performs *L'Allegro*', *Time Out New York*, August 2, 2010; http://www.timeout. com/newyork/dance/julie-worden, accessed April 17, 2013.

64   Sarah Kaufman, 'Mark Morris Dance Group Performs at George Mason Center for the Arts', *The Washington Post*, June 14, 2010.

65   Judith Mackrell, 'Soldiers, Stompers and Demons from Mesmerising Morris', *The Guardian*, October 29, 2009.

66   Interview with Matthew Rose, April 5, 2013. I am especially grateful to Rose for his expert clarification, as Rehearsal Director of MMDG, of relations between choreography and music in *Empire Garden*.

67   This is similar to Balanchine's choreography to the late, serial Stravinsky, where the rests in the score are clarified on stage: Jordan, *Stravinsky Dances: Re-Visions across a Century* (Alton, Hants: Dance Books, 2007), p. 214.

68   DKE stands for the Delta Kappa Epsilon fraternity.

69   Information from *Empire Garden* rehearsal, October 9, 2010.

70   See Stuart Feder, *The Life of Charles Ives* (Cambridge: Cambridge University Press, 1999), p. 86.

71   This is an expanded version of the introduction to Morris's *Rite* setting presented at 'Reassessing *The Rite*: A Centennial Conference, University of North Carolina at Chapel Hill', October 26, 2012. For a discussion of the history of danced *Rites* across a century, see Jordan, *Stravinsky Dances*, pp. 411-505. There is also an internet chronology of *Rites* (and other dances to Stravinsky's music): *Stravinsky the Global Dancer*, Jordan, with Larraine Nicholas, 2003, http://ws1.roehampton.ac.uk/stravinsky.

72   Ethan Iverson blog, 'Mixed Meter Mysterium', March 21, 2011, http://dothemath.typepad.com/dtm/mixed-meter-mysterium.html, accessed July 1, 2013.

73   Ethan Iverson quoted in Richard Scheinin, '"Rite of Spring"—century-old prog-rock precursor', *San José Mercury News*, May 30, 2013.

74   Interview with Morris.

75   Morris in interview with Lesser, June 4, 2013.

76   Interview with Morris.

77   Interview with Iverson, June 13, 2013.

78   Michel Georges-Michel, 'Les deux "Sacres du printemps"', *Comoedia*, December 11, 1920; Stravinsky and Robert Craft, *Expositions and Developments* (London: Faber and Faber, 1962), p. 144.

79   Alastair Macaulay: 'A Latter-Day American Answer to Stravinsky's "Rite of Spring"', *The New York Times*, June 16, 2013.

80   Morris in dress rehearsal, June 11, 2013.

81   Deborah Jowitt, 'For Eyes and Ears', *DanceBeat*, April 7, 2013, http://www.artsjournal.com/dancebeat/2013/04/for-eyes-and-ears/, accessed April 8, 2013.

82   For a discussion of Balanchine's use of repetition in big forms, see Jordan, *Moving Music: Dialogues with Music in Twentieth-Century Ballet* (London: Dance Books, 2000), pp. 128-50.

83   Morris reminded his audience of this point in a public interview with Jordan at Sadler's Wells Theatre, November 30, 2013.

84   For instance, to the more fluid, through-composed Villa-Lobos quartet, *Petrichor* seems to be one of Morris's least successful large-scale pieces. In relation to this point, Jordan has discussed Balanchine's form and narrative experiments in *Scotch Symphony* (Mendelssohn): in *Moving Music*, p. 149; also in *Divertimento from Le Baiser de la fée* (Stravinsky): in *Stravinsky Dances*, pp. 225-38.

CHAPTER 13

1   Examples of danced concertos include those choreographed by: Balanchine: *Concerto Barocco* (1941, Bach), *Ballet Imperial* (1941, Tchaikovsky), *Symphonie Concertante* (1947, Mozart); Bronislava Nijinska: *Chopin Concerto* (1937); Jerome Robbins, *Piano Concerto in G* (1975, Ravel); Kenneth MacMillan, *Concerto* (1966, Shostakovich); Alexei Ratmansky, *Concerto DSCH* (2008, Shostakovich).

2   Morris quoted in Acocella, *Mark Morris*, p. 163.

3   Jordan, *Moving Music: Dialogues with Music in Twentieth-Century Ballet* (London: Dance Books, 2000), p. 110.

4   Wye J. Allanbrook, *Rhythmic Gesture in Mozart: 'Le Nozze di Figaro' and 'Don Giovanni'* (Chicago and London: University of Chicago Press, 1983).

5   Morris quoted in Gia Kourlas, 'Who's Afraid of the Big, Bad Wolfgang?' *Time Out New York* (August 17-23, 2006), p. 98.

6   Charles Rosen, *The Classical Style* (New York: Viking Press, 1971), p. 324.

7   Richard Taruskin, 'Why Mozart Has Become an Icon for Today', *The New York Times*, September 9, 1990, H35-H40; Rose Rosengaard Subotnik, 'Evidence of a Critical World View in Mozart's Last Three Symphonies', in *Developing Variations: Style and Ideology in Western Music* (Minneapolis: University of Minnesota Press, 1991), pp. 98-111; Susan McClary, 'A Musical Dialectic from the Enlightenment: Mozart's Piano Concerto in G major, K. 453, Movement 2', *Cultural Critique*, 5 (1986), pp. 129-69; and Neal Zaslaw, *Mozart's Symphonies: Context, Performance Practice, Reception* (Oxford: Clarendon Press, 1989).

8   Morris quoted in Martin Morrow, 'Le freak c'est chic', CBC News: Arts and Entertainment, June 4, 2008, http://www.cbc.ca/news/arts/theatre/story/2008/06/04/f-mark-morris-luminato.html, accessed February 1, 2013.

9   The men make a brief appearance at the start of 'Eleven', and the women near the end of the slow movement of 'Double'.

10   Rosen, *The Classical Style* , pp. 6-7. Other discussions of concerto as drama include: Donald Francis Tovey, *Essays in Musical Analysis*, Vol. 3, *Concertos* (London: Oxford University Press, 1936), pp. 6-7; Leonard G. Ratner, *Classic Music: Expression, Form, and Style* (New York: Schirmer, 1980), pp. 297-305. Further discussions stem from the 1989 Michigan MozartFest, in Neal Zaslaw, ed., *Mozart's Piano Concertos: Text, Context, Interpretation* (Ann Arbor, Michigan: University of Michigan Press, 1996).

11   Tovey, *Essays in Musical Analysis*, pp. 6-7.

12   Heinrich Christoph Koch, *Versuch einer Anleitung zur Composition*, Vol. III (Leipzig, 1793), p. 332; quoted in translation by Jane R. Stevens, 'An Eighteenth-Century Description of Concerto First-Movement Form', *Journal of the American Musicological Society (JAMS)*. XXIV (1971), p. 94.

13   Stevens, 'An Eighteenth-Century Description', p. 94. See also Taruskin, 'Music in the Seventeenth and Eighteenth Centuries', *The Oxford History of Western Music*, Vol. 2 (Oxford: Oxford University Press, 2010), p. 621.

14   Taruskin, 'Music in the Seventeenth and Eighteenth Centuries', p. 606.

15   Allanbrook, 'Comic Issues in Mozart's Piano Concertos,' in Zaslaw, ed., *Mozart's Piano Concertos*, p. 85. The format suggested by Allanbrook links with V. Kofi Agawu's more formally-oriented reading that a mobile surface of fragments is at the core of Mozart's style: 'Mozart's Art of Variation: Remarks on the First Movement of K. 503', in Zaslaw, ed., *Mozart's Piano Concertos*, pp. 303-14.

16   There is also the 'learned counterpoint' topic, with liturgical overtones, in the 'Melancholy Octet' fugue in Handel's *L'Allegro* (see Ch. 6) and in the earlier Mozart fugue in *Fugue and Fantasy* that Morris used in tongue in cheek fashion (see Ch. 5). See also Allanbrook, *Rhythmic Gesture in Mozart*, p. 8.
17   Maile Okamura learnt Grant's role for the MMDG visit to Macau in 2012.
18   Interview with Lauren Grant, January 10, 2013.
19   Anne Carson, 'Variations on the Right to Remain Silent', from *A Public Space*, Issue 7, 2008, http://poems.com/special_features/prose/essay_carson.php, accessed February 1, 2013.
20   'The Brutality of Fact' is the subtitle of the book by David Sylvester, *Interviews with Francis Bacon* (London: Thames & Hudson, 1987); see specifically p. 48.
21   Carson, 'Variations on the Right to Remain Silent'.
22   On rare occasions, to save time, Morris has given a feeling image to a new person stepping into an existing role, and the image of self-protection is one of these: 'as if you're going to be horribly crushed by a falling building': interview with Morris.
23   Interview with Morris.
24   Morris said in interview that he worked on 'Eleven' and 'Double' at the same time.
25   Similarly, a weaving exit step from I/3 that fits the 3/4 musical metre crosses the 4/4 in II/1, and seems to accrue additional energy by doing so.
26   Interview with Grant, April 15, 2014.
27   It is important that baroque dance style of the mid-late eighteenth century overlaps with what is commonly known as the 'classical period' in music, the period to which Mozart belongs.
28   Interview with Morris.
29   Interview with Lauren Grant, January 10, 2013.
30   Grant explained in interview that she sometimes found herself questioning what this finger motif meant.
31   The movement occurs earlier, in the first part of the Larghetto, but to much less distinctive effect at this point.
32   Rosen, *Sonata Forms* [1980] (New York, London: W.W. Norton, 1988), pp. 123-6.
33   Interview with Morris.
34   DVD of rehearsal of *Mozart Dances*, prior to the PBS *Live From Lincoln Center* broadcast, August 14, 2007, in the MMDG archive.
35   This was indeed Morris's conception of the women.
36   Rosen, *The Classical Style*, p. 260; Cuthbert Girdlestone, *Mozart and His Piano Concertos*, 3rd ed. (New York: Dover, 1978), p. 489.
37   Morris said in interview that he first plotted when the solos would start and finish and choreographed them as individual dancers became available to rehearse.
38   Interview with Morris.
39   Allanbrook, 'Comic Issues...', p. 96; Tovey, *Essays in Musical Analysis*, p. 23.
40   I am grateful to Howard Friend for noting the connection here with *Così fan tutte*, December 30, 2012.
41   Girdlestone, *Mozart and His Piano Concertos*, p. 488.
42   Interview with Morris.
43   Morris in interview with Joan Acocella, *Mozart Dances* programme, 2006, p. 9.
44   Acocella, 'Mozart Moves: Mark Morris at Lincoln Center', *The New Yorker*, August 20, 2007, http://www.newyorker.com/magazine/2007/08/20/mozart-moves, accessed August 15, 2014.

45   Interview with Morris.
46   Allanbrook, 'Comic Issues...', pp. 101-2; Allanbrook, 'Mozart's Tunes and the
      Comedy of Closure', in James M. Morris, ed., *On Mozart* (Cambridge: Cambridge
      University Press, 1994), pp. 185-6.

PRESENT INTO FUTURE

1   Alastair Macaulay, 'An Old Love Story, Tinkered for the Times', *The New York
      Times*, August 8, 2014.

PERMISSIONS

Text Publications

Excerpts from 'Choreomusical Conversations: Facing a Double Challenge', *Dance Research Journal*, 43/1 (Summer, 2011), pp. 43-64.

In modified form, the article 'Mark Morris Marks Purcell: *Dido and Aeneas* as Danced Opera', *Dance Research*, 22/2 (Winter, 2011), pp. 167-213.

In modified form, the chapter 'Mark Morris Marks Music, Or: What Did He Make of Bach's *Italian Concerto?*', in Stephanie Schroedter, ed. *Bewegungen zwischen Hören und Sehen. Denkbewegungen zu Bewegungskünsten* (Wurzburg: Königshausen & Neumann, 2012), pp. 219-36.

Music

Béla Bartók: Fourth String Quartet
Reproduced by permission of Universal Edition (London) Ltd.
Rights for USA controlled by Boosey & Hawkes Inc.

Lou Harrison: *Rhymes With Silver*
© Copyright 2000 by Peermusic III Ltd
All Rights Reserved. Used by permission.

Charles Ives: Trio for Violin, Cello and Piano S.86
© Peermusic Classical
Reproduced by permission of Faber Music Ltd, London
All Rights Reserved.

Four Saints in Three Acts: Music by Virgil Thomson, Lyrics by Gertrude Stein
Copyright © 1933, 1948 by G. Schirmer, Inc. International copyright secured. All rights reserved. Used by permission.

Alexander Tcherepnin: Bagatelles, Op. 5 Copyright © Heugel SA.
International copyright secured. All rights reserved. Used by permission.

Igor Stravinsky: *Symphonies of Wind Instruments*
© Copyright 2001 by Boosey & Hawkes Music Publishers Ltd Reproduced by permission of Boosey & Hawkes Music Publishers Ltd.

Index

Compositions that have been used by Morris as scores for his dances are indexed under the titles of those dances rather than under the composer's name.

Lightning Source UK Ltd.
Milton Keynes UK
UKOW02n0347121115

262527UK00003B/32/P